Master Visual C++ 1.5

Master
Visual C++
1.5

Nathan Gurewich and

Ori Gurewich

A Division of Prentice Hall Computer Publishing
201 West 103rd Street, Indianapolis, Indiana 46290

SAMS
PUBLISHING

International Standard Book Number: 0-672-30468-6

Library of Congress Catalog Card Number: 93-87177

97   96   95   94   4   3   2   1

Interpretation of the printing code: the rightmost double-digit number is the year of the book's printing; the rightmost single-digit, the number of the book's printing. For example, a printing code of 94-1 shows that the first printing of the book occurred in 1994.

Composed in AGaramond and MCPdigital by Prentice Hall Computer Publishing

Printed in the United States of America

Trademarks

The text in this book is printed on recycled paper.

Overview

C

Contents

Acknowledgments

We would like to thank Greg Croy, Acquisitions Editor at Sams Publishing, for asking us to write this book.

Thanks also to Phil Paxton, the Development Editor of this book; to Robert Bogue, the Technical Editor; to the Production Editor, Katherine Stuart Ewing; and to the Copy Editors, Sean Medlock, Mitzi Foster Gianakos, and Kitty Wilson. Many thanks to Wayne Blankenbeckler and Keith Davenport, who helped in the creation of the CD for this book; and to Sharon Cox and Lynette Quinn at Sams.

We would also like to thank the Microsoft Corporation for supplying us with the various beta versions, enhancements, and commercial packages of Visual C++ and for providing us with technical information.

About the Authors

Ori Gurewich and **Nathan Gurewich** are the authors of several best-selling books in the areas of Visual Basic for Windows, C/C++ programming, multimedia programming, and client/server database design and programming.

Ori has an electrical engineering degree from Stony Brook University, New York. His background includes positions as senior software engineer and software consultant engineer for companies developing professional multimedia and communication software for DOS, Windows, and Windows NT.

Nathan has a master's degree in electrical engineering from Columbia University, New York City, New York, and a bachelor's degree in electrical engineering from Hofstra University, Long Island, New York. Since the introduction of the PC, the author has been involved in the design and implementation of commercial software packages for the PC. Nathan is an expert in the field of PC programming and PC software marketing.

Ori and Nathan can be contacted via CompuServe (CompuServe ID: 72072,312).

Introduction

What Do You Need to Know?

This book teaches you how to write Windows applications by using the Microsoft Visual C++ package. But wait a minute! Do you know how to use the C++ programming language? Well, if you don't know C++, Chapters 2 and 3 of this book teach you the essentials. In these chapters you'll learn C++ topics and concepts that are prerequisites for the rest of the book. The book assumes that you have some "regular" C programming experience.

The Book's CD

This book comes with a CD. On the CD you'll find all the book's programs, BMP files, WAV files, MIDI files, movie files, and other files that you'll need while reading this book.

To install the book's CD to your hard drive, follow these steps:

1. Start Windows.
2. Insert the CD into your CD-ROM drive.
3. Select Run from the Program Manager's File menu and execute the INSTALL.EXE program that resides in the root directory of the CD.
4. Follow the directions in the INSTALL.EXE program.

NOTE

The INSTALL program creates the directory C:\VCPROG and subdirectories below C:\VCPROG. During the course of this book you'll be instructed to execute various EXE programs. These programs are located in the subdirectory ORIGINAL. For example, in Chapter 20, "Menus," you'll learn how to write three applications: MyMenu.EXE, Grow.EXE and PicMenu.EXE. The MyMenu.EXE application and its source code files reside in the C:\VCPROG\ORIGINAL\CH20\MYMENU directory, the Grow.EXE application and its source code files reside in the C:\VCPROG\ORIGINAL\CH20\GROW directory, and the PicMenu.EXE application and its source code files reside in the C:\VCPROG\ORIGINAL\CH20\MyPic directory.

The \VCPROG\ORIGINAL directory is supplied so that you'll be able to execute the applications prior to writing them and compare the supplied source code files with the source code files that you'll generate.

While reading this book, you'll be instructed to write the code for the book's programs in the \VCPROG\PRACTICE directory. For example, in Chapter 20, you'll be instructed to write the MyMenu application in the \VCPROG\PRACTICE\CH20\MYMENU directory, the Grow application in the \VCPROG\PRACTICE\CH20\GROW directory, and the PicMenu application in the \VCPROG\PRACTICE\CH20\PICMENU directory.

How the Book Is Organized

The objective of this book is to teach you how to write Windows applications with the Visual C++ package. Here's how the book is organized:

In Chapters 2 and 3 you'll learn C++ topics. These chapters assume that you know how to write simple C DOS programs. The materials covered in these chapters are prerequisites for the rest of the book.

In Chapter 4 you'll learn how to write your first Visual C++ Windows application. In this chapter you'll learn how to use the visual tools of Visual C++.

In Chapter 5 you'll learn about the document class and how to store variables in it.

Chapter 6 teaches you how to write Windows applications that play WAV files through the PC speaker without a sound card.

In Chapter 7 you'll learn to design dialog boxes, and in Chapters 8, 9, 10, and 11 you'll learn how to implement basic Windows controls such as check boxes, scroll bars, list boxes, combo boxes, and radio buttons.

In Chapter 12 you'll learn the important topic of placing controls in your application's main window.

Almost every application requires reading and writing data to and from the disk, and in Chapters 13, 14, 15, and 16 you'll learn how this is accomplished in Visual C++.

In Chapter 17 you'll learn how to take advantage of the mouse from within your Visual C++ applications, and in Chapter 18 you'll learn how to handle the keyboard from within your Visual C++ applications.

In Chapter 19 you'll learn how to design Multiple Document Interface (MDI) applications.

In Chapter 20 you'll learn how to implement sophisticated menus, and in Chapter 21 you'll learn how to implement sophisticated toolbars and status bars.

In Chapters 22, 23, 24, and 25 you'll learn how to implement programs that use the popular multimedia technologies. These include programs that play video files, WAV files, MIDI files, and CD audio.

Chapter 26 teaches you how your applications can use the timer, and Chapter 27 teaches you how to implement animation programs.

Chapter 28 teaches you about the `OnIdle()` function, and Chapter 29 teaches you how to write applications that make use of advanced PC speaker topics.

Chapter 30 teaches you how to use the grid control (a spreadsheet-like application).

Chapter 31 covers displaying and printing topics.

Chapters 32 and 33 teach you how to incorporate advanced controls, such as three-dimensional buttons, into your Visual C++ applications.

Chapter 34 covers drawing topics.

Throughout the course of the book you'll learn how to use VBX controls (Visual Controls) that were created by others. In Chapter 35 you'll learn how to create your own VBX controls!

1

Why Visual C++?

Welcome to the fascinating world of
programming Windows applications
with the Microsoft Visual C++
package.

Currently, Windows is the most popular operating system for the PC, and consequently almost all vendors ship their PCs with a mouse and the Windows operating system already installed.

Why Use Windows? Why Use Visual C++?

There are several reasons why Windows became so popular in a relatively short time:

With Windows you can write device-independent programs. This means that while you write the application, you don't have to concern yourself with issues such as what types of printer, mouse, monitor, keyboard, sound card, CD drive, or other devices your users own. Your application should work fine no matter what hardware your users have. So does this mean, for example, that your user can use any sound card? Not at all! It is your user's responsibility to install the sound card into his or her PC. During the installation, Windows asks the user to install the appropriate drivers, and Windows either accepts or rejects the sound card. Windows will accept the sound card provided that the hardware and the software (drivers) your user receives from the sound card's vendor are implemented in accordance with Windows requirements. Once Windows accepts the sound card, the Windows applications that you write should work with that sound card. The same applies for other devices, such as the printer, the monitor, the CD drive, and so on.

A lot of code is already installed in your user's PC. Once Windows is installed, the PC contains a lot of Windows-related code. This code exists on your PC (the developer's PC) and on your users' PCs. This means that before you even start writing the first line of code, your user already has more than half of your program in his or her PC! Not only can you avoid writing this code, but you can avoid distributing it to your users as well (because your users already have this code in their Windows packages).

There's a standard user interface. The user interface mechanism is the same for all Windows applications. For example, without reading your application's documentation, users should know that they can use Run from Program Manager's File menu to run the application, and they can use the arrow icon that appears in the upper-right corner of your application's window to minimize the window. They also know about the OK and Cancel buttons, the About dialog box, and many other features of your programs before you even start writing them!

The preceding reasons to use Windows are applicable no matter what programming language you use to develop the application. The question is, why should you use Visual C++ to write Windows applications rather than the "regular" C with SDK for Windows? The answer to this question is discussed in the next section.

Visual C++: What Is That?

C++ is known as an *object-oriented* programming language. The *C++* in *Visual C++* means that you have to use C++ for writing the code. However, this book assumes you have *no* previous C++ experience. During the course of this book, you'll learn all the stuff you'll need to write powerful, professional Windows applications with the C++ programming language. This book does assume, however, that you have some previous experience with the "regular" C programming language. This book does not assume that you have any Windows programming experience. If you have some minimal C DOS programming experience, you'll do fine.

Now that you know the meaning of the *C++* in *Visual C++*, what is the meaning of *Visual?* It means that you'll accomplish many of your programming tasks by using the keyboard and the mouse to design and write your applications visually. You'll select controls, such as push buttons and scroll bars, with the mouse, drag them to your application, and size them. You'll actually be able to see your application as you build it (during design time). In other words, you'll be able to see how your application will look before you execute it. This is a great advantage because you can see your application without compiling/linking it (which saves you considerable time), and if you change your mind regarding placement and sizes of edit boxes, push buttons, and other controls, you can change them with the mouse.

ClassWizard: What Is That?

The most powerful feature of Visual C++ is a program called *ClassWizard.* ClassWizard is a program that writes code for you! In the industry, this type of program is often referred to as a *CASE* program. Of course, ClassWizard isn't a magic program; you have to tell it what you want it to write for you. For example, suppose you place a push button in your application's window with the mouse. Once you place the button, you want to write code that is executed whenever the user clicks that button. This is the time to use ClassWizard. By clicking various buttons in the ClassWizard window, you tell it to prepare all the overhead code. ClassWizard does this, and then it shows you where you should insert your own code. Thus, your job is to type your code in the area that ClassWizard prepares for you.

Visual C++ is an interesting and fun package to use, because with it you can develop sophisticated Windows applications in a very short time. So relax and prepare yourself for a pleasant journey!

> **NOTE**
>
> Before proceeding to the next chapter, make sure to install the book's CD, as outlined in the introduction.

2

Your First C++ DOS Program

In this chapter and the next you'll learn some basic C++ concepts and topics that are prerequisites for the subsequent chapters of this book.

What Is QuickWin?

Visual C++ comes with a program called *QuickWin*. With QuickWin you can generate DOS programs that are executed in a Windows shell. This means that the programs you write with QuickWin can use C statements such as `printf()`, but you execute these programs from within Windows.

> **NOTE**
>
> Use QuickWin to write C and C++ DOS programs that are executed in a Windows shell.

Why Learn QuickWin?

As stated, you can use QuickWin to write DOS programs that are executed in a Windows shell. The objective of this book is to teach you how to write C++ true Windows applications with the Visual C++ package. So the question is, why does this chapter teach QuickWin? The answer is that in order to use Visual C++ to write Windows applications, you need to know some C++ topics. As you know, even the simplest Windows program is long and contains several overhead files. Thus, it is much simpler to learn the basics of C++ by writing simple DOS programs than by writing Windows programs.

Writing a Simple DOS C++ Program

Now you'll write a simple C++ DOS program with Visual C++'s QuickWin feature.

> **NOTE**
>
> The purpose of this chapter and the next is to teach you C++ concepts and topics. These topics are prerequisites to the subsequent chapters of the book. This book assumes you have no previous C++ programming experience, so if you've never done C++ programming or you need to refresh your C++ knowledge, read this chapter and the next.
>
> If you already know C++ and feel that you can jump directly into the Visual C++ ocean, then feel free to just browse through this chapter and the next.

☐ Start Visual C++ by double-clicking the Visual C++ icon (see Figure 2.1).

Windows responds by running the Visual C++ program (see Figure 2.2).

Figure 2.1.
The Visual C++
program group.

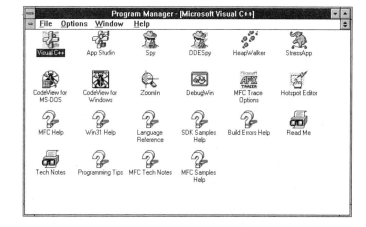

Figure 2.2.
The Microsoft
Visual C++
window.

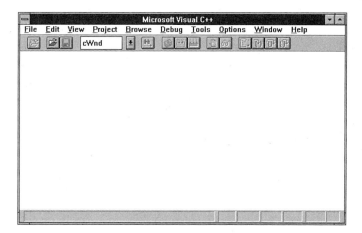

☐ Select New from the File menu (see Figure 2.3).

Visual C++ responds by opening a new window with the title "<1> UN-
TITLED.1" (see Figure 2.4). You will write the program's code in the <1>
UNTITLED.1 window.

Figure 2.3.
Opening a new file.

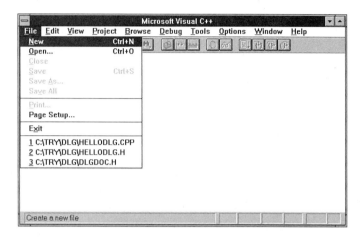

Figure 2.4.
The new window
that Visual C++
opens.

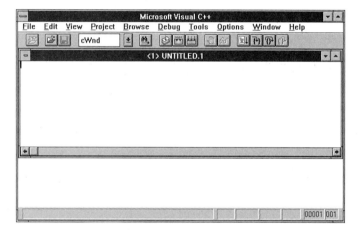

At this point, you have to tell Visual C++ that the program you're going to write is a QuickWin program (and not a true Windows program). Here's how you tell this to Visual C++:

☐ Select Project from the Options menu.

>   *Visual C++ responds by displaying the Project Options dialog box*
>   *(see Figure 2.5).*

As shown in Figure 2.5, the Project Type box contains the text "QuickWin application (.EXE)." This means that Visual C++ is currently set to generate QuickWin programs. If the Project Type box does not contain the text "QuickWin application (.EXE)":

☐ Click the down-arrow icon next to the Project Type box.

> *Visual C++ responds by displaying a drop-down list (see Figure 2.6).*

☐ Select the QuickWin application (.EXE) item.

☐ Set the Build Mode to Release. That is, click the Release radio button in the Build Mode box.

☐ Now your Project Options dialog box looks as shown in Figure 2.5.

Figure 2.5.
The Project Options
dialog box.

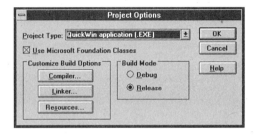

Figure 2.6.
The list of available
project types.

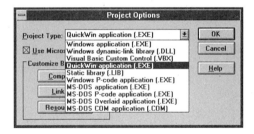

NOTE

As shown in Figure 2.5, you have to set the Build Mode to Release. When you do so, the EXE file you'll generate will be small. However, if you set the Build Mode to Debug, the resulting EXE file will be large, because it will contain additional code that's used for debugging purposes.

☐ Click the Project Option dialog box's OK button.

Now you're ready to write the program's C++ code. You will call this program Hello.CPP.

☐ Type the Hello program code in the <1> UNTITLED.1 window. The Hello.CPP program code is shown in Listing 2.1.

Listing 2.1. The Hello.CPP program.

```
/////////////////////////////
// Program Name: Hello.CPP
/////////////////////////////

////////////////////////////////////////////////////////////
// Program Description:
//
// This program illustrates the use of the cout operator.
////////////////////////////////////////////////////////////

//////////////
// #include
//////////////
#include <iostream.h>

/////////////////////////////
// Function Name: main()
/////////////////////////////
void main()
{

cout << "Hello, this is my first C++ program";

}
```

Now save your program:

☐ Select Save As from the File menu.

QuickWin responds by displaying the Save As dialog box (see Figure 2.7).

☐ Save your program as HELLO.CPP in the directory C:\VCPROG\PRACTICE\CH02.

Figure 2.7.
The Save As
dialog box.

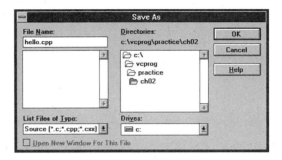

Compiling/Linking
the Hello.CPP Program

It's now time to compile/link your Hello.CPP program:

☐ Select Rebuild All HELLO.EXE from the Project menu.

QuickWin responds by compiling and linking the Hello.CPP program.

If you followed the instructions outlined in the previous sections and typed the code exactly as you were instructed, you see the window shown in Figure 2.8. This window is called the Output window. It contains the results of the compiling/linking process. (Naturally, when the Output window contains the message "0 error(s), 0 warning(s)," this window is referred to as the "happy window.")

Figure 2.8.
Visual C++'s
Output window.

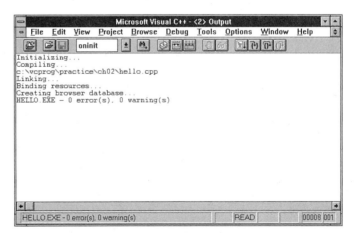

If you didn't get the 0 error(s) message, display the Hello.CPP file and make sure that you typed everything without any syntax errors.

To display the Hello.CPP window:

☐ Select the HELLO.CPP file from the Window menu.

Executing the Hello.EXE Program

You're now in a position to execute the Hello.EXE program.

☐ Select Execute HELLO.EXE from the Project menu.

QuickWin responds by executing the Hello.EXE program (see Figure 2.9).

*Figure 2.9.
The Hello.EXE
program.*

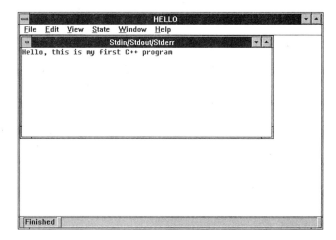

As shown in Figure 2.9, the output of the Hello.EXE program is displayed in a Stdin/Stdout/Stderr window. As implied by the name of this window, it serves as the means for accepting input from the user (Stdin). Of course, Hello.CPP doesn't require any input from the user, but any program that does require the user to type something during the execution of the program will let the user type in this window.

The Hello.EXE program displays the text:

```
Hello, this is my first C++ program.
```

This text is displayed in the Stdin/Stdout/Stderr window (hence, this window is also called the *Stdout window*).

If Hello.EXE had generated nasty error messages during its execution (such as Stack full, Not enough memory, division by zero), these messages would be displayed in the Stdin/Stdout/Stderr window (hence, this window is also called the Stderr window).

Putting it all together, the Stdin/Stdout/Stderr window serves the same role as the monitor during a regular DOS session.

To terminate the Hello.EXE program:

☐ Select Exit from the Hello program's File menu (see Figure 2.10).

As you can see, the Hello program contains a menu, even though you didn't write any code that implements this menu.

Figure 2.10.
Terminating the
Hello.EXE
program.

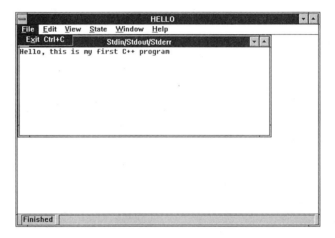

NOTE

You should be aware that EXE files generated by QuickWin aren't true DOS programs. In fact, if you exit to DOS, log into the `C:\VCPROG\PRACTICE\CH02` directory, and enter `HELLO  {Enter}`

You'll get a message:

`This program requires Microsoft Windows`

You should also know that the EXE files you generate with QuickWin are stand-alone EXE files. That is, your users do not have to own Visual C++. To

execute a program that was created with QuickWin, your user can double-click the HELLO.EXE file from the File Manager program or select Run from the Program Manager's File menu and select the file
C:\VCPROG\PRACTICE\CH02\HELLO.EXE.

Who Needs QuickWin?

The question is, who needs Visual C++'s QuickWin feature? Well, there are several uses for this feature. For example, you need it to demonstrate C++ topics without using all the overhead code that true Windows applications require.

Also, there are situations in which you'll need to write a small program that performs a certain task. For example, suppose you need to calculate the sum of all the odd integers from 1 to 100, and you have only two and a half minutes to accomplish this task. This is an ideal excuse to use QuickWin.

Examining the Hello.CPP Program's Code

To review the Hello.CPP program's code:

Note that the code (Listing 2.1) contains a lot of // characters. Yes, comments in C++ start with the // characters. For example, the following is a valid C++ comment:

```
// This is my comment.
```

Unlike comments in C, you don't have to terminate the comment with the comment characters.

So in C, you would write the following comment:

```
/*
   This is my comment.
   I can write here whatever I want.
*/
```

while in C++, this comment can be written as follows:

```
//
//   This is my comment.
//   I can write here whatever I want.
//
```

> **NOTE**
>
> Generally speaking, C is a subset of C++. Thus, everything that you know in C can be applied to your C++ programs. For example, the following is valid in a C++ program:
>
> ```
> // This is my comment.
> /* I can mix C and C++ syntax, */
> // because C is a subset of C++.
> ```

The Hello.CPP program starts by #including the iostream.h file:

```
#include <iostream.h>
```

The iostream.h file is necessary because it includes all the prototypes of the functions you use to stream characters to and from the input/output (I/O) device.

The next statements of the Hello.CPP program contain the main() function:

```
void main()
{

cout << "Hello, this is my first C++ program";

}
```

Just as in DOS C programs, DOS C++ programs require a main() function.

main() contains a single statement:

```
cout << "Hello, this is my first C++ program";
```

As you probably guessed, cout serves the same role as the printf() function in C. The << characters indicate the direction of the stream. Because the << characters point from the string to the cout, the characters will flow from the buffer of the string to the cout device (the screen).

As previously stated, C is a subset of C++. This means that you can use C's printf() function in C++.

☐ Open the Hello.CPP file. That is, open the Window menu and click the Hello.CPP item to display the Hello.CPP file. If the Window menu does not contain the Hello.CPP item, use the Open item from the File menu to load the Hello.CPP file from the C:\VCPROG\PRACTICE\CH02 directory.

☐ Modify the Hello.CPP file to look as follows:

```
/////////////////////////////
// Program Name: Hello.CPP
/////////////////////////////

/////////////////////////////////////////////////////////
// Program Description:
//
// This program illustrates the use of the cout operator.
/////////////////////////////////////////////////////////

//////////////
// #include
//////////////
#include <iostream.h>

/////////////////////////////
// Function Name: main()
/////////////////////////////
void main()
{

// cout << "Hello, this is my first C++ program";
printf ("Hello, this is my first C program");

}
```

☐ Save the `Hello.CPP` file (that is, select Save from the File menu).

Now compile/link the `Hello.CPP` program:

☐ Select Rebuild All HELLO.EXE from the Project menu.

  Visual C++ responds by displaying the error messages shown in Figure 2.11.

Figure 2.11.
The error messages that Visual C++ displays.

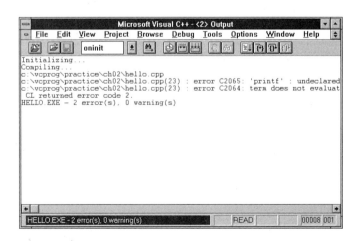

Errors? Why? From the errors you received, you may conclude that the compiler doesn't know the meaning of `printf()`. This makes sense, because you didn't `#include` the `stdio.h` file.

> **NOTE**
>
> During the compiling process, the compiler/linker displays errors (if any) in the Output window. To go directly to the line that causes the error, you can double-click the error message in the Output window.

☐ Add the following statement at the beginning of the `Hello.CPP` file:

```
#include <stdio.h>
```

☐ Select Rebuild All HELLO.EXE from the Project menu.

> *Visual C++ responds by compiling and linking the Hello.CPP program.*

☐ Select Execute HELLO.EXE from the Project menu.

> *Visual C++ responds by executing the Hello.EXE program. As expected, the program displays this message:*

```
Hello, this is my first C program
```

C++ Versus C

You learned in the previous sections that C++ uses a different comment syntax than C and that C++ uses the `cout` statement instead of the `printf()` function. Of course, these aren't the only differences between C and C++.

C++ was invented after several years of extensive C usage. People had used C for a long time, and this programming language proved itself to be reliable and convenient. The EXE files generated with the C programming language are short and are executed quickly. So why bother with a new programming language? Because people started to demand more from C. So in essence, C++ is the second version of the C programming language. This version contains all the enhancements that C programmers desired when they wrote their C programs. Naturally, the resulting C++ language is convenient and easy to use, and it produces small, fast EXE files, as does the C language.

You can take advantage of C++ for writing DOS programs, but probably the main advantage of using C++ is for writing Windows applications. If you've ever written

Windows applications with the C language, you know that the process involves typing a lot of code that just serves as the overhead for the application. There is nothing ingenious about that code, and it must appear in each and every C Windows application that you write. Does this make sense to you? By using C++, you can use something called classes. We'll get into the business of C++ classes soon enough, but for now you can think of them as program modules that you can easily plug into your programs. You can write the classes yourself, as well as purchase them from software vendors. For example, the Microsoft Visual C++ package comes with the *Microsoft Foundation Classes* (*MFC*). The MFC contains many useful code modules that are available for your C++ Windows applications. Throughout the book, you'll have chances to use many of the classes that come with the MFC.

Classes in C++

The most important concept in C++ is the concept of *classes*. C++ classes are similar to C structures. However, a C structure only defines the data that is associated with the structure. For example, the following is a C structure:

```
struct MYSTRUCT
{
int radius;
int color;
};
```

Once you declare the structure, you can use it from within your main(), as follows:

```
void main()
{
MYSTRUCT MyCircle;
...
...
...

MyCircle.radius = 10;
MyCircle.color = 255; /* 255 represents the red color */
...
...
...
}
```

As stated, the MyCircle structure has data associated with it (the radius and the color).

On the other hand, a class in C++ has data as well as functions associated with it. The data of the class are called *data members*, and the functions of the class are called *member functions*.

Declaring a Class

Before you can do anything with the class, your program must declare the class. Now you'll learn about the syntax used for declaring a class.

For practice, declare a class called `Circle`.

Here is the declaration of the `Circle` class:

```
class Circle
{
public:
  Circle();
  void SetRadius(void);
  void GetRadius(void);
  ~Circle();
private:
  void CalculateArea(void);
  int radius;
  int color;
};
```

To begin with, the class declaration has the following skeleton:

```
class Circle
{
........
........
........
Here you type the declaration of the class
........
........
........
};
```

The `class` keyword is an indication to the compiler that whatever is typed between the curly brackets ({}) belongs to the class declaration. Don't forget to include the semicolon (;) character at the end of the declaration.

The declaration of the class contains the declarations of data members (for example, `int radius`) as well as the declarations of the member functions' prototypes. In the previous `Circle` class declaration, the declaration contains two data members:

```
int radius;
int color;
```

and five prototypes of member functions:

```
Circle();
void SetRadius(void);
void GetRadius(void);
```

```
~Circle();
void CalculateArea(void);
```

The first and fourth prototypes look strange. The first prototype is

```
Circle();
```

It's the prototype of the *constructor* function. You'll learn later in this chapter about the role of the constructor function. But for now, you can examine the syntax that C++ uses for the constructor function. There are certain rules you must follow when writing the prototype of the constructor function:

- Every class declaration must include the prototype of the constructor function.

- The name of the constructor function must be the same name as the class, but with () after it. For example, if you declare a class called `Rectangle`, the declaration of this class must include the declaration of its constructor function, and the name of the constructor function must be `Rectangle()`. So the declaration of the `Rectangle` class will look as follows:

```
      class Rectangle
{
public:
  Rectangle(); // The constructor
...
...
...
private:
...
...
...
};
```

- Don't mention any returned value for the constructor function. That is, the constructor function must be of type `void`, but do not mention it.

    At this point you are probably asking yourself, "What are the `public` and `private` keywords that are mentioned in the class declaration?" These keywords indicate the visibility of the data members and member functions of the class. You'll learn about these keywords later in this chapter. However, for now, just remember the final rule:

- The constructor function must be under the `public` keyword.

As stated, the constructor function always has a return value of type void (even though you shouldn't mention it in the prototype). As you'll soon see, usually the constructor function has one or more parameters.

The Destructor Function

The destructor function is mentioned in the class declaration as follows:

```
class Circle
{
public:
     ......
     ......
     ......
     ~Circle(); // The destructor
private:
     ......
     ......
     ......
};
```

Note the ~ character that precedes the prototype of the destructor function. (The ~ character can be typed by pressing the SHIFT key together with the key to the left of the 1 key.)

When writing the prototype of the destructor function, follow these rules:

- The name of the destructor function must be the same name as the class, but preceded by the ~ character. For example, if you declare a class called Rectangle, the name of the destructor function must be ~Rectangle. So the declaration of the Rectangle class looks as follows:

```
    class Rectangle
{
public:
    Rectangle();  // The constructor
    .......
    .......
    .......
    ~Rectangle(); // The destructor
private:
    .......
    .......
    .......
};
```

- Don't mention any returned value for the destructor function. That is, the constructor function must be of type void, but do not mention it.
- The destructor function does not have any parameters.

The *Public* and *Private* Keywords

As you saw, you include the prototypes of the functions and the declarations of the data members under the public or the private sections of the class declaration.

The public and private keywords tell the compiler the accessibility of the functions and the data members. For example, the SetRadius() function is defined under the public section. This means that any function in the program can call the SetRadius() function. However, because the CalculateArea() function is declared under the private section, only member functions of the Circle class can call the CalculateArea() function. In a similar manner, because the Radius variable is declared under the private section, only member functions of the Circle class program can update or read the value of this variable directly. However, if you would have declared the Radius variable under the public section, any function in the program could access (read and update) the Radius variable. To summarize, the class declaration defines the accessibility of its member functions and data members with the public and private keywords.

> **NOTE**
>
> The class declaration defines the accessibility of its member functions and data members with the public and private keywords.

The Circle Program

So far you've learned about some important syntax topics in C++ (for example, the syntax of class declaration). You're now ready to write a program that makes use of a class. The program that you'll write is called Circle.CPP.

Follow these steps to write the Circle.CPP program:

☐ Select New from the File menu.

☐ Save the new (empty) file as Circle.CPP in the C:\VCPROG\PRACTICE\CH02 directory.

☐ Type the code shown in Listing 2.2 in the Circle.CPP window.

Don't forget to save your work:

☐ Select Save from Visual C++'s File menu.

Listing 2.2. The Circle.CPP program.

```
/////////////////////////////
// Program Name: Circle.CPP
/////////////////////////////

///////////////////////
// #include files
///////////////////////
#include <iostream.h>

// Declare the Circle class
class CCircle
{
public:
  CCircle( int r);    // Constructor
  void   SetRadius(int r);
  int    GetRadius(void);
  void   DisplayArea(void);
  ~CCircle();          // Destructor
private:
  float CalculateArea(void);
  int m_Radius;
  int m_Color;
};


/////////////////////////////
// The constructor function
/////////////////////////////
CCircle::CCircle ( int r )
{

// Set the radius
m_Radius = r;

}


/////////////////////////////
// The destructor function
/////////////////////////////
```

continues

Listing 2.2. continued

```
CCircle::~CCircle ()
{

}


/////////////////////////////////
// Function Name: DisplayArea()
/////////////////////////////////
void CCircle::DisplayArea ( void )
{

float fArea;

fArea = CalculateArea ( );

// Print the area
cout << "The area of the circle is: " << fArea;


}


/////////////////////////////////
// Function Name: CalculateArea()
/////////////////////////////////
float CCircle::CalculateArea ( void )
{

float f;

f = (float) (3.14 * m_Radius * m_Radius);

return f;

}


void main(void)
{
// Create an object of class Circle with
// radius equals to 10.
CCircle MyCircle ( 10 );

// Display the area of the circle
MyCircle.DisplayArea();

}
```

NOTE

Usually, a class name starts with the C character (for example, the CCircle class, the CRectangle class, and so on).

Data member names usually start with the characters m_ (for example, m_Radius, m_Colors).

This is not a Visual C++ requirement, but it helps you to identify names of classes and data members by inspection.

The Circle.CPP Program's Code

Reviewing the Circle.CPP program's code.

The program #includes the iostream.h file:

```
#include <iostream.h>
```

It's necessary to #include this file because the cout statement is utilized in this program.

The Circle.CPP program declares the CCircle class as follows:

```
class CCircle
{
public:
  CCircle( int r);        // Constructor
  void    SetRadius(int r);
  int     GetRadius(void);
  void    DisplayArea(void);
  ~CCircle();             // Destructor
private:
  float CalculateArea(void);
  int m_Radius;
  int m_Color;
};
```

The public section contains five prototypes. The first is the prototype of the constructor function:

```
CCircle( int r);       // Constructor
```

As always, the prototype of the constructor function does not mention the fact that the function is of type void. Note that the constructor function has the parameter int r.

Then there are three more prototypes:

```
void    SetRadius(int r);
int     GetRadius(void);
void    DisplayArea(void);
```

Remember that you'll be able to access these functions from any function in the program, because these functions are `public` member functions.

The fifth prototype under the `public` section is the prototype of the destructor function:

```
~CCircle();
```

Again, the prototype of the destructor function does not mention the fact that this function is of type `void`. Note that the ~ character precedes the name of the destructor function.

The `private` section of the `CCircle` class declaration contains the prototype of one function and the declaration of two data members:

```
private:
  float CalculateArea(void);
  int m_Radius;
  int m_Color;
```

Because `CalculateArea()` is declared under the `private` section of the `CCircle` class declaration, you will be able to access the `CalculateArea()` function only from within member functions of the `CCircle` class.

Now take a look at the `main()` function:

```
void main(void)
{

// Create an object of class CCircle with radius
// equals to 10.
CCircle MyCircle ( 10 );

// Display the area of the circle
MyCircle.DisplayArea();

}
```

The first statement in `main()` creates an *object* called `MyCircle` of class `CCircle`:

```
CCircle MyCircle ( 10 );
```

This statement causes the execution of the constructor function. At first glance, this notation of executing the constructor function might look strange. However, as you'll see later in this chapter, this notation makes sense. For now, just accept the fact that this is the way to execute the constructor function. As stated, the statement creates an object called MyCircle of class CCircle.

Before continuing to examine the main() function, take a look at the constructor function:

```
/////////////////////////////
// The constructor function
/////////////////////////////
CCircle::CCircle ( int r )
{

// Set the radius
m_Radius = r;

}
```

As committed in its prototype, the constructor function has one parameter, int r. Note the first line of the function:

```
CCircle::CCircle ( int r )
{
...
...
...
}
```

The name of the function is preceded by the text CCircle::. This means that the CCircle() function is a member function of the CCircle class.

The code in the constructor function consists of a single statement:

```
Radius = r;
```

r is the parameter that was passed to the constructor function. You created the MyCircle (in main()) as follows:

```
CCircle MyCircle ( 10 );
```

Thus, 10 is passed to the constructor function.

The statement in the constructor function sets the value of m_Radius to r:

```
m_Radius = r;
```

Putting it all together, after creating the MyCircle object in main(), the constructor function is executed, and the constructor function's code sets the value of m_Radius to 10. Recall that m_Radius was declared as a data member of the CCircle class. As such, any member function (public or private) of the CCircle class can read or update m_Radius.

Okay, an object MyCircle of class CCircle was created, and its data member m_Radius was set to 10 with the constructor function.

The next statement in main() executes the DisplayArea() member function:

```
MyCircle.DisplayArea();
```

Recall that you declared the DisplayArea() function in the public section of the CCircle class declaration. Thus, main() can indeed access the DisplayArea() function. Note the dot (.) operation that separates the name of the object MyCircle and the DisplayArea() function. It tells the compiler to execute the DisplayArea() function on the MyCircle object.

The DisplayArea() function displays the area of the MyCircle object. Take a look at this function's code:

```
void Circle::DisplayArea ( void )
{

float fArea;

fArea = CalculateArea ( );

// Print the area
cout << "The area of the circle is: " << fArea;

}
```

Again, the compiler knows that this function is a member function of the CCircle class, because the first line uses the CCircle:: notation. The function declares a local float variable called fArea:

```
float fArea;
```

and then the CalculateArea() function is executed:

```
fArea = CalculateArea ( );
```

Recall that CalculateArea() is a member function of the CCircle class. Thus, DisplayArea() can call the CalculateArea() function.

The CalculateArea() function returns the area of the circle as a float number, and the next statement in DisplayArea() uses cout to display the value of fArea:

```
cout << "The area of the circle is: " << fArea;
```

This statement streams the value of fArea and the string The area of the circle is: into the screen.

Take a look at the CalculateArea() function. Again, the first line of the CalculateArea() function uses the CCircle:: text to indicate that this function is a member function of the CCircle class:

```
float CCircle::CalculateArea ( void )
{

float f;

f = (float) (3.14 * m_Radius * m_Radius);

return f;

}
```

The CalculateArea() function declares a local variable, f:

```
float f;
```

and then the area of the circle is calculated and assigned to the f variable:

```
f = (float) (3.14 * m_Radius * m_Radius);
```

Note that CalculateArea() does not have any parameters. So how does this function know to substitute 10 for m_Radius? Because during the execution of the Circle program, the history of executing the function is traced. First main() creates the MyCircle object:

```
Circle MyCircle ( 10 );
```

This causes the execution of the constructor function, which causes the m_Radius of the MyCircle object to be equal to 10. Then main() executes the DisplayArea() function on the MyCircle object:

```
MyCircle.DisplayArea();
```

DisplayArea() executes the CalculateArea() function:

```
fArea = CalculateArea ( );
```

Putting it all together, CalculateArea() "knows" to use 10 for the value of m_Radius because CalculateArea() is executed due to the fact that DisplayArea() was executed on the MyCircle object. CalculateArea() can access m_Radius because CalculateArea() is a member function of the CCircle class, and m_Radius is a data member of the CCircle class.

The last statement in CalculateArea() returns the calculated area:

```
return f;
```

The destructor function looks as follows:

```
CCircle::~CCircle ()
{


}
```

The first line of the destructor function starts with the CCircle:: text, an indication that this function is a member function of the CCircle class.

There is no code in the destructor function. However, you should know that the destructor function is executed whenever the MyCircle object is destroyed. In the case of the Circle program, the MyCircle object is destroyed when the program terminates.

Note that the SetRadius() and GetRadius() functions weren't used in the Circle.CPP program. You'll have a chance to use these functions later in this chapter.

Compiling/Linking the Circle.CPP Program

☐ Select Project from the Options menu and make sure that the Project Type is set to QuickWin application (.EXE) and that the Build Mode is set to Release.

To compile and link the Circle.CPP program:

☐ Select Rebuild All CIRCLE.EXE from the Project menu.

Visual C++ responds by compiling and linking the Circle program.

Now execute the Circle.EXE program:

☐ Select Execute CIRCLE.EXE from the Project menu.

As shown in Figure 2.12, the Circle program displays the message The area of the circle is: 314.

☐ Select Exit from the File menu to terminate the Circle program.

☐ Select Close from the File menu to close the Circle.CPP window.

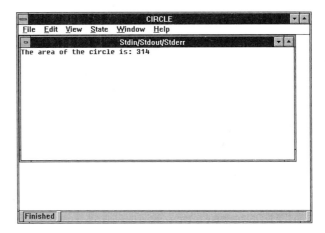

Figure 2.12.
The output of
the Circle.EXE
program.

The Circle2 Program

Summarizing what you've done in the Circle program: You declared a class called CCircle, you created an object MyCircle of class CCircle, and then you calculated and displayed the area of the MyCircle object.

Note that main() looks elegant and short; however, it doesn't demonstrate the object-oriented nature of C++. The Circle2 program demonstrates how you can create more than one object of class CCircle.

> **NOTE**
>
> C++ is known as an *OOP* language. OOP stands for *Object-Oriented Programming*. As you'll see in this and the following chapter, in C++ your program deals with objects.

The Circle2.CPP Program's Code

The Circle2.CPP program code appears in Listing 2.3.

Listing 2.3. The Circle2.CPP program.

```
/////////////////////////////
// Program Name: Circle2.CPP
/////////////////////////////
```

continues

Listing 2.3. continued

```
////////////////////
// #include files
////////////////////
#include <iostream.h>

// Declare the Circle class
class CCircle
{
public:
  CCircle( int r);      // Constructor
  void    SetRadius(int r);
  int     GetRadius(void);
  void    DisplayArea(void);
  ~CCircle();            // Destructor
private:
  float CalculateArea(void);
  int m_Radius;
  int m_Color;
};


/////////////////////////////
// The constructor function
/////////////////////////////
CCircle::CCircle ( int r )
{

// Set the radius
m_Radius = r;

}



/////////////////////////////
// The destructor function
/////////////////////////////
CCircle::~CCircle ()
{


}



///////////////////////////////
// Function Name: DisplayArea()
///////////////////////////////
void CCircle::DisplayArea ( void )
{
```

```
    float fArea;

    fArea = CalculateArea ( );

    // Print the area
    cout << "The area of the circle is: " << fArea;


}


/////////////////////////////////
// Function Name: CalculateArea()
/////////////////////////////////
float CCircle::CalculateArea ( void )
{

    float f;

    f = (float) (3.14 * m_Radius * m_Radius);

    return f;

}


void main(void)
{
// Create an object of class CCircle with
// radius equal to 10.
CCircle MyCircle ( 10 );


// Create an object of class CCircle with
// radius equal to 20.
CCircle HerCircle ( 20 );


// Create an object of class CCircle with
// radius equal to 30.
CCircle HisCircle ( 30 );


// Display the area of the circles
MyCircle.DisplayArea();
cout << "\n";
HerCircle.DisplayArea();
cout << "\n";
HisCircle.DisplayArea();
```

continues

Listing 2.3. continued

```
}
```

To review the code of the Circle2.CPP program:

Because the Circle2 program uses cout, you need to #include the iostream.h file:

```
#include <iostream.h>
```

Then the class declaration of the CCircle class appears:

```
class CCircle
{
public:
   CCircle( int r);      // Constructor
   void    SetRadius(int r);
   int     GetRadius(void);
   void    DisplayArea(void);
   ~CCircle();             // Destructor
private:
   float CalculateArea(void);
   int m_Radius;
   int m_Color;
};
```

Note that this is the same class declaration that appears in the Circle program discussed earlier in this chapter. The CCircle class also has the same constructor function as the Circle.CPP program, as well as the same destructor function, DisplayArea() function, and CalculateArea() function.

So in fact, the only thing different in the Circle2.CPP program is the code in the main() function:

```
void main(void)
{

// Create an object of class Circle with
// radius equal to 10.
CCircle MyCircle ( 10 );


// Create an object of class Circle with
// radius equal to 20.
CCircle HerCircle ( 20 );
```

```
// Create an object of class Circle with
// radius equal to 30.
CCircle HisCircle ( 30 );


// Display the area of the circles
MyCircle.DisplayArea();
cout << "\n";
HerCircle.DisplayArea();
cout << "\n";
HisCircle.DisplayArea();

}
```

The first statement in main() creates an object called MyCircle of class CCircle:

```
CCircle MyCircle ( 10 );
```

Note that the MyCircle object is created with its m_Radius data member equal to 10.

The next two statements create two more objects:

```
CCircle HerCircle ( 20 );
CCircle HisCircle ( 30 );
```

The HerCircle object is created with its m_Radius data member equal to 20, and the HisCircle object is created with its m_Radius data member equal to 30.

Now that these three objects are created, main() displays the areas of these circles by using the DisplayArea() member function on the corresponding circle objects:

```
MyCircle.DisplayArea();
cout << "\n";
HerCircle.DisplayArea();
cout << "\n";
HisCircle.DisplayArea();
```

Between the execution of the DisplayArea() functions, cout is used to print a carriage return/line feed character (\n) so that the areas will be displayed on different lines.

Take a look at the execution of the first DisplayArea() function:

```
MyCircle.DisplayArea();
```

When DisplayArea() is executed, it calls the CalculateArea() function. Recall that CalculateArea() makes use of the m_Radius data member. So which m_Radius will be used? The m_Radius of the MyCircle object will be used, because DisplayArea() works on the MyCircle object.

In a similar way, the statement

```
HerCircle.DisplayArea();
```

works on the HerCircle object. This means that when the CalculateArea() function is executed from DisplayArea(), the m_Radius of the HerCircle object will be used.

And of course, when displaying the area of the HisCircle object, the m_Radius of HisCircle will be used to calculate the area.

Compiling, Linking, and Executing the Circle2.CPP Program

To see your code in action:

☐ Select New from the File menu.

☐ Select Save As from the File menu and save your new window as Circle2.CPP in the directory C:\VCPROG\PRACTICE\CH02.

Now you have to type the Circle2.CPP program's code per Listing 2.3. Because most of the code already appears in the Circle.CPP program, use the Edit menu's Copy and Paste items to copy the Circle.CPP program's code to the Circle2.CPP program.

☐ Modify the main() function of Circle2.CPP so that it looks as shown in Listing 2.3.

☐ Save the Circle2.CPP file (by selecting Save from the File menu).

☐ Select Rebuild All CIRCLE2.CPP from the Project menu.

> *Visual C++ responds by compiling and linking the Circle2.CPP program.*

☐ Select Execute CIRCLE2.EXE from the Project menu.

> *Visual C++ responds by executing the Circle2.EXE program. As expected, the Circle2 program displays the areas of the three circle objects (see Figure 2.13).*

☐ Select Exit from the File menu to terminate the Circle2 program.

☐ You can now close all the open windows on the desktop by selecting Close from the File menu for each open window.

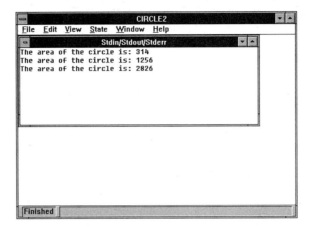

Figure 2.13.
The window of
the Circle2.EXE
program.

The Circle3.CPP Program

Note how short and elegant the Circle2 program's main() function is. It's easy to read, and more importantly, it's easy to maintain. For example, if you decide you need more accuracy in the calculation of the circle areas, you can change the CalculateArea() function's code. (For example, you can change 3.14 to 3.1415.)

If you type the class declaration in a file called CIRCLE.H, you can remove the CCircle class declaration from the Circle.CPP file and from the Circle2.CPP file, and you can replace that declaration with the statement

```
#include "CIRCLE.H"
```

Note that in both Circle.CPP and Circle2.CPP, m_Radius was set by the constructor function. However, you cannot change the value of m_Radius from within main(), because m_Radius was declared in the private section of the class declaration.

If you want to be able to change the value of m_Radius from within main(), you have to move the m_Radius declaration from the private section to the public section, as follows:

```
class Circle
{
public:
        Circle( int r);      // Constructor
  void  SetRadius(int r);
  int   GetRadius(void);
  void  DisplayArea(void);
        ~Circle();           // Destructor
  int m_Radius; // *** Here m_Radius is public  ***
```

```
private:
  float CalculateArea(void);
  // int m_Radius;
  int m_Color;
};
```

Then `main()` can read and write the value of `m_Radius`, as follows:

```
void main ( void)
{

// Create the MyCircle object with m_Radius equal to 10
CCircle MyCircle (10);

// Display the area of the circle
MyCircle.DisplayArea();
cout << "\n";

//Set the Radius of MyCircle to 20.
MyCircle.m_Radius = 20;

// Display the area of the circle
MyCircle.DisplayArea();

}
```

In a similar manner, you also can read the value of `m_Radius` from `main()`, as follows:

```
void main ( void)
{

// Create the MyCircle object with m_Radius equal to 10
CCircle MyCircle (10);

// Display the area of the circle
MyCircle.DisplayArea();
cout << "\n";

//Set the Radius of MyCircle to 20.
MyCircle.m_Radius = 20;

// Display the radius of the circle
cout << "The radius is: " << MyCircle.m_Radius;

}
```

There is nothing wrong with reading and updating the value of `m_Radius` directly from within `main()`. However, the recommended way of reading and writing important data members of a class is by using *access functions*. The access functions serve as focal points for reading and writing data into the data members. The advantage of using access functions is that they can perform additional tasks. For example, they can check whether the value assigned to m_Radius is a positive number.

NOTE

By using access functions, you can add more code that checks the validity of the data members.

The next program that you'll write is called Circle3.CPP. This program demonstrates how you can set and read the value of m_Radius with access functions.

Examining the Circle3.CPP Program's Code

The Circle3.CPP program is similar to the Circle.CPP and Circle2.CPP programs.

The Circle3.CPP program is shown in Listing 2.4.

Listing 2.4. The Circle3.CPP program.

```
/////////////////////////////
// Program Name: Circle3.CPP
/////////////////////////////

//////////////////////
// #include files
//////////////////////
#include <iostream.h>

// Declare the CCircle class
class CCircle
{
public:
  CCircle( int r);     // Constructor
  void    SetRadius(int r);
  int     GetRadius(void);
  void    DisplayArea(void);
  ~CCircle();          // Destructor
private:
  float CalculateArea(void);
  int m_Radius;
  int m_Color;
};
```

continues

Listing 2.4. continued

```
/////////////////////////
// The constructor function
/////////////////////////
CCircle::CCircle ( int r )
{

// Set the radius
m_Radius = r;

}


/////////////////////////
// The destructor function
/////////////////////////
CCircle::~CCircle ()
{


}


/////////////////////////////
// Function Name: SetRadius()
/////////////////////////////
void CCircle::SetRadius ( int r)
{

m_Radius = r;

}


/////////////////////////////
// Function Name: GetRadius()
/////////////////////////////
int CCircle::GetRadius ( void)
{

return m_Radius;

}

/////////////////////////////
// Function Name: DisplayArea()
/////////////////////////////
void CCircle::DisplayArea ( void )
{
```

```
    float fArea;

    fArea = CalculateArea ( );

    // Print the area
    cout << "The area of the circle is: " << fArea;


}


/////////////////////////////////
// Function Name: CalculateArea()
/////////////////////////////////
float CCircle::CalculateArea ( void )
{

    float f;

    f = (float) (3.14 * m_Radius * m_Radius);

    return f;

}


void main ( void)
{

    // Create the MyCircle object with
    // m_Radius equal to 10
    CCircle MyCircle (10);

    // Display the area of the circle
    MyCircle.DisplayArea();
    cout << "\n";

    //Set the m_Radius of MyCircle to 20.
    MyCircle.SetRadius (20);

    // Display the radius of the circle
    cout << "The Radius is: " << MyCircle.GetRadius();

}
```

As shown in Listing 2.4, the m_Radius data member in Circle3.CPP is in the private section. As such, main() cannot access this data member directly. For example, you can't have the following statement in main():

```
//Not allowed when m_Radius is private
MyCircle.m_Radius = 20;
```

Instead, two access functions are used. The SetRadius() member function is used to set the m_Radius data member, and the GetRadius() member function is used to read it. Recall that SetRadius() and GetRadius() are defined as public in the CCircle class declaration. This means that main() can use these functions as follows:

```
void main ( void)
{

// Create the MyCircle object with
// m_Radius equal to 10
CCircle MyCircle (10);

// Display the area of the circle
MyCircle.DisplayArea();
cout << "\n";

//Set the Radius of MyCircle to 20.
MyCircle.SetRadius (20);

// Display the radius of the circle
cout << "The Radius is: " << MyCircle.GetRadius();

}
```

The SetRadius() function sets the value of m_Radius:

```
void CCircle::SetRadius ( int r)
{

m_Radius = r;

}
```

And the GetRadius() function returns the value of m_Radius:

```
int CCircle::GetRadius ( void)
{

return m_Radius;

}
```

As previously stated, the `SetRadius()` and `GetRadius()` functions are called *access functions*. Typically, these functions contain additional code. For example, the `SetRadius()` function may include code that checks whether `m_Radius` is set within a certain range.

To see the Circle3.CPP program in action:

☐ Select New from the File menu.

☐ Select Save As from the File menu, and save your new file as `Circle3.CPP` in the directory `C:\VCPROG\PRACTICE\CH02`.

☐ Copy the `Circle2.CPP` file into the `Circle3.CPP` file (that is, use Copy and Paste from the Edit menu).

☐ Add the `SetRadius()` and `GetRadius()` functions to the `Circle3.CPP` file (see Listing 2.4 for the code of these functions).

☐ Modify the `main()` function of Circle3.CPP in accordance with Listing 2.4.

☐ Select Save from the File menu to save the `Circle3.CPP` file.

☐ Select Rebuild All CIRCLE3.EXE from the Project menu to compile/link the Circle3 program.

☐ Select Execute CIRCLE3.EXE from the Project menu.

The Circle3.EXE window appears, as shown in Figure 2.14.

Figure 2.14.
The Circle3.EXE
program.

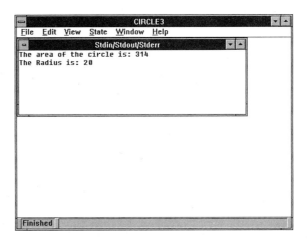

43

To terminate the Circle3 program:

☐ Select Exit from the File menu.

Overloaded Functions

In C++, you can use the same name for more than one function. For example, you can declare two SetRadius() functions in the class declaration of the CCircle class.

The Circle4.CPP program demonstrates how a program can have two different functions with the same name. Such functions are called *overloaded* functions.

The Circle4.CPP program is shown in Listing 2.5.

Listing 2.5. The Circle4.CPP program.

```
////////////////////////////////
// Program Name: Circle4.CPP
////////////////////////////////

////////////////////
// #include files
////////////////////
#include <iostream.h>

// Declare the CCircle class
class CCircle
{
public:
  CCircle( int r);     // Constructor

  void   SetRadius(int r);          // Overloaded
  void   SetRadius(int r, int c );  // Overloaded

  int    GetRadius(void);
  void   DisplayArea(void);
  ~CCircle();             // Destructor

  int m_Color;

private:
  float CalculateArea(void);
  int m_Radius;
  // int Color;
};
```

```
/////////////////////////
// The constructor function
/////////////////////////
CCircle::CCircle ( int r )
{

// Set the radius
m_Radius = r;
m_Color = 0;

}


/////////////////////////
// The destructor function
/////////////////////////
CCircle::~CCircle ()
{


}


///////////////////////////
// Function Name: SetRadius()
///////////////////////////
void CCircle::SetRadius ( int r)
{

m_Radius = r;
m_Color = 255;

}


///////////////////////////
// Function Name: SetRadius()
///////////////////////////
void CCircle::SetRadius ( int r, int c)
{

m_Radius = r;
m_Color = c;

}


///////////////////////////
// Function Name: GetRadius()
///////////////////////////
```

continues

Listing 2.5. continued

```cpp
int CCircle::GetRadius ( void)
{

return m_Radius;

}

///////////////////////////////
// Function Name: DisplayArea()
///////////////////////////////
void CCircle::DisplayArea ( void )
{

float fArea;

fArea = CalculateArea ( );

// Print the area
cout << "The area of the circle is: " << fArea;


}


///////////////////////////////
// Function Name: CalculateArea()
///////////////////////////////
float CCircle::CalculateArea ( void )
{

float f;

f = (float) (3.14 * m_Radius * m_Radius);

return f;

}


void main ( void)
{
// Create the MyCircle object with Radius equal to 10
CCircle MyCircle (10);

// Display the radius of the circle
cout << "The Radius is: " << MyCircle.GetRadius();
cout << "\n";
```

```
// Display the color of the circle
cout << "The Color of the circle is: " << MyCircle.m_Color;
cout << "\n";

//Set the Radius of MyCircle to 20.
MyCircle.SetRadius (20);

// Display the radius of the circle
cout << "The Radius is: " << MyCircle.GetRadius();
cout << "\n";

// Display the color of the circle
cout << "The Color of the circle is: " << MyCircle.m_Color;
cout << "\n";

// Use the other SetRadius() function
MyCircle.SetRadius (40, 100);

// Display the radius of the circle
cout << "The Radius is: " << MyCircle.GetRadius();
cout << "\n";

// Display the color of the circle
cout << "The Color of the circle is: " << MyCircle.m_Color;

}
```

Examining the Circle4.CPP Program's Code

The Circle4.CPP program #includes the iostream.h file (because it uses the cout statement):

```
#include <iostream.h>
```

And then the CCircle class is declared:

```
class CCircle
{
public:
  Circle( int r);     // Constructor

  void    SetRadius(int r);          // Overloaded
  void    SetRadius(int r, int c );  // Overloaded

  int     GetRadius(void);
  void    DisplayArea(void);
  ~Circle();              // Destructor
```

```
    int m_Color;

private:
  float CalculateArea(void);
  int m_Radius;
  // int m_Color;
};
```

This CCircle class is similar to the CCircle classes in the previous programs, except that the int m_Color data member has been moved from the private section to the public section. (This was done because you want to access m_Color from main(), and you don't want to write an access function such as GetColor().)

Also, the CCircle class declaration now has a set of overloaded functions:

```
void    SetRadius(int r);          // Overloaded
void    SetRadius(int r, int c );   // Overloaded
```

That is, the CCircle class has two SetRadius() functions, one with a single parameter (int r) and the other with two parameters (int r, int c).

The constructor function of this CCircle class is similar to the constructor functions that were introduced previously in this chapter, except that this constructor function also sets the value of m_Color to 0:

```
CCircle::CCircle ( int r )
{

// Set the radius
m_Radius = r;
m_Color = 0;

}
```

The destructor function is identical to the destructor function of the previous programs (it has no code in it).

One of the SetRadius() functions in Circle4.CPP sets m_Radius to the value that was passed to it, and it also sets m_Color to 255:

```
void CCircle::SetRadius ( int r)
{

m_Radius = r;
m_Color = 255;

}
```

The other SetRadius() function in Circle4.CPP sets m_Radius to the value that was passed to it, and it also sets the m_Color to the value that was passed to it:

```
void CCircle::SetRadius ( int r, int c)
{

m_Radius = r;
m_Color = c;

}
```

The GetRadius() function is identical to the GetRadius() functions of the previous programs:

```
int CCircle::GetRadius ( void)
{

return m_Radius;

}
```

Here is the main() function of Circle4.CPP:

```
void main ( void)
{

// Create the MyCircle object with
// Radius equal to 10
Circle MyCircle (10);

// Display the radius of the circle
cout << "The Radius is: " << MyCircle.GetRadius();
cout << "\n";

// Display the color of the circle
cout << "The Color of the circle is: " << MyCircle.m_Color;
cout << "\n";

//Set the Radius of MyCircle to 20.
MyCircle.SetRadius (20);

// Display the radius of the circle
cout << "The Radius is: " << MyCircle.GetRadius();
cout << "\n";

// Display the color of the circle
cout << "The Color of the circle is: " << MyCircle.m_Color;
cout << "\n";

// Use the other SetRadius() function
MyCircle.SetRadius (40, 100);

// Display the radius of the circle
cout << "The Radius is: " << MyCircle.GetRadius();
```

```
cout << "\n";

// Display the color of the circle
cout << "The Color of the circle is: " << MyCircle.m_Color;

}
```

The main() function starts by creating the MyCircle() object:

```
Circle MyCircle (10);
```

Recall that the constructor function is executed whenever an object is created. Because 10 is passed in this statement, the constructor function sets m_Radius of the MyCircle object to 10. It also sets m_Color to 0. So after creating the MyCircle object, the MyCircle object has m_Radius equal to 10 and m_Color equal to 0.

This is verified with the next two statements in main():

```
cout << "The Radius is: " << MyCircle.GetRadius();
cout << "\n";

cout << "The Color of the circle is: " << MyCircle.m_Color;
cout << "\n";
```

Note that m_Color can be accessed with MyCircle.m_Color because m_Color was moved to the public section in the CCircle class declaration.

As shown in Figure 2.15, the Circle4 program outputs the messages The Radius is: 10 and The Color of the circle is: 0.

Figure 2.15.
The Circle4.EXE
program.

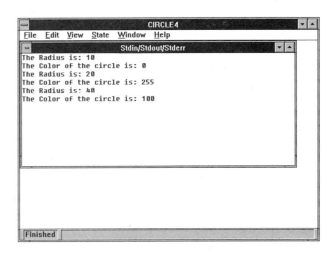

The next statement in main() sets the m_Radius data members of MyCircle to 20:

```
MyCircle.SetRadius (20);
```

The question is, which SetRadius() function will be executed? Remember that there are two SetRadius() functions! Well, the C++ compiler is smart. It knows that there are two SetRadius() functions, and because you specified only one parameter in this statement, it knows that you want to execute the SetRadius() function with the one parameter.

To verify that the compiler uses the SetRadius() function, which has one parameter, the next two statements in main() display the m_Radius and the m_Color:

```
cout << "The Radius is: " << MyCircle.GetRadius();
cout << "\n";

cout << "The Color of the circle is: " << MyCircle.m_Color;
cout << "\n";
```

As shown in Figure 2.15, the Circle4 program displays the messages The Radius is: 20 and The Color of the circle is: 255.

Indeed, m_Radius should be equal to 20 because you passed 20 as the parameter of SetRadius(), and m_Color should be equal to 255 because the SetRadius() function that was executed sets m_Color to 255.

The next statement in main() uses the other SetRadius() function:

```
MyCircle.SetRadius (40, 100);
```

The compiler knows that you mean to use the other SetRadius() function because you supplied two parameters for this function. The next two statements in main() display m_Radius and m_Color:

```
cout << "The Radius is: " << MyCircle.GetRadius();
cout << "\n";

cout << "The Color of the circle is: " << MyCircle.m_Color;
```

☐ As you can see from Figure 2.15, the Circle4 program displays the messages The Radius is: 40 and The Color of the Circle is: 100. Indeed, you supplied 40 as the first parameter of SetRadius() and 100 as its second parameter.

☐ Select Save As from the File menu and save the new file as Circle4.CPP in the directory C:\VCPROG\PRACTICE\CH02.

☐ Copy the contents of the `Circle3.CPP` file to the `Circle4.CPP` file and then modify the Circle4.CPP program in accordance with Listing 2.5.

☐ Save the Circle4.CPP program in the `C:\VCPROG\PRACTICE\CH02` directory (that is, select Save from the File menu).

☐ Select Rebuild All CIRCLE4.EXE from the Project menu.

   Visual C++ responds by compiling and linking the Circle4 program.

☐ Select Execute CIRCLE4.EXE from the Project menu.

The CIRCLE4.EXE window appears as shown in Figure 2.15.

To terminate the Circle4.EXE program:

☐ Select Exit from Circle4.EXE's File menu.

Declaring Variables in C++ Versus C

In C, you have to declare your variables at the beginning of the function. For example, the following `main()` declares the variable `i` at its beginning and then uses the variable 1,000 lines later:

```
void main(void)
{
i = 3;
.....
.....
.....
/* 1,000 lines of code */
.....
.....
.....

while (i<0)
     {
     ...
     ...
     ...
     }

}
```

In C++ you don't have to declare your variables at the beginning of the function. For example, that C `main()` function can be written in C++ as follows:

```
void main(void)
{
```

```
.....
.....
.....
// 1,000 lines of code
.....
.....
.....
int i =3;
while (i<0)
      {
      ...
      ...
      ...
      }

}
```

Of course, don't try to use the i variable before it is declared.

Default Parameters

Another convenient feature in C++ that doesn't exist in C is the concept of default parameters.

In C, you can declare the following function prototype:

```
int MyFunction (int a,
                int b,
                int c,
                int d);
```

and the actual function may look as follows:

```
int MyFunction (int a,
                int b,
                int c,
                int d)
{
...
...
...
}
```

If you execute MyFunction() from within main(), you must supply four parameters, because that's what you specified in the prototype of the function.

C++ is more liberal than C. The designers of C++ knew that although you specified four parameters for the MyFunction() function, in most cases you'll use the same values for some of the parameters of the function. Thus, in C++ you can specify default parameters in the prototype of MyFunction() as follows:

```
int MyFunction ( int a = 10,
                 int b = 20,
                 int c = 30,
                 int d = 40 );
```

And from `main()`, you can execute `MyFunction()` as follows:

```
main()
{
...
...
...
int iResult;
iResult = MyFunction();
...
...
...
}
```

Because you didn't supply any parameters for `MyFunction()`, the compiler will automatically interpret your statement as:

```
main()
{
...
...
...
int iResult;
iResult = MyFunction(10,
                     20
                     30
                     40);
...
...
...
}
```

In addition, you can override the default parameters, as follows:

```
main()
{
...
...
...
int iResult;
iResult = MyFunction(100,
                     200);
...
...
...
}
```

Because you didn't supply any third and fourth parameters to `MyFunction()`, the compiler will automatically interpret your statement as

```
main()
{
...
...
...
int iResult;
iResult = MyFunction(100,
                     200,
                     30,
                     40);
...
...
...
}
```

That is, you overrode the first and second parameters, and the compiler automatically substituted the third and fourth parameters (as indicated in the prototype of the function).

NOTE

When using a default parameter, you must use all the default parameters that appear after that parameter. For example, the following is not allowed:

```
void main(void)
{
...
...
...
int iResult;
iResult = MyFunction(100,
                      ,  // Not allowed
                     300
                     400);
...
...
...
}
```

That is, because you overrode the third parameter, you must specify a value for the second parameter as well.

Summary

In this chapter, you learned about the major differences between C and C++. As you can see, the C++ concepts aren't difficult. They represent the natural evolution of the C programming language. You can use C++ to write complex programs that are easy to write and understand.

Consider the following declaration of the CPersonGoToWork class:

```
class CPersonGoToWork
{
public:
      CPersonGoToWork(); // The constructor
    void WakeUp(void);
      void Wash(void);
      void Dress(void);
      void Eat(void);
      void TakeBus(void);
      void TakeCar(void);
      void TakeSubway(void);
      void TurnPCon(void);
      void TurnIrrigationOn(void);
      void CalibrateRadar(void);
    ~CPersonGoToWork(); // The destructor

private:
      .....
      .....
      .....
}
```

This class contains member functions that display cartoon characters doing something during the course of going to work. For example, the TakeCar() function displays a person getting into a car, and the TakeSubway() function displays a person taking a subway to work.

Consider the following main() program:

```
void main(void)
{
// Create an object called Jim
// for Mr. Jim Smart the programmer.
CPersonGoToWork Jim;

// Show Jim going to work.
Jim.WakeUp(void);
Jim.Wash(void);
Jim.Dress(void);
Jim.Eat(void);
Jim.TakeCar(void);
Jim.TurnPCon(void);
```

```
// Create an object called Jill
// for Ms. Jill Officer the police woman.
CPersonGoToWork Jill;

// Show Jill going to work.
Jill.WakeUp(void);
Jill.Wash(void);
Jill.Dress(void);
Jill.Eat(void);
Jill.TakeCar(void);
Jill.CalibrateRadar();


// Create an object called Don
// for Mr. Don Farmer the farmer.
CPersonGoToWork Don;

// Show Don going to work.
Don.WakeUp(void);
Don.Wash(void);
Don.Dress(void);
Don.Eat(void);
Don.TurnIrrigationOn(void);

}
```

As you can see, main() can be written in a matter of minutes, and it can be easily understood and maintained. Of course, the real work of writing such a program is writing the member functions, such as in the CPersonGoToWork class. But once the class is ready, writing main() is very easy! This is the main advantage of using Visual C++ to write Windows applications. The Microsoft Foundation Class (MFC) is supplied with the Visual C++ package. So in fact, the majority of your program is written already. All that you have to do is just understand the powerful member functions that exist in the MFC and apply them to your Windows applications.

The next chapter discusses other important C++ concepts. Then, starting with Chapter 4, "Your First True Windows Application," you'll learn how to write Windows applications.

3

Class Hierarchy and Other C++ Topics

In this chapter you'll learn about additional C++ topics that are prerequisites for the rest of the book.

As stated in the last chapter, you'll start writing true Windows applications in Chapter 4, "Your First True Windows Application." In this chapter, however, you'll learn the material by writing DOS QuickWin programs.

The Rect Program

Now you'll write the RECT.CPP program.

☐ Set the Project Type to QuickWin (select Project from the Options menu and set the Project Type to QuickWin Application (.EXE)).

☐ Select New from Visual C++'s File menu.

☐ Select Save As from the File menu and save the new file as Rect.CPP in the directory C:\VCPROG\PRACTICE\CH03.

☐ Type the code in Listing 3.1 in the RECT.CPP window.

☐ Select Rebuild All RECT.EXE from the Project menu.

   Visual C++ responds by compiling/linking the Rect program.

☐ Select Execute RECT.EXE from the Project menu.

   Visual C++ responds by executing the Rect.EXE program. As shown in Figure 3.1, the Rect.EXE program displays a message telling you the area of a rectangle.

Figure 3.1.
The Rect.EXE
program.

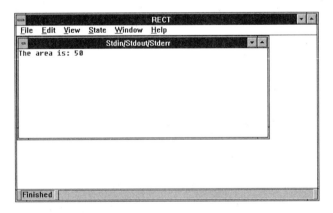

☐ Select Exit from the File menu to terminate the Rect.EXE program.

Listing 3.1. The Rect.CPP program.

```
//////////////////////////
// Program Name: Rect.CPP
//////////////////////////
```

```
///////////
// #include
///////////
#include <iostream.h>


/////////////////////////////////////
// The CRectangle class declaration
/////////////////////////////////////
class CRectangle
{
public:
      CRectangle(int w, int h);   // Constructor

      void DisplayArea (void);   // Member function

      ~CRectangle();             // Destructor

      int m_Width;   // Data member
      int m_Height;  // Data member

};


//////////////////////////////
// The constructor function
//////////////////////////////
CRectangle::CRectangle( int w, int h)
{

m_Width = w;
m_Height = h;

}


//////////////////////////////
// The destructor function
//////////////////////////////
CRectangle::~CRectangle()
{



}


//////////////////////////////////
// Function Name: DisplayArea()
//////////////////////////////////
```

continues

Listing 3.1. continued

```
void CRectangle::DisplayArea(void)
{

int iArea;

iArea = m_Width * m_Height;

cout << "The area is: " << iArea << "\n";

}

void main(void)
{

CRectangle MyRectangle ( 10, 5 );

MyRectangle.DisplayArea();


}
```

The Rect.CPP Program's Code

Reviewing the Rect.CPP program's code:

The program starts by #including the iostream.h file (because the cout statement is used):

```
#include <iostream.h>
```

And then the program declares the CRectangle class:

```
class CRectangle
{
public:
      CRectangle(int w, int h);  // Constructor

      void DisplayArea (void);   // Member function

      ~CRectangle();             // Destructor

      int m_Width;   // Data member
      int m_Height;  // Data member

};
```

The CRectangle class declaration contains its constructor function, destructor function, DisplayArea() function, and two data members.

The constructor function initializes the data members:

```
CRectangle::CRectangle( int w, int h)
{

m_Width = w;
m_Height = h;

}
```

There is no code in the destructor function. The DisplayArea() function calculates the area of the rectangle and displays it:

```
void CRectangle::DisplayArea(void)
{

int iArea;

iArea = m_Width * m_Height;

cout << "The area is: " << iArea << "\n";

}
```

main() creates an object called MyRectangle of class CRectangle:

```
CRectangle MyRectangle ( 10, 5 );
```

Because (10,5) is passed to the constructor function, the MyRectangle object has a width of 10 and a height of 5.

main() then displays the area of MyRectangle, as follows:

```
MyRectangle.DisplayArea();
```

As you can see, you can use the CRectangle class to calculate the area of the rectangle.

The CRectangle class has a limitation: you can't use it to calculate the area of other rectangles. For example, suppose that you want to calculate the area of a rectangle with a width of 20 and a height of 5. What would you do? The first thing that comes to mind is to add SetWidth() and SetHeight() member functions that set the values of m_Width and m_Height.

Thus, the `CRectangle` class declaration would look as follows:

```
/////////////////////////////////
// The CRectangle class declaration
/////////////////////////////////
class CRectangle
{
public:
      CRectangle(int w, int h);   // Constructor

      void DisplayArea (void);

      void SetWidth ( int w );
      void SetHeight ( int h );

      ~CRectangle();              // Destructor

      int m_Width;
      int m_Height;
};
```

And the `SetWidth()` and `SetHeight()` member functions might look as follows:

```
///////////////////////////////
// Function Name: SetWidth()
///////////////////////////////
void CRectangle::SetWidth(int w)
{

m_Width = w;

}
```

```
///////////////////////////////
// Function Name: SetHeight()
///////////////////////////////
void CRectangle::SetHeight(int h)
{

m_Height = h;

}
```

Your `main()` can then look as follows:

```
void main(void)
{
```

```
// Create the MyRectangle with width equal to 10
// and height equal to 5
CRectangle MyRectangle (10,5);

// Display the area
MyRectangle.DisplayArea();

// Change the width and height
MyRectangle.SetWidth(20);
MyRectangle.SetHeight(5);

// Display the area
MyRectangle.DisplayArea();

}
```

What If You Need Additional Member Functions?

There's nothing wrong with the previous implementation. However, this solution assumes that you own the source code of the CRectangle class and hence can modify it at any time. In reality, the software vendors do not supply you with the source code of the class! For one thing, they don't want you to have the source code because they want to protect their product. Also, they don't want you to mess with the source code of the class because you can do damage to the class by accident. For example, the MFC is a complex set of classes. Microsoft tested the classes and found them to be in working condition. By not supplying you with the source code of the classes, they're actually protecting you from yourself. You should be able to write Windows applications with the MFC without modifying the source code of the classes.

Nevertheless, in many cases you will need to add some of your own member functions, just as you need to add the SetWidth() and SetHeight() functions to the CRectangle class.

Class Hierarchy

To solve the problem discussed previously, the class hierarchy of C++ was introduced. Basically, the class hierarchy enables you to create a new class from the original class. The original class is called the *base* class, and the class that you create from the original class is called the *derived* class. The derived class inherits data members and member functions from its base class. Once you create the derived class, you can add member functions and data members to it.

Now you can create a class called `CNewRectangle` from the `CRectangle` class. (The base class will be `CRectangle`, and the derived class will be `CNewRectangle`.)

Listing 3.2 shows the Rect2.CPP program's code.

Listing 3.2. The Rect2.CPP program.

```
////////////////////////////
// Program Name: Rect2.CPP
////////////////////////////


////////////////
// #include
////////////////
#include <iostream.h>


//////////////////////////////////////////////////
// The CRectangle class declaration (base class)
//////////////////////////////////////////////////
class CRectangle
{
public:
     CRectangle(int w, int h);  // Constructor

     void DisplayArea (void);

     ~CRectangle();             // Destructor


     int m_Width;
     int m_Height;

};


//////////////////////////////////////////////////
// The declaration of the derived class CNewRectangle
//////////////////////////////////////////////////
class CNewRectangle : public CRectangle
{

public:
     CNewRectangle(int w, int h);  // Constructor
```

```
    void SetWidth (int w);
    void SetHeight (int h);


    ~CNewRectangle();               // Destructor

};


//////////////////////////////////////////////////
// The constructor function of CRectangle (base)
//////////////////////////////////////////////////
CRectangle::CRectangle( int w, int h)
{

cout << "In the constructor of the base class" << "\n";

m_Width = w;
m_Height = h;

}



//////////////////////////////////////////////////
// The destructor function of CRectangle (base)
//////////////////////////////////////////////////

CRectangle::~CRectangle()
{

cout << "In the destructor of the base class" << "\n";

}


////////////////////////////////////////////
// Function Name: DisplayArea() (base)
////////////////////////////////////////////
void CRectangle::DisplayArea(void)
{

int iArea;

iArea = m_Width * m_Height;

cout << "The area is: " << iArea << "\n";

}
```

continues

Listing 3.2. continued

```
/////////////////////////////////////////////////////
// The constructor function of CNewRectangle (derived)
/////////////////////////////////////////////////////
CNewRectangle::CNewRectangle( int w,
                              int h):CRectangle( w, h)
{

cout << "In the constructor of the derived class" << "\n";

}


/////////////////////////////////////////////////////
// The destructor function of CNewRectangle (derived)
/////////////////////////////////////////////////////
CNewRectangle::~CNewRectangle()

{

cout << "In the destructor of the derived class" << "\n";

}


////////////////////////////////////////
// Function Name: SetWidth() (derived)
////////////////////////////////////////
void CNewRectangle::SetWidth(int w)
{

m_Width = w;

}


////////////////////////////////////////
// Function Name: SetHeight() (derived)
////////////////////////////////////////
void CNewRectangle::SetHeight(int h)
{

m_Height = h;

}


void main(void)
{
```

```
CNewRectangle MyRectangle (10, 5);

MyRectangle.DisplayArea();


MyRectangle.SetWidth (100);
MyRectangle.SetHeight (20);


MyRectangle.DisplayArea();



}
```

The Rect2.CPP Program's Code

The Rect2.CPP program declares the CRectangle class exactly as it was declared in the Rect.CPP program:

```
class CRectangle
{
public:
       CRectangle(int w, int h);   // Constructor

       void DisplayArea (void);

       ~CRectangle();                // Destructor


     int m_Width;
     int m_Height;

};
```

The CRectangle class is used as the base class. Assume that you don't have the source code of this class, and therefore you can't add or delete any of its code.

The Rect2 program then declares a class called CNewRectangle. This class is derived from the CRectangle class:

```
//////////////////////////////////////////////////
// The declaration of the derived class CNewRectangle
//////////////////////////////////////////////////
class CNewRectangle : public CRectangle
{

public:
    CNewRectangle(int w, int h);   // Constructor
```

```
        void SetWidth (int w);
        void SetHeight (int h);

        ~CNewRectangle();                // Destructor

};
```

Note the first line of the declaration of the derived class:

```
class CNewRectangle : public CRectangle
{
....
....
....
};
```

The text : `public CRectangle` is an indication that `CNewRectangle` is derived from `CRectangle`.

The derived class has a constructor function, a destructor function, a `SetWidth()` function, and a `SetHeight()` function. As you'll soon see, the `CNewRectangle` class has all the "features" of the `CRectangle` class. For example, even though the data members `m_Width` and `m_Height` do not appear as data members of `CNewRectangle`, `CNewRectangle` inherits these data members from `CRectangle`. Also, even though `CNewRectangle` doesn't have the `DisplayArea()` function as one of its member functions, for all purposes you can regard `CNewRectangle` as if it had this member function. Why? Because `CNewRectangle` inherits the `DisplayArea()` function from its base class.

The constructor function of the base class sets the values of the data members of the class:

```
CRectangle::CRectangle( int w, int h)
{

cout << "In the constructor of the base class" << "\n";

m_Width = w;
m_Height = h;

}
```

Note that the `cout` statement is used in this constructor function so that you'll be able to tell during the execution of the program that this constructor function was executed.

Here is the destructor function of the base class:

```
CRectangle::~CRectangle()
```

```
{

cout << "In the destructor of the base class" << "\n";

}
```

Again, the cout statement is used so that during the execution of the program you'll be able to tell that this function was executed.

The DisplayArea() function of the base class calculates and displays the area:

```
void CRectangle::DisplayArea(void)
{

int iArea;

iArea = m_Width * m_Height;

cout << "The area is: " << iArea << "\n";

}
```

Now take a look at the constructor function of the derived class:

```
CNewRectangle::CNewRectangle(int w,
                            int h):CRectangle(w,h)
{

cout << "In the constructor of the derived class" << "\n";

}
```

The first line of this function includes the text

```
:CRectangle(w,h)
```

This means that when an object of class CNewRectangle is created, the constructor function of the base class is executed and the parameters (w,h) are passed to the constructor function of the base class.

The code in the constructor function of the derived class uses the cout statement so that during the execution of the program you'll be able to tell that this function was executed.

Here is the destructor function of the derived class:

```
CNewRectangle::~CNewRectangle()
{

cout << "In the destructor of the derived class" << "\n";

}
```

The cout statement is used again so that you'll be able to tell whenever this function is executed.

Here are the SetWidth() and SetHeight() functions of the derived class:

```
void CNewRectangle::SetWidth(int w)
{

m_Width = w;

}


void CNewRectangle::SetHeight(int h)
{

m_Height = h;

}
```

main() starts by creating an object of class CNewRectangle:

```
CNewRectangle MyRectangle (10, 5);
```

This statement creates the MyRectangle object of class CNewRectangle. However, because CNewRectangle is derived from CRectangle, you can use member functions from the base class:

```
MyRectangle.DisplayArea();
```

This statement executes the DisplayArea() member function of the base class (even though the derived class doesn't have this member function in its class declaration). This is possible because CNewRectangle inherited the member functions of CRectangle.

main() then uses the SetWidth() and SetHeight() member functions to set new values for m_Width and m_Height:

```
MyRectangle.SetWidth (100);
MyRectangle.SetHeight (20);
```

And finally, main() uses the DisplayArea() function to display the area of the rectangle:

```
MyRectangle.DisplayArea();
```

Now that you understand the Rect2.CPP program's code, watch it in action:

☐ Set the Project Type to QuickWin. That is, select Project from the Options menu and set the Project Type to QuickWin Application (.EXE).

☐ Select New from Visual C++'s File menu.

☐ Save your new file as RECT2.CPP in the directory C:\VCPROG\PRACTICE\CH03.

☐ Type the code found in Listing 3.2 in the RECT2.CPP window.

You can now compile/link and execute the Rect2.CPP program:

☐ Select Rebuild All RECT2.EXE from the Project menu.

☐ Select Execute RECT2.EXE from the Project menu.

The window of the Rect2.EXE program is shown in Figure 3.2.

Figure 3.2.
The Rect2.EXE
program.

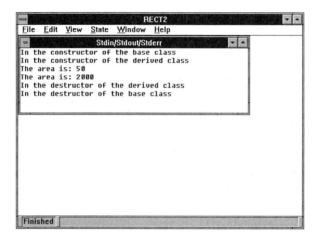

As you can see from Figure 3.2, the Rect2 program first executes the constructor function of the base class, and then it executes the constructor function of the derived class. This happens due to the statement

```
CNewRectangle MyRectangle(10, 5);
```

in main().

Per Figure 3.2, the Rect2 program then displays the area of a rectangle with a width of 10 and a height of 5.

Then Rect2 displays the area of a rectangle with a width of 100 and a height of 20.

And finally, when the main() function is completed, the MyRectangle object is destroyed. As you can see from Figure 3.2, the destructor function of the derived class was executed, and then the destructor function of the base class was executed.

Note from this discussion that the constructor function of the base class was executed, and then the constructor function of the derived class was executed. And when the object was destroyed, the destructor function of the derived class was executed and then the destructor function of the base class was executed.

Class Hierarchy Pictorial Representation

The class hierarchy relationship between CRectangle and CNewRectangle is shown in Figure 3.3.

Figure 3.3.
The class hierarchy
of CRectangle
and
CNewRectangle.

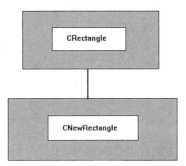

The relationship shown in Figure 3.3 is simple, and you probably don't even need a diagram to show this relationship. However, the class hierarchy can be as complex as you want it to be. For example, you may want to construct another derived class, called CNewNewRectangle, which is derived from the CNewRectangle class. In this case, the class declaration of CNewNewRectangle would look as follows:

```
class CNewNewRectangle: public CNewRectangle
{
....
....
....
};
```

In this declaration, CNewNewRectangle serves as the derived class, and CNewRectangle serves as the base class. Now you can declare another derived class with CNewNewRectangle as the base class. Figure 3.4 is a pictorial representation of a complex class hierarchy. You should be aware, however, that this class hierarchy isn't being demonstrated for academic reasons. In fact, as you'll see later in this book, the class hierarchy of the MFC is far more complex than the one shown in Figure 3.4.

Figure 3.4.
A complex class
hierarchy.

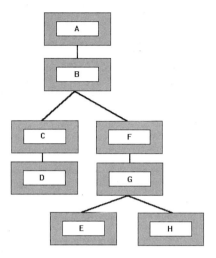

So how can you make use of a pictorial representation of a class hierarchy? By looking at the class hierarchy, you can tell which member functions you can execute. For example, by looking at Figure 3.4, you can tell that you can execute a member function that exists in class A on objects of classes B, C, D, E, F, G, and H. You can execute a member function that appears in class F on an object of classes G, E, and H. But you can't execute a member function that appears in class F on objects of classes A, B, C, and D.

Overriding a Member Function

Sometimes, you will find it necessary to override a particular member function. For example, suppose that you purchase the CRectangle class. You like this class, and you want to use it in your applications. The only problem is that you don't like the way the author of the CRectangle class wrote the DisplayArea() function. Can you override that function? Sure you can. The Rect3.CPP program demonstrates how this can be accomplished.

Because the Rect3.CPP program is very similar to the Rect2.CPP program, follow these steps to create the Rect3.CPP program:

☐ Open the Rect2.CPP file (select Open from Visual C++'s File menu).

☐ Select Save As from the File menu and save the file as Rect3.CPP in the directory C:\VCPROG\PRACTICE\CH03.

☐ Add another prototype function to the declaration of the CNewRectangle class. After you add the prototype, the declaration of the CNewRectangle class looks as follows:

```
///////////////////////////////////////////////////
// The declaration of the derived class CNewRectangle
///////////////////////////////////////////////////
class CNewRectangle : public CRectangle
{

public:
    CNewRectangle(int w, int h);  // Constructor

    void SetWidth (int w);
    void SetHeight (int h);

    void DisplayArea();

    ~CNewRectangle(); // Destructor

};
```

In this declaration, you added the prototype of the DisplayArea() function.

☐ Add the DisplayArea() function's code to the Rect3.CPP file. Here's the code for the DisplayArea() function of the derived class:

```
///////////////////////////////////////////
// Function Name: DisplayArea() (derived)
///////////////////////////////////////////
void CNewRectangle::DisplayArea(void)
{

int iArea;

iArea = m_Width * m_Height;

cout << "================== \n";
cout << "The area is: " << iArea << "\n";
cout << "================== \n";

}
```

As you can see, now the Rect3.CPP program has two DisplayArea() functions. One function is a member function of the CRectangle class (the base class), and the other one is a member function of the CNewRectangle class (the derived class).

main() remains exactly as it was in the Rect2.CPP program:

```
void main(void)
```

```
{

CNewRectangle MyRectangle (10, 5);

MyRectangle.DisplayArea();


MyRectangle.SetWidth (100);
MyRectangle.SetHeight (20);


MyRectangle.DisplayArea();

}
```

☐ Save your work (that is, select Save from the File menu).

☐ Select Rebuild All RECT3.EXE from the Project menu.

    Visual C++ responds by compiling/linking the Rect3 program.

☐ Select Execute RECT3.EXE from the Project menu.

    The Rect3.EXE window appears, as shown in Figure 3.5.

As shown in Figure 3.5, the output of Rect3 is the same as the output of Rect2, except that the areas are displayed with the `DisplayArea()` function of the derived class.

Figure 3.5.
The Rect3.EXE
program's window.

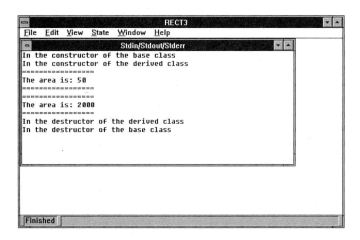

This means that when the

```
MyRectangle.DisplayArea();
```

statement is executed, the `DisplayArea()` function of the derived class is executed (not the `DisplayArea()` function of the base class).

Pointers to Objects

In many cases, it's more convenient to use pointers to objects. The Rect4.CPP program demonstrates this concept.

☐ Select Save As from the File menu and save the `Rect3.CPP` file as `Rect4.CPP` in the directory `C:\VCPROG\PRACTICE\CH03`.

☐ Modify the `main()` function of Rect4.CPP as follows:

```
void main(void)
{

CNewRectangle MyRectangle (10, 5);

CNewRectangle * pMyRectangle = &MyRectangle;

pMyRectangle->DisplayArea();


pMyRectangle->SetWidth (100);
pMyRectangle->SetHeight (20);


pMyRectangle->DisplayArea();

}
```

As you can see, `main()` creates an object `MyRectangle` of class `CNewRectangle`:

```
CNewRectangle MyRectangle (10, 5);
```

And then `main()` declares a pointer `pMyRectangle` of type `CNewRectangle`:

```
CNewRectangle * pMyRectangle = &MyRectangle;
```

In this statement, the address of the `MyRectangle` object is assigned to `pMyRectangle`.

The rest of the statements in `main()` are similar to the statements in the Rect3.CPP program's `main()` function. However, unlike `main()` in Rect3.CPP, `main()` in Rect4.CPP uses the pointer of the `MyRectangle` object to execute the member function. For example, here's how you execute the `DisplayArea()` function in Rect4.CPP:

```
pMyRectangle->DisplayArea();
```

and here's how you execute the `SetWidth()` and `SetHeight()` functions:

```
pMyRectangle->SetWidth (100);
pMyRectangle->SetHeight (20);
```

☐ Compile/link the Rect4.CPP program.

☐ Execute the Rect4.EXE program and verify that it produces the same results as the Rect3.CPP program (see Figure 3.5).

The *New* and *Delete* Operators

In the Rect4.CPP program, you created the `MyRectangle` object in `main()` as follows:

```
void main(void)
{

CNewRectangle MyRectangle (10, 5);

CNewRectangle * pMyRectangle = &MyRectangle;

pMyRectangle->DisplayArea();

...
...
...

}
```

In this `main()`, the object is destroyed when the `main()` function terminates. For example, you might create the object from within a function, such as

```
void MyFunction(void)
{

CNewRectangle MyRectangle (10, 5);

CNewRectangle * pMyRectangle = &MyRectangle;

pMyRectangle->DisplayArea();

...
...
...

}
```

Then, when `MyFunction()` terminates, the memory that was used to store the `MyRectangle` object is freed automatically.

As shown previously, the object is first created with the statement

```
CNewRectangle MyRectangle (10, 5);
```

and then the pointer to the object is created, as follows:

```
CNewRectangle * pMyRectangle = &MyRectangle;
```

Alternatively, you can use the new operator. The new operator is equivalent to the malloc() function in C.

The Rect5.CPP program demonstrates how you can use the new operator.

☐ Open the Rect4.CPP file and then select Save As from the File menu to save the file as RECT5.CPP in the directory C:\VCPROG\PRACTICE\CH03.

☐ Modify the main() function so that it looks as follows:

```
void main(void)
{

CNewRectangle* pMyRectangle;
pMyRectangle = new CNewRectangle(10,5);

pMyRectangle->DisplayArea();


pMyRectangle->SetWidth (100);
pMyRectangle->SetHeight (20);


pMyRectangle->DisplayArea();

delete pMyRectangle;
}
```

☐ To save your work, select Save from the File menu.

☐ Select Rebuild All RECT5.EXE from the Project menu.

☐ Select Execute RECT5.EXE from the Project menu.

The QuickWin window of Rect5.EXE appears, as shown in Figure 3.6.

Figure 3.6
The Rect5.EXE
program.

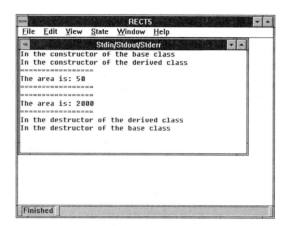

As shown in Figure 3.6, the output of Rect5.EXE is identical to the output of the Rect4.EXE program.

Take a look at the code for the `main()` function of the Rect5.CPP program.

A pointer, `pMyRectangle`, is declared as a pointer to an object of class `CNewRectangle`:

```
CNewRectangle* pMyRectangle;
```

Then the `new` operator is used to create a new object. The pointer of this new object is `pMyRectangle`:

```
pMyRectangle = new CNewRectangle(10,5);
```

The rest of the code in `main()` remains the same as it was in the Rect4.CPP program. For example, to execute the `DisplayArea()` member function on the object, you use the statement

```
pMyRectangle->DisplayArea();
```

The last thing that `main()` does is free the memory occupied by the object:

```
delete pMyRectangle;
```

Note that the `delete` operator must be used to free objects that were created with the `new` operator.

> **NOTE**
>
> If you use the new operator from within a function, the memory occupied by the pointer is freed automatically when the function terminates, because the pointer is just a local variable to the function. However, the pointer holds a memory address where the actual object is stored, and that memory is not freed when the function terminates! You must use the delete operator to free the memory occupied by the object.

> **NOTE**
>
> In the Rect5.CPP program, you created the object by using two statements in main():
>
> ```
> CNewRectangle* pMyRectangle;
> pMyRectangle = new CNewRectangle(10,5);
> ```
>
> Typically, in Visual C++ you'll see these two statements combined into one statement, as follows:
>
> ```
> CNewRectangle* pMyRectangle = new CNewRectangle(10,5);
> ```
>
> This statement is identical to the previous two statements.

What's It All About?

Congratulations! You've completed the quick C++ tutorial. Starting with the next chapter, you'll begin writing true C++ Windows applications. Visual C++ enables you to write powerful, sophisticated, professional applications in a short time. This is possible because Microsoft ships the Visual C++ package with a set of a powerful classes called the MFC. So as it turns out, learning Visual C++ amounts to knowing how to use the powerful member functions of the MFC. In addition, you can use Visual C++ to visually design your windows, dialog boxes, menus, bitmaps, and icons. That is, you use the mouse and a program called App Studio to design these visual objects. Visual C++ also includes a program called AppWizard. AppWizard writes the overhead code for you. A Windows application always requires several overhead files. These overhead files appear in every Windows application that you'll ever write. So instead of your having to type these repetitive, boring files, the AppWizard program writes them.

And finally, Visual C++ is equipped with a program called ClassWizard. As you saw in this chapter, once you know that a certain class is available (for example, the CRectangle class), you can derive other classes from it that inherit the data members and member functions of the base class. However, unlike the CRectangle and CNewRectangle classes that were discussed in this chapter, the classes of the MFC are extremely powerful, and the process of deriving classes from the MFC requires a lot of typing! But don't worry! ClassWizard takes care of this. When you use ClassWizard, the computer does the typing. It inserts the prototypes of the member functions into the declarations of the derived classes, and even starts writing the function for you. All you have to do is type your own specific code in the functions that ClassWizard prepares for you.

These wizard programs are what Visual C++ is all about, and during the course of this book you'll use them extensively.

4

Your First True Windows Application

In this chapter you'll write your first
true Windows application with
Visual C++. As you'll soon see,
writing a true Windows application
with Visual C++ is easy, because
a lot of the code is generated
automatically for you by Visual C++.

Writing a Visual C++ Windows application involves the following two steps:

1. The visual programming step
2. The code programming step

During the visual programming step, you design your application by using software tools that come with the Visual C++ package. With these tools, you design your application by using the mouse and the keyboard. You don't have to write any code in this step! You just have to know how to use the visual tools of the package to place objects (for example, menus, push buttons, scroll bars, and so on) in your application.

In the code programming step, you write code using the text editor that comes with the Visual C++ package. The code statements are written in the C++ programming language.

The SAY Application

In the following sections you'll find step-by-step instructions to create a simple Windows application called SAY.

Before you start writing the SAY application, execute SAY. It appears in your C:\vcProg\Original\CH04\Say directory. This way, you'll have a better understanding of what the SAY application is supposed to do.

To execute the SAY application:

☐ Select Run from Program Manager's File menu.

   Windows responds by displaying the Run dialog box.

☐ Type C:\vcProg\Original\CH04\SAY\SAY.EXE in the Command Line box and then click the OK button.

   Windows responds by executing the SAY application.

The main window of the SAY application appears, as shown in Figure 4.1.

As you can see from Figure 4.1, the SAY application has a menu bar with two popup menus, File and Help.

The File and Help popup menus are shown in Figures 4.2 and 4.3.

Figure 4.1.
The SAY
application's
main window.

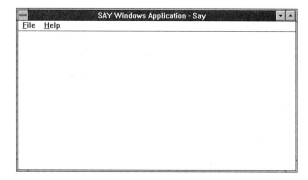

Figure 4.2.
The SAY
application's
File menu.

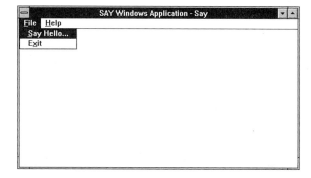

Figure 4.3.
The SAY
application's
Help menu.

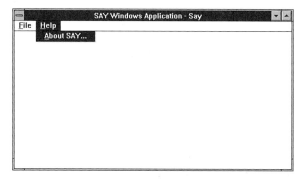

Experiment with the various menu items of the SAY application:

☐ Select Say Hello from the File menu.

> *The SAY application responds by displaying a Hello dialog box (see Figure 4.4).*

☐ Close the Hello dialog box by clicking its OK button.

Figure 4.4.
The SAY
application's Hello
dialog box.

☐ Select About SAY... from the Help menu.

> *The SAY application responds by displaying the About SAY dialog box*
> *(see Figure 4.5).*

☐ Close the About SAY dialog box by clicking its OK button.

Figure 4.5.
The SAY
application's About
dialog box.

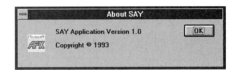

To terminate the SAY application:

☐ Select Exit from the File menu.

> *The SAY application responds by terminating.*

Okay, so you know what the SAY application is supposed to do. Now it's time to write the SAY application from scratch. In the following sections, you'll follow a set of step-by-step instructions to implement the SAY application.

Creating the Project of the SAY Application

The first thing to do when you design a new application is to create the project of the application.

To create the project of the SAY application:

☐ Double-click the Visual C++ icon in the Visual C++ group.

> *Windows responds by running the Visual C++ program. The main window*
> *of Visual C++ appears, as shown in Figure 4.6.*

☐ Select AppWizard from the Project menu.

> *Visual C++ responds by displaying the AppWizard dialog box*
> *(see Figure 4.7).*

Figure 4.6.
The Visual C++
main window.

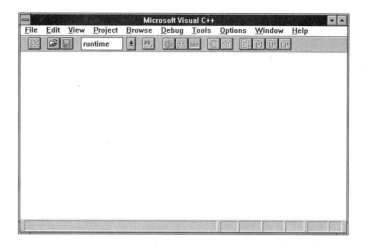

Figure 4.7.
The AppWizard
dialog box.

What is AppWizard? AppWizard is a very powerful *wizard* that writes for you the skeleton code of your application. Instead of writing overhead code every time you start writing a new application, AppWizard writes this overhead code for you.

NOTE

Whenever you begin writing a new application, start by running AppWizard. AppWizard creates the skeleton of your application; it creates all the necessary files and subdirectories for your new application.

To tell AppWizard the directory where you want to create the new application, do the following:

Use the directory list box (see Figure 4.7) to select the directory C:\vcProg\Practice\CH04.

That is, first double-click c:\ and then double-click vcprog and then double-click practice and finally double-click ch04.

Now your AppWizard window looks as shown in Figure 4.8.

> ### NOTE
>
> If you are using an earlier version of Visual C++, the dialog boxes that you'll see on your screen may be different from the dialog boxes that you see in this book. However, these differences are minor.

Figure 4.8.
The AppWizard window after selecting the directory
c:\vcProg\Practice\ch04.

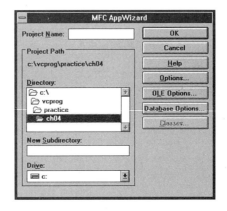

Now, do the following to tell AppWizard the name of the new application:

◻ Type say in the Project Name box.

AppWizard responds by creating the subdirectory SAY (see Figure 4.9). Now the full pathname of the application is as follows:

c:\vcProg\Practice\ch04\say\say.mak

say.mak *is the name of the project file that AppWizard creates.*

By leaving the check mark in the Generate Source Code check box, you're telling AppWizard to include comments in the code it generates.

Now AppWizard "knows" what kind of application you want to create.

☐ Click the OK button of the Options dialog box.

AppWizard responds by closing the Options dialog box.

You can now tell AppWizard to create the SAY application:

☐ Click the OK button of the AppWizard dialog box.

AppWizard responds by displaying the New Application Information dialog box (see Figure 4.11).

Figure 4.11.
The New
Application
Information dialog
box.

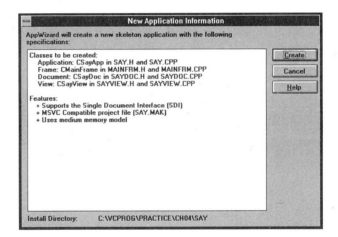

☐ Click the Create button.

AppWizard responds by creating all the skeleton files of the SAY application in the directory C:\vcPROG\Practice\CH04\SAY, *and then the main window of Visual C++ appears.*

Note that now the main window of Visual C++ has the title Microsoft Visual C++ - SAY.MAK. SAY.MAK is the project file of the SAY application.

What exactly did AppWizard do for you? If you examine your hard drive, you'll see that AppWizard created several files in your C:\vcPROG\Practice\CH04\SAY directory. These files are the "bones" (that is, the skeleton) of your application. Your job, with

Figure 4.9.
The AppWizard
window after
specifying the
directory and name
of the new
application.

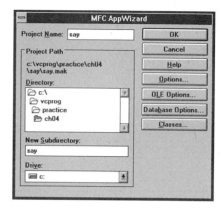

You've finished telling AppWizard the directory and name of the new applica
you want to create. Next you have to set various options for the new applicatio

☑ Click the Options button.

AppWizard responds by displaying the Options dialog box.

☐ Uncheck all the check boxes except the Generate Source Comments check
box.

Now your Options dialog box looks as shown in Figure 4.10.

Figure 4.10.
The Options dialog
box.

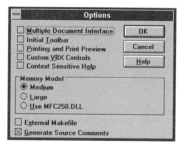

By unchecking the Multiple Document Interface option, you're telling AppWizard
that you aren't creating a Multiple Document Interface (MDI) application. MDI
applications are covered in Chapter 19, "Multiple Document Interface (MDI)."

Similarly, by unchecking the check boxes for the Initial Toolbar and Printing options, you're telling AppWizard not to include the skeleton code needed for a Toolbar
and for printing. (Toolbars and printing are covered in later chapters of this book.)

the aid of Visual C++, is to customize these files so that the SAY application does what it's supposed to do.

Running the SAY Application Before Customizing It

Before you start customizing the files of the SAY application, compile, link, and execute the SAY application in its current status. As you'll see, the skeleton files that AppWizard created have code in them that actually does something.

To compile and link the SAY application:

☒ Select Rebuild All SAY.EXE from the Project menu of Visual C++.

Visual C++ responds by compiling and linking the SAY application.

When Visual C++ finishes compiling/linking the application, you can run it:

☒ Select Execute SAY.EXE from the Project menu.

Visual C++ responds by executing the SAY application. The main window of the SAY application appears, as shown in Figure 4.12.

Figure 4.12.
The SAY application's main window (before customizing).

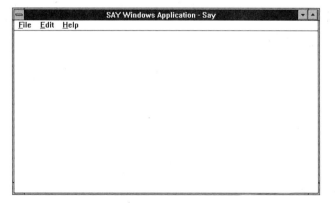

As you can see, the SAY application has a menu with three popup menus: File, Edit, and Help. These popup menus are shown in Figures 4.13, 4.14, and 4.15.

Figure 4.13.
The SAY
application's File
menu (before
customization).

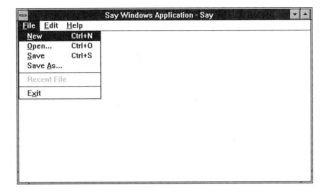

Figure 4.14.
The SAY
application's
Edit menu (before
customization).

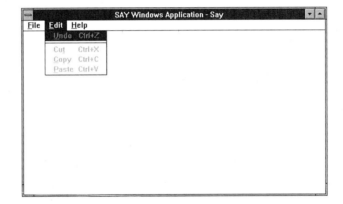

Figure 4.15.
The SAY
application's
Help menu (before
customization).

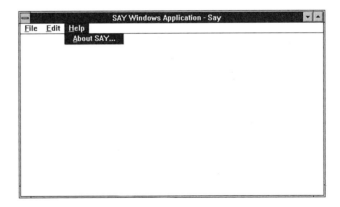

NOTE

Figure 4.13 shows that the File menu has the Recent File menu item. This menu item doesn't appear in earlier versions of Visual C++.

To terminate the SAY application:

✔ Select Exit from the File menu.

The SAY application responds by terminating.

Even though you haven't written a single line of code yet, you have a true working Windows application in your hands—a gift from AppWizard. Of course, this program isn't exactly what you want it to be. In the following sections, you will design the files for the SAY application so that it does what it's supposed to do.

As stated at the beginning of the chapter, the design process involves two steps:

1. The visual implementation step
2. The code writing step

The Visual Implementation of the SAY Application

Currently, the menu of the SAY application has three popup menus: File, Edit, and Help (see Figures 4.13, 4.14, and 4.15). Your objective is to customize the menu of the SAY application so that it looks like the one shown in Figures 4.2 and 4.3. Here's how you do that:

☒ Select App Studio from the Tools menu of Visual C++.

Visual C++ responds by running the App Studio program (see Figure 4.16).

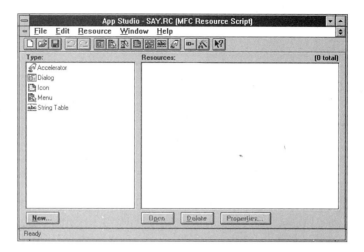

Figure 4.16.
App Studio.

As you can see from Figure 4.16, the title of App Studio's window is currently:

```
App Studio - SAY.RC [MFC Resource Script]
```

This means that right now, App Studio displays on the screen a visual representation of the file SAY.RC.

What is SAY.RC? It's one of the skeleton files that AppStudio created for you. SAY.RC is where the resources of the application are defined—things like menus, dialog boxes, icons, and so on.

> **NOTE**
>
> To visually design the resources of the application (menus, dialog boxes, and so on) you have to use App Studio. When you start App Studio, it displays a visual representation of the RC file of the application (SAY.RC). The RC file is where the resources of the application (menus, icons, dialog boxes, bitmaps, icons, and so on) are defined.

As you can see from Figure 4.16, the left side of the SAY.RC window (the Type list) lists types of resources (Accelerator, Bitmap, Dialog, and so on). Because now you want to design the menu of the application, you need to select the Menu item:

☒ Click the Menu item in the Type list.

App Studio responds by displaying the text IDR_MAINFRAME *in the right side of the SAY.RC window (see Figure 4.17).*

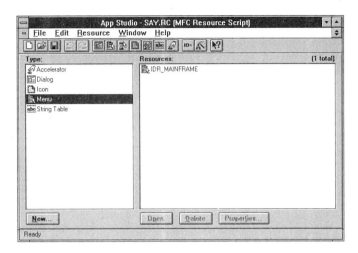

Figure 4.17.
Selecting the Menu
item from the Type
list.

IDR_MAINFRAME is the ID of the main menu of the application. This menu was already created by AppWizard. Your objective is to customize this menu for the SAY application.

To open the IDR_MAINFRAME menu in design mode, do the following:

☒ Double-click the IDR_MAINFRAME item.

> *App Studio responds by opening the menu of the SAY application*
> *(IDR_MAINFRAME) in design mode (see Figure 4.18).*

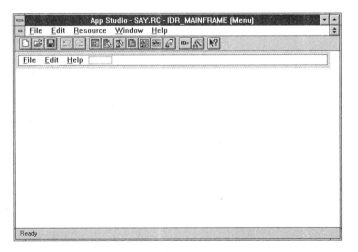

Figure 4.18.
The menu of the
SAY application
in design mode.

Note that now the title of App Studio's window is

```
App Studio - SAY.RC - IDR_MAINFRAME [Menu]
```

So just by looking at this title you can tell that you're now working on SAY.RC, and in particular you're designing the menu of the application—IDR_MAINFRAME.

As you can see from Figure 4.18, the menu currently has three popup menus: File, Edit, and Help.

Because the SAY application shouldn't have an Edit menu (see Figure 4.1), please remove it:

☒ Click the Edit item on the menu.

> *App Studio responds by popping the Edit popup menu (see Figure 4.19).*

Figure 4.19.
The application's
Edit popup menu.

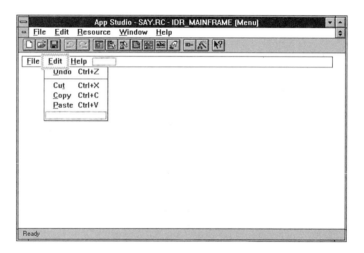

☒ Now, press the Delete key on your keyboard.

> *App Studio responds by displaying a dialog box warning you that you're about to delete an entire popup menu (see Figure 4.20).*

☒ Click the OK button of the dialog box.

> *App Studio responds by deleting the Edit popup. Now your menu looks as shown in Figure 4.21.*

Figure 4.20.
The warning that
App Studio displays
when you try to
delete an entire
popup menu.

Figure 4.21.
The menu of the
application after
removing the Edit
popup.

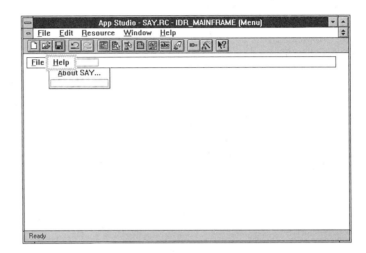

Now, modify the File popup menu so that it looks as shown in Figure 4.2.

☒ Click the File item.

App Studio responds by opening the File popup (see Figure 4.22).

Figure 4.22.
The File popup
menu.

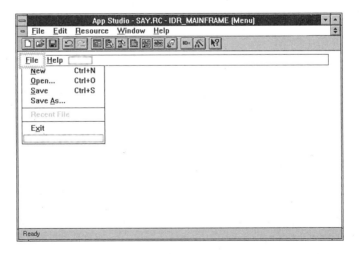

Currently, the File menu has the following items:

```
New
Save
Save As…

_____

Recent File

_____

Exit
```

As you can see from Figure 4.2, the only item you need from this list is the Exit item. You have to delete all the items from the File popup except the Exit item:

☒ To delete the New menu item, click it and then press the Delete key on your keyboard.

App Studio responds by removing the New item from the File popup.

☒ Use the same method to delete the rest of the items in the File menu, except the Exit item.

Your File popup looks as shown in Figure 4.23.

Figure 4.23.
The File popup
after removing all
the items except the
Exit item.

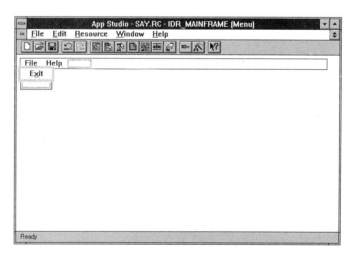

The File popup isn't ready yet. As you can see from Figure 4.2, the File popup should contain another menu item:

```
Say Hello…
```

Here's how you add this menu item:

▷ Double-click the blank item below the Exit item.

> *App Studio responds by displaying the Menu Item Properties dialog box (see Figure 4.24).*

Figure 4.24.
The Menu Item
Properties dialog
box.

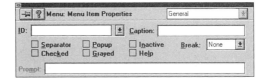

▷ Type &Say Hello... in the Caption box.

▷ When you finish typing, the menu item Say Hello... appears in the File popup below the Exit item, as shown in Figure 4.25.

Figure 4.25.
The new menu
item in the File
popup.

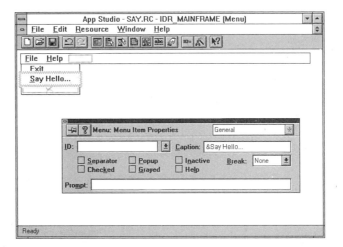

NOTE

The & character that prefixes the S in & Say Hello causes the character S to be underlined. This means that when the File popup is displayed during the execution of the program, pressing S produces results identical to selecting the Say Hello item. (The character & is located on the 7 key of your keyboard.)

As you can see from Figure 4.25, the Menu Item Properties dialog box also has an ID box. In Figure 4.25, the ID box is blank. You don't have to fill the ID of the menu item! App Studio does it for you:

☐ Double-click the Say Hello menu item.

> *App Studio responds by displaying the Menu Item Properties dialog box again, but this time App Studio has filled the ID box with* ID_FILE_SAYHELLO *(see Figure 4.26).*

Figure 4.26.
The ID that App Studio gives the Say Hello menu item.

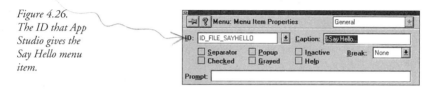

There's still one more thing to do before you finish the visual implementation of the menu. As you can see from Figure 4.2, the Exit menu item should be the second item in the File popup (not the first item).

To make the Exit item the second item in the File popup menu, do the following:

☐ Click the Exit item and drag it down until the mouse pointer is on the second item.

Now your File popup looks as shown in Figure 4.27.

Figure 4.27.
The File popup after making the Exit item the second item in the popup.

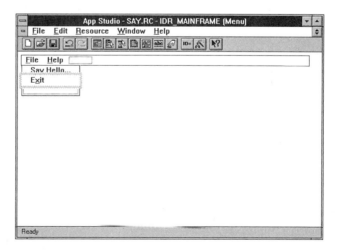

To save your work:

✗ ☒ Select Save from the File menu of App Studio.

> *App Studio responds by saving your design work in the file* SAY.RC.

That's it for the visual implementation of the SAY application. As you've seen, the visual implementation of a menu in Visual C++ is quite easy. You don't have to write any code; you just use the keyboard and mouse. In later chapters you'll learn how to visually implement other resources—for example, dialog boxes with objects such as push buttons, scroll bars, and radio buttons.

Look at What You've Accomplished So Far

Although you haven't finished designing the SAY application yet (that is, you haven't attached code to the menu), you can execute the application in its current status and see what you've accomplished so far.

First, you need to switch back to Visual C++ (currently, you're still running App Studio).

✗ ☒ Select Exit from the File menu of App Studio.

> *App Studio terminates, and the window of Visual C++ appears.*

> **NOTE**
>
> Another way to switch back to Visual C++ from App Studio is to press Ctrl+Esc (press the Ctrl and Esc keys simultaneously) and then select Microsoft Visual C++ from the Task List dialog box.

Now, compile and link the SAY application:

✗ ☒ Select Build SAY.EXE from the Project menu of Visual C++.

> *Visual C++ responds by compiling and linking the SAY application.*

> **NOTE**
>
> Visual C++ is a new and complex package, so you'll occasionally receive Fatal Error messages when you compile/link your applications, even though you

did everything right. In such cases, terminate Visual C++ and exit Windows. Then start Windows, start Visual C++, and select Rebuild All from the Project menu of Visual C++.

The Rebuild All item of the Project menu instructs Visual C++ to recompile all the files, even if the date and time stamps of the files indicate that they weren't changed since the last compile.

The Build item of the Project menu instructs Visual C++ to compile only those files that were changed since the last compile.

When Visual C++ finishes compiling/linking the application, you can run it:

☐ Select Execute SAY.EXE from the Project menu.

Visual C++ responds by executing the SAY application.

Experiment with the menu items of the SAY application.

As you can see, now the menu of the SAY application appears just as you designed it:

> The menu bar has two popups: File and Help.
> The Edit popup doesn't exist anymore.
> The File menu has only two items: Say Hello and Exit.

Note, however, that the Say Hello option in the File menu is dimmed (that is, it isn't available). Why? Because you haven't attached code to this menu item yet.

On the other hand, the About SAY option of the Help menu is available, because the code for this menu item was written by AppWizard when you created the project. The code for the Exit menu item was also written by AppWizard.

Now exit the SAY application:

☐ Select Exit from the File menu.

SAY responds by terminating.

Attaching Code to the SAY Application

As you've seen, the only item in the menu of the SAY application that doesn't have any code attached is the Say Hello menu item. The other menu items (Exit in the

File menu and About in the Help menu) already have code attached to them—a "gift" from AppWizard.

So here's how you attach code to the Say Hello menu item:

☒ Select App Studio from the Tools menu.

> *Visual C++ responds by running App Studio. App Studio appears with the SAY.RC window (see Figure 4.16).*

Because you want to attach code to the menu of the application:

☒ Select Menu from the Type list of SAY.RC.

> *App Studio responds by displaying the text* `IDR_MAINFRAME` *in the right side of the SAY.RC window (see Figure 4.17).*

☒ Double-click the `IDR_MAINFRAME` item.

> *App Studio responds by displaying the menu of the SAY application* (`IDR_MAINFRAME`) *in design mode (see Figure 4.18).*

To attach code to the Say Hello menu item of the File popup menu:

☒ Click the File popup menu to open it.

> *App Studio responds by opening the File popup.*

☒ Double-click the Say Hello item in the File popup.

> *App Studio responds by displaying the Menu Item Properties dialog box for the Say Hello menu item (see Figure 4.28).*

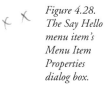

Figure 4.28.
The Say Hello menu item's Menu Item Properties dialog box.

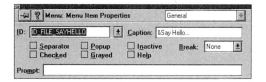

Make sure that the ID box in the Properties window contains the ID of the Say Hello menu item. That is, the ID should be `ID_FILE_SAYHELLO`, as shown in Figure 4.28.

NOTE

The preceding step may seem redundant at this point. After all, you double-clicked the Say Hello menu item, so the Properties window that pops up is the one for this menu item, and the ID should correspond to this menu item. However, as it turned out in earlier versions of Visual C++, App Studio occasionally gets confused and displays the wrong ID in the Properties window. If this is the case, use the arrow icon of the ID box to drop down a list of IDs and select the proper one (ID_FILE_SAYHELLO). Microsoft is aware of this problem, and it's anticipated that it will be corrected in future versions of Visual C++.

Select ClassWizard from the Resource menu of App Studio and make sure that the Message Maps tab at the top of the ClassWizard window is selected.

> *App Studio responds by displaying the window of ClassWizard (see Figure 4.29).*

Note that if you're using an earlier version of Visual C++, the ClassWizard window that you see on your screen may look different than the one shown in Figure 4.29. In particular, in earlier versions of Visual C++, the tabs Message Maps, Member Variables, OLE Automation, and Class Info tabs don't exist in the ClassWizard window.

Figure 4.29.
The ClassWizard window.

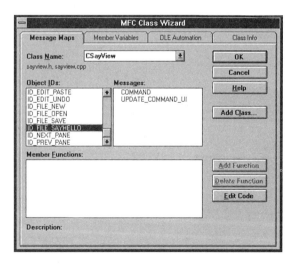

Now use ClassWizard to write the code that's automatically executed whenever the user selects Say Hello from the File menu.

As you can see from Figure 4.29, the middle section of the ClassWizard window has two list boxes:

- The Object IDs list box (on the left side of the window).
- The Messages list box (on the right side of the window).

The Object IDs list box is used to select the object to which you want to attach code. As you can see from Figure 4.29, currently ID_FILE_SAYHELLO is selected in the Objects IDs list box—that's because you're currently trying to attach code to the Say Hello item of the File menu.

The Messages list box contains messages that represent events that relate to the selected object. As you can see from Figure 4.29, two possible events relate to the ID_FILE_SAYHELLO menu item: COMMAND and UPDATE_COMMAND_UI. COMMAND represents the event, "User selected the menu item," and UPDATE_COMMAND_UI is discussed later in the book.

To summarize, in order to tell ClassWizard that you want to write code for the event "User selected Say Hello from the File menu," you need to select ID_FILE_SAYHELLO in the Object IDs list box, and then you need to select COMMAND in the Messages list box.

☒ Select COMMAND in the Messages list box (click the COMMAND item in the Messages list box).

> *Now your ClassWizard window looks as shown in Figure 4.30.*
> *ID_FILE_SAYHELLO is selected in the Object IDs list box, and COMMAND is selected in the Messages list box.*

So far you've selected ID_FILE_SAYHELLO from the Object IDs list and COMMAND from the Messages list. Now you have to select the class:

☐ Set the Class Name box of ClassWizard to CSayView.

> *Now the ClassWizard window looks as shown in Figure 4.30.*

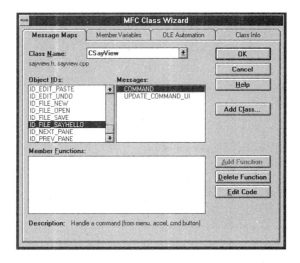

Figure 4.30.
Selecting COMMAND
in the Messages list
box.

NOTE

Typically, new users of Visual C++ forget to set the Class Name (as indicated in the preceding step).

In many cases, the default class name that appears in the ClassWizard window's class Name box is the class you'll use. However, as you'll see during the course of this book, you'll be instructed in many cases, to set the Class Name to a different class.

If the Class Name isn't set to the proper class, you'll receive many compiling and linking errors.

Next, you have to tell ClassWizard to add the function that corresponds to the event you just selected. That is, you have to tell ClassWizard to add the function that's executed automatically whenever the user selects Say Hello from the File menu.

To tell ClassWizard to add this function:

☒ Click ClassWizard's Add Function button.

ClassWizard responds by displaying the Add Member Function dialog box (see Figure 4.31).

Figure 4.31.
The Add Member
Function dialog
box.

As you can see from Figure 4.31, ClassWizard suggests naming the new function
OnFileSayhello().

☒ Click the OK button to accept the default name that ClassWizard suggests.

> *ClassWizard responds by adding the function* OnFileSayhello() *to the SAY
> application. This function is automatically executed whenever the user selects
> Say Hello from the File menu.*

Note that now the function OnFileSayhello() is listed in the Member Functions list
box of ClassWizard's window (see Figure 4.32).

Figure 4.32.
ClassWizard after
adding the function
OnFileSayhello().

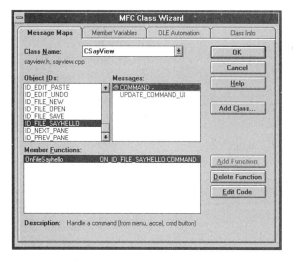

ClassWizard wrote only the code that declares the OnFileSayhello() function and
its skeleton. It's your job to write the code in the OnFileSayhello() function.

To write the code in the OnFileSayhello() function:

☒ Click ClassWizard's Edit Code button.

> *ClassWizard responds by switching back to Visual C++ and opening the file
> SAYVIEW.CPP. (The function OnFileSayhello() resides in the file
> SAYVIEW.CPP.) The function OnFileSayhello() is ready for you to edit (see
> Figure 4.33).*

Figure 4.33.
The
OnFileSayhello()
function.

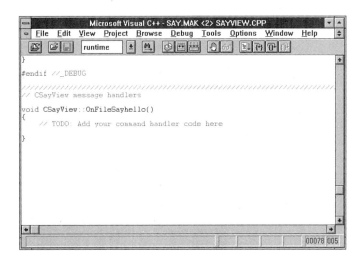

It's important to see the correlation between Figure 4.30 and Figure 4.33. Per Figure 4.30, you told ClassWizard the following:

Class Name:	CSayView
Object ID:	ID_FILE_SAYHELLO
Message:	COMMAND

After you clicked the Add Function button of ClassWizard, ClassWizard generated the code shown in Figure 4.33.

As you can see from Figure 4.33, ClassWizard generated a member function called `OnFileSayhello()` of class CSayView. In addition, ClassWizard also added all the other code that has to be written when you add a member function to a class. For example, ClassWizard added to the declaration of the CSayView class the prototype of the `OnFileSayhello()` function.

☒ Write code in the `OnFileSayhello()` function so that it looks as follows:

```
void CSayView::OnFileSayhello()
{
    // TODO: Add your command handler code here

    /////////////////////////////
    // MY CODE STARTS HERE //
    /////////////////////////////

    MessageBox ("Hello! Have a nice day!");
```

```
/////////////////////////
// MY CODE ENDS HERE //
/////////////////////////
```

}

Save your work!

☒ Select Save from the File menu of Visual C++.

> **NOTE**
>
> As shown previously, you have to type your code in an existing function. To make it easy to distinguish between code that Visual C++ wrote for you and code that you have to type, the following convention is used in this book:
>
> Code that you have to write is enclosed between the following comments:
>
> ```
> /////////////////////////
> // MY CODE STARTS HERE
> /////////////////////////
>
> ...............................
> ... Your code appears here ...
> ...............................
>
> /////////////////////////
> // MY CODE ENDS HERE
> /////////////////////////
> ```
>
> The MY CODE STARTS HERE and MY CODE ENDS HERE comments will help you distinguish between code that Visual C++ wrote for you and code that you have to type or modify.

The code you just typed is quite simple (one line):

```
MessageBox ("Hello! Have a nice day!");
```

It uses the MessageBox() function to display this message:

```
Hello! Have a nice day!
```

111

That's it! You've finished attaching code to the SAY application. Next, you'll execute it and see the code that you just wrote in action.

Executing the Final Version of the SAY Application

To compile and link the SAY application:

☒ Select Build SAY.EXE from the Project menu.

When Visual C++ finishes compiling/linking the application, you can run it:

☒ Select Execute SAY.EXE from the Project menu.

> *Visual C++ responds by executing the SAY application.*

☐ Experiment with the menu items of the SAY application.

As you can see, the menu item Say Hello in the File menu is available now. When you select this menu item, the SAY application displays a Hello message, as shown in Figure 4.4.

To terminate the SAY application:

☒ Select Exit from the File menu.

Creating Smaller EXE Files

If you inspect the size of your SAY.EXE file, you'll see that it's large (more than 1.1 megabytes). Don't worry about this huge size, because you can decrease it. SAY.EXE is so large because, by default, Visual C++'s compile/link options are set for debugging. To change these options from debugging mode to release mode, follow these steps:

☒ Select Project from the Options menu of Visual C++.

> *Visual C++ responds by displaying the Project Options dialog box.*

☒ Select the Release option in the Project Options dialog box by clicking the Release radio button.

> *Now your Project Options dialog box looks as shown in Figure 4.34.*

4

Figure 4.34.
The Project Options
dialog box with the
Release option
selected.

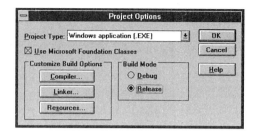

☒ Now, click the OK button of the Project Options dialog box.

From now on, whenever you compile/link the SAY application it will be small, because it won't include debugging information.

To generate the small SAY.EXE:

☒ Select Build SAY.EXE from the Project menu.

When Visual C++ finishes compiling/linking the application, you can inspect the new size of the resultant SAY.EXE file. You will see that SAY.EXE is much smaller—approximately 50,000 bytes long.

The Document Class and the View Class

As stated previously, when you created the SAY application with AppWizard, AppWizard created several files for you in the directory C:\vcPROG\Practice\CH04\SAY. You don't have to concern yourself with most of these files. That is, Visual C++ automatically maintains for you the code within these files.

However, pay special attention to four files, because quite often you have to write your own code in these files. In the SAY application these four files are as follows:

> SAYDOC.H—The Document class header file
> SAYDOC.CPP—The Document class implementation file
> SAYVIEW.H—The View class header file
> SAYVIEW.CPP—The View class implementation file

SAYDOC.H and SAYDOC.CPP are the files where the SAY application's Document class is defined. What's the Document class? You can think of it as the place where you define and initialize data (variables) that are used by your application. In the SAY application you didn't have to write any code in the SAYDOC.H and SAYDOC.CPP files, because the SAY application didn't need any variables.

SAYVIEW.H and SAYVIEW.CPP are the files where the View class for the SAY application is defined. What's the View class? It's where all the action takes place. The code you write in the View class (that is, in SAYVIEW.CPP) is the code that's responsible for what the user sees (views) on the screen.

In the SAY application, you already wrote code in the View class. You may have noticed that when you added the function OnFileSayhello() to the SAY application, ClassWizard placed the skeleton of this function in the file SAYVIEW.CPP (see Figure 4.33).

Note the first line of the OnFileSayhello() function:

```
void CSayView::OnFileSayhello()
{
.....
.....
.....
}
```

[handwritten annotation: void cMainFrame:: OnFile Sayhello() { messageBox(" Hello!, Have a nice day - Bill"); }]

As you can see from the first line, the OnFileSayhello() function is a member function of the CSayView class.

In the following chapter you'll write an application that stores data. Thus, unlike what you've done for the SAY application (where you wrote code only in the View class), you'll write code in both the View class and in the Document class.

> **NOTE**
>
> Note the way in which AppWizard named the SAY application's Document class and View class files:
>
> SAYDOC.H and SAYDOC.CPP (the Document class files)
>
> SAYVIEW.H and SAYVIEW.CPP (the View class files)
>
> The names begin with the characters of the application's name (SAY) and end with the characters of the class type (DOC for Document and VIEW for View). If the application name is long, ClassWizard truncates the

application's name. For example, if the application's name is *abcdefgh*, ClassWizard names the Doc and View class files as follows:

> `abcdeDOC.H` and `abcdeDOC.CPP` (the Document class files)

> `abcdeVW.H` and `abcdeVW.CPP` (the View class files)

Note that when the application filename is long, AppWizard ends the names of the View class files with VW (not VIEW).

5

Storing Variables in the Document Class

In this chapter you'll learn how to declare and initialize variables in the document class of an application.

As stated in the previous chapter, the *document class* is used for storage of data, and the *view class* is where all the action takes place (that is, where the data is viewed).

In the SAY application of the previous chapter, you didn't have to enter any code in the document class because you didn't have to maintain any data (variables).

To illustrate how to declare and initialize variables in the document class and then use these variables in the view class, you'll now write the VAR application. The VAR application declares and initializes a variable in the document class, and then the code in the view class uses this variable and displays its value.

The VAR Application

Before you start writing the VAR application, execute it. It appears in your `C:\vcProg\Original\CH05\VAR` directory. This way, you'll have a better understanding of what the VAR application is supposed to do.

To execute the VAR application:

☐ Select Run from the Program Manager's File menu.

Windows responds by displaying the Run dialog box.

☐ Type `C:\vcProg\Original\CH05\VAR\VAR.EXE` in the Command Line box and then click the OK button.

Windows responds by executing the VAR application (see Figure 5.1).

*Figure 5.1.
The VAR
application's
main window.*

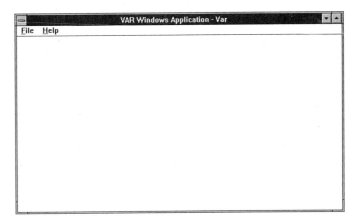

The VAR application has two popup menus: File and Help. These popup menus are shown in Figures 5.2 and 5.3.

Figure 5.2.
The VAR
application's
File menu.

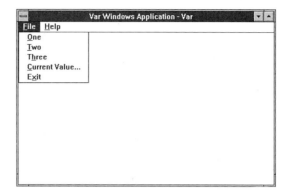

Figure 5.3.
The VAR
application's
Help menu.

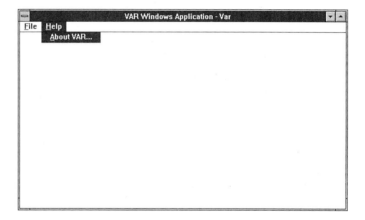

Experiment with the menu options of the File menu:

☐ Select Current Value from the File menu.

> *The VAR application responds by displaying a dialog box, as shown in Figure 5.4.*

Figure 5.4.
The Current Value
dialog box.

As you can see from Figure 5.4, the dialog box is telling you that the current value of the variable m_MyVar is "Zero."

☐ Click the OK button of the dialog box.

Now select One from the File menu.

The VAR application responds by displaying a dialog box telling you the value of m_MyVar has been changed to "One," as shown in Figure 5.5.

Figure 5.5.
The One
dialog box.

☐ Click the OK button of the dialog box.

☐ Select Current Value from the File menu again.

The VAR application responds by displaying a dialog box, as shown in Figure 5.6.

Figure 5.6.
The Current Value
dialog box after
*m_MyVar has been
changed to "One."*

As you can see from Figure 5.6, the dialog box tells you that the current value of the m_MyVar variable is "One."

In a similar manner, when you select the Two and Three options of the File menu, the VAR application changes the value of m_MyVar accordingly.

To exit from the VAR application:

☐ Select Exit from the File menu.

Now that you know what the VAR application should do, you can start writing it.

Creating the Project of the VAR Application

To create the project of the VAR application:

☐ Select AppWizard from the Project menu.

Visual C++ responds by running AppWizard.

☐ Use the Directory list box to select the directory C:\VCPROG\PRACTICE\CH05.

☐ Type VAR in the Project Name box.

Now your AppWizard dialog box looks as shown in Figure 5.7.

Figure 5.7.
The VAR
application's
AppWizard
dialog box.

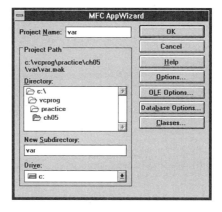

☐ Click the Options button and set the options as shown in Figure 5.8 (that is, uncheck all the check boxes except the Generate Source Comments check box).

Figure 5.8.
Setting the options
for the VAR
application.

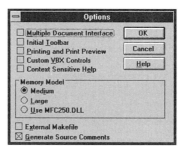

☐ Click the OK button of the Options dialog box and then click the OK button of the AppWizard dialog box and finally click the Create button of the New Application Information dialog box.

AppWizard responds by creating the VAR project and all the skeleton files of the VAR application.

To remove the debug options of the project (so you'll have a small EXE file):

☐ Select Project from the Options menu of Visual C++, click the Release radio button, and then click the OK button of the dialog box.

The Visual Implementation of the VAR Application

The VAR application should have a menu as shown in Figures 5.1, 5.2, and 5.3. Implement this menu:

☐ Select App Studio from the Tools menu of Visual C++.

> *Visual C++ responds by running App Studio.*

☐ Select the Menu item in the Type list and then double-click the IDR_MAINFRAME item in the Resources list.

> *Visual C++ responds by displaying the menu of the VAR application in design mode.*

☐ Design the menu so it looks as shown in Figures 5.1, 5.2, and 5.3.

NOTE

If you forget how to design a menu, refer to Chapter 4, "Your First True Windows Application." It includes a detailed description of how to design a menu.

To save your work:

☐ Select Save from the File menu of App Studio.

The visual implementation of the VAR application is completed. Next you'll write the application's code.

Writing the VAR Application's Code

The VAR application uses a variable called m_MyVar. You'll declare this variable in the document class of the application. The document class files of the VAR application are the following:

- `VARDOC.H`—The document class header file
- `VARDOC.CPP`—The document class code file

You'll declare the `m_MyVar` variable in `VARDOC.H`, and you'll initialize it in `VARDOC.CPP`.

Declaring the *m_MyVar* Variable

To declare the `m_MyVar` variable as a data member of the document class, follow these steps:

☐ Switch to Visual C++.

☐ Select Open from the File menu of Visual C++ and open the file `VARDOC.H`.

☐ Modify the class declaration of the document class `CVarDoc` so that it looks as follows:

> **NOTE**
>
> Remember: You only have to type the code that appears between the **MY CODE STARTS HERE** and **MY CODE ENDS HERE** comments. The rest of the code is already there.

```
class CVarDoc : public CDocument
{
protected: // create from serialization only
    CVarDoc();
    DECLARE_DYNCREATE(CVarDoc)

// Attributes
public:


    ////////////////////////
    // MY CODE STARTS HERE
    ////////////////////////

    CString m_MyVar;

    ////////////////////////
    // MY CODE ENDS HERE
    ////////////////////////


// Operations
public:
```

```
// Implementation
public:
    virtual ~CVarDoc();
    virtual void Serialize(CArchive& ar);
// overridden for document i/o
#ifdef _DEBUG
    virtual void AssertValid() const;
    virtual void Dump(CDumpContext& dc) const;
#endif

protected:
    virtual BOOL OnNewDocument();

// Generated message map functions
protected:
    //{{AFX_MSG(CVarDoc)
// NOTE - the ClassWizard will add and remove
// member functions here.
//    DO NOT EDIT what you see in these
//    blocks of generated code !
    //}}AFX_MSG
    DECLARE_MESSAGE_MAP()
};
```

The code you typed,

```
CString m_MyVar;
```

defines the variable m_MyVar as a string. Because you entered this declaration under the Public: keyword of the class declaration, m_MyVar is a public data member of the document class.

As discussed in the previous chapter, the **MY CODE STARTS HERE** and **MY CODE ENDS HERE** comments that enclose your code help you to distinguish easily between your own code and code Visual C++ has written for you.

To save the modified VARDOC.H file:

☐ Select Save from the File menu of Visual C++.

Initializing the *m_MyVar* Variable

To write the code that initializes the m_MyVar data member of the document class, follow these steps:

☐ Select Open from the File menu of Visual C++ and open the file VARDOC.CPP.

☐ Modify the constructor function of the document class CVarDoc so that it looks as follows:

```
CVarDoc::CVarDoc()
{
    // TODO: add one-time construction code here


    ///////////////////////
    // MY CODE STARTS HERE
    ///////////////////////

    // Initialize m_MyVar to "Zero".
    m_MyVar = "Zero";

    ///////////////////////
    // MY CODE ENDS HERE
    ///////////////////////

}
```

The statement

```
m_MyVar = "Zero";
```

fills the variable m_MyVar with the string "Zero". Thus, on starting the application (when the document object of the VAR application is created), the data member m_MyVar of the document object is initialized to "Zero".

To save the modified VARDOC.CPP file:

☐ Select Save from the File menu.

You've finished writing the code that declares and initializes the m_MyVar data member of the document class. Next, you'll attach code to the menu of the VAR application. This code will use the m_MyVar variable.

Attaching Code to the Menu for the VAR Application

You can start by attaching code to the Current Value item of the File menu. Recall that when the user selects Current Value from the File menu, the program should display the current value of m_MyVar (see Figure 5.4).

In the previous chapter, when you attached code to the Say Hello menu item of the SAY application, you did it by running ClassWizard from App Studio (that is, you selected ClassWizard from the Resource menu of App Studio). In this chapter you'll also use ClassWizard, but instead of running it from the Resource menu of App Studio, you'll run it from the menu of Visual C++. It doesn't matter from where you run ClassWizard—run it from wherever it's most convenient for you.

To attach code to the Current Value menu item, you need to add a member function to the view class of the application:

☐ Select ClassWizard from the Browse menu of Visual C++.

Visual C++ responds by displaying the ClassWizard dialog box.

☐ Set the Class Name box (at the top of ClassWizard's dialog box) to CVarView.

☐ Select the event:

Class Name:	CVarView
Object ID:	ID_FILE_CURRENTVALUE
Message:	COMMAND

☐ That is, select ID_FILE_CURRENTVALUE from the Object IDs list box, select COMMAND from the Messages list box, and set the Class Name to CVarView. (If your ClassWizard contains tabs at the top of its window, make sure the Message Maps tab is selected.)

> **NOTE**
>
> If you can't find ID_FILE_CURRENTVALUE in your Object IDs list box, you didn't save your work after adding the Current Value menu item in App Studio. If this is the case, switch back to App Studio and save your work (that is, select Save from the File menu of App Studio).

Recall that for menus, the message COMMAND corresponds to the event, "User selected a menu item." Thus, by selecting ID_FILE_CURRENTVALUE and COMMAND you're specifying the event, "User selected Current Value from the File menu."

Now your ClassWizard dialog box looks as shown in Figure 5.9.

Figure 5.9
ClassWizard after
selecting the eclass
CVasView, *the*
ID_FILE_
CURRENTVALUE,
and the meassage
COMMAND.

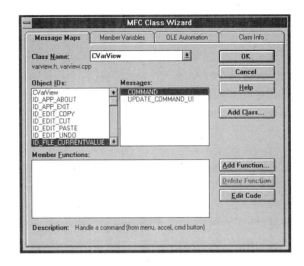

To tell ClassWizard to add the function for the event you selected:

☐ Click the Add Function button of ClassWizard.

> *ClassWizard responds by displaying the Add Member Function dialog box.*
> *ClassWizard suggests naming the new function* OnFileCurrentvalue.

☐ Click the OK button to accept the default name that ClassWizard suggests.

> *ClassWizard responds by adding the function* OnFileCurrentvalue() *to the*
> CVarView *class. This function is automatically executed whenever the user*
> *selects Current Value from the File menu.*

Note that now the function OnFileCurrentvalue() is listed in the Member Functions list box at the bottom of ClassWizard's window.

To write the OnFileCurrentvalue() function's code:

☐ Click the Edit Code button of ClassWizard.

> *ClassWizard responds by opening the file* VARVIEW.CPP *with the function*
> OnFileCurrentvalue() *ready for you to edit.*

☐ Add code to the OnFileCurrentvalue() function. After you type the code,
the function looks as follows:

```
void CVarView::OnFileCurrentvalue()
{
    // TODO: Add your command handler code here
```

```
/////////////////////
// MY CODE STARTS HERE
/////////////////////

// Get a pointer to the document class.
CVarDoc* pDoc = GetDocument();

// Display the current value of m_MyVar
MessageBox("Current value of m_MyVar is: "
                    + pDoc->m_MyVar);

/////////////////////
// MY CODE ENDS HERE
/////////////////////
```

}

To save your work:

☐ Select Save from the File menu of Visual C++.

To review the code you just typed:

```
The first statement,
CVarDoc* pDoc = GetDocument();
```

extracts the pointer (pDoc) of the document class of the application.

The next statement uses the MessageBox() function and the pDoc pointer to display the current value of m_MyVar:

```
MessageBox("Current value of m_MyVar is: "
                + pDoc->m_MyVar);
```

Note that the value of the m_MyVar data member of the document class is accessed with the expression

```
pDoc->m_MyVar
```

Although you haven't finished attaching code to all the menu items of the VAR application, you can look at the code of the OnFileCurrentvalue() function in action:

☐ Select Build VAR.EXE from the Project menu of Visual C++.

When Visual C++ completes compiling/linking the VAR application, run it:

☐ Select Execute VAR.EXE from the Project menu.

Visual C++ responds by executing the VAR application.

☐ Select Current Value from the File menu.

> *The VAR application responds by displaying a dialog box telling you that the current value of* m_MyVar *is* "Zero" *(see Figure 5.4).*

The initial value of the m_MyVar data member of the document class is "Zero", because that's how you initialized m_MyVar in the constructor of the document class.

To terminate the VAR application:

☐ Select Exit from the File menu.

Attaching Code to the Other Menu Items of the VAR Application

You still have to attach code to the One, Two, and Three menu items of the VAR application. Start with the One menu item. Recall that when the user selects One from the File menu, the program should assign the value "One" to the m_MyVar variable (see Figure 5.5).

To attach code to the One menu item of the File menu, you need to add a member function to the view class of the application:

☐ Select ClassWizard from the Browse menu of Visual C++.

☐ Set the Class Name box (at the top of ClassWizard's dialog box) to CVarView.

☐ Select the event:

> Object ID: ID_FILE_ONE
> Message: COMMAND

☐ That is, select ID_FILE_ONE from the Objects IDs list box and then select COMMAND from the Messages list box.

☐ Click the Add Function button in ClassWizard.

> *ClassWizard responds by displaying the Add Member Function dialog box. ClassWizard suggests naming the new function* OnFileOne.

☐ Click the OK button to accept the default name that ClassWizard suggests.

> *ClassWizard responds by adding the function* OnFileOne() *to the* CVarView *class. This function is automatically executed whenever the user selects One from the File menu.*

To write the `OnFileOne()` function's code:

☐ Click the Edit Code button of ClassWizard.

> *ClassWizard responds by opening the file* VARVIEW.CPP *with the function* `OnFileOne()` *ready for you to edit.*

☐ Write the code in the `OnFileOne()` function so that it looks as follows:

```
void CVarView::OnFileOne()
{
    // TODO: Add your command handler code here


    ////////////////////////
    // MY CODE STARTS HERE
    ////////////////////////

    // Get a pointer to the document class.
    CVarDoc* pDoc = GetDocument();

    // Change the value of m_MyVar to "One".
    pDoc->m_MyVar = "One";

    // Tell the user that m_MyVar was changed to "One".
    MessageBox("m_MyVar is now: " + pDoc->m_MyVar);

    ////////////////////////
    // MY CODE ENDS HERE
    ////////////////////////

}
```

Save your work:

☐ Select Save from the File menu.

To review the code you just typed:

The first statement in the `OnFileOne()` function is the same as the first statement in the `OnFileCurrentvalue()` function:

```
CVarDoc* pDoc = GetDocument();
```

This statement extracts the pointer (pDoc) of the document class.

The next statement uses the pDoc pointer to assign the value "One" to the m_MyVar data member of the document of the application:

```
pDoc->m_MyVar = "One";
```

Finally, a message box is displayed:

```
MessageBox("m_MyVar is now: " + pDoc->m_MyVar);
```

To complete the implementation of the VAR application, you still need to attach code to the Two and Three menu items of the File menu.

Follow these steps to attach code to the Two menu item:

☐ Select ClassWizard from the Browse menu of Visual C++.

☐ Set the Class Name box (at the top of ClassWizard's dialog box) to
  `CVarView`.

☐ Select the event:

  Object ID: `ID_FILE_TWO`
  Message: `COMMAND`

☐ That is, select `ID_FILE_TWO` from the Object IDs list box and then select `COMMAND` from the Messages list box.

☐ Click the Add Function button of ClassWizard.

  ClassWizard responds by displaying the Add Member Function dialog box. ClassWizard suggests naming the new function `OnFileTwo`.

☐ Click the OK button to accept the default name that ClassWizard suggests.

  ClassWizard responds by adding the function `OnFileTwo()` *to the* `CVarView` *class. This function is automatically executed whenever the user selects Two from the File menu.*

To write the `OnFileTwo()` function's code:

☐ Click the Edit Code button of ClassWizard.

  ClassWizard responds by opening the file `VARVIEW.CPP` *with the function* `OnFileTwo()` *ready for you to edit.*

☐ Write the code in the `OnFileTwo()` function so that it looks as follows:

```
void CVarView::OnFileTwo()
{
    // TODO: Add your command handler code here

    /////////////////////////
    // MY CODE STARTS HERE
    /////////////////////////
```

```
// Get a pointer to the document class.
CVarDoc* pDoc = GetDocument();

// Change the value of m_MyVar to "Two".
pDoc->m_MyVar = "Two";

// Tell the user that m_MyVar was changed to "One".
MessageBox("m_MyVar is now: " + pDoc->m_MyVar);

/////////////////////
// MY CODE ENDS HERE
/////////////////////
```

}

As you can see, the OnFileTwo() function's code is similar to the OnFileOne() function's code. The only difference is that now, the variable m_MyVar is assigned the string "Two" (not "One").

There is still one more menu item left: the Three menu item.

Follow these steps to attach code to the Three menu item:

☐ Select ClassWizard from the Browse menu of Visual C++.

☐ Set the Class Name box (at the top of ClassWizard's dialog box) to CVarView.

☐ Select the event:

> Object ID: ID_FILE_THREE
> Message: COMMAND

☐ That is, select ID_FILE_THREE from the Object IDs list box and then select COMMAND from the Messages list box.

☐ Click the Add Function button of ClassWizard.

> *ClassWizard responds by displaying the Add Member Function dialog box. ClassWizard suggests naming the new function OnFileThree.*

☐ Click the OK button to accept the default name that ClassWizard suggests.

> *ClassWizard responds by adding the function OnFileThree() to the CVarView class. This function is automatically executed whenever the user selects Three from the File menu.*

To write the OnFileThree() function's code:

☐ Click the Edit Code button of ClassWizard.

ClassWizard responds by opening the file VARVIEW.CPP *with the function* OnFileThree() *ready for you to edit.*

☐ Write the code in the OnFileThree() function so that it looks as follows:

```
void CVarView::OnFileThree()
{
    // TODO: Add your command handler code here

    /////////////////////////
    // MY CODE STARTS HERE
    /////////////////////////

    // Get a pointer to the document class.
    CVarDoc* pDoc = GetDocument();

    // Change the value of m_MyVar to "Three".
    pDoc->m_MyVar = "Three";

    // Tell the user that m_MyVar was changed to "Three".
    MessageBox("m_MyVar is now: " + pDoc->m_MyVar);

    /////////////////////
    // MY CODE ENDS HERE
    /////////////////////
}
```

As you can see, the OnFileThree() function is similar to the code's in the OnFileOne() and OnFileTwo() functions. The only difference is that now the variable m_MyVar is assigned the string "Three".

☐ Save your work! (Select Save from the File menu.)

You have finished writing the VAR application's code!

To see your code in action:

☐ Select Build VAR.EXE from the Project menu of Visual C++.

When Visual C++ completes compiling/linking the VAR application, run it:

☐ Select Execute VAR.EXE from the Project menu.

Visual C++ responds by executing the VAR application.

☐ Experiment with the One, Two, Three, and Current Value items of the File menu.

As you can see, the VAR application changes the value of the m_MyVar variable in accordance with your selection.

To terminate the VAR application:

☐ Select Exit from the File menu.

Why Should You Declare Variables in the Document Class?

In the VAR application, you defined the data member variable m_MyVar in the document class, and then you accessed this variable in the view class by using the function GetDocument().

In the following chapters, you'll see examples of applications that declare and define variables in the view class (without declaring variables in the document class).

So should you declare and define variables in the document class or in the view class? If you want your application to be a Multiple-View application, declare the variables in the document class. What is a Multiple-View application? It's an application that can load and display several views (windows) of the same document. In addition, if the user modifies the contents of one of the views, this modification automatically takes place in all the other views. To see a Multiple-View application in action:

☐ Start a Windows program that supports the Multiple-View feature. (For example, the word processor Microsoft Word for Windows supports this feature.)

☐ Open a new document.

☐ Type something in the document.

☐ Save the document as Try.DOC.

☐ Select Open from the File menu and load the same document again.

> *So now you should have two views (windows) of the same document on the desktop.*

☐ Arrange the documents so that they look as shown in Figure 5.10.

Figure 5.10.
Two views of the
same document in
Word for Windows.

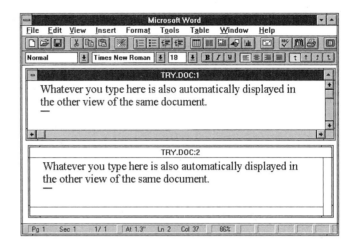

☐ Type something in one of the views.

> *As you can see, whatever you type in one of the views is automatically displayed in the other view!*

Now you know what Multiple-View is all about. You know that to create a Windows application that supports the Multiple-View feature, you'll need to store data in the document class. (Later in the book, you'll learn how to write Windows applications that support this feature.)

6

Playing WAV Files Through the PC Speaker

In this chapter you'll learn how to play
WAV files through the PC speaker
without any additional hardware (no
sound card is needed) and without any
drivers. If you browse through the table
of contents of this book, you'll notice
that there are several chapters dedicated
to multimedia. So why do we
introduce WAV playback at this point
in this book?

There are three reasons for introducing WAV playback now.

Many programming books start by introducing the Hello program, a program that displays the message "Hello World" on the screen. We would like to follow this tradition, but just displaying "Hello World" is no fun! The SayHello program that you'll write will actually speak in a human voice.

By learning this topic, you'll understand how to declare variables in the view class. (Recall that in Chapter 5, "Storing Variables in the Document Class," you declared variables in the document class.)

By learning this topic at this early stage, you'll be able to utilize this technology immediately and apply it to your programs.

Executing the SayHello Application

Before you write the SayHello application, try executing the copy of it that resides in your C:\VCPROG\ORIGINAL\CH06\SAYHELLO directory. This way you'll gain a better understanding of what the application is supposed to do.

To execute the SayHello application:

☐ Use the Run item from the Program Manager's File menu to execute
C:\VCPROG\ORIGINAL\CH06\SAYHELLO\SayHello.EXE.

Windows responds by executing the SayHello.EXE application.

The hourglass cursor appears, and then SayHello says, "Hello," through the PC speaker.

The main window of the SayHello application is shown in Figure 6.1.

*Figure 6.1.
The SayHello application's main window.*

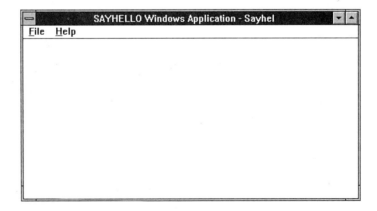

As shown in Figure 6.1, SayHello has a File menu and a Help menu. These menus are shown in Figures 6.2 and 6.3.

Figure 6.2.
The SayHello
program's File
menu.

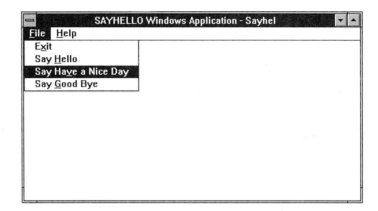

Figure 6.3.
The SayHello
program's Help
menu.

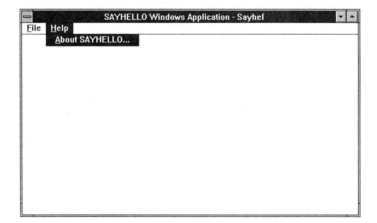

☐ Select the various items of the File menu. For example, select Say Have a Nice Day from the File menu.

SayHello responds by saying, "Have a Nice Day," through your PC's speaker.

☐ Experiment with the other Say items of the File menu.

As you can hear, SayHello says, "Hello," "Have a Nice Day," and "Good-bye."

On terminating the SayHello application, SayHello says, "It's been fun working with you." To hear this:

☐ Select Exit from the File menu or click the minus icon that appears at the upper-left corner of the window and then select Close from the System menu that pops up.

Creating the SayHello Project

To create the project of the SayHello application:

☐ Select AppWizard from the Project menu.

Visual C++ responds by executing AppWizard.

☐ Use the Directory list box to select the directory C:\vcProg\Practice\CH06.

☐ Type sayhello in the Project Name box.

Now your AppWizard dialog box looks as shown in Figure 6.4.

Figure 6.4.
The AppWizard
dialog box for the
SayHello
application.

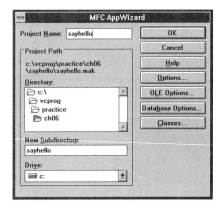

☐ Click the Options button and set the options as shown in Figure 6.5.

Figure 6.5.
Setting the options
for the SayHello
application.

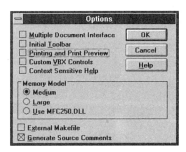

☐ Click the OK button in the Options dialog box, then click the OK button in the AppWizard dialog box, and finally click the Create button in the New Application Information dialog box.

AppWizard responds by creating the SayHello project and all the skeleton files of the SayHello application.

Set the project options for release:

☐ Select Project from the Options menu, click the Release radio button of the Build Mode, and then click the OK button.

Introduction to Dynamic Linked Libraries (DLLs)

A *Dynamic Linked Library (DLL)* is a library of functions that your Windows application can use. Typically, a DLL contains functions that are used by several Windows applications. You can write your own DLLs, or you can purchase third-party DLLs.

One example of a DLL is the TegoSND.DLL file. This file was copied to your C:\Windows directory when you installed the book's software. This DLL contains functions that you can use to play WAV files through the PC speaker. To use these functions from within your Visual C++ programs, you have to:

Tell the Visual C++ compiler the name of the DLL and the name of the functions that reside in the DLL.

Tell the Visual C++ compiler the prototypes of these functions.

Specifying the Name of the DLL and the Names of the Functions

As stated, you have to tell the Visual C++ compiler the name of the DLL and the names of the DLL functions that your application uses. You do that in the DEF file of the application. When you created the SayHello project, AppWizard automatically created the file SayHello.DEF.

☐ Select Open from the File menu and select the file
   C:\vcProg\Practice\CH06\SAYHELLO\SayHello.DEF.

> **NOTE**
>
> Take a look at the SayHello.DEF file. It contains various overhead statements. Unlike C/C++ statements, each statement doesn't terminate with the ; character. In fact, the ; character is used at the beginning of a comment line. That is, the ; character in the DEF file serves the same purpose as the // characters in C++.

☐ Add code to the SayHello.DEF file. After you add the code, the SayHello.DEF file looks as follows:

```
; sayhello.def : Declares the module parameters for the application.

NAME            SAYHELLO
DESCRIPTION     'SAYHELLO Windows Application'
EXETYPE         WINDOWS

CODE            PRELOAD MOVEABLE DISCARDABLE
DATA            PRELOAD MOVEABLE MULTIPLE

HEAPSIZE        1024    ; initial heap size
; Stack size is passed as argument
; to linker's /STACK option


;;;;;;;;;;;;;;;;;;;;;;;;;;
; MY CODE STARTS HERE
;;;;;;;;;;;;;;;;;;;;;;;;;;


;;;;;;;;;;;;;;;;;;;;;;;;;;;;;;;;;;;;;;;;;;;;;;;;
; sp_functions from the TegoSND.DLL library
;;;;;;;;;;;;;;;;;;;;;;;;;;;;;;;;;;;;;;;;;;;;;;;;

IMPORTS
TegoSND.sp_OpenSession
TegoSND.sp_PlaySnd
TegoSND.sp_MouseOn
TegoSND.sp_MouseOff
TegoSND.sp_CloseSession
```

```
;;;;;;;;;;;;;;;;;;;;;;;;;
; MY CODE ENDS HERE
;;;;;;;;;;;;;;;;;;;;;;;;;
```

The IMPORTS statement that you added is an instruction to the compiler, telling it that the lines after the IMPORTS statement list the functions that reside in a DLL. For example, the statement

```
TegoSND.sp_OpenSession
```

is an instruction to the compiler, telling it that the program might use a function called sp_OpenSession() from a DLL called TegoSND.DLL.

Specifying a DLL function in the DEF file doesn't mean that your program must make use of the function.

The TegoSND.DLL library contains other sp_ functions. However, because SayHello doesn't use these functions, you don't have to include them in the IMPORTS list. This is the reason for specifying only five sp_ functions in the SayHello.DEF file.

> **NOTE**
>
> The functions from the TegoSND.DLL library start with the characters sp_. For example, sp_OpenSession() is a function from the TegoSND.DLL library.

> **NOTE**
>
> As you can see, the DEF file contains many other statements. These statements were written by AppWizard. This is one of the advantages of using AppWizard; you don't have to write a repeated overhead code.

Specifying the Prototypes of the DLL's Functions

Because your application uses functions from the DLL, you must tell the compiler the prototypes of these functions. The prototypes of the functions from the TegoSND.DLL library reside in the file C:\vcProg\DLL\TegoSND.H. Thus, you have to #include this file in your SayHello.H file:

☐ Select Open from the File menu of Visual C++ and open the file
`C:\vcProg\Practice\CH06\SayHello\SayHello.H`.

☐ Add the `#include` statement at the beginning of the `SayHello.H` file so that it looks as follows:

```
// sayhello.h : main header file for the SAYHELLO
// application

#ifndef __AFXWIN_H__
    #error include 'stdafx.h' before including this file for PCH
#endif

#include "resource.h"          // main symbols

/////////////////////////
// MY CODE STARTS HERE
/////////////////////////

// Include the prototypes of the TegoSND.DLL functions
#include "c:\vcProg\DLL\TegoSND.H"

/////////////////////////
// MY CODE ENDS HERE
/////////////////////////
.....
.....
.....
```

Using the *extern "C"* Keyword

C++ is a much more powerful programming language than C. However, this doesn't mean that you can discard all your C stuff! C was around for many years, and millions of lines of code were written with it. To enable you to make use of these powerful C libraries, the designers of Visual C++ have included the `extern "C"` keyword in the language. To specify the prototypes of functions written with C, preface them with the `extern "C"` keyword:

```
extern "C"
{

...............................................
... Here you type the prototypes of functions  ...
... that were written with C.                  ...
...............................................

}
```

By using the extern "C" keyword, your Visual C++ programs can use libraries written with C.

Take a look at the file c:\vcProg\DLL\TegoSND.H; it includes the extern "C" statement:

```
/*=========================================================
 File name: TegoSND.h

 This is the h file of the TegoSND.DLL file.

 TegoSND.DLL contains sp_ functions for playing sound
 through the PC speaker without any drivers, and without
 any additional hardware.

 (C) Copyright TegoSoft Inc. 1992, 1993
 (R) All rights reserved.
 TegoSoft Inc.
 Box 389, Bellmore, NY 11710
 Phone:(516)783-4824
 =========================================================*/


/*=========================================================
 PROTOTYPES
 =========================================================*/
extern "C"
{

...................................
... Prototypes of sp functions .....
...................................

}
```

As you can see from the TegoSND.H file, the extern "C" keyword is used to specify that the sp_ functions were written with C.

Declaring a Variable in the View Class

The SayHello application has to use a variable (m_HelloSession) that is accessible by the member functions of the view class (CSayhelloView).

To declare the m_HelloSession variable as a data member of the view class CSayhelloView, follow these steps:

☐ Select Open from the File menu of Visual C++, and open the file
C:\vcProg\Practice\CH06\SayHello\sayhevw.h.

☐ Declare the integer m_HelloSession as a data member of the CSayhelloView
class. The CSayhelloView class is declared in the sayhevw.h file. After you
declare this variable, your CSayhelloView class looks as follows:

```
class CSayhelloView : public CView
{
protected: // create from serialization only
     CSayhelloView();
     DECLARE_DYNCREATE(CSayhelloView)

// Attributes
public:
     CSayhelloDoc* GetDocument();


     //////////////////////////
     // MY CODE STARTS HERE
     //////////////////////////

     // Declaring m_HelloSession as a data member
     // of the view class.
     int m_HelloSession;

     //////////////////////////
     // MY CODE ENDS HERE
     //////////////////////////


// Operations
public:

// Implementation
public:
     virtual ~CSayhelloView();
     virtual void OnDraw(CDC* pDC);
// overridden to draw this view
#ifdef _DEBUG
     virtual void AssertValid() const;
     virtual void Dump(CDumpContext& dc) const;
#endif

protected:

// Generated message map functions
protected:
```

```
//{{AFX_MSG(CSayhelloView)
// NOTE - the ClassWizard will add and remove member functions here.
//    DO NOT EDIT what you see in these blocks of generated code !
//}}AFX_MSG
    DECLARE_MESSAGE_MAP()
};
```

Opening a WAV Session

Before you can play WAV files, you must first open a WAV session with the file to be played. To open a WAV session, use the sp_OpenSession() function.

> **NOTE**
>
> Before playing a WAV file, you must open a WAV session with the sp_OpenSession() function.
>
> The returned value of sp_OpenSession() is an integer. This integer serves as the ID of the session.
>
> If the returned value is less than zero, the WAV session can't be opened (for example, the WAV file doesn't exist).
>
> The sp_OpenSession() function has one parameter. This parameter specifies the path and name of the WAV file to be opened.

You need to open the WAV file only once during the life of the program. Thus, a good place to open a WAV session is in the constructor function of the view class (because the constructor function is executed only once, when the view class is first created):

☐ Add code to the constructor function of the CSayhelloView class that resides in the SAYHEVW.CPP file. After you add the code, the CSayhelloView() constructor function looks as follows:

```
/////////////////////////////////////////////////////////
// CSayhelloView construction/destruction

CSayhelloView::CSayhelloView()
{
    // TODO: add construction code here
```

```
///////////////////////
// MY CODE STARTS HERE
///////////////////////

// Open a WAV session for Hello.WAV
char FileToOpen[255];
strcpy ( FileToOpen, "\\vcProg\\WAV\\Hello.WAV" );
m_HelloSession = sp_OpenSession ( FileToOpen );

// If WAV session can't be opened, display an error
// message box.
if ( m_HelloSession < 0 )
   {
   CString Message, Caption;
   Message = "Can't open the file: ";
   Message = Message + FileToOpen;
   Caption = "Error";
   MessageBox ( Message, Caption );
   }
 else
   {
   // The WAV session was opened successfully, so
   // play "Hello"
   sp_PlaySnd ( m_HelloSession,
                SP_START_OF_FILE,
                16000L);
   }

///////////////////////
// MY CODE ENDS HERE
///////////////////////
}
```

The code that you typed first declares the FileToOpen local string variable:

```
char FileToOpen[255];
```

and then the strcpy() function is used to fill this string with the path- and filename of the WAV file:

```
strcpy ( FileToOpen, "\\vcProg\\WAV\\Hello.WAV" );
```

Note that in the previous statement, the \\ characters are used (not the \ character). That is, just as in C, C++ requires that you use \\ when specifying the path of a file.

You then use the sp_OpenSession() function to open the WAV session:

```
m_HelloSession = sp_OpenSession ( FileToOpen );
```

The next statement is an if statement that checks whether the WAV session was opened successfully. If it wasn't, a message box is displayed:

```
CString Message, Caption;
Message = "Can't open the file: ";
Message = Message + FileToOpen;
Caption = "Error";
MessageBox ( Message, Caption );
```

This code declares two local strings (`Message` and `Caption`) of class `CString`. The `CString` class is part of the MFC that comes with Visual C++:

```
CString Message, Caption;
```

The next statement updates the `Message` string with the string `"Can't open the file:"`

```
Message = "Can't open the file: ";
```

Then the filename is added to the `Message` string:

```
Message = Message + FileToOpen;
```

Putting it all together, `Message` is now equal to

```
Can't open the file: \vcProg\WAV\Hello.WAV
```

Note how easy it is to manipulate strings of class `CString`. Instead of using the `strcpy()` and `strcat()` functions, you assign the string as in

```
Message = "Can't open the file: ";
```

and you add the strings as in

```
Message = Message + FileToOpen;
```

The next statement updates the `Caption` string with the string `"Error"`:

```
Caption = "Error";
```

Finally, the `MessageBox()` member function of the `CSayhelloView` class is executed:

```
MessageBox ( Message, Caption );
```

The first parameter of `MessageBox()` is the `Message` string, which appears as the message of the message box. The second parameter of `MessageBox()` is the `Caption` string, which appears as the caption of the message box.

Putting it all together, if `sp_OpenSession()` returns a value less than zero, the program displays the message box shown in Figure 6.6.

Figure 6.6.
The message box
that SayHello
displays if the WAV
session can't be
opened.

NOTE

`CSayhelloView` is a class derived from `CView`. `CView` is a class derived from `CWnd`. One of the member functions of `CWnd` is `MessageBox()`. Thus, `CSayhelloView` inherited the `MessageBox()` member function.

If `sp_OpenSession()` successfully opens the WAV file, the `else` is satisfied and the WAV file is played with the following statement:

```
sp_PlaySnd ( m_HelloSession,
             SP_START_OF_FILE,
             16000L);
```

As you can see, the `sp_PlaySnd()` function has three parameters. The first parameter is the session number that was returned from the `sp_OpenSession()` function.

The second parameter of the `sp_PlaySnd()` function is the starting point in the WAV file. For example, if you want to play from byte 3,000 to byte 5,000, use the statement

```
sp_PlaySnd ( m_HelloSession,
             3000L,
             5000L);
```

If you want to play from the beginning of the WAV file, you can supply `SP_START_OF_FILE` as the second parameter of the `sp_PlaySnd()` function.

The last parameter of `sp_PlaySnd()` is the last byte that will be played. As it turns out, the audio phrase, "Hello," is between byte 0 and byte 16,000 of the `Hello.WAV` file. This is the reason for supplying 16000 as the third parameter of the `sp_PlaySnd()` function.

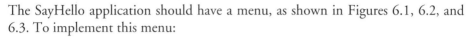

The Visual Implementation of the SayHello Program

Now you'll visually design the menu of the SayHello program.

The SayHello application should have a menu, as shown in Figures 6.1, 6.2, and 6.3. To implement this menu:

☐ Select App Studio from the Tools menu of Visual C++.

Visual C++ responds by running App Studio.

☐ Select the Menu item in the Type list and then double-click the IDR_MAINFRAME item in the Resources list.

Visual C++ responds by displaying the menu of the SayHello application in design mode.

☐ Design the menu so that it looks as shown in Figures 6.1, 6.2, and 6.3.

> **NOTE**
>
> If you forgot how to design a menu, refer to Chapter 4, "Your First True Windows Application." It includes a detailed description of how to design a menu.

To save your work:

☐ Select Save from the File menu of App Studio.

The visual implementation of the SayHello application is completed. Next, you will write the code of the SayHello application.

Attaching Code to the Say Hello Menu Item

When you select the Say Hello item from the File menu, the SayHello application should say, "Hello." Thus, you need to attach code to the Say Hello menu item that plays the "Hello" audio phrase through the PC speaker:

To attach code to the Say Hello menu item of the File menu, you need to add a member function to the view class of the application:

☐ Start ClassWizard. (You can start ClassWizard from either the Browse menu in Visual C++ or from the Resource menu in App Studio.)

☐ Set the Class Name box (at the top of ClassWizard's dialog box) to CSayhelloView.

☐ Select the event ID_FILE_SAYHELLO : COMMAND. (That is, select ID_FILE_SAYHELLO from the Object IDs list box and then select COMMAND from the Messages list box.)

☐ Click the Add Function button in ClassWizard.

ClassWizard responds by displaying the Add Member Function dialog box. ClassWizard suggests naming the new function OnFileSayhello().

☐ Click the OK button to accept the default name that ClassWizard suggests.

ClassWizard responds by adding the function OnFileSayhello() to the CSayhelloView class. This function is automatically executed whenever the user selects Say Hello from the File menu.

To write the OnFileSayhello() function's code, do the following:

☐ Click the Edit Code button in ClassWizard.

ClassWizard responds by opening the file SAYHEVW.CPP with the function OnFileSayhello() ready for you to edit.

☐ Add code to the OnFileSayhello() function so that it looks as follows:

```
void CSayhelloView::OnFileSayhello()
{
    // TODO: Add your command handler code here

    /////////////////////////
    // MY CODE STARTS HERE
    /////////////////////////

    // Play the audio phrase "Hello"
    sp_PlaySnd ( m_HelloSession,
                 SP_START_OF_FILE,
                 16000L );
```

```
///////////////////,
// MY CODE ENDS HERE
///////////////////
```

}

The code that you added to the `OnFileSayhello()` function consists of a single statement:

```
sp_PlaySnd ( m_HelloSession,
             SP_START_OF_FILE,
             16000L );
```

This statement plays the "Hello" audio section of the `Hello.WAV` file (that is, from byte location 0 to byte location 16,000).

Attaching Code to the Say Have a Nice Day Menu Item

In the following steps, you'll repeat the preceding steps to attach code to the Say Have a Nice Day menu item:

☐ Start ClassWizard.

☐ Set the Class Name box (at the top of ClassWizard's dialog box) to `CSayhelloView`.

☐ Select the event `ID_FILE_SAYHAVEANICEDAY : COMMAND`. (That is, select `ID_FILE_SAYHAVEANICEDAY` from the Object IDs list box and then select `COMMAND` from the Messages list box.)

☐ Click the Add Function button in ClassWizard.

   ClassWizard responds by displaying the Add Member Function dialog box. ClassWizard suggests naming the new function `OnFileSayhaveaniceday()`.

☐ Click the OK button to accept the default name that ClassWizard suggests.

   ClassWizard responds by adding the function `OnFileSayhaveaniceday()` *to the* `CSayhelloView` *class. This function is executed automatically whenever the user selects Say Have a Nice Day from the File menu.*

To write the `OnFileSayhaveaniceday()` function's code:

☐ Click the Edit Code button of ClassWizard.

   ClassWizard responds by opening the file `SAYHEVW.CPP` *with the function* `OnFileSayhaveaniceday()` *ready for you to edit.*

☐ Add code to the `OnFileSayhaveaniceday()` function so that it looks as follows:

```
void CSayhelloView::OnFileSayhaveaniceday()
{
    // TODO: Add your command handler code here


    //////////////////////
    // MY CODE STARTS HERE
    //////////////////////

    sp_PlaySnd ( m_HelloSession,
                 18000L,
                 50000L );

    //////////////////////
    // MY CODE ENDS HERE
    //////////////////////

}
```

The code that you typed plays the audio section (18,000–50,000) of the `Hello.WAV` file. How can you find out whether the audio phrase, "Have a Nice Day," resides between these byte locations? Use a WAV editor program. For example, Figure 6.7 shows the Quick Recorder program with the section, "Have a Nice Day," highlighted. As you can see, it's easy to distinguish the various audio sections that contain a human voice. The Quick Recorder program comes with the Microsoft sound system package. If you don't have this program, you can use any other WAV editor program. For example, you can use the Sound Recorder program that is shipped with Windows (it usually resides in the Accessories program group).

NOTE

To extract the byte locations of various audio sections, you can use the Sound Recorder program or the Media Player program. Both programs come with Windows. You can use them to extract the coordinates of audio sections in WAV files.

Usually, the coordinates of the audio sections that are extracted by using a WAV editor program are supplied in units of milliseconds. However, converting the time coordinates to byte coordinates is easy. All you have to know is the sampling rate of the WAV file. For example, if a certain WAV file was recorded at 11,025 Hz, the conversion from the time coordinate 100 milliseconds to its corresponding byte coordinate is

[Byte Coordinates] = 11,025 * 100 / 1000 = 1102.5

which tells you that 1103 is the byte coordinate corresponding to the time coordinate 100 milliseconds.

Figure 6.7.
The `Hello.WAV`
file with the "Have
a Nice Day" audio
section highlighted.

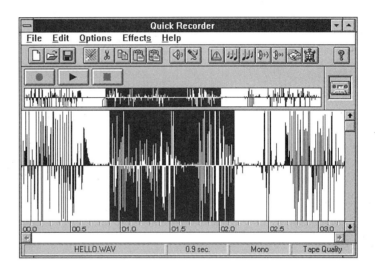

Attaching Code to the Say Good-Bye Menu Item

Now attach code to the Say Good-Bye menu item:

☐ Start ClassWizard.

☐ Set the Class Name box (at the top of ClassWizard's dialog box) to
`CSayhelloView`.

☐ Select the event `ID_FILE_SAYGOODBYE : COMMAND`. (That is, select
`ID_FILE_SAYGOODBYE` from the Object IDs list box and then select `COMMAND`
from the Messages list box.)

☐ Click the Add Function button of ClassWizard.

ClassWizard responds by displaying the Add Member Function dialog box. ClassWizard suggests naming the new function OnFileSaygoodbye()*.*

☐ Click the OK button to accept the default name that ClassWizard suggests.

ClassWizard responds by adding the function OnFileSaygoodbye() *to the* CSayhelloView *class. This function is automatically executed whenever the user selects Say Good-Bye from the File menu.*

To write the OnFileSaygoodbye() function's code:

☐ Click the Edit Code button of ClassWizard.

ClassWizard responds by opening the file SAYHEVW.CPP *with the function* OnFileSaygoodbye() *ready for you to edit.*

☐ Add code to the OnFileSaygoodbye() function so that it looks as follows:

```
void CSayhelloView::OnFileSaygoodbye()
{
    // TODO: Add your command handler code here


    /////////////////////////
    // MY CODE STARTS HERE
    /////////////////////////

    sp_PlaySnd ( m_HelloSession,
                 50000L,
                 SP_END_OF_FILE );


    /////////////////////////,
    // MY CODE ENDS HERE
    /////////////////////////

}
```

The OnFileSaygoodbye() function's code plays the audio section from byte location 50,000 to the end of the WAV file. These byte coordinates correspond to the audio section "Good-Bye."

Attaching Code to the Exit Point of the Program

There is one more thing to do to the SayHello program: it would be nice to have SayHello say, "It's been fun working with you," every time the user terminates the SayHello program.

The WAV file that contains the audio phrase, "It's been fun working with you," is \vcProg\WAV\ItsBeen1.WAV.

As you know by now, you must open a WAV session before playing the WAV file. The returned value from the sp_OpenSession() function for ItsBeen1.WAV is stored in a variable called m_ItsBeenSession. This variable should be declared in the class declaration of the CSayhelloView class. (Recall that you already declared the m_HelloSession variable in the CSayhelloView class declaration.)

☐ Add the variable m_ItsBeenSession to the CSayhelloView class declaration in the sayhevw.h file. After you add this variable, the view class declaration looks as follows:

```
class CSayhelloView : public CView
{
protected: // create from serialization only
    CSayhelloView();
    DECLARE_DYNCREATE(CSayhelloView)

// Attributes
public:
    CSayhelloDoc* GetDocument();

    /////////////////////////
    // MY CODE STARTS HERE
    /////////////////////////

    int m_HelloSession;
    int m_ItsBeenSession;

    /////////////////////////
    // MY CODE ENDS HERE
    /////////////////////////


// Operations
public:

// Implementation
public:
    virtual ~CSayhelloView();
    virtual void OnDraw(CDC* pDC);  // overridden to draw this view
#ifdef _DEBUG
    virtual void AssertValid() const;
    virtual void Dump(CDumpContext& dc) const;
#endif
```

```
protected:
// Generated message map functions
protected:
    //{{AFX_MSG(CSayhelloView)
    afx_msg void OnFileSayhello();
    afx_msg void OnFileSayhaveaniceday();
    afx_msg void OnFileSaygoodbye();
    //}}AFX_MSG
    DECLARE_MESSAGE_MAP()
};
```

☐ Add code that opens the ItsBeen1.WAV session in the constructor function of the CSayhelloView() class. This constructor function resides in the sayhevw.CPP file. After you add the code, the CSayhelloView() constructor function looks as follows:

```
CSayhelloView::CSayhelloView()
{
    // TODO: add construction code here

    /////////////////////////
    // MY CODE STARTS HERE
    /////////////////////////

    char FileToOpen[255];


    // Open the Hello.WAV session
    strcpy ( FileToOpen, "\\vcProg\\WAV\\Hello.WAV" );
    m_HelloSession = sp_OpenSession ( FileToOpen );

     // Open the ItsBeen1.WAV session
    strcpy ( FileToOpen, "\\vcProg\\WAV\\ItsBeen1.WAV" );
    m_ItsBeenSession = sp_OpenSession ( FileToOpen );

    // If Hello WAV session can not be opened,
    // display a message box.
    if ( m_HelloSession < 0 )
        {
        CString Message, Caption;
        Message = "Can't open the file: ";
        Message = Message + FileToOpen;
        Caption = "Error";
        MessageBox ( Message, Caption );
        }
      else
        {
        // Play the Hello audio section.
        sp_PlaySnd ( m_HelloSession,
```

```
                    SP_START_OF_FILE,
                    16000L);
     }


  // If It's been WAV session can not be opened,
  // display a message box.
  if ( m_ItsBeenSession < 0 )
     {
     CString Message, Caption;
     Message = "Can't open the file: ";
     Message = Message + FileToOpen;
     Caption = "Error";
     MessageBox ( Message, Caption );
     }


  /////////////////////
  // MY CODE ENDS HERE
  /////////////////////

}
```

The code that you added uses sp_OpenSession() to open the ItsBeen1.WAV file.

Now that the WAV session is open, you have to call the sp_PlaySnd() function to play the ItsBeen1.WAV file at a point in the program that is executed whenever the program terminates.

Can you think of a point in the program that is executed whenever the user closes the window of the SayHello application? You guessed it! That point is in the destructor function of the view class of the application (the destructor of the CSayhelloView class).

☐ Open the sayhevw.CPP file and add code to the destructor function of the CSayhelloView class. After you add the code, the destructor function looks as follows:

```
CSayhelloView::~CSayhelloView()
{

    /////////////////////////
    // MY CODE STARTS HERE
    /////////////////////////

    sp_PlaySnd ( m_ItsBeenSession,
                 SP_START_OF_FILE,
                 SP_END_OF_FILE );
```

159

```
///////////////////,
// MY CODE ENDS HERE
///////////////////
```

```
}
```

The code you typed calls the sp_PlaySnd() function:

```
sp_PlaySnd ( m_ItsBeenSession,
             SP_START_OF_FILE,
             SP_END_OF_FILE );
```

The second and third parameters (SP_START_OF_FILE and SP_END_OF_FILE) indicate that the entire WAV file should be played. The first parameter is m_ItsBeenSession. This is the value that was returned when the ItsBeen1.WAV file was opened.

Closing the Sound Sessions

The TegoSND.DLL library lets your application open as many WAV sessions as it needs. For example, SayHello opens two sessions, m_HelloSession and m_ItsBeenSession. However, when you no longer need the sessions, you must close them to free memory for the system. To close a sound session, you have to execute the sp_CloseSession() function. Thus, in the following steps you'll close the two sessions that you opened.

To close the WAV sessions in the destructor function of the view class:

☐ Type the sp_CloseSession() statements in the destructor function of the CSayhelloView class in the sayhevw.CPP file. After you type these statements, the destructor function looks as follows:

```
CSayhelloView::~CSayhelloView()
{

    /////////////////////////
    // MY CODE STARTS HERE
    /////////////////////////

    sp_PlaySnd ( m_ItsBeenSession,
                 SP_START_OF_FILE,
                 SP_END_OF_FILE );

    sp_CloseSession ( m_HelloSession );
    sp_CloseSession ( m_ItsBeenSession );
```

```
//////////////////////,
// MY CODE ENDS HERE
//////////////////////
```

}

The sp_CloseSession() has a single parameter, which is the session number of the WAV session to be closed.

Now you can compile, link, and execute the SayHello application:

☐ Select Rebuild All SAYHELLO.EXE from the Project menu.

   Visual C++ responds by compiling and linking the SayHello application.

☐ Select Execute SAYHELLO.EXE from the Project menu.

   Visual C++ responds by executing the SayHello application.

☐ Experiment with the SayHello application and verify its proper operation.

NOTE

The TegoSND.DLL library supplied with the book's software is the limited version of the DLL. With it, you can play only the WAV files supplied with the book's software. To play any other WAV file (for example, your voice), you need to purchase the full version of the TegoSND.DLL library. You can get it directly from TegoSoft, Inc. at this address:

TegoSoft, Inc.
Box 389
Bellmore, NY 11710
ATTN: TegoSND.DLL for Visual C++
Phone: (516)783–4824

The price of the full-version DLL is $29.95, plus $5.00 for shipping and handling.

Summary

In this chapter you learned how to use some of the sp_ functions of the TegoSND.DLL library. However, you learned only how to play the audio sections of a WAV file.

During the course of this book you'll learn how to use additional sp_ functions and how to display animation (moving graphics and text) in synchronization with the playback, as well as other interesting sound-related tasks.

7

Designing Your First Dialog Box

In this chapter you'll learn how to implement an important Windows feature—dialog boxes. As you know, every Windows application communicates with the user via dialog boxes. Thus, knowing how to incorporate dialog boxes into your applications is important.

Writing an Application That Includes a Dialog Box

Now you'll write an application that has a custom-made dialog box in it. The application is called DIA.

Before you start writing this application, execute the copy of it that resides in your `C:\VCPROG\ORIGINAL\CH07\DIA` directory.

To execute the DIA application:

☐ In Windows, select Run from the Program Manager's File menu.

   Windows responds by displaying the Run dialog box.

☐ Type `C:\vcProg\Original\CH07\DIA\DIA.EXE` in the Command Line box and then click the OK button.

   Windows responds by executing the DIA application.

The main window of the DIA application appears, as shown in Figure 7.1.

Figure 7.1.
The DIA
application's main
window.

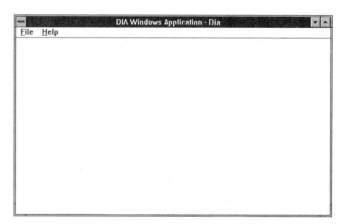

The DIA application has two popup menus: File and Help. These menus are shown in Figures 7.2 and 7.3.

Figure 7.2.
The DIA
application's File
menu.

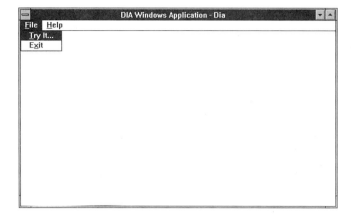

Figure 7.3.
The DIA
application's Help
menu.

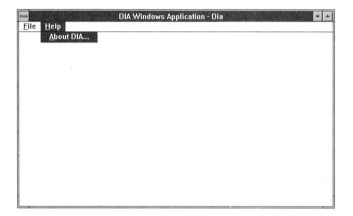

☐ Select Try It from the File menu.

> *The DIA application responds by displaying a dialog box, as shown in*
> *Figure 7.4.*

Figure 7.4.
The DIA
application's dialog
box.

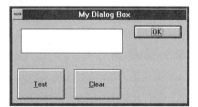

As you can see from Figure 7.4, the dialog box has an OK button, a Test button, a Clear button, and an edit box.

Experiment with the buttons of the dialog box:

☐ Click the Test button.

> *The DIA application responds by displaying the text, "THIS IS A TEST" in the edit box (see Figure 7.5).*

Figure 7.5.
The DIA
application's dialog
box after clicking
the Test button.

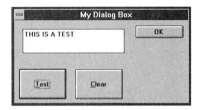

☐ Now, click the Clear button.

> *DIA responds by clearing the text in the edit box.*

To close the dialog box:

☐ Click the OK button.

To exit from the DIA application:

☐ Select Exit from the File menu.

Now that you know what the DIA application should do, you can start learning to write it.

Creating the Project of the DIA Application

To create the project of the DIA application:

☒ Select AppWizard from the Project menu.

> *Visual C++ responds by running AppWizard.*

☒ Use the Directory list box to select the directory C:\VCPROG\PRACTICE\CH07.

☒ Type dia in the Project Name box.

Your AppWizard dialog box looks as shown in Figure 7.6.

Figure 7.6.
The AppWizard
dialog box for the
DIA application.

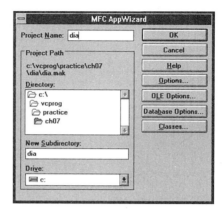

☒ Click the Options button and set the options as shown in Figure 7.7 (that is, uncheck all the check boxes except the Generate Source Comments check box).

Figure 7.7.
Setting the options
for the DIA
application.

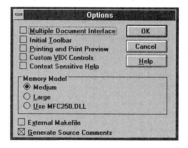

☒ Click the OK button in the Options dialog box and then click the OK button in the AppWizard dialog box and click the Create button in the New Application Information dialog box.

> *AppWizard responds by creating the DIA project and all the skeleton files of the DIA application.*

To remove the debug options of the project (so that you'll have a small file):

☒ Select Project from the Options menu of Visual C++, click the Release radio button, and then click the OK button of the dialog box.

The Visual Implementation of the DIA Application

The DIA application has a menu, a custom dialog box, and an About dialog box. Now you'll use the visual tools of Visual C++ to implement these resources.

The Visual Implementation of the Menu

The DIA application should have a menu, as shown in Figures 7.1, 7.2, and 7.3. To implement this menu:

☒ Select App Studio from the Tools menu of Visual C++.

> *Visual C++ responds by running App Studio.*

☒ Select the Menu item in the Type list and then double-click the IDR_MAINFRAME item in the Resources list.

> *Visual C++ responds by displaying the DIA application's menu in design mode.*

☒ Design the menu so that it looks as shown in Figures 7.1, 7.2, and 7.3.

To save your work:

☒ Select Save from the File menu of App Studio.

The visual implementation of the DIA application menu is complete.

The Visual Implementation of the Dialog Box

You'll now visually design the DIA application's dialog box.

☒ Select DIA.RC [MFC Resource Script] from the Window menu of App Studio.

> *App Studio responds by displaying the [MFC Resource Script] window.*

Because you now want to visually design a dialog box:

☒ Select the Dialog item in the Type list.

> *App Studio responds by displaying in the Resources list the names of the dialog boxes that the DIA application currently has (see Figure 7.8).*

Figure 7.8.
The list of dialog
boxes.

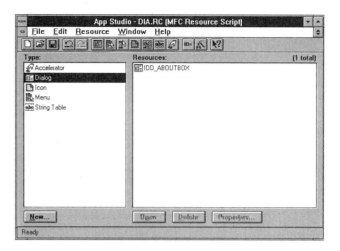

As shown in Figure 7.8, only one dialog box (IDD_ABOUTBOX) is listed in the Resources list. This means that the DIA application currently has only one dialog box: the About dialog box, which was created by AppWizard.

To create a new dialog box:

☐ Click the New button of App Studio's window (below the Type list).

> *App Studio responds by displaying the New Resource dialog box (see Figure 7.9).*

Figure 7.9.
The New Resource
dialog box.

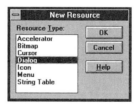

Because you're trying to create a dialog box:

☐ Make sure that the Dialog item is selected in the New Resource window and then click the OK button.

> *App Studio responds by displaying a new dialog box, ready for you to design (see Figure 7.10).*

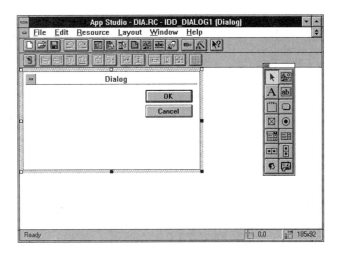

Figure 7.10.
The new dialog box
in design mode.

As you can see from Figure 7.10, App Studio already placed two push buttons in the dialog box—an OK button and a Cancel button. These two buttons are "gifts" from App Studio.

Using ClassWizard to Generate a Class for the Dialog Box

Before you start customizing the new dialog box (that is, making it look like Figure 7.4), you need to create a class for it.

Naturally, the declaration of this class will have to contain many lines of code. For example, this class will have to include member functions that display the dialog box, member functions that initialize the dialog box, and many other member functions. Sure, you can write this class by yourself; however, Visual C++ comes with a class called CDialog. This class is exactly what you need. It contains all the member functions and data members that a dialog box should have. Instead of writing your own dialog box class, you'll derive your class from the CDialog MFC class that comes with Visual C++.

Creating a derived class for the dialog box is easy because ClassWizard will write all the necessary code for you. All you have to do is tell ClassWizard the name of the derived class and the name of the base class. ClassWizard will write the declaration of the derived class for you.

Here's how you create a new class for your dialog box:

Select ClassWizard from the Resource menu of App Studio.

ClassWizard responds by displaying the Add Class dialog box (see Figure 7.11).

Figure 7.11.
The Add Class
dialog box.

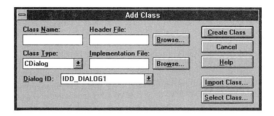

As shown in Figure 7.11, the Class Type is CDialog. That is, ClassWizard knows that you're trying to create a derived class for a dialog box, so it suggests using the base class, CDialog.

The Class Name box in Figure 7.11 is currently empty. Here's where you'll type the name of the derived class that you're creating now:

Type CMyDlg in the Class Name box of the Add Class dialog box.

Now your Add Class dialog box looks as shown in Figure 7.12. Note that ClassWizard filled the Header file and Implementation File boxes with mydlg.h and mydlg.cpp, respectively. These files are automatically created by ClassWizard to define the derived class CMyDlg.

Figure 7.12.
The Add Class
dialog box after
specifying the new
class name.

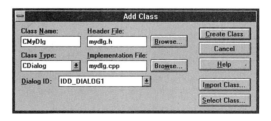

Click the Create Class button of the Add Class dialog box.

ClassWizard responds by displaying the ClassWizard dialog box (see Figure 7.13). (If you are using an earlier version of Visual C++, the ClassWizard dialog box will look a little differently.)

CMyDlg : public CDialog

Figure 7.13.
The ClassWizard
dialog box.

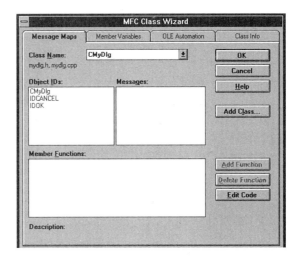

☒ Click the OK button of the ClassWizard dialog box.

That's it! You've completed creating a class for your dialog box. You named this class CMyDlg, and you derived it from the base class CDialog. As you can see from Figure 7.12, ClassWizard created two files for this class:

mydlg.h—the header file (where the class is defined)
mydlg.cpp—the program file of the class (where the member functions of the class are written)

The Visual Implementation of the Dialog Box

Now that you have a class for the new dialog box, you can customize its appearance so that it looks as shown in Figure 7.4.

As you can see from Figure 7.4, the dialog box shouldn't contain a Cancel button, so remove it:

☒ Click the Cancel button.

App Studio responds by enclosing the Cancel button with a rectangular frame.

☒ Press the Delete key on your keyboard.

App Studio responds by deleting the Cancel button from the dialog box. Now your dialog box looks as shown in Figure 7.14.

Figure 7.14.
The dialog box after
deleting the Cancel
button.

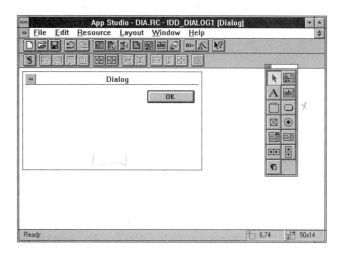

Placing a New Push Button in the Dialog Box

As shown in Figure 7.4, the dialog box should contain three push buttons:

> An OK button
> A Test button
> A Clear button

The OK button is implemented already (a gift from App Studio). It's your job to place the Test and Clear buttons.

Start with the Test button:

☐ Click the push button icon that appears in the Tool Box window (see Figure 7.15).

Note that in Figure 7.15, the push button icon appears as the third icon from the top, in the right column.

☐ Drag the Tool Box push button icon to the dialog box. Place it as shown in Figure 7.16.

Figure 7.15.
App Studio's Tool
Box window.

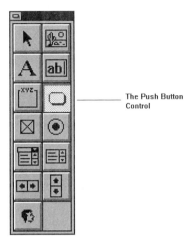

The Push Button
Control

Figure 7.16.
Placing a new push
button in the dialog
box.

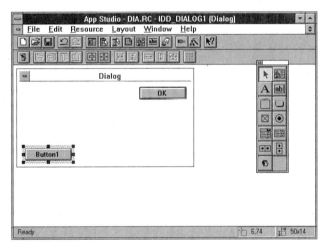

When you place a new control (for example, a push button) in the dialog box, App Studio automatically assigns to it a unique ID. You don't have to concern yourself with the value of this ID. However, you should be aware of a small problem. The following section discusses this problem and how to solve it.

Problem When Placing the First Control in the Dialog Box

When you place the first control in the dialog box (for example, the push button that you placed), App Studio assigns to it the same ID as the ID of the dialog box.

This will cause you problems later on, because App Studio confuses the dialog box with the control.

To verify that App Studio assigned the button (you placed) the same ID as the dialog box:

⊠ Select Symbols from the Edit menu of App Studio.

App Studio responds by displaying the Symbol Browser dialog box (see Figure 7.17).

Figure 7.17.
The Symbol Browser dialog box, with
IDC_BUTTON1
highlighted.

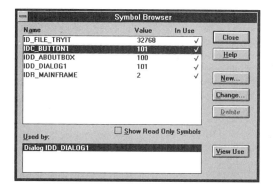

In Figure 7.17, the ID number assigned to the dialog box (IDD_DIALOG1) has the same value as the ID assigned to the button (IDC_BUTTON1). That is, both IDD_DIALOG1 and IDC_BUTTON1 have the value 101, which will cause problems later on, because App Studio will confuse the dialog box with the button.

NOTE

Starting with Visual C++ Version 1.5, this problem doesn't exist. That is, App Studio assigns a unique number to the controls that you add to your dialog boxes. Thus, if you are using Visual C++ Version 1.5 or later, the Symbol Browser dialog box (Figure 7.17) will indicate that the ID of the button is 1000 (not 101).

If you are using Visual C++ version 1.0, use the following trick to fix this problem:

⊠ Close the Symbol Browser dialog box (click the Close button of the Symbol Browser dialog box).

⬜ Delete the new button that you placed in the dialog box (click the Button1 button and then press the Delete key on your keyboard).

Now your dialog box looks as shown in Figure 7.14.

⬜ Now place a new button in the dialog box, exactly as you did before (that is, click the Push Button icon in the Tool Box window and place the button in the form as shown in Figure 7.16).

Now your dialog box looks as shown in Figure 7.18.

Figure 7.18.
The dialog box
with a new button.

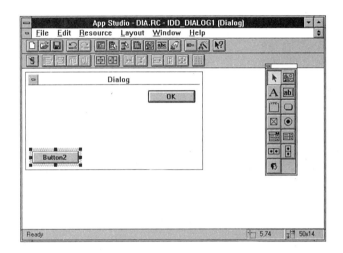

As shown in Figure 7.18, the caption of the new button is now Button2, not Button1.

To verify that the new button doesn't have the same ID number as that of the dialog box:

⬜ Select Symbols from the Edit menu of App Studio.

App Studio responds by displaying the Symbol Browser dialog box (see Figure 7.19).

Figure 7.19.
The Symbol
Browser dialog box,
with
IDC_BUTTON2
highlighted.

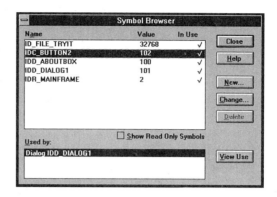

As you can see from Figure 7.19, now the ID number of the button (IDC_BUTTON2) is different from the ID of the dialog box (IDD_DIALOG1). The ID value of the button is 102, not 101 (as it was before).

To close the Symbol Browser dialog box, click the Close button.

To summarize, when you place the first control in the dialog box, App Studio assigns the new control the same ID number as that of the dialog box. This will cause you problems later on, because App Studio will confuse the dialog box with the control. To solve this problem, delete the first control that you place and then place another control. The new control will have a unique ID value.

This problem does not exist with Visual C++ Version 1.5 or later.

Changing the Properties of the New Push Button

Currently, the caption of the push button is Button2. As shown in Figure 7.4, the caption of this button should be Test. Here is how you change the caption of the button from Button2 to Test:

☐ Double-click the Button2 button.

App Studio responds by displaying the Push Button Properties dialog box (see Figure 7.20).

Figure 7.20.
The Push Button
Properties dialog
box.

As you can see from Figure 7.20, the Caption box contains the text, "Button2." You want to change the Caption property to "Test":

◻ Click the Caption box and type &Test.

> **NOTE**
>
> The & character that prefixes the T in &Test causes the character T to be underlined. This means that when the dialog box is displayed during the execution of the program, pressing Alt+T produces the same results as clicking the Test button. (The character & is located on the 7 key of your keyboard.)

Your dialog box looks as shown in Figure 7.21.

Figure 7.21.
Changing the
caption of Button1
to Test.

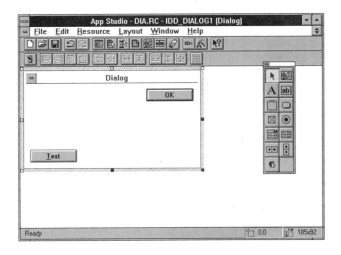

As you can see from Figure 7.4, the Test button should be larger than the one in Figure 7.21. To enlarge the Test button:

☒ Select the Test button and then drag its handles until the button is at the required size. (The handles are the solid squares on the rectangle that encloses the button.)

The enlarged Test button is shown in Figure 7.22.

Figure 7.22.
The Test button
after enlarging.

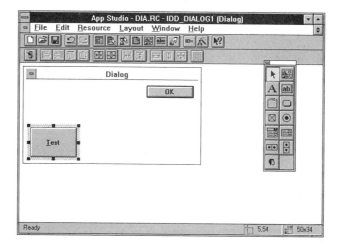

Currently, the ID constant of the Test button is IDC_BUTTON2. It would be better if the ID of the Test button had a friendlier name, a name that would identify it as the ID of the Test button (for example, IDC_TEST_BUTTON).

To change the ID name of the Test button from IDC_BUTTON2 to IDC_TEST_BUTTON:

☒ Double-click the Test button.

> *App Studio responds by displaying the Push Button Properties dialog box. Currently, the ID box contains the text IDC_BUTTON2. You want to change it to IDC_TEST_BUTTON:*

☒ Click the ID box and type IDC_TEST_BUTTON.

From now on, App Studio will refer to the Test button as IDC_TEST_BUTTON.

As shown in Figure 7.4, the dialog box should also contain a Clear button:

☐ Place a new button next to the Test button and resize it to match the size of the Test button.

Change the properties of the new button as follows:

- Double-click the new button.
- Set the Caption property to &Clear.
- Set the ID property to IDC_CLEAR_BUTTON.

Now your dialog box looks as shown in Figure 7.23.

Figure 7.23.
The dialog box
with the Test and
Clear buttons.

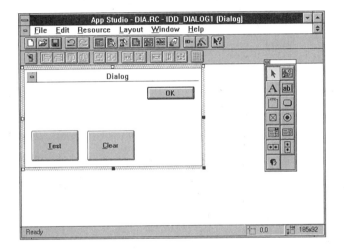

Changing the Title of the Dialog Box

As you can see from Figure 7.4, the title of the dialog box should be My Dialog Box. Currently, the title is Dialog (see Figure 7.23). To change the title of the dialog box:

- Double-click anywhere in a free area of the dialog box.

  App Studio responds by displaying the Dialog Properties dialog box.

- Change the Caption box from Dialog to My Dialog Box (see Figure 7.24).

  App Studio responds by changing the title (caption) of the dialog box to My Dialog Box (see Figure 7.25).

Figure 7.24.
The Dialog
Properties window
of the dialog box
with a new Caption
property.

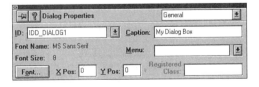

Figure 7.25.
The dialog box
with its new
caption.

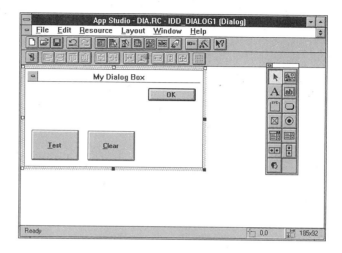

NOTE

As you can see from Figure 7.24, the ID name of the dialog box is
`IDD_DIALOG1`. From now on, we'll refer to this dialog box as `IDD_DIALOG1`.

Adding an Edit Box to the Dialog Box

Your dialog box isn't ready yet. As you can see from Figure 7.4, there's one more
control to place in the dialog box: an edit box.

Here's how you add an edit box to the dialog box:

▢ Click the edit box icon in the Tool box (see Figure 7.26) and drag it to the
dialog box. (The edit box icon is shown in Figure 7.26 as the second icon
from the top in the right column.)

▢ Enlarge the edit box until it looks as shown in Figure 7.27.

Figure 7.26.
The edit box icon.

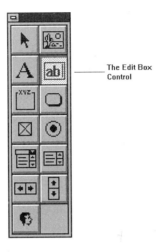

The Edit Box
Control

Figure 7.27.
The dialog box
with the edit box
in it.

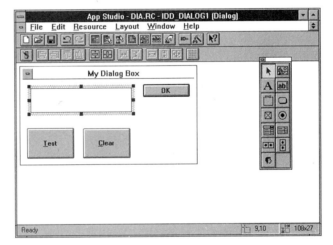

Connecting a Variable to the Edit Box

Now you'll connect a variable to the edit box. Later, when you write the application's code, you'll use this variable to read and write data from and to the edit box. For example, if the name of the variable is m_MyEditBox, the statement

```
m_MyEditBox = "Hello";
```

updates the edit box with the string "Hello".

Similarly, the statement

```
MyString = m_MyEditBox;
```

fills the variable MyString with the current contents of the edit box.

The variable that you connect to the edit box is a data member of the CMyDlg class (the class of the dialog box).

To connect the edit box to a variable:

☐ Double-click the edit box.

App Studio responds by displaying the Properties window of the edit box (see Figure 7.28).

Figure 7.28.
The Properties
window of the
edit box.

☐ Select ClassWizard from the Resource menu of App Studio.

App Studio responds by displaying the ClassWizard window (see Figure 7.29).

Note that the Class Name box of Figure 7.29 contains the text CMyDlg. Also note that the ID of the edit box (IDC_EDIT1) is selected in the Object IDs list. (If you're using an earlier version of Visual C++, the ClassWizard window looks different than the one shown in Figure 7.29.)

Figure 7.29.
The ClassWizard
window.

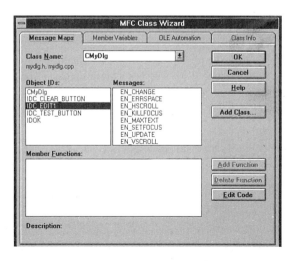

⊠ If your ClassWizard window looks as shown in Figure 7.29, click the Member Variables tab (at the top of the ClassWizard window).

☐ Make sure `IDC_EDIT1` is selected and then click the Add Variables button. If you are using Visual C++ Version 1.0, click the Edit Variable button (ClassWizard will respond by displaying the Edit Member Variables dialog box shown in Figure 7.30) and then click the Add Variable button.

Visual C++ responds by displaying the Add Member Variable dialog box (see Figure 7.31).

Figure 7.30.
The Edit Member Variables dialog box (Visual C++ Version 1.0).

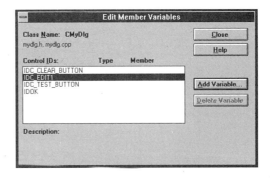

Figure 7.31.
The Add Member Variable dialog box.

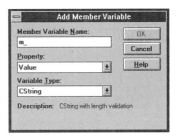

As you can see from Figure 7.31, ClassWizard is waiting for some information from you. ClassWizard already set the Property and the Variable Type of the variable. All you have to do is name the variable. ClassWizard suggests starting the name of the variable with the characters `m_`. Now type the rest of the variable name:

☑ Name the variable `m_MyEditBox` (see Figure 7.32) and then click the OK button.

ClassWizard responds by returning to the ClassWizard window (see Figure 7.33). (If you're using Visual C++ Version 1.0, click the OK button and then click the Close button to return to the ClassWizard window.)

Figure 7.32.
Naming the
variable of the edit
box.

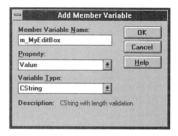

Figure 7.33.
The ClassWizard
window showing
the variable of the
edit box.

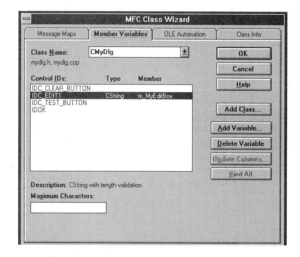

Now the edit box IDC_EDIT1 is associated with the variable m_MyEditBox. This variable is a data member of the class CMyDlg. In the following sections you'll use the m_MyEditBox data member to place text in the edit box.

Saving Your Work

Congratulations! You've completed the visual design of the DIA application (the menu and the dialog box).

To save your work:

☐ Select Save from the File menu of App Studio.

Attaching Code to the DIA Application

In the following sections you'll attach code to the menu of the application and to the dialog box.

Attaching Code to the Try It Menu Item

Recall that when you select Try It from the File menu, the DIA application should display the dialog box that you designed.

Follow these steps to attach code to the Try It menu item:

- [ ] Start ClassWizard (recall that you can start ClassWizard from the Resource menu of App Studio or from the Browse menu of Visual C++).

- [ ] If you are using Visual C++ Version 1.5 or higher, make sure that the Message Maps tab is selected at the top of the ClassWizard window.

- [x] Set the Class Name box (at the top of ClassWizard's dialog box) to `CDiaView.`

- [x] Select the event:

Object ID:	`ID_FILE_TRYIT`
Message:	`COMMAND`

- [ ] That is, select `ID_FILE_TRYIT` from the Object IDs list box and then select `COMMAND` from the Messages list box.

- [x] Click the Add Function button of ClassWizard.

  ClassWizard responds by displaying the Add Member Function dialog box. ClassWizard suggests naming the new function `OnFileTryit`.

- [x] Click the OK button to accept the default name that ClassWizard suggests.

  ClassWizard responds by adding the function `OnFileTryit()` *to the* `CDiaView` *class. This function is executed automatically whenever the user selects Try It from the File menu.*

NOTE

In the preceding discussion, you were given step-by-step instructions to add the `OnFileTryit()` function. As you can see, describing these steps is lengthy and inefficient.

From now on, a more efficient notation will be used to instruct you to add a function. The notation will list the class name, the object ID, the message, and the function name. For example, the previous lengthy step-by-step instructions would be replaced with a one-step instruction:

Use ClassWizard to add a function for the event:

Class Name:	`CDiaView`
Object ID:	`ID_FILE_TRYIT`
Message:	`COMMAND`
Function Name:	`OnFileTryit()`

To write the `OnFileTryit()` function's code:

☐ Click the Edit Code button of ClassWizard.

   ClassWizard responds by opening the file `DIAVIEW.CPP` *with the function* `OnFileTryit()` *ready for you to edit.*

☐ Edit the `OnFileTryit()` function that you added to the `DIAVIEW.CPP` file. After you edit the function, your `OnFileTryit()` function looks as follows:

```
void CDiaView::OnFileTryit()
{
    // TODO: Add your command handler code here


    ////////////////////////
    // MY CODE STARTS HERE
    ////////////////////////

    // Create an object of class CMyDlg
    CMyDlg dlg;

    // Display the dialog box.
    dlg.DoModal();
```

```
/////////////////////
// MY CODE ENDS HERE
/////////////////////
```

}

To review the code you just typed:

The first statement,

```
CMyDlg dlg;
```

creates an object of class CMyDlg. Recall that CMyDlg is the class name of the dialog box you created during the visual design.

The next statement uses the member function DoModal() of the CMyDlg class to display the dialog box:

```
dlg.DoModal();
```

DoModal() is a powerful member function of the CMyDlg class that actually displays the dialog box. Note that you didn't have to write the DoModal() function's code, because when you created the CMyDlg class you derived it from the MFC class CDialog (see Figure 7.12); the CDialog MFC class contains the DoModal() member function.

If you try to compile the DIAVIEW.CPP file, you'll get a compiling error. Why? Because in the previous code you used the class CMyDlg, but CMyDlg isn't known in DIAVIEW.CPP. Thus, you must #include "MyDlg.h" (the header file of the CMyDlg class) at the beginning of the DIAVIEW.CPP file:

☐ Add the #include "MyDlg.h" statement at the beginning of the DIAVIEW.CPP file. After you add this #include statement, the beginning of the DIAVIEW.CPP looks as follows:

```
// diaview.cpp : implementation of the CDiaView class
//

#include "stdafx.h"
#include "dia.h"

#include "diadoc.h"
#include "diaview.h"

#ifdef _DEBUG
#undef THIS_FILE
static char BASED_CODE THIS_FILE[] = __FILE__;
#endif
```

```
//////////////////////
// MY CODE STARTS HERE
//////////////////////

#include "MyDlg.h"

//////////////////////
// MY CODE ENDS HERE
//////////////////////
......
......
......
```

Save your work:

Select Save from the File menu of Visual C++.

Executing the DIA Application

Although you haven't finished writing the DIA application, execute it and see what you have accomplished so far:

▢ Select Rebuild All DIA.EXE from the Project menu of Visual C++.

Visual C++ responds by compiling and linking the DIA application.

> **NOTE**
>
> The Project menu includes items called Build DIA.EXE and Rebuild All DIA.EXE. If you select the Rebuild All item, Visual C++ will compile all the DIA files (even these files that weren't changed since the last compile).
>
> The Build menu item compiles only the files that have been changed since the last compile. Naturally, using the Build item will save you time. However, in some cases, the Visual C++ program gets "confused," and files that should be compiled aren't. (This little problem should be corrected in future versions of Visual C++.)

To execute the DIA.EXE application:

▢ Select Execute DIA.EXE from the Project menu.

Visual C++ responds by executing the DIA application.

Experiment with the Try It item of the File menu:

☑ Select Try It from the File menu.

> *The DIA application responds by displaying the dialog box that you visually designed (see Figure 7.4).*

☑ Click the Test button of the dialog box.

As you can see, nothing happens. Why? Because you haven't attached code to the Test button.

☑ Click the Clear button of the dialog box.

Again, nothing happens, because you haven't attached code to the Clear button.

☑ Try to click the mouse outside the dialog box but in the DIA application's window.

> *DIA responds by beeping, because the dialog box is modal (you used the* `DoModal()` *function), and as such, the dialog box must be closed before the program can respond to any clicking outside the dialog box.*

☑ Click in the edit box and type something (but do not press the Enter key).

As you can see, you can type characters in the Edit box.

☑ Click the OK button of the dialog box.

> *The DIA application responds by closing the dialog box.*

Who attached code to the OK button? This was a gift from Visual C++. (Recall that App Studio placed the OK button automatically for you.)

☑ Select Exit from the File menu to terminate the DIA application.

Attaching Code to the Test Button of the Dialog Box

Recall that when the user clicks the Test button of the dialog box, the DIA application should display the text, "This is a test," in the Edit box (see Figure 7.5).

Follow these steps to attach code to the Test button:

☑ Use ClassWizard to add a function for the event:

Object ID:	IDC_TEST_BUTTON
Message:	BN_CLICKED
Class Name:	CMyDlg
Function Name:	OnClickedTestButton()

NOTE

Starting with Visual C++ Version 1.5, the name of the function that ClassWizard suggests is OnTestButton(). Visual C++ Version 1.0, however, suggests the name OnClickedTestButton().

In other words, in the new versions, Microsoft decided to omit the word Clicked from the name of the functions that ClassWizard suggests.

NOTE

The message BN_CLICKED corresponds to the event:

```
User clicked the button
```

The button object also has the message BN_DOUBLECLICKED, which corresponds to the event:

```
User double-clicked the button
```

Edit the OnTestButton() function that you added to the MYDLG.CPP file. After you edit the function, your OnTestButton() function looks as follows:

```
void CMyDlg::OnTestButton()
{
// TODO: Add your control notification handler code here

        ///////////////////////
        // MY CODE STARTS HERE
        ///////////////////////

        // Fill the edit box with text.
        m_MyEditBox = "THIS IS A TEST";
        UpdateData(FALSE);

        ///////////////////////
        // MY CODE ENDS HERE
        ///////////////////////

}
```

Now review the code that you just typed:

The first statement,

```
m_MyEditBox = "THIS IS A TEST";
```

fills the variable of the edit box with the string, `"THIS IS A TEST"`. Recall that you connected the variable `m_MyEditBox` to the edit box during the visual implementation of the dialog box.

Note that just filling the `m_MyEditBox` variable with a string is not enough to update the contents of the edit box. To transfer the contents of the `m_MyEditBox` variable to the edit box (that is, to the screen), you need to use the `UpdateData()` function. Thus, the next statement in the function is as follows:

```
UpdateData(FALSE);
```

> **NOTE**
>
> Specifying `FALSE` as the argument of the `UpdateData()` function causes the `UpdateData()` function to update the edit box (from the variable to the screen).
>
> Specifying `TRUE` as the argument of the `UpdateData()` function causes the `UpdateData()` function to transfer the contents of the edit box to the `m_MyEditBox` variable (from the screen to the variable).

Save your work:

☐ Select Save from the File menu.

Attaching Code to the Clear Button

Recall that when the user clicks the Clear button of the dialog box, the DIA application should clear the text in the Edit box.

Follow these steps to attach code to the Clear button:

☐ Use ClassWizard to add a function for the event:

Class Name:	CMyDlg
Object ID:	IDC_CLEAR_BUTTON
Message:	BN_CLICKED
Function Name:	OnClearButton()

☐ Edit the `OnClearButton()` function that you added to the `MYDLG.CPP` file.
   After you edit the function, it looks as follows:

```
void CMyDlg::OnClearButton()
{
// TODO: Add your control notification handler code here

    ////////////////////////
    // MY CODE STARTS HERE
    ////////////////////////

    // Fill the edit box with null.
    m_MyEditBox = "";
    UpdateData(FALSE);

    ////////////////////////
    // MY CODE ENDS HERE
    ////////////////////////

}
```

As you can see, the `OnClearButton()` function's code is like the `OnTestButton()` function's code. The only difference is that now the `m_MyEditBox` variable is filled with a null string:

```
m_MyEditBox = "";
```

```
UpdateData(FALSE);
```

This clears the contents of the edit box.

That's it! You've finished writing the DIA application!

Save your work:

☑ Select Save from the File menu.

Executing the Finished DIA Application

To see the code that you attached to the Test and Clear buttons:

☐ Select Rebuild All DIA.EXE from the Project menu of Visual C++.

☐ Execute the DIA application.

☐ Select Try It from the File menu and experiment with the Test and Clear buttons.

When you click the Test button, the text, "THIS IS A TEST," appears in the edit box, and when you click the Clear button, the edit box is cleared.

Note that if you click the Test button, click the OK button to close the dialog box and then select Try It from the File menu again, the dialog box doesn't appear with the text, "THIS IS A TEST." In other words, the dialog box doesn't maintain its own data! In the next chapter you'll learn how to implement dialog boxes that do maintain their own data.

8

Dialog Boxes: Check Boxes

In this chapter you'll learn how to use check boxes in your dialog boxes. As you know, check boxes serve an important role in the Windows user-interface mechanism.

The CHKBOX Application

Before you start writing the CHKBOX application, execute the copy of it that resides in your `\VCPROG\ORIGINAL\CH08\CHKBOX` directory.

To execute the CHKBOX application:

☐ Use Run from the Program Manager's File menu to execute
`C:\VCPROG\ORIGINAL\CH08\CHKBOX\ChkBox.EXE`.

> *Windows responds by executing the CHKBOX application. The main window of* `CHKBOX.EXE` *appears, as shown in Figure 8.1.*

Figure 8.1.
The CHKBOX
application's main
window.

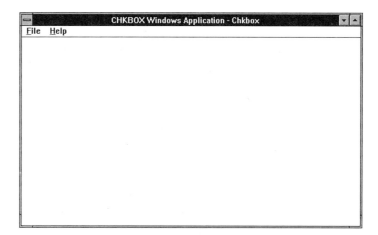

The CHKBOX application has two popup menus, File and Help. These popup menus are shown in Figures 8.2 and 8.3.

Figure 8.2.
The CHKBOX application's File menu.

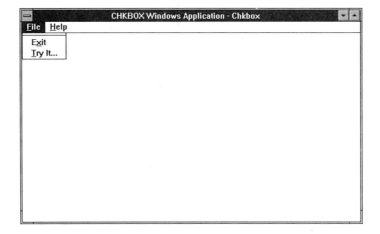

Figure 8.3.
The CHKBOX application's Help menu.

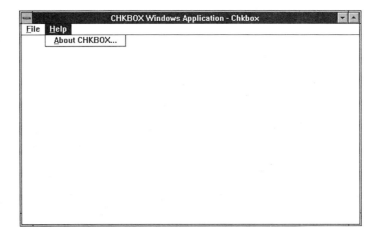

☐ Select Try It from the File menu.

> *CHKBOX responds by displaying the dialog box shown in Figure 8.4.*
> *Although the text isn't shown in Figure 8.4, initially the box contains the text,*
> *"I was updated in* CMyDlg(). *"*

Figure 8.4.
The CHKBOX
application's dialog
box.

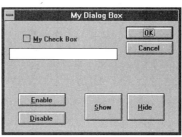

☐ Click the My Check Box check box.

> *CHKBOX responds by placing a check mark in the check box and displaying the text, "My Check Box is checked," in the edit box.*

☐ Click the My Check Box check box again.

> *CHKBOX responds by removing the check mark from the check box and displaying the text, "My Check Box is not checked," in the edit box.*

☐ Click the OK button of the dialog box.

> *CHKBOX responds by closing the dialog box.*

☐ Click in the text box, use the arrow and Delete keys to erase the current contents of the edit box and then type something in the edit box.

☐ Click the OK button in the dialog box.

☐ Select Try It from the File menu again.

> *CHKBOX responds by displaying the dialog box again.*

As you can see, the contents of the edit box are the same as they were before you clicked the OK button in the dialog box.

☐ Type something new in the edit box and then click the Cancel button in the dialog box.

☐ Select Try It from the File menu again.

> *CHKBOX responds by displaying the dialog box again.*

As you can see, the contents of the edit box aren't the same as they were before you clicked the Cancel button. That is, the contents of the edit box are maintained only if you click the OK button.

Try the other buttons in the dialog box. As you can see, the Disable button makes the check box unavailable (dimmed), and the Enable button makes it available. Similarly, the Hide button makes the check box invisible, and the Show button makes it visible.

☐ Click the OK button of the dialog box and then select Exit from the File menu to terminate the CHKBOX application.

Now that you know what the CHKBOX application should do, you can begin learning how to write it.

Creating the Project of the CHKBOX Application

To create the project of the CHKBOX application:

☐ Select AppWizard from the Project menu.

Visual C++ responds by running AppWizard.

☐ Select the directory C:\VCPROG\PRACTICE\CH08 from the Directory list box.

☐ Type chkbox in the Project Name box.

Now your AppWizard dialog box looks as shown in Figure 8.5.

Figure 8.5.
The AppWizard
dialog box for the
CHKBOX
application.

☐ Click the Options button and set the options as shown in Figure 8.6 (that is, uncheck all the check boxes except the Generate Source Comments check box).

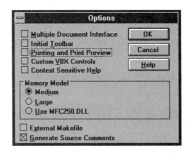

Figure 8.6.
Setting the options
for the CHKBOX
application.

☐ Click the OK button in the Options dialog box and then click the OK button in the AppWizard dialog box and finally click the Create button in the New Application Information dialog box.

> *AppWizard responds by creating the CHKBOX project and all the skeleton files of the CHKBOX application.*

To remove the debug options of the project (so that you'll have a small EXE file):

☐ Select Project from the Options menu of Visual C++, click the Release radio button, and then click the OK button of the dialog box.

The Visual Implementation of the CHKBOX Application

The CHKBOX application has a menu, a custom dialog box, and an About dialog box. In the following sections you'll visually design the menu and the custom dialog box.

The Visual Implementation of the CHKBOX Application's Menu

The CHKBOX application should have a menu, as shown in Figures 8.1, 8.2, and 8.3. To implement this menu:

☐ Select App Studio from the Tools menu of Visual C++.

> *Visual C++ responds by running App Studio.*

☐ Select the Menu item from the Type list and then double-click the IDR_MAINFRAME item in the Resources list.

Visual C++ responds by displaying the menu of the CHKBOX application in design mode.

☐ Design the menu so that it looks as shown in Figures 8.1, 8.2, and 8.3.

To save your work:

☐ Select Save from the File menu of App Studio.

The visual implementation of the CHKBOX application's menu is completed.

The Visual Implementation of the Dialog Box

Now you'll implement visually the custom dialog box of the CHKBOX application:

☐ Display the CHKBOX.RC window in App Studio (that is, select CHKBOX.RC from the Window menu in App Studio).

☐ Click the Dialog item in the Type list that appears on the left side of the App Studio window.

App Studio responds by displaying the list of dialog boxes that the CHKBOX application currently has. Because currently there's only one dialog box (the About dialog box), App Studio displays the text IDD_ABOUTBOX *on the right side of the App Studio window.*

Because you now want to design a new dialog box:

☐ Click the New button of App Studio.

App Studio responds by displaying the New Resource dialog box.

☐ Make sure that the Dialog item is selected and then click the OK button.

App Studio responds by displaying a new dialog box.

Creating a Class for the Dialog Box

Now create a class for the dialog box:

☐ Select ClassWizard from the Resource menu of App Studio.

☐ Make sure that the Class Type is set to `Cdialog` and then type `CMyDlg` in the Class Name box and then click the Create Class button.

Class Wizard responds by creating the CMyDlg *class (which is derived from the* CDialog *class) and displaying the ClassWizard dialog box.*

☐ Click the OK button of the ClassWizard dialog box.

Changing the Caption of the Dialog Box

Currently, the caption of the dialog box is "Dialog." To change the caption to "My Dialog Box":

☐ Double-click in a free area of the dialog box. (A free area is an area that doesn't contain any controls.)

App Studio responds by displaying the Properties window of the dialog box.

☐ Change the Caption property to My Dialog Box.

The following sections describe how to add controls to the dialog box. When you finish adding the controls, your dialog box looks as shown in Figure 8.4.

Placing a Check Box in the Dialog Box

☐ If you are using Visual C++ Version 1.0, place a button in the dialog box and then press the Delete key to delete this control. (As explained in Chapter 7, "Designing Your First Dialog Box," this causes App Studio to assign a unique ID to all subsequent controls.)

☐ Place a check box in the dialog box. (That is, drag the check box icon from the Tools window into the dialog box. The check box icon is shown in Figure 8.7.)

Figure 8.7.
The Tools window.

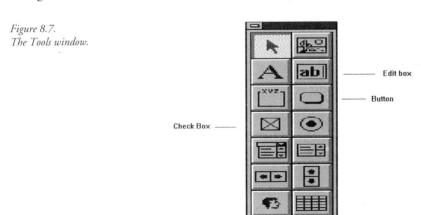

☐ Enlarge the check box by dragging its handles to the right. (Make the check box approximately the size shown in Figure 8.4.)

☐ Double-click in the check box.

App Studio responds by displaying the Properties window of the check box.

☐ Change the Caption property of the check box to &My Check Box.

☐ Change the ID of the check box to IDC_MY_CHECK_BOX.

Attaching a Variable to the Check Box

In this section you'll attach a variable to the check box. Here's how you attach (connect) a variable to the check box:

☐ Click in the check box and then select ClassWizard from the Resource menu.

☐ Make sure that IDC_MY_CHECK_BOX is selected from the Object IDs list, click the Member Variables folder index that appears on the top of the dialog box, and then click the Add Variable button.

ClassWizard responds by displaying the Add Member Variable dialog box.

As you can see, ClassWizard suggests giving the variable a name that starts with the characters m_.

☐ Type the name of the variable in the Member Variable Name box and then click the OK button. The name of the variable should be m_CheckBoxStatus.

Class Wizard responds by returning to the ClassWizard dialog box.

☐ Click the OK button of the ClassWizard dialog box.

You successfully attached the m_CheckBoxStatus variable to the check box. This variable holds the status of the check box.

Note that if you're using Visual C++ Version 1.0, the procedure for attaching a variable to a control is slightly different from the one described here.

Placing an Edit Box in the Dialog Box

☐ Place an edit box in the dialog box. (That is, drag the edit box icon from the Tools window to the dialog box. The edit box icon is shown in Figure 8.7.) Place the edit box as shown in Figure 8.4.

☐ Enlarge the edit box by dragging its handles until it's the size as shown in Figure 8.4.

☐ Double-click in the edit box.

App Studio responds by displaying the Properties window of the edit box.

☐ Change the ID of the edit box to `IDC_MY_EDIT_BOX`.

Attaching a Variable to the Edit Box

Now you'll attach a variable to the edit box that you placed in the dialog box. Here's how you attach (connect) a variable to the edit box:

☐ Make sure that `IDC_MY_EDIT_BOX` is selected from the Object IDs list, click the Member Variables folder index that appears at the top of the dialog box, and then click the Add Variable button.

ClassWizard responds by displaying the Add Member Variable dialog box.

As you can see, ClassWizard suggests giving the variable a name that starts with the characters m_.

☐ Set the name of the variable in the Member Variable Name box to `m_EditBoxContents` and then click the OK button.

Class Wizard responds by returning to the ClassWizard dialog box.

☐ Click the OK button of the ClassWizard dialog box.

You successfully attached the `m_EditBoxContents` variable to the edit box. This variable holds the contents of the edit box.

To save the work that you have done so far:

☐ Select Save from the File menu.

Placing Buttons in the Dialog Box

In the preceding sections you placed a check box and an edit box in the dialog box. Now you'll place four buttons in it, as shown in Figure 8.4.

To make room for the buttons, you have to enlarge the dialog box:

☐ Click in a free area of the dialog box.

☐ Enlarge the dialog box by dragging its bottom handle downward.

Here's how you place the Enable button:

☐ Drag the button icon from the Tools window to the dialog box.

Change the Caption property and the ID of the button as follows:

☐ Double-click the button.

> *App Studio responds by displaying the Properties window of the button.*

☐ Change the Caption property of the button to &Enable.

☐ Change the ID of the button to IDC_ENABLE.

Now place the other buttons in the dialog box:

☐ Place a second button in the dialog box.

☐ Set the Caption property of the button to &Disable and set the ID of the button to IDC_DISABLE.

☐ Place a third button in the dialog box.

☐ Set the Caption property of the button to &Show and set the ID of the button to IDC_SHOW.

☐ Place a fourth button in the dialog box.

☐ Set the Caption property of the button to &Hide and set the ID of the button to IDC_HIDE.

Drag and size the four buttons that you placed in the dialog box as shown in Figure 8.4.

That's it, you've completed the visual implementation of the dialog box.

To save your work:

☐ Select Save from the File menu of App Studio.

Notation Used for the Visual Implementation

As you can see, it took several pages to describe in detail the visual implementation of the menu and dialog box. As you practice and become experienced with the visual implementation, no doubt you'll find these detailed steps a nuisance rather than a help. Thus, in subsequent chapters, you'll be instructed to visually implement menus and dialog boxes through tables.

The menu for the CHKBOX application is shown in Table 8.1.

Table 8.1. The menu for the CHKBOX application.
Figures relating to menu: 8.1, 8.2, 8.3

Menu Item
&File
E&xit
&Try It...
&Help
&About CHKBOX....

The table starts by listing the figures that relate to the menu:

Figures relating to menu: 8.1, 8.2, 8.3

This means that you should consult these figures when implementing the menu.

The main section of the table lists the menu bar and the menu items. For example, Table 8.1 shows that the leftmost item on the menu bar is &File because this is the first item in the table. The item to the right of the &File item in the menu bar is &Help. This is evident from Table 8.1, because &File and &Help aren't indented to the right in the table. The menu items under &File are E&xit and &Try It.... This is evident from Table 8.1, because these items are located under the &File item, and they are indented in the table. Similarly, &About CHKBOX... is the menu item of the &Help menu, because &About CHKBOX... appears under the &Help item, and it's indented to the right.

The contents of the CHKBOX application's dialog box are shown in Table 8.2.

Table 8.2. The CHKBOX application's dialog box.

Class Name:	CMyDlg (CDialog)
Figure:	8.4
OK button:	Yes
Cancel button:	Yes

Object	Property	Setting
Dialog box	ID	IDD_DIALOG1
	Caption	My Dialog Box
Check Box	ID	IDC_MY_CHECK_BOX
	Caption	&My Check Box
	Variable	m_CheckBoxStatus (BOOL)
Edit Box	ID	IDC_MY_EDIT_BOX
	Variable	m_EditBoxContents (CString)
Push Button	ID	IDC_ENABLE
	Caption	&Enable
Push Button	ID	IDC_DISABLE
	Caption	&Disable
Push Button	ID	IDC_SHOW
	Caption	&Show
Push Button	ID	IDC_HIDE
	Caption	&Hide

The table starts by displaying the following:

Class Name:	CMyDlg (CDialog)
Figure:	8.4
OK button:	Yes
Cancel button:	Yes

The notation

Class Name: CMyDlg (CDialog)

means that you need to create a class called CMyDlg for the dialog box and that the CMyDlg class is a derived class from the CDialog class.

The notation

Figure: 8.4

means that you should consult Figure 8.4 when placing and sizing the controls.

The notation

OK button:	Yes
Cancel button:	Yes

means that you shouldn't delete the OK and Cancel buttons.

The rest of the table describes the dialog box and its contents. For example, the first object in the table is

Dialog Box	ID	IDD_DIALOG1
	Caption	My Dialog Box

This means that you need to set the ID of the dialog box to IDD_DIALOG1 and the Caption property to My Dialog Box.

The second object in the table is

Check Box	ID	IDC_MY_CHECK_BOX
	Caption	&My Check Box
	Variable	m_CheckBoxStatus (BOOL)

This means that you should place a check box control in the dialog box (per Figure 8.4), you should set the ID of the check box to IDC_MY_CHECK_BOX, you should set the Caption property of the check box to &My Check Box, and you should attach a variable (of type BOOL) called m_CheckBoxStatus to the check box.

Note that in almost all cases, you should accept the default variable type that ClassWizard suggests for the variable you are typing. For example, ClassWizard suggests the type BOOL for the variable of the check box and the CString type for the variable of the edit box.

Attaching Code to the Try It Menu Item of the ChkBox Application

You'll now attach code to the Try It menu item. Recall that when you select the Try It menu item from the File menu, the CHKBOX application should display the dialog box.

☐ Use ClassWizard to add a function for the event:

Class Name:	CChkboxView
Object ID:	ID_FILE_TRYIT
Message:	COMMAND
Function Name:	OnFileTryit()

Make sure that in the preceding step, the Class Name of the ClassWizard dialog box is set to CChkboxView.

☐ Edit the OnFileTryit() function that you added to the CHKBOVW.CPP file. After you edit the function, it looks as follows:

```
void CChkboxView::OnFileTryit()
{
    // TODO: Add your command handler code here

    //////////////////////////
    // MY CODE STARTS HERE
    //////////////////////////

    CMyDlg dlg;

    dlg.DoModal();

    //////////////////////////
    // MY CODE ENDS HERE
    //////////////////////////

}
```

To review the code you typed:

The statement

```
CMyDlg dlg;
```

creates an object dlg, of class CMyDlg.

Creating the dlg object doesn't display the dialog box. To display the dialog box, you use the DoModal() member function:

```
dlg.DoModal();
```

DoModal() is a member function of the CDialog class. Recall that when you created the CMyDlg dialog box (during the visual design), you specified CDialog as the base class. Thus, CMyDlg is derived from the CDialog class, and because dlg is an object of class CMyDlg, you can use DoModal() on the dlg object.

If you try to compile the CHKBOVW.CPP file now, you'll get an error message. Why? Because the class CMyDlg isn't known in CHKBOVW.CPP. ClassWizard declared the class declaration of CMyDlg in the file MyDlg.h. Thus, you must #include MyDlg.h at the beginning of the CHKBOVW.CPP file:

☐ Add the #include statement at the beginning of the CHKBOVW.CPP file as follows:

```
// chkbovw.cpp : implementation of the CChkboxView class
//

#include "stdafx.h"
#include "chkbox.h"

#include "chkbodoc.h"
#include "chkbovw.h"

#ifdef _DEBUG
#undef THIS_FILE
static char BASED_CODE THIS_FILE[] = __FILE__;
#endif

/////////////////////////
// MY CODE STARTS HERE
/////////////////////////

#include "MyDlg.h"

/////////////////////////
// MY CODE ENDS HERE
/////////////////////////

. . . . .
. . . . .
. . . . .
```

Compiling, Linking, and Executing the CHKBOX Application

Although you haven't completed writing the CHKBOX application, compile, link, and execute it.

☐ Select Rebuild All CHKBOX.EXE from the Project menu.

☐ Execute the CHKBOX application.

☐ Select Try It from the File menu.

CHKBOX responds by displaying the dialog box.

☐ Click the check box.

CHKBOX responds by placing a check mark in the check box.

☐ Click the OK button.

CHKBOX responds by closing the dialog box.

☐ Select Try It from the File menu again.

CHKBOX responds by displaying the dialog box. However, the check box doesn't have a check mark in it.

This is because you created the dlg object in the OnFileTryit() function, so every time the user clicks the Try It menu item, the dlg object is created. The initial value of the check box is unchecked, and hence every time you display the dialog box, the check box appears unchecked.

In other words, the scope of the dlg object is during the life of the OnFileTryit() function (because dlg is a local object in this function). You need to create the dlg object elsewhere in the program so that the data members of the dlg object won't vanish.

Making the *dlg* Object a Data Member of the View Class

Now you'll create the dlg object in the view class. This way, the dlg object is created only when the CChkboxView object is created (that is, only once during the life of the CHKBOX application).

☐ Modify the OnFileTryit() function (in CHKBOVW.CPP) so that it looks as follows:

```
void CChkboxView::OnFileTryit()
{
    // TODO: Add your command handler code here


    /////////////////////////
    // MY CODE STARTS HERE
    /////////////////////////
```

211

```
        dlg.DoModal();

        /////////////////////
        // MY CODE ENDS HERE
        /////////////////////

}
```

As you can see, now `OnFileTryit()` doesn't create the `dlg` object. That is, you removed the statement

```
CMyDlg dlg;
```

The `CChkboxView` class is declared in the `CHKBOVW.H` file. To make the `dlg` object a data member of the `CChkboxView` class:

☐ Open the `CHKBOVW.H` file and add the `dlg` object as a data member of the `CChkboxView` class. After you modify the declaration of the `CChkboxView` class, it looks as follows:

```
class CChkboxView : public CView
{
protected: // create from serialization only
        CChkboxView();
        DECLARE_DYNCREATE(CChkboxView)

// Attributes
public:
        CChkboxDoc* GetDocument();

        /////////////////////////
        // MY CODE STARTS HERE
        /////////////////////////

        CMyDlg dlg;

        /////////////////////
        // MY CODE ENDS HERE
        /////////////////////


// Operations
public:

// Implementation
public:
        virtual ~CChkboxView();
        virtual void OnDraw(CDC* pDC);  // overridden to draw this view
#ifdef _DEBUG
        virtual void AssertValid() const;
```

```
    virtual void Dump(CDumpContext& dc) const;
#endif

protected:

// Generated message map functions
protected:
    //{{AFX_MSG(CChkboxView)
    afx_msg void OnFileTryit();
    //}}AFX_MSG
    DECLARE_MESSAGE_MAP()
};
```

The code you typed declares dlg as an object of class CMyDlg. Because dlg is now a data member of the CChkboxView class, all the data members of the dlg object (such as m_EditBoxContents) are maintained as long as the view object (of class CChkboxView) exists. Note that the view object is created automatically. That is, unlike the dlg object of class CMyDlg that you created, the view object of CChkboxView class was created automatically when the application started.

If you compile the ChkBox application now you'll get an error message, because the CMyDlg class is unknown in the file CHKBOVW.H. So #include the file MyDlg.h (which contains the class declaration of CMyDlg) at the beginning of the CHKBOVW.H file as follows:

```
// chkbovw.h : interface of the CChkboxView class
//
/////////////////////////////////////////////////////////////////


/////////////////////////
// MY CODE STARTS HERE
/////////////////////////

#include "MyDlg.h"

/////////////////////////
// MY CODE ENDS HERE
/////////////////////////
.....
.....
.....
```

If you compile CHKBOX now you'll get an error message, because the class CMyDlg is currently declared twice: once in the #include "MyDlg.h" in CHKBOVW.CPP and once in the #include "MyDlg.h" in CHKBOVW.H. Because CMyDlg no longer appears in CHKBOVW.CPP, you can remove the #include "MyDlg.h" statement from it:

☐ Remove the statement #include "MyDlg.h" from the CHKBOVW.CPP file.

Compiling, Linking, and Executing the ChkBox Application

Now compile, link, and execute the CHKBOX application:

☐ Select Rebuild All CHKBOX.EXE from the Project menu.

☐ Execute the CHKBOX application.

☐ Select Try It from the File menu.

> *CHKBOX responds by displaying the dialog box.*

☐ Click the check box.

> *CHKBOX responds by placing a check mark in the check box.*

☐ Type something in the edit box.

☐ Click the OK button.

> *CHKBOX responds by closing the dialog box.*

☐ Select Try It from the File menu again.

> *CHKBOX responds by displaying the dialog box. Now the check box has a check mark in it! Also, the edit box still contains the characters that you typed in it.*

Recall that during the visual implementation of the dialog box, you created a variable for the check box and a variable for the edit box. These variables (data members of the CMyDlg class) store the status of the check box and the contents of the edit box.

Attaching Code to the Check Box

Now you'll attach code to the check box. This code should be executed whenever the user clicks the check box. Recall that when the check box is clicked, the edit box should display a message ("My Check Box is checked" or "My Check Box is not checked").

☐ Use ClassWizard to add a function for the event:

Class Name:	CMyDlg
Object ID:	IDC_MY_CHECK_BOX
Message:	BN_CLICKED
Function Name:	OnClicked

214

☐ Edit the OnMyCheckBox() function that you added to the MYDLG.CPP file to look like the following:

```
void CMyDlg::OnMyCheckBox()
{
    // TODO: Add your control notification handler code here

///////////////////////
// MY CODE STARTS HERE
///////////////////////

// Update the variables, based on the contents of the
// controls.
UpdateData ( TRUE );


// Based on the value of the check box variable,
// update the variable of the edit box.
if ( m_CheckBoxStatus == 1 )
    m_EditBoxContents = "My Check Box is checked.";


if ( m_CheckBoxStatus == 0 )
    m_EditBoxContents = "My Check Box is not checked.";

// Update the contents of the controls based on the values
// of the variables,
UpdateData ( FALSE );

///////////////////////
// MY CODE ENDS HERE
///////////////////////


}
```

The code you typed uses the UpdateData() function:

```
UpdateData ( TRUE );
```

When the parameter of UpdateData() is TRUE, the contents of the controls are transferred to the controls' variables. Thus, when you click the check box, the OnMyCheckBox() function is executed, and because the first statement in this function is UpdateData(TRUE), the data member m_CheckBoxStatus is updated with a new value. (Of course, UpdateData(TRUE) also updates m_EditBoxContents with the contents of the edit box, but you don't care about that here.)

Now that m_CheckBoxStatus is updated with the status of the check box, the if statements check the value of m_CheckBoxStatus, and based on its value, m_EditBoxContents is updated:

```
if ( m_CheckBoxStatus == 1 )
    m_EditBoxContents = "My Check Box is checked.";


if ( m_CheckBoxStatus == 0 )
    m_EditBoxContents = "My Check Box is not checked.";
```

At this point, the value of m_EditBoxContents is updated with "My Check Box is checked" or with "My Check Box is not checked."

Note that just changing the value of m_EditBoxContents does not change the contents of the edit box. To transfer the contents of m_EditBoxContents to the edit box, you use the UpdateData() function with FALSE as its parameter:

```
UpdateData ( FALSE );
```

When FALSE is the parameter of UpdateData(), data is transferred from the variables of the controls to the controls themselves. This means that the contents of m_EditBoxContents are transferred to the edit box.

NOTE

The UpdateData(TRUE) function is used to transfer data from the controls to the variables of the controls, and UpdateData(FALSE) is used to transfer data from the variables of the controls to the controls themselves.

Compiling, Linking, and Executing the ChkBox Application

☐ Rebuild the CHKBOX application.

☐ Execute the CHKBOX application.

☐ Select Try It from the File menu.

　　CHKBOX responds by displaying the dialog box.

☐ Click the check box.

> *CHKBOX responds by placing a check mark in the check box and by displaying the text "My Check Box is checked" in the edit box.*

☐ Click the check box again.

> *CHKBOX responds by removing the check mark from the check box and by displaying the text "My Check Box is not checked" in the edit box.*

☐ Click the OK button in the dialog box.

> *CHKBOX responds by closing the dialog box.*

☐ Select Try It from the File menu.

> *CHKBOX responds by displaying the dialog box. As you can see, the last status of the dialog box's controls appears.*

☐ Close the dialog box and then terminate the ChkBox application.

NOTE

Three ways to close the dialog box are

Click the OK button.

Click the Cancel button.

Click the minus icon that appears on the upper-left corner of the dialog box and then select Close from the system menu that pops up. Closing the dialog box this way is the same as clicking the Cancel button.

Enabling and Disabling the Check Box

Sometimes you'll need to disable the check box. For example, consider a game application in which the user must decide whether the application should use the sound card. If the user checks the check box, the application uses the sound card, but if the user unchecks the check box, it doesn't. If your program discovers that the system doesn't have a sound card, the check box should be displayed as unavailable (dimmed).

The Enable and Disable buttons in ChkBox demonstrate how you can enable and disable the check box from within your code.

Attaching Code to the Disable Button

Recall that when you click the Disable button, the check box should be unavailable (dimmed).

☐ Use ClassWizard to add a function for the event:

Class Name:	CMyDlg
Object ID:	IDC_DISABLE
Message:	BN_CLICKED
Function Name:	OnDisable()

☐ Edit the OnDisable() function that you added to the MYDLG.CPP file so that it looks as follows:

```
void CMyDlg::OnDisable()
{
     // TODO: Add your control notification handler code here

//////////////////////
// MY CODE STARTS HERE
//////////////////////

GetDlgItem(IDC_MY_CHECK_BOX)->EnableWindow(FALSE);

//////////////////////
// MY CODE ENDS HERE
//////////////////////

}
```

The GetDlgItem() function returns the handler of the control that's mentioned in its parameter. For example, GetDlgItem(IDC_MY_CHECK_BOX) returns the handler of the check box. IDC_MY_CHECK_BOX is the ID of the check box (used in the resource file ChkBox.RC, and throughout the program) and is convenient to use. However, Windows uses the pointer of the check box's handler. The GetDlgItem() function returns that pointer.

Once you extract the pointer, you can execute the EnableWindow() function as follows:

```
GetDlgItem(IDC_MY_CHECK_BOX)->EnableWindow(FALSE);
```

When you supply FALSE as the parameter of EnableWindow(), the control is dimmed.

Attaching Code to the Enable Button

Recall that when the Enable button is clicked, the check box should be available (not dimmed).

☐ Use ClassWizard to add a function for the event:

Class Name:	CMyDlg
Object ID:	IDC_ENABLE
Message:	BN_CLICKED
Function Name:	OnEnable()

☐ Edit the OnEnable() function that you added to the MYDLG.CPP file so that it looks as follows:

```
void CMyDlg::OnEnable()
{
    // TODO: Add your control notification handler code here


////////////////////////
// MY CODE STARTS HERE
////////////////////////

GetDlgItem(IDC_MY_CHECK_BOX)->EnableWindow(TRUE);

////////////////////////
// MY CODE ENDS HERE
////////////////////////

}
```

The code that you added uses the GetDlgItem() function to extract the pointer of the IDC_MY_CHECK_BOX check box and executes the EnableWindow() function with TRUE as its parameter. This causes the check box to be available (undimmed).

Compiling, Linking, and Executing the CHKBOX Application

☐ Rebuild the CHKBOX application.

☐ Execute the CHKBOX application.

☐ Select Try It from the File menu.

   CHKBOX responds by displaying the dialog box.

☐ Click the Disable button.

CHKBOX responds by disabling the check box.

☐ Click the Enable button.

CHKBOX responds by enabling the check box.

☐ Close the dialog box and then terminate the ChkBox application.

Making the Check Box Visible or Invisible

Sometimes you'll need to make the check box invisible. The Hide and Show buttons in CHKBOX demonstrate how you can make the check box visible or invisible from within your code.

Attaching Code to the Hide Button

Recall that when you click the Hide button, the check box should become invisible.

☐ Use ClassWizard to add a function for the event:

Class Name:	CMyDlg
Object ID:	IDC_HIDE
Message:	BN_CLICKED
Function Name:	OnHide()

☐ Edit the OnHide() function that you added to the MYDLG.CPP file. After you edit the function, it looks as follows:

```
void CMyDlg::OnHide()
{
    // TODO: Add your control notification handler code here

/////////////////////
// MY CODE STARTS HERE
/////////////////////

GetDlgItem(IDC_MY_CHECK_BOX)->ShowWindow(SW_HIDE);

/////////////////////
// MY CODE ENDS HERE
/////////////////////

}
```

The code that you typed uses the GetDlgItem() function to extract the pointer of the My Check Box check box and executes the ShowWindow() function with its parameter equal to SW_HIDE. This causes the check box to become invisible.

Attaching Code to the Show Button

Recall that when you click the Show button, the check box should become visible.

☐ Use ClassWizard to add a function for the event:

Class Name:	CMyDlg
Object ID:	IDC_SHOW
Message:	BN_CLICKED
Function Name:	OnShow()

☐ Edit the OnShow() function that you added to the MYDLG.CPP file. After you edit the function, it looks as follows:

```
void CMyDlg::OnShow()
{
    // TODO: Add your control notification handler code here

/////////////////////
// MY CODE STARTS HERE
/////////////////////

GetDlgItem(IDC_MY_CHECK_BOX)->ShowWindow(SW_SHOW);

/////////////////////
// MY CODE ENDS HERE
/////////////////////

}
```

The code that you typed uses the GetDlgItem() function to extract the pointer of the My Check Box check box and executes the ShowWindow() function with its parameter equal to SW_SHOW. This causes the check box to become visible.

Compiling, Linking, and Executing the ChkBox Application

☐ Rebuild the ChkBox application.

☐ Execute the ChkBox application.

☐ Select Try It from the File menu.

    ChkBox responds by displaying the dialog box.

☐ Click the Hide button.

    ChkBox responds by making the check box invisible.

☐ Click the Show button.

    ChkBox responds by making the check box visible.

☐ Close the dialog box and then terminate the ChkBox application.

Setting Initial Status Settings for the Check Box

Sometimes you'll want your check box to appear with certain predefined initial conditions when you first display the dialog box. For example, currently the check box is unchecked when the dialog box is displayed for the first time. To add code that causes the check box to be checked when the dialog box appears:

☐ Use ClassWizard to add a function for the event:

Class Name:	CMyDlg
Object ID:	CMyDlg
Message:	WM_INITDIALOG
Function Name:	OnInitDialog()

☐ Edit the OnInitDialog() function that you added to the MYDLG.CPP file. After you edit the function, it looks as follows:

```
BOOL CMyDlg::OnInitDialog()
{
    CDialog::OnInitDialog();

    // TODO: Add extra initialization here

    /////////////////////////
    // MY CODE STARTS HERE
    /////////////////////////

    m_CheckBoxStatus = 1;
    m_EditBoxContents = "I was updated inside OnInitDialog()";

    UpdateData(FALSE);
```

```
//////////////////////
// MY CODE ENDS HERE
//////////////////////

    return TRUE;  // return TRUE  unless you set the focus
                  // to a control
}
```

The code that you typed updates the initial value of m_CheckBoxStatus with 1 (checked), and it updates m_EditBoxContents with a string.

UpdateData() is then executed to transfer the contents of the variables to their corresponding controls:

```
UpdateData(FALSE);
```

Something is wrong with the preceding implementation, however. The OnInitDialog() function is executed whenever the program executes the dlg.DoModal() function.

In other words, whenever the user selects Try It from the File menu, the OnFileTryit() function is executed. The OnFileTryIt() function executes the dlg.DoModal() function, which executes the OnInitDialog() function. This means that every time the user selects Try It, the dialog box appears with the check box checked and with the string, I was updated inside OnInitDialog() in the edit box.

To see this in action:

☐ Select Rebuild All CHKBOX.EXE from the Project menu.

☐ Execute the ChkBox application.

☐ Select Try It from the File menu.

> *ChkBox responds by displaying the dialog box. As you can see, the check box is checked, and the edit box contains the string, "I was updated inside* OnInitDialog()*."*

☐ Change the status of the check box and then click the OK button.

> *ChkBox responds by closing the dialog box.*

☐ Select Try It again.

ChkBox responds by displaying the dialog box again. However, the values of the check box and the edit box weren't saved. The check box is still checked, and the edit box still contains the string "I was updated inside `OnInitDialog( )`*," because the* `OnInitDialog( )` *function is executed whenever you select Try It from the File menu (that is, whenever* `DoModal( )` *is executed).*

Deleting the *OnInitDialog()* Function

Obviously, `OnInitDialog( )` isn't the appropriate place to set the initial status of the check box.

To remove the `OnInitDialog( )` function:

☐ Run ClassWizard and delete the function `OnInitDialog( )` (that is, select the class `CMyDlg` in the Class Name box, make sure that `CMyDlg` is selected in the Object IDs list and `WM_INITDIALOG` is selected in the Messages list, and click the Delete Function button).

ClassWizard responds by displaying a dialog box reminding you that it's your responsibility to actually remove the function from `MyDlg.CPP`. *(Class Wizard removes all other code that has to be removed, but you have to remove the actual function.)*

☐ Click the Yes button to confirm that you understand you have to manually remove the `OnInitDialog( )` function from `MyDlg.CPP`.

☐ Click the OK button in the ClassWizard dialog box, load `MyDlg.CPP`, and remove the `OnInitDialog( )` function.

NOTE

Remove the whole function, including the first and last lines of the function:

```
BOOL CMyDlg::OnInitDialog()      <— REMOVE THIS LINE
{                                <— REMOVE THIS LINE

....                             <— REMOVE THIS LINE
....                             <— REMOVE THIS LINE
....                             <— REMOVE THIS LINE

}                                <— REMOVE THIS LINE
```

Initializing the Dialog Box

Where should you put the initialization code? Well, you need to put it at a point in the program that's executed only once during the life of the program. Can you think of such a place? Sure you can, in the constructor function of the CMyDlg class. Recall that you already placed the statement

```
CMyDlg dlg;
```

in the class declaration of the CChkboxView class.

This means that the dlg object is created only once during the life of the ChkBox application.

☐ Open the MyDlg.CPP file and note that the constructor function of the CMyDlg class is currently as follows:

```
CMyDlg::CMyDlg(CWnd* pParent /*=NULL*/)
    : CDialog(CMyDlg::IDD, pParent)
{
    //{{AFX_DATA_INIT(CMyDlg)
    m_CheckBoxStatus = FALSE;
    m_EditBoxContents = "";
    //}}AFX_DATA_INIT
}
```

As you can see, ClassWizard set the default value of m_CheckBoxStatus to FALSE (unchecked) and the value of m_EditBoxContents to null.

☐ Modify the preceding constructor function as follows:

```
CMyDlg::CMyDlg(CWnd* pParent /*=NULL*/)
    : CDialog(CMyDlg::IDD, pParent)
{
    //{{AFX_DATA_INIT(CMyDlg)

    /////////////////////////
    // MY CODE STARTS HERE
    /////////////////////////

    m_CheckBoxStatus = 1;
    m_EditBoxContents = "I was updated inside CMyDlg()";

    /////////////////////////
    // MY CODE ENDS HERE
    /////////////////////////

    //}}AFX_DATA_INIT
}
```

☐ Select Rebuild All CHKBOX.EXE from the Project menu.

☐ Execute the ChkBox application.

☐ Select Try It from the File menu.

> *CHKBOX responds by displaying the dialog box. As you can see, the check box is checked, and the text in the edit box is* `I was updated inside CMyDlg().`

Changing the Initial Settings of the Check Box Visually

In the previous section, you established the initial settings by writing code in the constructor function of `CMyDlg()`. There's an alternative way of setting the initial settings of the check box—visually.

To see how this is done:

☐ Start App Studio.

☐ Display the dialog box in its design mode.

☐ Double-click the My Check Box check box.

> *App Studio responds by displaying the Check Box Properties window (see Figure 8.8).*

Figure 8.8.
The Check Box
Properties window.

As shown in Figure 8.8, the Visible check box is checked. To make the check box invisible:

☐ Uncheck the Visible check box.

☐ Save the CHKBOX.RC file by selecting Save from the File menu of App Studio.

If you examine the CHKBOX.RC file, you'll see the lines

```
CONTROL          "&My Check Box",IDC_MY_CHECK_BOX,"Button",
                 BS_AUTOCHECKBOX | WS_TABSTOP,10,5,65,10
```

These lines define IDC_MY_CHECK_BOX as a check box control that is 10 pixels from the left edge of the dialog box, 5 pixels from the top edge, 65 pixels wide, and 10 pixels high. (In your CHKBOX.RC file, the coordinates of the check box may be different, because you probably placed the check box control at a slightly different location in the dialog box.) The NOT WS_VISIBLE parameter was added because you unchecked the Visible check box of My Check Box. This parameter causes the check box to be invisible. Later in the program you can make the check box visible (for example, by pressing the Show button).

The preceding discussions about CHKBOX.RC were included to show you the effect of unchecking the Visible check box in the Check Box Properties window. However, you don't need to examine or modify the CHKBOX.RC file. After all, this is App Studio's job.

Dialog Boxes: Scroll Bars

In this chapter you'll learn how to
use scroll bars in your dialog boxes.
As you know, scroll bars serve an
important role in the Windows user
interface mechanism.

The SPEED Application

Before you start writing the SPEED application, execute the copy of it that resides in your `C:\VCPROG\ORIGINAL\CH09\SPEED` directory.

To execute the SPEED application:

☐ Use the Run item from the Program Manager's File menu to execute
   `C:\VCPROG\ORIGINAL\CH09\SPEED\Speed.EXE`.

   Windows responds by executing the Speed.EXE application. The main window of Speed.EXE appears, as shown in Figure 9.1.

Figure 9.1.
The SPEED application's main window.

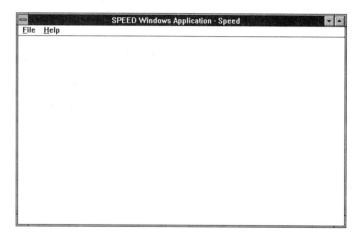

The SPEED application has two popup menus: File and Help. These popop menus are shown in Figures 9.2 and 9.3.

☐ Select Current Speed from the File menu.

   SPEED responds by displaying the current speed (see Figure 9.4).

Figure 9.2.
The SPEED
application's File
menu.

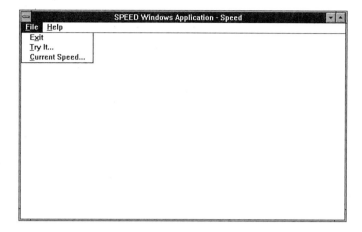

Figure 9.3.
The SPEED
application's Help
menu.

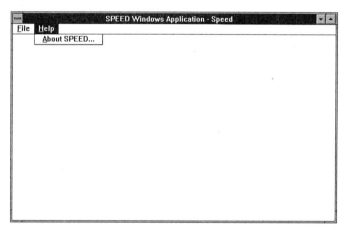

Figure 9.4.
Displaying the
current speed.

☐ Select Try it from the File menu.

SPEED responds by displaying the dialog box shown in Figure 9.5. As you can see, the current speed is set to 50.

Figure 9.5.
The SPEED
application's
dialog box.

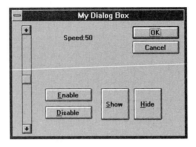

☐ Change the scroll bar's thumb position (for example, click the arrow icons of the scroll bar, click between the thumb and the arrow icon, or drag the thumb of the scroll bar).

SPEED responds by displaying a number that represents the new position of the scroll bar.

☐ Click the OK button in the dialog box.

SPEED responds by closing the dialog box.

☐ Select Current Speed from the File menu.

SPEED responds by displaying the current speed. As you can see, the displayed current speed is the same speed that you set with the dialog box's scroll bar.

Try the other buttons in the dialog box. As you can see, the Disable button makes the scroll bar unavailable (dimmed), and the Enable button makes the scroll bar available. Similarly, the Hide button makes the scroll bar invisible, and the Show button makes the scroll bar visible.

☐ Click the OK button in the dialog box and then select Exit from the File menu to terminate the SPEED application.

☐ Experiment with the SPEED application. In particular, note that if you close the dialog box by clicking its Cancel button, the current setting of the scroll bar isn't saved. However, if you close the dialog box by clicking the OK button, the current setting of the scroll bar is saved.

☐ Select Exit from the File menu to terminate the SPEED application.

Now that you know what the SPEED application should do, you can begin to write it.

Creating the Project of the SPEED Application

To create the project of the SPEED application:

☐ Select AppWizard from the Project menu.

> *Visual C++ responds by running AppWizard.*

☐ Use the Directory list box to select the directory C:\VCPROG\PRACTICE\CH09.

☐ Type speed in the Project Name box.

Now your AppWizard dialog box looks as shown in Figure 9.6.

Figure 9.6.
The AppWizard
dialog box for the
SPEED applica-
tion.

☐ Click the Options button and set the options as shown in Figure 9.7 (that is, uncheck all the check boxes except the Generate Source Comments check box).

☐ Click the OK button in the Options dialog box and then click the OK button in the AppWizard dialog box and finally click the Create button in the New Application Information dialog box.

> *AppWizard responds by creating the SPEED project and all the skeleton files of the SPEED application.*

233

To remove the debug options of the project (so that you'll have a small EXE file):

☐ Select Project from the Options menu in Visual C++, click the Release radio button, and then click the OK button in the dialog box.

Figure 9.7.
Setting the options
for the SPEED
application.

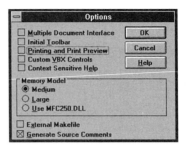

The Visual Implementation of the SPEED Application

The SPEED application has a menu, a custom dialog box, and an About dialog box. In the following sections you'll visually design the menu and the custom dialog box of the SPEED application.

The Visual Implementation of the SPEED Application's Menu

The SPEED application should have a menu as shown in Figures 9.1, 9.2, and 9.3.

☐ Use App Studio to implement the menu of the SPEED application per Table 9.1.

Table 9.1. The menu of the SPEED application.
Figures relating to menu: 9.1, 9.2, 9.3

Menu Item
&File
E&xit
&try It...
&Current Speed
&Help
&About SPEED...

To save your work:

☐ Select Save from the File menu of App Studio.

The visual implementation of the SPEED application's menu is completed.

The Visual Implementation of the Dialog Box

Now you'll visually implement the dialog box of the SPEED application:

☐ Implement the SPEED application's dialog box per Table 9.2.

Table 9.2. The SPEED application's dialog box.

Class Name:		CMyDlg
Figure:		9.5
OK button:		Yes
Cancel button:		Yes

Object	Property	Setting
Class Name:		CMyDlg (derived from Cdialog)
	Figure:	9.5
	OK button:	Yes
	Cancel button:	Yes
Dialog box	ID	IDD_DIALOG1
	Caption	My Dialog Box
Vertical	ID	IDC_SCROLL_SPEED
Scroll bar		
Label	ID	IDC_SPEED_LABEL
	Caption	Speed:
Push Button	ID	IDC_ENABLE
	Caption	&Enable
Push Button	ID	IDC_DISABLE
	Caption	&Disable
Push Button	ID	IDC_SHOW
	Caption	&Show
Push Button	ID	IDC_HIDE
	Caption	&Hide

NOTE

As specified in the header of Table 9.2, you have to use ClassWizard to create a dialog box class called `CMyDlg`. This class is derived from the `CDialog` class. Typically, new users of Visual C++ forget this important step. Naturally, if you forget, you'll get plenty of compiling and linking errors.

NOTE

The icon for the Label control in the Tools Window is shown in Figure 9.8.

Figure 9.8.
The Label control
icon in the Tools
Window.

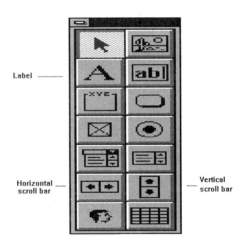

That's it! You've completed the visual implementation of the dialog box.

To save your work:

☐ Select Save from the File menu.

Declaring the Dialog Box Object as a Data Member of the View Class

Now you'll declare the dialog box as an object `dlg` of type `CMyDlg`. You'll create this object as a data member of the view class.

☐ Open the SPEEDVW.H file and modify the declaration of the `CSpeedView` class. After you modify the declaration, it looks as follows:

```
class CSpeedView : public CView
{
protected: // create from serialization only
     CSpeedView();
     DECLARE_DYNCREATE(CSpeedView)

// Attributes
public:
     CSpeedDoc* GetDocument();


     /////////////////////
     // MY CODE STARTS HERE
     /////////////////////

     // Create a dialog box object of class CMyDlg
     CMyDlg dlg;

     /////////////////////
     // MY CODE ENDS HERE
     /////////////////////


// Operations
public:

// Implementation
public:
virtual ~CSpeedView();
virtual void OnDraw(CDC* pDC);
// overridden to draw this view
#ifdef _DEBUG
     virtual void AssertValid() const;
     virtual void Dump(CDumpContext& dc) const;
#endif

protected:

// Generated message map functions
protected:
//{{AFX_MSG(CSpeedView)
// NOTE - the ClassWizard will add and remove member
// functions here.
// DO NOT EDIT what you see in these blocks of
// generated code !
//}}AFX_MSG
DECLARE_MESSAGE_MAP()
};
```

Because the CMyDlg class is unknown in the file SPEEDVW.H, you have to #include the file MyDlg.h (which contains the class declaration of CMyDlg) at the beginning of the SPEEDVW.H file.

☐ Add the #include "MyDlg.h" statement at the beginning of the SPEEDVW.H file.

After you #include this statement, the beginning of the SPEEDVW.H file looks as follows:

```
// speedvw.h : interface of the CSpeedView class
//
/////////////////////////////////////////////////////

//////////////////////
// MY CODE STARTS HERE
//////////////////////

// Because the declaration of the CSpeedView class
// contains the creation of the dlg object of type
// CMyDlg, the MyDlg.h file must be #included.

#include "MyDlg.h"

//////////////////////
// MY CODE ENDS HERE
//////////////////////

. . . . .
. . . . .
. . . . .
```

Attaching Code to the SPEED Application's Try It Menu Item

You'll now attach code to the Try It menu item. Recall that when you select the Try It menu item, the SPEED application displays the dialog box.

☐ Use ClassWizard to add a function for the event:

Class Name:	CSpeedView
Object ID:	ID_FILE_TRYIT
Message:	COMMAND
Function Name:	OnFileTryit()

When you add the OnFileTryIt() function, make sure to set Class Name to CSpeedView as indicated previously. Typically, new users of Visual C++ forget to set the Class Name, which will generate plenty of compiling and linking errors.

☐ Edit the OnFileTryit() function that you added to the SPEEDVW.CPP file. After you edit the function, your OnFileTryit() function looks as follows:

```
void CSpeedView::OnFileTryit()
{
    // TODO: Add your command handler code here


    ////////////////////////
    // MY CODE STARTS HERE
    ////////////////////////

    // Display the dialog box.
    // Note that DoModal() is a member function
    // of the CWnd class.
    // dlg is an object of the CMyDlg class, and CMyDlg
    // class is derived from the CDialog class which is
    // derived from the CWnd class.
    // Thus, you can execute DoModal() on the dlg object.

    dlg.DoModal();

    ////////////////////////
    // MY CODE ENDS HERE
    ////////////////////////

}
```

In the preceding code, you display the dialog box by using the DoModal() function:

```
dlg.DoModal();
```

The DoModal() function is a member function of the CWnd class. dlg is an object of the CMyDlg class. The CMyDlg class is derived from the CDialog class, which is derived from the CWnd class. Thus, you can execute DoModal() on the dlg object. Of course, dlg is accessible from the OnFileTryIt() function, because dlg is a data member of the CSpeedView class, and OnFileTryIt() is a member function of the CSpeedView class.

Although you haven't completed writing the SPEED application, compile, link, and execute it.

☐ Select Rebuild All SPEED.EXE from the Project menu.

☐ Execute the SPEED application.

☐ Select Try It from the File menu.

SPEED responds by displaying the dialog box.

☐ Click the scroll bar.

As you can see, nothing happens! This is because you need to write code to make the scroll bar operational. (Also, no other buttons except the OK and Cancel buttons are working yet, because you haven't attached code to them.)

Attaching Code to the Scroll Bar

Now you'll attach code to the scroll bar. This code should be executed whenever the user clicks the scroll bar. Recall that when a user clicks the scroll bar, the label control should display the position of the scroll bar, and the thumb of the scroll bar should move to its new position.

During the visual implementation of the ChkBox application in Chapter 8, "Dialog Boxes: Check Boxes," you were instructed to attach variables to the edit box and the check box. In Table 9.2, you weren't instructed to attach a variable to the scroll bar! Why? Well, with ClassWizard you can't attach variables to scroll bars. Thus, it's your responsibility to attach variables manually to the scroll bar. What variables should you use? A scroll bar should have three variables associated with it:

- The current position of the scroll bar's thumb
- The minimum value that the extreme top of the scroll bar represents
- The maximum value that the extreme bottom of the scroll bar represents

These variables should be defined in the class declaration of the `CMyDlg` class (which resides in `MyDlg.h`):

☐ Define the variables of the scroll bar in the `CMyDlg` class declaration as follows:

```
class CMyDlg : public CDialog
{
// Construction
public:
     CMyDlg(CWnd* pParent = NULL); // standard constructor

     /////////////////////////
     // MY CODE STARTS HERE
     /////////////////////////

     // Declare data members that are used as
     // the Scroll bars variables.
```

```
    int m_ScrollPosition; // Current position
    int m_ScrollMin;      // Minimum posistion
    int m_ScrollMax;      // Maximum position

    ///////////////////////
    // MY CODE ENDS HERE
    ///////////////////////
```

```
// Dialog Data
    //{{AFX_DATA(CMyDlg)
    enum { IDD = IDD_DIALOG1 };
// NOTE: the ClassWizard will add data members here
//}}AFX_DATA
```

```
// Implementation
protected:
// DDX/DDV support
virtual void DoDataExchange(CDataExchange* pDX);
```

```
// Generated message map functions
//{{AFX_MSG(CMyDlg)
// NOTE: the ClassWizard will add member functions here
//}}AFX_MSG
    DECLARE_MESSAGE_MAP()
};
```

The scroll bar variables that you declared are data members of the CMyDlg class. Because you created the dialog object dlg in the view class (CSpeedView), the scroll bar variables are accessible from the member functions of the view class.

Initializing the Scroll Bar's Variables

In the previous section you declared the scroll bar's variables. To initialize these variables:

☐ Add initialization code in the constructor function of the CMyDlg class (in MyDlg.CPP) as follows:

```
CMyDlg::CMyDlg(CWnd* pParent /*=NULL*/)
    : CDialog(CMyDlg::IDD, pParent)
{
//{{AFX_DATA_INIT(CMyDlg)
// NOTE: the ClassWizard will add member initialization here
//}}AFX_DATA_INIT

    ///////////////////////
    // MY CODE STARTS HERE
    ///////////////////////
```

```
    // Initialize the data members
    m_ScrollPosition = 50;
    m_ScrollMin = 0;
    m_ScrollMax = 100;

    /////////////////////
    // MY CODE ENDS HERE
    /////////////////////
}
```

The code you typed sets the variable m_ScrollPosition to 50 and the range of the scroll bar to (0, 100). In other words, the current position of the scroll bar's thumb is set to the middle of the scroll bar.

Okay, you set the scroll bar's range variables to (0, 100), and you set the position of the scroll bar's thumb to the middle of the range. This has no effect on the appearance of the scroll bar, however, because you still haven't made any connections between these variables and the appearance of the scroll bar.

Initializing the Scroll Bar

Because you now want to initialize the appearance of the dialog box, you have to attach code to the OnInitDialog() function:

☐ Use ClassWizard to add a function for the event:

Class Name:	CMyDlg
Object ID:	CMyDlg
Message:	WM_INITDIALOG
Function Name:	OnInitDialog()

☐ Edit the OnInitDialog() function that you added to the MyDlg.CPP file so that it looks as follows:

```
BOOL CMyDlg::OnInitDialog()
{
    CDialog::OnInitDialog();

    // TODO: Add extra initialization here


    /////////////////////
    // MY CODE STARTS HERE
    /////////////////////
```

```
// Extract the pointer of the scroll bar.
CScrollBar* pSB =
        (CScrollBar*) GetDlgItem ( IDC_SCROLL_SPEED);

// Set the range of the scroll bar.
pSB -> SetScrollRange (m_ScrollMin,
                         m_ScrollMax );

// Set the position of the scroll bar.
pSB -> SetScrollPos ( m_ScrollPosition );


// Declare local variables
CString LabelContents;
char sPos[25];

// Convert the current position from an
// integer to a string.
itoa ( m_ScrollPosition, sPos, 10 );

// Update the variable of the label.
LabelContents = (CString) "Speed:" + sPos ;

// Update the caption of the label
SetDlgItemText(IDC_SPEED_LABEL, LabelContents);


/////////////////////
// MY CODE ENDS HERE
/////////////////////


// return TRUE  unless you set the focus to a control
return TRUE;
}
```

The first statement extracts the pointer of the scroll bar by using the GetDlgItem()
function and supplying IDC_SCROLL_SPEED as its parameter:

```
// Extract the pointer of the scroll bar.
CScrollBar* pSB =
  (CScrollBar*) GetDlgItem ( IDC_SCROLL_SPEED);
```

The pointer that's extracted (pSB) is of type CScrollBar. Note that GetDlgItem() is a
member function of the CWnd class. You can use GetDlgItem() from OnInitDialog()
because OnInitDialg() is a member function of CMyDlg, which is derived from Cdialog,
which is derived from CWnd.

Once pSB is extracted, the SetScrollRange() member function is executed:

```
// Set the range of the scroll bar.
pSB -> SetScrollRange (m_ScrollMin,
                       m_ScrollMax );
```

The first parameter of SetScrollRange() is m_ScrollMin, and the second parameter is m_ScrollMax. Recall that you set m_ScrollMin to 0 and m_ScrollMax to 100. Putting it together, the SetScrollRange() function sets the range of the scroll bar to (0, 100).

SetScrollRange() is a member function of the class CWnd. You can use SetScrollRange() from within OnInitDialog() (a member function of CDialog) because the CDialog class is a derived class from CWnd, and CMyDlg is a derived class from CDialog.

The next statement in OnInitDialog() sets the position of the scroll bar to m_ScrollPosition:

```
// Set the position of the scroll bar.
pSB -> SetScrollPos ( m_ScrollPosition );
```

This statement places the thumb of the scroll bar at a position indicated by m_ScrollPosition. For example, if m_ScrollPosition is equal to 50, the thumb of the scroll bar is placed at the middle of the scroll bar (because you already set the range to [0, 100]). Note that SetScrollPos() is a member function of CWnd, so you can use it from within OnInitDialog().

> **NOTE**
>
> To execute the member functions (for example, SetScrollRange(), SetScrollPos()), you used the statements
>
> ```
>     pSB -> SetScrollRange (m_ScrollMin,
>                            m_ScrollMax );
> ```
>
> and
>
> ```
>     pSB -> SetScrollPos ( m_ScrollPosition );
> ```
>
> Recall that at the beginning of the OnInitDialog() function you extracted the pointer of the scroll bar (pSB) as follows:
>
> ```
>     CScrollBar* pSB =
>        (CScrollBar*) GetDlgItem ( IDC_SCROLL_SPEED);
> ```

If you aren't used to pointer notation, these statements might look strange. However, they're no different from the statement

```
dlg.DOModal();
```

In this statement, the `DoModal()` member function is executed on the `dlg` object.

In the statement

```
pSB -> SetScrollPos ( m_ScrollPosition );
```

the `SetScrollPos()` member function is executed on the scroll bar. Which scroll bar? The scroll bar with a pointer equal to `pSB` (and you extracted this pointer by using the `GetDlgItem()` member function with its parameter equal to `SB_SCROLL_SPEED`).

The next two statements declare two local variables:

```
CString LabelContents;
char sPos[25];
```

Then the integer `m_ScrollPosition` is converted to a string (`sPos`) by using the C/C++ function `itoa()`:

```
itoa ( m_ScrollPosition, sPos, 10 );
```

`itoa()` is a regular (not an MFC function) C/C++ function that converts integers to ASCII (hence the name *itoa()*). The first parameter of `itoa()` is the integer to be converted, the second parameter is the name of the string that will be updated by `itoa()`, and the third parameter is the radix. When converting base 10 numbers (that is, regular integers), the third parameter should be 10.

Now that the current position, `sPos`, is available as a string, you can prepare the `LabelContents` variable:

```
LabelContents = (CString) "Speed:" + sPos ;
```

For example, if the variable `m_ScrollPosition` is currently equal to 50, the previous statements convert this integer to a string, `sPos`, that is equal to "50", and the variable `LabelContents` is set to "Speed:50".

Finally, the caption of the label is updated with the contents of the LabelContents variable:

```
SetDlgItemText(IDC_SPEED_LABEL, LabelContents);
```

The SetDlgItemText() function (a member function of CWnd) sets the caption of the label control by supplying the ID of the label as its first parameter, and the caption as its second parameter.

To summarize, the code you typed in OnInitDialog() sets the range of the scroll bar, and then the thumb of the scroll bar is placed at m_ScrollPosition. As you'll soon see, m_ScrollPosition will be updated so that it always contains the current position of the scroll bar. Finally, the caption of the label is set to reflect the position of the scroll bar.

Compiling, Linking, and Executing the SPEED Application

Although you haven't completed writing the SPEED application, you can compile, link, and execute it so that you can see the initialization in action:

☐ Select Rebuild All SPEED.EXE from the Project menu in Visual C++.

☐ Select Execute SPEED.EXE from the Project menu.

☐ Select Try It from the File menu.

> *SPEED responds by displaying the dialog box. As you can see, the scroll bar's thumb appears at its middle position, and the caption of the label is "Speed:50". The code that you wrote in OnInitDialog() works.*

Of course, moving the thumb of the scroll bar doesn't have any effect yet (because you haven't written any code to accomplish that).

Next, you'll write code that is executed whenever the user drags and moves the thumb.

☐ Close the dialog box and then terminate the SPEED application.

Detecting Scroll Bar Clicking

Now you'll write code that is executed whenever the user drags and moves the thumb of the scroll bar.

☐ Use ClassWizard to add a function for the event:

Class Name:	CMyDlg
Object ID:	CMyDlg
Message:	WM_VSCROLL
Function Name:	OnVScroll()

☐ Edit the `OnVScroll()` function that you added to the `MyDlg.CPP` file so that it looks as follows:

```
void CMyDlg::OnVScroll(UINT nSBCode,
                       UINT nPos,
                       CScrollBar* pScrollBar)
{
// TODO: Add your message handler
// code here and/or call default

        ///////////////////////
        // MY CODE STARTS HERE
        ///////////////////////

        // Declare local variables
        CString LabelContents;
        char sPos[25];

        switch (nSBCode)
             {
             case SB_THUMBPOSITION:

                   // Set the scroll bar to its new position.
                   pScrollBar->SetScrollPos ( nPos );


                   // Update the caption of the label.
                   itoa ( nPos, sPos, 10 );
                   LabelContents = (CString) "Speed:" + sPos ;

                   SetDlgItemText( IDC_SPEED_LABEL,
                                   LabelContents );
                   break;

             } // end of switch

        ///////////////////////
        // MY CODE ENDS HERE
        ///////////////////////


CDialog::OnVScroll(nSBCode, nPos, pScrollBar);
}
```

This code defines two local variables:

```
CString LabelContents;
char sPos[25];
```

A switch is then used to determine which code will be executed, based on the value of nSBCode. nSBCode is a variable that was supplied as the first parameter to the OnVScroll() function. This parameter indicates what was clicked on the scroll bar. As you know, you can click the scroll bar at a variety of places.

When nSBCode is equal to SB_THUMBPOSITION, the user has dragged the thumb of the scroll bar. SB_THUMBPOSITION is generated when the user releases the thumb.

Thus, the code in the SB_THUMBPOSITION case of the switch is executed when the user releases the thumb:

```
switch (nSBCode)
    {
    case SB_THUMBPOSITION:
        ............................................
        ... This code is executed when the user   ...
        ... releases the thumb of the scroll bar. ...
        ............................................
        break;
    }
```

The first statement in the SB_THUMBPOSITION case sets the scroll bar to its new position by using the statement

```
pScrollBar->SetScrollPos ( nPos );
```

Note that now you don't have to extract the pointer of the scroll bar, pScrollBar, because it was supplied as the third parameter of the OnVScroll() function.

The parameter of SetScrollPos() is nPos. This variable was supplied as the second parameter of the OnVScroll() function, and it's an integer that represents the new location of the scroll bar's thumb.

To update the caption of the label control, the C/C++ function itoa() is used to convert the integer nPos to the string sPos:

```
itoa ( nPos, sPos, 10 );
```

The new caption of the label control is prepared and stored in the local variable LabelContents:

```
LabelContents = (CString) "Speed:" + sPos ;
```

and finally the caption of the label is updated by using the `SetDlgItemText()` member function:

```
SetDlgItemText( IDC_SPEED_LABEL,
                LabelContents );
```

Compiling, Linking, and Executing the SPEED Application

Although you haven't completed writing the SPEED application, you can compile, link, and execute it:

☐ Select Rebuild All SPEED.EXE from the Project menu in Visual C++.

☐ Select Execute SPEED.EXE from the Project menu.

☐ Select Try It from the File menu.

  SPEED responds by displaying the dialog box.

☐ Drag the thumb of the scroll bar.

  SPEED responds by changing the caption of the label only when you release the thumb (because in the switch, you only took care of the `SB_THUMBPOSITION` *case).*

☐ Click the OK button.

  SPEED responds by closing the dialog box.

☐ Select Try It again.

  SPEED responds by displaying the dialog box again. However, the last position of the scroll bar was not maintained, because you haven't written the code that accomplishes that.

☐ Close the dialog box and then terminate the SPEED application.

> **NOTE**
>
> In the SPEED application the only scroll bar that appears in the dialog box is the `IDC_SCROLL_SPEED` scroll bar. Thus, whenever `OnVScroll()` is executed, it means that the `IDC_SCROLL_SPEED` was clicked. If your dialog box contains more than one scroll bar, your code must determine which scroll bar was

clicked. This can be done by comparing the pointer that appears as the third parameter of OnVScroll() with the pointer that is extracted with the GetDlgItem() function.

For example, the following is the format of the OnVScroll() function when there are two scroll bars in the dialog box:

```
void CMyDlg::OnVScroll(UINT nSBCode,

                       UINT nPos,

                       CScrollBar* pScrollBar)
{
// TODO: Add your message handler code here

// and/or call default


    ////////////////////////
    // MY CODE STARTS HERE
    ////////////////////////


    if ( GetDlgItem(IDC_SCROLL_NUMBER_1) == pScrollBar )
       {
       switch (nSBCode)
               {
               case SB_THUMBPOSITION:
                    .....................................
                    ... Here is the code for scroll #1 ...
                    .....................................
                    break;

               }
       }


    if ( GetDlgItem(IDC_SCROLL_NUMBER_2) == pScrollBar )
       {
       switch (nSBCode)
               {
               case SB_THUMBPOSITION:
                    .....................................
                    ... Here is the code for scroll #2 ...
```

```
                    ....................................
                    break;
                }
            }


        /////////////////////
        // MY CODE ENDS HERE
        /////////////////////


        CDialog::OnVScroll(nSBCode, nPos, pScrollBar);
}
```

That is, in the preceding code the pointers of the scroll bars are extracted (with GetDlgItem()), and the extracted pointers are compared with the pointer that was supplied as the third parameter of OnVScroll().

Maintaining the Status of the Scroll Bar

Now you'll attach code that maintains the status of the scroll bar. That is, if you change the position of the scroll bar's thumb, close the dialog box by pressing the OK button, and then display the dialog box again, the thumb will appear in the same position it was in when you closed the dialog box.

The variable that maintains the position of the scroll bar is m_ScrollPosition. Recall that you declared this variable as a data member of the CMyDlg class.

☐ Use ClassWizard to add a function for the event:

Class Name:	CMyDlg
Object ID:	IDOK
Message:	BN_CLICKED
Function Name:	OnOK()

☐ Edit the OnOK() function that you added to the MyDlg.CPP file so that it looks as follows:

```
void CMyDlg::OnOK()
{
    // TODO: Add extra validation here

    /////////////////////
    // MY CODE STARTS HERE
    /////////////////////
```

```
// Extract the pointer of the scroll bar whose
// ID is IDC_SCROLL_SPEED
CScrollBar* pSB =
    (CScrollBar*) GetDlgItem ( IDC_SCROLL_SPEED);

// Extract the thumb position of the scroll bar, and
// assign it to the m_ScrollPosition data member.
m_ScrollPosition = pSB -> GetScrollPos ();

//////////////////////
// MY CODE ENDS HERE
//////////////////////



    CDialog::OnOK();

}
```

Note that the last statement, CDialog::OnOK();, was written by ClassWizard. This statement closes the dialog box.

The code you typed extracts the pointer of the scroll bar:

```
CScrollBar* pSB =
    (CScrollBar*) GetDlgItem ( IDC_SCROLL_SPEED);
```

Now that the pointer of the scroll bar (pSB) is known, the member function GetScrollPos() is executed. The variable m_ScrollPosition is updated with the returned value from GetScrollPos():

```
m_ScrollPosition = pSB -> GetScrollPos ();
```

To summarize, every time the user clicks the OK button, the m_ScrollPosition variable is updated with the current position of the scroll bar's thumb.

Compiling, Linking, and Executing the SPEED Application

☐ Select Rebuild All SPEED.EXE to compile and link the SPEED program.

☐ Select Execute SPEED.EXE from the Project menu.

☐ Select Try It from the File menu.

SPEED responds by displaying the dialog box.

☐ Drag the thumb of the scroll bar to a new location.

SPEED responds by changing the caption of the label to reflect the thumb's new position.

☐ Click the OK button of the dialog box.

☐ Select Try It from the File menu.

SPEED responds by displaying the dialog box, with the thumb in the same position it was in when you closed the dialog box.

☐ Experiment with the SPEED application and then terminate the SPEED application.

Detecting Other Scroll Bar Clicking

Now you can add more cases to the switch of the OnVScroll() function that resides in the MyDlg.CPP file. These cases correspond to the various clicking events the scroll bar should respond to.

☐ Edit the OnVScroll() function of the MyDlg.CPP file so that it looks as follows:

```
void CMyDlg::OnVScroll( UINT nSBCode,
                        UINT nPos,
                        CScrollBar* pScrollBar)
{
// TODO: Add your message handler code here
// and/or call default

///////////////////////
// MY CODE STARTS HERE
///////////////////////

CString LabelContents;
char sPos[25];
int iCurrent;

switch (nSBCode)
     {
     case SB_THUMBPOSITION:
          // Set the scroll bar to its new position.
          pScrollBar->SetScrollPos ( nPos );


          // Update the caption of the label.
          itoa ( nPos, sPos, 10 );
          LabelContents = (CString) "Speed:" + sPos ;
```

```
        SetDlgItemText(IDC_SPEED_LABEL,LabelContents);
        break;

case SB_LINEDOWN:

        // Get the current position
        iCurrent = pScrollBar->GetScrollPos();


        // Increase current position
        // by 1 (if possible)
        iCurrent = iCurrent + 1;

        if ( iCurrent >= m_ScrollMax )
            iCurrent = m_ScrollMax;

        // Set scroll bar to its new position.
        pScrollBar->SetScrollPos ( iCurrent );


        // Update the caption of the label.
        itoa ( iCurrent, sPos, 10 );

        LabelContents = (CString) "Speed:" + sPos ;

        SetDlgItemText(IDC_SPEED_LABEL,LabelContents);
        break;

case SB_LINEUP:

        // Get the current position
        iCurrent = pScrollBar->GetScrollPos();


        // Decrease current position
        // by 1 (if possible)
        iCurrent = iCurrent - 1;

        if ( iCurrent <= m_ScrollMin )
            iCurrent = m_ScrollMin;

        // Set scroll bar to its new position.
        pScrollBar->SetScrollPos ( iCurrent );


        // Update the caption of the label.
        itoa ( iCurrent, sPos, 10 );
        LabelContents = (CString) "Speed:" + sPos ;
```

```
        SetDlgItemText(IDC_SPEED_LABEL,LabelContents);
        break;

case SB_PAGEDOWN:

        // Get the current position.
        iCurrent = pScrollBar->GetScrollPos();

        // Increase scroll bar (if possible).
        iCurrent = iCurrent + 1;

        if ( iCurrent >= m_ScrollMax )
            iCurrent = m_ScrollMax;


        // Set scroll bar to its new position.
        pScrollBar->SetScrollPos ( iCurrent );


        // Update the caption of the label.
        itoa ( iCurrent, sPos, 10 );
        LabelContents = (CString) "Speed:" + sPos ;

        SetDlgItemText(IDC_SPEED_LABEL,LabelContents);
        break;

case SB_PAGEUP:

        // Get the current position.
        iCurrent = pScrollBar->GetScrollPos();

        // Decrease scroll bar (if possible).
        iCurrent = iCurrent - 1;

        if ( iCurrent <= m_ScrollMin )
            iCurrent = m_ScrollMin;


        // Set scroll bar to its new position.
        pScrollBar->SetScrollPos ( iCurrent );


        // Update the caption of the label.
        itoa ( iCurrent, sPos, 10 );
        LabelContents = (CString) "Speed:" + sPos ;

        SetDlgItemText(IDC_SPEED_LABEL,LabelContents);
        break;

    }
```

```
///////////////////
// MY CODE ENDS HERE
///////////////////
```

```
CDialog::OnVScroll(nSBCode, nPos, pScrollBar);

}
```

First you typed the declaration of a new local variable:

```
int iCurrent;
```

The SB_LINEDOWN case is executed whenever the user clicks the down-arrow icon that appears at the bottom of the scroll bar.

In this case, the GetScrollPos() member function is executed to extract the current position of the scroll bar's thumb:

```
iCurrent = pScrollBar->GetScrollPos();
```

So now iCurrent contains the current position of the thumb of the scroll bar.

Then the value of iCurrent is increased by one:

```
iCurrent = iCurrent + 1;
```

Because the value of the current position of the scroll bar's thumb shouldn't be greater than m_ScrollMax, an if statement is executed to limit the value of iCurrent:

```
if ( iCurrent >= m_ScrollMax )
    iCurrent = m_ScrollMax;
```

Then the SetScrollPos() member function is executed to set the thumb of the scroll bar to its new position:

```
pScrollBar->SetScrollPos ( iCurrent );
```

Finally, the caption of the label control is updated:

```
itoa ( iCurrent, sPos, 10 );
```

```
LabelContents = (CString) "Speed:" + sPos ;
```

```
SetDlgItemText(IDC_SPEED_LABEL,LabelContents);
```

To summarize, whenever the user clicks the down-arrow icon of the scroll bar, the thumb of the scroll bar is increased by one unit.

The *SB_LINEUP* Case

The SB_LINEUP case is executed whenever the user clicks the up-arrow icon that appears on the top of the scroll bar. The code under the SB_LINEUP is identical to the code under the SB_LINEDOWN case, except that under the SB_LINEUP case, the position of the scroll bar's thumb is decreased by one (instead of increased it by one):

```
// Decrease current position by 1 (if possible)
iCurrent = iCurrent - 1;

if ( iCurrent <= m_ScrollMin )
    iCurrent = m_ScrollMin;
```

The *SB_PAGEDOWN* Case

The SB_PAGEDOWN case is executed whenever the user clicks in between the thumb and the down-arrow icon of the scroll bar. The code under this case is identical to the code under the SB_LINEDOWN case. Note that some programmers like to increase the position of the scroll bar's thumb under this case by more than one unit. For example, to increase the thumb position by 10 percent for each click between the thumb and the down-arrow icon of the scroll bar, use the following code under the SB_PAGEDOWN case:

```
case SB_PAGEDOWN:

        // Get the current position.
         iCurrent = pScrollBar->GetScrollPos();

        // Increase scroll bar (if possible).
        iCurrent =
           iCurrent + (int)((m_ScrollMax - m_ScrollMin)*0.1);

        if ( iCurrent >= m_ScrollMax )
            iCurrent = m_ScrollMax;

        // Set scroll bar to its new position.
        pScrollBar->SetScrollPos ( iCurrent );


        //  Update the caption of the label.
        itoa ( iCurrent, sPos, 10 );
        LabelContents = (CString) "Speed:" + sPos ;

        SetDlgItemText(IDC_SPEED_LABEL,LabelContents);
        break;
```

If implemented this way, SB_PAGEDOWN causes the thumb to move in large increments, and SB_LINEDOWN causes the scroll bar to move in small increments.

The *SB_PAGEUP* Case

The SB_PAGEUP case is executed whenever the user clicks the up-arrow icon that appears at the top of the scroll bar. The code under this case is identical to the code under the SB_PAGEDOWN case, except that under this case, the thumb's current position is decreased (instead of increased).

Compiling, Linking, and Executing the SPEED Program

Now compile, link, and execute the SPEED program:

☐ Select Rebuild All SPEED.EXE from the Project menu.

☐ Select Execute SPEED.EXE from the Project menu.

Experiment with the SPEED program (change the scroll bar thumb's position by clicking at various points on the scroll bar).

The *SB_THUMBTRACK* Case of the Scroll Bar

Note that as you drag the thumb of the scroll bar, the caption of the label control doesn't change. Why? Because there's one more important case that you haven't included in the switch.

☐ Add the following case in the switch of the OnVScroll() function that resides in the MyDlg.CPP program:

```
case SB_THUMBTRACK:

    // Set scroll bar to its new position.
    pScrollBar->SetScrollPos ( nPos );

    //  Update the caption of the label.
    itoa ( nPos, sPos, 10 );
    LabelContents = (CString) "Speed:" + sPos ;
    SetDlgItemText(IDC_SPEED_LABEL,LabelContents);
    break;
```

The code under the SB_THUMBTRACK case is executed whenever the user moves the thumb of the scroll bar (that is, by dragging it).

☐ Compile, link, and execute the SPEED program. Notice that as you move the thumb of the scroll bar, the caption of the label control changes immediately (that is, you don't have to release the mouse).

As you drag the thumb, the program is fast enough to execute the code. However, you have to be careful when using the SB_THUMBTRACK case. For example, suppose that the response of changing the thumb's position involves executing an extremely large function. Currently, when you drag the thumb, the only code that is executed is that which changes the caption of the label control. The PC is capable of executing this and immediately responds to the next SB_THUMBTRACK message. However, if you want additional tasks to be executed whenever the thumb's position is changed, and these tasks take a long time to execute, the PC won't be able to keep up with the thumb position. In this case, the user will notice that the program doesn't respond to the thumb's movement. It's therefore best in these cases not to include the SB_THUMBTRACK case. For example, in Word for Windows, as you drag the thumb of a document's vertical scroll bar, the document doesn't scroll until you release the thumb.

Displaying the Current Speed from the Menu

In practice, you'll design a dialog box so that the user can enter various data. Later in the program, the value that the user entered is used. This is the reason for declaring the dlg object as a data member of the view class (the CSpeedView class).

To demonstrate how your program can use the value of the scroll bar that was set in the dialog box:

☐ Use ClassWizard to add a function for the event:

Class Name:	CSpeedView
Object ID:	ID_FILE_CURRENTSPEED
Message:	COMMAND
Function Name:	OnFileCurrentspeed()

NOTE

You were instructed in the previous step to use ClassWizard to add a function to the COMMAND event of ID_FILE_CURRENTSPEED. In the early versions of Visual C++, if you use ClassWizard from the Browse menu of Visual C++, you won't see this ID in the IDs list! However, if you select App Studio from the Tools menu, display the menu in its design mode, and then select ClassWizard from the Resource menu, the ID FILE CURRENT SPEED appears in the IDs list, and you can add the OnFileCurrentspeed() function.

So if you don't see a particular menu ID in the IDs list, switch to App Studio, select the menu, and run ClassWizard from the Resource menu. It's expected that this problem will be corrected in future versions of Visual C++.

☐ Edit the OnFileCurrentspeed() function that you added to the MyDlg.CPP file so that it looks as follows:

```
void CSpeedView::OnFileCurrentspeed()
{
    // TODO: Add your command handler code here

    ////////////////////////
    // MY CODE STARTS HERE
    ////////////////////////

    // Local variables
    CString Message;
    char Current[25];

    // Prepare the message
    itoa ( dlg.m_ScrollPosition, Current, 10 );
    Message = (CString) "Current Speed is: " +  Current;

    // Display the message
    MessageBox ( Message, "Current Speed", MB_OK);


    ////////////////////////
    // MY CODE ENDS HERE
    ////////////////////////

}
```

The code you typed declares two local variables:

```
CString Message;
char Current[25];
```

The itoa() C/C++ function then converts the member data of the dlg dialog box object to the string Current:

```
itoa ( dlg.m_ScrollPosition, Current, 10 );
```

and then the `CString` Message is prepared:

```
Message = (CString) "Current Speed is: " + Current;
```

Finally, the `MessageBox()` function is used to display the `Message` variable:

```
MessageBox ( Message, "Current Speed", MB_OK);
```

To compile and link the SPEED application:

Select Rebuild All SPEED.EXE from the Project menu in Visual C++.

Execute the SPEED application:

☐ Select Execute SPEED.EXE from the Project menu.

☐ Select Try It from the File menu.

> *SPEED responds by displaying the dialog box.*

☐ Change the position of the scroll bar and then click the OK button.

☐ Select Current Speed from the File menu.

> *SPEED responds by displaying the current speed as you set it in the dialog box.*

Experiment with the SPEED application and then terminate it.

Disabling, Enabling, Hiding, and Showing the Scroll Bar

As shown in Figure 9.5, the dialog box contains the buttons Enable, Disable, Hide, and Show.

Now you'll write code that's executed when these buttons are clicked. This code illustrates how you can enable/disable and show/hide a scroll bar.

☐ Use ClassWizard to add a function for the event:

```
Class Name:      CMyDlg
Object ID:       IDC_ENABLE
Message:         BN_CLICKED
Function Name:   OnEnable()
```

☐ Edit the `OnEnable()` function that you added to the `MyDlg.CPP` file so that it looks as follows:

```
void CMyDlg::OnEnable()
{
// TODO: Add your control notification handler code here

    /////////////////////////
    // MY CODE STARTS HERE
    /////////////////////////

    // Enable the scroll bar
    GetDlgItem(IDC_SCROLL_SPEED)->EnableWindow(TRUE);

    /////////////////////////
    // MY CODE ENDS HERE
    /////////////////////////

}
```

The code you typed extracts the pointer of the scroll bar by using the `GetDlgItem()` function with `IDC_SCROLL_SPEED` as its parameter, and it executes the `EnableWindow()` with `TRUE` as its parameter. This causes the scroll bar to be enabled (undimmed).

☐ Use ClassWizard to add a function for the event:

Class Name:	CMyDlg
Object ID:	IDC_DISABLE
Message:	BN_CLICKED
Function Name:	OnDisable()

☐ Edit the `OnDisable()` function that you added to the `MyDlg.CPP` file so that it looks as follows:

```
void CMyDlg::OnDisable()
{
// TODO: Add your control notification handler code here

    /////////////////////////
    // MY CODE STARTS HERE
    /////////////////////////

    // Disable the scroll bar
    GetDlgItem(IDC_SCROLL_SPEED)->EnableWindow(FALSE);

    /////////////////////////
    // MY CODE ENDS HERE
    /////////////////////////

}
```

The code you typed extracts the pointer of the scroll bar by using the GetDlgItem() function with IDC_SCROLL_SPEED as its parameter and executes the EnableWindow() function with FALSE as its parameter. This causes the scroll bar to be disabled (dimmed).

☐ Use ClassWizard to add a function for the event:

Class Name:	CMyDlg
Object ID:	IDC_HIDE
Message:	BN_CLICKED
Function Name:	OnHide()

☐ Edit the OnHide() function that you added to the MyDlg.CPP file so that it looks as follows:

```
void CMyDlg::OnHide()
{
// TODO: Add your control notification handler code here

    /////////////////////
    // MY CODE STARTS HERE
    /////////////////////

    // Hide the scroll bar
    GetDlgItem(IDC_SCROLL_SPEED)->ShowWindow(SW_HIDE);

    /////////////////////
    // MY CODE ENDS HERE
    /////////////////////

}
```

The code you typed extracts the pointer of the scroll bar by using the GetDlgItem() function with IDC_SCROLL_SPEED as its parameter and executes the ShowWindow() function with SW_HIDE as its parameter. This causes the scroll bar to be invisible.

☐ Use ClassWizard to add a function for the event:

Class Name:	CMyDlg
Object ID:	IDC_SHOW
Message:	BN_CLICKED
Function Name:	OnShow()

☐ Edit the OnShow() function that you added to the MyDlg.CPP file so that it looks as follows:

```
void CMyDlg::OnShow()
{
// TODO: Add your control notification handler code here

        /////////////////////////
        // MY CODE STARTS HERE
        /////////////////////////

        // Un-hide the scroll bar
        GetDlgItem(IDC_SCROLL_SPEED)->ShowWindow(SW_SHOW);

        /////////////////////////
        // MY CODE ENDS HERE
        /////////////////////////

}
```

The code you typed extracts the pointer of the scroll bar by using the GetDlgItem() function with IDC_SCROLL_SPEED as its parameter and executes the ShowWindow() with SW_SHOW as its parameter. This causes the scroll bar to be visible.

To compile and link the SPEED application:

☐ Select Rebuild All SPEED.EXE from the Project menu in Visual C++.

Execute the SPEED application:

☐ Select Execute SPEED.EXE from the Project menu.

☐ Select Try It from the File menu and experiment with the various buttons in the dialog box.

10

Dialog Boxes: List and Combo Boxes

In this chapter you'll learn how to use list and combo boxes from within your dialog boxes. As you know, list and combo boxes serve an important role in the Windows user-interface mechanism.

The *MyList* Application

Before you start writing the MyList application by yourself, execute a copy of the MyList application that resides in your `C:\VCPROG\ORIGINAL\CH10\MYLIST` directory.

To execute the MyList application:

☐ Use Run from Program Manager's File menu to execute
`C:\VCPROG\ORIGINAL\CH10\MYLIST\MyList.EXE`.

> *Windows responds by executing the MyList application. The main window of* `MyList.EXE` *appears as shown in Figure 10.1.*

Figure 10.1.
The MyList
application's
main window.

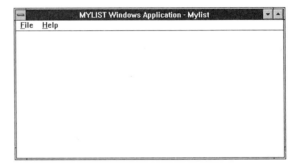

The MyList application has two popup menus: File and Help. These popup menus are shown in Figures 10.2 and 10.3.

Figure 10.2.
The MyList
application's
File menu.

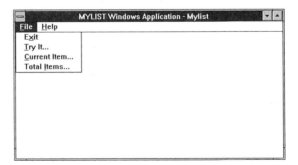

Figure 10.3.
The MyList
application's
Help menu.

☐ Select Try It from the File menu.

>   *MyList responds by displaying a dialog box (see Figure 10.4).*

Figure 10.4.
The MyList
application's
dialog box.

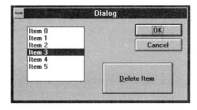

Experiment with the list box by selecting different items.

☐ Select Item 0 and then close the dialog box by clicking the OK button.

☐ Select Current Item from the File menu.

>   *MyList responds by displaying a message indicating that the current selection*
>   *is Item 0 (see Figure 10.5).*

Figure 10.5.
Displaying the
current selection.

267

☐ Click the OK button of the message box and then select Try It from the File menu.

MyList responds by displaying the dialog box. As you can see, the list box is the same as it was before you closed the dialog box with the OK button.

☐ Click the Delete Item button.

MyList responds by deleting an item from the list box.

☐ Click the Delete Item button a few more times.

MyList responds by deleting an item for each click. (However, MyList doesn't let you delete the first item in the list.)

☐ Click the OK button to close the dialog box.

☐ Select Total Items from the File menu.

MyList responds by displaying the total number of items in the list box.

Experiment with the MyList application and then select Exit from the File menu.

Now that you know what the MyList application should do, you can write it.

Creating the Project of the MyList Application

To create the project of the MyList application:

☐ Select AppWizard from the Project menu.

Visual C++ responds by running AppWizard.

☐ Use the Directory list box to select the directory
`C:\VCPROG\PRACTICE\CH10`.

☐ Type `mylist` in the Project Name box.

Now your AppWizard dialog box looks as shown in Figure 10.6.

☐ Click the Options button and set the options as shown in Figure 10.7. (That is, uncheck all the check boxes except the Generate Source Comments check box.)

Figure 10.6.
The MyList
application's
AppWizard
dialog box.

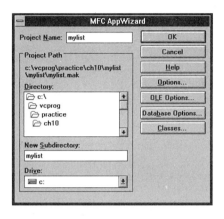

Figure 10.7.
Setting the options
for the MyList
application.

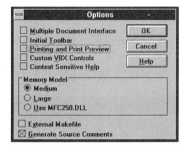

☐ Click the OK button in the Options dialog box and then click the OK
  button in the AppWizard dialog box and finally click the Create button in
  the New Application Information dialog box.

> *AppWizard responds by creating the MyList project and all the skeleton files of
> the MyList application.*

To remove the debug options of the project (so that you'll have a small EXE file):

☐ Select Project from the Options menu in Visual C++, click the Release radio
  button, and then click the OK button in the dialog box.

The Visual Implementation of the MyList Application

The MyList application has a menu, a custom dialog box, and an about dialog box.
In the following sections you'll visually design the menu and the custom dialog box
of the MyList application.

The Visual Implementation of the Menu of the MyList Application

The MyList application should have a menu as shown in Figures 10.1, 10.2, and 10.3. Implement this menu:

☐ Use App Studio to implement the menu of the MyList application per Table 10.1.

Table 10.1. The menu of the MyList application.
Figures relating to menu: 10.1, 10.2, 10.3

Menu Item
&File
E&xit
&Try It...
&Current Item...
Total &Items...
&Help
&About MYLIST...

To save your work:

☐ Select Save from the File menu of App Studio.

The visual implementation of the MyList application's menu is complete.

The Visual Implementation of the Dialog Box

Now you'll visually implement the dialog box of the MyList application:

Use App Studio to implement the MyList application's dialog box, per Table 10.2.

Table 10.2. The MyList application's dialog box.

Class Name:	CMyDlg
Figure:	10.4
OK button:	Yes
Cancel button:	Yes

Object	Property	Setting
Dialog box	ID	IDD_DIALOG1
List Box	ID	IDC_LIST1
	Variable	m_SelectedItem CString)
Push Button	ID	IDC_DELETE_ITEM
	Caption	&Delete Item

NOTE: The list box icon in the Tools Window is shown in Figure 10.8.

Figure 10.8.
The list box control
icon in the Tools
Window.

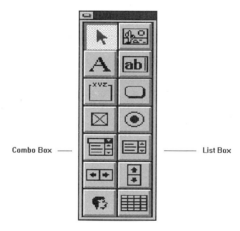

Combo Box ——— ——— List Box

That's it! You've completed the visual implementation of the dialog box.

To save your work:

☐ Select Save from the File menu.

Declaring the Dialog Box Object as a Data Member of the View Class

Now you'll create an object called dlg of class CMyDlg. CMyDlg is a class derived from the CDialog class. You visually designed CMyDlg during the visual implementation of the dialog box.

☐ Open the MYLISVW.H file and modify the declaration of the CMylistView class. After you modify the CMylistView class declaration, it looks as follows:

```
class CMylistView : public CView
{
protected: // create from serialization only
    CMylistView();
    DECLARE_DYNCREATE(CMylistView)

// Attributes
public:
    CMylistDoc* GetDocument();


    ////////////////////////
    // MY CODE STARTS HERE
    ////////////////////////

    // Create an object dlg (a dialog box)
    // of class CMyDlg.
    CMyDlg dlg;

    ////////////////////////
    // MY CODE ENDS HERE
    ////////////////////////


// Operations
public:

// Implementation
public:
    virtual ~CMylistView();
// overridden to draw this view
    virtual void OnDraw(CDC* pDC);
#ifdef _DEBUG
    virtual void AssertValid() const;
    virtual void Dump(CDumpContext& dc) const;
#endif

protected:

// Generated message map functions
protected:
```

```
//{{AFX_MSG(CMylistView)
// NOTE - the ClassWizard will add and remove member
//        functions here.
//    DO NOT EDIT what you see in these blocks of
//    generated code !
    //}}AFX_MSG
    DECLARE_MESSAGE_MAP()

};
```

Because the CMyDlg class is unknown in the file MYLISVW.H, you have to #include the file MyDlg.h (which contains the class declaration of CMyDlg) at the beginning of the MYLISVW.H file.

Add the #include "MyDlg.h" statement at the beginning of the MYLISVW.H file so that it will look as follows:

```
// mylisvw.h : interface of the CMylistView class
//
/////////////////////////////////////////////////////////////////////

////////////////////////
// MY CODE STARTS HERE
////////////////////////

#include "MyDlg.h"

////////////////////////
// MY CODE ENDS HERE
////////////////////////


.....
.....
.....
```

Save your work:

☐ Select Save from the File menu.

Attaching Code to the Try It Menu Item of the MyList Application

Now you'll attach code to the Try It menu item. Recall that when you select the Try It menu item, the MyList application should display the dialog box.

☐ Use ClassWizard to add a function for the event:

Class Name:	`CMylistView`
Object ID:	`ID_FILE_TRYIT`
Message:	`COMMAND`
Function Name:	`OnFileTryit()`

NOTE: Make sure you're adding the `OnFileTryit()` function to the class `CMylistView`.

☐ Edit the `OnFileTryit()` function that you added to the `MYLISVW.CPP` file so that it looks as follows:

```
void CMylistView::OnFileTryit()
{
    // TODO: Add your command handler code here

    /////////////////////////
    // MY CODE STARTS HERE
    /////////////////////////

    // Display the dlg dialog box.
    dlg.DoModal();

    /////////////////////////
    // MY CODE ENDS HERE
    /////////////////////////

}
```

In this code, you display the dialog box by using the `DoModal()` function:

```
dlg.DoModal();
```

Compiling, Linking, and Executing the MyList Application

Even though you haven't finished writing the MyList application, compile, link, and execute it so that you can see how the list box looks in runtime.

☐ Select Rebuild All MYLIST.EXE application from the Project menu.

☐ Execute the MyList application.

☐ Select Try It from the File menu.

> *MyList responds by displaying the dialog box. Of course, there are no items in the list box (because you haven't written the code that sets the items in it).*

☐ Close the dialog box and then select Exit to terminate the MyList application.

Declaring the Variables of the List Box

The MyList application uses four variables for the list box:

> m_SelectedItem—This string variable holds the string of the currently selected (highlighted) item in the list box. Recall that you declared this variable during the visual implementation of the dialog box (Table 10.2).
> m_CurrentSelectedItem —This integer variable holds the index of the currently selected item in the list box. The index of the first item in the list is 0, the index of the second item in the list is 1, and so on. (You haven't declared this variable yet.)
> m_TotalItems—This variable holds the total number of items in the list box. For example, if there are 6 items in the list, m_TotalItems is equal to 6. (You haven't declared this variable yet.)
> m_Item[6]—This array of strings holds the contents of the list box's items. Because the MyList application will never have more than 6 items in the list, the size of the array is set to 6. (You haven't declared this variable yet.)

☐ Declare m_CurrentSelectedItem, m_TotalItems, and m_Item[] as data members of the CMyDlg class that resides in the MyDlg.h file. After you declare these variables, the class declaration of CMyDlg looks as follows:

```
class CMyDlg : public CDialog
{
// Construction
public:
    CMyDlg(CWnd* pParent = NULL); // standard constructor

    /////////////////////////
    // MY CODE STARTS HERE
    /////////////////////////

    int m_CurrentSelectedItem;
    int m_TotalItems;
    CString m_Item[6];

    /////////////////////////
    // MY CODE ENDS HERE
    /////////////////////////


// Dialog Data
    //{{AFX_DATA(CMyDlg)
    enum { IDD = IDD_DIALOG1 };
    CString   m_SelectedItem;
    //}}AFX_DATA
```

```
// Implementation
protected:
// DDX/DDV support
    virtual void DoDataExchange(CDataExchange* pDX);

    // Generated message map functions
    //{{AFX_MSG(CMyDlg)
    // NOTE: the ClassWizard will add member functions here
    //}}AFX_MSG
    DECLARE_MESSAGE_MAP()
};
```

Save your work:

☐ Select Save from the File menu.

Initializing the Variables of the List Box

Now you'll write code that initializes the variables of the list box.

☐ Edit the constructor function of the CMyDlg class that resides in the MyDlg.CPP file so that it looks as follows:

```
CMyDlg::CMyDlg(CWnd* pParent /*=NULL*/)
    : CDialog(CMyDlg::IDD, pParent)
{

    ///////////////////////
    // MY CODE STARTS HERE
    ///////////////////////

    m_CurrentSelectedItem = 3;

    m_TotalItems = 6;

    m_Item[0] = "Item 0";
    m_Item[1] = "Item 1";
    m_Item[2] = "Item 2";
    m_Item[3] = "Item 3";
    m_Item[4] = "Item 4";
    m_Item[5] = "Item 5";

    ///////////////////////
    // MY CODE ENDS HERE
    ///////////////////////

    //{{AFX_DATA_INIT(CMyDlg)
    m_SelectedItem = "";
    //}}AFX_DATA_INIT

}
```

The m_CurrentSelectedItem variable is set to 3. As you'll see later, when you display the dialog box for the first time, the list box will have its m_Item[3] item highlighted.

The m_TotalItems variable is set to 6. This variable is updated when items are deleted so that it always contains the current total number of items in the list box.

The m_Item[] array holds the contents of the list box's items. Thus, m_Item[0] is equal to Item 0, m_Item[1] is equal to Item 1, and so on.

Setting the Items of the List Box

In the previous section you initialized the variables that are associated with the list box. Of course, initializing the m_Item[] array doesn't cause the list box to display these items. Here's how you set the list box's items:

☐ Use ClassWizard to add a function for the event:

Class Name:	CMyDlg
Object ID:	CMyDlg
Message:	WM_INITDIALOG
Function Name:	OnInitDialog()

☐ Edit the OnInitDialog() function that you added to the MYDLG.CPP file so that it looks as follows:

```
BOOL CMyDlg::OnInitDialog()
{
   CDialog::OnInitDialog();

   // TODO: Add extra initialization here


   ////////////////////////
   // MY CODE STARTS HERE
   ////////////////////////


   // Update the m_TotalItem variable.
   m_TotalItems = 6;

   // Fill the 6 items of the list box.
   for (int i=0; i<=5; i++ )
       {
       SendDlgItemMessage(IDC_LIST1,
                         LB_ADDSTRING,
                         0,
                 (LPARAM)(LPSTR)(const char *)m_Item[i]);
```

```
                }

        // Highlight an item in the list.
        SendDlgItemMessage(IDC_LIST1,
                            LB_SETCURSEL,
                            m_CurrentSelectedItem,
                            0);


        /////////////////////
        // MY CODE ENDS HERE
        /////////////////////


        // return TRUE  unless you set the focus to a control
        return TRUE;

        }
```

The code you typed updates m_TotalItems:

```
m_TotalItems = 6;
```

Recall that you updated m_TotalItems in the constructor function of CMyDlg. This was done so that if the user selects Total Items from the File menu (before ever opening the dialog box), the program will display the correct number of items in the list (that is, 6). You also need to update m_TotalItems in OnInitDialog(), because every time the Delete Item is clicked, the program must reduce m_TotalItems by 1. However, every time the user selects Try It from the File menu, the dialog should appear with 6 items in it. Thus, when the dialog box is displayed (that is, when you execute OnInitDialog()), m_TotalItems must be updated to 6.

The next section you typed in OnInitDialog() uses a for() loop to set the items of the list box with the members of the m_Item[] array:

```
for (int i=0; i<=5; i++ )
    {
     SendDlgItemMessage(IDC_LIST1,
                        LB_ADDSTRING,
                        0,
              (LPARAM)(LPSTR)(const char *)m_Item[i]);
    }
```

This is accomplished by using the SendDlgItemMessage() member function. The first parameter of this function is IDC_LIST1, which is the ID of the list box. The second, third, and fourth parameters of the SendDlgItemMessage() function make up the message that is sent to the list box. The second parameter, LB_ADDSTRING, tells the list box to add an item to the list. Of course, the list box must know what string to use. The actual string is supplied by the fourth parameter:

```
(LPARAM)(LPSTR)(const char *)m_Item[i];
```

When the `for()` loop is executed for the first time, `i` is equal to 0, so the fourth parameter is

```
(LPARAM)(LPSTR)(const char *)m_Item[0];
```

Thus, during the first iteration of the `for()` loop, the string `m_Item[0]` is added as an item to the list box.

During the second iteration of the `for()` loop, `i` is equal to 1. This means that the fourth parameter is

```
(LPARAM)(LPSTR)(const char *)m_Item[1]
```

The loop continues until all the items in the list are filled.

To summarize, the `for()` loop fills the 6 items of the list box with the contents of the `m_Item[]` array.

Note the casting of the fourth parameter. It converts the member of the array to `const char*`, it then converts it to `LPSTR`, and finally it converts it to `LPARAM`. This is done to comply with the data type of the `SendDlgItemMessage()` function's fourth parameter, which expects a `LPARAM` data type as its fourth parameter.

Now, what about the third parameter of the `SendDlgItemMessage()` function? You typed 0 as the third parameter of this function. The `SendDlgItemMessage()` function is used to send all types of messages to the controls, and the value of the third parameter depends on the type of message that is being sent. When sending the message `LB_ADDSTRING`, the third parameter isn't used, and therefore you supplied 0 for it.

The next statement in the `OnInitDialog()` function highlights one of the items in the list box. Which item? The item with an index equal to `m_CurrentSelectedItem`. For example, if currently `m_CurrentSelectedItem` is equal to 0, the statement:

```
SendDlgItemMessage(IDC_LIST1,
                   LB_SETCURSEL,
                   m_CurrentSelectedItem,
                   0);
```

causes `Item 0` to be highlighted in the list box.

The first parameter of `SendDlgItemMessage()` indicates which control will receive the message. Because you supplied `IDC_LIST1` as the first parameter, the list box will receive this message. The second parameter is `LB_SETCURSEL`. As implied by its name, `LB_SETCURSEL` "tells" the list box to highlight one of its items (the item whose index is provided as the third parameter).

When the `LB_SETCURSEL` message is sent, the fourth parameter of `SendDlgItemMessage()` isn't used, so you supply 0 as its value.

NOTE

You can send many messages to the list box with the `SendDlgItemMessage()` function. To make it easy to remember, Microsoft uses the following notation for the IDs of the messages: When using `SendDlgItemMessage()` to send a message to a list box, the name of the message starts with the characters `LB_`.

Examples:

```
LB_ADDSTRING
LB_SETCURSEL
```

Compiling, Linking, and Executing the MyList Application

Even though you haven't finished writing the MyList application, compile, link, and execute it so that you can see the initialization in action:

☐ Select Rebuild All MYLIST.EXE application from the Project menu.

☐ Select Execute MYLIST.EXE from the Project menu.

☐ Select Try It from the File menu.

> *MyList responds by displaying the dialog box. As you can see, the list box is filled with the members of the* `m_Item[]` *array. Item 3 is highlighted, because you set* `m_CurrentSelectedItem` *to 3.*

☐ Highlight the second item in the list box.

☐ Close the dialog box by clicking the OK button and then select Try It to display the dialog box again.

As you can see, the last status of the list box wasn't maintained.

☐ Close the dialog box and then terminate the MyList application.

Maintaining the Status of the List Box

Now you'll add code that maintains the status of the list box. When you click the OK button in the dialog box to close it, m_CurrentSelectedItem should be changed to a value that represents the currently selected item in the list box. This means that you have to type your code in the function that's executed whenever the user clicks the OK button.

☐ Use ClassWizard to add a function for the event:

Class Name:	CMyDlg
Object ID:	IDOK
Message:	BN_CLICKED
Function Name:	OnOK()

☐ Edit the OnOK() function that you added to the MYDLG.CPP file so that it looks as follows:

```
void CMyDlg::OnOK()
{
    // TODO: Add extra validation here

    /////////////////////////
    // MY CODE STARTS HERE
    /////////////////////////

    // Update m_CurrentSelectedItem with the currently
    // highlighted item.
    m_CurrentSelectedItem =
        (int) SendDlgItemMessage(IDC_LIST1,
                                 LB_GETCURSEL,
                                 0,
                                 0);

    /////////////////////////
    // MY CODE ENDS HERE
    /////////////////////////

    CDialog::OnOK();

}
```

The code that you typed sends a message to the list box:

```
m_CurrentSelectedItem =
    (int) SendDlgItemMessage(IDC_LIST1,
                             LB_GETCURSEL,
                             0,
                             0);
```

281

Again, to send a message to the list box, the SendDlgItemMessage() member function is used. The first parameter is IDC_LIST1 because you are sending the message to the list box. The second parameter is the LB_GETCURSEL message. As implied by its name, this message tells the list box to return the index number of the currently highlighted (selected) item. The third and fourth parameters aren't used, so you supply 0 for each of these parameters.

The currently selected item is returned from the SendDlgItemMessage() function and is assigned to the m_CurrentSelectedItem variable. Note that the (int) casting is used, because SendDlgItemMessage() returns a data type LRESULT, but m_SelectedItem is an integer. The (int) casting tells the compiler to convert the returned value (which is of type LRESULT) to an integer.

To summarize, whenever the user clicks the OK button, the m_CurrentSelectedItem variable is updated with a number that represents the highlighted item in the list box. Recall that the code you typed in the OnInitDialog() function sets the currently selected item to an item corresponding to the value of m_CurrentSelectedItem. So the next time the user selects Try It, the DoModal() function will be executed, and therefore the OnInitDialog() function will be executed. OnInitDialog() will highlight the appropriate item.

Compiling, Linking, and Executing the MyList Application

Even though you haven't finished writing the MyList application, compile, link, and execute it so that you can see in action the code that you typed:

☐ Select Rebuild All MYLIST.EXE application from the Project menu.

☐ Select Execute MYLIST.EXE from the Project menu.

☐ Select Try It from the File menu.

☐ Highlight the second item in the list box.

☐ Close the dialog box by clicking the OK button and then select Try It to display the dialog box again.

As you can see, the last status of the list box was maintained.

Close the dialog box and then terminate the MyList application.

Displaying the Value of the Selected Item from the Menu

Typically, the dialog box is used to set various values of the controls, and then the program makes use of these values. You'll now learn how to write code that makes use of the list box's setting. The code that you'll write will cause the currently selected item in the list box to be displayed whenever the user selects Current Item from the File menu.

☐ Use ClassWizard to add a function for the event:

Class Name:	CMylistView
Object ID:	ID_FILE_CURRENTITEM
Message:	COMMAND
Function Name:	OnFileCurrentitem()

☐ Edit the OnFileCurrentitem() function that you added to the MYLISVW.CPP file so that it looks as follows:

```
void CMylistView::OnFileCurrentitem()
{
    // TODO: Add your command handler code here

    ////////////////////////
    // MY CODE STARTS HERE
    ////////////////////////

    MessageBox ( "The current selected item is: " +
                dlg.m_SelectedItem );

    ////////////////////////
    // MY CODE ENDS HERE
    ////////////////////////
}
```

The code you typed is executed whenever the user selects Current Item from the File menu. It consists of a single statement:

```
MessageBox ( "The current selected item is: " +
            dlg.m_SelectedItem );
```

This statement displays a message box that indicates which item is currently selected in the list box. Note that dlg.m_SelectedItem is the CString data member that you connected to the list box during the visual implementation.

NOTE

You can get information (help) concerning the prototype of the `MessageBox()` function as follows:

> Highlight the word "`MessageBox`" in the code you typed (that is, double-click the mouse on any of the characters of "`MessageBox`").
>
> Press F1.
>
> Visual C++ responds by displaying a dialog box. (Depending on the particular version that you're using, Visual C++ may or may not display this dialog box.) This dialog box "asks" you to specify whether you want help with the `MessageBox()` function that exists in the SDK Windows 3.1 API library or the `MessageBox()` member function that belongs to the MFC. If this dialog box appears, select the Microsoft Foundation Class (MFC) library option and then click the OK button. In this case, you want the `MessageBox()` function from the MFC.

Figure 10.9 shows the help window of the `MessageBox()` member function. As you can see from Figure 10.9, `MessageBox()` is a member function of the `CWnd` class. `CView` is a derived class from the class `CWnd`. `CMylistView` is a derived class from `CView`. Putting it all together, you can use the MFC `MessageBox()` from within the `OnFileCurrentitem()` function (because `OnFileCurrentitem()` is a member function of the `CMylistView` class).

The Help program of Visual C++ responds by displaying the help window for the `MessageBox()` function from the MFC (see Figure 10.9). As you can see from the prototype of this function, you have to specify the first parameter (the message that will be displayed). However, it's your option whether or not to specify the second parameter (the caption of the message box) and the third parameter. This is because in C++, a function can have default values for its parameters. If you don't specify any values for the second and third parameters, `MessageBox()` uses the default values that are mentioned in its prototype.

Figure 10.9.
The help window
that Visual C++
displays when
you ask for
information
about the
MessageBox()
MFC function.

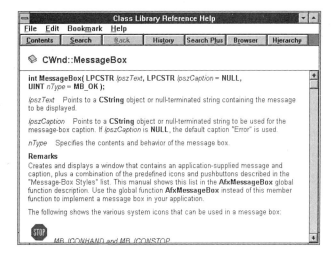

NOTE

In the previous note, you were told that CWnd is the base class of the CView class.

You can verify this as follows:

Select Foundation Classes from the Help menu of Visual C++.

Visual C++ responds by displaying the MFC Help window shown in Figure 10.10.

Click the Application Architecture Hierarchy item.

Visual C++ responds by displaying the hierarchy shown in Figure 10.11. As shown, CWnd is the base class of CView.

To close the Help window:

Click in a free area of the Help window, click the window's minus icon and select Close from the system menu that pops up.

Figure 10.10.
The MFC Help
window.

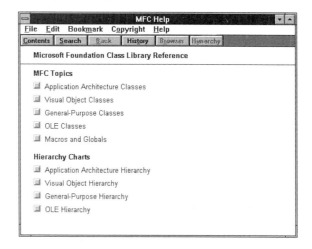

Figure 10.11.
The Application
Architecture
Hierarchy.

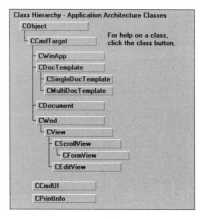

Compiling, Linking, and Executing the MyList Application

Even though you haven't finished writing the MyList application, compile, link, and execute it so that you can see in action the code you typed:

☐ Select Rebuild All MYLIST.EXE application from the Project menu.

☐ Select Execute MYLIST.EXE from the Project menu.

☐ Select Try It from the File menu.

MyList responds by displaying the dialog box.

☐ Highlight the second item in the list box.

☐ Close the dialog box by clicking the OK button and then select Current
Item from the File menu.

> *MyList responds with a message box that indicates the currently selected item
> in the list box.*

☐ Close the dialog box and then terminate the MyList application.

Deleting Items from the List Box

In some applications, you may want to delete items from the list box during runtime.
(You can also add items to the list box during runtime by using the
`SendDlgItemMessage()` function with the `LB_ADDSTRING` message, as you did in
the `OnInitDialog()` function.)

Here's how you attach code to the Delete Item button. This code will delete an item
from the list box whenever the user clicks the Delete button:

☐ Use ClassWizard to add a function for the event:

Class Name:	`CMyDlg`
Object ID:	`IDC_DELETE_ITEM`
Message:	`BN_CLICKED`
Function Name:	`OnDeleteItem()`

NOTE: Make sure that you're adding this function to the `CMyDlg` class.

☐ Edit the `OnDeleteItem()` function that you added to the `MYDLG.CPP` file so
that it looks as follows:

```
void CMyDlg::OnDeleteItem()
{
// TODO: Add your control notification handler code here

        /////////////////////////
        // MY CODE STARTS HERE
        /////////////////////////

        // Delete item 1 from the list box.
        SendDlgItemMessage(IDC_LIST1,
                           LB_DELETESTRING,
                           1,
                           0);

        /////////////////////////
        // MY CODE ENDS HERE
        /////////////////////////

}
```

The code you typed uses the `SendDlgItemMessage()` function to send the `LB_DELETESTRING` message to the list box:

```
SendDlgItemMessage(IDC_LIST1,
                   LB_DELETESTRING,
                   1,
                   0);
```

The first parameter indicates that the message should be sent to the list box (`IDC_LIST1`), the second parameter is the `LB_DELETESTRING` message, and the third parameter is the item to be deleted. For example, to delete the first item in the list box, you would supply 0 as the third parameter. The code that you typed supplies 1 as the third parameter of the `SendDlgItemMessage()` function. This means that the second item in the list will be deleted.

When the `LB_DELETESTRING` message is sent, the fourth parameter of the `SendDlgItemMessage()` function isn't used, so you supply 0 as its value.

Compile, link, and execute the application so that you can see the code of the Delete button in action:

☐ Select Rebuild All MYLIST.EXE application from the Project menu.

☐ Select Execute MYLIST.EXE from the Project menu.

☐ Select Try It from the File menu.

    MyList responds by displaying the dialog box.

☐ While Item 0 is selected, click the Delete Item button.

    MyList responds by deleting Item 1. Now the list box contains the items:

    Item 0
    Item 2
    Item 3
    Item 4
    Item 5

It's important to understand that from the point of view of the list box, Item 0 still has index 0, Item 2 now has index 1, Item 3 now has index 2, and so on. In other words, because you deleted an item, the list box updated the indexes of its remaining items. To verify this:

☐ Highlight Item 2 in the list box.

☐ Click the OK button and then select Current Item from the File menu.

MyList responds by displaying a message that says that the currently selected item in the list box is Item 1. That is, the string Item 2 in the list box is now the second item in the list box, so its index is 1.

☐ Select Try It from the File Menu again.

MyList responds by displaying the dialog box with all 6 items in the list box.

☐ Highlight the second item from the top of the list.

☐ Click the Delete button.

MyList responds by deleting the second item. As you can see, nothing is selected in the list box now because the second item was highlighted prior to the deletion.

☐ Click the OK button to close the dialog box.

☐ Select Current Item from the File menu.

MyList responds by displaying the message box with the text, "The current selected item is:" in it, with no number after the colon.

This of course makes sense because the statement that displays that string is

```
MessageBox ( "The current selected item is: " +
            dlg.m_SelectedItem );
```

and currently `dlg.m_SelectedItem` is null (because nothing is selected in the list box).

Displaying the Total Number of Items

Now you'll attach code so that the user can select Total Items from the menu to display the total in the list box.

Recall that one of the data member variables you declared in the declaration of the `CMyDlg` class (which is in `MYDLG.H`) is `m_TotalItems` and that you initialized this variable to 6 in the constructor function of `CMyDlg` (in `MyDlg.CPP`). This variable is used to store the total number of items in the list box. You set the initial value of this variable to 6, because initially, there are 6 items in the list box. The only place in the program where the total number of items in the list box is changed is the `OnDeleteItem()` function, which is called when the user clicks the Delete Item button.

Edit the `OnDeleteItem()` function that you added to the `MYDLG.CPP` file so that it looks as follows:

```
void CMyDlg::OnDeleteItem()
{
// TODO: Add your control notification handler code here

    //////////////////////////
    // MY CODE STARTS HERE
    //////////////////////////

    // Delete item 1 from the list box.
    SendDlgItemMessage(IDC_LIST1,
                        LB_DELETESTRING,
                        1,
                        0);


    // Update the m_TotalItems variable with the total
    // number of items.
    m_TotalItems =
        (int) SendDlgItemMessage(IDC_LIST1,
                                  LB_GETCOUNT,
                                  0,
                                  0);

    //////////////////////////
    // MY CODE ENDS HERE
    //////////////////////////

}
```

The code you added updates the `m_TotalItems` variable with the returned value of the `SendDlgItemMessage()` function:

```
m_TotalItems =
    (int) SendDlgItemMessage(IDC_LIST1,
                              LB_GETCOUNT,
                              0,
                              0);
```

The first parameter of the `SendDlgItemMessage()` function is `IDC_LIST1` (because you're sending a message to the list box).

The second parameter is `LB_GETCOUNT`, which "tells" the list box to report the number of items.

You supply 0 for the third and fourth parameters because they aren't used when the `LB_GETCOUNT` message is sent.

To display the total number of items, you need to attach code to the Total Items menu item:

☐ Use ClassWizard to add a function for the event:

Class Name:	CMYLISTView
Object ID:	ID_FILE_TOTALITEMS
Message:	COMMAND
Function Name:	OnFileTotalitems())

NOTE: Make sure you're adding this function to the `CMylsitView` class.

☐ Edit the `OnFileTotalitems()` function that you added to the MYLISVW.CPP file so that it looks as follows:

```
void CMylistView::OnFileTotalitems()
{
// TODO: Add your command handler code here

    ///////////////////////
    // MY CODE STARTS HERE
    ///////////////////////

    char sTotalItems[10];

    itoa ( dlg.m_TotalItems, sTotalItems, 10);

    CString Message;

    Message =
        "Total Number of items is: " + (CString)sTotalItems;

    MessageBox ( Message );

    ///////////////////////
    // MY CODE ENDS HERE
    ///////////////////////

}
```

The code you added declares a local variable, sTotalItems:

```
char sTotalItems[10];
```

Then the `itoa()` function is used to convert the integer `dlg.m_TotalItems` to the string sTotalItems:

```
itoa ( dlg.m_TotalItems, sTotalItems, 10);
```

The `Message` `CString` is declared:

`CString Message;`

Then `Message` is prepared:

```
Message =
"Total Number of items is: " + (CString)sTotalItems;
```

Finally, the `MessageBox()` member function is executed to display the contents of `Message`:

`MessageBox ( Message );`

To see the code you typed in action:

☐ Select Rebuild All MYLIST.EXE application from the Project menu.

☐ Select Execute MYLIST.EXE from the Project menu.

☐ Select Try It from the File menu.

> *MyList responds by displaying the dialog box.*

☐ Click the Delete Item button.

> *MyList responds by deleting Item 1. Now the list box contains 5 items.*

☐ Close the dialog box and then select Total Items from the File menu.

> *MyList responds by displaying a message box that displays the fact that there are five items in the list box.*

Now you can return to the dialog box, delete any number of items, select Total Items from the File menu, and confirm that the message box displays the number of items that remain in the list box.

The MyCombo Application

A combo box is similar to a list box. The difference is that with a combo box users can select an item from a list of items (just as in a list box) as well as typing their own text. It's called a combo box because it's a combination of a list box and an edit box.

The MyCombo application demonstrates how to incorporate a combo box control into your dialog boxes.

Before you start writing the MyCombo application, execute a copy of the MyCombo application that resides in your `C:\VCPROG\ORIGINAL\CH10\MYCOMBO` directory.

To execute the MyCombo application:

☐ Use the Run item from the File menu of the Program Manager to execute
`C:\VCPROG\ORIGINAL\CH10\MYCOMBO\MyCombo.EXE`.

> *Windows responds by executing the MyCombo application. The main
> window of* `MyCombo.EXE` *appears as shown in Figure 10.12.*

*Figure 10.12.
The MyCombo
application's
main window.*

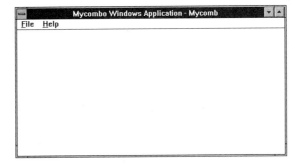

The MyCombo application has two popup menus: File and Help. These popup menus
are shown in Figures 10.13 and 10.14.

*Figure 10.13.
The MyCombo
application's
File menu.*

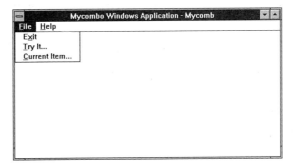

*Figure 10.14.
The MyCombo
application's
Help menu.*

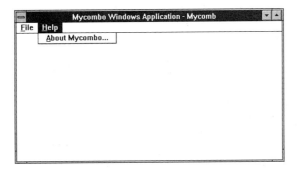

293

☐ Select Try It from the File menu.

MyCombo responds by displaying a dialog box (see Figure 10.15).

Figure 10.15.
The MyCombo
application's dialog.

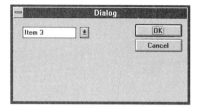

Experiment with the MyCombo application and then select Exit from the File menu.

Now that you know what the MyCombo application should do, you can write it.

Creating the Project of the MyCombo Application

To create the project of the MyCombo application:

☐ Select AppWizard from the Project menu.

Visual C++ responds by running AppWizard.

☐ Use the Directory list box to select the directory
`C:\VCPROG\PRACTICE\CH10`.

☐ Type `mycombo` in the Project Name box.

Now your AppWizard dialog box looks as shown in Figure 10.16.

Figure 10.16.
The MyCombo
application's
AppWizard dialog
box.

☐ Click the Options button and set the options as shown in Figure 10.17 (that is, uncheck all the check boxes except the Generate Source Comments check box).

Figure 10.17.
Setting the options
of the MyCombo
application.

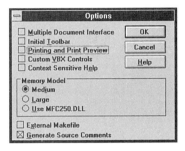

☐ Click the OK button of the Options dialog box and then click the OK button of the AppWizard dialog box and finally click the Create button of the New Application Information dialog box.

AppWizard responds by creating the MyCombo project and all the skeleton files of the MyCombo application.

To remove the debug options of the project (so that you'll have a small EXE file):

☐ Select Project from the Options menu of Visual C++, click the Release radio button, and then click the OK button of the dialog box.

The Visual Implementation of the MyCombo Application

The MyCombo application has a menu, a custom dialog box, and an About dialog box. In the following sections you'll visually design the menu and the custom dialog box of the MyCombo application.

The Visual Implementation of the Menu of the MyCombo Application

The MyCombo application should have a menu as shown in Figures 10.12, 10.13, and 10.14. To implement this menu:

☐ Use App Studio to implement the menu of the MyCombo application per Table 10.3.

Table 10.3. The MyCombo application menu.
   Figures relating to menu: 10.12, 10.13, 10.14

Menu Item
`&File`
`E&xit`
`&Try It...`
`&Current Item...`
`&Help`
`&About Mycombo...`

To save your work:

☐ Select Save from the File menu of App Studio.

The visual implementation of the menu of the MyCombo application is completed.

The Visual Implementation of the Custom Dialog Box

Now you'll visually implement the MYCOMBO application's dialog box.

☐ Implement the dialog box of the MyCombo application per Table 10.4.

Table 10.4. The dialog box of the MyCombo application.

Class Name:	`CMyDlg`
Figure:	10.15
OK button:	Yes
Cancel button:	Yes

Object	*Property*	*Setting*
Dialog box	ID	`IDD_DIALOG1`
Combo box	ID	`IDC_COMBO1`
	Variable	`m_SelectedItem` (of type `CString`)

NOTE: The icon of the combo box control in the Tools Window is shown in Figure 10.8.

> **NOTE**
>
> When you size the combo box, you have to size two separate entities in it:
>
> The edit box of the combo box.
>
> The list box of the combo box.
>
> You can change the width of the edit box by dragging its handles to the right and left.
>
> To make the list box longer, you have to:
>
> > Click the arrow icon of the combo box.
> >
> > App Studio responds by dropping down an empty list.
> >
> > Drag the handle of the list to increase/decrease the length of the list.

That's it! You've completed the visual implementation of the dialog box.

To save your work:

☐ Select Save from the File menu.

As you'll soon see, the MyCombo application is similar to the MyList application discussed earlier in this chapter.

Declaring the Dialog Box Object as a Data Member of the View Class

Now you'll create an object dlg of class CMyDlg. You'll create this object as a data member of the view class (the CMycomboView class).

☐ Open the MYCOMVW.H file and modify the declaration of the CMycomboView class so that it looks as follows:

```
class CMycomboView : public CView
{
protected: // create from serialization only
    CMycomboView();
    DECLARE_DYNCREATE(CMycomboView)
```

```
// Attributes
public:
    CMycomboDoc* GetDocument();

    /////////////////////////
    // MY CODE STARTS HERE
    /////////////////////////

    // Create a dlg object of class CMyDlg
    CMyDlg dlg;

    /////////////////////////
    // MY CODE ENDS HERE
    /////////////////////////


// Operations
public:

// Implementation
public:
    virtual ~CMycomboView();
    virtual void OnDraw(CDC* pDC);
// overridden to draw this view
#ifdef _DEBUG
    virtual void AssertValid() const;
    virtual void Dump(CDumpContext& dc) const;
#endif

protected:

// Generated message map functions
protected:
//{{AFX_MSG(CMycomboView)
// NOTE - the ClassWizard will add and remove
// member functions here.
//    DO NOT EDIT what you see in these blocks
//    of generated code !
    //}}AFX_MSG
    DECLARE_MESSAGE_MAP()
};
```

Because the CMyDlg class is unknown in the file MYCOMVW.H, you have to #include the file MyDlg.h (which contains the class declaration of CMyDlg) at the beginning of the MYCOMVW.H file.

☐ Add the #include "MyDlg.h" statement at the beginning of the MYCOMVW.H file.

After you #include this file, the beginning of the MYCOMVW.H file looks as follows:

```
// mycomvw.h : interface of the CMycomboView class
//
/////////////////////////////////////////////////////////

/////////////////////
// MY CODE STARTS HERE
/////////////////////

#include "MyDlg.h"

/////////////////////
// MY CODE ENDS HERE
/////////////////////

.....
.....
.....
```

Attaching Code to the Try It Menu Item of the MyCombo Application

Now you'll attach code to the Try It menu item. Recall that when you select the Try It menu item, the MYCOMBO application should display the dialog box.

☐ Use ClassWizard to add a function for the event:

Class Name:	CMycomboView
Object ID:	ID_FILE_TRYIT
Message:	COMMAND
Function Name:	OnFileTryit()

NOTE: Make sure to add the function to the CMycomboView class.

☐ Edit the OnFileTryit() function that you added to the MYCOMVW.CPP file so that it looks as follows:

```
void CMycomboView::OnFileTryit()
{
    // TODO: Add your command handler code here

    /////////////////////
    // MY CODE STARTS HERE
    /////////////////////

    // Display the dialog box.
    dlg.DoModal();
```

```
////////////////////
// MY CODE ENDS HERE
////////////////////
```

}

By using the DoModal() function, the code you typed displays the dialog box.

Compiling, Linking, and Executing the MyCombo Application

Even though you haven't finished writing the MyCombo application, compile, link, and execute it so that you can see how the combo box behaves:

☐ Select Rebuild All MYCOMBO.EXE application from the Project menu.

☐ Execute the MyCombo.EXE application.

☐ Select Try It from the File menu.

   MyCombo responds by displaying the dialog box. Of course, the combo box contains no items (because you haven't written the code that sets the items for it).

☐ Experiment with the combo box by typing something in the edit box of the combo box and by dropping down the list box of the combo box.

☐ Click the OK button in the dialog box to close it.

☐ Select Try It from the File menu again.

   MyCombo responds by displaying the dialog box with the edit box filled with the text that existed before you closed the dialog box with the OK button.

☐ Close the dialog box and then select Exit to terminate the MyCombo application.

Declaring the Variables of the Combo Box

The MyCombo application uses three variables for the combo box:

   m_SelectedItem—This variable holds the current selection in the edit box of the combo box. Recall that you connected this variable to the combo box during the visual implementation of the dialog box.

m_Item[10]—This array holds the contents of the list of the combo box. (You haven't declared this variable.)

m_CurrentSelectedItem—This variable holds the index of the selected item in the list. For example, when m_CurrentSelectedItem is equal to 0, the first item of the list is highlighted. When m_CurrentSelectedItem is equal to 1, the second item in the list is highlighted, and so on. (You haven't declared this variable yet.)

☐ Declare the m_CurrentSelectedItem variable and the m_Item[] array as data members of the CMyDlg class that resides in the MyDlg.h file so that it looks as follows:

```
class CMyDlg : public CDialog
{
// Construction
public:
    CMyDlg(CWnd* pParent = NULL); // standard constructor

    //////////////////////
    // MY CODE STARTS HERE
    //////////////////////

    int m_CurrentSelectedItem;
    CString m_Item[6];

    //////////////////////
    // MY CODE ENDS HERE
    //////////////////////


// Dialog Data
    //{{AFX_DATA(CMyDlg)
    enum { IDD = IDD_DIALOG1 };
    CString m_SelectedItem;
    //}}AFX_DATA

// Implementation
protected:
    virtual void DoDataExchange(CDataExchange* pDX);
// DDX/DDV support

// Generated message map functions
//{{AFX_MSG(CMyDlg)
// NOTE: the ClassWizard will add member functions here
//}}AFX_MSG
    DECLARE_MESSAGE_MAP()
};
```

Initializing the Variables of the Combo Box

Now you'll write code that initializes the m_CurrentSelectedItem variable and the m_Item[] array of the combo box.

☐ Edit the constructor function of the CMyDlg class that resides in the MyDlg.CPP file so that it looks as follows:

```
CMyDlg::CMyDlg(CWnd* pParent /*=NULL*/)
    : CDialog(CMyDlg::IDD, pParent)
{
    //{{AFX_DATA_INIT(CMyDlg)
    m_SelectedItem = "";
    //}}AFX_DATA_INIT

    /////////////////////////
    // MY CODE STARTS HERE
    /////////////////////////

    m_CurrentSelectedItem = 3;

    m_Item[0] = "Item 0";
    m_Item[1] = "Item 1";
    m_Item[2] = "Item 2";
    m_Item[3] = "Item 3";
    m_Item[4] = "Item 4";
    m_Item[5] = "Item 5";

    /////////////////////////
    // MY CODE ENDS HERE
    /////////////////////////

}
```

m_CurrentSelectedItem is set to 3 because you want to highlight Item 3 when the dialog box is first displayed.

The m_Item[] array holds the items of the list box. Thus, m_Item[0] is equal to Item 0, m_Item[1] is equal to Item 1, and so on.

Setting the Items of the Combo Box's List

In the previous section you initialized the array that holds the items of the combo box's list box. Of course, initializing the array doesn't cause the list to display these items. Here's how you set the items of the list:

☐ Use ClassWizard to add a function for the event:

Class Name: CMyDlg
Object ID: CMyDlg

Message: WM_INITDIALOG
Function Name: OnInitDialog()

☐ Edit the OnInitDialog() function that you added to the MYDLG.CPP file so that it looks as follows:

```cpp
BOOL CMyDlg::OnInitDialog()
{
    CDialog::OnInitDialog();

    // TODO: Add extra initialization here

    ///////////////////////
    // MY CODE STARTS HERE
    ///////////////////////

    // Fill the items of the list.
    for (int i=0; i<=5; i++ )
        {
        SendDlgItemMessage(IDC_COMBO1,
                        CB_ADDSTRING,
                        0,
            (LPARAM)(LPSTR)(const char *)m_Item[i]);
        }

    // Set the selected item to the third item.
    SendDlgItemMessage(IDC_COMBO1,
                    CB_SETCURSEL,
                    m_CurrentSelectedItem,
                    0);

    ///////////////////////
    // MY CODE ENDS HERE
    ///////////////////////


    return TRUE;
    // return TRUE unless you set the focus to a control

}
```

The code you typed uses a for() loop to set the members of the list with the member of the m_Item[] array:

```cpp
for (int i=0; i<=5; i++ )
    {
    SendDlgItemMessage(IDC_COMBO1,
                    CB_ADDSTRING,
                    0,
        (LPARAM)(LPSTR)(const char *)m_Item[i]);
    }
```

This is accomplished by using the SendDlgItemMessage() member function. The first parameter of this function is IDC_COMBO1, which is the ID of the combo box.

The second, third, and fourth parameters of this function make up the message sent to the combo box's list box.

The second parameter, CB_ADDSTRING, "tells" the combo box to add an item to the list. Of course, the list box must know what string to use. The actual string is supplied as the fourth parameter:

```
(LPARAM)(LPSTR)(const char *)m_Item[i]);
```

To summarize, the for() loop fills the six items of the list box with the contents of the m_Item[] array.

The next statement in the OnInitDialog() function highlights Item 3 in the list box (because you initialized m_CurrentSelectedItem to 3):

```
SendDlgItemMessage(IDC_COMBO1,
                   CB_SETCURSEL,
                   m_CurrentSelectedItem,
                   0);
```

Note that highlighting an item in the list causes that item to be displayed in the edit box of the combo list. (This is done automatically by the combo box.)

☐ Select Rebuild All MYCOMBO.EXE application from the Project menu.

☐ Select Execute MYCOMBO.EXE from the Project menu.

☐ Select Try It from the File menu.

> *MyCombo responds by displaying the dialog box. As you can see, the list box is filled with the members of the m_Item[] array, Item 3 in the list is highlighted, and the edit box is filled with the contents of the highlighted item in the list.*

☐ Highlight the second item in the list.

> *The combo box responds by displaying the contents of the highlighted item in the edit box.*

☐ Close the dialog box by clicking the OK button and then select Try It to display the dialog box again.

As you can see, the last status of the combo box isn't maintained.

☐ Close the dialog box and then terminate the MyCombo application.

Maintaining the Status of the Combo Box

Now you'll add code that maintains the status of the combo box. That is, when you display the dialog box, the status of the combo box should be the same as it was before the dialog box's OK button was clicked.

☐ Use ClassWizard to add a function for the event:

Class Name:	CMyDlg
Object ID:	IDOK
Message:	BN_CLICKED
Function Name:	OnOK()

☐ Edit the OnOK() function that you added to the MYDLG.CPP file so that it looks as follows:

```
void CMyDlg::OnOK()
{
// TODO: Add extra validation here


/////////////////////////
// MY CODE STARTS HERE
/////////////////////////

m_CurrentSelectedItem =
        (int) SendDlgItemMessage(IDC_COMBO1,
                                 CB_GETCURSEL,
                                 0,
                                 0);

if ( m_CurrentSelectedItem == CB_ERR )
    {
      MessageBox (
        "Nothing is selected in the list. Forcing Item 3" );

      // Set the selected item to the third item.
      m_CurrentSelectedItem = 3;

    }

/////////////////////
// MY CODE ENDS HERE
/////////////////////

CDialog::OnOK();

}
```

The `OnOK()` function uses `SendDlgItemMessage()` to extract the currently selected item in the list box:

```
m_CurrentSelectedItem =
        (int) SendDlgItemMessage(IDC_COMBO1,
                                 CB_GETCURSEL,
                                 0,
                                 0);
```

The first parameter in `SendDlgItemMessage()` is `IDC_COMBO1` because you're sending the message to the combo box. The second parameter is `CB_GETCURSEL`, which "tells" the combo box to report back the currently selected item. The third and forth parameters aren't used, and therefore they must be 0.

If the user clicks an item from the list, the combo box reacts as follows:

1. The clicked item is highlighted, and the edit box is filled with that item.
2. `m_SelectedItem` (the variable that you connected to the combo box during the visual implementation) is updated with the highlighted string.

If the user clicks in the edit box and then types something in it, the combo box reacts as follows:

1. No item in the list is selected.
2. `m_SelectedItem` (the variable that you connected to the combo box during the visual implementation) is updated with the characters that were typed in the edit box.

Recall that the `OnOK()` function is executed whenever the user clicks the OK button. The `if()` statement you typed in `OnOK()` checks to determine whether there's a highlighted item in the list. It accomplishes that by checking the value returned from the `SendDlgItemMessage()` function:

```
if ( m_CurrentSelectedItem == CB_ERR )
  {

  MessageBox (
    "Nothing is selected in the list. Forcing Item 3");

  // Set the selected item to the third item.
  m_CurrentSelectedItem = 3;

  }
```

If the returned value from `m_CurrentSelectedItem()` is equal to `CB_ERR`, there's no item selected in the list. In this case, the statements of the `if()` are executed. These statements display a message with the `MessageBox()` function, and then m_CurrentSelectedItem is set to 3. Thus, the next time the dialog box is displayed, Item 3 will be highlighted. Why did you use the MessageBox() function? Just to prove that whenever there's not a highlighted item in the list, CB_ERR is returned from the SendDlgItemMessage() function when the CB_GETCURSEL message is sent.

☐ Select Rebuild All MYCOMBO.EXE application from the Project menu.

☐ Select Execute MYCOMBO.EXE from the Project menu.

☐ Select Try It from the File menu.

> *MyCombo responds by displaying the dialog box. As you can see, the list box is filled with the members of the* m_Item[] *array, Item 3 is highlighted, and the edit box is filled with the contents of the highlighted item in the list.*

☐ Click in the edit box of the combo box and then click the OK button.

> *The combo box responds by displaying a message box that tells you nothing is currently selected in the list.*

☐ Close the dialog box by clicking the OK button and then select Try It to display the dialog box again.

> *The combo box responds by displaying the dialog box with* Item 3 *highlighted in the list (because you forced* Item 3 *in the* if() *statements of the* OnOK() *function).*

☐ Select Item 5 from the list and then click the OK button.

☐ Select Try It from the File menu again.

> *MyCombo responds by displaying the dialog box with* Item 5 *highlighted in the list. That is, MyCombo maintains the status of the combo box as it was before the OK button of the dialog box was clicked.*

NOTE

In this section you learned that whenever the list of the combo box doesn't contain any highlighted item, the SendDlgItemMessage() function with CB_GETCURSEL message as its parameter returns CB_ERR.

In a similar manner, a regular list box returns LB_ERR when none of its items are highlighted.

Completing the MyCombo Application

You'll now complete the MyCombo application. Recall that the reason you let the user select (or type) a string with the combo box is to select an item. After the user selects (or types) a string, the rest of the program should read and make use of this string. The MyCombo application demonstrates this by displaying the value of the selected string whenever Current Item is selected from the menu. Here's how to accomplish that:

☐ Use ClassWizard to add a function for the event:

Class Name:	CMycomboView
Object ID:	ID_FILE_CURRENTITEM
Message:	COMMAND
Function Name:	OnFileCurrentitem()

NOTE: Make sure to add the function to the CMycomboView class.

☐ Edit the OnFileCurrentitem() function that you added to the MYCOMVW.CPP file so that it looks as follows:

```
void CMycomboView::OnFileCurrentitem()
{
// TODO: Add your command handler code here

////////////////////////
// MY CODE STARTS HERE
////////////////////////

MessageBox ( "The current selection in the combo box is: "+
             dlg.m_SelectedItem);

////////////////////////
// MY CODE ENDS HERE
////////////////////////

}
```

The code you typed uses the MessageBox() to display the value of dlg.m_SelectedItem. This variable contains the selected string that was clicked or typed in the combo box.

☐ Select Rebuild All MYCOMBO.EXE application from the Project menu.

☐ Execute the MyCombo application.

Experiment with the MyCombo application and verify its operation. In particular, note that when you type something in the edit box and then click the OK button, the message box that the Current Item displays contains the text that you typed in the edit box.

11

Dialog Boxes: Radio Buttons

In this chapter you will learn how to
use radio buttons from within dialog
boxes. As you know, radio buttons
serve an important role in the
Windows user interface mechanism.

The MyRadio Application

Before you begin writing the MyRadio application by yourself, execute the copy of the MyRadio application that resides in your `C:\VCPROG\ORIGINAL\CH11\MYRADIO` directory.

To execute the MyRadio application:

☐ Use Run from the Program Manager's File menu to execute
`C:\VCPROG\ORIGINAL\CH11\MYRADIO\MyRadio.EXE`.

> *Windows responds by executing the MyRadio application. The main window of* `MyRadio.EXE` *appears as shown in Figure 11.1.*

Figure 11.1.
The MyRadio
application's main
window.

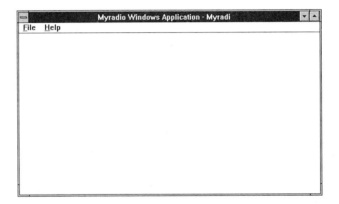

The MyRadio application has two popup menus: File and Help. These popup menus are shown in Figures 11.2 and 11.3.

Figure 11.2.
The MyRadio
application's File
menu.

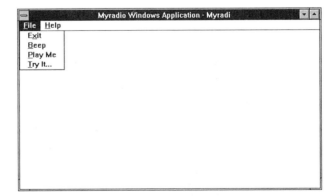

Figure 11.3.
The MyRadio
application's Help
menu.

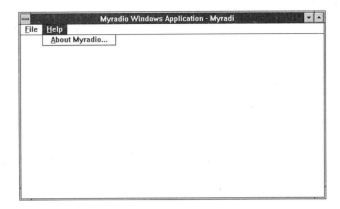

☐ Select Try It from the File menu.

MyRadio responds by displaying a dialog box (see Figure 11.4).

Figure 11.4.
The MyRadio
application's dialog
box.

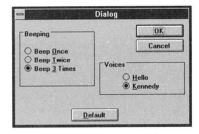

As you can see, the dialog box contains two groups of radio buttons. One group is called *Beeping*, and the other group is called *Voices*. The Beeping group has three radio buttons:

Beep Once
Beep Twice
Beep 3 Times

The Voices group has two radio buttons:

Hello
Kennedy

☐ Click the various radio buttons of the Beeping group and notice that within the Beeping group you can select only one radio button at any time.

☐ Select the Beep Twice button from the Beeping group.

☐ Click the various radio buttons of the Voices group and notice that within the Voices group you can select only one radio button at any time.

☐ Select the Kennedy radio button from the Voices group.

☐ Close the dialog box by clicking the OK button.

☐ Select Beep from the File menu.

> *MyRadio responds by beeping in accordance with the setting of the radio button in the Beeping group. (Because you set the Beep Twice radio button, the program beeps twice.)*

☐ Select Play Me from the File menu.

> *MyRadio responds by playing a voice through the PC speaker.*

The voice that is played corresponds to the radio button that you set in the Voices group. Because you set the Kennedy radio button, the program plays a portion of a famous speech by President Kennedy:

> So my fellow Americans,
> ask not what your country can do for you,
> ask what you can do for your country.
> (People cheering)

☐ Experiment with the other radio buttons of the dialog box and note that the setting of these buttons determines which audio file will be played when Play Me from the File menu is selected, and the settings determine the number of beeps that will be heard when Beep from the File menu is executed.

☐ Click the Default button.

> *MyRadio responds by selecting the third radio button in the Beeping group and the second radio button in the Voices group.*

☐ Experiment with the MyRadio application and then select Exit from the File menu.

Now that you know what the MyRadio application should do, you can write it.

Creating the Project of the MyRadio Application

To create the project of the MyRadio application:

☐ Select AppWizard from the Project menu.

Visual C++ responds by running AppWizard.

☐ Use the Directory list box to select the directory C:\VCPROG\PRACTICE\CH11.

☐ Type myradio in the Project Name box.

Now your AppWizard dialog box looks as shown in Figure 11.5.

Figure 11.5.
The MyRadio
application's
AppWizard dialog
box.

☐ Click the Options button and set the options as shown in Figure 11.6 (that is, uncheck all the check boxes except the Generate Source Comments check box).

☐ Click the OK button of the Options dialog box and then click the OK button of the AppWizard dialog box, and finally, click the Create button of the New Application Information dialog box.

AppWizard responds by creating the MyRadio project and all the skeleton files of the MyRadio application.

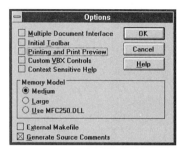

Figure 11.6.
Setting the options
for the MyRadio
application.

To remove the debug options of the project (so that you'll have a small EXE file):

☐ Select Project from the Options menu of Visual C++, click the Release radio button, and then click the OK button of the dialog box.

The Visual Implementation of the MyRadio Application

The MyRadio application has a menu, a custom dialog box, and an About dialog box. In the following sections, you'll visually design the menu and the custom dialog box of the MyRadio application.

The Visual Implementation of the Menu of the MyRadio Application

The MyRadio application should have a menu as shown in Figures 11.1, 11.2, and 11.3. To implement this menu:

☐ Use App Studio to implement the menu of the MyRadio application per Table 11.1.

Table 11.1. The menu of the MyRadio application.
Figures relating to menu: 11.1, 11.2, 11.3

Menu Item
&File
E&xit
&Beep
&Play Me

Menu Item
&Try It...
&Help
&About MyRadio...

To save your work:

☐ Select Save from the File menu of App Studio.

The visual implementation of the menu of the MyRadio application is completed.

The Visual Implementation of the Dialog Box

Now you'll visually implement the dialog box of the MyRadio application.

☐ Implement the dialog box of the MyRadio application per Table 11.2.

Table 11.2. The dialog box of the MyRadio application.

Class Name:	CMyDlg (of class CDialog)
Figure:	11.4
OK button:	Yes
Cancel button:	Yes

Object	Property	Setting
Dialog box	ID	IDD_DIALOG1
Push button	ID	IDC_DEFAULT
	Caption	&Default
Static frame	ID	IDC_STATIC_BEEPING
	Caption	Beeping
Radio button	ID	IDC_RADIO_BEEP1
	Caption	Beep &Once
	Group	Checked
	Variable	m_BeepStatus
	Type	int
	Note: In the Beeping group	

continues

Table 11.2. continued

Object	Property	Setting
Radio button	ID	IDC_RADIO_BEEP2
	Caption	Beep &Twice
	Group	Not checked
	Note: In the Beeping group	
Radio button	ID	IDC_RADIO_BEEP3
	Caption	Beep &3 Times
	Group	Not checked
	Note: In the Beeping group	
Static frame	ID	IDC_STATIC_VOICES
	Caption	Voices
Radio button	ID	IDC_RADIO_HELLO
	Caption	&Hello
	Variable	m_VoiceStatus
	Type	int
	Group	Checked
	Note: In the Voices group	
Radio button	ID	IDC_RADIO_KENNEDY
	Caption	&Kennedy
	Group	Not checked
	Note: In the Voices group	

NOTE

The icons of the radio button and the static frame in the Tools Window are shown in Figure 11.7.

Figure 11.7.
The icons of the
static frame and
radio button in the
Tools Window.

Static Frame ——

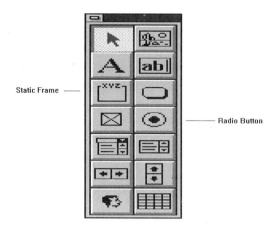

—— Radio Button

Here is how you implement the Beeping group that is mentioned in Table 11.2:

☐ Place three radio buttons in the dialog box.

☐ Place a static frame in the dialog box.

☐ Enclose the three radio buttons with the static frame.

(To size the static frame, you have to click the periphery of the frame and drag its handles.)

☐ Double click the Beep Once radio button and check its Group property check box.

NOTE

As indicated in Table 11.2, the Group properties of the Beep Twice and Beep 3 Times radio buttons shouldn't be checked. In other words, you should check the Group property of only the first radio button in the group.

☐ Change the IDs and the captions of the radio buttons and the static frame in accordance with Table 11.2.

☐ As indicated in Table 11.2, attach the variable `m_BeepStatus` of type `int` to the `IDC_RADIO_BEEP1` radio button.

NOTE

As indicated in Table 11.2, don't attach variables to the other radio buttons of the Beeping group. That is, only the first button in the group is attached to a variable. As you'll learn later in this chapter, Visual C++ knows that this variable is connected to the other radio buttons in this group.

You now have a group that contains three radio buttons—the Beeping group.

☐ Repeat the previous steps to create the Voices group of two radio buttons. Don't forget that only the Hello button—the first button in the group—is connected with a variable and its Group property should be checked.

NOTE

The Static frame is also called a *Group box.*

NOTE

Creating groups of radio buttons is a simple, straightforward process, but it requires some practice. The main thing to note about a group of radio buttons is that, in a group, no more than one radio button can be selected at any time.

Once you complete the visual implementation, it is a good idea to check your implementation before attaching any code to the program. Here is how you check your visual implementation:

Select Test from the Resource menu of App Studio.

App Studio responds by displaying the dialog box.

Click the various radio buttons and make sure that you can select only one button in each group. Make sure that selecting a button in the Beeping group doesn't affect any of the buttons in the Voices group and that selecting any of the buttons in the Voices group doesn't affect any of the buttons in the Beeping group.

If the test fails, delete the radio buttons and the static frames, start placing these objects all over again, and perform the test again.

To terminate a test:

Click the Cancel button of the dialog box.

NOTE

As you can see, the Test feature is a useful test. That is, if something is wrong with your visual implementation, you'd better know it (and fix it) now!

The test feature is useful for checking the group/radio buttons' functionality, as well as for examining the appearance of the dialog box.

As stated, to terminate the test, you have to click the Cancel button of the dialog box. But what if you implement a dialog box that doesn't have a Cancel button? To terminate the test of such a dialog box, click the minus icon that appears on the upper-left corner of the dialog box and select Close from the system menu that pops up.

That's it! You've completed the visual implementation of the dialog box.

To save your work:

☐ Select Save from the File menu.

Declaring the Dialog Box Object as a Data Member of the View Class

You'll now declare an object `dlg` of class `CMyDlg`. You'll create this object as a data member of the view class (the `CMyradioView` class).

☐ Open the `MYRADVW.H` file and modify the declaration of the `CMyradioView` class. After the modification, the `CMyradioView` class declaration looks as follows:

```
class CMyradioView : public CView
{
protected: // create from serialization only
                CMyradioView();
                DECLARE_DYNCREATE(CMyradioView)

// Attributes
public:
                CMyradioDoc* GetDocument();
```

319

```
/////////////////////
// MY CODE STARTS HERE
/////////////////////

// Create an object dlg (a dialog box) of class CMyDlg.
CMyDlg dlg;

/////////////////////
// MY CODE ENDS HERE
/////////////////////



// Operations
public:

// Implementation
public:
                virtual ~CMyradioView();
                virtual void OnDraw(CDC* pDC);
// overridden to draw this view
#ifdef _DEBUG
                virtual void AssertValid() const;
                virtual void Dump(CDumpContext& dc) const;
#endif

protected:

// Generated message map functions
protected:
                //{{AFX_MSG(CMyradioView)
// NOTE - the ClassWizard will add and remove member functions here.
// DO NOT EDIT what you see in these blocks of generated code !
                //}}AFX_MSG
                DECLARE_MESSAGE_MAP()
};
```

Because the CMyDlg class is unknown in the file MYRADVW.H, you have to #include the file MyDlg.h (that contains the class declaration of CMyDlg) at the beginning of the MYRADVW.H file.

☐ Add the #include "MyDlg.h" statement at the beginning of the MYRADVW.H file.

After you #include this statement, the beginning of the MYRADVW.H file looks as follows:

```
// myradvw.h : interface of the CMyradioView class
//
```

```
/////////////////////////////////////////////////////////////

//////////////////////
// MY CODE STARTS HERE
//////////////////////

#include "MyDlg.h"

//////////////////////
// MY CODE ENDS HERE
//////////////////////
.....
.....
.....
```

Attaching Code to the Try It Menu Item of the MyRadio Application

You'll now attach code to the Try It menu item. Recall that when the Try It menu item is selected, the MyRadio application should display the dialog box.

☐ Use ClassWizard to add a function for the event:

Class Name:	CMyradioView
Object ID:	ID_FILE_TRYIT
Message:	COMMAND
Function Name:	OnFileTryit()

NOTE: In the preceding, make sure that you are adding the function to the CMyradioView class.

☐ Edit the OnFileTryit() function that you added to the MYRADVW.CPP file. After you edit the function, your OnFileTryit() function looks as follows:

```
void CMyradioView::OnFileTryit()
{
                // TODO: Add your command handler code here

    //////////////////////
    // MY CODE STARTS HERE
    //////////////////////

    // Display the dlg dialog box.
    dlg.DoModal();
```

```
/////////////////////
// MY CODE ENDS HERE
/////////////////////
```

}

In the preceding code, you display the dialog box `dlg` by using the `DoModal()` function:

```
dlg.DoModal();
```

Compiling, Linking, and Executing the MyRadio Application

Although you haven't completed writing the MyRadio application, compile, link, and execute it so that you can see how the radio buttons behave:

☐ Select Rebuild All MYRADIO.EXE from the Project menu.

☐ Execute the MyRadio application.

☐ Select Try It from the File menu.

MyRadio responds by displaying the dialog box.

☐ Experiment with the various radio buttons and notice that only one radio button can be selected in each group at any one time.

☐ Close the dialog box by clicking the OK button and then select Try It from the File menu.

MyRadio responds by displaying the dialog box again. As you can see, the status of the radio buttons is maintained. This is due to the `m_BeepStatus` *and* `m_VoiceStatus` *variables that you attached to the radio buttons.*

☐ Take a look at the constructor function of `CMyDlg` in the `MyDlg.CPP` file:

```
CMyDlg::CMyDlg(CWnd* pParent /*=NULL*/)
        CDialog(CMyDlg::IDD, pParent)
{
        //{{AFX_DATA_INIT(CMyDlg)
        m_BeepStatus = -1;
                m_VoiceStatus = -1;
                //}}AFX_DATA_INIT
}
```

As you can see, Visual C++ initialized these two variables for you. A value of −1 means that none of the radio buttons are selected. A value of 0 means that the first radio button in the group is selected, a value of 1 means that the second radio button in the group is selected, and so on. If when creating the dialog box you want the initial status of the groups to be different, change the values of the m_BeepStatus and m_VoiceStatus variables.

Indeed, because Visual C++ initialized these two variables to –1, when displaying the dialog box for the first time, none of the radio buttons are selected.

> **NOTE**
>
> Visual C++ updates the values of m_BeepStatus and m_VoiceStatus automatically. This means that if the user closes the dialog box by clicking the OK button, the values of these variables are updated in accordance with the setting of the radio buttons. If the user closes the dialog box by clicking the Cancel button, the values of these variables remain the same as they were when the dialog box was opened.
>
> After closing the dialog box, the dlg object is not destroyed because the dlg object is a data member of the View (CMyradioView) class.

Implementing a Default Behavior

Typically, you want to implement a default behavior for the dialog box. That is, your user will be able to display the dialog box and customize the behavior of the application by selecting various settings in the dialog box. However, if your user doesn't display the dialog box and customize the behavior of the application, the application should behave in accordance with some default settings that you have to set. Suppose that the default of the MyRadio application should be as follows:

> The Beep 3 Times radio button should be selected.
> The Kennedy radio button should be selected.

You have to specify this default behavior by changing the code of the constructor function of CMyDlg in the MyDlg.CPP file.

To implement this default setting:

☐ Modify the constructor function of CMyDlg in the MyDlg.CPP file as follows:

```
CMyDlg::CMyDlg(CWnd* pParent /*=NULL*/)
            : CDialog(CMyDlg::IDD, pParent)
```

```
{
                        //{{AFX_DATA_INIT(CMyDlg)

    /////////////////////////
    // MY CODE STARTS HERE
    /////////////////////////

    m_BeepStatus  = 2; // Third radio button
    m_VoiceStatus = 1; // Second radio button


    /////////////////////////
    // MY CODE ENDS HERE
    /////////////////////////

    //}}AFX_DATA_INIT
}
```

☐ Compile, link, and execute the MyRadio application, and notice that when the dialog box is displayed for the first time, the radio buttons appear as you set them in the constructor function CMyDlg().

Providing Your User with a Default Button

Many Windows applications provide the user with a Default button. That is, the user is able to change the various settings of the dialog box. However, the user can click the Default button to return the dialog box to its original settings.

You'll now attach code to the Default button.

☐ Use ClassWizard to add a function for the event:

Class Name:	CMyDlg
Object ID:	IDC_DEFAULT
Message:	BN_CLICKED
Function Name:	OnDefault()

NOTE: Make sure you're adding the function to the CMyDlg class.

☐ Edit the OnDefault() function that you added to the MYDLG.CPP file. After you edit the function, your OnDefault() function looks as follows:

```
void CMyDlg::OnDefault()
{
    // TODO: Add your control notification handler code here


    /////////////////////////
    // MY CODE STARTS HERE
    /////////////////////////


    // Set the default values for the variables of
    // the radio buttons.
    m_BeepStatus  = 2; // Third radio button
    m_VoiceStatus = 1; // Second radio button

    // Update the screen with the values of the variables.
    UpdateData (FALSE );

    ///////////////////////
    // MY CODE ENDS HERE
    ///////////////////////


}
```

The code that you typed updates the variables of the radio buttons with the default values

```
    m_BeepStatus  = 2;
    m_VoiceStatus = 1;
```

and then the screen is updated, so it will correspond to the values of the variables, as follows:

```
UpdateData (FALSE );
```

To see the Default button in action:

☐ Compile, link, and execute the MyRadio application.

☐ Change the settings of the radio buttons.

☐ Click the Default button.

> *MyRadio responds by returning the status of the radio buttons to their default settings.*

☐ Close the dialog box and then select Exit from the File menu to terminate the MyRadio application.

Using the Settings of the Radio Buttons

Typically, the dialog box is used to set the various status of the controls, and the program uses the values set in the dialog box. You'll now learn how to write code that uses the radio buttons' settings. The code you'll write will cause the correct number of beeps and the playback of the correct voice when the user selects Beeping and Voices from the File menu.

☐ Use ClassWizard to add a function for the event:

Class Name:	`CMyradioView`
Object ID:	`ID_FILE_BEEP`
Message:	`COMMAND`
Function Name:	`OnFileBeep()`

NOTE: Make sure that you add the above function to the `CMyradioView` class.

☐ Edit the `OnFileBeep()` function that you added to the `MYRADVW.CPP` file. After you edit `OnFileBeep()`, it looks as follows:

```
void CMyradioView::OnFileBeep()
{
                // TODO: Add your command handler code here

        ///////////////////////
        // MY CODE STARTS HERE
        ///////////////////////

        // User selected Beep from the File menu, so beep.
        DWORD start;
        switch (dlg.m_BeepStatus)
                {
                case 0:
                        // Beep
                        MessageBeep(-1);
                        break;
                case 1:
                        // Beep
                        MessageBeep(-1);

                        // 1 second delay
                        start = GetTickCount();
                        while ( GetTickCount() < start + 1000 )
                                ;
```

```
            // Beep
            MessageBeep(-1);
            break;
        case 2:
            // Beep
            MessageBeep(-1);

            // 1 second delay
            start = GetTickCount();
            while ( GetTickCount() < start + 1000 )
                ;

            // Beep
            MessageBeep(-1);

            // 1 second delay
            start = GetTickCount();
            while ( GetTickCount() < start + 1000 )
                ;

            // Beep
            MessageBeep(-1);
            break;
    }

/////////////////////
// MY CODE ENDS HERE
/////////////////////

}
```

The code that you typed uses the switch statement to examine the value of m_BeepStatus. If m_BeepStatus is equal to 0, the Beep Once radio button is selected, and the program will beep once (by using the MessageBeep() function). If the value of m_BeepStatus is equal to 1, the Beep Twice radio button is selected, and the program will beep twice. Note that between the two beeps, a delay is implemented as follows:

```
// 1 second delay
start = GetTickCount();
while ( GetTickCount() < start + 1000 )
        ;
```

This delay updates the value of the local variable start with the returned value of the GetTickCount() function. GetTickCount() returns the number of milliseconds that elapsed since Windows started. The while loop compares the value of GetTickCount() with the value of start. Eventually, the returned value from GetTickCount() will be greater than start+1000, and the while loop will terminate. So to summarize, the program stays in the while loop for 1 second (1000 milliseconds).

In a similar manner, the code under `case 2:` beeps 3 times, and there is a 1 second delay in between the beeps.

To see the preceding code in action:

☐ Compile, link, and execute the MyRadio program.

☐ Select Try It from the File menu, select a radio button in the Beeping group, close the dialog box by clicking the OK button, and then select Beep from the File menu.

> *MyRadio responds by beeping. It beeps in accordance with the selection of the radio button that you selected in the Beeping group.*

Implementing the Play Me Menu

The last thing you have to do is implement the Play Me menu item. Recall that when Play Me is selected from the File menu, the MyRadio application should play a WAV file. The WAV file to be played depends on the particular radio button that is selected in the Voices group.

Playing WAV files through the PC speaker requires the use of sp_ functions that reside in TegoSND.DLL. To be able to use these functions from your Visual C++ programs, you have to do the following:

1. Tell the Visual C++ compiler the name of the DLL and the name of the functions that reside in the DLL.

2. Tell the Visual C++ compiler the prototypes of these functions.

Specifying the Names of the DLL and Functions

As stated, you have to tell the Visual C++ compiler the name of the DLL and the names of the functions that your application uses from the DLL. You do that in the DEF file of the application. (Recall that one of the files created by Visual C++ when you created the MyRadio project is the `MyRadio.DEF` file.)

☐ Select Open from the File menu and select the file `C:\vcProg\Practice\CH11\MYRADIO\MyRadio.DEF`.

☐ Add code in the `MyRadio.DEF` file. After you add the code, the `MyRadio.DEF` file looks as follows:

```
; myradio.def : Declares the module parameters for the application.

NAME          MYRADIO
DESCRIPTION   'MYRADIO Windows Application'
EXETYPE       WINDOWS

CODE          PRELOAD MOVEABLE DISCARDABLE
DATA          PRELOAD MOVEABLE MULTIPLE

HEAPSIZE      1024    ; initial heap size
; Stack size is passed as argument to linker's /STACK option


;;;;;;;;;;;;;;;;;;;;;;;;
; MY CODE STARTS HERE
;;;;;;;;;;;;;;;;;;;;;;;;

;;;;;;;;;;;;;;;;;;;;;;;;;;;;;;;;;;;;;;;;;;;;;;;
; sp_ functions from the TegoSND.DLL library
;;;;;;;;;;;;;;;;;;;;;;;;;;;;;;;;;;;;;;;;;;;;;;;

IMPORTS
TegoSND.sp_OpenSession
TegoSND.sp_PlaySnd
TegoSND.sp_MouseOn
TegoSND.sp_MouseOff
TegoSND.sp_CloseSession

;;;;;;;;;;;;;;;;;;;;;;;;
; MY CODE ENDS HERE
;;;;;;;;;;;;;;;;;;;;;;;;
```

The IMPORTS statement that you added tells the compiler that the lines following the IMPORTS statement list the functions that reside in a DLL. For example, the statement

```
TegoSND.sp_PlaySnd
```

is an instruction to the compiler, telling it that the program might use a function called sp_PlaySnd() from a DLL called TegSND.DLL.

Specifying the Prototypes of the DLL's Functions

Because your application uses functions from the DLL, you must tell the compiler the prototypes of these functions. The prototypes of the functions from the TegoSND.DLL library reside in the file C:\vcProg\DLL\TegoSND.H. Thus, you have to #include this file in your MYRADIO.H file:

☐ Select Open from the File menu of Visual C++ and open the file
`C:\vcProg\Practice\CH11\MYRADIO\MYRADIO.H`.

☐ Add the #include statement at the beginning of the MYRADIO.H file. After you add the #include statement, the beginning of your MYRADIO.H file looks as follows:

```
// myradio.h : main header file for the MYRADIO application
//

#ifndef __AFXWIN_H__
#error include 'stdafx.h' before including this file for PCH
#endif

#include "resource.h"        // main symbols


////////////////////////
// MY CODE STARTS HERE
////////////////////////

#include "\vcProg\DLL\TegoSND.H"

////////////////////////
// MY CODE ENDS HERE
////////////////////////

.....
.....
.....
```

Your program can now use the sp_ functions from the Tego SND.DLL library (that are mentioned in the DEF File).

> **NOTE**
>
> During the compiling/linking process, the file TegoSND.DLL may or may not reside in your \Windows directory. In other words, the compiler doesn't use the DLL during compilation time. However, during runtime, the DLL must reside in the \Windows directory.
>
> If you installed the book's CD, the file TegoSND.DLL was copied into your \Windows directory.

Opening the WAV Files

The MyRadio application uses two WAV files:

```
C:\vcProg\WAV\Hello.WAV
C:\vcProg\WAV\8Kenned3.WAV
```

Thus, MyRadio needs to use the sp_OpenSession() function to open sessions for these two WAV files.

The variables that hold the session numbers are

m_HelloSession. This variable holds the session number of the Hello.WAV file.

m_KennedySession. This variable holds the session number of the 8Kenned3.WAV file.

Because the preceding two variables are to be accessible by the member functions of the view class (CMyradioView), you have to declare these variables as data members of the view class (CMyradioView):

☐ Declare the integers m_HelloSession and m_KennedySession in the CMyradioView class that resides in the MYRADVW.H file. After you declare these variables, your CMyradioView class declaration looks as follows:

```
class CMyradioView : public CView
{
protected: // create from serialization only
                CMyradioView();
                DECLARE_DYNCREATE(CMyradioView)

// Attributes
public:
                CMyradioDoc* GetDocument();


        /////////////////////////
        // MY CODE STARTS HERE
        /////////////////////////

        // Create an object dlg (a dialog box) of class CMyDlg.
        CMyDlg dlg;

        // Declare the variables that hold the session numbers.
        int m_HelloSession;
        int m_KennedySession;
```

```
//////////////////////
// MY CODE ENDS HERE
//////////////////////


// Operations
public:

// Implementation
public:
                virtual ~CMyradioView();
                virtual void OnDraw(CDC* pDC);
// overridden to draw this view
#ifdef _DEBUG
                virtual void AssertValid() const;
                virtual void Dump(CDumpContext& dc) const;
#endif

protected:

// Generated message map functions
protected:
                //{{AFX_MSG(CMyradioView)
                afx_msg void OnFileTryit();
                afx_msg void OnFileBeep();
                //}}AFX_MSG
                DECLARE_MESSAGE_MAP()
};
```

You only need to open the WAV files once during the life of the program. Thus, a good place to open a WAV session is in the constructor function of the view class:

☐ Type code in the constructor function of the CMyradioView class that resides in the MYRADVW.CPP file. After you type the code, the CMyradioView() constructor function looks as follows:

```
///////////////////////////////////////////////////////////////
// CMyradioView construction/destruction

CMyradioView::CMyradioView()
{
                // TODO: add construction code here

    //////////////////////
    // MY CODE STARTS HERE
    //////////////////////

    // Declare local variables
    char FileToOpen[255];
    CString Message, Caption;
```

```
 // Open a WAV session for Hello.WAV
 strcpy ( FileToOpen, "\\vcProg\\WAV\\Hello.WAV" );
 m_HelloSession = sp_OpenSession ( FileToOpen );

  // If WAV session can't be opened, display an error
  // message box.
 if ( m_HelloSession < 0 )
    {
    Message = "Can't open the file: ";
    Message = Message + FileToOpen;
    Caption = "Error";
    MessageBox ( Message, Caption );
    }

 // Open a WAV session for 8Kenned3.WAV
 strcpy ( FileToOpen, "\\vcProg\\WAV\\8Kenned3.WAV" );
 m_KennedySession = sp_OpenSession ( FileToOpen );

  // If WAV session can't be opened, display an error
  // message box.
 if ( m_KennedySession < 0 )
    {
    Message = "Can't open the file: ";
    Message = Message + FileToOpen;
    Caption = "Error";
    MessageBox ( Message, Caption );
    }

 ////////////////////
 // MY CODE ENDS HERE
 ////////////////////

}
```

The code you typed declares the local variables:

```
char FileToOpen[255];
CString Message, Caption;
```

and then the `strcpy()` function is used to fill the `FileToOpen` string with the path and filename of the WAV file:

```
strcpy ( FileToOpen, "\\vcProg\\WAV\\Hello.WAV" );
```

You then use the `sp_OpenSession()` function to open the WAV session:

```
m_HelloSession = sp_OpenSession ( FileToOpen );
```

The parameter of the `sp_` is `FileToOpen`, which is the WAV file that will be played.

The next statement is an `if` that checks whether the WAV session was opened successfully. If the WAV session wasn't opened successfully, a message box is displayed:

```
Message = "Can't open the file: ";
Message = Message + FileToOpen;
Caption = "Error";
MessageBox ( Message, Caption );
```

The next group of statements opens a WAV session for the `8Kenned3.WAV` file.

Whenever the user selects Play Me from the File menu, MyRadio should play the WAV file that corresponds to the radio button that is selected in the Voices group. Thus, attach the following code to the Play Me menu item:

☐ Use ClassWizard to add a function for the event:

Class Name:	`CMyradioView`
Object ID:	`ID_FILE_PLAYME`
Message:	`COMMAND`
Function Name:	`OnFilePlayme()`

NOTE: In the preceding, make sure that you are adding the function to the `CMyradioView` class.

☐ Edit the `OnFilePlayme()` function that you added to the `MYRADVW.CPP` file. After you edit the function, it looks as follows:

```
void CMyradioView::OnFilePlayme()
{
                // TODO: Add your command handler code here


        /////////////////////////
        // MY CODE STARTS HERE
        /////////////////////////

        switch (dlg.m_VoiceStatus)
              {
              case 0:
                   sp_PlaySnd (m_HelloSession,
                               SP_START_OF_FILE,
                               SP_END_OF_FILE );
                   break;
```

```
case 1:
        sp_PlaySnd (m_KennedySession,
                    SP_START_OF_FILE,
                    SP_END_OF_FILE );
        break;

    }

//////////////////////
// MY CODE ENDS HERE
//////////////////////
}
```

The code you typed uses a switch to check the value of dlg.m_VoiceStatus. If m_VoiceStatus is equal to 0, it means that the first radio button in the Voices group is selected, and thus the Hello.WAV file is played by using the sp_PlaySnd() function. And if the value of m_VoiceStatus is 1, it means that the second radio button in the Voices group is selected, and therefore the 8Kenned3.WAV file is played.

Save your work:

☐ Select Save from the File menu.

☐ Compile/link the MyRadio application.

☐ Execute the MyRadio application and verify its operation.

Closing the Sound Sessions and Saying Good-Bye

Don't forget to close the sound sessions that you opened. Of course, a good place to execute the sp_CloseSession() function is in the destructor function of the view class:

☐ Type the sp_CloseSession() statements in the destructor function of the CMyradioView class that resides in the MYRADIO.CPP file. After you type these statements, the destructor function looks as follows:

```
CMyradioView::~CMyradioView()
{

    //////////////////////
    // MY CODE STARTS HERE
    //////////////////////

    sp_PlaySnd ( m_HelloSession,
                 52160L,
                 SP_END_OF_FILE );
```

```
sp_CloseSession ( m_HelloSession );
sp_CloseSession ( m_KennedySession );


///////////////////////,
// MY CODE ENDS HERE
///////////////////////

}
```

The code that you typed plays the audio section from byte location 52,160 to the end of the WAV file:

```
sp_PlaySnd ( m_HelloSession,
             52160L,
             SP_END_OF_FILE );
```

This audio section contains the audio, "Good-bye."

And finally, the sp_CloseSession() function is executed twice to close the two WAV sessions.

12

Placing Controls Inside the Main Window

So far in this book, you've placed controls (for example, push buttons, edit boxes, and so on) in dialog boxes, but you haven't placed controls in the main window of the application.

In this chapter you will write an application that has controls in its main window.

The TEST Application

Now you'll write the TEST application. The TEST application is an example of an application that has controls in its main window.

Before you start writing the TEST application, execute the copy of this application that resides in your `C:\VCPROG\ORIGINAL\CH12\TEST` directory.

To execute the DIA application:

☐ In Windows, select Run from Program Manager's File menu.

Windows responds by displaying the Run dialog box.

☐ Type `C:\vcProg\Original\CH12\TEST\TEST.EXE` in the Command Line box and then click the OK button.

Windows responds by executing the TEST application. The main window of TEST.EXE appears as shown in Figure 12.1.

*Figure 12.1.
The TEST
application's main
window.*

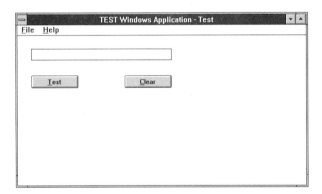

As you can see from Figure 12.1, the main window of the application contains three controls: an edit box, a Test button, and a Clear button.

☐ Experiment with the buttons of the application.

When you click the Test button, the text, "THIS IS A TEST" appears in the edit box. When you click the Clear button, the text in the edit box is cleared.

The TEST application has two popup menus: File and Help. These popup menus are shown in Figures 12.2 and 12.3.

Figure 12.2.
The TEST
application's File
menu.

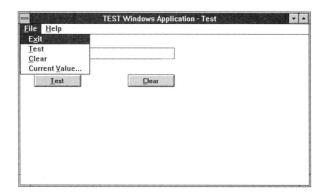

Figure 12.3.
The TEST
application's Help
menu.

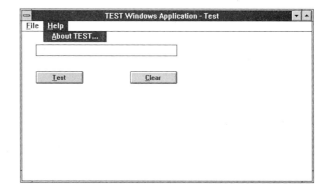

As you can see from Figure 12.2, the File menu has four items:

```
Exit
Test
Clear
Current value...
```

☐ Experiment with the Test and Clear menu items of the File menu.

As you can see, the Test and Clear menu items have the same functionality as the Test and Clear buttons.

☐ Select the Current Value menu item.

> *The TEST application responds by displaying a message box that shows the current contents of the edit box.*

To exit from the TEST application:

☐ Select Exit from the File menu.

Now that you know what the TEST application should do, start writing it.

Creating the TEST Application Project

To create the project of the TEST application:

☐ Select AppWizard from the Project menu.

  Visual C++ responds by running AppWizard.

☐ Use the Directory list box to select the directory C:\VCPROG\PRACTICE\CH12.

☐ Type test in the Project Name box.

Now your AppWizard dialog box looks as shown in Figure 12.4.

Figure 12.4.
The TEST
application's
AppWizard
dialog box.

☐ Click the Options button and set the options as shown in Figure 12.5 (that is, uncheck all the check boxes except the Generate Source Comments check box).

Figure 12.5.
Setting the options
for the TEST
application.

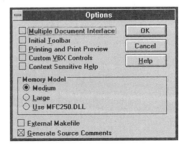

☐ Click the OK button of the Options dialog box and then click the OK button of the AppWizard dialog box and finally click the Create button of the New Application Information dialog box.

AppWizard responds by creating the TEST project and all the skeleton files of the TEST application.

To remove the debug options of the project (so that you'll have a small EXE file):

☐ Select Project from the Options menu of Visual C++, click the Release radio button, and then click the OK button of the dialog box.

Removing the View Class that AppWizard Created

The easiest way to place objects in the main window of the application is to design a dialog box with App Studio, create a class for this dialog box, and then set the view class of the application to the class of the dialog box.

Before you create the new view class, remove the current view class:

☐ Use the Windows File Manager (or DOS Shell) to delete the two view class files of the TEST application:

Delete C:\VCPROG\PRACTICE\CH12\TEST\TESTVIEW.CPP.
Delete C:\VCPROG\PRACTICE\CH12\TEST\TESTVIEW.H.

☐ Select ClassWizard from the Browse menu of Visual C++.

ClassWizard responds by displaying a dialog box informing you that the files of the view class do not exist (see Figure 12.6).

Figure 12.6.
ClassWizard informs you that the view class files are missing.

☐ Click the OK button of the dialog box.

ClassWizard responds by displaying the Repair Class Information dialog box (see Figure 12.7).

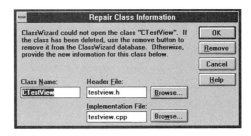

Figure 12.7.
The Repair Class
Information
dialog box.

☐ Click the Remove button of the Repair Class Information dialog box.

> *ClassWizard responds by removing the view class from the application and by displaying the main dialog box of ClassWizard.*

☐ Click the OK button of ClassWizard's dialog box.

You've just finished removing the view class of the TEST application.

In the following sections you'll create a dialog box, you'll create a class for this dialog box, and you'll make this class the new view class of the application.

Creating a New View Class for the Application

In the preceding steps, you deleted the view class of the application. Now you will create a new view class for the application. This new view class will be connected to a dialog box that you'll design by yourself with App Studio. As a result, the dialog box you'll design will become the main window of the application.

What class can be connected to a dialog box and then serve as the view class of your application? This class is called CFormView.

In the following steps, you'll design a dialog box, and then you'll connect this dialog box to a class derived from CFormView.

Designing the Dialog Box

Designing the dialog box that will serve as the main window of the application is as easy as designing a regular dialog box (that is, you use App Studio). The only difference is that you have to set some of the properties settings of the dialog box in a special way.

Follow these steps to create a new dialog box and to set its properties settings:

☐ Select App Studio from the Tools menu of Visual C++.

☐ Create a new dialog box with App Studio. (That is, highlight Menu in the Type list, click the New button, and then click the OK button from the New Recourse dialog box that pops up.)

☐ Double-click in a free area of the new dialog box.

App Studio responds by displaying the Properties window of the dialog box (see Figure 12.8).

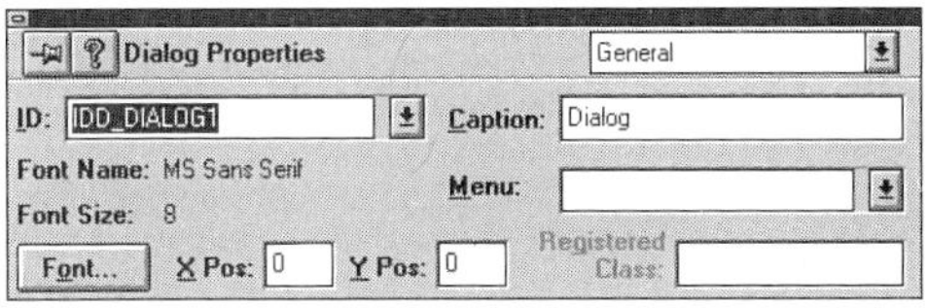

Figure 12.8.
The Properties
window of the new
dialog box.

As shown in Figure 12.8, the drop-down list box that appears in the upper-right corner of the Properties windows is currently set to General. Now you'll set this drop-down list to Styles.

☐ Select Styles from the drop-down list box that is located at the upper-right corner of the Properties window.

App Studio responds by displaying the Styles properties of the dialog box.

☐ Select Child in the Style box.

☐ Select None in the Border box.

☐ Uncheck the Visible property (that is, remove the check mark from the Visible check box).

Now the Styles properties of the dialog box looks as shown in Figure 12.9.

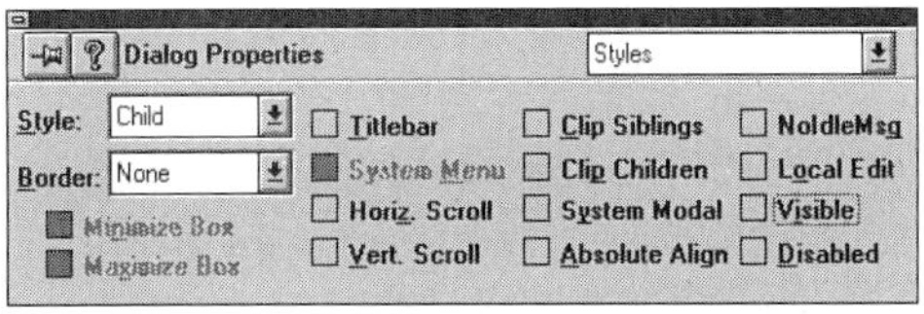

Figure 12.9.
Setting the styles of
the dialog box.

☐ Select General from the drop-down list box at the upper-right corner of the Properties window and make sure that the Caption box is empty.

You've finished setting the special settings for the dialog box. These settings are necessary because the dialog box will serve as the main window of the application (that is, it isn't a regular dialog box).

Next, you'll connect the dialog box to a class derived from CFormView.

Connecting the Dialog Box to a Class Derived from *CFormView*

Now you'll connect the dialog box that you designed to a class derived from CFormView. This class will be the view class of the application. As a result, the main window of the application will be your dialog box.

So here is how you connect the dialog box to a class derived from CFormView:

☐ Select ClassWizard from the Resource menu of App Studio.

> *ClassWizard responds by displaying the Add Class dialog box as shown in Figure 12.10.*

Figure 12.10.
The Add Class
dialog box.

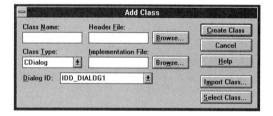

☐ Type CTestView in the Class Name box

NOTE

It's important that you name the class CTestView, because this was the original name of the view class of the application. This way, you will not have to alter any files of the application that refer to the view class name. Also, by naming the new view class with the "regular" view class name, you avoid confusing this class with other classes. That is, in the future you will always be able to tell that CTestView is the view class of the application.

Note that if you don't name the class CTestView, you'll get many compiling errors.

☐ Set the Class Type to `CFormView`.

> **NOTE**
>
> Typically, new users of Visual C++ forget to set the Class Type to `CFormView`.
>
> Note that if you don't set Class Type to `CFormView`, you'll get many compiling errors.

Now your Add Class dialog box looks as shown in Figure 12.11.

Figure 12.11.
Adding a new class.

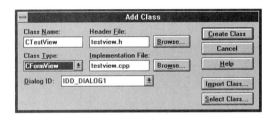

☐ Click the Create Class button.

ClassWizard responds by creating the new class and by displaying ClassWizard's main window.

☐ Click the OK button of ClassWizard's window to go back to App Studio.

You have finished creating the new view class of the application. This view class is a derived class from the MFC `CFormView` class and is connected to the dialog box you designed. Thus, the main window of the application will be the dialog box you designed.

The Visual Implementation of the Dialog Box

Now you can visually design the dialog box.

☐ Delete the OK button and the Cancel button.

☐ Place an edit box and two push buttons in the dialog box as shown in Figure 12.1.

> **NOTE**
>
> Before you place the first control, don't forget to place a push button and then delete the push button so that the first control won't have the same ID number as the ID number of the dialog box. (See the discussion in the *Problem When Placing the First Control in the Dialog Box* section of Chapter 7, "Designing Your First Dialog Box.") As mentioned in Chapter 7, this problem doesn't exist in later versions of Visual C++.

☐ Use ClassWizard to connect the edit box to a CString variable. Name the variable _MyEditBox.

☐ Set the Caption property of the first button to &Test.

☐ Set the ID of the first button to IDC_TEST_BUTTON.

☐ Set the Caption property of the second button to &Clear.

☐ Set the ID of the second button to IDC_CLEAR_BUTTON.

Now your dialog box looks as shown in Figure 12.12.

Figure 12.12.
The Test
application's
dialog box.

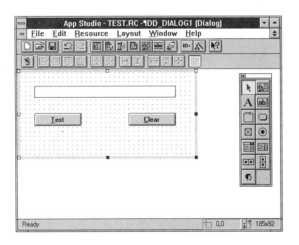

☐ To save your work, select Save from the File menu of App Studio.

You have finished designing the dialog box!

The Visual Implementation of the Menu

The TEST application should have a menu as shown in Figures 12.1, 12.2, and 12.3. The following text illustrates how to implement this menu.

☐ Use App Studio to implement the menu of the TEST application per Table 12.1.

Table 12.1. The menu of the TEST application.
Figures relating to menu: 12.1, 12.2, 12.3

Menu Item
&File
E&xit
&Test
&Clear
Current &Value...
&Help
&About TEST...

NOTE

This note applies only if you're using Visual C++ Version 1.0. (If you're using a later version of Visual C++, disregard this note).

When you implement the menu in Version 1.0, you have to associate the application's menu with the new view class (CTestView) you created.

While the menu is displayed in design mode in App Studio, select ClassWizard from the Resource menu.

ClassWizard responds by displaying the Select Class dialog box that asks you to select a class to be associated with the menu (see Figure 12.13).

Select the CTestView class and then click the OK button.

ClassWizard responds by associating the CTestView class with the menu and by displaying ClassWizard's main window.

Click the OK button of ClassWizard to go back to App Studio.

As stated, if you are using a later version of Visual C++, you don't have to perform the preceding steps.

Figure 12.13.
The Select Class
dialog box
(Version 1.0).

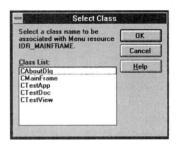

To save your work:

☐ Select Save from the File menu of App Studio.

The TEST application's visual implementation is complete.

Executing the TEST Application

Although you haven't completed writing the TEST application, execute it and see what you have accomplished so far.

☐ Select Rebuild All TEST.EXE from the Project menu of Visual C++.

   Visual C++ responds by compiling and linking the TEST application.

To execute the TEST.EXE application:

☐ Select Execute TEST.EXE from the Project menu.

   Visual C++ responds by executing the TEST application. As you can see, the
   dialog box you designed appears as the main window of the application (see
   Figure 12.1).

Of course, when you click the Test and Clear buttons, nothing happens because you haven't attached code to these buttons.

The Test and Clear menu items of the File popup menu are dimmed (unavailable) because you haven't attached any code to them.

To terminate the TEST application:

☐ Select Exit from the File menu.

Attaching Code to the Test Button

Recall that when the user clicks the Test button, the TEST application should display the text, "THIS IS A TEST," in the Edit box.

Follow these steps to attach code to the Test button:

☐ Use ClassWizard to add a function for the event:

Class Name:	CTestView
Object ID:	IDC_TEST_BUTTON
Message:	BN_CLICKED
Function Name:	OnTestButton()

Don't forget to set the Class Name to CTestView.

NOTE

The function you just added is a member function of the view class (the CTestView class). Recall that in previous chapters, the function you added to a button was a member function of the dialog box class (for example, CMyDlg). However, in the TEST application, there is no dialog box class.

NOTE

In Visual C++ version 1.0, ClassWizard suggests the name OnClickedTestButton().

☐ Edit the OnTestButton() function that you added to the TESTVIEW.CPP file. After editing the function, your OnTestButton() function should look as follows:

```
void CTestView::OnTestButton()
{
// TODO: Add your control notification handler code here

      /////////////////////////
      // MY CODE STARTS HERE
      /////////////////////////
```

```
// Fill the edit box with text.
m_MyEditBox = "THIS IS A TEST";
UpdateData(FALSE);

//////////////////////
// MY CODE ENDS HERE
//////////////////////

}
```

To review the code that you just typed:

The first statement,

```
m_MyEditBox = "THIS IS A TEST";
```

fills the variable of the edit box with the string "THIS IS A TEST." Recall that you connected the variable m_MyEditBox to the edit box during the visual implementation of the dialog box.

The next statement,

```
UpdateData(FALSE);
```

transfers the contents of the m_MyEditBox variable to the edit box (that is, to the screen).

Attaching Code to the Clear Button

Recall that when the user clicks the Clear button, the TEST application should clear the text in the Edit box.

Follow these steps to attach code to the Clear button:

☐ Use ClassWizard to add a function for the event:

Class Name:	CTestView
Object ID:	IDC_CLEAR_BUTTON
Message:	BN_CLICKED
Function Name:	OnClearButton()

☐ Edit the OnClearButton() function that you added to the TESTVIEW.CPP file. After editing the function, your OnClearButton() function should look as follows:

```
void CTestView::OnClearButton()
{
// TODO: Add your control notification handler code here
```

```
///////////////////////
// MY CODE STARTS HERE
///////////////////////

// Fill the edit box with null.
m_MyEditBox = "";
UpdateData(FALSE);

///////////////////////
// MY CODE ENDS HERE
///////////////////////
}
```

As you can see, the code of the OnClearButton() is similar to the code of the OnTestButton(). The only difference is that the m_MyEditBox variable is filled with the following null string:

```
m_MyEditBox = "";
UpdateData(FALSE);
```

This clears the contents of the edit box.

Attaching Code to the Test Menu Item

Recall that when the user selects Test from the File menu, the TEST application should do exactly as it does when the user clicks the Test button (that is, display the text, "THIS IS A TEST," in the edit box).

Follow these steps to attach code to the Test menu item:

☐ Use ClassWizard to add a function for the event:

Class Name:	CTestView
Object ID:	ID_FILE_TEST
Message:	COMMAND
Function Name:	OnFileTest()

NOTE

In the preceding step you were instructed to use ClassWizard to add the OnFileTest() function in the class CTestView for the ID_FILE_TEST menu item. If you start ClassWizard from the Browse menu of Visual C++ and don't see the ID_FILE_TEST item in the Object IDs list, do the following:

Select App Studio from the Tools menu, select the menu of the application in App Studio's window, and then select ClassWizard from the Resource menu of App Studio.

Typically, new users of Visual C++ add the function to the wrong class. Remember, you're instructed to add the function to the CTestView class. That is, set Class Name to CTestView.

☐ Edit the OnFileTest() function that you added to the TESTVIEW.CPP file. After editing the function, your OnFileTest() function should look as follows:

```
void CTestView::OnFileTest()
{
// TODO: Add your command handler code here

        /////////////////////////
        // MY CODE STARTS HERE
        /////////////////////////

        OnTestButton();

        /////////////////////////
        // MY CODE ENDS HERE
        /////////////////////////

}
```

As you can see, the code of the OnFileTest() function is simple. It executes the OnTestButton() function:

```
OnTestButton();
```

Thus, selecting Test from the File menu has the same effect as clicking the Test button. Of course, OnTestButton() is accessible from within the OnFileTest() function, because both functions are member functions of the CTestView class.

Attaching Code to the Clear Menu Item

Recall that when the user selects Clear from the File menu, the TEST application should do exactly as it does when the user clicks the Clear button (that is, clear the contents of the edit box).

Follow these steps to attach code to the Clear menu item:

☐ Use ClassWizard to add a function for the event:

Class Name:	CTestView
Object ID:	ID_FILE_CLEAR
Message:	COMMAND
Function Name:	OnFileClear()

☐ Note that in the preceding, you're instructed to add a function to the CTestView class. So make sure to set Class Name in the ClassWizard window to CTestView. If you don't see this event in the Message list, access ClassWizard from the Resources menu of App Studio.

☐ Edit the OnFileClear() function that you added to the TESTVIEW.CPP file. After you edit the function, your OnFileClear() function looks as follows:

```
void CTestView::OnFileClear()
{
    // TODO: Add your command handler code here


    /////////////////////////
    // MY CODE STARTS HERE
    /////////////////////////

    OnClearButton();

    /////////////////////////
    // MY CODE ENDS HERE
    /////////////////////////

}
```

As you can see, the code of the OnFileClear() function executes the OnClearButton() function:

```
OnClearButton();
```

Thus, selecting Clear from the File menu has the same effect as clicking the Clear button.

Attaching Code to the Current Value Menu Item

Recall that when the user selects Current Value from the File menu, the TEST application should display a message box with the current value of m_MyEditBox.

Follow these steps to attach code to the Current Value menu item:

☐ Use ClassWizard to add a function for the event:

Class Name:	CTestView
Object ID:	ID_FILE_CURRENTVALUE
Message:	COMMAND
Function Name:	OnFileCurrentvalue()

☐ Note that in the preceding, you were instructed to add the function to the CTestView class. So make sure to set Class Name in the window of ClassWizard to CTestView. If you don't see this event in the Message list, access ClassWizard from the Resources menu of App Studio.

☐ Edit the OnFileCurrentvalue() function that you added to the TESTVIEW.CPP file. After you edit the function, your OnFileCurrentvalue() function looks as follows:

```
void CTestView::OnFileCurrentvalue()
{
        // TODO: Add your command handler code here

        /////////////////////////
        // MY CODE STARTS HERE
        /////////////////////////

        // Display the current contents of the edit box.
        UpdateData(TRUE);
        MessageBox("Current value of m_MyEditBox = "
                        + m_MyEditBox);

        /////////////////////////
        // MY CODE ENDS HERE
        /////////////////////////

}
```

The first statement of the OnFileCurrentvalue() function

```
UpdateData(TRUE);
```

updates the variables of the controls (m_MyEditBox) with the current values displayed in the controls.

The next statement,

```
MessageBox("Current value of m_MyEditBox = "+ m_MyEditBox;
```

displays the contents of the `m_MyEditBox` variable (that is, the current contents of the edit box).

Don't forget to save your work:

☐ Select Save from the File menu.

Executing the Finished TEST Application

To see the code you attached to the buttons and to the menu items of the TEST application:

☐ Select Rebuild All TEST.EXE from the Project menu of Visual C++.

☐ Execute the TEST application.

☐ Experiment with the buttons and menu items of the application.

When you click the Test button (or select Test from the File menu), the text, "THIS IS A TEST," appears in the edit box, and when you click the Clear button (or select Clear from the File menu), the edit box is cleared. When you select Current Value from the File menu, the current contents of the edit box are displayed in a message box.

13

Using Serialization to Write and Read Data to and from Files

So far, you've written applications that you
can use to display and edit data on-screen,
but none of these applications save the data.
For example, you can type data into edit
boxes, set check boxes, and set radio
buttons, but all the data you've entered
is gone forever once you terminate
the application.

In this chapter you'll write an application to edit data and save it in a file. Then the user can quit the application and load the saved data the next time the application is run. As you'll see soon, writing an application that reads and writes data to the disk is quite easy with Visual C++.

In this chapter you'll also learn how to use the document class for storing the application's data. That is, in the applications you wrote in previous chapters, you wrote code only in the application's view class files. In this chapter you'll learn how to separate the document class from the view class, you'll use the document class to store the application's data, and you'll use the view class for viewing (displaying) the document's data.

At the end of the chapter you'll learn how to use App Studio to modify the application's string table so that changes are made to the application's default characteristics, such as the title of the application's main window.

The MEMO Application

Now you'll write the MEMO application, an example of an application that reads and writes data to the disk.

Before you start writing the MEMO application, execute it. A copy of this application resides in your `C:\VCPROG\ORIGINAL\CH13\MEMO` directory.

To execute the MEMO application:

☐ In Windows, select Run from the Program Manager's File menu.

Windows responds by displaying the Run dialog box.

☐ Type `C:\vcProg\Original\CH13\MEMO\MEMO.EXE` in the Command Line box and then click the OK button.

Windows responds by executing the MEMO application. The main window of `MEMO.EXE` *looks as in Figure 13.1.*

As you can see from Figure 13.1, the main window of the application displays a blank memo form ready for typing. The title of the window is `Memo for Windows - Untitled`.

The MEMO application has two popup menus, File and Help. These popup menus are shown in Figures 13.2 and 13.3.

Figure 13.1.
The MEMO
application's
main window.

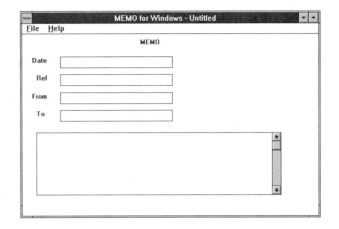

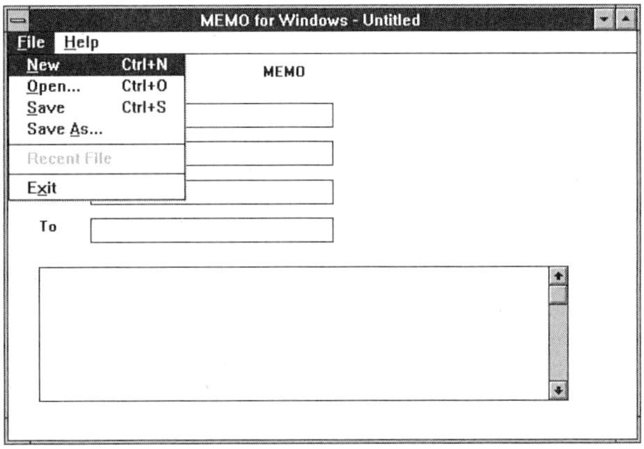

Figure 13.2.
The MEMO
application's File
popup menu.

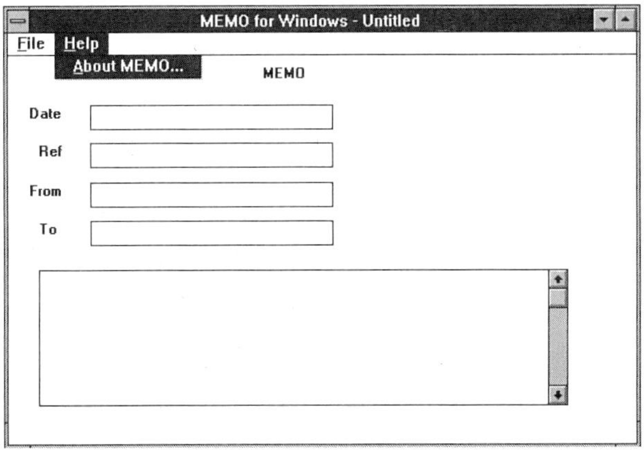

Figure 13.3.
The MEMO
application's Help
popup menu.

☐ Fill the memo's blank fields. Figure 13.4 shows the memo form after it's completed.

Figure 13.4.
A completed
memo form.

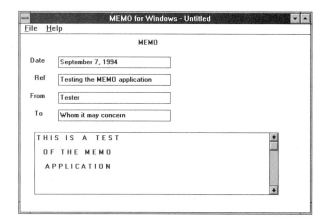

☐ Select Save from the MEMO application's File menu.

> *The MEMO application responds by displaying the File Save As dialog box (see Figure 13.5).*

Figure 13.5.
The MEMO
application's File
Save As dialog box.

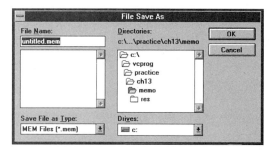

☐ Save the file as TRY.MEM (the default filename is untitled.mem, so change it to TRY.MEM and then click the OK button).

> *The MEMO application responds by saving your memo in the file TRY.MEM and changing the window's title to* Memo for Windows - TRY.MEM.

To verify that indeed your memo is saved in the file TRY.MEM:

☐ Exit the MEMO application.

☐ Execute the MEMO application again.

☐ Select Open from the MEMO application's File menu.

The MEMO application responds by displaying the File Open dialog box (see Figure 13.6).

Figure 13.6.
The MEMO
application's File
Open dialog box.

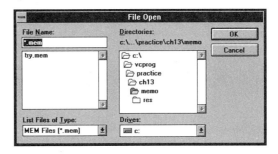

☐ Select the file TRY.MEM.

The MEMO application responds by displaying the TRY.MEM memo file on the screen.

Experiment with the other menu items of the File menu (New and Save As). As you can see, all the File menu items behave as you would expect them to behave in a standard Windows application.

To exit from the MEMO application:

☐ Select Exit from the File menu.

Now that you know what the MEMO application should do, you can start writing it.

Creating the Project of the MEMO Application

To create the project of the MEMO application:

☐ Select AppWizard from the Project menu.

Visual C++ responds by running AppWizard.

☐ Use the Directory list box to select the directory C:\VCPROG\PRACTICE\CH13.

□ Type memo in the Project Name box.

Now your AppWizard dialog box looks as shown in Figure 13.7.

Figure 13.7.
The AppWizard
dialog box for
the MEMO
application.

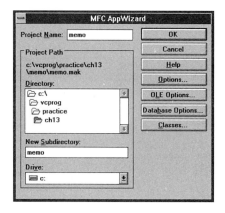

□ Click the Options button and set the options as shown in Figure 13.8 (that is, uncheck all the check boxes except the Generate Source Comments check box).

Figure 13.8.
Setting the options
for the MEMO
application.

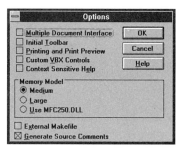

□ Click the OK button of the Options dialog box and then click the OK button of the AppWizard dialog box and finally click the Create button of the New Application Information dialog box.

AppWizard responds by creating the MEMO project and all the skeleton files of the MEMO application.

To remove the debug options of the project (so that you'll have a small EXE file):

□ Select Project from Visual C++'s Options menu, click the Release radio button, and then click the OK button of the dialog box.

Creating the Application's Form

As shown in Figure 13.1, the main window of the MEMO application should contain a data entry form for a memo.

To implement this form, you will replace the current view class of the application with a new view class derived from the CFormView class (just as you did in Chapter 12, "Placing Controls Inside the Main Window").

Follow these steps to create the application's form:

☐ Use the Windows File Manager (or DOS Shell) to delete the two files of the MEMO application's view class:

Delete C:\VCPROG\PRACTICE\CH13\MEMO\MEMOVIEW.CPP.
Delete C:\VCPROG\PRACTICE\CH13\MEMO\MEMOVIEW.H.

☐ Select ClassWizard from Visual C ++'s Browse menu.

ClassWizard responds by displaying a dialog box that indicates the files in the view class don't exist.

☐ Click the dialog box's OK button.

☐ Click the Remove button of the Repair Class Information dialog box.

☐ Click the OK button of ClassWizard's dialog box.

You've just finished removing the view class of the MEMO application.

In the following steps, you'll create a dialog box, create a CFormView type class for this dialog box, and make this class the new view class of the application:

☐ Select App Studio from the Tools menu of Visual C++.

☐ Create a new dialog box with App Studio.

☐ Double-click in a free area of the new dialog box.

☐ Select Styles from the drop-down list box at the upper-right corner of the Properties window.

Set the Styles properties of the dialog box as follows:

☐ Select Child in the Style box.

☐ Select None in the Border box.

☐ Uncheck the Visible property (that is, remove the check mark from the Visible check box).

☐ Select General from the drop-down list box at the upper-right corner of the Properties window and make sure that the Caption box is empty.

Now, connect the dialog box to a class derived from `CFormView`:

☐ Select ClassWizard from the Resource menu of App Studio.

ClassWizard responds by displaying the Add Class dialog box.

☐ Type `CMemoView` in the Class Name box.

☐ Set the Class Type to `CFormView`.

☐ Click the Create Class button.

☐ Make sure that the Header File box is filled with `memoview.h` and that the Implementation File box is filled with `memoview.cpp`.

☐ Click the OK button in ClassWizard's window to go back to App Studio.

You've finished creating the new view class of the application. This view class is a derived class from the MFC `CFormView` class and is connected to the dialog box you created. Thus, the main window of the application will be the dialog box that you created.

The Visual Implementation of the Dialog Box

☐ Implement the dialog box of the MEMO application per Table 13.1.

Table 13.1. The dialog box of the MEMO application.

Class Name:	`CMemoView`
Figure:	13.1
OK button:	No
Cancel button:	No

Object	Property	Setting
Dialog Box	ID	`IDD_DIALOG1`
Label	ID	`IDC_STATIC`
	Caption	`MEMO`
Label	ID	`IDC_STATIC`
	Caption	Date
Edit Box	ID	`IDC_DATE`
	Variable	`m_Date`
	Type	`CString`

Object	Property	Setting
Label	ID	`IDC_STATIC`
	Caption	`Ref`
Edit Box	ID	`IDC_REF`
	Variable	`m_Ref`
	Type	`CString`
Label	ID	`IDC_STATIC`
	Caption	`From`
Edit Box	ID	`IDC_FROM`
	Variable	`m_From`
	Type	`CString`
Label	ID	`IDC_STATIC`
	Caption	`To`
Edit Box	ID	`IDC_TO`
	Variable	`m_To`
	Type	`CString`
Edit Box	ID	`IDC_MEMO`
	Variable	`m_Memo`
	Type	`CString`

Now your dialog box looks as shown in Figure 13.9.

Figure 13.9.
The dialog box
of the MEMO
application.

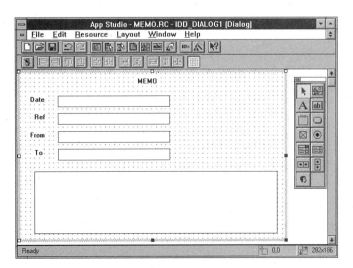

Save your work:

☐ Select Save from the File menu of App Studio.

You've finished designing the dialog box.

The Visual Implementation of the Menu

The MEMO application should have a menu, as shown in Figures 13.1, 13.2, and 13.3.

Implementing this menu is easy, because all you have to do is delete the Edit popup menu. The File popup menu and Help popup menu that AppWizard generated for you are exactly what you need for the MEMO application.

☐ Use App Studio to delete the Edit popup of the menu.

To save your work:

☐ Select Save from the File menu of App Studio.

The visual implementation of the MEMO application's menu is completed.

Executing the MEMO Application

Even though you haven't finished writing the MEMO application yet, try executing it to see what you've accomplished so far.

☐ Compile and link the MEMO application.

To execute the MEMO.EXE application:

☐ Select Execute MEMO.EXE from the Project menu.

> *Visual C++ responds by executing the MEMO application. As you can see, the dialog box you designed appears as the main window of the application (see Figure 13.1).*

Experiment with the memo form:

☐ Type something in the Date, Ref, From, and To fields. Note that you can move from one field to another by pressing the Tab key.

☐ Type something in the memo edit box (the large edit box at the bottom of the form) and then try to press the Enter key.

As you can see, there's a small problem when the cursor is in the memo edit box. When you press the Enter key, nothing happens. That is, the keyboard cursor doesn't move to the next line in the edit box as it should. The following section describes the solution to this problem.

To exit the MEMO application:

☐ Select Exit from the File menu.

NOTE

Although you haven't written any code for opening and saving memo files, the menu items of the File menu have some functionality. For example, if you select Open from the File menu, a File Open dialog box appears. Of course, when you select a file, it isn't loaded, because you haven't written code to accomplish that.

Be careful with the Save and Save As menu items. Even though you haven't written code for the Save and Save As menu items, they write data to the disk. For example, if you have a file TRY.TXT that has some data in it and you select TRY.TXT from Save As in the File menu, the original TRY.TXT is overwritten by a new, blank TRY.TXT.

Changing the Properties of the Memo Edit Box

As you've just seen, when you press the Enter key while your cursor is in the memo edit box, nothing happens. You have to change the properties of the memo edit box so that when you press the Enter key, a carriage return is inserted in the edit box.

☐ Start App Studio.

☐ Open the IDD_DIALOG1 dialog box.

☐ Double-click in the IDC_MEMO edit box.

☐ Select Styles from the drop-down list box at the upper-right corner of the Properties window.

Set the Styles properties of the IDC_MEMO edit box as follows:

☐ Place a check mark in the Multiline check box.

☐ Place a check mark in the Want Return check box.

☐ Place a check mark in the Vert. Scroll check box (this will provide the edit box with a vertical scroll bar).

☐ Now the Style properties window of your IDC_MEMO edit box looks as in Figure 13.10.

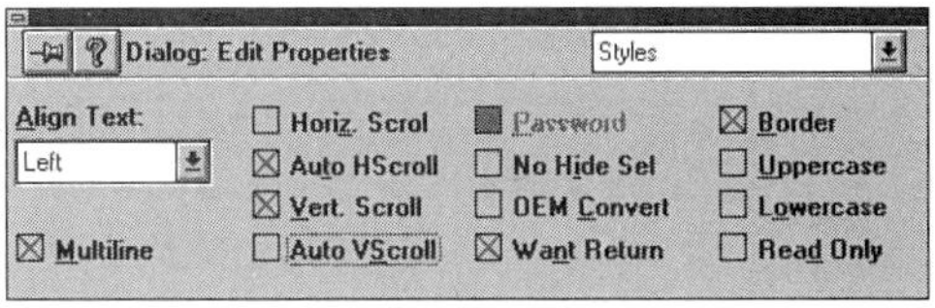

Figure 13.10.
Setting the Style
properties of
the IDC_MEMO
edit box.

Save your work:

☐ Select Save from the File menu of App Studio.

To see the effects of these settings on the program:

☐ Switch back to Visual C++.

☐ Compile and link the MEMO application.

☐ Select Execute MEMO.EXE from the Project menu.

Experiment with the memo edit box. As you can see, when you press the Enter key when the cursor is in the memo edit box, the program responds by inserting a carriage return in the edit box, which moves the keyboard cursor to the next line.

To terminate the MEMO application:

☐ Select Exit from the File menu.

The Document Class of the MEMO Application

In a well organized Visual C++ application, the document class is used to hold the application's data, and the view class is used to display the data and to enable the user to edit it.

In all the applications that you've written so far (except Chapter 5, "Storing Variables in the Document Class"), you haven't stored any data in the document class. The MEMO application illustrates how you can use the document class for storing the application's data.

As you'll soon see, storing the data of the application in the document class is useful, because it enables you to read and write data into files easily.

Recall that during the visual implementation of the dialog box you created five variables:

m_Date	(the variable for the IDC_DATE edit box)
m_Ref	(the variable for the IDC_REF edit box)
m_From	(the variable for the IDC_FROM edit box)
m_To	(the variable for the IDC_TO edit box)
m_Memo	(the variable for the IDC_MEMO edit box)

Because you connected the dialog box to the view class of the application, these variables are data members of the view class.

Now add five data members to the document class. These variables should have the same names as the five data members of the view class. The document class of the MEMO application is CMemoDoc, and the declaration of this class is inside the header file MEMODOC.H.

☐ Open the file MEMODOC.H and add code to it that defines the five variables (m_Date, m_Ref, m_From, m_To, and m_Memo) as public data members of the CMemoDoc class. Declare each of these variables as type CString. After you write this code, the CMemoDoc class declaration looks as follows:

```
class CMemoDoc : public CDocument
{
protected: // create from serialization only
    CMemoDoc();
    DECLARE_DYNCREATE(CMemoDoc)

// Attributes
public:

    /////////////////////////
    // MY CODE STARTS HERE
    /////////////////////////

    CString m_Date;
    CString m_Ref;
    CString m_From;
    CString m_To;
    CString m_Memo;

    /////////////////////////
    // MY CODE ENDS HERE
    /////////////////////////
```

```
// Operations
public:

// Implementation
public:
    virtual ~CMemoDoc();
    virtual void Serialize(CArchive& ar);
// overridden for document i/o
#ifdef _DEBUG
    virtual void AssertValid() const;
    virtual void Dump(CDumpContext& dc) const;
#endif

protected:
    virtual BOOL OnNewDocument();

// Generated message map functions
protected:
    //{{AFX_MSG(CMemoDoc)
// NOTE - the ClassWizard will add and remove
// member functions here.
//    DO NOT EDIT what you see in these
// blocks of generated code !
    //}}AFX_MSG
    DECLARE_MESSAGE_MAP()
};
```

Save your work:

☐ Select Save from the File menu of Visual C++.

You've finished declaring the data members of the document class. Next, you will initialize these variables.

Initializing the Data Members of the Document Class

When the user starts the application or selects New from the File menu, the data members of the document class should be initialized to null. Why? Because whenever a new memo is created, you want it to be blank (see Figure 13.1).

The document class has a member function called OnNewDocument(). Whenever a new document is created (when either the application begins or the user selects New from the File menu), this member function is executed automatically. Thus, the code that initializes the data members of the document class should be written inside this function.

☐ Open the file MEMODOC.CPP and edit the OnNewDocument() function as follows:

```
BOOL CMemoDoc::OnNewDocument()
{
    if (!CDocument::OnNewDocument())
        return FALSE;

    // TODO: add reinitialization code here
    // (SDI documents will reuse this document)

    /////////////////////////
    // MY CODE STARTS HERE
    /////////////////////////

    // Make the memo blank.
    m_Date = "";
    m_Ref  = "";
    m_From = "";
    m_To   = "";
    m_Memo = "";

    /////////////////////////
    // MY CODE ENDS HERE
    /////////////////////////


    return TRUE;
}
```

The code that you just added to the OnNewDocument() function assigns null strings to the five data members of the document class. Thus, when the user starts the application or selects New from the File menu, the five data members of the document class are initialized to null.

Of course, you can initialize the variables to any other value. For example, you can write code that retrieves today's date and then stores this value in the m_Date data member.

To save your work:

☐ Select Save from Visual C++'s File menu.

Initializing the Data Members of the View Class

The code that you wrote in the OnNewDocument() member function of the document class initializes the data members of the document class. But what about the data members of the view class? After all, they're important because they represent what the user sees (views) on the screen. You need to initialize the data members of the view class inside the `OnInitialUpdate()` member function of the view class.

The `OnInitialUpdate()` member function of the view class is executed automatically:

- On starting the application
- When the user selects New from the File menu
- When the user selects Open from the File menu

The code that you write in the `OnInitialUpdate()` function updates the data members of the view class with the current values of the data members of the document class. Thus, whenever the user starts the application, creates a new memo file, or opens an existing memo file, the data members of the view class are updated with data members of the document class.

Visual C++ didn't write the declaration and skeleton of the `OnInitialUpdate()` function. Instead of depending on Visual C++, you have to declare this function and write its skeleton. Here's how you do that:

☐ Open the file MEMOVIEW.H and add code to it that defines the function `OnInitialUpdate()` as a member function of the `CMemoView` class. After you write this code, the `CMemoView` class declaration looks as follows:

```
class CMemoView : public CFormView
{
    DECLARE_DYNCREATE(CMemoView)
protected:
    CMemoView();
// protected constructor used by dynamic creation


    /////////////////////////
    // MY CODE STARTS HERE
    /////////////////////////

    virtual void OnInitialUpdate();

    /////////////////////////
    // MY CODE ENDS HERE
    /////////////////////////


// Form Data
public:
    //{{AFX_DATA(CMemoView)
    enum { IDD = IDD_DIALOG1 };
```

```
        CString     m_Date;
        CString     m_Ref;
        CString     m_From;
        CString     m_To;
        CString     m_Memo;
        //}}AFX_DATA

// Attributes
public:

// Operations
public:

// Implementation
protected:
        virtual ~CMemoView();
        virtual void DoDataExchange(CDataExchange* pDX);
// DDX/DDV support
        // Generated message map functions
        //{{AFX_MSG(CMemoView)
// NOTE - the ClassWizard will add and remove member
// functions here.
        //}}AFX_MSG
        DECLARE_MESSAGE_MAP()
};
```

Now write the `OnInitialUpdate()` function's code:

☐ Open the file `MEMOVIEW.CPP` and add the `OnInitialUpdate()` function to the
end of the file so that it looks as follows:

```
/////////////////////////////////////////////////////
// CMemoView message handlers

//////////////////////////
// MY CODE STARTS HERE
//////////////////////////

void CMemoView::OnInitialUpdate()
{

  // Get a pointer to the document.
  CMemoDoc* pDoc = (CMemoDoc*) GetDocument();

  // Update the data members of the view class with the
  // current values of the data members of document class.
  m_Date = pDoc->m_Date;
  m_Ref   = pDoc->m_Ref;
  m_From = pDoc->m_From;
  m_To    = pDoc->m_To;
  m_Memo = pDoc->m_Memo;
```

```
   // Update the screen with the new values of the variables.
   UpdateData(FALSE);

}

/////////////////////
// MY CODE ENDS HERE
/////////////////////
```

The following text reviews the code for the OnInitialUpdate() function:

The first statement,

```
CMemoDoc* pDoc = (CMemoDoc*) GetDocument();
```

extracts pDoc (the pointer for the document class).

Then the data members of the view class are updated with the current values of the document:

```
m_Date = pDoc->m_Date;
m_Ref  = pDoc->m_Ref;
m_From = pDoc->m_From;
m_To   = pDoc->m_To;
m_Memo = pDoc->m_Memo;
```

Finally, the UpdateData() function is used to transfer the new values of the variables to the screen:

```
UpdateData(FALSE);
```

If you try to compile the MEMOVIEW.CPP file now, you'll get a compiling error. Why? Because in this code you referred to the CMemoDoc class, but the CMemoDoc class isn't known in the MEMOVIEW.CPP file. Thus, you must #include MEMODOC.H (the header file of the CMemoDoc class) at the beginning of the MEMOVIEW.CPP file.

☐ Add the #include "memodoc.h" statement at the beginning of the MEMOVIEW.CPP file (immediately before the #include statement of the memoview.h file). After adding this #include statement, the beginning of the MEMOVIEW.CPP file looks as follows:

```
// memoview.cpp : implementation file
//

#include "stdafx.h"
#include "memo.h"
```

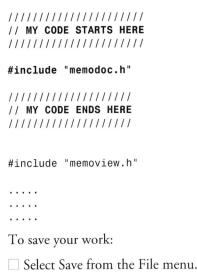
```
////////////////////
// MY CODE STARTS HERE
////////////////////

#include "memodoc.h"

////////////////////
// MY CODE ENDS HERE
////////////////////


#include "memoview.h"
```

. . . . .
. . . . .
. . . . .

To save your work:

☐ Select Save from the File menu.

So what have you accomplished so far? You wrote the code that initializes the data members of the document and the code that initializes the data members of the view class.

Updating the Data Members of the Document Class

Whenever the user edits the memo form of the application, the data members of the document class should be updated with the new values that the user types. For example, if the IDC_DATE edit box is currently empty, and the user types in it the character A, the data member m_Date of the document class should be updated with A.

Who's responsible for updating the data members of the document class? You! Whenever the user changes a data member of the view class, you have to update the corresponding data member in the document class with the new value.

In the MEMO application, the view class has five data members:

m_Date	The variable for the IDC_DATE edit box
m_Ref	The variable for the IDC_REF edit box
m_From	The variable for the IDC_FROM edit box
m_To	The variable for the IDC_TO edit box
m_Memo	The variable for the IDC_MEMO edit box

Whenever the user changes any of these variables (that is, when the user types something in an edit box), the application's code should update the corresponding data member in the document class. Here's how you do that:

☐ Use ClassWizard to add a function for the event:

Class Name:	CMemoView
Object ID:	IDC_DATE
Message:	EN_CHANGE
Function Name:	OnChangeDate()

> **NOTE**
>
> The message EN_CHANGE corresponds to the event, "User changed the contents of the edit box."
>
> Thus, whenever the user changes the IDC_DATE edit box, the OnChangeDate() function is executed automatically.

☐ Edit the OnChangeDate() function that you added to the MEMOVIEW.CPP file as follows:

```
void CMemoView::OnChangeDate()
{
// TODO: Add your control notification handler code here

    /////////////////////////
    // MY CODE STARTS HERE
    /////////////////////////

    // Update the variables of the controls with the current
    // values inside the controls.
    UpdateData(TRUE);

    // Get a pointer to the document.
    CMemoDoc* pDoc = (CMemoDoc*) GetDocument();

    // Update the m_Date data member of the document class.
    pDoc->m_Date = m_Date;

    // Set the Modified flag of the document class to TRUE.
    pDoc->SetModifiedFlag();
```

```
//////////////////////
// MY CODE ENDS HERE
//////////////////////
```

}

To review the code you just typed:

The first statement in the function,

```
UpdateData(TRUE);
```

updates the variables of the controls with the current values in the controls.

The next statement,

```
CMemoDoc* pDoc = (CMemoDoc*) GetDocument();
```

extracts pDoc (the pointer for the document class).

The next statement,

```
pDoc->m_Date = m_Date;
```

updates the m_Date data member of the document class with the new contents of the IDC_DATE edit box.

The last statement in the function is

```
pDoc->SetModifiedFlag();
```

This statement executes a member function of the document class called SetModifiedFlag(). The SetModifiedFlag() function sets the Modified flag in the document class to TRUE. This flag indicates that data has been changed by the user.

When the user saves the document (by selecting either Save or Save As from the File menu), the Modified flag is automatically set to FALSE. You don't have to write the code that sets the Modified flag to FALSE. This code is a gift from Visual C++.

If the Modified flag is set to TRUE and the user tries to quit the application or load a new file, the application displays a warning message informing the user that the file hasn't been saved. Again, you don't have to write the code that displays this warning message; it's a gift from Visual C++.

Putting it all together: whenever the user changes the IDC_DATE edit box, the OnChangeDate() function is executed. The code that you wrote in the OnChangeDate() function transfers the new contents of the edit box to the m_Date data member of the document class. In addition, the OnChangeDate() function sets a Modified flag in the document class to indicate that data has been changed by the user.

In a similar manner, you need to attach code to the other edit boxes of the memo form:

☐ Use ClassWizard to add a function for the event:

Class Name:	CMemoView
Object ID:	IDC_REF
Message:	EN_CHANGE
Function Name:	OnChangeRef()

☐ Edit the OnChangeRef() function that you added to the MEMOVIEW.CPP file. After you edit the OnChangeRef() function, it looks as follows:

```
void CMemoView::OnChangeRef()
{
// TODO: Add your control notification handler code here

    /////////////////////////
    // MY CODE STARTS HERE
    /////////////////////////

    // Update the variables of the controls with the current
    // values inside the controls.
    UpdateData(TRUE);

    // Get a pointer to the document.
    CMemoDoc* pDoc = (CMemoDoc*) GetDocument();

    // Update the m_Ref data member of the document class.
    pDoc->m_Ref = m_Ref;

    // Set the Modified flag of the document class to TRUE.
    pDoc->SetModifiedFlag();

    /////////////////////////
    // MY CODE ENDS HERE
    /////////////////////////

}
```

☐ Use ClassWizard to add a function for the event:

Class Name:	CMemoView
Object ID:	IDC_FROM
Message:	EN_CHANGE
Function Name:	OnChangeFrom()

☐ Edit the OnChangeFrom() function that you added to the MEMOVIEW.CPP file as
follows:

```
void CMemoView::OnChangeFrom()
{
// TODO: Add your control notification handler code here

    /////////////////////////
    // MY CODE STARTS HERE
    /////////////////////////

    // Update the variables of the controls with the current
    // values inside the controls.
    UpdateData(TRUE);

    // Get a pointer to the document.
    CMemoDoc* pDoc = (CMemoDoc*) GetDocument();

    // Update the m_From data member of the document class.
    pDoc->m_From = m_From;

    // Set the Modified flag of the document class to TRUE.
    pDoc->SetModifiedFlag();

    /////////////////////////
    // MY CODE ENDS HERE
    /////////////////////////

}
```

☐ Use ClassWizard to add a function for the event:

Class Name:	CMemoView
Object ID:	IDC_TO
Message:	EN_CHANGE
Function Name:	OnChangeTo()

☐ Edit the OnChangeTo() function that you added to the MEMOVIEW.CPP file.
After you edit the OnChangeTo() function, it looks as follows:

```
void CMemoView::OnChangeTo()
{
// TODO: Add your control notification handler code here

    /////////////////////////
    // MY CODE STARTS HERE
    /////////////////////////
```

```
    // Update the variables of the controls with the current
    // values inside the controls.
    UpdateData(TRUE);

    // Get a pointer to the document.
    CMemoDoc* pDoc = (CMemoDoc*) GetDocument();

    // Update the m_To data member of the document class.
    pDoc->m_To = m_To;

    // Set the Modified flag of the document class to TRUE.
    pDoc->SetModifiedFlag();

    /////////////////////////
    // MY CODE ENDS HERE
    /////////////////////////
}
```

☐ Use ClassWizard to add a function for the event:

Class Name:	CMemoView
Object ID:	IDC_MEMO
Message:	EN_CHANGE
Function Name:	OnChangeMemo()

☐ Edit the OnChangeMemo() function that you added to the MEMOVIEW.CPP file. After you edit the OnChangeMemo() function, it looks as follows:

```
void CMemoView::OnChangeMemo()
{
    // TODO: Add your control notification handler code here


    /////////////////////////
    // MY CODE STARTS HERE
    /////////////////////////

    // Update the variables of the controls with the current
    // values inside the controls.
    UpdateData(TRUE);

    // Get a pointer to the document.
    CMemoDoc* pDoc = (CMemoDoc*) GetDocument();

    // Update the m_Memo data member of the document class.
    pDoc->m_Memo = m_Memo;

    // Set the Modified flag of the document class to TRUE.
    pDoc->SetModifiedFlag();
```

```
///////////////////
// MY CODE ENDS HERE
///////////////////
```

}

You've finished attaching code to all the edit boxes of the memo form.

To save your work:

☐ Select Save from the File menu.

Review what you've accomplished so far:

1. You wrote the code that initializes the data members of the document class.

2. You wrote the code that initializes the data members of the view class.

3. You wrote the code that updates the data members of the document class whenever the user changes the data members of the view class (that is, whenever the user changes the contents of the memo form's edit boxes).

Next, you'll write the code that enables the user to write and read data to and from the disk.

> **NOTE**
>
> Okay, you wrote enough code! To make sure that you typed the correct code, compile/link the application:
>
> Select Build MEMO.EXE from the Project menu, and make sure there are no compiling/linking errors.
>
> Don't execute the application. The only reason that you're instructed to compile/link the program is to verify that you entered the code correctly.

Writing and Reading Data to and from Files

When the user selects Save or Save As from the File menu, the application ought to write the data members of the document class into a file. When the user selects Open from the File menu, the application ought to read the data from the file that the user selects and assign this data to the data members of the document class.

Accomplishing these tasks is easy. It's easy because most of the code that accomplishes these tasks has already been written by Visual C++.

The document class of the application (CMemoDoc) has a member function called Serialize(), which is executed automatically when the user selects Save, Save As, or Open from the File menu. All you have to do is customize the Serialize() function for the Memo application.

The Serialize() member function of the CMemoDoc class looks as follows:

```
/////////////////////////////////////////////////////////
// CMemoDoc serialization

void CMemoDoc::Serialize(CArchive& ar)
{
    if (ar.IsStoring())
    {
        // TODO: add storing code here
    }
    else
    {
        // TODO: add loading code here
    }
}
```

As you can see, the code in the Serialize() function consists of a simple if statement that checks for the condition

```
if (ar.IsStoring())
```

In this code, ar is the parameter of the Serialize() function and represents the archive (that is, the file) that you're trying to read (or write). If the user selects Save or Save As from the File menu, the condition of the if statement is satisfied and the code under the if is executed. If the user selects Open from the File menu, the condition of the if statement isn't satisfied, and the code under the else is executed.

Thus, your job is

1. To write the code that writes data to the file under the if.

2. To write the code that reads the data from the file under the else.

The code for writing and reading data to and from the file is easy to write. Follow these steps to write this code:

☐ Open the file MEMODOC.CPP and edit the Serialize() function. When you finish editing the Serialize() function, it looks as follows:

```
/////////////////////////////////////////////////////////
// CMemoDoc serialization

void CMemoDoc::Serialize(CArchive& ar)
{
     if (ar.IsStoring())
     {
          // TODO: add storing code here

          /////////////////////////
          // MY CODE STARTS HERE
          /////////////////////////

          // Write to the file.
          ar << m_Date;
          ar << m_Ref;
          ar << m_From;
          ar << m_To;
          ar << m_Memo;

          /////////////////////////
          // MY CODE ENDS HERE
          /////////////////////////

     }
     else
     {
          // TODO: add loading code here

          /////////////////////////
          // MY CODE STARTS HERE
          /////////////////////////

          // Read from the file.
          ar >> m_Date;
          ar >> m_Ref;
          ar >> m_From;
          ar >> m_To;
          ar >> m_Memo;

          /////////////////////////
          // MY CODE ENDS HERE
          /////////////////////////

     }
}
```

To review the code that you just typed:

The code that's responsible for saving the data in the file (the code under the if) is

```
ar << m_Date;
ar << m_Ref;
ar << m_From;
ar << m_To;
ar << m_Memo;
```

The insertion operator (<<) indicates that you want to save data in the file. For example, the statement

```
ar << m_Date;
```

stores the data member m_Date of the document class in the file. In what file? Well, it depends on what the user did. As mentioned before, the Serialize() member function of the document class is executed automatically whenever the user selects Open, Save, or Save As from the File menu. If, for example, the user selects Save As and then selects the file TRY.MEM from the Save As dialog box, the previous statement stores the m_Date variable in the TRY.MEM file. (So think of ar as the file that the user selected).

NOTE

ar is the archive object (an object of class CArchive) corresponding to the file that the user selected. The CArchive class will be discussed in more detail in Chapter 15, "Customizing Serialization."

The code that's responsible for loading the data from the file into the variables (the code under the else) is

```
ar >> m_Date;
ar >> m_Ref;
ar >> m_From;
ar >> m_To;
ar >> m_Memo;
```

The extractor operators (>>) indicate that you want to load data from the file into the variable. For example, the statement,

```
ar >> m_Date;
```

fills the data member `m_Date` of the document class with data from the file. From what file? Again, it depends on what the user did. If, for example, the user selects Open from the File menu and then the user selects the file `TRY.MEM` (from the Open File dialog box), the preceding statement fills the `m_Date` variable with data from the `TRY.MEM` file.

Note that the order in which you extract the data must be the same order used for saving the data. For example, if you save data to the file with these statements:

```
ar << Var1;
ar << Var2;
ar << Var3;
```

you must extract the data from the file into the variables in the same order:

```
ar >> Var1;
ar >> Var2;
ar >> var3;
```

NOTE

In the previous code you used the insertion (>>) and extractor (<<) operators on several lines. You can also use these operators on a single line. For example, these three statements:

```
ar << Var1;
ar << Var2;
ar << Var3;
```

are equivalent to this single statement:

```
ar << Var1 << var2 << << var3;
```

Similarly, these three statements:

```
ar >> Var1;
ar >> Var2;
ar >> Var3;
```

are equivalent to this single statement:

```
ar >> Var1 >> Var2 >> Var3;
```

Executing the MEMO Application

You have finished writing most of the code for the MEMO application. To see your code in action:

☐ Compile and link the MEMO application.

To execute the MEMO.EXE application:

☐ Select Execute MEMO.EXE from the Project menu.

> *Visual C++ responds by executing the MEMO application. The main window of the application appears with a blank memo form. The title of the window is* MEMO Windows Application - Memo.

☐ Fill the blank form with data.

☐ Select Save from the File menu and save your memo as TRY.MEM.

> *The MEMO application responds by saving your memo in the file* TRY.MEM *and by changing the title of the window to* MEMO Windows Application - TRY.MEM.

☐ Experiment with all the other menu items of the File menu.

As you can see, all the File menu items behave as you would expect them to behave in a standard Windows application. For example, if you modify the memo form and try to exit from the application without saving the memo, the application prompts you with a warning message. Recall that you didn't have to write the code that displays this warning message. All you had to do was set the Modified flag of the document class (using the SetModifiedFlag() function) to TRUE whenever the user made changes to the form.

Also note that the File menu maintains a Most Recently Used (MRU) file list (see Figure 13.11). The MRU list in the File menu lists the most recent files that the user worked with. When the user clicks one of the files in the MRU list, the file is opened. Again, you didn't have to write any code for this useful feature. Note that the application stores the names of the most recently used files in its INI file, which resides in your Windows directory (for example, C:\WINDOWS\MEMO.INI).

To exit from the MEMO application:

☐ Select Exit from the File menu.

In the following section you'll enhance the MEMO application.

Figure 13.11.
The File menu with
a Most Recently
Used (MRU)
file list.

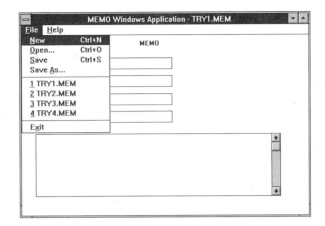

Enhancing the MEMO Application

You'll enhance the MEMO application in two ways:

Change the application window's title from `MEMO Windows Application -
[filename]` to `Memo for Windows - [filename]` (where `[filename]` is the
name of the file that's currently open). This means that whenever user starts
the application and whenever the user selects New from the File menu, the
application window title will be `Memo for Windows - Untitled`.
Change the default file type that is displayed in the Save As and Open dialog
boxes, from *.* to *.MEM.

This means that whenever the user selects Open or Save As from the dialog box, the
default files that will be displayed in the File list box will have a .MEM file extension.

Follow the following steps to implement these enhancements:

☐ Select App Studio from the Tools menu of Visual C++.

Visual C++ responds by displaying the MEMO.RC window.

☐ Select String Table from the Type list (see Figure 13.12) and then double-
click the `String Segment:0` item in the Resources list.

App Studio responds by displaying the String Table Editor (see Figure 13.13).

As you can see from Figure 13.13, the string with the ID of `IDR_MAINFRAME` is currently highlighted, and the current value of this string is

`MEMO Windows Application\nMemo\nMEMO Document`

Figure 13.12.
Selecting String
Table from the
Type list.

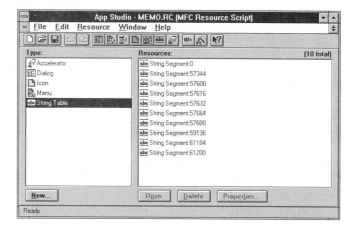

Figure 13.13.
The String
Table Editor.

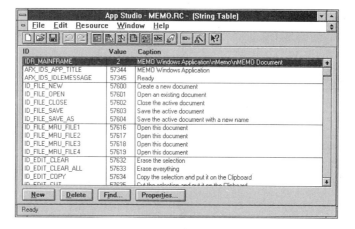

The \n in the string serves as a separator between substrings. Thus, the previous string is made of three substrings:

```
MEMO Windows Application
Memo
MEMO Document
```

The first substring represents the title of the application's main window. Recall that your objective is to change the application's main window title to Memo for Windows. The second substring represents the default document name, which appears in the main window title when the user starts the application or selects New from the File menu. Recall that your objective is to change this value to Untitled.

The third substring represents the document type name of the application.

Besides the previous three substrings, you can add to the IDR_MAINFRAME string two more substrings that represent the default document type that is displayed in the Save As dialog box and Open File dialog box of the application. For example, if you add to \nMEM Files (*.mem)\n.mem the IDR_MAINFRAME string when the user selects Save As or Open from the File menu, the files listed in the File Name list box have the extension .mem, and the files that appear in the Save File as Type box are MEM files (*.mem).

Figure 13.14 shows the File Save As dialog box listing files with extension .mem. The text MEM Files (*.mem) appears in the File Type box.

Figure 13.14.
The File Save As
dialog box listing
files with the .mem
extension.

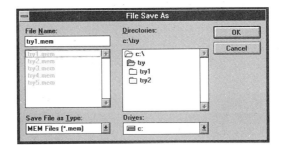

Now that you know what each of the substrings of the IDR_MAINFRAME string represents, you can customize the IDR_MAINFRAME string for the MEMO application:

☐ Double-click the IDR_MAINFRAME string.

> *App Studio responds by displaying the String Properties window for the*
> *IDR_MAINFRAME string (see Figure 13.15).*

Figure 13.15.
The String
Properties
window for the
IDR_MAINFRAME
string.

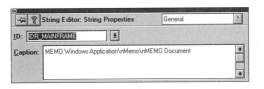

The value of the string is displayed in the Caption box.

☐ Change the value of the string to:

MEMO for Windows\nUntitled\nMEMO Document

\nMEM Files (*.mem)\n.mem

389

NOTE: The preceding text should be typed on a single line without pressing the Enter key. AppWizard will wrap the line when it is too long.

Your String Properties window for the IDR_MAINFRAME string looks as shown in Figure 13.16.

Figure 13.16.
The String
Properties window
with a new string
value.

Save your work:

☐ Select Save from the File menu of App Studio.

Executing the Final Version of the MEMO Application

To see the effects of the modification that you made to the IDR_MAINFRAME string:

☐ Compile and link the MEMO application.

☐ Execute the MEMO application.

> *Now the main window of the application appears with the title* Memo for Windows - Untitled.

☐ Fill the blank memo form with data.

☐ Select Save from the File menu.

> *The MEMO application responds by displaying a Save As dialog box. Now the Save As dialog box lists files with .mem extensions.*

☐ Save your memo form as: TRY.MEM

> *The MEMO application responds by saving the memo form to the file* TRY.MEM *and by changing the title of the application window to* Memo for Windows - TRY.MEM.

☐ Select New from the File menu.

> *The MEMO application responds by displaying a blank memo form and by changing the title of the application window to* Memo for Windows - Untitled.

So as you can see, you've enhanced the MEMO application significantly by customizing the IDR_MAINFRAME string using App Studio.

NOTE

In the MEMO application, you serialized CString data members of the document class. That is, the MEMO application's code writes and reads CString data members of the document class (for example, m_Memo) to and from the files by utilizing the Serialize() function of the document class. Can you serialize other types of variables? Yes, you can! However, you should know that an int variable can't be serialized. So whenever you need to serialize integers, serialize a long type instead.

If you try to serialize an integer, as in

```
ar << m_MyInteger;
```

where m_MyInteger is an integer, you will get the compiling error

```
'operator <<' is ambiguous
```

14

Using Serialization to Write and Read Lists to and from Files

In this chapter you'll learn how to serialize lists. First you'll learn how to create and maintain a list of objects, and then you'll learn how to serialize the list (that is, how to read and write the list to and from files).

> **NOTE**
>
> This chapter isn't a typical chapter, because it requires you to type a substantial amount of code before you see any action. Therefore, you'll be instructed throughout the tutorial to compile/link (but not to execute) the application. The sole purpose of this compiling/linking is to verify that you entered the code without typographical errors.
>
> Although this chapter is more complex than other chapters in this book, it's worth your efforts, because maintaining a list of objects is a powerful and useful feature that can be incorporated into serious Windows applications.
>
> You can use the steps presented in this chapter (for maintaining a list of objects) as a framework for your future projects.

The PHN Application

Now you'll write the PHN application. The PHN application is an example of an application that reads and writes a list of objects to and from files by using serialization; it enables the user to maintain a list of phone numbers, for example.

Before you start writing the PHN application, execute a copy of it. A copy of this application resides in your C:\VCPROG\ORIGINAL\CH14\PHN directory.

To execute the PHN application:

☐ In Windows, select Run from Program Manager's File menu.

> *Windows responds by displaying the Run dialog box.*

☐ Type C:\vcProg\Original\CH14\PHN\PHN.EXE in the Command Line box and then click the OK button.

> *Windows responds by executing the PHN application. The main window of PHN.EXE appears as shown in Figure 14.1.*

As you can see from Figure 14.1, the main window of the application displays a blank record of a phone entry form ready for you to edit. The title of the window is Phone for Windows - Untitled.

The PHN application has two popup menus: File and Help. These popup menus are shown in Figures 14.2 and 14.3.

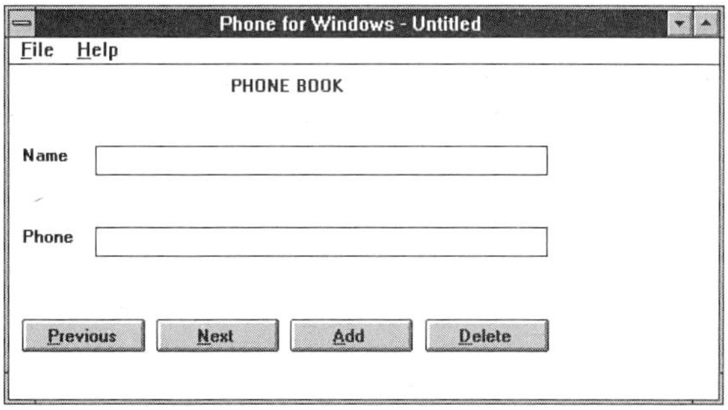

Figure 14.1.
The PHN
application's
main window.

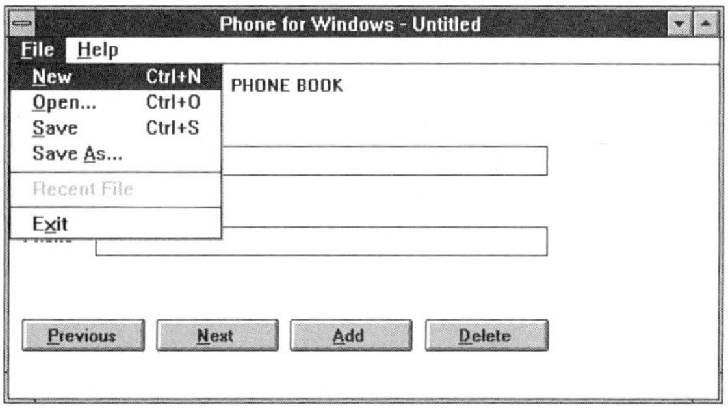

Figure 14.2.
The PHN
application's
File popup menu.

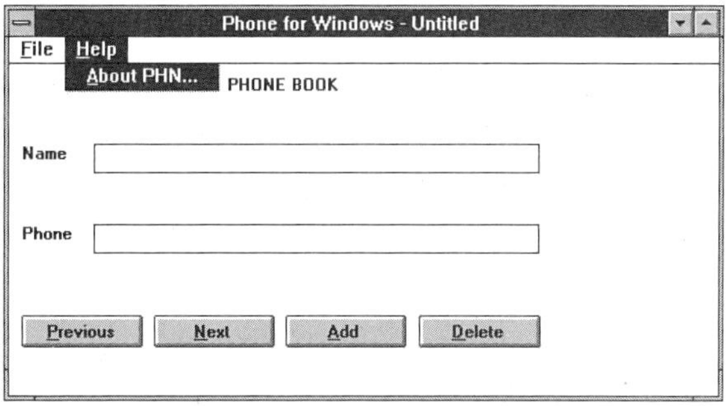

Figure 14.3.
The PHN
application's
Help popup menu.

☐ Fill the Name and Phone fields of the blank phone entry form. Figure 14.4 shows the phone entry form after it was filled.

Figure 14.4.
A completed
phone entry form.

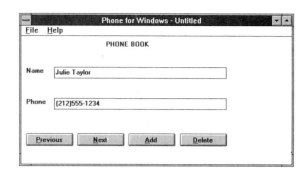

☐ Click the Add button of the Phone entry form.

The PHN application responds by adding a new blank record.

☐ Fill the Name and Phone fields of the new record with new data.

☐ Repeat the previous steps to add several other records.

You can now experiment with the other buttons of the PHN application:

☐ Experiment with the Next and Previous buttons to navigate among the records you added.

☐ As you can see, when you click the Next button, the next record is displayed, and when you click the Previous button, the previous record is displayed.

☐ Experiment with the Delete button: Use the Next and Previous buttons to display any record and then click the Delete button.

The PHN application responds by deleting the record you displayed.

To save the list of phone numbers that you entered into a file:

☐ Select Save from the File menu.

The PHN application responds by displaying the File Save As dialog box (see Figure 14.5).

☐ Save your phone list as PHONE1.PHN.

The PHN application responds by saving your phone list in the file PHONE1.PHN and by changing the title of the application window to Phone for Windows - PHONE1.PHN.

Experiment with the other menu items in the File menu (New, Open, and Save As). As you can see, all the File menu items behave as you would expect them to behave in a standard Windows application.

To exit from the PHN application:

☐ Select Exit from the File menu.

Now that you know what the PHN application should do, you can write it.

Figure 14.5.
The PHN
application's
Save As dialog box.

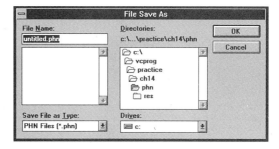

Creating the Project of the PHN Application

To create the project of the PHN application:

☐ Select AppWizard from the Project menu.

Visual C++ responds by running AppWizard.

☐ Use the Directory list box to select the directory C:\VCPROG\PRACTICE\CH14.

☐ Type phn in the Project Name box.

Now your AppWizard dialog box looks as shown in Figure 14.6.

Figure 14.6.
The AppWizard
dialog box for the
PHN application.

☐ Click the Options button and set the options as shown in Figure 14.7 (that is, uncheck all the check boxes except the Generate Source Comments check box).

Figure 14.7.
Setting the options
for the PHN
application.

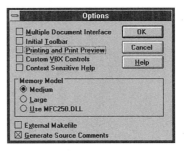

☐ Click the OK button of the Options dialog box and then click the OK button of the AppWizard dialog box and finally click the Create button of the New Application Information dialog box.

> *AppWizard responds by creating the PHN project and all the skeleton files of the PHN application.*

To remove the debug options of the project (so that you'll have a small EXE file):

☐ Select Project from the Options menu of Visual C++, click the Release radio button, and then click the OK button of the dialog box.

Creating the Form of the Application

As shown in Figure 14.1, the main window of the PHN application should contain a data form for entering a name and a phone number.

To implement this form you'll replace the current view class of the application with a new view class derived from the CFormView class.

Follow these steps to create the form of the application:

☐ Use the Windows File Manager (or DOS Shell) to delete the two files of the view class of the PHN application:

    Delete C:\VCPROG\PRACTICE\CH14\PHN\PHNVIEW.CPP.
    Delete C:\VCPROG\PRACTICE\CH14\PHN\PHNVIEW.H.

☐ Select ClassWizard from the Browse menu of Visual C++.

> *ClassWizard responds by displaying a dialog box telling you that the files of the view class don't exist.*

☐ Click the OK button of the dialog box.

☐ Click the Remove button of the Repair Class Information dialog box.

☐ Click the OK button of ClassWizard's dialog box.

You've just finished removing the view class of the PHN application.

In the following steps you'll create a dialog box, you'll create a `CFormView` type class for this dialog box, and you'll make this class the new view class of the application:

☐ Select App Studio from the Tools menu of Visual C++.

☐ Create a new dialog box with App Studio.

☐ Double-click in a free area of the new dialog box.

☐ Select Styles from the drop-down list box at the upper-right corner of the Properties window.

Set the Styles properties of the dialog box as follows:

☐ Select Child in the Style box.

☐ Select None in the Border box.

☐ Uncheck the Visible property (that is, remove the check mark from the Visible check box).

☐ Select General from the drop-down list box at the upper-right corner of the Properties window and make sure that the Caption box is empty.

Now, connect the dialog box to a class derived from `CFormView`:

☐ Select ClassWizard from the Resource menu of App Studio.

> *ClassWizard responds by displaying the Add Class dialog box.*

☐ Type `CPhnView` in the Class Name box.

☐ Set the Class Type to `CFormView`.

☐ Make sure the Header File box is set to `phnview.h`.

☐ Make sure the Implementation File box is set to `phnview.cpp`.

☐ Click the Create Class button.

☐ Click the OK button of ClassWizard's window to go back to App Studio.

You've finished creating the new view class of the application. This view class is a derived class from the MFC `CFormView` class and it's connected to the dialog box that you created. Thus, the main window of the application will be the dialog box that you created.

The Visual Implementation of the Dialog Box

☐ Design the dialog box of the PHN application (that you created previously) per Table 14.1.

Table 14.1. The PHN application's dialog box.

Class Name:	CPhnView
Figure:	14.8
OK button:	No
Cancel button:	No

Object	Property	Setting
Dialog Box	ID	IDD_DIALOG1
Label	ID	IDC_STATIC
	Caption	PHONE BOOK
Label	ID	IDC_STATIC
	Caption	Name
Edit Box	ID	IDC_NAME
	Variable	m_Name
	Variable Type	CString
Label	ID	IDC_STATIC
	Caption	Phone
Edit Box	ID	IDC_PHONE
	Variable	m_Phone
	Variable Type	CString
Push Button	ID	IDC_PREVIOUS_BUTTON
	Caption	&Previous
Push Button	ID	IDC_NEXT_BUTTON
	Caption	&Next
Push Button	ID	IDC_ADD_BUTTON
	Caption	&Add
Push Button	ID	IDC_DELETE_BUTTON
	Caption	&Delete

Your dialog box looks as the one shown in Figure 14.8.

Figure 14.8.
The PHN
application's
dialog box.

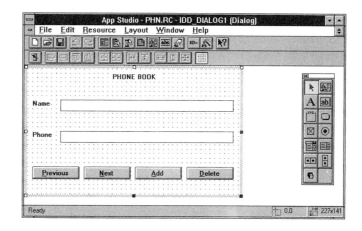

Save your work:

☐ Select Save from the File menu of App Studio.

You finished designing the form of the application!

The Visual Implementation of the Menu

The PHN application should have a menu, as shown in Figures 14.1, 14.2, and 14.3.

Implementing this menu is easy, because all you have to do is just delete the Edit popup menu. The File and Help popup menus that AppWizard generated for you, are exactly what you need for the PHN application.

☐ Use App Studio to delete the Edit popup of the menu.

To save your work:

☐ Select Save from the File menu of App Studio.

The visual implementation of the PHN application's menu bar is complete.

Executing the PHN Application

Although you haven't completed writing the PHN application, execute it and see what you've accomplished so far:

☐ Select Rebuild All PHN.EXE from the Project menu of Visual C++.

Visual C++ responds by compiling and linking the PHN application.

☐ Select Execute PHN.EXE from the Project menu.

Visual C++ responds by executing the PHN application. As you can see, the dialog box that you designed appears as the main window of the application (see Figure 14.1).

Of course, none of the buttons in the dialog box are working because you haven't written any code yet. In the following sections you'll write the code of the PHN application.

To exit the PHN application:

☐ Select Exit from the File menu.

Declaring the Phone Class

You want the PHN application to store a list of people's names and phone numbers. Thus, you need to create a class that will be used to store a person's name and a phone number. You'll name this class CPhone, and you'll declare it with two data members: m_Name and m_Phone. Both of these data members will be defined as CString types.

You'll define the CPhone class as a derived class from the MFC class CObject. This is necessary because later in this chapter, you will write code that serializes the data members of the CPhone class—and in order to serialize a class, it must be a derived class from the MFC CObject class.

In the following steps you'll create the CPhone class. You'll create two new files: PHONE.H and PHONE.CPP. You'll declare the CPhone class inside PHONE.H, and you'll write the functions of the CPhone class (for example, the constructor function) in PHONE.CPP.

To create the PHONE.H file:

☐ Select New from the File menu of Visual C++.

Visual C++ responds by opening a new file.

☐ Type the following code in the new file:

```
/////////////////////////
// MY CODE STARTS HERE
/////////////////////////
```

```
// PHONE.H
//
// Header file for the CPhone class.


// CPhone class declaration.
class CPhone : public CObject
{

public:

    // Constructor
    CPhone();

    // Data members
    CString m_Name;
    CString m_Phone;
};

/////////////////////
// MY CODE ENDS HERE
/////////////////////
```

☐ Select Save As from the File menu and save the file as PHONE.H (in the
   C:\VCPROG\PRACTICE\CH14\PHN directory).

Note that the constructor function of the CPhone class is declared without any arguments. That's because later you'll want to be able to serialize the CPhone class, and
one of the constructor functions of a serializable class must be declared with no arguments. Of course, if you want, you can add more constructor functions to the class
(overload functions) that do take parameters.

To create PHONE.CPP:

☐ Select New from the File menu.

   Visual C++ responds by opening a new file.

☐ Type the following code in the new file:

```
/////////////////////////
// MY CODE STARTS HERE
/////////////////////////

// PHONE.CPP
//
// Implementation file of the CPhone class.

#include "stdafx.h"
#include "phone.h"
```

```
// Constructor.
CPhone::CPhone()
 {
    m_Name  = "";
    m_Phone = "";
 }


/////////////////////
// MY CODE ENDS HERE
/////////////////////
```

☐ Select Save As from the File menu and save the file as PHONE.CPP (in the C:\VCPROG\PRACTICE\CH14\PHN directory).

To summarize what you did in the preceding steps:

1. You created a class CPhone with two CString data members: m_Name and m_Phone.
2. You declared the CPhone class as a derived class from the MFC CObject class. This is necessary because you want to be able to serialize the CPhone class, and thus CPhone must be derived from CObject.
3. You declared the constructor function of the CPhone class with no arguments. This is necessary also because you will want to be able to serialize the CPhone class, and a serializeable class must have a constructor function that has no arguments. As stated previously, if you wish you can add additional constructor functions to the CPhone class that do have arguments.

Adding the *PHONE.CPP* File to the PHN Project

In the previous steps, you created two new files, PHONE.H and PHONE.CPP. The PHONE.CPP file must be included in the project of the application (PHN.MAK) so that Visual C++ will compile PHONE.CPP whenever needed.

Follow these steps to add PHONE.CPP into the PHN.MAK project:

☐ Select Edit from the Project menu.

Visual C++ responds by displaying the Edit - PHN.MAK dialog box (see Figure 14.9).

The list at the bottom of the dialog box (the Files In Project list) contains all the files currently included in the PHN.MAK project.

To add the PHONE.CPP file to the list:

☐ Select PHONE.CPP from the list below the File Name box and then click the Add button.

> *Visual C++ responds by adding the* PHONE.CPP *file to the Files In Project list.*

☐ Click the Close button of the dialog box.

> *Visual C++ responds by adding the* PHONE.CPP *to the project.*

Figure 14.9.
The Edit -
PHN.MAK
dialog box.

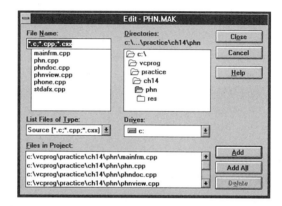

NOTE

Okay, you've written enough code for now! To make sure that you typed the correct code, compile/link the application:

Select Rebuild All PHN.EXE from the Project menu and make sure there are no compiling/linking errors.

Don't execute the application. The only reason you're compiling/linking the program is to verify that you entered the code correctly.

The Document Class of the PHN Application

As you know, the document class of the application should hold the application's data. The question is, what is the PHN application's data? Recall that the PHN application should maintain a list of names and phone numbers. You already defined the CPhone class with two data members, m_Name and m_Phone. So now you can declare a list of objects of class CPhone. Each object in this list will store the name and phone number of a particular person. You'll declare this list as a data member of the document class.

The MFC *CObList* Class

The MFC CObList class is a useful and powerful class you can use with great ease to maintain a list of objects. After you declare an object of class CObList, you can use member functions of the CObList class to maintain a list of objects (for example, add objects to the list, delete objects from the list, and so on).

In the PHN application you will create an object of class CObList to maintain a list of CPhone objects. You'll name this list m_PhoneList, and you'll make m_PhoneList a data member of the document class. Thus, the document class of the application will store a list of names and phone numbers.

Follow these steps to declare m_PhoneList as a data member of the document class:

☐ Open the file PHNDOC.H and add to the CPhnDoc class declaration the m_PhoneList data member. Declare m_PhoneList as an object of class CObList and make it a public data member of CPhnDoc. After you write this declaration, the CPhnDoc class declaration looks as follows:

```
// phndoc.h : interface of the CPhnDoc class
//
/////////////////////////////////////////////////////

class CPhnDoc : public CDocument
{
protected: // create from serialization only
    CPhnDoc();
    DECLARE_DYNCREATE(CPhnDoc)

// Attributes
public:

    ////////////////////////
    // MY CODE STARTS HERE
    ////////////////////////

    CObList m_PhoneList;

    ////////////////////////
    // MY CODE ENDS HERE
    ////////////////////////
```

```
// Operations
public:

// Implementation
public:
    virtual ~CPhnDoc();
    virtual void Serialize(CArchive& ar);
// overridden for document i/o
#ifdef _DEBUG
    virtual void AssertValid() const;
    virtual void Dump(CDumpContext& dc) const;
#endif

protected:
    virtual BOOL OnNewDocument();

// Generated message map functions
protected:
    //{{AFX_MSG(CPhnDoc)
        // NOTE - the ClassWizard will add and
// remove member functions here.
        //     DO NOT EDIT what you see in these
// blocks of generated code !
    //}}AFX_MSG
    DECLARE_MESSAGE_MAP()
};
```

Note that m_PhoneList is declared as a public data member (that is, it's declared below the public: keyword) because, as you'll see later in the chapter, the view class must have access to m_PhoneList. Alternatively, you can declare m_PhoneList as private, but then you'll need to write a public access function (for example, GetPhoneList()) that will return the address of m_PhoneList.

Save your work:

☐ Select Save from the File menu of Visual C++.

You've finished declaring the data member of the document class. Next, you will initialize this data member.

Initializing the Data Member of the Document Class

In the previous steps you added the data member m_PhoneList to the document class. You declared m_PhoneList as an object of class CObList. Thus, m_PhoneList can store a list of objects. At this point, m_PhoneList is empty. That is, it doesn't have any objects in it.

As you learned in the previous chapter, a good place to initialize the data members of the document class is in the OnNewDocument() member function of the document class. That's because OnNewDocument() is executed automatically whenever a new document is created (either when the application begins or whenever the user selects New from the File menu).

☐ Open the file PHNDOC.CPP and edit the OnNewDocument() function. After editing this function, your OnNewDocument() function looks as follows:

```
BOOL CPhnDoc::OnNewDocument()
{
    if (!CDocument::OnNewDocument())
        return FALSE;

    // TODO: add reinitialization code here
    // (SDI documents will reuse this document)


    ///////////////////////////
    // MY CODE STARTS HERE
    ///////////////////////////

    // Create an object of class CPhone.
    CPhone* pPhone  = new CPhone();
    pPhone->m_Name  = "";
    pPhone->m_Phone = "";

    // Add the new object to the m_PhoneList list.
    m_PhoneList.AddHead(pPhone);

    ///////////////////////
    // MY CODE ENDS HERE
    ///////////////////////


    return TRUE;
}
```

To review the code you just entered in the OnNewDocument() function:

The first statement,

```
CPhone* pPhone  = new CPhone();
```

creates an object of class CPhone and assigns the address of this object to the pPhone pointer. Therefore, pPhone contains the address of the new CPhone object.

The next two statements assign null to the pPhone object:

```
pPhone->m_Name  = "";
pPhone->m_Phone = "";
```

Note that these statements aren't really necessary, because the constructor function of the CPhone class already assigned null values to the m_Name and m_Phone data members. However, you write these statements anyway because they make the code easier to read (that is, these statements emphasize the fact that now m_Name and m_Phone are blank).

The last statement in the OnNewDocument() function is

```
m_PhoneList.AddHead(pPhone);
```

This statement uses the AddHead() member function of the CObList class to add the new CPhone object that you created to the m_PhoneList list. Thus, whenever a new document is created (for example, on starting the application), a blank CPhone object is added to the m_PhoneList list.

> **NOTE**
>
> The AddHead() member function of the CObList class adds an object to the "head" (that is, to the beginning) of the list. Pass to this function the address of the object that you want to add to the list.
>
> Example:
>
> ```
> MyList.AddHead(pMyObject);
> ```

If you try to compile the PHNDOC.CPP file now, you'll get a compiling error. Why? Because in this code you referred to the CPhone class but the CPhone class is not known in the PHNDOC.CPP file. Thus, you must #include PHONE.H (the header file of the CPhone class) at the beginning of the PHNDOC.CPP file:

☐ Add the #include "phone.h" statement at the beginning of the PHNDOC.CPP file (immediately before the #include statement of the phndoc.h file). After adding this #include statement, the beginning of the PHNDOC.CPP file looks as follows:

```
// phndoc.cpp : implementation of the CPhnDoc class
//

#include "stdafx.h"
#include "phn.h"
```

```
/////////////////////
// MY CODE STARTS HERE
/////////////////////

#include "phone.h"

/////////////////////
// MY CODE ENDS HERE
/////////////////////


#include "phndoc.h"
.......
.......
.......
```

Save your work:

☐ Select Save from the File menu of Visual C++.

> **NOTE**
>
> To make sure you typed the correct code, compile/link the application:
>
> Select Build PHN.EXE from the Project menu and make sure there are no compiling/linking errors.
>
> Don't execute the application. The only reason you're compiling/linking the program is to verify that you entered the code correctly.

Deleting the Objects of the *m_PhoneList* List

You need to delete (from memory) the objects that are listed in the `m_PhoneList` list, whenever any of the following three events takes place:

- User exits the application
- User starts a new document (that is, selects New from the File menu)
- User opens an existing document (that is, user selects Open from the File menu)

The `DeleteContents()` member function of the document class is executed automatically whenever one of these three events takes place. Thus, the `DeleteContents()` function is a good place to write the code that deletes the objects listed in the `m_PhoneList` list.

Visual C++ did not write the declaration and skeleton of the `DeleteContents()` function. You have to declare this function and write its skeleton. Here's how you do that:

☐ Open the file `PHNDOC.H` and add code to it that defines the function `DeleteContents()` as a member function of the `CPhnDoc` class. After you write this code, the `CPhnDoc` class declaration looks as follows:

NOTE

In the following listing, there are two sections of MY CODE STARTS HERE.

```
/////////////////////
MY CODE STARTS HERE
/////////////////////
. . . . . .
. . . . . .
. . . . . .
/////////////////////
MY CODE ENDS HERE
/////////////////////
```

You already typed the first section so now just add the second section.

```cpp
class CPhnDoc : public CDocument
{
protected: // create from serialization only
    CPhnDoc();
    DECLARE_DYNCREATE(CPhnDoc)

// Attributes
public:

    /////////////////////
    // MY CODE STARTS HERE
    /////////////////////

    CObList m_PhoneList;

    /////////////////////
    // MY CODE ENDS HERE
    /////////////////////
```

```
// Operations
public:

// Implementation
public:
    virtual ~CPhnDoc();
    virtual void Serialize(CArchive& ar);
// overridden for document i/o
#ifdef _DEBUG
    virtual void AssertValid() const;
    virtual void Dump(CDumpContext& dc) const;
#endif

protected:
    virtual BOOL OnNewDocument();

    /////////////////////////
    // MY CODE STARTS HERE
    /////////////////////////

    virtual void DeleteContents();

    /////////////////////////
    // MY CODE ENDS HERE
    /////////////////////////

// Generated message map functions
protected:
    //{{AFX_MSG(CPhnDoc)
        // NOTE - the ClassWizard will add
//and remove member functions here.
        //    DO NOT EDIT what you see in
// these blocks of generated code !
    //}}AFX_MSG
    DECLARE_MESSAGE_MAP()
};
```

Save your work:

☐ Select Save from the File menu.

Now write the code of the DeleteContents() function:

☐ Open the file PHNDOC.CPP and add to the end of the file the
DeleteContents() function. After you write this function, the
end of the PHNDOC.CPP file looks as follows:

```
/////////////////////////
// MY CODE STARTS HERE
/////////////////////////
```

```
void CPhnDoc::DeleteContents()
{

    // Remove all the items in the list and free the
    // memory occupied by the listed objects.
    while ( !m_PhoneList.IsEmpty() )
          {
          delete m_PhoneList.RemoveHead();
          }
}
```

```
////////////////////
// MY CODE ENDS HERE
////////////////////
```

As you can see, the DeleteContents() function uses a while() loop to delete all the objects that are listed in the m_PhoneList list:

```
while ( !m_PhoneList.IsEmpty() )
      {
      delete m_PhoneList.RemoveHead();
      }
```

The IsEmpty() member function of the CObList class returns TRUE if the list is empty. Thus, the while() condition,

```
!m_PhoneList.IsEmpty()
```

is satisfied as long as the list isn't empty.

The statement in the while() loop,

```
delete m_PhoneList.RemoveHead();
```

does two things:

> It removes the head item (the first item) of the m_PhoneList list.
> It frees (deletes) the memory that was occupied by the object that the head item listed.

The RemoveHead() member function removes the first item from the list and returns the address of the removed object. Thus, in this statement, the delete operator deletes the memory that was occupied by the removed object.

Note that the RemoveHead() function does more than just remove the head item. It also updates the new locations of the remaining items in the list. That is, item number 2 in the list now becomes item number 1, item number 3 becomes item number 2, and so on.

> **NOTE**
>
> To make sure you typed the correct code, compile/link the application:
>
> Select Build PHN.EXE from the Project menu and make sure that there are no compiling/linking errors.
>
> Don't execute the application. The only reason you're compiling/linking the program is to verify that you entered the code correctly.

The View Class of the PHN Application

In the following sections you will write the code of the view class of the PHN application.

Declaring the Data Members of the View Class

So far the view class has two data members: m_Name (the variable of the IDC_NAME edit box) and m_Phone (the variable of the IDC_PHONE edit box). You created these data members during the visual implementation of the application when you designed the application's form.

Now you'll declare two additional data members: m_pList and m_position.

m_pList will be used to store the address of the m_PhoneList data member of the document class.

m_position will be used to store the element number of the item that's currently displayed. That is, at any given time, the form of the application will display a particular object from the objects listed in m_PhoneList, and m_position will point to the item that's currently displayed.

Follow these steps to declare m_pList and m_position:

☐ Open the file PHNVIEW.H and add code to the class declaration of CPhnView that defines m_pList and m_position as data members. After you write this code, the CPhnView class declaration looks as follows:

```
class CPhnView : public CFormView
{
    DECLARE_DYNCREATE(CPhnView)
protected:
    CPhnView();
// protected constructor used by dynamic creation


    ///////////////////////
    // MY CODE STARTS HERE
    ///////////////////////

    POSITION m_position; // Current position in DOC list.
    CObList* m_pList;    // Pointer to the DOC list.

    ///////////////////////
    // MY CODE ENDS HERE
    ///////////////////////


// Form Data
public:
    //{{AFX_DATA(CPhnView)
    enum { IDD = IDD_DIALOG1 };
    CString    m_Name;
    CString    m_Phone;
    //}}AFX_DATA

// Attributes
public:

// Operations
public:

// Implementation
protected:
    virtual ~CPhnView();
    virtual void DoDataExchange(CDataExchange* pDX);
// DDX/DDV support
    // Generated message map functions
    //{{AFX_MSG(CPhnView)
        // NOTE - the ClassWizard will add and
// remove member functions here.
    //}}AFX_MSG
    DECLARE_MESSAGE_MAP()
};
```

Initializing the Data Members of the View Class

Recall from the previous chapter that you write the code which initializes the data members of the view class in the OnInitialUpdate() member function of the view class. The OnInitialUpdate() function is executed automatically:

- On starting the application
- When the user selects New from the File menu
- When the user selects Open from the File menu

The code you write in the OnInitialUpdate() function updates the m_Name and m_Phone data members of the view class with the values of the object that's at the head position (at the beginning) of the list.

Visual C++ didn't write the declaration and skeleton of the OnInitialUpdate() function for you. You have to declare this function and write its skeleton. Here's how you do that:

☐ Open the file PHNVIEW.H and add code to it that defines the function OnInitialUpdate() as a member function of the CPhnView class. After you write this code, the CPhnView class declaration looks as follows:

```
class CPhnView : public CFormView
{
    DECLARE_DYNCREATE(CPhnView)
protected:
    CPhnView();
// protected constructor used by dynamic creation


    ////////////////////////
    // MY CODE STARTS HERE
    ////////////////////////

    virtual void OnInitialUpdate();

    POSITION m_position;    // Current position in DOC list.
    CObList* m_pList;       // Pointer to the DOC list.

    ////////////////////////
    // MY CODE ENDS HERE
    ////////////////////////


// Form Data
public:
```

```
//{{AFX_DATA(CPhnView)
enum { IDD = IDD_DIALOG1 };
CString     m_Name;
CString     m_Phone;
//}}AFX_DATA
```

```
// Attributes
public:
```

```
// Operations
public:
```

```
// Implementation
protected:
    virtual ~CPhnView();
    virtual void DoDataExchange(CDataExchange* pDX);
// DDX/DDV support
    // Generated message map functions
    //{{AFX_MSG(CPhnView)
        // NOTE - the ClassWizard will add and
// remove member functions here.
    //}}AFX_MSG
    DECLARE_MESSAGE_MAP()
};
```

Now write the code of the OnInitialUpdate() function:

☐ Open the file PHNVIEW.CPP and add to it (at the end of the file) the OnInitialUpdate() function. After you write this function, the end of the PHNVIEW.CPP file looks as follows:

```
/////////////////////////
// MY CODE STARTS HERE
/////////////////////////

void CPhnView::OnInitialUpdate()
{

  // Get a pointer to the document.
  CPhnDoc* pDoc = (CPhnDoc*) GetDocument();

  // Get the address of m_PhoneList of the document class.
  m_pList = &(pDoc->m_PhoneList);

  // Get head position.
  m_position = m_pList->GetHeadPosition();


  // Update m_Name and m_Phone with values from the list.
  CPhone* pPhone = (CPhone*)m_pList->GetAt(m_position);
```

417

```
m_Name  = pPhone->m_Name;
m_Phone = pPhone->m_Phone;

// Update the screen with the new values of the variables.
UpdateData(FALSE);

// Place the cursor inside the IDC_NAME edit box.
((CDialog*) this)->GotoDlgCtrl(GetDlgItem(IDC_NAME));

}

//////////////////////
// MY CODE ENDS HERE
//////////////////////
```

To review the code of the OnInitialUpdate() function:

The first statement,

```
CPhnDoc* pDoc = (CPhnDoc*) GetDocument();
```

extracts pDoc (the pointer for the document class).

Then the address of m_PhoneList of the document class is assigned to the pointer m_pList:

```
m_pList = &(pDoc->m_PhoneList);
```

From now on, m_pList will be used to access m_PhoneList of the document class. Recall that you declared m_pList as a data member of the view class. Thus, it will be visible in all the other member functions of the view class.

Then m_position is initialized to the head position (the first position) of the list:

```
m_position = m_pList->GetHeadPosition();
```

Again, because you also declared m_position as a data member of the view class, it will be visible in all the other functions of the view class.

Then the m_Name and m_Phone data members of the view class are updated with the values in the list that correspond to the position m_position:

```
CPhone* pPhone = (CPhone*)m_pList->GetAt(m_position);
m_Name  = pPhone->m_Name;
m_Phone = pPhone->m_Phone;
```

Because currently, m_position is the head position, these three statements update m_Name and m_Phone with the values of the first object in the list. Note that in this code, the statement

```
CPhone* pPhone = (CPhone*)m_pList->GetAt(m_position);
```

uses the GetAt() member function of the CObList class to update pPhone (pointer of class CPhone) with the address of element m_position of the list. That is, GetAt() returns the address of the object in position m_position.

After updating m_Name and m_Phone, the UpdateData() function is used to transfer the new values of these variables to the screen:

```
UpdateData(FALSE);
```

Finally, the last statement in the OnInitialUpdate() function places the cursor inside the IDC_NAME edit box:

```
((CDialog*) this)->GotoDlgCtrl(GetDlgItem(IDC_NAME));
```

Thus, whenever the user starts the application, selects New from the File menu, or selects Open from the File menu (that is, whenever the OnInitialUpdate() function is executed), the cursor appears in the IDC_NAME edit box.

If you try to compile the PHNVIEW.CPP file now, you will get a compiling error. Why? Because in this code you referred to the CPhone class and to the CPhnDoc class, but these classes aren't known in the PHNVIEW.CPP file. Thus, you must #include PHONE.H (the header file of the CPhone class) and PHNDOC.H at the beginning of the PHNVIEW.CPP file:

☐ Add the statements #include "phone.h" and #include "phndoc.h" at the beginning of the PHNVIEW.CPP file (immediately before the #include statement of the phnview.h file). After adding these #include statements, the beginning of the PHNVIEW.CPP file should look as follows:

```
// phnview.cpp : implementation file
//

#include "stdafx.h"
#include "phn.h"

////////////////////////
// MY CODE STARTS HERE
////////////////////////

#include "phone.h"
#include "phndoc.h"

////////////////////////
// MY CODE ENDS HERE
////////////////////////
```

419

```
#include "phnview.h"

. . . . . .
. . . . . .
. . . . . .
```

To save your work:

☐ Select Save from the File menu.

NOTE

To make sure that you typed the correct code, compile\link the application:

Select Build PHN.EXE from the Project menu and make sure there are no compiling\linking errors.

Don't execute the application. The only reason you're compiling\linking the program is to verify that you entered the code correctly.

Updating the Data Members of the Document Class

Whenever the user edits the IDC_NAME or IDC_PHONE edit boxes, the data members of the document class should be updated accordingly. For example, if m_position currently points to the fifth item in the list and the user types something in the IDC_NAME edit box, the data member m_Name of the fifth object in the list m_PhoneList (in the document class) should be updated with the same value that the user typed.

So you need to write code that detects when the user types something in the IDC_NAME and IDC_PHONE edit boxes and then changes the m_PhoneList data member of the document class accordingly. Here is how you do that:

☐ Use ClassWizard to add a function for the event:

Class Name:	CPhnView
Object ID:	IDC_NAME
Message:	EN_CHANGE
Function Name:	OnChangeName()

Make sure to add the OnChangeName() function to the CPhnView class.

☐ Edit the OnChangeName() function that you added to the PHNVIEW.CPP file.

After editing the function, your OnChangeName() function looks as follows:

```
void CPhnView::OnChangeName()
{
// TODO: Add your control notification handler code here


    /////////////////////////
    // MY CODE STARTS HERE
    /////////////////////////

    // Update controls variables with screen contents.
    UpdateData(TRUE);

    // Get a pointer to the document.
    CPhnDoc* pDoc = (CPhnDoc*) GetDocument();

    // Update the document.
    CPhone* pPhone = (CPhone*)m_pList->GetAt(m_position);
    pPhone->m_Name = m_Name;

    // Set the Modified flag to TRUE.
    pDoc->SetModifiedFlag();

    /////////////////////////
    // MY CODE ENDS HERE
    /////////////////////////

}
```

To review the code you just typed:

The first statement in the function,

```
UpdateData(TRUE);
```

updates the variables of the controls with the current values in the controls.

The next statement,

```
CPhnDoc* pDoc = (CPhnDoc*) GetDocument();
```

extracts pDoc (the pointer for the document class).

The next two statements,

```
CPhone* pPhone = (CPhone*)m_pList->GetAt(m_position);
pPhone->m_Name = m_Name;
```

update the `m_Name` data member of the object that's listed at position `m_position` of the list. Recall that `GetAt(m_position)` returns the address of the object in position `m_position`.

The last statement in the function is

```
pDoc->SetModifiedFlag();
```

This statement executes the `SetModifiedFlag()` member function of the document class to set the Modified flag to `TRUE`, signaling that the document's data was modified. Recall from the previous chapter that when the Modified flag is set to `TRUE` and the user tries to quit the application or to load a new file, the application displays a warning message informing the user that the file hasn't been saved.

In a similar manner, you need to attach code to the `IDC_PHONE` edit box:

☐ Use ClassWizard to add a function for the event:

Class Name:	`CPhnView`
Object ID:	`IDC_PHONE`
Message:	`EN_CHANGE`
Function Name:	`OnChangePhone()`

Make sure to add the `OnChangePhone()` function to the `CPhnView` class.

☐ Edit the `OnChangePhone()` function that you added to the `PHNVIEW.CPP` file.
   After editing the function, your `OnChangePhone()` function looks as follows:

```
void CPhnView::OnChangePhone()
{
// TODO: Add your control notification handler code here



    /////////////////////////
    // MY CODE STARTS HERE
    /////////////////////////

    // Update controls variables with screen contents.
    UpdateData(TRUE);

    // Get a pointer to the document.
    CPhnDoc* pDoc = (CPhnDoc*) GetDocument();

    // Update the document.
    CPhone* pPhone = (CPhone*)m_pList->GetAt(m_position);
```

```
    pPhone->m_Phone = m_Phone;

    // Set the Modified flag to TRUE.
    pDoc->SetModifiedFlag();

    ///////////////////////
    // MY CODE ENDS HERE
    ///////////////////////

}
```

As you can see, OnChangePhone() function is similar to the OnChangeName() function. The only difference is that now m_Phone is updated, not m_Name.

You've finished attaching code to the IDC_NAME and IDC_PHONE edit boxes. Now, whenever the user changes these edit boxes, m_PhoneList of the document class will be updated accordingly.

To save your work:

☐ Select Save from the File menu.

To review what you've accomplished so far:

> You've written the code that initializes the data members of the document class.
> You've written the code that initializes the data members of the view class.
> You've written the code that updates the data members of the document class whenever the user changes the data members of the view class (that is, whenever the user changes the contents of the form's edit boxes).

In the following sections you will attach code to the Previous, Next, Add, and Delete buttons.

NOTE

To make sure that you typed the correct code, compile/link the application:

Select Build PHN.EXE from the Project menu and make sure there are no compiling/linking errors.

Do not execute the application. The only reason you're compiling/linking the program is to verify that you entered the code correctly.

Attaching Code to the Previous Button

Whenever the user clicks the Previous button, `m_position` should be updated with the previous position in the list and the `IDC_NAME` and `IDC_PHONE` edit boxes should be updated accordingly.

Follow these steps to attach code to the Previous button:

☐ Use ClassWizard to add a function for the event:

Class Name:	`CPhnView`
Object ID:	`IDC_PREVIOUS_BUTTON`
Message:	`BN_CLICKED`
Function Name:	`OnPreviousButton()`

NOTE: Make sure to add the `OnPreviousButton()` function to the `CPhnView` class.

☐ Edit the `OnPreviousButton()` function that you added to the `PHNVIEW.CPP` file. After editing the function, your `OnPreviousButton()` function should look as follows:

```
void CPhnView::OnPreviousButton()
{
// TODO: Add your control notification handler code here

//////////////////////////
// MY CODE STARTS HERE
//////////////////////////

// Declare a Temporary POSITION variable.
POSITION temp_pos;

// Update temp_pos with the current position of the list.
temp_pos = m_position;

// Update temp_pos with the previous position.
m_pList->GetPrev(temp_pos);

if (temp_pos == NULL)
    {
    // No previous element.
    MessageBox("Bottom of file encountered!",
               "Phone for Windows");
    }
else
    {
    // Update m_position, m_Name, and m_Phone.
    m_position = temp_pos;
```

```
        CPhone* pPhone = (CPhone*)m_pList->GetAt(m_position);
        m_Name  = pPhone->m_Name;
        m_Phone = pPhone->m_Phone;
        UpdateData (FALSE);
        }

    // Place the cursor inside the IDC_NAME edit box.
    ((CDialog*) this)->GotoDlgCtrl(GetDlgItem(IDC_NAME));

    /////////////////////
    // MY CODE ENDS HERE
    /////////////////////


}
```

To review the code for the OnPreviousButton() function:

The first statement,

```
POSITION temp_pos;
```

declares a temporary variable temp_pos (of type POSITION). You need this temporary temp_pos variable, because you want to update the "real" POSITION variable, m_position, only after you're sure that a previous position exists. That is, if the current position is the head position (the first position in the list), there is no previous position.

The next statement updates temp_pos with the value of m_position:

```
temp_pos = m_position;
```

So now temp_pos contains the current position in the list.

The next statement uses the GetPrev() member function of the CObList class to update temp_pos with the previous position in the list (if there is one):

```
m_pList->GetPrev(temp_pos);
```

Note that the GetPrev() function changes the value of the variable that's passed to it. So now temp_pos points to the previous position. If there is no previous position (that is, the current position is the head position), GetPrev() updates temp_pos with NULL.

The next block of statements is an if-else that checks for the value of temp_pos:

```
if (temp_pos == NULL)
    {
    // No previous element.
    MessageBox("Bottom of file encountered!",
            "Phone for Windows");
```

```
    }
else
    {
    // Update m_position, m_Name, and m_Phone.
    m_position = temp_pos;
    CPhone* pPhone = (CPhone*)m_pList->GetAt(m_position);
    m_Name  = pPhone->m_Name;
    m_Phone = pPhone->m_Phone;
    UpdateData (FALSE);
    }
```

If `temp_pos` is NULL, it means that there is no previous position (that is, the current position is the head position), so the user is prompted with a "Bottom of file encountered" message:

```
MessageBox("Bottom of file encountered!",
           "Phone for Windows");
```

If however, `temp_pos` is not NULL, the code under the `else` is executed:

```
m_position = temp_pos;
CPhone* pPhone = (CPhone*)m_pList->GetAt(m_position);
m_Name  = pPhone->m_Name;
m_Phone = pPhone->m_Phone;
UpdateData (FALSE);
```

The first statement,

```
m_position = temp_pos;
```

updates `m_position` with the value of `temp_pos` (which is the previous position in the list).

The next statement updates `pPhone` with the address of the object pointed to by `m_position`:

```
CPhone* pPhone = (CPhone*)m_pList->GetAt(m_position);
```

and then the data members of the view class are updated with the values of the data members from the document class:

```
m_Name  = pPhone->m_Name;
m_Phone = pPhone->m_Phone;
```

The next statement,

```
UpdateData (FALSE);
```

transfers the new values of `m_Name` and `m_Phone` to the screen.

The last statement in the OnPreviousButton() function is

```
((CDialog*) this)->GotoDlgCtrl(GetDlgItem(IDC_NAME));
```

This statement places the cursor in the IDC_NAME edit box. Thus, after the Previous button is clicked, the cursor appears in the IDC_NAME edit box.

Don't forget to save your work:

☐ Select Save from the File menu.

Attaching Code to the Next Button

Whenever the user clicks the Next button, m_position should be updated with the next position in the list, and the IDC_NAME and IDC_PHONE edit boxes should be updated accordingly.

Follow these steps to attach code to the Next button:

☐ Use ClassWizard to add a function for the event:

Class Name:	CPhnView
Object ID:	IDC_NEXT_BUTTON
Message:	BN_CLICKED
Function Name:	OnNextButton()

Make sure to add the OnNextButton() function to the CPhnView class.

☐ Edit the OnNextButton() function that you added to the PHNVIEW.CPP file. After you edit the function, it looks as follows:

```
void CPhnView::OnNextButton()
{
// TODO: Add your control notification handler code here

    /////////////////////////
    // MY CODE STARTS HERE
    /////////////////////////

    // Declare a temporary POSITION variable.
    POSITION temp_pos;

    // Update temp_pos with the current position of the list.
    temp_pos = m_position;

    // Update temp_pos with the next position.
    m_pList->GetNext(temp_pos);
```

```
    if (temp_pos == NULL)
        {
        // No next element.
        MessageBox("End of file encountered!",
                   "Phone for Windows");
        }
    else
        {
        // Update m_position, m_Name, and m_Phone.
        m_position = temp_pos;
        CPhone* pPhone = (CPhone*)m_pList->GetAt(m_position);
        m_Name  = pPhone->m_Name;
        m_Phone = pPhone->m_Phone;
        UpdateData (FALSE);
        }

    // Place the cursor inside the IDC_NAME edit box.
    ((CDialog*) this)->GotoDlgCtrl(GetDlgItem(IDC_NAME));

    ////////////////////////
    // MY CODE ENDS HERE
    ////////////////////////


}
```

As you can see, the OnNextButton() is similar to the OnPreviousButton() function. The only difference is that in OnNextButton() you use the GetNext() member function of the CObList class, not the GetPrevious() function.

Save your work:

☐ Select Save from the File menu.

NOTE

To make sure that you typed the correct code, link the application:

Select Build PHN.EXE from the Project menu and make sure that there are no compiling/linking errors.

Don't execute the application. The only reason you're compiling/linking the program is to verify that you entered the code correctly.

Attaching Code to the Add Button

Whenever the user clicks the Add button, a new blank object should be added to the tail of the list (that is, to the end), and m_position should be updated accordingly.

Follow these steps to attach code to the Add button:

☐ Use ClassWizard to add a function for the event:

Class Name:	CPhnView
Object ID:	IDC_ADD_BUTTON
Message:	BN_CLICKED
Function Name:	OnAddButton()

Make sure to add the OnAddButton() function to the CPhnView class.

☐ Edit the OnAddButton() function that you added to the PHNVIEW.CPP file. After you edit the function, it looks as follows:

```
void CPhnView::OnAddButton()
{
// TODO: Add your control notification handler code here

    /////////////////////////
    // MY CODE STARTS HERE
    /////////////////////////

    // Update m_Name, m_Phone and the screen with blanks.
    m_Name  = "";
    m_Phone = "";
    UpdateData (FALSE);

    // Create a new object of class CPhone.
    CPhone* pPhone  = new CPhone();
    pPhone->m_Name  = m_Name;
    pPhone->m_Phone = m_Phone;

    // Add the new object to the tail of the list, and
    // update m_position with the new position.
    m_position = m_pList->AddTail(pPhone);

    // Get a pointer to the document.
    CPhnDoc* pDoc = (CPhnDoc*) GetDocument();

    // Set the Modified flag to TRUE.
    pDoc->SetModifiedFlag();

    // Place the cursor inside the IDC_NAME edit box.
    ((CDialog*) this)->GotoDlgCtrl(GetDlgItem(IDC_NAME));
```

```
/////////////////////
// MY CODE ENDS HERE
/////////////////////
```

```
}
```

To review the code for the OnAddButton() function:

The first two statements,

```
m_Name  = "";
m_Phone = "";
```

update the data members m_Name and m_Phone of the view class with blanks.

The next statement,

```
UpdateData (FALSE);
```

transfers the new values of m_Name and m_Phone to the screen.

Then a new object (pPhone) of class CPhone is created and its data members are initialized:

```
CPhone* pPhone    = new CPhone();
pPhone->m_Name    = m_Name;
pPhone->m_Phone   = m_Phone;
```

So now the data members of pPhone are also blanks.

The next statement in the function is

```
m_position = m_pList->AddTail(pPhone);
```

This statement uses the AddTail() member function of the CObList class to add the pPhone object to the tail of the list. Note that the returned value of the AddTail() function is the new position of the added object. Thus, after executing this statement, m_position is updated with the position of the pPhone object, which is the new tail position of the list.

The next statement,

```
CPhnDoc* pDoc = (CPhnDoc*) GetDocument();
```

extracts pDoc (the pointer for the document class).

Then pDoc is used to execute the SetModifiedFlag() member function of the document class:

```
pDoc->SetModifiedFlag();
```

This is done to signal that the document data has been changed.

The last statement in the function is

```
((CDialog*) this)->GotoDlgCtrl(GetDlgItem(IDC_NAME));
```

This statement places the cursor in the IDC_NAME edit box. Thus, after you click the Add button, the cursor will always appear in the IDC_NAME edit box.

Don't forget to save your work:

☐ Select Save from the File menu.

Attaching Code to the Delete Button

Whenever the user clicks the Delete button, the item in the list that is pointed to by m_position should be removed.

Follow these steps to attach code to the Delete button:

☐ Use ClassWizard to add a function for the event:

Class Name:	CPhnView
Object ID:	IDC_DELETE_BUTTON
Message:	BN_CLICKED
Function Name:	OnDeleteButton()

Make sure to add the OnDeleteButton() function to the CPhnView class.

☐ Edit the OnDeleteButton() function you added to the PHNVIEW.CPP file. After you edit the OnDeleteButton() function, it looks as follows:

```
void CPhnView::OnDeleteButton()
{
// TODO: Add your control notification handler code here

    ///////////////////////
    // MY CODE STARTS HERE
    ///////////////////////

    // Save the old pointer for deletion.
    CObject* pOld;
    pOld = m_pList->GetAt( m_position );
```

431

```
// Remove the element from the list.
m_pList->RemoveAt( m_position );

// Delete the object from memory.
delete pOld;

// If the list is now completely empty, add a blank item.
if ( m_pList->IsEmpty() )
   OnAddButton();

// Get a pointer to the document.
CPhnDoc* pDoc = (CPhnDoc*) GetDocument();

// Set the Modified flag to TRUE.
pDoc->SetModifiedFlag();

// Display the first item of the list.
OnInitialUpdate();

//////////////////////
// MY CODE ENDS HERE
//////////////////////

}
```

To review the code for the OnDeleteButton() function:

The first two statements are

```
CObject* pOld;
pOld = m_pList->GetAt( m_position );
```

These statements save the address of the object to be deleted in the pointer pOld.

Then the object to be deleted is removed from the list by using the RemoveAt() member function of the CObList class:

```
m_pList->RemoveAt( m_position );
```

Note that the RemoveAt() function doesn't delete the object from memory. It merely removes the object from the list.

The next statement actually deletes the object from memory:

```
delete pOld;
```

Then the IsEmpty() member function of the CObList class is used to check whether the list is completely empty:

```
if ( m_pList->IsEmpty() )
   OnAddButton();
```

If the list is completely empty, the `OnAddButton()` function (which you wrote earlier) is called so that the list will have one blank object.

The next statement in the function,

```
CPhnDoc* pDoc = (CPhnDoc*) GetDocument();
```

extracts `pDoc` (the pointer for the document class).

Then `pDoc` is used to execute the `SetModifiedFlag()` member function of the document class:

```
pDoc->SetModifiedFlag();
```

This is done to signal that the document data has been changed.

The last statement in the function is

```
OnInitialUpdate();
```

This statement calls the `OnInitialUpdate()` function (which you wrote earlier) so that the first object in the list will be displayed.

Don't forget to save your work:

☐ Select Save from the File menu.

Executing the PHN Application

Although you haven't written the code that writes and reads the list to and from the disk, you've finished writing most of the code. That is, you've finished writing the code that enables the user add items to the list, navigate between items in the list, and delete items in the list.

To see this code in action:

☐ Select Build `PHN.EXE` from the Project menu of Visual C++.

> *Visual C++ responds by compiling and linking the PHN application.*

☐ Select Execute `PHN.EXE` from the Project menu.

> *Visual C++ responds by executing the application.*

Experiment with the application:

☐ Add several names and phone numbers to the list with the Add button and try the Previous, Next, and Delete buttons.

As you can see, you can add items to the list, you can delete items from the list, and you can navigate between the items in the list. In the following sections, you will write the code that will enable the user to write and read the list to and from files.

To terminate the PHN application:

☐ Select Exit from the File menu.

Serializing the List

In the following sections you will write the code that serializes the m_PhoneList list. That is, you will utilize the Serialize() function of the CObList class to write and read the m_PhoneList list to and from files.

Adding Overhead Code to *PHONE.H* and *PHONE.CPP*

To support the serialization of the m_PhoneList list, you must add some overhead code in the CPhone class files (PHONE.H and PHONE.CPP). Why in the code of the CPhone class? Because m_PhoneList lists objects of class CPhone.

☐ Open the file PHONE.H and add code to it so that it will look as follows:

```
///////////////////////
// MY CODE STARTS HERE
///////////////////////

// PHONE.H
//
// Header file for the CPhone class.


// CPhone class declaration.
class CPhone : public CObject
{
    // Needed for serialization.
    DECLARE_SERIAL(CPhone)

public:

    // Constructor
    CPhone();

    // Data members
    CString m_Name;
```

```
    CString m_Phone;

    // The Serialize() function.
    virtual void Serialize(CArchive& ar);

};
```

```
/////////////////////
// MY CODE ENDS HERE
/////////////////////
```

That is, you have to add at the beginning of the CPhone class declaration the DECLARE_SERIAL statement, and you have to add the prototype of the Serialize() member function.

Save the modifications that you made to PHONE.H:

☐ Select Save from the File menu.

Now, modify the PHONE.CPP file:

☐ Open the file PHONE.CPP, and add code so that it will look as follows:

```
/////////////////////////
// MY CODE STARTS HERE
/////////////////////////

// PHONE.CPP
//
// Implementation file of the CPhone class.


#include "stdafx.h"
#include "phone.h"

// Needed for serialization.
IMPLEMENT_SERIAL(CPhone, CObject, 0)

// Constructor.
CPhone::CPhone()
{
    m_Name  = "";
    m_Phone = "";
}
```

```
// Serialize function of the CPhone class.
void CPhone::Serialize(CArchive& ar)
{
    if (ar.IsStoring())
        {
        ar << m_Name << m_Phone;
        }
    else
        {
        ar >> m_Name >> m_Phone;
        }
}

//////////////////////
// MY CODE ENDS HERE
//////////////////////
```

That is, you have to add the IMPLEMENT_SERIAL statement at the beginning of the file (immediately after the #include phone.h statement), and you have to add the serialize() function.

Save the modifications that you made to PHONE.CPP:

☐ Select Save from the File menu.

To review the code you added to PHONE.H and PHONE.CPP:

Inside the declaration of CPhone (in PHONE.H) you wrote the statement

```
// Needed for serialization.
DECLARE_SERIAL(CPhone)
```

DECLARE_SERIAL is a macro that is needed for serialization. Note that this macro takes one parameter—the name of the class.

You also added the prototype of the Serialize() function to the CPhone class declaration:

```
// The Serialize() function.
virtual void Serialize(CArchive& ar);
```

This prototype is necessary because you want to serialize a list of objects of class CPhone. Thus, the CPhone class itself must have a Serialize() function.

You added this statement to the beginning of the file PHONE.CPP:

```
// Needed for serialization.
IMPLEMENT_SERIAL(CPhone, CObject, 0)
```

IMPLEMENT_SERIAL is another macro that is needed for serialization. Note that this macro takes three parameters. The first parameter is the name of the class (CPhone),

the second parameter is the name of the base class (CObject), and the third parameter is the version number of the application. You can specify any value you wish for
the version number. The version number that you specify will be written into the
file when you'll serialize the data into the file.

Inside PHONE.CPP you wrote the code of the Serialize() function of the CPhone class:

```
// Serialize function of the CPhone class.
void CPhone::Serialize(CArchive& ar)
{
    if (ar.IsStoring())
        {
        ar << m_Name << m_Phone;
        }
    else
        {
        ar >> m_Name >> m_Phone;
        }
}
```

As you can see, the Serialize() function of the CPhone class resembles the
Serialize() function of the document class, which you saw in the previous chapter.
The code under the if,

```
ar << m_Name << m_Phone;
```

is responsible for writing the data members m_Name and m_Phone into the file, and the
code under the else,

```
ar >> m_Name >> m_Phone;
```

is responsible for reading the contents of the file into the data members m_Name and
m_Phone.

NOTE

To be able to use the Serialize() member function of a CObList class list
(for example, m_PhoneList), there are several overheads that you have to
perform:

> The objects that the list lists must be objects of a class that's
> derived from the MFC CObject class. That's why when you
> declared the CPhone class you declared it as a derived class from
> the MFC class CObject.

The class of the objects that the list lists (for example, CPhone) must have a constructor function with no arguments. That's why when you declared the CPhone class, you declared its constructor function with no arguments. If you wish, you can add additional constructor functions to the CPhone class that do have arguments.

You must declare and write the Serialize() member function of the class of the objects that the list lists (for example, CPhone::Serialize()).

When you write the code of the class of the objects that the list lists (for example, CPhone), you must use the IMPLEMENT_SERIAL and DECLARE_SERIAL macros.

Calling the List's *Serialize()* Function

Okay, so you finished writing all the overhead code necessary for serializing the list. Now, it's finally time to serialize the m_PhoneList list. That is, it's time to call the Serialize() member function of m_PhoneList.

The question is, from where should you call this function? Recall that the Serialize() function of the document class is executed automatically whenever the user selects Save, Save As, or Open from the File menu. Thus, you should call the Serialize() function of m_PhoneList from the Serialize() function of the document class.

This way, whenever the user selects Save or Save As from the File menu, m_PhoneList will be saved into the file that the user selected. Also, whenever the user selects Open from the File menu, m_PhoneList will be filled with the list that's stored in the file that the user opened.

Follow these steps to write the code that calls the Serialize() function of m_PhoneList:

☐ Open the file PHNDOC.CPP and modify the Serialize() function of the document class so that it will look as follows:

```
/////////////////////////////////////////////////////
// CPhnDoc serialization

void CPhnDoc::Serialize(CArchive& ar)
{
```

```
if (ar.IsStoring())
{
     // TODO: add storing code here
}
else
{
     // TODO: add loading code here

}
```

```
/////////////////////
// MY CODE STARTS HERE
/////////////////////
```

```
m_PhoneList.Serialize(ar);
```

```
/////////////////////
// MY CODE ENDS HERE
/////////////////////
```

```
}
```

As you can see, you didn't have to write any code under the `if` and `else` of the document `Serialize()` function (as you did in the previous chapter). Instead you wrote the statement

```
m_PhoneList.Serialize(ar);
```

at the end of the function. You do that because you want to run the `Serialize()` function of `m_PhoneList`. The `Serialize()` function of `m_PhoneList` will do all the work for you; it will serialize all the objects listed in `m_PhoneList` to or from the file that the user selected.

Note that you pass the parameter `ar` to the `Serialize()` function of `m_PhoneList`. Recall that `ar` is the archive object that corresponds to the file the user selected. You need to pass `ar` because the serialize function of `m_PhoneList` must "know" which file the user selected.

Note that you didn't have to write the code of the `Serialize()` function of `m_PhoneList`. In fact, you can't edit the code of this `Serialize()` function because `m_PhoneList` is an object of the MFC class `CObList` and you cannot modify the code of an MFC class.

The question is, what does the `Serialize()` function of the `CObList` class (`PhoneList.Serialize()`) do?

The statement

```
m_PhoneList.Serialize()
```

will execute the `Serialize()` function of each of the objects that are listed in `m_PhoneList`. Because `m_PhoneList` lists objects of class `CPhone`, the previous statement will cause the execution of the `Serialize()` function of the `CPhone` class for each of the objects that's listed in `m_PhoneList`.

Don't forget to save the changes that you made to `PHNDOC.CPP`:

☐ Select Save from the File menu.

Executing the PHN Application

You've finished writing the code that serializes the `m_PhoneList` list to/from files.

To see this code in action:

☐ Select Build PHN.EXE from the Project menu of Visual C++.

  Visual C++ responds by compiling and linking the PHN application.

☐ Select Execute PHN.EXE from the Project menu.

  Visual C++ responds by executing the application.

Experiment with the application:

☐ Add several names and phone numbers to the list.

☐ Select Save from the File menu and save your list as `TRY.PHN`.

☐ Experiment with the other File menu options (Save As, Open, and New).

As you can see, you can save lists of names and phone numbers in files, and you can load saved lists from files.

To terminate the PHN application:

☐ Select Exit from the File menu.

The Final Touch

There are several cosmetic enhancements that you can apply to the PHN application:

☐ Use App Studio's String Table editor to modify the IDR_MAINFRAME string to:

```
Phone for Windows\nUntitled\nPHONE Document\nPHN Files (*.phn)\n.phn
```

> **NOTE**
>
> If you forgot how to use the String Table editor, refer to the end of Chapter 13, where this topic is discussed via a detailed step-by-step example.

The PHN application is now complete! You can build and execute it to verify that the changes you just made to the IDR_MAINFRAME string work.

15

Customizing Serialization

In the previous two chapters you learned
about the process of serialization. In
Chapter 13, "Using Serialization to Write
and Read Data to and from Files," you
wrote a program that serializes data
members of the document class, and in
Chapter 14, "Using Serialization to Write
and Read Lists to and from Files," you
wrote a program that serializes a list of
objects. In this chapter you will learn
how to customize serialization.

The *CArchive* Class

Recall from the previous two chapters that the parameter of the Serialize() function is an object of class CArchive. For example, a typical Serialize() function of the document class looks as follows:

```
void CTryDoc::Serialize(CArchive& ar)
{
    if (ar.IsStoring())
    {

/////////////////////
// MY CODE STARTS HERE
/////////////////////

ar << m_Var1 << m_Var2 << m_Var3;

/////////////////////
// MY CODE ENDS HERE
/////////////////////

    }
    else
    {

/////////////////////
// MY CODE STARTS HERE
/////////////////////

ar >> m_Var1 >> m_Var2 >> m_Var3;

/////////////////////
// MY CODE ENDS HERE
/////////////////////

    }
```

The parameter of the Serialize() function (ar) is an archive object (an object of class CArchive) and it corresponds to a file. In the case of the document class, ar corresponds to the file that the user selects from the File menu. For example, if the user selects Open from the File menu and then selects the file MyFile.TXT, the code for the application (code that Visual C++ wrote for you) is executed automatically. This code creates a CArchive object that corresponds to the MyFile.TXT file and passes this CArchive object to the Serialize() function of the document class.

Sometimes you'll find it useful to create and customize a CArchive object by your-self, such as in cases where you don't want the user to select the file, but rather you want to serialize data to or from a specific file.

The ARCH application illustrates how you can create and customize a CArchive object by yourself.

The ARCH Application

Now you'll write the ARCH application. The code that you'll write creates an object of class CArchive and uses this object to write and read data to and from a file.

Before you start writing the ARCH application, execute the copy of it in your C:\VCPROG\ORIGINAL\CH15\ARCH directory.

To execute the ARCH application:

☐ Use the Run item from the File menu of the Program Manager to execute C:\VCPROG\ORIGINAL\CH15\ARCH\ARCH.EXE.

> *Windows responds by executing the ARCH application. The main window of* ARCH.EXE *appears, as shown in Figure 15.1.*

Figure 15.1.
The ARCH
application's
main window.

Arch Windows Application - Arch
<u>F</u>ile   <u>H</u>elp
Variable 1: [   ]
Variable 2: [   ]
[<u>S</u>ave To File TRY.TRY]   [<u>L</u>oad From File TRY.TRY]

As you can see from Figure 15.1, the main window of the application displays a blank form with two fields (Variable 1 and Variable 2) and two push buttons (Save To File TRY.TRY and Load From File TRY.TRY).

The ARCH application has two popup menus, File and Help. These popup menus are shown in Figures 15.2 and 15.3.

Figure 15.2.
The ARCH
application's
File popup
menu.

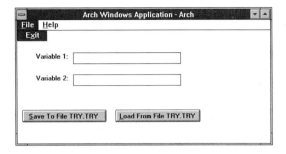

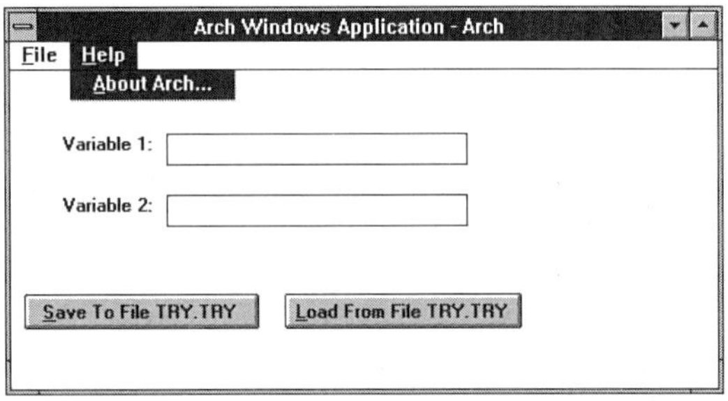

Figure 15.3.
The ARCH
application's
Help popup
menu.

☐ Fill the Variable 1 and Variable 2 fields of the blank entry form with any string values you like.

☐ Click the Save To File TRY.TRY button.

The ARCH application responds by saving the two strings you typed into the file TRY.TRY.

To verify that the strings are saved:

☐ Delete the contents of the two fields and then click the Load From File TRY.TRY button.

The ARCH application responds by loading the contents of the file TRY.TRY into the Variable 1 and Variable 2 fields. As you can see, the two fields are now filled with the values that you saved.

To terminate the ARCH application:

☐ Select Exit from the File menu.

Now that you know what the ARCH application is supposed to do, you can start writing it.

Creating the Project of the ARCH Application

To create the project of the ARCH application:

☐ Select AppWizard from the Project menu.

> *Visual C++ responds by running AppWizard.*

☐ Use the Directory list box to select the directory `C:\VCPROG\PRACTICE\CH15`.

☐ Type `arch` in the Project Name box.

Now your AppWizard dialog box looks as shown in Figure 15.4.

*Figure 15.4.
The ARCH
application's
AppWizard
dialog box.*

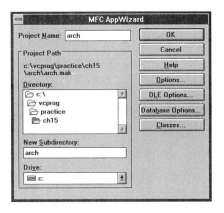

☐ Click the Options button and set the options as shown in Figure 15.5 (that is, uncheck all the check boxes except the Generate Source Comments check box).

*Figure 15.5.
Setting the options
for the ARCH
application.*

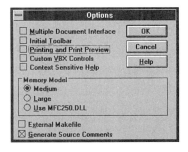

☐ Click the OK button in the Options dialog box, click the OK button in the AppWizard dialog box, and click the Create button in the New Application Information dialog box.

AppWizard responds by creating the ARCH project and all the skeleton files of the ARCH application.

To remove the debug options of the project (so that you'll have a small EXE file):

☐ Select Project from the Options menu in Visual C++, click the Release radio button, and then click the OK button in the dialog box.

Creating the Form of the Application

As shown in Figure 15.1, the main window of the ARCH application should contain a data entry form for entering two strings.

To implement this form you'll replace the current view class of the application with a new view class derived from the CFormView class.

Follow these steps to create the form of the application:

☐ Use the File Manager in Windows (or DOS Shell) to delete the two view class files in the ARCH application:

Delete C:\VCPROG\PRACTICE\CH15\ARCH\ARCHVIEW.CPP.
Delete C:\VCPROG\PRACTICE\CH15\ARCH\ARCHVIEW.H.

☐ Select ClassWizard from the Browse menu in Visual C++.

ClassWizard responds by displaying a dialog box telling you that the files in the view class don't exist.

☐ Click the OK button in the dialog box.

☐ Click the Remove button in the Repair Class Information dialog box.

☐ Click the OK button in ClassWizard's dialog box.

You've just finished removing the view class of the ARCH application.

In the following steps you'll create a dialog box, you'll create a CFormView type class for this dialog box, and you'll make this class the new view class of the application.

☐ Select App Studio from the Tools menu in Visual C++.

☐ Create a new dialog box with App Studio.

☐ Double-click in a free area of the new dialog box.

☐ Select Styles from the drop-down list box at the upper-right corner of the Properties window.

Set the Styles properties of the dialog box as follows:

☐ Select Child in the Style box.

☐ Select None in the Border box.

☐ Uncheck the Visible property (that is, remove the check mark from the Visible check box).

☐ Select General from the drop-down list box at the upper-right corner of the Properties window and make sure that the Caption box is empty.

Now, connect the dialog box to a class derived from CFormView:

☐ Select ClassWizard from the Resource menu in App Studio.

   ClassWizard responds by displaying the Add Class dialog box.

☐ Type CArchView in the Class Name box.

☐ Set the Class Type to CFormView.

☐ Make sure that the Header File box is filled with archview.h and that the Implementation File box is filled with archview.cpp.

☐ Click the Create Class button.

☐ Click the OK button in ClassWizard's window to go back to App Studio.

You've finished creating the new view class of the application. This view class is a derived class from the MFC `CFormView` class, and it's connected to the dialog box that you created. Thus, the main window of the application will be the dialog box you created.

The Visual Implementation of the Dialog Box

☐ Design the dialog box of the ARCH application per Table 15.1.

Table 15.1. The ARCH application's dialog box.

Class Name:	`CArchView`
Figure:	15.6
OK Button:	No
Cancel Button:	No

Object	Property	Setting
Dialog Box	ID	`IDD_DIALOG1`
Label	ID	`IDC_STATIC`
	Caption	`Variable 1:`
Edit Box	ID	`IDC_VAR1`
	Variable	`m_Var1`
	Type	`CString`
Label	ID	`IDC_STATIC`
	Caption	`Variable 2:`
Edit Box	ID	`IDC_VAR2`
	Variable	`m_Var2`
	Type	`CString`
Push Button	ID	`IDC_SAVE_BUTTON`
	Caption	`&Save To File TRY.TRY`
Push Button	ID	`IDC_LOAD_BUTTON`
	Caption	`&Load From File TRY.TRY`

Your dialog box should now look as shown in Figure 15.6.

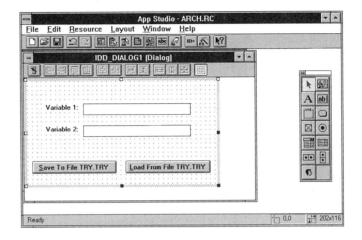

Figure 15.6.
The ARCH
application's
dialog box.

Save your work:

☐ Select Save from the File menu in App Studio.

You've finished designing the form of the application!

The Visual Implementation of the Menu

The ARCH application should have a menu, as shown in Figures 15.1, 15.2, and 15.3.

☐ Use App Studio to implement the menu of the ARCH application per Table 15.2.

Table 15.2. The ARCH application's menu.
Figures relating to menu: 15.1, 15.2, 15.3

Menu Item
&File
E&xit
&Help
&About Arch...

To save your work:

☐ Select Save from the File menu in App Studio.

The visual implementation of the ARCH application's menu is complete.

Executing the ARCH Application

Even though you haven't finished writing the ARCH application, execute it to see what you've accomplished so far:

☐ Select Rebuild All ARCH.EXE from the Project menu in Visual C++.

>*Visual C++ responds by compiling and linking the ARCH application.*

☐ Select Execute ARCH.EXE from the Project menu.

>*Visual C++ responds by executing the ARCH application. As you can see, the dialog box that you designed appears as the main window of the application (see Figure 15.1).*

Of course, none of the buttons in the dialog box are working because you haven't written any code yet. In the following sections you'll attach code to the two buttons in the form.

To exit the ARCH application:

☐ Select Exit from the File menu.

Attaching Code to the Save Button

Whenever the user clicks the Save To File TRY.TRY button, the contents of the two edit boxes (IDC_VAR1 and IDC_VAR2) should be serialized into the file TRY.TRY.

Follow these steps to attach code to the Save button:

☐ Use ClassWizard to add a function for the event:

Class Name:	CArchView
Object ID:	IDC_SAVE_BUTTON
Message:	BN_CLICKED
Function Name:	OnSaveButton()

Make sure to add the OnSaveButton() function to the CArchView class.

☐ Edit the OnSaveButton() function that you added to the ARCHVIEW.CPP file.

After you edit the OnSaveButton() function, it looks as follows:

```
void CArchView::OnSaveButton()
{
// TODO: Add your control notification handler code here

    ///////////////////////
    // MY CODE STARTS HERE
    ///////////////////////

    // Update m_Var1 and m_Var2 with the screen contents.
    UpdateData(TRUE);

    // Create the file TRY.TRY.
    CFile f;
    f.Open("TRY.TRY", CFile::modeCreate | CFile::modeWrite );

    // Create an archive object.
    CArchive ar( &f, CArchive::store );

    // Serialize m_Var1 and m_Var2 into the archive.
    ar << m_Var1 << m_Var2;

    // Close the archive
    ar.Close();

    // Close the file.
    f.Close();

    ///////////////////////
    // MY CODE ENDS HERE
    ///////////////////////

}
```

To review the code for the OnSaveButton() function:

The first statement,

```
UpdateData(TRUE);
```

updates the variables of the edit boxes (m_Var1 and m_Var2) with the current values displayed in the edit boxes.

The next two statements create the file TRY.TRY:

```
CFile f;
f.Open("TRY.TRY", CFile::modeCreate | CFile::modeWrite );
```

The first statement creates an object of class CFile, called f, and the second statement uses the Open() member function of the CFile class to create the TRY.TRY file. The CFile class will be discussed in more detail in the next chapter.

The next statement creates an object of class CArchive, called ar:

```
CArchive ar( &f, CArchive::store );
```

As you can see, this statement passes two parameters to the constructor of CArchive. The first parameter is the address of the CFile object associated with the archive. In this statement the first parameter is &f, the address of the CFile object of the TRY.TRY file. Thus, the archive object ar will be associated with the file TRY.TRY.

The second parameter in this statement specifies the mode of the archive object. An archive object can be created for storage purposes (to save variables into the archive) or for loading purposes (to load data from the archive into variables). In this statement, the second parameter is

```
CArchive::store
```

Thus, the archive object ar will be used for storage purposes. You want to use ar for storage purposes because you want the m_Var1 and m_Var2 variables to be saved into the archive whenever the user clicks the Save button.

Now that you have an archive object associated with the file TRY.TRY, and this archive object is in a storage mode, you can serialize variables into TRY.TRY. The next statement in the function serializes the two data members, m_Var1 and m_Var2, into TRY.TRY:

```
ar << m_Var1 << m_Var2;
```

The next statement uses the Close() member function of the CArchive class to close the ar archive:

```
ar.Close();
```

The last statement uses the Close() member function of the CFile class to close the file associated with the f object (TRY.TRY):

```
f.Close();
```

Don't forget to save your work:

☐ Select Save from the File menu.

Attaching Code to the Load Button

Whenever the user clicks the Load From File TRY.TRY button, the contents of the two edit boxes (IDC_VAR1 and IDC_VAR2) should be filled with the values stored in the file TRY.TRY.

Follow these steps to attach code to the Load button:

☐ Use ClassWizard to add a function for the event:

Class Name:	CArchView
Object ID:	IDC_LOAD_BUTTON
Message:	BN_CLICKED
Function Name:	OnLoadButton()

Make sure to add the OnLoadButton() function to the CArchView class.

☐ Edit the OnLoadButton() function that you added to the ARCHVIEW.CPP file as follows:

```
void CArchView::OnLoadButton()
{
    // TODO: Add your control notification handler code here

    /////////////////////////
    // MY CODE STARTS HERE
    /////////////////////////

    // Open the file TRY.TRY.
    CFile f;
    if ( f.Open("TRY.TRY", CFile::modeRead)== FALSE )
        return;

    // Create an archive object.
    CArchive ar( &f, CArchive::load );

    // Serialize data from the archive into m_Var1 and m_Var2.
    ar >> m_Var1 >> m_Var2;

    // Close the archive
    ar.Close();

    // Close the file.
    f.Close();

    // Update screen with the new values of m_Var1 and m_Var2.
    UpdateData(FALSE);
```

```
/////////////////////
// MY CODE ENDS HERE
/////////////////////
```

```
}
```

To review the code for the OnLoadButton() function:

The first two statements open the file TRY.TRY in read mode:

```
CFile f;
if ( f.Open("TRY.TRY", CFile::modeRead)== FALSE )
    return;
```

The first statement,

```
CFile f;
```

creates an object of class CFile, called f.

The second statement,

```
if ( f.Open("TRY.TRY", CFile::modeRead)== FALSE )
    return;
```

is an if statement that uses the Open() member function of the CFile class to try to open the TRY.TRY file in read mode. If the returned value of the Open() function is FALSE, it means that the file can't be opened, in which case the if condition is satisfied and the function is terminated with the return statement. As stated before, the CFile class will be discussed in more detail in the next chapter.

The next statement creates an object of class CArchive, called ar:

```
CArchive ar( &f, CArchive::load );
```

As you can see, this statement passes two parameters to the constructor of CArchive. The first parameter is the address of the CFile object that is associated with the archive. In this statement the first parameter is &f, the address of the CFile object of the TRY.TRY file. Thus, the archive object ar will be associated with the file TRY.TRY.

The second parameter in the preceding statement specifies the mode of the archive object. As stated before, an archive object can be created for storage purposes (to save variables into the archive) or for loading purposes (to load data from the archive into variables). In this statement, the second parameter is

```
CArchive::load
```

Thus, the archive object ar will be used for loading purposes. You want to use ar for loading purposes because you want to load data from the archive into the m_Var1 and m_Var2 variables whenever the user clicks the Load button.

Now that you have an archive object that is associated with the file TRY.TRY, and this archive object is in a loading mode, you can serialize data from TRY.TRY into variables. The next statement in the function serializes data from TRY.TRY into the two data members, m_Var1 and m_Var2:

```
ar >> m_Var1 >> m_Var2;
```

The next statement,

```
ar.Close();
```

uses the Close() member function of the CArchive class to close the ar archive.

The next statement,

```
f.Close();
```

uses the Close() member function of the CFile class to close the file associated with the f object (TRY.TRY).

The last statement in the OnLoadButton() function,

```
UpdateData(FALSE);
```

updates the screen (that is, the two edit boxes) with the new values of m_Var1 and m_Var2.

Don't forget to save your work:

☐ Select Save from the File menu.

Executing the Finished ARCH Application

You've finished writing the code for the ARCH application.

To test your code:

☐ Select Build ARCH.EXE from the Project menu in Visual C++.

☐ Select Execute ARCH.EXE from the Project menu.

Visual C++ responds by executing the application.

Experiment with the Save and Load buttons. As you can see, when you click the Save button, the contents of the two edit boxes are saved, and when you click the Load button, the edit boxes are filled with the saved data.

16

Writing and Reading Data (Without Serialization) to and from Files

In this chapter you'll learn how to
write and read data to and from files.
Unlike the programs in the previous
chapters that use serialization, the
programs in this chapter don't;
instead, they utilize
the MFC class CFile.

So far in this book, you've used the default icon that Visual C++ assigns as the icon for the application. In this chapter you'll also learn how to attach your own icons to the application.

The FileIt Application

The FileIt application utilizes the MFC class `CFile` to write and read data to and from a file. Before you start writing the FileIt application by yourself, execute a copy of the FileIt application that resides in your `C:\VCPROG\ORIGINAL\CH16\FILEIT` directory.

To execute the FileIt application:

☐ Use Run from the Program Manager's File menu to execute
  `C:\VCPROG\ORIGINAL\CH16\FILEIT\FileIt.EXE`.

  Windows responds by executing the FileIt application. The main window of
  `FileIt.EXE` *appears, as shown in Figure 16.1.*

Figure 16.1.
The FileIt
application's
main window.

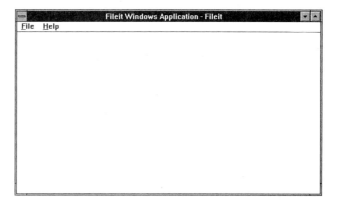

The FileIt application has two popup menus: File and Help. These popup menus are shown in Figures 16.2 and 16.3.

Figure 16.2.
The FileIt
application's
File menu.

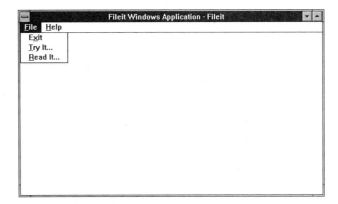

Figure 16.3.
The FileIt
application's
Help menu.

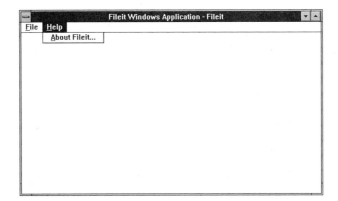

☐ Select Try It from the File menu.

> *FileIt responds by displaying a dialog box (see Figure 16.4).*

Figure 16.4.
The FileIt
application's
dialog box.

As you can see, the dialog box contains an edit box and a push button labeled Save It As MyFile.TXT.

☐ Click inside the edit box and type something.

☐ Click the Save It As MyFile.TXT button.

> *FileIt responds by creating the file*
> `C:\vcProg\Practice\CH16\FILEIT\MyFile.TXT`.
> *This text file contains the text you typed in the edit box.*

To verify that this is indeed the case:

☐ Switch to the Notepad program that comes with Windows (it's usually inside the Accessories group).

☐ Load the file `C:\vcProg\Practice\CH16\FILEIT\MyFile.TXT`.

As you can see, this file contains the text you typed in the edit box.

☐ Click either the OK or Cancel button of the dialog box to close it.

☐ Select Read It from the File menu.

> *FileIt responds by reading the* `MyFile.TXT` *file and displaying its contents.*

☐ Experiment with the FileIt application and then select Exit from the File menu.

Note that when selecting About FileIt from the Help menu, FileIt responds by displaying the standard About dialog box. The icon that appears in the dialog box is the regular Microsoft AFX icon. Later in this chapter you'll also learn to insert a more appropriate icon into the About dialog box.

Now that you know what FileIt does, you can write it.

Creating the Project of the FileIt Application

To create the project of the FileIt application:

☐ Select AppWizard from the Project menu.

> *Visual C++ responds by running AppWizard.*

☐ Use the Directory list box to select the directory `C:\VCPROG\PRACTICE\CH16`.

☐ Type `fileit` in the Project Name box.

Your AppWizard dialog box should now look as shown in Figure 16.5.

Figure 16.5.
The FileIt
application's
AppWizard
dialog box.

☐ Click the Options button and set the options as shown in Figure 16.6 (that is, uncheck all the check boxes except the Generate Source Comments check box).

Figure 16.6.
Setting the options
for the FileIt
application.

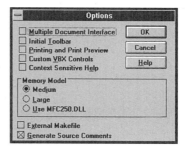

☐ Click the OK button of the Options dialog box and then click the OK button of the AppWizard dialog box and finally click the Create button of the New Application Information dialog box.

> *AppWizard responds by creating the FileIt project and all the skeleton files of the FileIt application.*

To remove the debug options of the project (so you'll have a small EXE file):

☐ Select Project from the Options menu of Visual C++, click the Release radio button, and then click the OK button of the dialog box.

The Visual Implementation of the FileIt Application

The FileIt application has a menu, a custom dialog box, and an About dialog box. In the following sections you'll visually design the menu and the FileIt application's custom dialog box.

The Visual Implementation of the FileIt Application's Menu Bar

The FileIt application should have a menu, as shown in Figures 16.1, 16.2, and 16.3.

☐ Use App Studio to implement the menu of the FileIt application per Table 16.1.

Table 16.1. The FileIt application's menu bar.
Figures relating to menu: 16.1, 16.2, 16.3

Menu Item
&File
E&xit
&Try It...
&Read It...
&Help
&About Fileit...

To save your work:

☐ Select Save from the File menu of App Studio.

The visual implementation of the FileIt application's menu is complete.

The Visual Implementation of the Dialog Box

Now you'll visually implement the dialog box of the FileIt application:

☐ Implement the dialog box of the FileIt application per Table 16.2.

Table 16.2. The FileIt application's dialog box.

Class Name:	CMyDlg (of class CDialog)
Figure:	16.4
OK Button:	Yes
Cancel Button:	Yes

Object	Property	Setting
Dialog Box	ID	IDD_DIALOG1
Push Button	ID	IDC_SAVE_IT
	Caption	&Save It As MyFile.TXT
Edit Box	ID	IDC_EDIT1
	Variable	m_EditBoxContents
	Type	CString

That's it! You've completed the visual implementation of the dialog box.

To save your work:

☐ Select Save from the File menu.

Declaring the Dialog Box Object as a Data Member of the View Class

Now you'll create an object, dlg, of class CMyDlg. You'll declare this object as a data member of the view class (the CFileitView class).

☐ Open the FILEIVW.H file and modify the declaration of the CFileitView class. After you modify the CFileitView class declaration, it looks as follows:

```
{
protected: // create from serialization only
    CFileitView();
    DECLARE_DYNCREATE(CFileitView)

// Attributes
public:
    CFileitDoc* GetDocument();

    ////////////////////////
    // MY CODE STARTS HERE
    ////////////////////////
```

465

```
    // Create an object dlg (a dialog box) of class CMyDlg.
    CMyDlg dlg;

    ////////////////////
    // MY CODE ENDS HERE
    ////////////////////


// Operations
public:

// Implementation
public:
    virtual ~CFileitView();
    virtual void OnDraw(CDC* pDC);
// overridden to draw this view
#ifdef _DEBUG
    virtual void AssertValid() const;
    virtual void Dump(CDumpContext& dc) const;
#endif

protected:

// Generated message map functions
protected:
    //{{AFX_MSG(CFileitView)
// NOTE - the ClassWizard will add and remove
// member functions here.
// DO NOT EDIT what you see in these blocks
// of generated code !
    //}}AFX_MSG
    DECLARE_MESSAGE_MAP()
};
```

Because the CMyDlg class is unknown in the file FILEIVW.H, you have to #include the file MyDlg.h (which contains the class declaration of CMyDlg) at the beginning of the FILEIVW.H file:

☐ Add the #include "MyDlg.h" statement at the beginning of the FILEIVW.H file.

☐ After #including this file, the beginning of the FILEIVW.H file should look as follows:

```
// fileivw.h : interface of the CFileitView class
//
/////////////////////////////////////////////////////////
```

```
/////////////////////
// MY CODE STARTS HERE
/////////////////////

#include "MyDlg.h"

/////////////////////
// MY CODE ENDS HERE
/////////////////////
```

```
......
......
......
```

Attaching Code to the FileIt Application's Try It Menu Item

You'll now attach code to the Try It menu item. Recall that when the user selects the Try It menu item, the FileIt application should display the dialog box.

☐ Use ClassWizard to add a function for the event:

Class Name:	`CFileitView`
Object ID:	`ID_FILE_TRYIT`
Message:	`COMMAND`
Function Name:	`OnFileTryit()`

NOTE: Make sure that you're adding the function to the `CFileitView` class.

☐ Edit the `OnFileTryit()` function that you added to the `FILEIVW.CPP` file.
After you edit the `OnFileTryit()` function, it looks as follows:

```
void CFileitView::OnFileTryit()
{
    // TODO: Add your command handler code here

    /////////////////////
    // MY CODE STARTS HERE
    /////////////////////

    // Display the dlg dialog box.
    dlg.DoModal();

    /////////////////////
    // MY CODE ENDS HERE
    /////////////////////

}
```

467

In this code, you display the dialog box dlg by using the DoModal() function:

```
dlg.DoModal();
```

Compiling, Linking, and Executing the FileIt Application

Although you haven't finished writing the FileIt application, compile, link, and execute it so that you can verify that everything you've typed so far is working.

☐ Select Rebuild All FileIt.EXE from the Project menu.

☐ Execute the FileIt application.

☐ Select Try It from the File menu.

FileIt responds by displaying the dialog box.

☐ Type something in the edit box.

☐ Click the OK button.

FileIt responds by closing the dialog box.

Because you connected the edit box with the variable m_EditBoxContents, the program automatically updates the m_EditBoxContents variable with the contents of the edit box. To verify that FileIt indeed maintains the contents of the edit box:

☐ Select Try It from the File menu.

FileIt responds by displaying the dialog box. The contents of the edit box are the same as they were before you closed the dialog box with the OK button.

☐ Close the dialog box and then select Exit from the File menu to terminate the FileIt application.

Providing Your User with a Save Button

The text that you type in the edit box can be saved to a file by clicking the Save It As MyFile.TXT button. As implied by its caption, this button causes the contents of the edit box to be saved to the MyFile.TXT file (in the current directory). Now you'll attach code to this button:

☐ Use ClassWizard to add a function for the event:

Class Name:	CMyDlg
Object ID:	IDC_SAVE_IT
Message:	BN_CLICKED
Function Name:	OnSaveIt()

In the preceding, make sure that you're adding the function to the CMyDlg class.

☐ Edit the OnSaveIt() function that you added to the MYDLG.CPP file. After you edit the OnSaveIt() function, it looks as follows:

```
void CMyDlg::OnSaveIt()
{
// TODO: Add your control notification handler code here

    //////////////////////////
    // MY CODE STARTS HERE
    //////////////////////////

    // Create an object TheFile of class CFile
    CFile TheFile;

    // Prepare the file for creation OR writing
    TheFile.Open ( "MyFile.TXT",
                CFile::modeCreate|CFile::modeWrite );


    // Update the value of m_EditBoxContents
    UpdateData (TRUE);

    // Write into the TheFile
    TheFile.Write ( m_EditBoxContents,
                    m_EditBoxContents.GetLength() );

    // Close the file
    TheFile.Close();

    //////////////////////////
    // MY CODE ENDS HERE
    //////////////////////////

}
```

The *CFile* MFC Class

The code you typed previously creates an object called TheFile of class CFile:

```
CFile TheFile;
```

469

What is the CFile class, and why do you need to create an object of this class? Because this class has a lot of "goodies" (useful member functions) in it that enable you to manipulate files with great ease.

The code you typed then uses the Open() member function of CFile to create MyFile.TXT:

```
TheFile.Open ( "MyFile.TXT",
              CFile::modeCreate|CFile::modeWrite );
```

The first parameter of Open() is the name of the file that you want to create or write into, and the second parameter is

```
CFile::modeCreate | CFile::modeWrite
```

These constants tell the Open() function to create the file (CFile::modeCreate) if it doesn't already exist and to open the file(CFile::modeWrite) for writing if it does exist. (Note that the OR operator (¦) is used between the two constants.)

The OnSaveIt() function then uses the UpdateData() function to update the variable m_EditBoxContents with the contents of the edit box:

```
UpdateData (TRUE);
```

> **NOTE**
>
> As you know, Visual C++ automatically updates the value of m_EditBoxContents. So why do you have to do the updating now? Because the automatic updating of m_EditBoxContents is performed after the user clicks the OK button. However, at this point in the program, the m_EditBoxContents hasn't been updated yet.

Now that m_EditBoxContents is updated with the contents of the edit box, you can use the Write() member function of the CFile class to write data into the MyFile.TXT:

```
TheFile.Write ( m_EditBoxContents,
                m_EditBoxContents.GetLength() );
```

The first parameter of the Write() function is the data you want to write into the MyFile.TXT file. The second parameter is the length of the data you want to write into the file. Note that the length is specified as:

```
m_EditBoxContents.GetLength()
```

Because the m_EditBoxContents variable is of type CString, you can use CString's GetLength() member function to extract the length of m_EditBoxContents.

To summarize, the Write() function writes the contents of the m_EditBoxContents into the MyFile.TXT file.

And finally, MyFile.TXT is closed by using the Close() member function of the CFile class:

```
TheFile.Close();
```

> **NOTE**
>
> The TheFile object is local to the OnSaveIt() function. This means that when the OnSaveIt() function is terminated, the TheFile object is destroyed (because the destructor function of the CFile class is executed). Thus, the statement TheFile.Close(); isn't really needed.
>
> Once the TheFile object is destroyed (or the TheFile.Close() function is executed), you can't perform any file manipulations on the file.

To see the Save It As MyFile.TXT button in action:

☐ Compile, link, and execute the FileIt application.

☐ Write something in the edit box.

☐ Click the Save It As MyFile.TXT button.

> *FileIt responds by saving the contents of the edit box into the MyFile.TXT file.*

☐ Verify that indeed the data was written into the C:\vcProg\Practice\CH16\FileIt\MyFile.TXT file by using Notepad to open the file and examining its contents.

☐ Close the dialog box and then select Exit from the File menu to terminate the FileIt application.

Reading the *MyFile.TXT* File

You've successfully written code that writes data into the MyFile.TXT file. You'll now attach code to the Read It menu item. The code you'll write will cause the FileIt program to read the data of MyFile.TXT and display it whenever the user selects Read It from the File menu.

☐ Use ClassWizard to add a function for the event:

Class Name:	CFileitView
Object ID:	ID_FILE_READIT
Message:	COMMAND
Function Name:	OnFileReadit()

Make sure you add the function to the CFileitView class.

☐ Edit the OnFileReadit() function that you added to the FILEIVW.CPP file. After you edit the OnFileReadit() function, it looks as follows:

```
void CFileitView::OnFileReadit()
{
// TODO: Add your command handler code here

    /////////////////////////
    // MY CODE STARTS HERE
    /////////////////////////

    UINT BytesRead;
    char FromFile[1000];


    // Create an object readMe of class CFile
     CFile readMe("MyFile.TXT",
                 CFile::modeRead );

    // Read the file into FromFile
    BytesRead = readMe.Read ( FromFile,
                              200 );


    // Add a null terminator
    FromFile[BytesRead] = 0;

    // Display it
    MessageBox ( FromFile );

    /////////////////////////
    // MY CODE ENDS HERE
    /////////////////////////


}
```

The code you typed declares two local variables,

```
UINT BytesRead;
char FromFile[1000];
```

and then an object `readMe` of class `CFile` is created:

```
CFile readMe("MyFile.TXT",
             CFile::modeRead );
```

Note that in this object creation statement, the first parameter is

```
"MyFile.TXT"
```

which is the name of the file from which data will be read and the second parameter specifies that the file is to be read.

The `Read()` member function of `CFile` is executed:

```
BytesRead = readMe.Read ( FromFile,
                          200 );
```

The first parameter of the `Read()` function specifies the name of the buffer that will hold the read data, and the second parameter is the maximum number of bytes that will be read.

The actual number of bytes read is returned from the `Read()` function and is assigned to the `BytesRead` variable.

The `OnFileReadit()` function then attaches a null-terminator character to the `FromFile` buffer:

```
FromFile[BytesRead] = 0;
```

And finally, the read data is displayed with the `MessageBox()` function:

```
MessageBox ( FromFile );
```

Note that the null terminator was attached to the `FromFile` buffer, because the `MessageBox()` function expects a null-terminated string as its parameter.

☐ Compile, link and execute the FileIt application, and verify its operation.

The SeekIt Application

One of the most important member functions of the `CFile` class is the `Seek()` function. You can use this function to position the file pointer at any desired location. Thus, your program will be able to read any number of bytes from any desired location in the file. The SeekIt application demonstrates how you can use the `Seek()` function to determine the sampling rate of a WAV file.

The Sampling Rate of a WAV File

A WAV file is a standard sound file used by Windows to play sound. A WAV file can be recorded at various sampling rates. For example, you can record a WAV file at a sampling rate of 8,000 Hz. To play back the WAV file, the program that plays the WAV file must determine the sampling rate at which the WAV file was recorded. Every WAV file begins with a header section. This header section contains information about the WAV file, including the sampling rate.

You can display a WAV file by using the DOS DEBUG program shipped with DOS:

☐ Exit Windows to a DOS shell (that is, double-click the MS-DOS icon that resides inside the Main group).

> *Windows responds by exiting to a DOS shell.*

☐ At the DOS prompt, type Debug C:\Windows\TADA.WAV and press the Enter key.

The preceding command line "assumes" that your Windows directory is C:\Windows, that the TADA.WAV file resides in your Windows directory, that your PATH includes your DOS directory, and that the DEBUG.EXE program resides in your DOS directory.

> *DOS responds by executing the DEBUG program with the TADA.WAV file, and you'll see the - character displayed.*

The - character is an indication that Debug is waiting for a command from you.

☐ Type D {Enter}.

> *DEBUG responds by displaying the first 128 bytes of the TADA.WAV file (see Figure 16.7).*

Figure 16.7.
Displaying the first
128 bytes of
TADA.WAV.

```
C:\WINDOWS>debug tada.wav
-d
2D9B:0100  52 49 46 46 94 6C 00 00-57 41 56 45 66 6D 74 20  RIFF.l..WAVEfmt
2D9B:0110  10 00 00 00 01 00 01 00-22 56 00 00 22 56 00 00  ........"V.."V..
2D9B:0120  01 00 08 00 64 61 74 61-70 6C 00 00 80 80 80 80  ....datapl......
2D9B:0130  80 80 80 80 80 80 80 80-80 80 80 80 80 80 80 80  ................
2D9B:0140  80 80 80 80 80 80 80 80-80 80 80 80 80 80 80 80  ................
2D9B:0150  80 80 80 80 80 80 80 80-80 80 80 80 80 80 80 80  ................
2D9B:0160  80 80 80 80 80 80 80 80-80 80 80 80 80 80 80 80  ................
2D9B:0170  80 80 80 80 80 80 80 80-80 80 80 80 80 80 80 80  ................
-
```

As shown in Figure 16.7, the first byte of the TADA.WAV byte is 52, the second byte is 49, and so on. As stated, these bytes represent information about the WAV file. The two bytes of interest are the 25th and 26th bytes. As shown in Figure 16.7, the 25th byte is 22, and the 26th byte is 56. (In Figure 16.7, these two bytes are circled.)

What is the meaning of these two bytes? To understand their meaning, you have to reverse their order. Thus, these two bytes become

56 22

5622 (hex) is equal to

```
5*16*16*16 + 6*16+16 + 2*16 + 2 =
  20480    +   1536  + 32   + 2 = 22050
```

So to summarize, 5622 (hex) is the same as 22,050 (decimal). Thus, the TADA.WAV was recorded at 22,050 Hz.

To exit DEBUG:

☐ Type Q {Enter}.

> *DEBUG responds by returning to the DOS prompt.*

To return to Windows:

☐ Type EXIT {Enter}.

Figure 16.8 shows the result of displaying the first 128 bytes of the C:\vcProg\WAV\8Kenned3.WAV file. As shown, the 25th and 26th bytes of this file are 11 and 2B. Reversing these two bytes produces

2B 11

which represents the value

```
2*16*16*16 + 11 *16*16 + 1*16 + 1 =
  8192     +   2816    +  16  + 1 = 11025
```

Figure 16.8.
Displaying the first
128 bytes of
8Kenned3.WAV.

```
C:\VCPROG\WAV>debug 8kenned3.wav
-d
2D9B:0100  52 49 46 46 1A 02 02 00-57 41 56 45 66 6D 74 20  RIFF....WAVEfmt
2D9B:0110  10 00 00 00 01 00 01 00-11 2B 00 00 11 2B 00 00  .........+...+..
2D9B:0120  01 00 08 00 64 61 74 61-F6 01 02 00 7A 80 7A 80  ....data...z.z.
2D9B:0130  7A 80 8A 8A 8A 8A 8A 8A-8A 8A 8A 8A 8A 8A 8A 8A  z...............
2D9B:0140  8A 8A 8A 8A 8A 8A 8A 8A-8A 8A 8A 8A 8A 8A 8A 8A  ................
2D9B:0150  8A 8A 8A 8A 8A 8A 8A 8A-8A 8A 8A 8A 8A 8A 8A 8A  ................
2D9B:0160  8A 8A 8A 8A 8A 8A 8A 8A-8A 8A 8A 8A 8A 8A 8A 8A  ................
2D9B:0170  8A 8A 8A 8A 8A 8A 8A 8A-8A 8A 8A 8A 8A 8A 8A 8A  ................
```

To summarize, the `8Kenned3.WAV` file was recorded at 11,025 Hertz.

The SeekIt application displays the sampling rate of the `DING.WAV` file (`DING.WAV` is shipped with Windows, and it resides in your `/Windows` directory).

Executing the SeekIt Application

Before writing the SeekIt program, execute it:

To execute the SeekIt application:

☐ Use Run from the Program Manager's File menu to execute
`C:\VCPROG\ORIGINAL\CH16\SEEKIT\SeekIt.EXE`.

> *Windows responds by executing the SeekIt application. The main window of* `SeekIt.EXE` *appears, as shown in Figure 16.9.*

Figure 16.9.
The SeekIt
application's
main window.

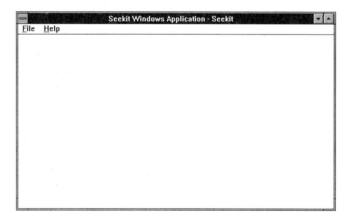

The SeekIt application has two popup menus: File and Help. These popup menus are shown in Figures 16.10 and 16.11.

Figure 16.10.
The SeekIt
application's
File menu.

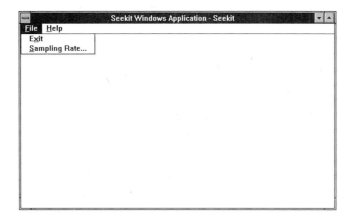

Figure 16.11.
The SeekIt
application's
Help menu.

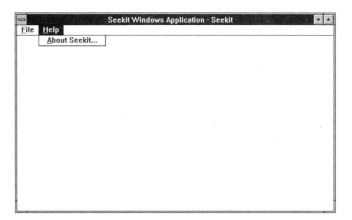

☐ Select Sampling Rate from the File menu.

SeekIt responds by displaying the sampling rate (see Figure 16.12).

Figure 16.12.
The sampling rate
that the SeekIt
application displays.

You can verify that this is indeed the case by using DEBUG.

☐ Close the dialog box and then select Exit from the File menu.

Now that you know what the SeekIt application does, write it.

Creating the Project of the SeekIt Application

To create the project of the SeekIt application:

☐ Select AppWizard from the Project menu.

  Visual C++ responds by running AppWizard.

☐ Use the Directory list box to select the directory C:\vcPROG\PRACTICE\CH16.

☐ Type seekit in the Project Name box.

Your AppWizard dialog box should now look as shown in Figure 16.13.

*Figure 16.13.
The AppWizard
dialog box for the
SeekIt application.*

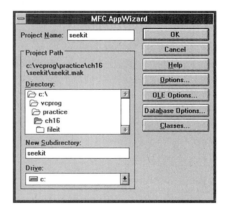

☐ Click the Options button and set the options as shown in Figure 16.14 (that is, uncheck all the check boxes except the Generate Source Comments check box).

Figure 16.14.
Setting the options
for the SeekIt
application.

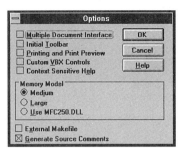

☐ Click the OK button of the Options dialog box and then click the OK
button of the AppWizard dialog box and finally click the Create button of
the New Application Information dialog box.

AppWizard responds by creating the SeekIt project and all the skeleton files of the
SeekIt application.

To remove the debug options of the project (so that you'll have a small EXE file):

☐ Select Project from the Options menu of Visual C++, click the Release radio
button, and then click the OK button of the dialog box.

The Visual Implementation of the SeekIt Application

The SeekIt application has a menu and an About dialog box. In the following sections you'll visually design the SeekIt application's menu. (The only dialog box that
SeekIt has is the About dialog box. This dialog box was prepared by Visual C++.)

The Visual Implementation of the SeekIt Application's Menu

The SeekIt application should have a menu as shown in Figures 16.9, 16.10,
and 16.11.

☐ Use App Studio to implement the SeekIt application's menu bar per
Table 16.3.

Table 16.3. The SeekIt application's menu.
Figures relating to menu: 16.9, 16.10, 16.11

Menu Item
&File
E&xit
&Sampling Rate...
&Help
&About Seekit...

To save your work:

☐ Select Save from the File menu of App Studio.

The visual implementation of the menu of the SeekIt application is complete.

Modifying the About Dialog Box

Now you'll modify the About dialog box. As shown in Figure 16.15, the default icon of the About dialog box is the Microsoft AFX icon.

Figure 16.15.
The About dialog box with its default AFX icon.

Replace this icon with the C:\vcProg\Icon\Sampling.ico icon (see Figure 16.16). After the modification, the About SeekIt application's dialog box looks as shown in Figure 16.17.

> **NOTE**
>
> The icon that appears in the About SeekIt dialog box is presented for cosmetic reasons only. You should assign an icon that is related to the topic of the application. For example, the topic of the SeekIt application is sampling rate. Thus, the icon in the About dialog box is Sampling.ICO, which represents an audio sample.

Note that this icon also appears as the SeekIt application's icon when the window of the application is minimized (see Figure 16.18). As you can see, now the user can easily identify the SeekIt application when its window is minimized.

Figure 16.16.
The Sampling.ICO
icon.

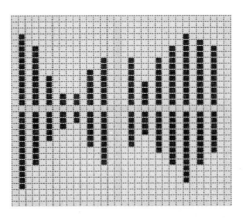

Figure 16.17.
The About SeekIt
dialog box with the
Sampling.ICO
icon.

Figure 16.18.
Minimizing the
window of the
SeekIt application.

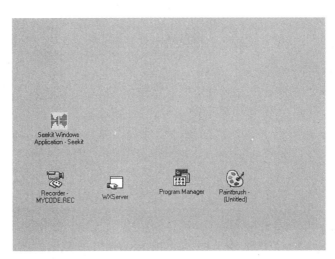

Here is how you create the icon of the SeekIt application:

☐ Select App Studio from the Tools menu of Visual C++.

☐ Select the Icon item on the left side of the window, select IDR_MAINFRAME on the right side of the window, and then click the Delete button located on the bottom of the window.

> *App Studio responds by deleting the IDR_MAINFRAME icon.*

☐ Click the New button (in the lower-left side of the window).

> *App Studio responds by displaying the New Resource dialog box (see Figure 16.19).*

Figure 16.19.
The New Resource
dialog box.

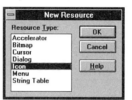

☐ Make sure that the Icon item is selected and click the OK button.

> *App Studio responds by displaying the IDI_ICON1 (Icon) window (see Figure 16.20). You can draw your own icon or use an existing icon. In the case of the SeekIt application you want to use the existing icon Sampling.ICO.*

Now you'll copy the Sampling.ICO icon into the IDI_ICON1 that you created in the previous step.

Figure 16.20.
The IDI_ICON1
window.

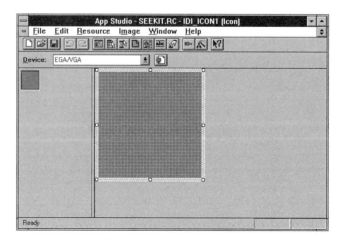

☐ Select Open from the File menu and select the file C:\vcProg\Icon\Sampling.ICO. (Note that to select an icon file, you have to set the Lists File of Type box in the Open dialog box to *.ICO).

App Studio responds by loading the Sampling.ICO *file.*

☐ Make sure that the icon you loaded (Sampling.ICO) is selected (enclosed with a frame) and select Copy from the Edit menu. (To select the icon, click in the left or right portion of the window but not inside the icon.)

App Studio responds by copying the Sampling.ICO icon to the Clipboard.

☐ Select IDI_ICON1 from the Window menu.

App Studio responds by making the IDI_ICON1 *the active menu.*

☐ Select Paste from the Edit menu.

App Studio responds by copying the contents of the Clipboard into the IDI_ICON1 *window (see Figure 16.21).*

Figure 16.21.
The IDI_ICON1
window showing
the Sampling.ICO
icon.

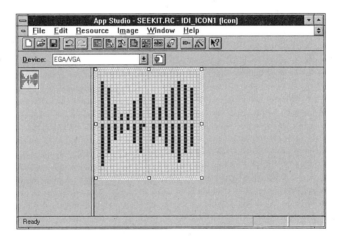

To switch back to the SeekIt.RC file:

☐ Select SEEKIT.RC from the Window menu.

App Studio displays the SEEKIT.RC window (see Figure 16.22).

As you can see, the window contains a new icon—the IDI_ICON1 icon.

Figure 16.22.
The SeekIt.RC
window.

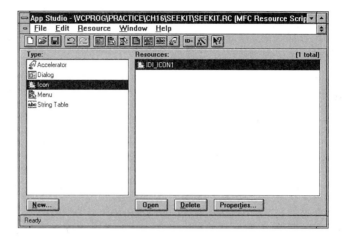

☐ Make sure the IDI_ICON1 is selected on the right side of the SEEKIT.RC window and then click the Properties button (on the bottom of the window).

> *App Studio responds by displaying the Icon Properties window (see Figure 16.23).*

Figure 16.23.
The Icon Properties
window.

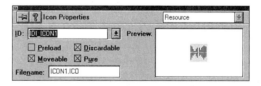

Visual C++ uses IDR_MAINFRAME as the icon's ID. Thus, you need to change the ID from IDI_ICON1 to IDR_MAINFRAME:

☐ Click the down-arrow icon that appears on the right side of the Properties window's ID box and select the IDR_MAINFRAME item.

The final Icon Properties window is shown in Figure 12.24.

Figure 16.24.
The new
IDR_MAINFRAME
icon.

To save your work:

☐ Select Save from the File menu of Visual C++.

Although you haven't finished writing the SeekIt application, execute it so that you can see the new `IDR_MAINFRAME` icon in action:

☐ Compile/link the SeekIt application and then execute it.

☐ Select About SeekIt from the Help menu.

> *SeekIt responds by displaying its About SeekIt dialog box, as shown in Figure 16.17. As you can see, the Sampling.ICO appears as the icon of the About SeekIt dialog box.*

☐ Click the OK button of the About SeekIt dialog box and then minimize the window of the SeekIt application.

> *The icon of the SeekIt application (the Sampling.ICO icon) appears as shown in Figure 16.18.*

☐ Restore the window of the SeekIt application and select Exit from the File menu to terminate the application.

Attaching Code to the SeekIt Application's Sampling Rate Menu Item

Now you'll attach code to the Sampling Rate menu item. Recall that when the Sampling Rate menu item is selected, the SeekIt application should display the sampling rate of the `DING.WAV` file.

☐ Use ClassWizard to add a function for the event:

Class Name:	CSeekitView
Object ID:	ID_FILE_SAMPLINGRATE
Message:	COMMAND
Function Name:	OnFileSamplingrate()

Make sure that you add the function to the `CSeekitView` class.

☐ Edit the `OnFileSampligrate()` function that you added to the `SEEKIVW.CPP` file. After editing the function, your `OnFileSamplingrate()` function should look as follows:

```
void CSeekitView::OnFileSamplingrate()
{
```

```
  // TODO: Add your command handler code here

//////////////////////
// MY CODE STARTS HERE
//////////////////////

char BytesRead[2];

unsigned int *ptrMyInteger;
unsigned int  MyInteger;
char sSamplingRate[10];
CString Message;

 // Create an object (for reading the .WAV file)
 CFile theWAVfile ("C:\\Windows\\DING.WAV",
                     CFile::modeRead ) ;

// Seek to byte number 24 (base 0)
theWAVfile.Seek ( 24, CFile::begin );

// Read 2 bytes from the .WAV file
theWAVfile.Read ( BytesRead, 2 );


ptrMyInteger = (unsigned int *)&BytesRead[0];

MyInteger = *ptrMyInteger;

// Display the sampling rate
itoa ( MyInteger, sSamplingRate, 10 );
Message =
(CString)"The sampling rate of DING.WAV is: " +
                        sSamplingRate ;

MessageBox (Message);


////////////////////
// MY CODE ENDS HERE
////////////////////

}
```

The code you typed starts by declaring various local variables:

```
char BytesRead[2];

unsigned int *ptrMyInteger;
unsigned int  MyInteger;
char sSamplingRate[10];
CString Message;
```

An object, `theWAVfile`, of class `CFile` is created:

```
CFile theWAVfile ("C:\\Windows\\DING.WAV",
                   CFile::modeRead ) ;
```

Note that the first parameter in this object creation statement is `C:\\Windows\\DING.WAV` and the second parameter is `CFile::modeRead`. This means that the `DING.WAV` file is opened for reading.

The next statement utilizes the `Seek()` member function of `CFile` to seek the file to byte 24:

```
theWAVfile.Seek ( 24, CFile::begin );
```

You're interested in reading the 25th and 26th bytes of the `DING.WAV` file. When seeking the file, byte 0 is considered the first byte of the file, byte 1 the second byte, and so on. This is the reason for supplying 24 as the first parameter of the `Seek()` function. The second parameter of the `Seek()` function is `CFile::begin`.

These parameters tell the `Seek()` function to count 24 bytes from the beginning of the file.

The next statement uses the `Read()` member function to read two bytes into the `BytesRead` buffer:

```
theWAVfile.Read ( BytesRead, 2 );
```

Which two bytes will be read? The two bytes starting with the current file position. Because you set the current file position to 24 (with the `Seek()` function), the two bytes that will be read are byte 24 and byte 25. (Because byte 24 is actually the 25th byte and byte 25 is actually the 26th byte, the two bytes to be read are the two bytes that contain the sampling rate.)

The next statements are byte manipulations to fill the integer `MyInteger` with an integer that contains the sampling rate represented by the two read bytes.

```
ptrMyInteger = (unsigned int *)&BytesRead[0];
```

`ptrMyInteger` is assigned with the address of the buffer that contains the read bytes.

Then the value stored in the address pointed to by `ptrMyInteger` is assigned to `MyInteger`:

```
MyInteger = *ptrMyInteger;
```

This means that `MyInteger` now contains the value of the read data in the form of an integer.

To display the integer, the `itoa()` function is used:

```
itoa ( MyInteger, sSamplingRate, 10 );
```

The `CString Message` is constructed:

```
Message =
(CString)"The sampling rate of DING.WAV is: " +
                        sSamplingRate ;
```

And finally the `MessageBox()` function is executed:

```
MessageBox (Message);
```

> **NOTE**
>
> When you use the `Seek()` function with `CFile:begin` as its second parameter, the `Seek()` function positions the file to a certain number of bytes from the beginning of the file.
>
> For example, the statement
>
> ```
> theWAVfile.Seek (100, CFile::begin);
> ```
>
> seeks the file 100 bytes from the beginning of the file.
>
> In a similar manner, you can supply as the second parameter of the `Seek()` function the value
>
> ```
> CFile::current
> ```
>
> or the value
>
> ```
> CFile::end
> ```
>
> When you supply `CFile::current` as the second parameter of `Seek()` the `Seek()` function will position the file a certain number of bytes from the current position. For example, the following statements,
>
> ```
> theWAVfile.Seek(100, CFile::begin);
> theWAVfile.Seek(-25, CFile::current);
> theWAVfile.Seek(200, CFile::current);
> ```
>
> set the position of the file 100 bytes from its beginning and then 25 bytes backward from the current position (that is, back to byte 75) and then 200 bytes forward from the current position.

The statement

```
theWAVfile (-100, CFile::end);
```

sets the file 100 bytes backward from the end of the file.

☐ Compile, link, and execute the SeekIt application, verifying its operation. When you select Sampling Rate from the File menu, the program should display the sampling rate of DING.WAV as shown in Figure 16.25.

Figure 16.25.
Displaying the
sampling rate of the
DING.WAV file.

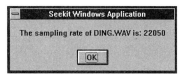

17

The Mouse

In this chapter you'll learn how to
detect and respond to mouse events
from within your programs.

As you know, the mouse is the recommended input device for Windows. You've already learned how to attach code to mouse-clicking events on controls. For example, in a previous chapter you attached code to the BN_CLICKED event that occurs whenever the user clicks the left mouse button.

In this chapter you'll attach code to other mouse events.

The MyMouse Application

Before you start writing the MyMouse application, execute the copy of it that resides in your C:\VCPROG\ORIGINAL\CH17\MyMouse directory.

To execute the MyMouse application:

☐ Use the Run item from the Program Manager's File menu to execute
  C:\VCPROG\ORIGINAL\CH17\MYMOUSE\MyMouse.EXE.

> *Windows responds by executing* MyMouse.EXE. *The main window of*
> MyMouse.EXE *appears, as shown in Figure 17.1.*

Figure 17.1.
The MyMouse
application's main
window.

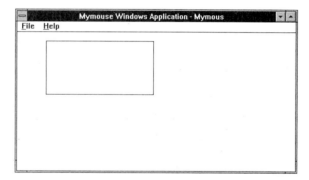

The MyMouse application has two popup menus, File and Help. These popup menus are shown in Figures 17.2 and 17.3.

☐ Press the Ctrl key and then while holding it down push the left mouse
  button.

MyMouse responds by displaying the following in the edit box (see Figure 17.4):

```
[v] Left Mouse Down
[v] Ctrl
[ ] Right Button down
[ ] SHIFT
```

The preceding means the program detected that the Ctrl key was pressed down at the time you pushed the left mouse button.

Figure 17.2.
The MyMouse
application's File
menu.

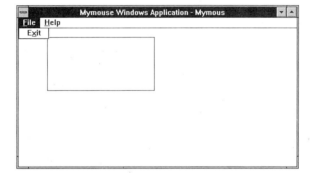

Figure 17.3.
The MyMouse
application's Help
menu.

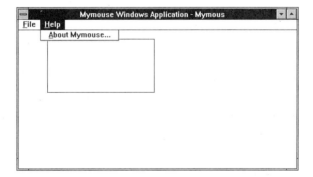

☐ Experiment with the MyMouse program by first pressing the Ctrl key and/or the SHIFT key and/or the right mouse button and then by pushing the left mouse button. MyMouse displays the status of these keys in the edit box. Note that you can't write in the edit box. That is, the edit box is a read-only control in the MyMouse application.

Figure 17.4.
Displaying the
status of Ctrl,
SHIFT, and the
right mouse button.

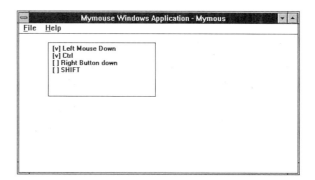

> **NOTE**
>
> The MyMouse application doesn't detect when only the right mouse button
> is clicked. MyMouse will detect the clicking of the right mouse button
> provided that you
>
> > Push the right mouse button.
> >
> > While holding down the right mouse button, push down the left mouse
> > button.
>
> Similarly, MyMouse doesn't detect when the SHIFT or Ctrl keys are pressed,
> unless the left mouse button is held down.

Now that you know what MyMouse does, you can write it.

Creating the Project of the MyMouse Application

To create the project of the MyMouse application:

☐ Select AppWizard from the Project menu.

> *Visual C++ responds by running AppWizard.*

☐ Use the Directory list box to select the directory C:\VCCPROG\PRACTICE\CH17.
Type mymouse in the Project Name box.

Your AppWizard dialog box looks as shown in Figure 17.5.

Figure 17.5.
The AppWizard
dialog box for the
MyMouse
application.

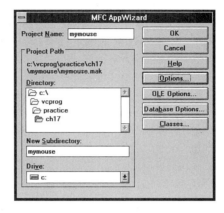

☐ Click the Options button and set the options as shown in Figure 17.6
(uncheck all the check boxes except the Generate Source Comments check
box).

Figure 17.6.
Setting the options
for the MyMouse
application.

☐ Click the OK button of the Options dialog box and then click the OK
button of the AppWizard dialog box and finally click the Create button of
the New Application Information dialog box.

> *AppWizard responds by creating the MyMouse project and all the skeleton
> files of the MyMouse application.*

To remove the debug options of the project (so you'll have a small EXE file):

☐ Select Project from Visual C++'s Options menu, click the Release radio
button, and then click the OK button of the dialog box.

Creating the Form of the Application

As shown in Figure 17.1, the main window of the application ought to contain an edit box.

To implement this form you'll replace the current view class of the application with a new view class derived from the CFormView class.

Follow these steps to create the form of the application:

☐ Use the Windows File Manager (or DOS Shell) to delete the MyMouse application's two view class files:

Delete C:\VCPROG\PRACTICE\CH17\MyMouse\MYMOUVW.CPP.
Delete C:\VCPROG\PRACTICE\CH17\MyMouse\MYMOUVW.H.

☐ Select ClassWizard from Visual C++'s Browse menu.

> *ClassWizard responds by displaying a dialog box telling you that the files of the view class don't exist.*

☐ Click the OK button of the dialog box.

☐ Click the Remove button of the Repair Class Information dialog box.

☐ Click the OK button of ClassWizard's dialog box.

You've just finished removing the view class of the application.

In the following steps you'll create a dialog box, you'll create a CFormView type class for this dialog box, and you'll make this class the new view class of the application.

☐ Select App Studio from Visual C++'s Tools menu.

☐ Create a new dialog box with App Studio.

☐ Double-click in a free area of the new dialog box.

☐ Select Styles from the drop-down list box in the upper-right corner of the Properties window.

Set the Styles properties of the dialog box as follows:

☐ Select Child in the Style box.

☐ Select None in the Border box.

☐ Uncheck the Visible property (that is, remove the check mark from the Visible check box).

☐ Select General from the drop-down list box in the upper-right corner of the Properties window and make sure that the Caption box is empty.

Now, connect the dialog box to a class derived from `CFormView`:

☐ Select ClassWizard from App Studio's Resource menu.

> *ClassWizard responds by displaying the Add Class dialog box.*

☐ Type `CMymouseView` in the Class Name box.

☐ Set the Class Type to `CFormView`.

☐ Change the Header File box in the Add Class dialog box to `mymouvw.h`.

☐ Change the Implementation File box inside the Add Class dialog box to `mymouvw.cpp`.

NOTE

The make file that Visual C++ uses for compiling/linking the MyMouse application expects the name of the view class files to be `mymouvw.h` and `mymouvw.cpp`. Recall that these are the two files you deleted.

This is the reason why you changed the header filename and implementation filename in the above steps to `mymouvw.h` and `mymouvw.cpp`.

Also, the class name must be `CMymouseView`, because this was the original view class name that Visual C++ used and some of the code that Visual C++ wrote uses this name.

☐ Click the Create Class button.

☐ Click the OK button of ClassWizard's window to go back to App Studio.

You've finished creating the new view class of the application. This view class is a derived class from the MFC `CFormView` class, and it's connected to the dialog box you created. Thus, the main window of the application will be the dialog box that you created.

To save your work:

☐ Select Save from App Studio's File menu.

The Visual Implementation of the Dialog Box

As shown in Figure 17.1, the window of the MyMouse application should have an edit box in it.

☐ Delete the OK and Cancel buttons of the dialog box.

Place an edit box in the dialog box. Make the size of the edit box the same as the size of the edit box shown in Figure 17.8. (Later in this chapter you'll be instructed to increase the size of the edit box.) The edit box IDC_EDIT1 that you placed in the dialog box should be a read-only edit box. This way the user will be able to read the contents of the edit box, but won't be able to type in it.

To make the IDC_EDIT1 edit box read-only:

☐ Double-click the edit box to display its Properties window.

☐ Make sure that the upper-right combo box of the Properties window contains the word "General" and then check the Disabled check box (put an X in the Disabled box).

☐ Use ClassWizard to connect the edit box (IDC_EDIT1) with a variable. The variable should have the following specifications:

> Variable name m_EditBoxContents of class CString.

Save your work by selecting Save from App Studio's File menu.

Compiling, Linking, and Executing the MyMouse Application

You haven't finished writing the MyMouse application. Nevertheless, compile and link it. This way you'll verify that all the operations you've performed so far were without error.

NOTE

If you're new to Visual C++, you might have accidentally skipped one of the previously listed steps, typed the wrong filename in the Add Class dialog box, typed the wrong class name, or made another error that will cause compiling/linking errors. Naturally, you want to catch the errors at this early stage of the project.

If you do get a compiling/linking error, the best thing to do is start the project over again. That is, close the App Studio application, close the Visual C++ application, delete the MyMouse directory, restart Visual C++, and start the project again.

The Visual Design of the Menu Bar

Now you'll visually design the MyMouse application's menu.

☐ Use App Studio to implement the MyMouse application's menu per Table 17.1.

Table 17.1. The MyMouse application's menu.
Figures relating to menu: 17.1, 17.2, 17.3

Menu Item
&File
E&xit
&Help
&About Mymouse...

To save your work:

☐ Select Save from App Studio's File menu.

The visual implementation of the MyMouse application's menu is completed.

NOTE

You can compile/link the application by selecting Build MYMOUSE.EXE from Visual C++'s Project menu. When selecting the Build item, the compiler compiles only these files that were changed since the last compile (unlike the Rebuild All item that compiles all the CPP files). As you can see, even though you made changes to the application's menu, the compile/link process takes little time. This is because when you change the application's menu, you only change the contents of the application's RC file (`MyMouse.RC`). The changes made to the RC file don't require recompilation of the program files. Instead, Visual C++ must only bind the resources, a process that takes a short time.

☐ Compile/link the MyMouse application.

☐ Execute the MyMouse application and verify its proper operation. Of course, at this point the MyMouse application doesn't display anything in the edit box, because you haven't written any code to do that. Note that you can't type anything in the edit box.

☐ Select Exit from the File menu to terminate the MyMouse application.

You can now proceed to visually design the MyMouse application.

Attaching Code to the *OnLButtonDown()* Function

You'll now attach code that will be executed whenever the user pushes down the left mouse button.

Use ClassWizard to add a function for the event:

Class Name:	CMymouseView
Object ID:	CMyMouseView
Message:	WM_LBUTTONDOWN
Function Name:	OnLButtonDown()

NOTE: Make sure that you add the function to the `CMymouseView` class (see Figure 17.7).

☐ Edit the `OnLButtonDown()` function that you added to the `MYMOUVW.CPP` file. After you edit the function, your `OnLButtonDown()` function looks as follows:

```
void CMymouseView::OnLButtonDown(UINT nFlags, CPoint point)
{
// TODO: Add your message handler code here and/or call default
```

```
/////////////////////
// MY CODE STARTS HERE
/////////////////////

MessageBeep(-1);

/////////////////////
// MY CODE ENDS HERE
/////////////////////


    CFormView::OnLButtonDown(nFlags, point);
}
```

The code you typed uses the MessageBeep(-1) function to beep.

As you can see, this demonstrates the operation of the OnLButtonDown() function by executing the MessageBeep(-1). In other words, whenever you click the left mouse button, the MyMouse application should beep.

Figure 17.7.
Adding the
OnLButton
Down( ) *function.*

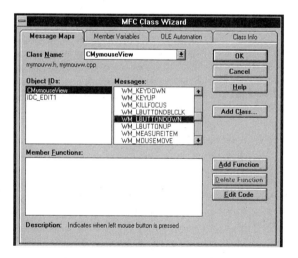

NOTE

The trick of beeping for the purpose of testing whether the code is attached to the proper function is quite useful. However, as you gain more experience with Visual C++ and write more complex applications, you'll soon discover that this trick doesn't always work, because Windows sometimes generates a beep when certain errors occur (such as clicking the left mouse button when it is in an invalid area). Suppose that you compile the MyMouse application, execute it, and discover that whenever you click the left mouse button, the PC beeps. Does the beeping occur because of the `MessageBeep(-1)` statement that you inserted in the `OnLButtonDown()` function, or maybe the beeping occurs because every time you click the mouse, Windows generates a beeping error?

In the case of the MyMouse application, you can trust that the beeping will occur because of the clicking of the mouse. However, in more complex applications, you might want to resort to other testing mechanisms. An alternative way of testing whether a certain code you typed is being executed is to insert the `MessageBox()` statement. For example, you may consider replacing the `MessageBeep(-1)` statement with the statement:

```
MessageBox ("I'm inside the OnLButtonDown() function" );
```

This method of quick testing works in many situations, but even this method won't work all the time. For example, if there's something wrong with your program, inserting the `MessageBox()` might cause the program to behave in additionally unpredictable ways.

In addition, once a message box is displayed with the `MessageBox()` function, you have to click the message box's OK button to close it.

Don't forget that you can always resort to playing WAV files through the PC speaker. For example, you can record and insert the statement

```
sp_PlaySnd( m_TestingSession,
          SP_FILE_STARTS_HERE,
          SP_FILE_ENDS_HERE);
```

instead of the `MessageBeep(-1)` statement. This method of testing doesn't utilize the display as the `MessageBox()` does and it doesn't conflict with the beep that Windows might generate.

☐ Compile/link the MyMouse application.

☐ Execute the MyMouse application and verify that every time you push the left mouse button, the PC beeps. This proves that the `OnLButtonDown()` function is executed whenever you push the left mouse button.

☐ Change the `MessageBeep()` statement to the statement

```
MessageBox ("I'm Here!");
```

☐ Compile/link and execute the MyMouse application and verify that every time you push the left mouse button, the application displays the message, "I'm Here!" in the message box.

☐ Experiment with the MyMouse application and then select Exit from the File menu.

Attaching Code to the *Left Button Up* Event

The term *click* means that two separate events occur. The first event is pushing down the mouse button, and the second event is releasing it.

In the previous section you attached code to the pushing-the-left-button event. Here's how you attach code to the event of releasing the left mouse button:

☐ Use ClassWizard to add a function for the event:

Class Name:	CMymouseView
Object ID:	CMyMouseView
Message:	WM_LBUTTONUP
Function Name:	OnLButtonUp()

Make sure that you're adding the function to the CMymouseView class.

☐ Edit the OnLButtonUp() function that you added to the MYMOUVW.CPP file. After you edit the OnLButtonUp() function, it looks as follows:

```
void CMymouseView::OnLButtonUp(UINT nFlags, CPoint point)
{
// TODO: Add your message handler code here and/or call default

        //////////////////////
        // MY CODE STARTS HERE
        //////////////////////

        m_EditBoxContents = "Left button of mouse is up";
        UpdateData(FALSE);

        //////////////////////
        // MY CODE ENDS HERE
        //////////////////////


        CFormView::OnLButtonUp(nFlags, point);
}
```

The code that you typed updates the variable of the edit box with the string

```
Left button of mouse is up
```

and then the UpdateData(FALSE) function is executed. This means that whenever the user releases the left mouse button, the edit box displays the contents of the m_EditBoxContents string.

☐ Modify the OnLButtonDown() function that resides in the MYMOUVW.CPP file. After the modification, your OnLButtonDown() function looks as follows:

```
void CMymouseView::OnLButtonDown(UINT nFlags, CPoint point)
{
// TODO: Add your message handler code here and/or call
// default

    /////////////////////////
    // MY CODE STARTS HERE
    /////////////////////////

    m_EditBoxContents = "Left button of mouse is down";
    UpdateData(FALSE);

    /////////////////////////
    // MY CODE ENDS HERE
    /////////////////////////


    CFormView::OnLButtonDown(nFlags, point);
}
```

The code that you typed displays the string

```
Left button of mouse is down
```

whenever the user pushes the left mouse button.

☐ Compile/Link and execute the MyMouse application.

☐ Push and hold down the left mouse button while the mouse pointer is in the MyMouse application's window.

> *MyMouse responds by displaying the text* Left button of mouse is down *in the edit box. (see Figures 17.8 and 17.9).*

Figure 17.8.
The string in the
edit box when the
left mouse button
is up.

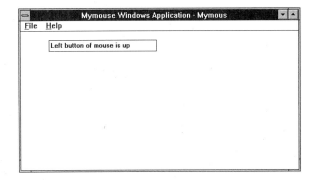

Figure 17.9.
The string in the
edit box when the
left mouse button is
down.

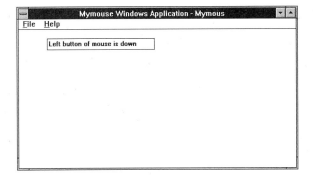

Who Receives the Messages?

When the left mouse button is released, Windows sends the message WM_LBUTTONUP.
The question is, what receives the message? Well, it depends on where the mouse
pointer was located when the left mouse button was released. If the mouse pointer
was in the window of the MyMouse application, Windows sends the message
WM_LBUTTONUP to the MyMouse application. If the left mouse button was released
outside the MyMouse window, however, MyMouse doesn't receive the message. You
can easily verify that by following these steps:

☐ Push and hold down the left mouse button while the mouse pointer is inside
the MyMouse window.

☐ While the left mouse button is down, move the mouse until the mouse
pointer is outside the MyMouse window and then release the mouse button.

*As you can see, the contents of the edit box don't reflect the fact that the left
mouse button was released. Because the left mouse button was released outside
the MyMouse window, Windows didn't send the* WM_LBUTTONUP *message to
MyMouse. This means that the* OnLButtonUp() *message wasn't executed.*

> **NOTE**
>
> Experiment with the MyMouse application and note that if you release the left mouse button in the rectangle that encloses the menu bar, Windows doesn't send the WM_LBUTTONUP message to MyMouse. In other words, Windows sends the WM_LBUTTONUP message to MyMouse only if the left mouse button is released in the area enclosed by the bottom edge of the menu bar and the left, right, and bottom edges of the window's frame. This area is called the *client area*.
>
> In a similar manner, Windows sends the WM_LBUTTONDOWN message to MyMouse only if the left mouse button is pushed while the mouse pointer is in the client area.

The Parameters of the *OnLButtonDown()* Function

Take a look at the parameters of the OnLButtonDown() function:

```
void CMymouseView::OnLButtonDown(UINT nFlags, CPoint point)
{
...
...
...
}
```

The parameters are nFlags and point.

These parameters provide you with additional information about the event. In particular, the point parameter contains the location of the mouse pointer when the left mouse button was pushed. The nFlags parameter contains information regarding the status of the right mouse button, the SHIFT key, and the Ctrl key at the time the left mouse button was pushed.

The value of nFlags can be tested as follows:

If nFlags & MK_CONTROL is equal to MK_CONTROL, the user pushed the left mouse button while the Ctrl key was pressed.

If nFlags & MK_SHIFT is equal to MK_SHIFT, the user pushed the left mouse button while the SHIFT key was pressed.

If nFlags & MK_RBUTTON is equal to MK_RBUTTON, the user pushed the left mouse button while the right mouse button was pushed down.

☐ Modify the OnLButtonDown() function. After the modification, your OnLButtonDown() function in the MYMOUVW.CPP file looks as follows:

```
void CMymouseView::OnLButtonDown(UINT nFlags, CPoint point)
{
// TODO: Add your message handler code here and/or call default

    ///////////////////////
    // MY CODE STARTS HERE
    ///////////////////////

    char LFCR[3]; // Variable to hold LF+CR

    LFCR[0] = 13;   // CR
    LFCR[1] = 10;   // LF
    LFCR[2] = 0;

    // Update the variable of the edit box.
    m_EditBoxContents =
        (CString)" [v] Left Mouse Down " + LFCR;


    // Was the Ctrl key pressed?
    if ( (nFlags & MK_CONTROL) == MK_CONTROL )
       m_EditBoxContents =
              m_EditBoxContents + " [v] Ctrl " + LFCR;
    else
       m_EditBoxContents =
              m_EditBoxContents + " [ ] Ctrl " + LFCR;

    // Was the mouse right button pressed?
    if ( (nFlags & MK_RBUTTON) == MK_RBUTTON )
       m_EditBoxContents =
              m_EditBoxContents + " [v] Right Button down "
       + LFCR;
    else
       m_EditBoxContents =
              m_EditBoxContents + " [ ] Right Button down "
       + LFCR;

    // Was the SHIFT key pressed?
    if ( (nFlags & MK_SHIFT) == MK_SHIFT )
       m_EditBoxContents =
         m_EditBoxContents + " [v] SHIFT ";
    else
       m_EditBoxContents =
         m_EditBoxContents + " [ ] SHIFT ";

    // Update the screen with the new
```

```
    // value of m_EditBoxContents.
    UpdateData(FALSE);

    ///////////////////////
    // MY CODE ENDS HERE
    ///////////////////////


    CFormView::OnLButtonDown(nFlags, point);
}
```

This code declares a local variable called LFCR:

```
char LFCR[3]; // Variable to hold LF+CR
```

This variable is updated with the values of the carriage return character (13), the line feed character (10), and the string null terminator (0):

```
LFCR[0] = 13;   // CR
LFCR[1] = 10;   // LF
LFCR[2] = 0;
```

The variable m_EditBoxContents is then updated:

```
m_EditBoxContents =
    (CString)" [v] Left Mouse Down " + LFCR;
```

Note that the CString casting is used in this statement. This is necessary, because the statement adds strings to m_EditBoxContents, which is a CString class. When adding strings as in this statement, at least one of the strings must be of class CString. If none of the added strings is of class CString, you have to cast one of the strings as CString. (If you don't use the casting, you'll get a compiling error, "Can't add two pointers.")

The next statements use if to determine whether the Ctrl, SHIFT, and right mouse button were pressed while the left mouse button was pushed. Here is the if statement that determines whether the Ctrl key was pressed:

```
if ( (nFlags & MK_CONTROL) == MK_CONTROL )
   m_EditBoxContents =
      m_EditBoxContents + " [v] Ctrl " + LFCR;
else
   m_EditBoxContents =
      m_EditBoxContents + " [ ] Ctrl " + LFCR;
```

If the if condition is satisfied, m_EditBoxContents will be equal to

```
[v] Left Mouse Down
[v] Ctrl
```

If the `if` condition isn't satisfied, `m_EditBoxContents` will be equal to

```
[v] Left Mouse Down
[ ] Ctrl
```

Note that the contents of `m_EditBoxContents` will be spread over two lines because of the carriage return/line feed.

In a similar manner, the next `if` statement checks to see whether the SHIFT key was pressed at the time the left mouse button was clicked, and the last `if` statement checks to see whether the right mouse button was pushed at the time the left mouse button was clicked.

The MyMouse application didn't check whether the middle button was pushed. If you write an application that makes use of the middle mouse button, use the following `if` statement:

```
if ( (nFlags & MK_MBUTTON) == MK_MBUTTON )
   {
   Here you write the code that should
   be executed whenever the left button
   of the mouse is pushed while the middle
   button was down.
   }
```

The last statement uses the `UpdateData(FALSE)` function to transfer the contents of `m_EditBoxContents` to the edit box:

```
UpdateData(FALSE);
```

Due to the insertion of the carriage return/line feed between the strings, the edit box should display the string on multiple lines. Thus, you should enlarge the edit box:

☐ Use App Studio to increase the size of the edit box to look as shown in Figure 17.13.

If you compile/link and execute the MyMouse application, you'll discover that the strings the edit box is supposed to display aren't displayed on multiple lines! Why? Because you didn't set the Multiple Lines property of the edit box. Here's how you set the Multiple Lines property of the edit box:

☐ Start App Studio and display the dialog box in its design mode.

☐ Double-click the edit box.

App Studio responds by displaying the Properties window of the edit box.

☐ Click the arrow icon next to the combo box in the upper-right corner of the Properties window and change the setting to Style.

☐ Place an X in the Multiline check box.

☐ Select Save from App Studio's File menu.

Currently, you have code in the OnLButtonUp() function (in the MYMOUVW.CPP file). Recall that you used ClassWizard to add this function, and then you typed code in this function. At this point, you don't need this function anymore, so you can delete it:

☐ Start ClassWizard from Visual C++'s Browse menu.

☐ In ClassWizard's dialog box, select CMymouseView as the Class Name, CMymouseView as the Project ID, and WM_LBUTTONUP as the message in the Messages list. Your ClassWizard dialog box should now look as shown in Figure 17.10.

Figure 17.10.
Preparing to
delete the
OnLButtonUp()
function.

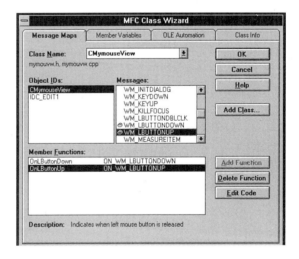

☐ Click the Delete Function button.

ClassWizard responds by displaying the message box shown in Figure 17.11.

This message box tells you that ClassWizard will delete the function, but you'll have to do some manual work.

Figure 17.11.
The message box
that ClassWizard
displays when you
delete a function.

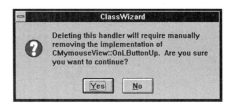

☐ Click the OK button of the message box and then click the OK button of the ClassWizard dialog box.

You now have to manually remove the `OnLButtonUp()` function:

☐ Open the file `MYMOUVW.CPP` and delete the `OnLButtonUp()` function.

NOTE

You have to delete the entire function—including its first line—not just the code inside it.

```
void CMymouseView::          <— DELETE THIS LINE
     OnLButtonUp(UINT nFlags,  <— DELETE THIS LINE
               CPoint point)   <— DELETE THIS LINE
{                            <— DELETE THIS LINE
.......                      <— DELETE THIS LINE
.......                      <— DELETE THIS LINE
.......                      <— DELETE THIS LINE
}                            <— DELETE THIS LINE
```

You've just learned the meaning of the `OnLButtonDown()` function's `nFlags` parameter. As you can imagine, Visual C++ has hundreds of other event-related functions. Are you supposed to remember the meanings of the parameters of all the functions? Not at all! Remember that the `OnLButtonDown()` function is executed whenever the left mouse button is down. (This isn't hard to remember, because the name of the function implies its purpose.) To figure out what the meanings of the functions' parameters are

☐ Double-click any of the characters of the `OnLButtonDown()` function in `MYMOUVW.CPP`.

Visual C++ responds by highlighting the `OnLButtonDown()` *characters.*

☐ Press F1.

Visual C++ responds by displaying the Help window for this function (see Figure 17.12).

This Help window tells you everything you need to know about the parameters of the function.

☐ Close the Help window by clicking the minus icon located in the upper-right corner of the Help window and then select Close from the system menu that pops up.

Figure 17.12.
The OnLButton
Down() *function's*
Help window.

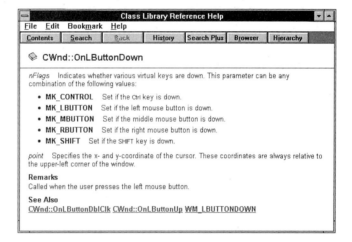

The MyMouse application is ready to be compiled, linked, and tested:

☐ Compile/link the application and then execute it.

The MyMouse window appears, as shown in Figure 17.13.

Experiment with the MyMouse application.

☐ For example, press and hold the SHIFT key and the right mouse button and then push the left mouse button.

MyMouse responds by displaying the corresponding strings in the edit box (see Figure 17.14). Note that there's a v for the SHIFT key and for the right mouse button. But there is no v for the Ctrl key, because you didn't press the Ctrl key.

Figure 17.13.
The MyMouse
window.

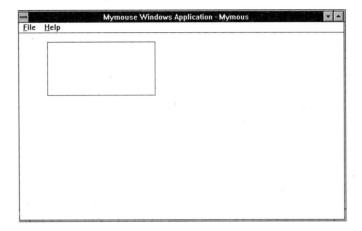

Figure 17.14.
The edit box
showing that the
right mouse button
and the SHIFT key
have been pressed at
the same time as the
left mouse button.

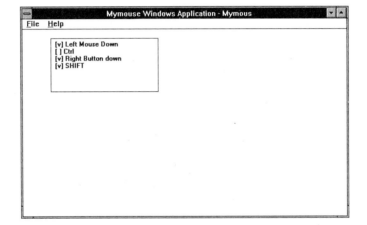

NOTE

The `OnLButtonDown()` function detects the fact that the SHIFT, Ctrl, or the right mouse button are held down when the left mouse button is pressed, provided that you pressed the SHIFT, Ctrl, or right mouse button prior to pressing the left mouse button.

For example, if you press the SHIFT key and only then press the left mouse button, `OnLButtonDown()` will report that the SHIFT key and the left mouse button have been pressed. However, if you push the left mouse button and then press the SHIFT key, the `OnLButtonDown()` function won't report that the SHIFT key has been pressed. This makes sense, because the `OnLButtonDown()` function is executed when you push the left mouse button. Nothing you press after that will be detected.

This is an important fact that should be included in your program's documentation. For example, suppose that you want to write a program that performs a certain operation whenever the user presses the SHIFT key and then pushes the left mouse button. Your code may look as follows:

```
void CMymouseView::OnLButtonDown(UINT nFlags, CPoint point)
{
// TODO: Add your message handler code here and/or call
// default

    ////////////////////////
    // MY CODE STARTS HERE
    ////////////////////////


    if ( (nFlags & MK_SHIFT) == MK_SHIFT )
       {
       Here is the code that is executed
       whenever the user presses the SHIFT
       key, and while holding the SHIFT key,
       then presses the left button of the
       mouse.
       }


    ///////////////////////
    // MY CODE ENDS HERE
    ///////////////////////


    CFormView::OnLButtonDown(nFlags, point);
}
```

Note that the `OnLButtonUp()` function has identical parameters as the `OnLButtonDown()` function.

The Point Parameter of the *OnLButtonUp()* and *OnLButtonDown()* Functions

As you saw, the OnLButtonDown() and OnLButtonUp() functions have point as their second parameter. This parameter contains the coordinates of the mouse pointer when the event takes place. This is a useful piece of information.

The WhereAmI Application

The next application you write in this chapter is called the WhereAmI application and demonstrates how you can use the point parameter.

Before you start writing the WhereAmI application, execute a copy of the WhereAmI application that resides in your C:\VCPROG\ORIGINAL\CH17\WhereAmI directory. To execute the WhereAmI application:

☐ Use Run from the Program Manager's File menu to execute
   C:\VCPROG\ORIGINAL\CH17\WHEREAMI\WhereAmI.EXE.

   Windows responds by executing WhereAmI. *The main window of*
   WhereAmI.EXE *appears, as shown in Figure 17.15.*

Figure 17.15.
The WhereAmI
application's main
window.

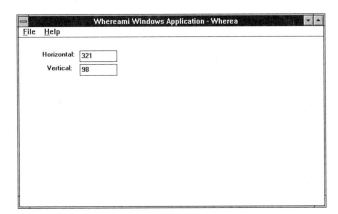

The WhereAmI application has two popup menus, File and Help. These popup menus are shown in Figures 17.16 and 17.17.

Figure 17.16.
The WhereAmI
application's File
menu.

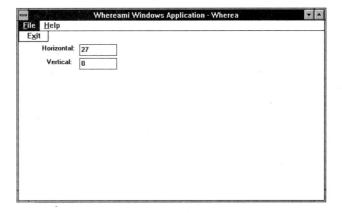

Figure 17.17.
The WhereAmI
application's Help
menu.

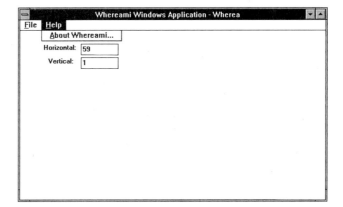

☐ Move the mouse in the window of the WhereAmI application.

> *WhereAmI responds by displaying the coordinates of the mouse pointer. In Figure 17.18, the center of the black dot represents the mouse pointer position. As shown, the coordinates of this point are 275 pixels from the left edge of the window and 139 pixels from the top edge of the window.*

Experiment with the WhereAmI application and then select Exit from the File menu to terminate the application.

Figure 17.18.
*Placing the mouse
pointer at
coordinates
(275,139).*

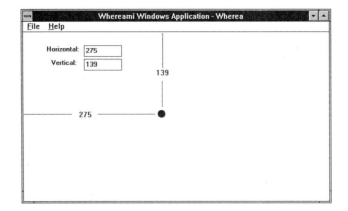

Creating the Project of the WhereAmI Application

To create the project of the WhereAmI application:

☐ Select AppWizard from the Project menu.

  Visual C++ responds by running AppWizard.

☐ Use the Directory list box to select the directory `C:\vcCPROG\PRACTICE\CH17`.

☐ Type `whereami` in the Project Name box.

Now your AppWizard dialog box looks as shown in Figure 17.19.

Figure 17.19.
*The AppWizard
dialog box for the
WhereAmI
application.*

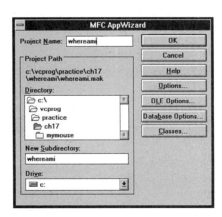

☐ Click the Options button and set the options as shown in Figure 17.20 (uncheck all the check boxes except the Generate Source Comments check box).

Figure 17.20. Setting the options for the WhereAmI application.

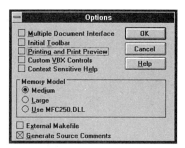

☐ Click the OK button of the Options dialog box and then click the OK button of the AppWizard dialog box and finally click the Create button of the New Application Information dialog box.

> *AppWizard responds by creating the WhereAmI project and all the skeleton files of the WhereAmI application.*

To remove the debug options of the project (so you'll have a small EXE file):

☐ Select Project from Visual C++'s Options menu, click the Release radio button, and then click the OK button of the dialog box.

Creating the Form of the Application

As shown in Figure 17.15, the main window of the application should contain two edit boxes and two labels.

To implement this form you'll replace the current view class of the application with a new view class derived from the CFormView class.

Follow these steps to create the form of the application:

☐ Use the Windows File Manager (or DOS Shell) to delete the two view class files of the WhereAmI application:

```
Rom C:\VCPROG\PRACTICE\CH17\WhereAmI\WhereVW.CPP.
Rom C:\VCPROG\PRACTICE\CH17\WhereAmI\WhereVW.H.
```

☐ Select ClassWizard from Visual C++'s Browse menu.

> *ClassWizard responds by displaying a dialog box telling you that the view class files don't exist.*

☐ Click the OK button of the dialog box.

☐ Click the Remove button of the Repair Class Information dialog box.

☐ Click the OK button of ClassWizard's dialog box.

You've just finished removing the view class of the application.

In the following steps you'll create a custom dialog box, you'll create a CFormView type class for this dialog box, and you'll make this class the new view class of the application:

☐ Select App Studio from Visual C++'s Tools menu.

☐ Create a new dialog box with App Studio.

☐ Double-click in a free area of the new dialog box.

☐ Select Styles from the drop-down list box at the upper-right corner of the Properties window.

Set the Styles properties of the dialog box as follows:

☐ Select Child from the Style box.

☐ Select None from the Border box.

☐ Uncheck the Visible property (remove the check mark from the Visible check box).

☐ Select General from the drop-down list box at the upper-right corner of the Properties window and make sure that the Caption box is empty.

Now connect the dialog box to a class derived from CFormView:

☐ Select ClassWizard from App Studio's Resource menu.

> *ClassWizard responds by displaying the Add Class dialog box.*

☐ Type CWhereamiView in the Class Name box.

☐ Set the Class Type to CFormView.

☐ Change the Header File box in the Add Class dialog box to wherevw.h.

☐ Change the Implementation File box in the Add Class dialog box to wherevw.cpp.

519

☐ Click the Create Class button.

☐ Click the OK button of ClassWizard's window to go back to App Studio.

You've finished creating the new view class of the application. This view class is a derived class from the MFC `CFormView` class, and it's connected to the dialog box that you created. Thus, the main window of the application will be the dialog box that you created.

To save your work:

☐ Select Save from App Studio's File menu.

The Visual Design of the Dialog Box

Implement the WhereAmI application's dialog box per Table 17.2. When you finish designing the dialog box, it looks as shown in Figure 17.21.

Table 17.2. The dialog box (main window) of the WhereAmI application.

Class Name:	`CWhereamiView` (of type `CFormView`)
OK button:	No
Cancel button:	No

Figure relating to the dialog box: 17.21

Object	Property	Setting
Dialog Box	ID	`IDD_DIALOG1`
Label	ID	`IDC_STATIC`
	Caption	`Horizontal:`

Object	Property	Setting
Edit Box	ID	IDC_HORIZ
	Variable	m_Horiz
	Type	CString
	Disabled	Yes
Label	ID	IDC_STATIC
	Caption	Vertical:
Edit Box	ID	IDC_VERT
	Variable	m_Vert
	Type	CString
	Disabled	Yes

Figure 17.21.
The WhereAmI
dialog box (in
design mode).

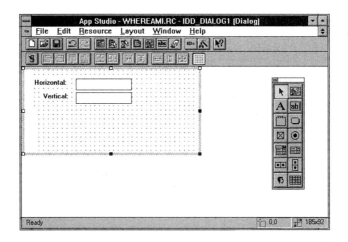

That's it! You've completed the visual implementation of the dialog box.

To save your work:

☐ Select Save from App Studio's File menu.

The Visual Design of the Menu

Now you'll visually design the WhereAmI application's menu.

Use App Studio to implement the WhereAmI application's menu per Table 17.3.

521

Table 17.3. The WhereAmI application's menu.
Figures relating to menu: 17.15, 17.16, 17.17

Menu Item
&File
E&xit
&Help
&About Whereami...

To save your work:

☐ Select Save from App Studio's File menu.

The visual implementation of the WhereAmI application's menu is completed.

Compiling, Linking, and Executing the WhereAmI Application

You haven't finished writing the WhereAmI application yet. Nevertheless, compile and link it to verify that all the operations you've written so far perform without errors.

☐ Compile/link the WhereAmI application.

☐ Execute the WhereAmI application and verify its proper operation. Of course, at this point the WhereAmI application doesn't display anything in the edit boxes because you haven't written any code to do that. Note that you can't type anything in the edit boxes because you set their Disabled properties.

☐ Select Exit from the File menu to terminate the WhereAmI application.

Responding to Mouse Events

Now that you've completed performing the visual design and all the overhead tasks, you can actually start attaching code to the WM_MOUSEMOVE event. WM_MOUSEMOVE is the message that Windows sends to WhereAmI whenever the mouse is moved into the client area of WhereAmI.

☐ Use ClassWizard to add a function for the event:

Class Name:	CWhereamiView
Object ID:	CWhereamiView
Message:	WM_MOUSEMOVE
Function Name:	OnMouseMove()

☐ Edit the OnMouseMove() function that you added to the WHEREVW.CPP file. After you edit the OnMouseMove() function, it looks as follows:

```
void CWhereamiView::OnMouseMove(UINT nFlags, CPoint point)
{
// TODO: Add your message handler code here and/or call default


        /////////////////////////
        // MY CODE STARTS HERE
        /////////////////////////
        char XPosition[10];
        char YPosition[10];

        itoa ( point.x, XPosition, 10 );
        itoa ( point.y, YPosition, 10 );

        m_Horiz = XPosition;
        m_Vert = YPosition;

        UpdateData(FALSE);

        /////////////////////
        // MY CODE ENDS HERE
        /////////////////////

        CFormView::OnMouseMove(nFlags, point);
}
```

The first two statements declare two local variables:

```
char XPosition[10];
char YPosition[10];
```

Then the itoa() function is executed to convert the x coordinate point.x to the string XPosition and to convert the y coordinate point.y to the string YPosition.

```
itoa ( point.x, XPosition, 10 );
itoa ( point.y, YPosition, 10 );
```

The variables of the edit boxes are then updated with the values of XPosition and YPosition:

```
m_Horiz = XPosition;
m_Vert = YPosition;
```

And finally, the UpdateData(FALSE) function is executed to update the edit boxes with the values of their variables:

```
UpdateData(FALSE);
```

☐ Compile/link and execute the WhereAmI application and verify its operation.

The DrawIt Application

The next application is called DrawIt. This application draws lines in accordance with mouse movement. When the user moves the mouse, Windows generates the WM_MOUSEMOVE message from time to time, but not for every move of the mouse. This makes sense, because if Windows sent a message for every movement of the mouse, you wouldn't be able to execute any program while you moved the mouse, because the CPU would be busy constantly processing the WM_MOUSEMOVE message. The DrawIt application demonstrates this concept.

Determining Mouse Movement

As stated, Windows doesn't send the WM_MOUSEMOVE message for each movement of the mouse. Instead, Windows checks the status of the mouse periodically. In each check, the current mouse coordinates are compared with the mouse coordinates from the last check. If the coordinates are different, Windows concludes that the mouse was moved, and it generates the WM_MOUSEMOVE message. This process is shown in Figure 17.22.

Figure 17.22.
Checking for mouse movement at times t1, t2, t3, t4, and t5.

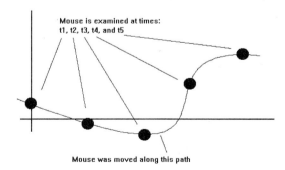

The curvy line in Figure 17.22 is the actual path of the mouse. However, due to the fact that it is impractical to process each pixel movement of the mouse, Windows generates the WM_MOUSEMOVE messages only at t1, t2, t3, t4, and t5.

So from the point of view of the application, the mouse moved only five times (because the application received only five WM_MOUSEMOVE messages). In most cases, the fact that not every pixel movement is detected doesn't have serious effects on the performance of the application.

As you'll soon see, when you draw a circle with the DrawIt application, the circle is drawn in accordance with the mouse movement. The quality of the circle depends on how fast you move the mouse. If you move the mouse slowly, you'll be able to draw a smooth shape (such as the shape shown on the left side of Figure 17.23). On the other hand, if you draw the circle quickly, the circle won't be smooth (as shown on the right side of Figure 17.23).

Figures 17.23.
Drawing shapes
with DrawIt. The
left shape was
drawn slowly; the
right shape was
drawn quickly.

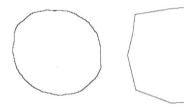

Before you start writing the DrawIt application, execute the copy of the DrawIt application that resides in your C:\VCPROG\ORIGINAL\CH17\DrawIt directory.

To execute the DrawIt application:

☐ Use Run from the Program Manager's File menu to execute
   C:\VCPROG\ORIGINAL\CH17\DRAWIT\DrawIt.EXE.

   Windows responds by executing the DrawIt application. The main window of
   DrawIt.EXE *appears, as shown in Figure 17.24.*

The DrawIt application has two popup menus, File and Help. These popup menus are shown in Figures 17.25 and 17.26.

Figure 17.24.
The DrawIt
application's main
window.

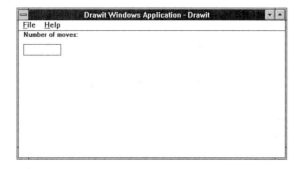

Figure 17.25.
The DrawIt
application's File
menu.

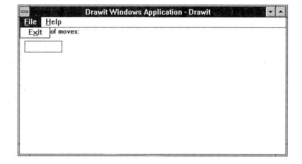

Figure 17.26.
The DrawIt
application's Help
menu.

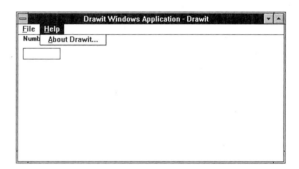

☐ Hold down the left mouse button and move the mouse around in the window of the DrawIt application.

> *DrawIt responds by drawing lines in accordance with the mouse movements (see Figure 17.27).*

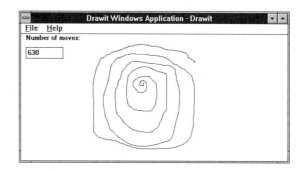

Figure 17.27.
Drawing with the
DrawIt applica-
tion.

Experiment with the DrawIt application and then select Exit from the File menu to terminate the application.

Creating the Project of the DrawIt Application

To create the project of the DrawIt application:

☐ Select AppWizard from the Project menu.

> *Visual C++ responds by running AppWizard.*

☐ Use the Directory list box to select the directory C:\VCPROG\PRACTICE\CH17. Type drawit in the Project Name box.

Now your AppWizard dialog box looks as shown in Figure 17.28.

Figure 17.28.
The AppWizard
dialog box for the
DrawIt applica-
tion.

☐ Click the Options button and set the options as shown in Figure 17.29 (uncheck all the check boxes except the Generate Source Comments check box).

Figure 17.29.
Setting the options
for the DrawIt
application.

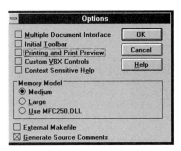

☐ Click the OK button of the Options dialog box and then click the OK button of the AppWizard dialog box and finally click the Create button of the New Application Information dialog box.

AppWizard responds by creating the DrawIt project and all the skeleton files of the DrawIt application.

To remove the debug options of the project (so you'll have a small EXE file):

☐ Select Project from Visual C++'s Options menu, click the Release radio button, and then click the OK button of the dialog box.

Creating the Form of the Application

As shown in Figure 17.24, the main window of the application should contain an edit box and a label.

To implement this form you'll replace the current view class of the application with a new view class derived from the CFormView class.

Follow these steps to create the form of the application:

☐ Use the Windows File Manager (or DOS Shell) to delete the two view class files of the DrawIt application:

Delete `C:\VCPROG\PRACTICE\CH17\DrawIt\DRAWIVW.CPP`.
Delete `C:\VCPROG\PRACTICE\CH17\DrawIt\DRAWIVW.H`.

☐ Select ClassWizard from Visual C++'s Browse menu.

ClassWizard responds by displaying a dialog box telling you that the view class files don't exist.

☐ Click the OK button of the dialog box.

☐ Click the Remove button of the Repair Class Information dialog box.

☐ Click the OK button of ClassWizard's dialog box.

You've just finished removing the view class of the application.

In the following steps you'll create a dialog box, you'll create a `CFormView` type class for this dialog box, and you'll make this class the new view class of the application:

☐ Select App Studio from Visual C++'s Tools menu.

☐ Create a new dialog box with App Studio.

☐ Double-click in a free area of the new dialog box.

☐ Select Styles from the drop-down list box at the upper-right corner of the Properties window.

Set the Styles properties of the dialog box as follows:

☐ Select Child in the Style box.

☐ Select None in the Border box.

☐ Uncheck the Visible property (remove the check mark from the Visible check box).

☐ Select General from the drop-down list box at the upper-right corner of the Properties window and make sure the Caption box is empty.

Now connect the dialog box to a class derived from `CFormView`:

☐ Select ClassWizard from App Studio's Resource menu.

ClassWizard responds by displaying the Add Class dialog box.

☐ Type `CDrawitView` in the Class Name box.

☐ Set the Class Type to `CFormView`.

☐ Change the Header File box in the Add Class dialog box to `drawivw.h`.

☐ Change the Implementation File box in the Add Class dialog box to `drawivw.cpp`.

☐ Click the Create Class button.

☐ Click the OK button of ClassWizard's window to go back to App Studio.

You've finished creating the new view class of the application. This view class is a derived class from the MFC `CFormView` class, and it's connected to the dialog box that you created. Thus, the main window of the application will be the dialog box that you created.

To save your work:

☐ Select Save from App Studio's File menu.

The Visual Design of the Dialog Box

Implement the dialog box of the WhereAmI application per Table 17.4. When you complete designing the dialog box, it should look as shown in Figure 17.24.

Table 17.4. The DrawIt application's dialog box (main window).

Class Name:	`CDrawitView`
Figure:	17.24
OK button:	No
Cancel button:	No

Object	Property	Setting
Dialog Box	ID	`IDD_DIALOG1`
Label	ID	`IDC_STATIC`
	Caption	`Number of moves:`
Edit Box	ID	`IDC_EDIT1`
	Variable	`m_NumberOfMoves`
	Type	`long`
	Disabled	Yes

NOTE

Up until now, you've attached a `CString` variable to the edit box.

The DrawIt application needs to increment the variable of the edit box. Thus, it's more convenient to make this variable a numeric type (not a `CString` type). Note that in Table 17.4, you were instructed to make the `m_NumberOfMoves` long (not a `CString`).

That's it! You've completed the visual implementation of the dialog box.

To save your work:

☐ Select Save from App Studio's File menu.

The Visual Design of the Menu

Now you'll visually design the menu of the DrawIt application.

Use App Studio to implement the menu per Table 17.5.

Table 17.5. The DrawIt application's menu.
Figures relating to menu: 17.24, 17.25, 17.26

Menu Item
&File
E&xit
&Help
&About Drawit...

To save your work:

☐ Select Save from App Studio's File menu.

The visual implementation of the DrawIt application's menu is completed.

Compiling, Linking, and Executing the DrawIt Application

You haven't finished writing the DrawIt application. Nevertheless, compile and link it to verify that all the operations perform without errors.

☐ Compile/link the DrawIt application.

☐ Execute the DrawIt application and verify its proper operation. Of course, at this point the DrawIt application doesn't display in the edit box any important information, because you haven't written any code that would do that. Note that you can't type in the edit box.

☐ Select Exit from the File menu to terminate the DrawIt application.

Responding to Mouse Events

Now that you've completed the visual design, you can start attaching code that implements the same job that the pencil tool of Paintbrush accomplishes.

☐ Use ClassWizard to add a function for the event:

Class Name:	CDrawitView
Object ID:	CDrawitView
Message:	WM_MOUSEMOVE
Function Name:	OnMouseMove()

☐ Edit the OnMouseMove() function that you added to the DRAWIVW.CPP file. After you edit the OnMouseMove() function, it looks as follows:

```
void CDrawitView::OnMouseMove(UINT nFlags, CPoint point)
{
// TODO: Add your message handler code here and/or call default

        ////////////////////////
        // MY CODE STARTS HERE
        ////////////////////////


    if ( (nFlags & MK_LBUTTON) == MK_LBUTTON )
        {
        // This code is executed provided that:
        // 1. The mouse moved inside the client area.
        // 2. The left button of the mouse was pushed down.

        // Create a dc object
        CClientDC dc(this);

        // Draw a pixel
        dc.SetPixel(point.x, point.y, RGB(0,0,0));

        // Increment the counter
        m_NumberOfMoves++;

        // Update the screen
        UpdateData(FALSE);
```

```
        }
////////////////////
// MY CODE ENDS HERE
////////////////////

        CFormView::OnMouseMove(nFlags, point);
}
```

The code under the `if` will be executed only if the mouse moved while the left mouse button was pushed down:

```
if ( (nFlags & MK_LBUTTON) == MK_LBUTTON )
   {
   // This code is executed provided that:
   // 1. The mouse moved inside the client area.
   // 2. The left button of the mouse was pushed down.
   ...
   ...
   ...
   }
```

The code under the `if` creates a `dc` object:

```
CClientDC dc(this);
```

The *dc* stands for *device context*. What's a device context? Think of it as your software drawing tool. In other words, the device context serves as the Paintbrush program for drawing from within your programs. However, instead of drawing by clicking the mouse on one of the Paintbrush tools and then drawing with the mouse, you perform your drawing by using the member functions of `dc`. As you can see, `dc` is an object of class `CClientDC`.

> **NOTE**
>
> With the object `dc` you can perform many drawing operations. Think of it as your own drawing tool to be used within your programs. To use the tools of the `dc` object, apply the member functions of the `CClientDC` class to the `dc` object as follows:
>
> ```
> dc.SetPixel(point.x, point.y, RGB(0,0,0));
> ```

The next statement uses the `SetPixel()` member function:

```
dc.SetPixel(point.x, point.y, RGB(0,0,0));
```

The `SetPixel()` function draws a single pixel. The x coordinate of the pixel is `point.x`, and the y coordinate is `point.y`. Recall that `point` is one of the parameters of the

`OnMouseMove()` function. The third parameter of the `SetPixel()` function specifies the color of the pixel that will be drawn.

> **NOTE**
>
> `RGB` stands for Red Green Blue. The three parameters of `RGB()` specify the mixing formula of the color that `RGB()` returns. The first parameter specifies the amount of red in the final color, the second parameter specifies the amount of green in the final color, and the third parameter specifies the amount of blue in the final color. Each parameter of `RGB()` can have a value between 0 and 255.
>
> **Examples:**
>
> RGB (255,   0,   0)   represents the color red
> RGB (0,   255,   0)   represents the color green
> RGB (0,   0,   255) represents the color blue
> RGB (0,   0,   0)   represents the color black
> RGB (255, 255, 255) represents the color white
>
> As you can see, you can figure out the basic colors by inspection. To figure out the final color produced by other values, you would probably need to have a Ph.D. degree in optical physics.

To summarize, the code you typed draws a pixel at the current location of the mouse pointer, provided that the mouse was moved and the left mouse button was pressed down.

The next statement in the `OnMouseMove()` function increments the value of `m_NumberOfMoves`:

`m_NumberOfMoves++;`

And finally, the `UpdateData(FALSE)` function is executed to update the contents of the edit box with the value of its variable:

`UpdateData(FALSE);`

So to summarize, the number that's displayed in the edit box represents the number of times that the code in the `if` block was executed. Or the number in the edit box represents the number of pixels that were drawn.

☐ Compile/link and execute the DrawIt application and verify its operation. Push the left mouse button and then move the mouse in the client area of DrawIt.

DrawIt responds by drawing pixels in black (see Figure 17.30).

Figure 17.30.
Drawing pixels
with the DrawIt
program.

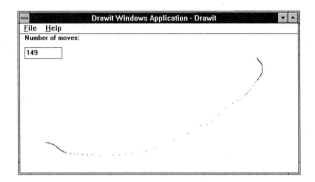

Figure 17.30 shows that 149 pixels were drawn. Note that the line in Figure 17.30 was drawn slowly at the beginning and then quickly and then slowly again.

When you're writing a drawing program, you realistically can't expect the user to move the mouse slowly. Thus, your program has to "cheat." Instead of drawing a pixel for each WM_MOUSEMOVE message, the program draws a line between the mouse's current location and its last location.

Implement the drawing by using the connecting-points-with-straight-lines technique. This technique requires the use of two variables: m_PrevX and m_PrevY. These variables hold the coordinate of the starting point of the line.

☐ Open the DrawiVW.H file.

☐ Modify the DrawiVW.H file and add the m_PrevX and m_PrevY data members to the CDrawitView class. After the addition of these two variables, the CDrawitView class declaration looks as follows:

```
class CDrawitView : public CFormView
{
    DECLARE_DYNCREATE(CDrawitView)
protected:
    CDrawitView();
// protected constructor used by dynamic creation

// Form Data
public:
    //{{AFX_DATA(CDrawitView)
    enum { IDD = IDD_DIALOG1 };
    long      m_NumberOfMoves;
    //}}AFX_DATA
```

```
// Attributes
public:

        ///////////////////////
        // MY CODE STARTS HERE
        ///////////////////////

        int m_PrevX;
        int m_PrevY;

        ///////////////////////
        // MY CODE ENDS HERE
        ///////////////////////


........
........
........
};
```

☐ Modify the code of the OnMouseMove() function in the DrawiVW.CPP file. After you modify this file, the OnMouseMove() function looks as follows:

```
void CDrawitView::OnMouseMove(UINT nFlags, CPoint point)
{
// TODO: Add your message handler code here and/or call default

        ///////////////////////
        // MY CODE STARTS HERE
        ///////////////////////


    if ( (nFlags & MK_LBUTTON) == MK_LBUTTON )
        {
        // This code is executed provided that:
        // 1. The mouse moved inside the client area.
        // 2. The left button of the mouse was pushed down.

        // Create a dc object
        CClientDC dc(this);

        // dc.SetPixel(point.x, point.y, RGB(0,0,0));

        dc.MoveTo(m_PrevX, m_PrevY);
        dc.LineTo(point.x, point.y);
        m_PrevX = point.x;
        m_PrevY = point.y;

        // Increment the counter
        m_NumberOfMoves++;

        // Update the screen
```

```
        UpdateData(FALSE);

    }

    ///////////////////////
    // MY CODE ENDS HERE
    ///////////////////////

        CFormView::OnMouseMove(nFlags, point);
}
```

The code that you typed creates the dc object of class CClientDC:

```
CClientDC dc(this);
```

The SetPixel() statement is commented out:

```
// dc.SetPixel(point.x, point.y, RGB(0,0,0));
```

and instead, the MoveTo() member function of the CClientDC class is executed on the dc object:

```
dc.MoveTo(m_PrevX, m_PrevY);
```

The MoveTo() function sets the current position to the coordinate (m_PrevX, m_PrevY). The current position is a coordinate used in several drawing functions (that is. the CClientDC member functions). You may think of the current position as an imaginary point that exists in the client area. The current position is affected by several drawing functions. For example, when the user uses the drawing function to draw a line from one point to another, the current position is updated automatically. The new coordinates of the current position are the coordinates of the drawn line's end point.

The MoveTo() function forces the coordinates of the current position to the coordinate specified by its parameters.

The next statement executes the LineTo() member function of the CClientDC class:

```
dc.LineTo(point.x, point.y);
```

As implied by its name, the LineTo() function draws a straight line. The question is, what are the coordinates of the starting and ending points of the line?

The coordinates of the ending point of the line are (point.x, point.y), as specified by the parameters of the LineTo() function. The coordinates of the starting point of the line are the coordinates of the current position. Because you set (m_PrevX, m_PrevY) as the current position (with the MoveTo() function), the line is drawn from (m_PrevX, m_PrevY) to (point.x, point.y).

As stated, once the `LineTo()` function completes drawing the line, the coordinates of the current position are updated automatically to the coordinates of the end point of the line, which are (`point.x`, `point.y`).

The code that you typed then updates the values of `m_PrevX` and `m_PrevY` with the coordinates of the end points of the line:

```
m_PrevX = point.x;
m_PrevY = point.y;
```

The rest of the code in the `OnMouseMove()` function increments the variable of the edit box by 1. This code is identical to the code that existed in the previous version of the DrawIt application.

To summarize, the next time the DrawIt application is executed, a line will be drawn from the end point of the previous line to the current position of the mouse. If the two points are close to each other, you won't notice that the two points are actually connected with a straight line.

The straight lines are drawn provided that the mouse moved while the left mouse button was held down. The whole process of drawing starts when the left mouse button is pushed down. Thus, the `OnLButtonDown()` function should be used to set the starting point of the first line of the drawing:

☐ Use ClassWizard to add a function for the event:

Class Name:	CDrawitView
Object ID:	CDrawitView
Message:	WM_LBUTTONDOWN
Function Name:	OnLButtonDown()

Make sure that you add the function to the `CDrawitView` class.

☐ Edit the `OnLButtonDown()` function that you added to the `DRAWIVW.CPP` file. After you edit the `OnLButtonDown()` function, it looks as follows:

```
void CDrawitView::OnLButtonDown(UINT nFlags, CPoint point)
{
    // TODO: Add your message handler code here and/or call default

    /////////////////////////
    // MY CODE STARTS HERE
    /////////////////////////
```

```
m_PrevX = point.x;

m_PrevY = point.y;

/////////////////////
// MY CODE ENDS HERE
/////////////////////
```

```
CFormView::OnLButtonDown(nFlags, point);
}
```

The code that you typed sets the values of m_PrevX and m_PrevY with the coordinates of the mouse pointer. Because immediately after the execution of this function, the OnMouseMove() function is executed and the line is drawn from the point where the mouse pointer was located when the left mouse button was pushed down.

☐ Compile/link the DrawIt application.

☐ Execute the DrawIt application and draw something. As you can see, now DrawIt works like the pencil tool of Paintbrush. Figure 17.31 is an example of how the DrawIt program was used as a pencil.

Figure 17.31.
Drawing with the
DrawIt application.

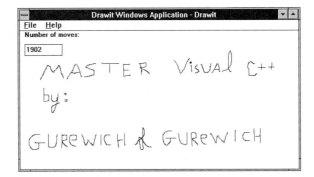

> **NOTE**
>
> When designing drawing applications such as the DrawIt application, it's better not to include the label control in the client area, because the user will be able to draw on the label. On the other hand, the user won't be able to draw over a control such as the edit box. Figure 17.32 illustrates this point.

Figure 17.32.
Drawing over the
label control (but
not over the edit
box control).

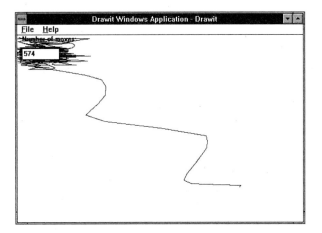

18

The Keyboard

In this chapter, you'll learn how to detect and respond to keyboard events from within your Visual C++ programs.

The prime function of the keyboard is to type characters (the mouse can't do that). Typically, you use the edit box control to receive characters from the keyboard. As you know, the edit control already contains all the code that enables you to type characters into it. However, the keyboard is also used to perform functions other than typing. For example, you can write code that performs certain operations when the user presses the arrow keys or other keys of the keyboard.

Generally speaking, the user should be able to perform all the major operations of the application (except typing) by using the mouse. However, a well-designed Windows application should enable the user to operate the application by using the keyboard as well.

The MyKey Application

Before you start writing the MyKey application, execute a copy of the MyKey application that resides in your `C:\VCPROG\ORIGINAL\CH18\MyKey` directory.

To execute the MyKey application:

☐ Use Run from the Program Manager's File menu to execute
`C:\VCPROG\ORIGINAL\CH18\MYKEY\MyKey.EXE`.

> *Windows responds by executing the MyKey application. The main window of* `MyKey.EXE` *appears, as shown in Figure 18.1.*

Figure 18.1.
The MyKey
application's
main window.

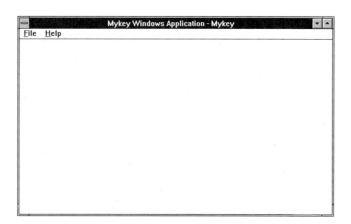

The MyKey application has two popup menus: File and Help. These popup menus are shown in Figures 18.2 and 18.3.

Figure 18.2.
The MyKey
application's
File menu.

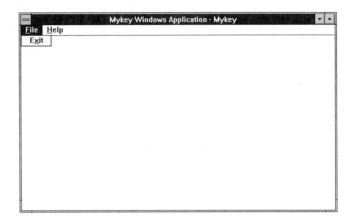

Figure 18.3.
The MyKey
application's
Help menu.

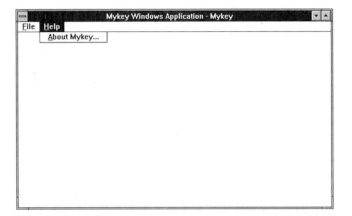

☐ Make sure that the Caps Lock key is off and then press the left arrow key.

> *MyKey responds by displaying a message box, telling you that you pressed the left arrow key while the Caps Lock key is off (see Figure 18.4).*

☐ Press the Caps Lock key and then press the left arrow key.

> *MyKey responds by displaying a message box, telling you that you pressed the left arrow key while the Caps Lock key was on.*

☐ Make sure that the Caps Lock key is off and then press the F1 key.

> *MyKey responds by displaying a message box, telling you that you pressed the F1 key while the Caps Lock key is off.*

☐ Press the Caps Lock key and then press the F1 key.

MyKey responds by displaying a message box, telling you that you pressed the F1 key while the Caps Lock key is on.

And now to the fun part of the MyKey application:

☐ Press any of the digits (0–9).

MyKey responds by telling you—through the PC speaker—which key you pressed.

☐ Experiment with the MyKey application and then select Exit from the File menu to terminate the MyKey application.

Figure 18.4.
The message box
that the MyKey
application displays.

Now that you know what MyKey should do, you can write it.

Creating the Project of the MyKey Application

To create the project of the MyKey application:

☐ Select AppWizard from the Project menu.

Visual C++ responds by running AppWizard.

☐ Use the Directory list box to select the directory C:\vcCPROG\PRACTICE\CH18.

☐ Type mykey in the Project Name box.

Now your AppWizard dialog box looks as shown in Figure 18.5.

☐ Click the Options button and set the options as shown in Figure 18.6 (that is, uncheck all the check boxes except the Generate Source Comments check box).

Figure 18.5.
The AppWizard
dialog box for the
MyKey application.

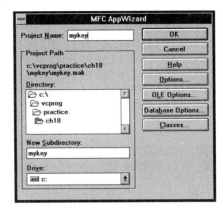

Figure 18.6.
Setting the options
for the MyKey
application.

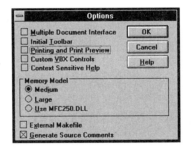

☐ Click the OK button of the Options dialog box and then click the OK
button of the AppWizard dialog box and finally click the Create button of
the New Application Information dialog box.

*AppWizard responds by creating the MyKey project and all the skeleton files of
the MyKey application.*

To remove the debug options of the project (so that you'll have a small EXE file):

☐ Select Project from the Options menu of Visual C++, click the Release radio
button, and then click the OK button of the dialog box.

The Visual Design of the Menu

Now visually design the menu of the MyKey application.

☐ Use App Studio to implement the menu of the MyKey application per
Table 18.1.

Table 18.1. The MyKey application's menu.
Figures relating to menu: 18.1, 18.2, 18.3

Menu Item
&File
E&xit
&Help
&About Mykey...

To save your work:

☐ Select Save from the File menu of App Studio.

The visual implementation of the menu of the MyKey application is completed.

To save your work:

☐ Select Save from the File menu of App Studio.

Note that the MyKey application doesn't have a custom dialog box. It has only an About dialog box.

Processing Keyboard Messages

When the user presses a key on the keyboard, Windows sends a message that corresponds to this event. The question is, who receives this message? The answer is that Windows sends the message to the object that currently has the *input focus*.

> **NOTE**
>
> Windows sends keyboard related messages to the object with the input focus. Thus, whenever the user presses keys on the keyboard, Windows sends the messages that correspond to these events to the object that currently has the input focus.

Now you'll attach code that will be executed whenever the user presses a key on the keyboard.

☐ Use ClassWizard to add a function for the event:

Class Name:	CMykeyView
Object ID:	CMykeyView
Message:	WM_KEYDOWN
Function Name:	OnKeyDown()

In the preceding step, make sure that you are adding the function to the `CMykeyView` class (see Figure 18.7).

Figure 18.7.
Adding the
`OnKeyDown()`
function.

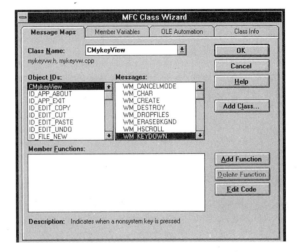

☐ Edit the `OnKeyDown()` function that you added to the `MYKEYVW.CPP` file. After you edit the function, your `OnKeyDown()` function should look as follows:

```
void CMykeyView::OnKeyDown(UINT nChar,
                           UINT nRepCnt,
                           UINT nFlags)
{
// TODO: Add your message handler
// code here and/or call default

/////////////////////////
// MY CODE STARTS HERE
/////////////////////////

switch (nChar)
{
case VK_LEFT:
```

```
MessageBox ("I detected that you pressed the left arrow");
break;

case VK_RIGHT:

MessageBox ("I detected that you pressed the right arrow");
break;

}

//////////////////////
// MY CODE ENDS HERE
//////////////////////


CView::OnKeyDown(nChar, nRepCnt, nFlags);
}
```

When the title of the MyKey window is highlighted, it means that this window has the input focus. If this window has a control in it, the control is called a *child window*. When the child window has the input focus, Windows sends the keyboard related messages to the child window. MyKey has no child windows, so Windows sends the keyboard related messages to the window of MyKey.

The code you typed uses a `switch` to detect and analyze the `WM_KEYDOWN` message. The `OnKeyDown()` function has three parameters. These parameters provide information about the message that was received. One of these parameters is `nChar`. This parameter contains the ID of the key that was pressed. The first `case` under the `switch` is

```
case VK_LEFT:

 MessageBox ("I detected that you pressed the left arrow");
 break;
```

As implied by its name, `VK_LEFT` is the ID of the left arrow key. To summarize, when the `WM_KEYDOWN` message is received with `nChar` equals to `VK_LEFT`, it means that the user pressed the left arrow key.

In a similar manner, the code you typed checks to see whether the pressed key was the right arrow key (`VK_RIGHT`).

☐ Compile/link the My key program and then execute it.

☐ Experiment with the MyKey application by pressing the left and right arrow keys.

> *MyKey responds by displaying the corresponding message box. When you press the right arrow key, MyKey displays the message:*

```
I detected that you pressed the right arrow
```

and when you press the left arrow key, MyKey responds by displaying the message:

```
I detected that you pressed the left arrow
```

☐ Terminate the MyKey application by selecting Exit from the File menu.

Other Virtual Keys

You detected the left and right arrow keys by checking whether nChar is equal to VK_LEFT or VK_RIGHT. These keys are called virtual keys (hence the characters VK_ at the beginning of their IDs). The left and right arrow keys (as well as other keys such as the Page Up and Page Down) are nonprintable keys.

The OnKeyDown() function can detect both printable and nonprintable keys. When a nonprintable key is pressed, you can detect the value of the key by examining the value of nFlags (the third parameter of OnKeyDown()).

☐ Modify the OnKeyDown() function. After the modification, this function looks as follows:

```
void CMykeyView::OnKeyDown(UINT nChar,
                           UINT nRepCnt,
                           UINT nFlags)
{
// TODO: Add your message handler code
// here and/or call default

//////////////////////
// MY CODE STARTS HERE
//////////////////////

switch (nChar)
{

case VK_LEFT:
 MessageBox ("I detected that you pressed the left arrow");
 break;

case VK_RIGHT:
 MessageBox ("I detected that you pressed the right arrow");
 break;

}
```

```
if ( nChar == 'A' || nChar == 'a' )
    MessageBox (" You pressed the 'A' key ");



/////////////////////
// MY CODE ENDS HERE
/////////////////////


CView::OnKeyDown(nChar, nRepCnt, nFlags);
}
```

The code you added to `OnKeyDown()` uses a message box to display a message whenever the `'A'` or `'a'` keys are pressed.

☐ Compile/link the MyKey application and execute it.

☐ Press the `'A'` key.

> *MyKey responds by displaying a message box telling you that you pressed the*
> `'A'` *key.*

NOTE

The `WM_KEYDOWN` message can be used to detect the pressing of printable and nonprintable keys.

The `WM_CHAR` can also be used for detecting the pressing of keys. However, the `WM_CHAR` message does not detect the keys listed in Table 18.2. (The `WM_CHAR` message is discussed later in this chapter.)

Table 18.2 lists the IDs that are used for detecting nonprintable keys with the `OnKeyDown()` function. For example, as shown in Table 18.2, `VK_RIGHT` represents the right arrow key, and `VK_LEFT` represents the left arrow key.

Table 18.2. Nonprintable keys that are detected by the `OnKeyDown()` function.

ID	*Key*
VK_CLEAR	The 5 key on the numeric pad when Num Lock is off
VK_SHIFT	SHIFT
VK_CONTROL	Ctrl
VK_PAUSE	Pause

ID	Key
VK_CAPITAL	Caps Lock
VK_PRIOR	Page Up
VK_NEXT	Page Down
VK_END	End
VK_HOME	Home
VK_LEFT	Left arrow
VK_UP	Up arrow
VK_RIGHT	Right arrow
VK_DOWN	Down arrow
VK_INSERT	Insert
VK_DELETE	Delete
VK_F1	F1
VK_F2	F2
VK_F3	F3
VK_F4	F4
VK_F5	F5
VK_F6	F6
VK_F7	F7
VK_F8	F8
VK_F9	F9
VK_F10	F10
VK_F11	F11
VK_F12	F12
VK_NUMLOCK	Num Lock
VK_SCROLL	Scroll Lock

Checking for the Ctrl Key

As you can see, the OnKeyDown() function can detect the pressing of the nonprintable keys. For example, the following code fragment is used to detect whether the End key or the Ctrl key was pressed:

```
void CMykeyView::OnKeyDown(UINT nChar,
                           UINT nRepCnt,
                           UINT nFlags)
{
// TODO: Add your message handler
// code here and/or call default
```

551

```
/////////////////////
// MY CODE STARTS HERE
/////////////////////

switch (nChar)
{
...
...
...
case VK_END:
 MessageBox ("I detected that you pressed the End key");
 break;

case VK_CONTROL:
 MessageBox ("I detected that you pressed the Ctrl key");
 break;

}

/////////////////////
// MY CODE ENDS HERE
/////////////////////

CView::OnKeyDown(nChar, nRepCnt, nFlags);
}
```

But how would you detect the pressing of Ctrl+End? (Recall that many Windows applications make use of such key combinations. For example, to go immediately to the end of a document in Microsoft Word for Windows, you have to press Ctrl+End). This is accomplished by using the `GetKeyState()` member function.

☐ Modify the `OnKeyDown()` function. After the modification, your `OnKeyDown()` function looks as follows:

```
void CMykeyView::OnKeyDown(UINT nChar,
                           UINT nRepCnt,
                           UINT nFlags)
{
// TODO: Add your message handler code
// here and/or call default

      /////////////////////
      // MY CODE STARTS HERE
      /////////////////////

      switch (nChar)
      {

      case VK_HOME:
```

```
        if ( GetKeyState(VK_CONTROL) & 0x8000 )
            {
            MessageBox ("You pressed Ctrl-Home");
            }
        else
            {
            MessageBox ("You pressed Home");
            }
        break;

    case VK_END:

        if ( GetKeyState(VK_CONTROL) & 0x8000 )
            {
            MessageBox ("You pressed Ctrl-End");
            }
        else
            {
            MessageBox ("You pressed End");
            }
        break;

    }

    /////////////////////
    // MY CODE ENDS HERE
    /////////////////////


    CView::OnKeyDown(nChar, nRepCnt, nFlags);
}
```

The code you typed uses an `if...else` statement to detect if the key was pressed with or without the Ctrl key. The parameter of the `GetKeyState()` function contains the virtual key code that is examined. Thus, to examine if the Ctrl key (`VK_CONTROL`) was pressed at the same time as the Home key (`VK_HOME`), you use the following `if...else` statement:

```
case VK_HOME:

    if ( GetKeyState(VK_CONTROL) & 0x8000 )
        {
        MessageBox ("You pressed Ctrl-Home");
        }
    else
        {
        MessageBox ("You pressed Home");
        }
    break;
```

In the preceding code, the case `VK_HOME` condition is satisfied if the Home key was pressed. The `if` statement is satisfied provided that the user pressed Ctrl. So putting it all together, the statement under the `if` is executed whenever the user presses Ctrl+Home. Note that the `if` statement ANDs `VK_CONTROL` with `0x8000`. If the result of this ANDing isn't 0, it means that the Ctrl key was pressed.

In a similar manner, you typed code that examines whether the End key was pressed at the same time as the Ctrl key.

☐ Compile/link the MyKey program and execute it.

☐ Press the Home key.

> *MyKey responds by displaying a message box indicating that you pressed the Home key.*

☐ Press and hold the Ctrl key and also press the Home key.

> *MyKey responds by displaying a message box indicating that you pressed the Ctrl+Home key.*

☐ Repeat the preceding steps for testing the End and the Ctrl+End keys.

☐ Terminate the MyKey application by selecting Exit from the File menu.

Checking for Other Combinations of Keys

As stated, the `GetStateKey(VK_CONTROL)` function tells you whether the Ctrl key was pressed at the same time as another key.

In a similar manner, you can use `GetStateKey(VK_SHIFT)` to test whether a key was pressed at the same time as the SHIFT (`VK_SHIFT`) key.

☐ Modify the `OnKeyDown()` function. When you complete modifying the `OnKeyDown()` function, it looks as follows:

```
void CMykeyView::OnKeyDown(UINT nChar,
                           UINT nRepCnt,
                           UINT nFlags)
{
// TODO: Add your message handler code
// here and/or call default

    /////////////////////////
    // MY CODE STARTS HERE
    /////////////////////////
```

```
    switch (nChar)
    {

    case VK_F1:

        if ( GetKeyState(VK_SHIFT) & 0x8000 )
            {
            MessageBox ("You pressed SHIFT-F1");
            }
        else
            {
            MessageBox ("You pressed F1");
            }
        break;

    case VK_LEFT:

        if ( GetKeyState(VK_SHIFT) & 0x8000 )
            {
            MessageBox ("You pressed SHIFT-Left arrow");
            }
        else
            {
            MessageBox ("You pressed Left arrow");
            }
        break;

    }

    ////////////////////////
    // MY CODE ENDS HERE
    ////////////////////////


    CView::OnKeyDown(nChar, nRepCnt, nFlags);
}
```

The code you typed checks whether the SHIFT key was pressed at the same time as the F1 key or the left arrow key.

☐ Compile/link the MyKey program and execute it.

☐ Press the F1 key.

MyKey responds by displaying a message box indicating that you pressed the F1 key.

☐ Press and hold the SHIFT key and also press the F1 key.

MyKey responds by displaying a message box indicating that you pressed the SHIFT+F1 key.

☐ Repeat the preceding steps to test the left arrow and the SHIFT+left arrow keys.

☐ Terminate the MyKey application by selecting Exit from the File menu.

Checking the Status of the Caps Lock, Num Lock, Scroll Lock, and Insert Keys

Several keys on the keyboard are toggled. For example, pressing the Caps Lock causes the keyboard to be in a non-Caps Lock state (when you type characters, they appear as lowercase characters). Pressing the Caps Lock key again causes the keyboard to be in a Caps Lock state (when you type characters, they appear as capitalized characters). If you press the Caps Lock key again, the keyboard returns to its non-Caps Lock state. Other toggling keys are the Num Lock, Scroll Lock, and Insert keys. The following modification to the OnKeyDown() function demonstrates how you can detect the state of these toggling keys.

☐ Modify the OnKeyDown() function. After the modification, your OnKeyDown() function looks as follows:

```
void CMykeyView::OnKeyDown(UINT nChar,
                           UINT nRepCnt,
                           UINT nFlags)
{
// TODO: Add your message handler code
// here and/or call default


//////////////////////////
// MY CODE STARTS HERE
//////////////////////////

switch (nChar)
{

case VK_F1:

  if ( GetKeyState(VK_CAPITAL) & 0x0001 )
     {
      MessageBox ("You pressed F1. Caps Lock = ON");
     }
  else
     {
```

```
    MessageBox ("You pressed F1. Caps Lock = OFF");
    }
break;

case VK_LEFT:

if ( GetKeyState(VK_CAPITAL) & 0x0001 )
{
MessageBox ("You pressed the Left arrow. Caps Lock = ON");
}
else
{
MessageBox ("You pressed the Left arrow. Caps Lock = OFF");
}
break;

}

////////////////////
// MY CODE ENDS HERE
////////////////////


     CView::OnKeyDown(nChar, nRepCnt, nFlags);
}
```

The code you typed ANDs VK_CAPITAL with 0x0001, and based on the result, it concludes the state of Caps Lock key:

```
if ( GetKeyState(VK_CAPITAL) & 0x0001 )
    {
     MessageBox ("You pressed F1. Caps Lock = ON");
    }
else
    {
    MessageBox ("You pressed F1. Caps Lock = OFF");
    }
```

☐ Compile/link the MyKey program and execute it.

☐ Press the F1 key.

> *MyKey responds by displaying a message box indicating that you pressed the F1 key and the status of the Caps Lock key.*

☐ Press the Caps Lock and then press the F1 key.

> *MyKey responds by displaying a message box indicating that you pressed the F1 key and the status of the Caps Lock key.*

☐ Repeat the preceding steps for testing the left arrow and the Caps Lock keys.

☐ Terminate the MyKey application by selecting Exit from the File menu.

In a similar manner, you can check for the status of the Num Lock key (by using `GetKeyStatus(VK_NUMLOCK)`), the status of the Scroll Lock (by using `GetKeyStatus(VK_SCROLL)`), and the status of the Insert key (by using `GetKeyStatus(VK_INSERT)`).

NOTE

You haven't read about the Print Screen key and the Alt key in this chapter. These keys are considered to be system keys. Usually, these keys are processed by Windows.

The *WM_CHAR* Message

As stated, the `WM_KEYDOWN` message can be used for processing both printable and nonprintable keys. On the other hand, the `WM_CHAR` message cannot be used for detecting the keys listed in Table 18.2.

☐ Use ClassWizard to add a function for the event:

Class Name:	CMykeyView
Object ID:	CMykeyView
Message:	WM_CHAR
Function Name:	OnChar()

NOTE: Make sure you're adding the function to the `CMykeyView` class (see Figure 18.8).

☐ Edit the `OnChar()` function that you added to the `MYKEYVW.CPP` file. After editing the function, your `OnChar()` function looks as follows:

```
void CMykeyView::OnChar(UINT nChar,
                        UINT nRepCnt,
                        UINT nFlags)
{
// TODO: Add your message handler
// code here and/or call default
```

```
/////////////////////
// MY CODE STARTS HERE
/////////////////////

if (nChar<32)
    {
    MessageBeep(-1);
    }
else
    {
    CClientDC dc (this);

    dc.TextOut (10, 10, "      ");
    dc.TextOut (10, 10, nChar);
    }

/////////////////////
// MY CODE ENDS HERE
/////////////////////


        CView::OnChar(nChar, nRepCnt, nFlags);
```

Figure 18.8.
Adding the
OnChar()
function.

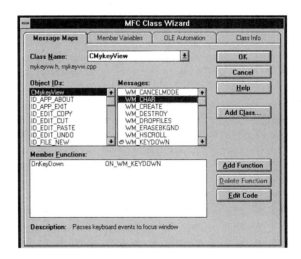

```
}
```

The code you typed uses an `if` statement to check whether `nChar` (the third parameter of `OnChar()`) is less than 32:

```
if (nChar<32)
    {
    MessageBeep(-1);
    }
```

If `nChar` is less than 32, the pressed key is a control character (for example, Enter or Tab), and the statement in the `if` block beeps.

If the `if` condition isn't satisfied, the `else` is executed.

Under the `else`, a `dc` object of class `CClientDC` is created as follows:

```
CClientDC dc (this);
```

The `TextOut()` function is executed to print several spaces on the monitor (to erase previous printing), and then the `TextOut()` function is executed again to print (at coordinate (10, 10)) the character that was pressed:

```
dc.TextOut (10, 10, "      ");
dc.TextOut (10, 10, nChar);
```

☐ Compile/link the MyKey application and execute it.

☐ Experiment with the MyKey application by pressing a printable key on the keyboard and verify that the character that corresponds to the key you pressed is displayed on your monitor.

Just for Fun (or Education)

The last enhancement that you'll make to the MyKey application is to play the audio of the digit that corresponds to the digit key the user presses.

Implementing such a program can be useful for applications that teach how to type, programs that teach the alphabet, and game programs.

Because the application uses `sp_` functions from the `TegoSND.DLL`, you have to `#include` the `c:\vcProg\DLL\TegoSND.DLL` file:

☐ Open the file `MyKey.H` and `#include` the `TegoSND.h` file at its beginning. After the modification, the `MyKey.H` file looks as follows:

```
// mykey.h : main header file for the MYKEY application
```

```
//

#ifndef __AFXWIN_H__
#error include 'stdafx.h' before including this file for PCH
#endif

#include "resource.h"        // main symbols


///////////////////////
// MY CODE STARTS HERE
///////////////////////

#include "\vcProg\DLL\TegoSND.H"

///////////////////////
// MY CODE ENDS HERE
///////////////////////

......
......
......
```

☐ Modify the MyKey.DEF file. After the modification, the MyKey.DEF file looks
   as follows:

```
; mykey.def : Declares the module parameters
; for the application.

NAME          MYKEY
DESCRIPTION   'MYKEY Windows Application'
EXETYPE       WINDOWS

CODE          PRELOAD MOVEABLE DISCARDABLE
DATA          PRELOAD MOVEABLE MULTIPLE

HEAPSIZE    1024    ; initial heap size
; Stack size is passed as argument to linker's /STACK option


;;;;;;;;;;;;;;;;;;;;;;;;;;;
; MY CODE STARTS HERE
;;;;;;;;;;;;;;;;;;;;;;;;;;;


;;;;;;;;;;;;;;;;;;;;;;;;;;;;;;;;;;;;;;;;;;;;;;;;;;;;
; sp_ functions from the TegoSND.DLL library
;;;;;;;;;;;;;;;;;;;;;;;;;;;;;;;;;;;;;;;;;;;;;;;;;;;;

IMPORTS
TegoSND.sp_OpenSession
TegoSND.sp_PlaySnd
TegoSND.sp_MouseOn
TegoSND.sp_MouseOff
```

```
TegoSND.sp_CloseSession

;;;;;;;;;;;;;;;;;;;;;;;;;;;
; MY CODE ENDS HERE
;;;;;;;;;;;;;;;;;;;;;;;;;;;
```

The session number that will be used for the WAV file is m_NumbersSession. Thus, you have to include this data member in the declaration of the view class:

☐ Open the MyKeyVW.H file and modify it. After the modification, your MyKeyVW.H file looks as follows:

```
class CMykeyView : public CView
{
protected: // create from serialization only
    CMykeyView();
    DECLARE_DYNCREATE(CMykeyView)

// Attributes
public:
    CMykeyDoc* GetDocument();

    /////////////////////////
    // MY CODE STARTS HERE
    /////////////////////////

    int m_NumbersSession;

    /////////////////////////
    // MY CODE ENDS HERE
    /////////////////////////


// Operations
public:

// Implementation
public:
    virtual ~CMykeyView();
    virtual void OnDraw(CDC* pDC);
 // overridden to draw this view
#ifdef _DEBUG
    virtual void AssertValid() const;
    virtual void Dump(CDumpContext& dc) const;
#endif

protected:

// Generated message map functions
protected:
```

```
//{{AFX_MSG(CMykeyView)
afx_msg void OnKeyDown(UINT nChar,
                       UINT nRepCnt,
                       UINT nFlags);
afx_msg void OnChar(UINT nChar,
                    UINT nRepCnt,
                    UINT nFlags);
//}}AFX_MSG
DECLARE_MESSAGE_MAP()
};
```

Now, open a WAV session for the file C:\vcProg\WAV\Numbers.WAV:

☐ Modify the constructor function of the view class. After the modification, the constructor function (in the MyKeyVW.CPP file) looks as follows:

```
/////////////////////////////////////////////////////
// CMykeyView construction/destruction

CMykeyView::CMykeyView()
{
    // TODO: add construction code here

    ///////////////////////
    // MY CODE STARTS HERE
    ///////////////////////

    char FileToOpen[255];


    // Open the WAV session
    strcpy ( FileToOpen, "\\vcProg\\WAV\\Numbers.WAV" );
    m_NumbersSession = sp_OpenWaveSession ( m_hWnd,
                                            FileToOpen );


// If WAV session can not be opened, display message box.
    if ( m_NumbersSession < 0 )
       {
       CString Message, Caption;
       Message = "Can't open the file: ";
       Message = Message + FileToOpen;
       Caption = "Error";
       MessageBox ( Message, Caption );
       }


    ///////////////////////
    // MY CODE ENDS HERE
    ///////////////////////
```

}

☐ Modify the destructor function of the view class. After the modification, the constructor function of the view class (in the MyKeyVW.CPP file) should look as follows:

```
CMykeyView::CMykeyView()
{
// TODO: add construction code here


       /////////////////////////
       // MY CODE STARTS HERE
       /////////////////////////


       char FileToOpen[255];


       // Open the WAV session
       strcpy ( FileToOpen, "\\vcProg\\WAV\\Numbers.WAV" );
       m_NumbersSession = sp_OpenSession ( FileToOpen );

// If WAV session can not be opened, display message box.
   if ( m_NumbersSession < 0 )
      {
        CString Message, Caption;
        Message = "Can't open the file: ";
        Message = Message + FileToOpen;
        Caption = "Error";
        MessageBox ( Message, Caption );
      }


       /////////////////////////
       // MY CODE ENDS HERE
       /////////////////////////
```

}

☐ Modify the destructor function of the view class. After the modification, the destructor function of the view class (in the MyKeyVW.CPP file) should look as follows:

```
CMykeyView::~CMykeyView()
{

       /////////////////////////
       // MY CODE STARTS HERE
```

```
//////////////////////

sp_CloseSession ( m_NumbersSession );

//////////////////////,
// MY CODE ENDS HERE
//////////////////////
```

}

☐ Modify the OnChar() function in the MyKeyVW.CPP file. After the modification, the OnChar() function looks as follows:

```
void CMykeyView::OnChar(UINT nChar,
                        UINT nRepCnt,
                        UINT nFlags)
{
// TODO: Add your message handler code here
// and/or call default

    //////////////////////
    // MY CODE STARTS HERE
    //////////////////////

    if (nChar<32)
      {
      MessageBeep(-1);
      }
    else
      {
      CClientDC dc (this);

      dc.TextOut (10, 10, "      ");
      dc.TextOut (10, 10, nChar);
      }


    switch (nChar)
     {

        case '0':
            sp_PlaySnd( m_NumbersSession,
                        1667,
                        8525 );
            break;

        case '1':
            sp_PlaySnd( m_NumbersSession,
                        10100,
                        16754 );
```

```
        break;

case '2':
        sp_PlaySnd( m_NumbersSession,
                    20673,
                    26942 );
        break;

  case '3':
        sp_PlaySnd( m_NumbersSession,
                    30270,
                    38500 );
        break;

  case '4':
        sp_PlaySnd( m_NumbersSession,
                    42030,
                    51830 );
        break;

  case '5':
        sp_PlaySnd( m_NumbersSession,
                    53390,
                    61000 );
        break;


  case '6':
        sp_PlaySnd( m_NumbersSession,
                    64360,
                    72200 );
        break;

  case '7':
        sp_PlaySnd( m_NumbersSession,
                    75530,
                    85720 );
        break;

  case '8':
        sp_PlaySnd( m_NumbersSession,
                    87680,
                    93950 );
        break;

  case '9':
        sp_PlaySnd( m_NumbersSession,
                    98060,
                    106492 );
        break;
```

```
    }

    ////////////////////
    // MY CODE ENDS HERE
    ////////////////////

    CView::OnChar(nChar, nRepCnt, nFlags);
}
```

The code you added to the OnChar() function uses a switch to examine the value of nChar:

```
switch (nChar)
{

    case '0':
        sp_PlaySnd( m_NumbersSession,
                    1667,
                    8525 );
        break;

    case '1':
        sp_PlaySnd( m_NumbersSession,
                    10100,
                    16754 );
        break;

    ...
    ...
    ...
```

The first case under the switch checks whether nChar is equal to the character '0'. If it's equal to '0', the sp_PlaySnd() function is executed. The first parameter is m_NumbersSession (the session number for the Numbers.WAV file).

The second and third parameters specify the beginning and end points of the audio section "Zero" in the WAV file.

Similarly, the other cases under the switch examine nChar, and the corresponding audio section is played.

Note that the virtual key codes (the value of nChar) for the letters A to Z and the digits 0 to 9 are their corresponding ASCII values. For example, to test the virtual key code for the digit 0, you used case '0', and to test the virtual key code for the digit 1, you used case '1'.

☐ Compile/link the MyKey application and execute it to verify its operation.

19

Multiple Document Interface (MDI)

In this chapter, you'll learn what
Multiple Document Interface
(MDI) applications are and how to
write such applications. Other
important topics covered in this
chapter include *multiple views* and
splitter windows.

What Is a Multiple Document Interface (MDI) Application?

A Multiple Document Application (MDI) is an application that enables the user to maintain several documents at one time. All the applications you've written so far are Single Document Interface (SDI) applications, because at any given time, the user could work with only one document. For example, the MEMO application you wrote in Chapter 13, "Using Serialization to Write and Read Data to and from Files," enables the user to work with one document at a time. When the user opens a new memo (by selecting New or Open from the File menu), the currently open memo is closed, and only then is the new memo opened.

In this chapter you will write an MDI application. When the user selects Open or New from the File menu, the currently open documents will remain open, and the new document will also be opened. Each document will have its own window, and the user will be able to move from one window to another. All these windows will be in the main window of the application.

The MDI application that you will write in this chapter will also support multiple views for the same document. That is, the user is allowed to open the same document several times and view the same document in different windows.

The PAD Application

Now you'll write the PAD application. The PAD application is an example of an MDI application. As you will soon see, most of the steps necessary for writing an MDI application are identical to the steps you took in building an SDI application. Thus, for the most part, the steps you'll take in building the PAD application will be the same as the steps you took when you built the MEMO application in Chapter 13.

Before you start writing the PAD application, execute the copy of it in your C:\VCPROG\ORIGINAL\CH19\PAD directory.

To execute the PAD application:

☐ Use Run from Program Manager's File menu to execute C:\VCPROG\ORIGINAL\CH19\PAD\PAD.EXE.

> *Windows responds by executing the PAD application. The main window of* PAD.EXE *appears, as shown in Figure 19.1.*

Figure 19.1.
The PAD
application's
main window.

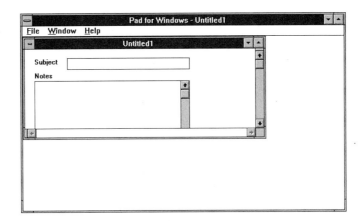

As you can see from Figure 19.1, the main window of the application has another window in it. This window is called a *child window*; that is, it's the *child* of the application's main window.

The title of the main window is Pad for Windows - Untitled1 and the title of the child window is Untitled1.

The Untitled1 window contains a data entry form with two fields: Subject and Notes.

☐ Fill the fields in the Untitled1 window as shown in Figure 19.2.

Figure 19.2.
Filling the fields
of the form.

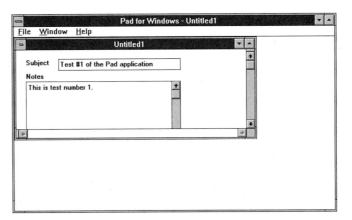

Now, save the Untitled1 document:

☐ Select Save from the File menu and save the Untitled1 document as
TRY1.PAD.

> *The PAD application responds by saving your entries into the file TRY1.PAD.*

Note that now the titles of the main window and the child window have changed
(see Figure 19.3). The title of the main window is now Pad for Windows - TRY1.PAD
and the title of the child window is now TRY1.PAD.

Figure 19.3.
The PAD
application after
saving a document
as TRY1.PAD.

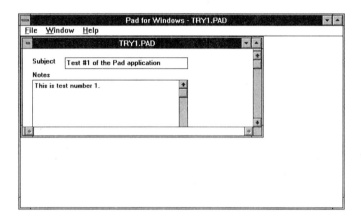

Because the PAD application is an MDI application, you can open more documents:

☐ Select New from the File menu.

> *The PAD application responds by opening a new document. The title of the*
> *new document's window is Untitled2 (see Figure 19.4).*

Figure 19.4.
The PAD
application
with two open
documents.

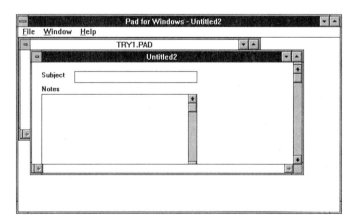

Fill the fields of the new document as follows:

☐ Type Test #2 in the Subject field.

☐ Type This is test number 2 of the Pad application in the Notes field.

☐ Select Save from the File menu and save the new document as TRY2.PAD.

Now your PAD application looks as shown in Figure 19.5.

Figure 19.5.
The PAD
application with
two documents.

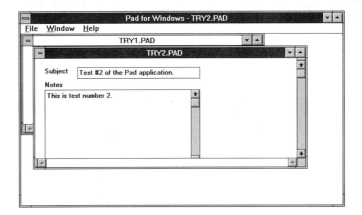

The Window menu of the PAD application (see Figure 19.6) has some interesting options.

Figure 19.6.
The PAD
application's
Window menu.

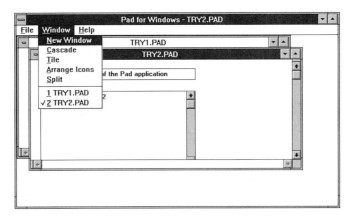

Experiment with the PAD application's Window menu options:

☐ Select Tile from the Window menu.

> *The PAD application responds by arranging the windows of* TRY1.PAD *and* TRY2.PAD *in tile format (see Figure 19.7).*

Figure 19.7.
Displaying the
child windows
in tile format.

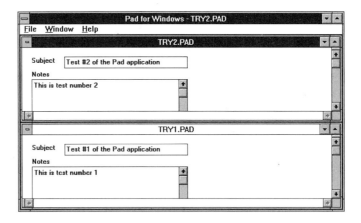

To rearrange the child windows back in cascade format:

☐ Select Cascade from the Window menu.

> *The PAD application responds by rearranging the child windows in cascade format (see Figure 19.5).*

Another nice feature that the PAD application supports is displaying multiple views for the same document. To see how you can open multiple views into a single document, follow these steps:

☐ Select the window of the TRY1.PAD document (that is, click anywhere on the window of TRY1.PAD or select TRY1.PAD from the Window menu).

☐ Select New Window from the Window menu.

> *The PAD application responds by opening another view (another window) for* TRY1.DOC *(see Figure 19.8).*

Figure 19.8.
Two views of the
same document.

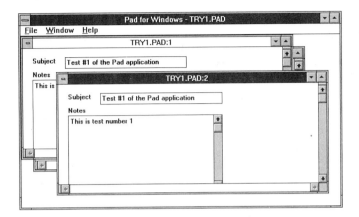

As you can see, now the document TRY1.PAD has two views (two child windows). One window has the title TRY1.PAD:1 and the other window has the title TRY1.PAD:2. If you change the contents of either of these windows, the contents of the other window are updated automatically. To see this automatic updating in action:

☐ Rearrange the TRY1.PAD:1 and TRY1.PAD:2 windows as shown in Figure 19.9. That is, move and size these two windows so that you'll be able to see the Notes fields of both windows.

Figure 19.9.
Rearranging the
two windows of
TRY1.PAD.

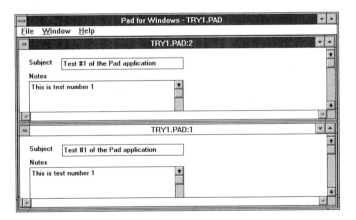

☐ Now type something in one of the TRY1 windows.

> *As soon as you type something in one window of TRY1.PAD, the other window of TRY1.PAD is updated automatically (see Figure 19.10).*

Figure 19.10.
The two windows
of TRY1.PAD *after*
typing something in
one of them.

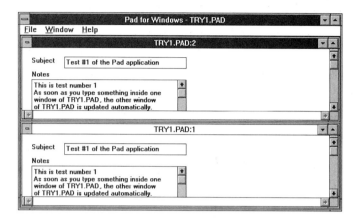

Why is the ability to see several views of the same document useful? The answer is that sometimes, when you have an extremely long document, you need to work on several sections of the same document at the same time. In such cases you can open several views (windows) of the same document and display in each window a different section of the document.

Another useful feature the PAD application supports is a splitter window. A splitter window enables the user to display several views of a document in one window. To see a splitter window in action, follow these steps:

☐ Select the window of the TRY2.PAD document (that is, click anywhere on the window of TRY2.PAD or select TRY2.PAD from the Window menu).

☐ Maximize the window of TRY2.DOC (by clicking the up-arrow icon that appears in the upper-right corner of the window of TRY2.DOC).

Now the window of TRY2.PAD looks as shown in Figure 19.11.

As shown in Figure 19.11, the window of TRY2.PAD has two small split boxes. One split box is located at the top of the window's vertical scroll bar, and the other split box is located at the extreme left of the window's horizontal scroll bar.

Figure 19.11.
The window of
TRY2.PAD after
maximizing it.

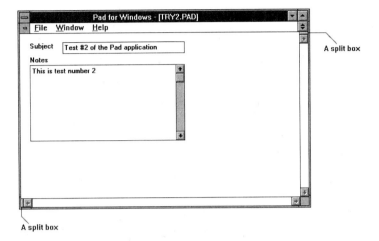

☐ To split the window of TRY2.PAD vertically, drag the split box located at the top of the vertical scroll bar to the middle of the scroll bar and then release the mouse button.

As soon as you release the mouse button, the window of TRY2.PAD splits into two parts (see Figure 19.12).

Figure 19.12.
Vertically splitting
the window of
TRY2.PAD into
two parts.

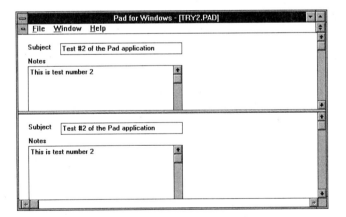

If you try to type something in one section of the split window, the other section of the window will be updated automatically.

Now you can split the window of TRY2.PAD further by using the split box located at the left side of the horizontal scroll bar:

☐ Drag the split box located at the extreme left side of the horizontal scroll bar to the middle of the scroll bar and then release the mouse button.

As soon as you release the mouse button, the window of TRY2.PAD splits into two more parts (see Figure 19.13).

Figure 19.13.
Splitting the
window of
TRY2.PAD
into four parts.

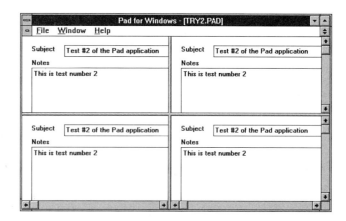

Again, if you try to type something in any of the split window's sections, the other three sections will be updated automatically.

In addition to using the split boxes to split a window, you can also use the Split option in the Window menu. To see the Windows menu's Split option in action:

☐ Select New from the File menu.

The PAD application responds by opening a new document.

☐ Fill the Subject and Notes fields of the new document with any data.

☐ Now select Split from the Window menu.

The PAD application responds by displaying a horizontal axis and a vertical axis (see Figure 19.14).

Figure 19.14.
Splitting a window
with the Split
option of the
Window menu.

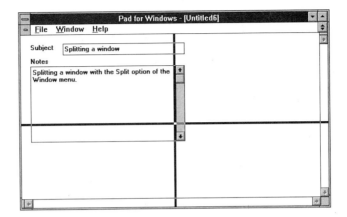

Note that as you move the mouse, the intersection point of the two axes moves accordingly.

☐ Move the mouse until the two axes divide the window as you desire and then click the mouse.

> *The PAD application responds by splitting the window in accordance with the point at which you clicked the mouse.*

You have finished experimenting with the New Window, Cascade, Tile, and Split options of the Window menu. There is still one more menu option in the Window menu that you didn't try: Arrange Icons.

To see the Arrange Icons menu option in action:

☐ Minimize all the child windows that are currently open on the desktop by clicking the down-arrow icon that appears at the upper-right corner of each of the child windows.

Figure 19.15 shows the main window of the PAD application with five minimized child windows.

☐ Drag the minimized child windows to various random locations in the main window of the application.

Figure 19.15.
The main window
of the PAD appli-
cation with five
minimized child
windows.

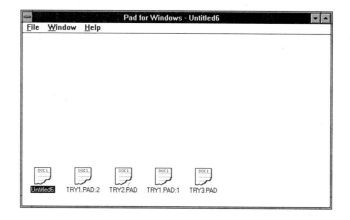

Figure 19.16 shows the minimized child windows placed at various random locations.

Figure 19.16.
Minimized child
windows scattered
at random locations
in the application's
main window.

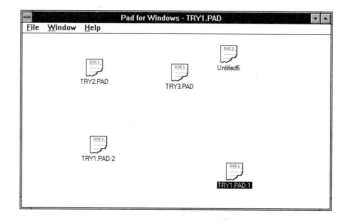

☐ Now select Arrange Icons from the Window menu.

> *The PAD application responds by arranging the minimized child windows at the bottom of the window (see Figure 19.15).*

Now that you're familiar with the options of the Window menu, you can experiment with the options of the File menu.

☐ Experiment with the various options of the File menu.

> *As you can see, the File menu of the application works as you would expect any standard Windows application to work.*

Note that at any given time, you can select only one child window and the operations that you perform apply to this child window. For example, if the window of TRY1.PAD is currently selected and you select Save from the File menu, TRY1.PAD will be saved.

Note that the PAD application actually has two sets of menu bars. One menu bar is displayed whenever there is at least one child window in the application's main window. This menu bar is shown in Figure 19.17 with the File popup open. The other menu bar is displayed when the application's main window contains no child windows (that is, the user closed all the child windows). This menu bar is shown in Figure 19.18 with the File popup open.

Figure 19.17.
The application's
menu bar when
at least one child
window is open.

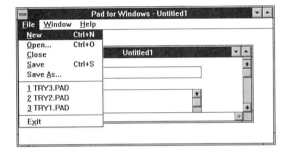

Figure 19.18.
The application's
menu bar when no
child windows are
open.

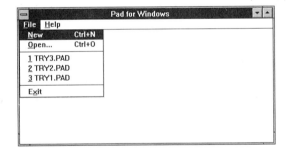

As you can see from Figure 19.18, when no child windows are in the main window of the application, the menu bar doesn't have a Window popup, and the File popup doesn't have the Close, Save, and Save As menu items.

To exit from the PAD application:

☐ Select Exit from the File menu.

You may think that because the PAD application supports such powerful features as previously described, the code you will have to write is more involved than the code you had to write in previous chapters (for example, the MEMO application in Chapter 13). However, this isn't the case! For the most part, the steps that you'll take while building the PAD application will be the same as the steps you took when you built the MEMO application in Chapter 13.

Now that you know what the PAD application should do, you can start writing it.

Creating the Project of the PAD Application

To create the project of the PAD application:

☐ Select AppWizard from the Project menu.

> *Visual C++ responds by running AppWizard.*

☐ Use the Directory list box to select the directory C:\VCPROG\PRACTICE\CH19.

☐ Type pad in the Project Name box.

Your AppWizard dialog box should now look as shown in Figure 19.19.

Figure 19.19.
The AppWizard
dialog box for the
PAD application.

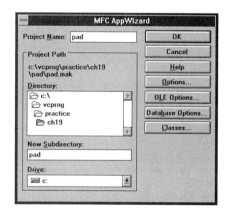

☐ Click the Options button and set the options as shown in Figure 19.20.

WARNING

Because you want the PAD application to be an MDI application, the Multiple Document Interface check box must be checked. As you can see from Figure 19.20, the Multiple Document Interface check box is indeed checked.

Figure 19.20.
Setting the PAD
application's
options.

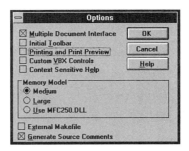

□ Click the OK button of the Options dialog box and then click the OK button of the AppWizard dialog box and finally click the Create button of the New Application Information dialog box.

AppWizard responds by creating the PAD project and all the skeleton files of the PAD application.

To remove the debug options of the project (so that you'll have a small EXE file):

□ Select Project from the Options menu of Visual C++, click the Release radio button, and then click the OK button of the dialog box.

Creating the Form of the Application

As shown in Figure 19.1, a child window of the PAD application should contain a data entry form with two fields: Subject and Notes.

To implement this form you'll replace the current view class of the application with a new view class derived from the `CFormView` class—just as you did when you designed SDI applications (for example, the MEMO application in Chapter 13).

Follow these steps to create the form of the application:

□ Use the Windows File Manager (or DOS Shell) to delete the two view class files of the PAD application:

Delete `C:\VCPROG\PRACTICE\CH19\PAD\PADVIEW.CPP`.
Delete `C:\VCPROG\PRACTICE\CH19\PAD\PADVIEW.H`.

☐ Select ClassWizard from the Browse menu of Visual C++.

ClassWizard responds by displaying a dialog box telling you that the files of the view class don't exist.

☐ Click the OK button of the dialog box.

☐ Click the Remove button of the Repair Class Information dialog box.

☐ Click the OK button of ClassWizard's dialog box.

You have just finished removing the view class of the PAD application.

In the following steps you'll create a dialog box, you'll create a `CFormView` type class for this dialog box, and you'll make this class the new view class of the application:

☐ Select App Studio from the Tools menu of Visual C++.

☐ Create a new dialog box with App Studio.

☐ Double-click in a free area of the new dialog box.

☐ Select Styles from the drop-down list box at the upper-right corner of the Properties window.

Set the Styles properties of the dialog box as follows:

☐ Select Child in the Style box.

☐ Select None in the Border box.

☐ Uncheck the Visible property (that is, remove the check mark from the Visible check box).

☐ Select General from the drop-down list box at the upper-right corner of the Properties window and make sure that the Caption box is empty.

Now connect the dialog box to a class derived from `CFormView`:

☐ Select ClassWizard from the Resource menu of App Studio.

ClassWizard responds by displaying the Add Class dialog box.

☐ Type `CPadView` in the Class Name box.

☐ Set the Class Type to `CFormView`.

☐ Make sure that the Header File box is filled with `padview.h`.

☐ Make sure that the Implementation File box is filled with `padview.cpp`.

☐ Click the Create Class button.

☐ Click the OK button of ClassWizard's window to go back to App Studio.

You've finished creating the new view class of the application. This view class is a derived class from the MFC `CFormView` class and is connected to the dialog box you created. Thus, each of the child windows of the PAD application will be the dialog box you created.

The Visual Implementation of the Dialog Box

☐ Implement the dialog box of the PAD application per Table 19.1.

Table 19.1. The dialog box of the PAD application.

Class Name:	CPadView (of type CFormView)
Figure:	19.21
OK button:	No
Cancel button:	No

Object	Property	Setting
Dialog Box	ID	IDD_DIALOG1
Label	ID	IDC_STATIC
	Caption	Subject
Edit Box	ID	IDC_SUBJECT
	Variable	m_Subject
	Variable Type	CString
Label	ID	IDC_STATIC
	Caption	Notes
Edit Box	ID	IDC_NOTES
	Variable	m_Notes
	Variable Type CString	
	Multiline Yes	
	Want Return Yes	
	Vert. Scroll Yes	

585

NOTE

Table 19.1 specifies that the Multiline, Want Return, and Vert. Scroll style properties of the IDC_NOTES edit box should be set. Recall from Chapter 13 that the Multiline and Want Return settings will enable the user to press the Enter key while typing in the edit box, and the Vert. Scroll setting will provide the edit box with a vertical scroll bar. If you forgot how to set these properties, follow these steps:

Double-click in the IDC_NOTES edit box.

Select Styles from the drop-down list box at the upper-right corner of the Properties window.

Set the Styles properties of the IDC_NOTES edit box as follows:

Place a check mark in the Multiline check box.

Place a check mark in the Want Return check box.

Place a check mark in the Vert. Scroll check box (this will provide the edit box with a vertical scroll bar).

Now your dialog box looks as shown in Figure 19.21.

Figure 19.21.
The dialog box
of the PAD
application.

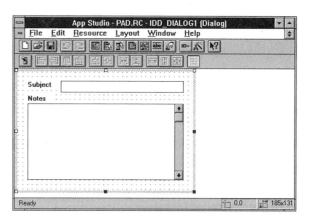

Save your work:

☐ Select Save from the File menu of App Studio.

586

You've finished designing the dialog box. This dialog box will appear in each of the child windows of the application.

The Visual Implementation of the Menus

As stated earlier, the PAD application has two menus. One menu is displayed when at least one child window is in the main window of the application (see Figure 19.17), and the other menu is displayed when no child windows are in the application's main window (see Figure 19.18).

Now use App Studio to customize these menus:

☐ Display the PAD.RC (MFC Resource Script) window in App Studio by selecting PAD.RC from the Window menu of App Studio or by selecting App Studio from the Tools menu of Visual C++.

☐ Select Menu in the Type list of App Studio's window.

App Studio responds by listing in the Resources list the names of the PAD application's menus (see Figure 19.22).

Figure 19.22.
The two menus
of the PAD
application.

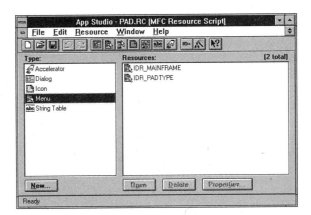

As you can see from Figure 19.22, the names of the PAD application's menus are IDR_MAINFRAME and IDR_PADTYPE.

IDR_MAINFRAME is the menu displayed when no child windows are in the application's main window. IDR_PADTYPE is the menu displayed when at least one child window is in the application's main window. Both of these menus were designed by Visual C++. Your job is to customize them (if necessary) for the particular application you're designing.

Now take a look at the IDR_MAINFRAME menu:

☐ Double-click IDR_MAINFRAME in the Resources list.

App Studio responds by displaying the IDR_MAINFRAME menu in design mode (see Figure 19.23).

Figure 19.23.
The
IDR_MAINFRAME
menu of the PAD
application.

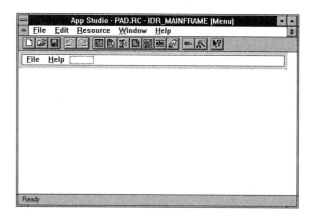

You don't have to customize the IDR_MAINFRAME menu for the PAD application; the way Visual C++ created the IDR_MAINFRAME menu is exactly what you need for the PAD application.

Now take a look at the IDR_PADTYPE menu:

☐ Select PAD.RC (MFC Resource Script) from the Window menu of App Studio.

App Studio responds by displaying the PAD.RC window (see Figure 19.22).

☐ Double-click IDR_PADTYPE in the Resources list.

App Studio responds by displaying the IDR_PADTYPE menu in design mode (see Figure 19.24).

Customizing this menu for the PAD application is easy, because all you have to do is delete the Edit popup menu. The File and Help popup menus that Visual C++ generated for you are exactly what you need for the PAD application.

☐ Use App Studio to delete the Edit popup of the IDR_PADTYPE menu.

To save your work:

☐ Select Save from the File menu of App Studio.

The visual implementation of the two menus of the PAD application is completed.

Figure 19.24.
The
IDR_PADTYPE
menu of the PAD
application.

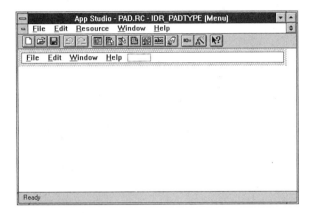

Executing the PAD Application

Even though you haven't written a single line of code for the PAD application, execute it and see your visual design in action:

☐ Select Rebuild All PAD.EXE from the Project menu of Visual C++.

Visual C++ responds by compiling and linking the PAD application.

To execute the PAD.EXE application:

☐ Select Execute PAD.EXE from the Project menu.

Visual C++ responds by executing the PAD application. The main window of the application appears with one child window in it. This child window has the two fields (Subject and Notes) that you designed.

Now you can experiment with various menu options of the application. However, do not experiment with the Save and Save As options of the File menu. Although, you haven't written any code that writes data, these menu options have some functionality, and if you aren't careful, you can accidentally overwrite important files.

NOTE

Although you haven't written any code for opening and saving files, the menu items of the File menu have some functionality. For example, if you select Open from the File menu, a File Open dialog box appears. Of course once you select a file, nothing will be loaded because you haven't written code to accomplish that.

Be careful with the Save and Save As menu items! Although you haven't written any code that writes data into files, the Save and Save As menu items write data. For example, if you have a file, TRY.TXT, that contains some data, and you select the file TRY.TXT from Save As in the File menu, the original TRY.TXT will be overwritten by a new blank TRY.TXT.

Experiment with the menu of the PAD application:

☐ Select New from the File menu to add a new child window in the application's main window.

☐ Repeat the previous step to add a few more child windows.

Experiment with the various options of the Window menu:

☐ Select Tile from the Window menu.

> *The PAD application responds by arranging the child windows in tile format.*

☐ Select Cascade from the Window menu.

> *The PAD application responds by rearranging the child windows in cascaded format.*

Now try the Arrange Icons option:

☐ Minimize all the child windows that are currently open on the desktop by clicking the down-arrow icon that appears at the upper-right corner of each of the child windows.

☐ Drag the minimized child windows to various random locations in the main window of the application.

☐ Now select Arrange Icons from the Window menu.

> *The PAD application responds by arranging the minimized child windows at the bottom of the window.*

As you can see, although you haven't written a single line of code, the PAD application already has a lot of functionality. That's because Visual C++ already wrote a lot of code for you.

In the following sections you'll write code that will add more life to the PAD application. You will write the code that enables the user to save documents into files and load documents from files.

Later in the chapter you will also write the code that enables the user to view the same document in several windows and the code that enables the user to split a window into several views.

To exit the PAD application:

☐ Select Exit from the File menu.

The Document Class of the PAD Application

Just as you used the document class for storing the data of the application in SDI applications (for example, the MEMO application in Chapter 13), so also will you use the document class for storing the application's data in the PAD application.

Recall that during the visual implementation of the dialog box you created two variables:

> m_Subject (the variable of the IDC_SUBJECT edit box)
> m_Notes (the variable of the IDC_NOTES edit box)

Because you connected the dialog box to the view class of the application, these variables are data members of the view class.

Now add two data members to the document class. These variables will have the same names as the two data members of the view class. (Note that you don't have to name the data members of the document class with the same names as the data members of the view class, but using the same names makes the program easy to read and understand.)

The document class of the PAD application is CPadDoc, and the declaration of this class is in the header file PADDOC.H.

☐ Open the file PADDOC.H and add code to it that defines the two variables
m_Subject and m_Notes as public data members of the CPadDoc class. Declare

each of these variables as type CString. After you write this code, the CPadDoc class declaration looks as follows:

```
class CPadDoc : public CDocument
{
protected: // create from serialization only
     CPadDoc();
     DECLARE_DYNCREATE(CPadDoc)

// Attributes
public:

     /////////////////////////
     // MY CODE STARTS HERE
     /////////////////////////

     CString m_Subject;
     CString m_Notes;

     ////////////////////////
     // MY CODE ENDS HERE
     ////////////////////////

// Operations
public:

// Implementation
public:
     virtual ~CPadDoc();
     virtual void Serialize(CArchive& ar);    // overridden for document
i/o
#ifdef _DEBUG
     virtual void AssertValid() const;
     virtual void Dump(CDumpContext& dc) const;
#endif

protected:
     virtual BOOL OnNewDocument();

// Generated message map functions
protected:
     //{{AFX_MSG(CPadDoc)
          // NOTE - the ClassWizard will add and remove
          //        member functions here.
          // DO NOT EDIT what you see in these blocks of
          // generated code !
     //}}AFX_MSG
     DECLARE_MESSAGE_MAP()
};
```

Save your work:

☐ Select Save from the File menu of Visual C++.

You finished declaring the data members of the document class. Next you will initialize these variables.

Initializing the Data Members of the Document Class

When the application is started, and whenever the user selects New from the File menu, the data members of the document class should be initialized to null. Why? Because whenever a new document is created you want it to be blank (see Figure 19.1).

Recall from Chapter 13 that the code which initializes the data members of the document class should be written in the OnNewDocument() member function of the document class. That's because OnNewDocument() is executed automatically whenever a new document is created (for example, when the user selects New from the File menu).

☐ Open the file PADDOC.CPP and edit the OnNewDocument() function. After you edit this function, your OnNewDocument() function looks as follows:

```
BOOL CPadDoc::OnNewDocument()
{
    if (!CDocument::OnNewDocument())
        return FALSE;

    // TODO: add reinitialization code here
    // (SDI documents will reuse this document)


    ////////////////////////
    // MY CODE STARTS HERE
    ////////////////////////

    // Make the new document blank.
    m_Subject = "";
    m_Notes   = "";

    ////////////////////////
    // MY CODE ENDS HERE
    ////////////////////////

    return TRUE;
}
```

The code you just added to the OnNewDocument() function assigns null strings to the two data members of the document class. Thus, whenever a new document is created (for example, when the user selects New from the File menu), the two data members of the document class are initialized to null.

Of course, you can initialize the variables to any other value. For example, you can initialize the m_Subject variable to "Miscellaneous", as in m_Subject = "Miscellaneous";.

As a result, whenever a new document is created, the default text in the Subject field will be "Miscellaneous".

To save your work:

☐ Select Save from the File menu of Visual C++.

Initializing the Data Members of the View Class

Recall from Chapter 13 that you write the code that initializes the data members of the view class in the OnInitialUpdate() member function of the view class. The OnInitialUpdate() function is executed automatically:

On starting the application
When the user selects New from the File menu
When the user selects Open from the File menu

The code you write in the OnInitialUpdate() function should update the m_Subject and m_Notes data members of the view class with the corresponding data members of the document class.

Visual C++ did not write the declaration and skeleton of the OnInitialUpdate() function. You have to declare this function and write its skeleton yourself. To do that:

☐ Open the file PADVIEW.H and add code to it that defines the function OnInitialUpdate() as a member function of the CPadView class. After you write this code, the CPadView class declaration looks as follows:

```
class CPadView : public CFormView
{
    DECLARE_DYNCREATE(CPadView)
protected:
    CPadView(); // protected constructor used by dynamic creation
```

```
/////////////////////
// MY CODE STARTS HERE
/////////////////////

    virtual void OnInitialUpdate();

/////////////////////
// MY CODE ENDS HERE
/////////////////////


// Form Data
public:
    //{{AFX_DATA(CPadView)
    enum { IDD = IDD_DIALOG1 };
    CString     m_Subject;
    CString     m_Notes;
    //}}AFX_DATA

// Attributes
public:

// Operations
public:

// Implementation
protected:
    virtual ~CPadView();
    virtual void DoDataExchange(CDataExchange* pDX);
    // Generated message map functions
    //{{AFX_MSG(CPadView)
        // NOTE - the ClassWizard will add and remove member
        //        functions here.
    //}}AFX_MSG
    DECLARE_MESSAGE_MAP()
};
```

Now write the `OnInitialUpdate()` function's code:

☐ Open the file PADVIEW.CPP and add the `OnInitialUpdate()` function to the end of the file. After you write this function, the end of the PADVIEW.CPP file looks as follows:

```
/////////////////////////////////////////////////////////
// CPadView message handlers

/////////////////////
// MY CODE STARTS HERE
/////////////////////
```

```
void CPadView::OnInitialUpdate()
{

    // Get a pointer to the document.
    CPadDoc* pDoc = (CPadDoc*) GetDocument();

    // Update the data members of the view class with the
    // current values of the document class data members.
    m_Subject = pDoc->m_Subject;
    m_Notes   = pDoc->m_Notes;

    // Update the screen with the new values.
    UpdateData(FALSE);

}

///////////////////////
// MY CODE ENDS HERE
///////////////////////
```

Review the OnInitialUpdate() function's code.

The first statement,

```
CPadDoc* pDoc = (CPadDoc*) GetDocument();
```

extracts pDoc (the pointer for the document class).

Then the data members of the view class are updated with the current values of the document:

```
m_Subject = pDoc->m_Subject;
m_Notes   = pDoc->m_Notes;
```

Finally, the UpdateData() function is used to transfer the new values of m_Subject and m_Notes to the screen:

```
UpdateData(FALSE);
```

If you try to compile the PADVIEW.CPP file now, you'll get a compiling error. Why? Because in the previous code you referred to the CPadDoc class, but the CPadDoc class isn't known in the PADVIEW.CPP file. Thus, you must #include PADDOC.H (the header file of the CPadDoc class) at the beginning of the PADVIEW.CPP file:

☐ Add the #include "paddoc.h" statement at the beginning of the PADVIEW.CPP file (immediately before the #include statement of the PADVIEW.H file). After you add this #include statement, the beginning of the PADVIEW.CPP file looks as follows:

```
// padview.cpp : implementation file
//

#include "stdafx.h"
#include "pad.h"

///////////////////////
// MY CODE STARTS HERE
///////////////////////

#include "paddoc.h"

///////////////////////
// MY CODE ENDS HERE
///////////////////////

#include "padview.h"
....
....
....
```

To save your work:

☐ Select Save from the File menu.

So what have you accomplished so far? You wrote the code that initializes the data members of the document class, and you wrote the code that initializes the data members of the view class.

NOTE

Okay, you've written enough code! To make sure that you've typed the correct code, compile/link the application.

Select Build PAD.EXE from the Project menu and make sure that there are no compiling/linking errors.

Don't execute the application. The only reason to compile/link the program is to verify that you entered the code correctly.

Updating the Data Members of the Document Class

Whenever the user edits the IDC_SUBJECT and IDC_NOTES edit boxes, the corresponding data members of the document class should be updated with the new values that the user types. For example, if the user changes the contents of the IDC_SUBJECT edit box, the data member m_Subject of the document class should be updated with the m_Subject data member of the view class (because the m_Subject data member of the view class is the variable of the IDC_SUBJECT edit box).

So you need to write code that detects when the user types something in the IDC_SUBJECT and IDC_NOTES edit boxes and then changes corresponding data members of the document class accordingly. Here is how you do that:

☐ Use ClassWizard to add a function for the event:

Class Name:	CPadView
Object ID:	IDC_SUBJECT
Message:	EN_CHANGE
Function Name:	OnChangeSubject()

☐ Edit the OnChangeSubject() function that you added to the PADVIEW.CPP file. After editing the function, your OnChangeSubject() function looks as follows:

```
void CPadView::OnChangeSubject()
{
// TODO: Add your control notification handler code here

    ////////////////////////
    // MY CODE STARTS HERE
    ////////////////////////

    // Update the variables of the controls with the
    // current values inside the controls.
    UpdateData(TRUE);

    // Get a pointer to the document.
    CPadDoc* pDoc = (CPadDoc*) GetDocument();

    // Update the m_Subject data member of the document class.
    pDoc->m_Subject = m_Subject;

    // Set the Modified flag of the document class to TRUE.
    pDoc->SetModifiedFlag();

    ////////////////////////
    // MY CODE ENDS HERE
    ////////////////////////

}
```

Review the code you just typed.

The first statement in the function,

```
UpdateData(TRUE);
```

updates the variables of the controls with the current values in the controls.

The next statement,

```
CPadDoc* pDoc = (CPadDoc*) GetDocument();
```

extracts pDoc (the pointer for the document class).

The next statement,

```
pDoc->m_Subject = m_Subject;
```

updates the m_Subject data member of the document class with the new contents of the IDC_SUBJECT edit box.

The last statement in the function is

```
pDoc->SetModifiedFlag();
```

This statement executes the SetModifiedFlag() member function of the document class to set the Modified flag to TRUE, signaling that the document's data was modified. Recall from Chapter 13 that when the Modified flag is set to TRUE and the user tries to quit the application, it will display a warning message informing the user that the file hasn't been saved.

In a similar manner, you now need to attach code to the IDC_NOTES edit box.

☐ Use ClassWizard to add a function for the event:

Class Name:	CPadView
Object ID:	IDC_NOTES
Message:	EN_CHANGE
Function Name:	OnChangeNotes()

☐ Edit the OnChangeNotes() function that you added to the PADVIEW.CPP file. After you edit the function, your OnChangeNotes() function looks as follows:

```
void CPadView::OnChangeNotes()
{
// TODO: Add your control notification handler code here

    /////////////////////////
    // MY CODE STARTS HERE
    /////////////////////////
```

```
// Update the variables of the controls with the
// current values inside the controls.
UpdateData(TRUE);

// Get a pointer to the document.
CPadDoc* pDoc = (CPadDoc*) GetDocument();

// Update the m_Notes data member of the document class.
pDoc->m_Notes = m_Notes;

// Set the Modified flag of the document class to TRUE.
pDoc->SetModifiedFlag();

//////////////////////
// MY CODE ENDS HERE
//////////////////////

}
```

As you can see, the OnChangeNotes() function is similar to the OnChangeSubject() function. The only difference is that now m_Notes is updated (not m_Subject).

You have finished attaching code to the IDC_SUBJECT and IDC_NOTES edit boxes. Now whenever the user changes these edit boxes, the corresponding data members of the document class will be updated.

Don't forget to save your work:

☐ Select Save from the File menu.

To review what you have accomplished so far:

You wrote the code that initializes the data members of the document class.
You wrote the code that initializes the data members of the view class.
You wrote the code that updates the data members of the document class whenever the user changes the data members of the view class (that is, when the user changes the contents of the edit boxes).

Next you will write the code that enables the user to save documents in files and load documents from files.

Writing and Reading Data to and from Files

Just as you brought to life the Open, Save, and Save As menu options of the File menu in previous chapters, so now all you have to do is write code in the

`Serialize()` function of the document class. Follow these steps to write the code in the document class `Serialize()` function:

☐ Open the file PADDOC.CPP and modify the `Serialize()` function of the document class until it looks as follows:

```
void CPadDoc::Serialize(CArchive& ar)
{
    if (ar.IsStoring())
    {
        // TODO: add storing code here

        /////////////////////////
        // MY CODE STARTS HERE
        /////////////////////////

        // Write to the file.
        ar << m_Subject << m_Notes;

        /////////////////////////
        // MY CODE ENDS HERE
        /////////////////////////

    }
    else
    {
        // TODO: add loading code here


        /////////////////////////
        // MY CODE STARTS HERE
        /////////////////////////

        // Read from the file.
        ar >> m_Subject >> m_Notes;

        /////////////////////////
        // MY CODE ENDS HERE
        /////////////////////////

    }
}
```

The code you typed in the `Serialize()` function serializes the m_Subject and m_Notes data members of the document class to and from the file that the user selects from the File menu.

> **NOTE**
>
> You have finished writing most of the PAD application's code. As you can see, even though the PAD application is an MDI application, all the steps you have taken so far are the same as the steps you took when you built an SDI application (for example, the MEMO application in Chapter 13). The only difference is that when you started the PAD application, you checked the Multiple Document Interface option in AppWizard (see Figure 19.20).

Executing the PAD Application

You have finished writing most of the PAD application's code. To see your code in action:

☐ Select Build PAD.EXE from the Project menu of Visual C++.

Visual C++ responds by compiling and linking the PAD application.

☐ Select Execute PAD.EXE from the Project menu.

Visual C++ responds by executing the PAD application. The application's main window appears with a child window in it. The title of the main window is Pad Windows Application - Pad 1.

The title of the child window is Pad1.

☐ Experiment with all the PAD application's menu options.

Notice that all the menu options of the PAD application are working. However, there are still a few enhancements that you need to apply to the PAD application.

In the following sections you'll enhance the PAD application in three ways:

> You will use App Studio's string editor to change the application windows' titles and the default document type that appears in the Save As and Open dialog boxes.
> You will add code that enables the user to display multiple views of the same document.
> You will add code that enables the user to split a window into several views.

To exit from the PAD application:

☐ Select Exit from the File menu.

Using App Studio's String Editor to Enhance the PAD Application

Now you'll use App Studio's string editor to change the following characteristics of the PAD application:

1. Change the title of the application's window from `Pad Windows Application - [filename]` to `Pad for Windows - [filename]`, where `[filename]` is the name of the document whose window is currently selected.

2. Change the default filename displayed in the application window's title when a new document is created from `Pad` to `Untitled`.

3. Change the default file type displayed in the Save As and Open dialog boxes from `*.*` to `*.PAD`. This means that when the user selects Open or Save As from the File menu, the default files displayed in the File list box will have a .PAD file extension.

To implement these enhancements:

☐ Select App Studio from the Tools menu of Visual C++.

Visual C++ responds by displaying the `PAD.RC` *window.*

☐ Select String Table from the Type list (see Figure 19.25) and then double-click the `String Segment:0` item in the Resources list.

App Studio responds by displaying the String Table Editor (see Figure 19.26).

Figure 19.25.
Selecting String
Table from the
Type list.

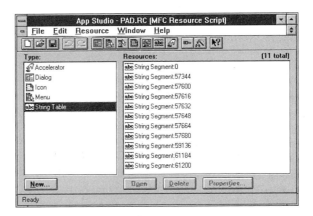

Figure 19.26.
The String
Table Editor.

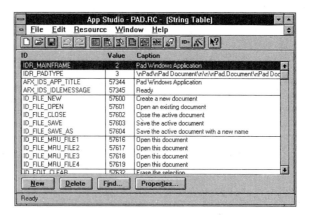

Recall that in previous chapters when you used the String Table Editor, you had to customize only one string—the IDR_MAINFRAME string. However, because the PAD application is an MDI application, now you need to customize two strings: IDR_MAINFRAME and IDR_PADTYPE. As you can see from Figure 19.26, IDR_MAINFRAME is the first string in the list, and IDR_PADTYPE is the second string in the list.

Why do you need to customize two strings? The first string, IDR_MAINFRAME, applies when the application's main window is empty (that is, when there are no open child windows). The second string, IDR_PADTYPE, applies when the application's main window contains at least one child window.

As you can see from Figure 19.26, the current value of the IDR_MAINFRAME string is Pad Windows Application.

This string represents the left portion of the main window title. Because you want the left portion of the main window title to be Pad for Windows (as shown in Figure 19.1), you need to change the IDR_MAINFRAME string as follows:

☐ Double-click the IDR_MAINFRAME string.

> *App Studio responds by displaying the Properties window of the*
> *IDR_MAINFRAME string.*

☐ Change the Caption property of the IDR_MAINFRAME string to Pad for Windows (see Figure 19.27).

Figure 19.27.
Changing the
IDR_MAINFRAME
string.

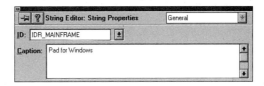

Next you need to customize the IDR_PADTYPE string. The current value of the IDR_PADTYPE string is

```
\nPad\nPad Document\n\n\nPad.Document\nPad Document
```

Recall that the \n within the string serves as a separator between substrings. Thus, the previous string is made of the following substrings:

```
NULL
Pad
Pad Document
NULL
NULL
Pad.Document
Pad Document
```

The first \n means that the first substring is NULL.

From these seven substrings, those of interest to you right now are the first five.

The first substring represents the left portion of the main window title. This substring is set to NULL, because the title of the main window is already specified in the IDR_MAINFRAME string (as Pad for Windows).

The second substring represents the default document name that appears in the main window title (the right portion of the title) when the user starts the application or when the user selects New from the File menu. Currently the value of this substring is Pad, and you want to change it to Untitled. The third substring represents the document type name of the application.

The fourth and fifth substrings represent the default document type displayed in the Save As and Open File dialog boxes of the application. For example, if you set the fourth substring to PAD Files (*.pad) and the fifth substring to pad, when the user selects Save As or Open from the File menu, the files listed in the Open and Save As dialog boxes have the extension pad and the text that appears in the File Type box will be PAD Files (*.pad).

Figure 19.28 shows the Save As dialog box listing files with the extension .pad. The text PAD Files (*.pad) appcars in the Save File as Type box.

Figure 19.28.
The Save As dialog
box listing files with
a .pad extension.

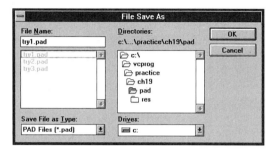

Now you can customize the IDR_PADTYPE string:

☐ Double-click the IDR_PADTYPE string.

> *App Studio responds by displaying the String Properties window of the*
> *IDR_PADTYPE string.*

Change the Caption property of the IDR_PADTYPE string to \nUntitled\nPad
Document\nPAD Files (*.pad)\n.pad\nPad.Document\nPad Document.

NOTE

Be sure to type the string on one line. Because the string is long, App Studio
will wrap the string on two lines.

Now your String Properties window for the IDR_PADTYPE string looks as shown in
Figure 19.29.

Figure 19.29.
Changing the
IDR_PADTYPE
string.

To save your work:

☐ Select Save from the File menu of App Studio.

To see the effects of the modification you made to the IDR_MAINFRAME and IDR_PADTYPE
strings:

☐ Select Build PAD.EXE from the Project menu of Visual C++.

☐ Execute the PAD application.

As you can see, the main window of the application appears with the title `Pad for Windows - Untitled1` and the title of the child window is `Untitled1`.

☐ Fill the blank form of the `Untitled1` window with data.

☐ Select Save from the File menu.

> *The PAD application responds by displaying a Save As dialog box. As you can see, the Save As dialog box lists files with the* `.pad` *extension.*

☐ Save your document as `TRY.PAD`.

The PAD application responds by saving the document into the file `TRY.PAD` and by changing the title of the application window to `Pad for Windows - TRY.PAD`.

The PAD application also changes the title of the child window to `TRY.PAD`. You have enhanced the PAD application significantly by simply customizing the `IDR_MAINFRAME` and `IDR_PADTYPE` strings using App Studio.

To terminate the PAD application:

☐ Select Exit from the File menu.

Multiple Views of the Same Document

Currently the PAD application doesn't support multiple viewing of the same document. As discussed at the beginning of this chapter, multiple viewing of the same document means the user is able to open several windows for the same document, and when the user changes the data in one of the windows, the data in the rest of the windows (of the same document) is updated automatically.

To verify that currently the PAD application doesn't support multiple viewing, try the following experiment:

☐ Execute the PAD application.

Fill the fields of the `Untitled1` window as follows:

☐ Type `Test` in the Subject field.

☐ Type `Testing multiple views of the same document` in the Notes field.

607

☐ Select Save from the File menu and save the new document as TEST.PAD.

☐ Select New Window from the Window menu.

The PAD application responds by opening another view (another window) for
TEST.PAD.

☐ Select Tile from the Window menu.

Now your PAD application looks as shown in Figure 19.30.

Figure 19.30.
Two views of
TEST.PAD.

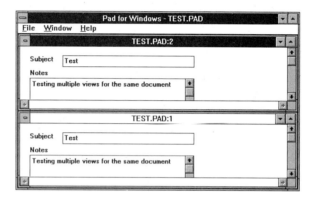

As you can see, the document TEST.PAD has two views (two child windows). One window has the title TEST.PAD:1, and the other window has the title TEST.PAD:2.

☐ Try to type something in one of the windows of TEST.PAD.

When you type something in one view of TEST.PAD, the other view is not updated! So currently, the PAD application does not support multiple viewing of the same document.

In the following sections, you'll add code to the PAD application so that when the user changes one view of a document, all the other views of the same document will be updated automatically.

☐ Terminate the PAD application.

The *UpdateAllViews()* and *OnUpdate()* Functions

Whenever the user changes the contents of the IDC_SUBJECT and IDC_NOTES edit boxes (that is, the user types something in one of these edit boxes), you want to update all the views of the particular document that the user is currently changing. You do that by calling the UpdateAllViews() member function of the document class.

What does the `UpdateAllViews()` function do? It notifies all the views of the modified document that they need to be updated by calling the `OnUpdate()` member function of the view class for each view that should be updated.

So your job is

> To write the code that calls `UpdateAllViews()` whenever the user changes any view (that is, when the user types something in an edit box).
> To write the `OnUpdate()` member function of the view class.

Calling the *UpdateAllViews()* Function

As stated previously, whenever the user changes a view of a particular document (that is, the user types something in the IDC_SUBJECT edit box or IDC_NOTES edit box) you need to call the `UpdateAllViews()` member function of the document class.

You call the `UpdateAllViews()` function from the `OnChangeSubject()` and `OnChangeNotes()` member functions of the view class. Recall that you wrote these two functions earlier. `OnChangeSubject()` is executed whenever the user changes the IDC_SUBJECT edit box, and `OnChangeNotes()` is executed whenever the user changes the IDC_NOTES edit box.

Follow these steps to modify the `OnChangeSubject()` and `OnChangeNotes()` functions:

☐ Open the file PADVIEW.CPP and add the statement

```
// Update all the other views of the same document.
pDoc->UpdateAllViews(this);
```

to the end of the `OnChangeSubject()` function. After you add this statement, your `OnChangeSubject()` function looks as follows:

```
void CPadView::OnChangeSubject()
{
// TODO: Add your control notification handler code here

    /////////////////////////
    // MY CODE STARTS HERE
    /////////////////////////

    // Update the variables of the controls with the
    // current values inside the controls.
    UpdateData(TRUE);

    // Get a pointer to the document.
    CPadDoc* pDoc = (CPadDoc*) GetDocument();
```

```
// Update the m_Subject data member of the document class.
pDoc->m_Subject = m_Subject;

// Set the Modified flag of the document class to TRUE.
pDoc->SetModifiedFlag();

// Update all the other views of the same document.
pDoc->UpdateAllViews(this);

/////////////////////
// MY CODE ENDS HERE
/////////////////////

}
```

The statement you just added,

```
pDoc->UpdateAllViews(this);
```

calls the UpdateAllViews() member function of the document class. The parameter
this is passed to tell UpdateAllViews() which view is the current one (the this keyword is a pointer to the current view object). This way, UpdateAllWindows() updates
all the views of the current document except the current view. For example, if the
user changes the IDC_SUBJECT edit box in a certain view of the document TRY.DOC,
UpdateAllViews() updates all the other views of TRY.DOC. There is no need for
UpdateAllWindows() to update the current view, because the current view has already
updated itself.

Similarly, you also need to modify the OnChangeNotes() function.

☐ Add the statement

```
// Update all the other views of the same document.
pDoc->UpdateAllViews(this);
```

to the end of the OnChangeNotes() function. After you add this statement, your
OnChangeNotes() function looks as follows:

```
void CPadView::OnChangeNotes()
{
// TODO: Add your control notification handler code here

    /////////////////////
    // MY CODE STARTS HERE
    /////////////////////

    // Update the variables of the controls with the
    // current values inside the controls.
    UpdateData(TRUE);
```

```
// Get a pointer to the document.
CPadDoc* pDoc = (CPadDoc*) GetDocument();

// Update the m_Notes data member of the document class.
pDoc->m_Notes = m_Notes;

// Set the Modified flag of the document class to TRUE.
pDoc->SetModifiedFlag();

// Update all the other views of the same document.
pDoc->UpdateAllViews(this);

/////////////////////
// MY CODE ENDS HERE
/////////////////////

}
```

The *OnUpdate()* Member Function of the View Class

As a result of the code you wrote previously, when the user changes one of the edit boxes in any view of a particular document, the OnUpdateAllViews() member function of the document class will be executed. The OnUpdateAllViews() function will update the contents of the other views (of the same document) by calling the OnUpdate() member function of the view class. Thus, you need to write the OnUpdate() function.

Visual C++ didn't write the declaration and skeleton of the OnUpdate() function. You have to declare this function and write its skeleton. Here is how you do that:

☐ Open the file PADVIEW.H and add code to it that defines the function OnUpdate() as a member function of the CPadView class. After you write this code, the CPadView class declaration looks as follows:

```
class CPadView : public CFormView
{
    DECLARE_DYNCREATE(CPadView)
protected:
    CPadView();  // protected constructor used by dynamic creation

    /////////////////////////
    // MY CODE STARTS HERE
    /////////////////////////

    virtual void OnInitialUpdate();
```

```
           virtual void OnUpdate(CView* pSender,
                                 LPARAM lHint,
                                 CObject* pHint);

       /////////////////////
       // MY CODE ENDS HERE
       /////////////////////

// Form Data
public:
       //{{AFX_DATA(CPadView)
       enum { IDD = IDD_DIALOG1 };
       CString     m_Subject;
       CString     m_Notes;
       //}}AFX_DATA

// Attributes
public:

// Operations
public:

// Implementation
protected:
       virtual ~CPadView();
       virtual void DoDataExchange(CDataExchange* pDX);
       // Generated message map functions
       //{{AFX_MSG(CPadView)
       afx_msg void OnChangeSubject();
       afx_msg void OnChangeNotes();
       //}}AFX_MSG
       DECLARE_MESSAGE_MAP()
};
```

Now write the OnUpdate() function's code.

☐ Open the file PADVIEW.CPP and add the OnUpdate() function to the end of the file. After you write this function, the end of the PADVIEW.CPP file looks as follows:

```
/////////////////////
// MY CODE STARTS HERE
/////////////////////

void CPadView::OnUpdate(CView* pSender,
                        LPARAM lHint,
                        CObject* pHint)
{
```

```
        // Get a pointer to the document.
        CPadDoc* pDoc = (CPadDoc*) GetDocument();

        // Update the view with the current document values.
        m_Subject = pDoc->m_Subject;
        m_Notes   = pDoc->m_Notes;

        // Update the screen with the new variables values.
        UpdateData(FALSE);

}

/////////////////////
// MY CODE ENDS HERE
/////////////////////
```

To review the OnUpdate() function's code:

The first statement,

```
CPadDoc* pDoc = (CPadDoc*) GetDocument();
```

extracts pDoc (the pointer for the document class).

Then the data members of the view class are updated with the current values of the document:

```
m_Subject = pDoc->m_Subject;
m_Notes   = pDoc->m_Notes;
```

Finally, the UpdateData() function is used to transfer the new values of m_Subject and m_Notes to the screen:

```
UpdateData(FALSE);
```

That's it! You've finished writing all the necessary code for multiple viewing of the same document.

Executing the PAD Application

To see in action the code that you just entered:

☐ Select Build PAD.EXE from the Project menu.

☐ Execute the PAD.EXE application.

Now verify that the PAD application supports multiple viewing of the same document:

☐ Select Open from the File menu to open the document TEST.PAD that you created earlier.

☐ Select New Window from the Window menu.

> *The PAD application responds by opening another view (another window) for* TEST.PAD.

☐ Arrange the two windows of TEST.PAD so that you'll be able to see the fields in both windows (see Figure 19.30).

☐ Try to type something in one of the windows of TEST.PAD.

As you can see, when you type something in one view of TEST.PAD, the other view is updated automatically!

You can now add as many views as you wish for the TEST.PAD document. You'll see that when you change one view, all the other views are updated automatically.

☐ Terminate the PAD application.

Splitter Windows

Recall from the beginning of the chapter that the PAD application should support the splitter window feature. That is, each of the child windows in the application's main window should have two small split boxes located on the horizontal and vertical scroll bars of the window (see Figure 19.11). When the user drags these split boxes, the window splits into several views (see Figures 19.12 and 19.13).

To provide the user with this powerful feature, you need to use ClassWizard to create a splitter class and then modify the main application source file of the application (PAD.CPP) to use this class. After you do that, the child windows of the application will have the two small split boxes.

To create the splitter class with ClassWizard follow these steps:

☐ Start ClassWizard from the Browse menu of Visual C++.

☐ Click the Add Class button in ClassWizard's dialog box.

> *ClassWizard responds by displaying the Add Class dialog box.*

☐ Type CMySplit in the Class Name box.

☐ Set the Class Type to splitter.

Now your Add Class dialog box looks as shown in Figure 19.31.

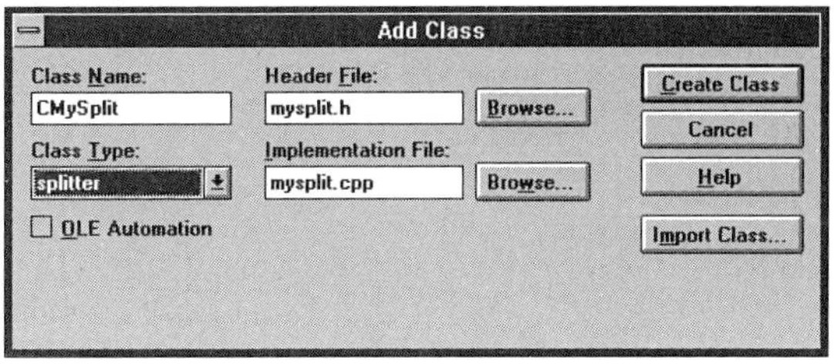

Figure 19.31.
Adding a splitter
class.

☐ Click the Create Class button of the Add Class dialog box and then click the
OK button of ClassWizard's dialog box.

ClassWizard responds by creating the splitter class CMySplit. Note that the
header file of this class is MYSPLIT.H and the implementation file of this class
is MYSPLIT.CPP (see Figure 19.31).

Now you need to modify the main application source file of the application (PAD.CPP)
so that it will use the splitter class you created.

☐ Open the file PAD.CPP and look for the InitInstance() function.

One of the statements in the InitInstance() function is

```
pDocTemplate = new CMultiDocTemplate(
    IDR_PADTYPE,
    RUNTIME_CLASS(CPadDoc),
    RUNTIME_CLASS(CMDIChildWnd), // standard MDI child frame
    RUNTIME_CLASS(CPadView));
```

This statement uses the CMultiDocTemplate() function with four parameters.

☐ Change the third parameter in the previous statement from
    RUNTIME_CLASS(CMDIChildWnd), // standard MDI child frame to
    RUNTIME_CLASS(CMySplit), // the splitter class.

After making this modification, the previous statement looks as follows:

```
pDocTemplate = new CMultiDocTemplate(
    IDR_PADTYPE,
    RUNTIME_CLASS(CPadDoc),
    RUNTIME_CLASS(CMySplit),      // the splitter class.
    RUNTIME_CLASS(CPadView));
```

Because the statement that you just modified refers to the CMySplit class, you need
to #include the header file of the CMySplit class (mysplit.h) at the beginning of
PAD.CPP:

☐ Add the #include "mysplit.h" statement at the beginning of the PAD.CPP file (immediately before the #include statement of the mainfrm.h file). After you add this #include statement, the beginning of the PAD.CPP file looks as follows:

```
// pad.cpp : Defines the class behaviors for the application.
//

#include "stdafx.h"
#include "pad.h"

/////////////////////////
// MY CODE STARTS HERE
/////////////////////////

#include "mysplit.h"

/////////////////////////
// MY CODE ENDS HERE
/////////////////////////

#include "mainfrm.h"
#include "paddoc.h"
#include "padview.h"
```

That's all you need to do! Now, the PAD application supports the splitter window feature.

To see your code in action:

☐ Select Build PAD.EXE from the Project menu.

☐ Execute the PAD.EXE application.

> *As you can see, now the child window that is displayed in the main window (Untitled1) has small split boxes on the horizontal and vertical scroll bars of the window (see Figure 19.11).*

☐ Drag the split boxes of the vertical and horizontal scroll bars of the window and notice how the window splits (see Figures 19.12 and 19.13).

☐ Terminate the PAD application.

Adding the Split Option to the Window Menu

Recall from the beginning of the chapter that besides using the split boxes, the user also should be able to split a child window by using the Split option of the Window menu (see Figure 19.6). Currently the Window menu of the PAD application doesn't include this menu item.

To add the Split option to the Window menu, you need to use App Studio. You don't have to write any code.

Follow these steps to add the Split option to the Window menu:

☐ Use App Studio to modify the `IDR_PADTYPE` menu.

☐ Add a new item to the Window popup.

☐ Set the Caption property of the new item to `&Split`.

☐ Set the ID of the new item to `ID_WINDOW_SPLIT`.

The properties window of your Split menu item looks as shown in Figure 19.32.

Figure 19.32.
The Properties
window of the
Split menu item.

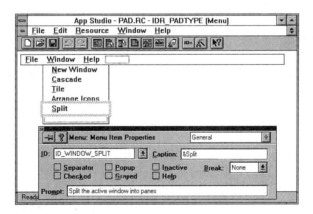

Note that you must name the ID of the Split menu item as `ID_WINDOW_SPLIT`, because the application code (code that Visual C++ wrote for you) associates this constant with the action of splitting the window.

Don't forget to save your work:

☐ Select Save from the File menu of App Studio.

Executing the Final Version of the PAD Application

To see the effects of adding the Split menu item:

☐ Select Build PAD.EXE from the Project menu.

☐ Execute the PAD.EXE application and experiment with the Split option of the Window menu.

As you can see, the Split menu item works!

20

Menus

So far, you've learned how to implement simple menus. In this chapter you'll learn advanced menu topics: how to implement accelerator keys, how to implement submenus, how to place and remove check marks in menu items, how to dim (gray) and undim menu items, how to take advantage of the `UPDATE_COMMAND_UI` message, how to add menu items during the execution of an application, and how to implement a menu that contains a bitmap picture.

The MyMenu Application

Before you start writing the MyMenu application, execute the copy of it that resides in your `C:\VCPROG\ORIGINAL\CH20\MyMenu` directory.

To execute the MyMenu application:

☐ Use the Run from Program Manager's File menu to execute
   `C:\VCPROG\ORIGINAL\CH20\MYMENU\MyMenu.EXE`.

> *Windows responds by executing the MyMenu application. The main window of `MyMenu.EXE` appears, as shown in Figure 20.1.*

Figure 20.1.
The MyMenu application's main window.

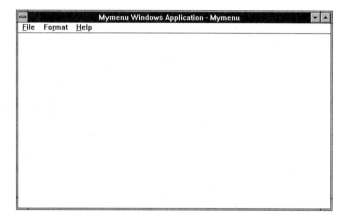

The MyMenu application has three popup menus: File, Format, and Help. These popup menus are shown in Figures 20.2, 20.3, and 20.4.

☐ Select the Format menu.

> *MyMenu responds by displaying the Format menu. As you can see, the Size menu item is unavailable (dimmed), and the Italic menu item is available.*

To make the Size menu item available:

☐ Select the Bold item from the File menu.

> *MyMenu responds by displaying a message box telling you that you selected Bold from the File menu.*

Figure 20.2.
The MyMenu
application's File
menu.

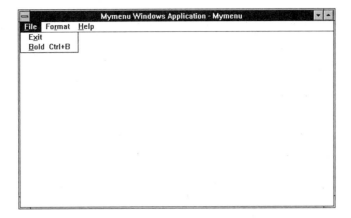

Figure 20.3.
The MyMenu
application's
Format menu.

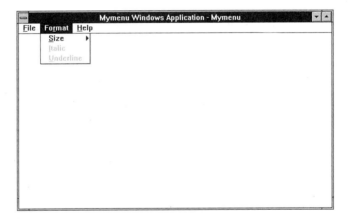

Figure 20.4.
The MyMenu
application's Help
menu.

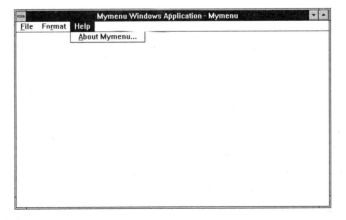

☐ Click the OK button of the message box and then select the Format menu again.

> *MyMenu responds by displaying the Format menu. However, now the Size menu item is available. From now on, the Size menu item will be available throughout the life of the MyMenu application.*

☐ Select Size from the Format menu.

> *MyMenu responds by displaying the menu shown in Figure 20.5. The check mark displayed to the left of the Size point 2 menu item is an indication that the Size point 2 is currently selected in the program.*

Figure 20.5.
The menu that
MyMenu displays
when you select Size
from the Format
menu.

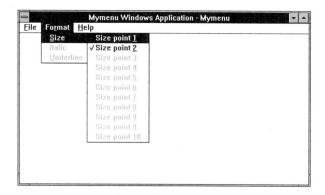

Figure 20.6.
The message box
that MyMenu
displays after you
select Format->Size
->Size point 1.

☐ Select Size point 1 from the menu.

> *MyMenu responds by displaying a message box (see Figure 20.6). The message box tells you the sequence of menus that have been selected.*

☐ Click the OK button of the message box and then select the Size menu item from the Format menu again.

> *MyMenu responds by displaying the Size menu again. However, now Size point 1 has a check mark, and Size point 2 doesn't.*

Experiment with the Size menu by selecting Size point 1 and Size point 2. Notice that when you select the Size menu again, the check mark appears next to the item that was selected last.

As you saw, the Size menu was initially unavailable. You had to select Bold from the File menu to make it available.

Note the text `Ctrl+B` that appears to the right of the Bold menu item (see Figure 20.2). Ctrl+B is called an *accelerator key*. It accelerates the process of selecting Bold. That is, instead of selecting the File menu and then selecting Bold from it, you can simply press Ctrl+B on your keyboard.

☐ Press Ctrl+B.

> *MyMenu responds in the same manner as it would if you had selected Bold from the File menu. To prove that this is the case, take a look at the Format menu. It contains the Italic menu item.*

☐ Select Bold from the File menu and then select the Format menu.

> *MyMenu responds by displaying the Format menu. The status of the Italic item is the opposite of what it was before you selected Bold. (If the Italic item was available before you selected Bold, now it's dimmed, and vice versa.)*

☐ Select Bold from the File menu and verify that the status of the Italic menu item toggles.

☐ Now select Bold by pressing Ctrl+B, and note that the status of the Italic item toggles.

☐ Experiment with the MyMenu application, and then select Exit from the File menu to terminate it.

Now that you know what MyMenu should do, you can write it.

Creating the Project of the MyMenu Application

To create the project of the MyMenu application:

☐ Select AppWizard from the Project menu.

> *Visual C++ responds by running AppWizard.*

☐ Use the Directory list box to select the directory C:\VCPROG\PRACTICE\CH20.

☐ Type mymenu in the Project Name box.

Now your AppWizard dialog box looks as shown in Figure 20.7.

Figure 20.7.
The AppWizard
dialog box for the
MyMenu
application.

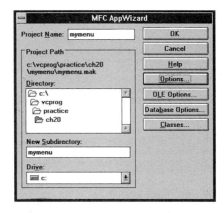

☐ Click the Options button and set the options as shown in Figure 20.8 (that
is, uncheck all the check boxes except the Generate Source Comments check
box).

Figure 20.8.
Setting the options
for the MyMenu
application.

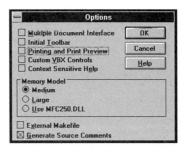

☐ Click the OK button of the Options dialog box and click the OK button of
the AppWizard dialog box and finally click the Create button of the New
Application Information dialog box.

AppWizard responds by creating the MyMenu project and all the skeleton files
of the MyMenu application.

To remove the debug options of the project (so you'll have a small EXE file):

☐ Select Project from Visual C++'s Options menu, click the Release radio button, and then click the OK button of the dialog box.

The Visual Design of the Menu

Now you'll visually design the menu of the MyMenu application.

☐ Use App Studio to implement the MyMenu application's menu per Table 20.1. (As shown in the table, this isn't the final menu of the MyMenu application. You'll be instructed later in this chapter to add the Format menu.)

Table 20.1. The MyMenu application's menu.

Menu Item
&File
E&xit
&Bold
&Help
&About Mymenu...

To save your work:

☐ Select Save from the File menu of App Studio.

The visual implementation of the menu of the MyMenu application is complete.

To save your work:

☐ Select Save from the File menu of App Studio.

NOTE: The MyMenu application doesn't have a custom dialog box. It only has an About dialog box.

Attaching Code to a Menu Item

Attaching code to a menu item is easy. (You've done it many times so far in this book.) Now you'll attach code to the Bold menu item. This code will be executed whenever the user selects the Bold item from the File menu.

☐ Use ClassWizard to add a function for the event:

Class Name:	CMymenuView
Object ID:	ID_FILE_BOLD
Message:	COMMAND
Function Name:	OnFileBold()

NOTE: Make sure that you're adding the function to the CMymenuView class.

As shown in Figure 20.9, with Visual C++ you can attach a function to either the COMMAND message or the UPDATE_COMMAND_UI message. The UPDATE_COMMAND_UI message is discussed later in this chapter.

Figure 20.9.
Adding the
OnFileBold()
function.

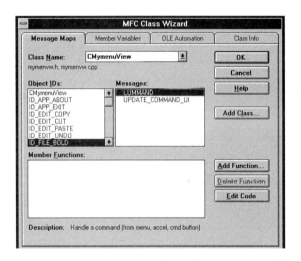

☐ Edit the OnFileBold() function that you added to the MYMENVW.CPP file.
  After you edit the OnFileBold() function, it looks as follows:

```
void CMymenuView::OnFileBold()
{
// TODO: Add your command handler code here

    ////////////////////////
    // MY CODE STARTS HERE
    ////////////////////////

    CString sMessage;

    sMessage = "I'm inside OnFileBold() ";

    MessageBox ( sMessage );
```

```
/////////////////////
// MY CODE ENDS HERE
/////////////////////
```

}

The code that you typed displays the message, "I'm inside OnFileBold()," whenever the user clicks the Bold menu item. Of course, a real application wouldn't display this message box, but would instead carry out the operation corresponding to the selected menu item. For example, in a word processing program, the user would highlight text and then select Bold from the menu to apply bold font to the highlighted text.

☐ Compile/link and execute the MyMenu application.

☐ Select Bold from the File menu.

> *MyMenu responds by displaying the message box shown in Figure 20.10. This proves that* OnFileBold() *was executed.*

Figure 20.10.
The message box
that MyMenu
displays when Bold
is selected from the
File menu.

☐ Select Exit from the File menu to terminate the MyMenu application.

Adding Accelerator Keys to the Menu

Many Windows applications attach *accelerator keys* to menu items. As implied by its name, an accelerator key enables the user to execute a menu item's code by pressing a combination of keys, instead of going through the procedure of opening the menu and then selecting the item from the menu.

Here's how you attach an accelerator key to the Bold menu item:

☐ Start App Studio.

☐ Display the menu in its design mode.

☐ Double-click the Bold menu item of the File menu.

> *App Studio responds by displaying the Properties window of the Bold menu item.*

☐ Change the caption to &Bold\tCtrl+B. (The "\t" serves as a Tab character.)

The Properties window of this menu item should look as shown in Figure 20.11.

Figure 20.11.
Changing the
caption of the Bold
menu item.

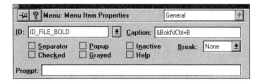

If you compile/link and execute the MyMenu application now, in the File menu you'll see the text Ctrl+B to the right of the Bold menu item. However, pressing Ctrl+B won't pop up the Bold menu, because all you did was change this item's caption. To actually add the Ctrl+B accelerator key to the Bold menu item:

☐ Select MYMENU.RC from the Window menu of App Studio,

> *App Studio responds by displaying the visual presentation of the* MYMENU.RC *file (see Figure 20.12).*

Figure 20.12.
Creating an
accelerator key.

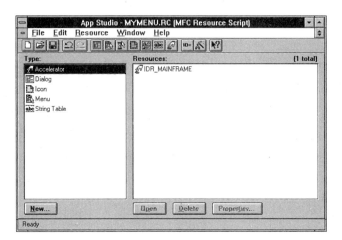

☐ Select the Accelerator item in the Type list of the MYMENU.RC window (see Figure 20.12), and then double-click the IDR_MAINFRAME item in the Resources list.

> *App Studio responds by displaying the Accelerator window.*

As you can see from Figure 20.13, Visual C++ has already assigned a variety of accelerator keys to the MyMenu application. For example, the Ctrl+Z key combination is assigned to the Undo item of the Edit menu. (You removed the Edit menu when you implemented the menu of MyMenu, but the accelerator key assignment remains.)

*Figure 20.13.
The
IDR_MAINFRAME
(Accelerator)
window.*

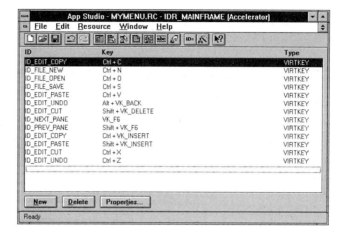

☐ Click the New button to add a new accelerator key.

> *App Studio responds by displaying the Properties window of your new
> accelerator key (see Figure 20.14).*

*Figure 20.14.
The empty Property
window of the new
accelerator key.*

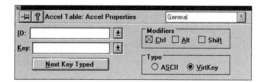

Now you'll fill the Property window seen in Figure 20.14 so that the new accelerator
key will be associated with the Bold menu item.

☐ Type ID_FILE_BOLD in the ID box. (Recall that the ID of the Bold menu
item is ID_FILE_BOLD.)

NOTE

As shown in Figure 20.15, App Studio will automatically add the numerical
value of the ID. You just have to type ID_FILE_BOLD or drop down the list of
the IDs and select ID_FILE_BOLD from the list.

☐ Type B in the Key box (because you want the accelerator key to be Ctrl+B).

☐ Make sure that the Ctrl check box in the Modifiers frame is checked and that the Alt and Shift check boxes aren't checked, because the accelerator key you are now attaching is a Ctrl key (Ctrl+B).

☐ Make sure that the VirtKey radio button is selected in the Type frame.

☐ Now the complete Property window looks as shown in Figure 20.15.

Figure 20.15.
The complete
Property window of
the new accelerator
key.

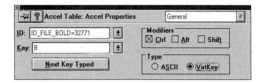

To save your work:

☐ Select Save from the File menu of App Studio.

As you can see from Figure 20.16, the Accelerator window now contains the Ctrl+B accelerator key.

Figure 20.16.
The Accelerator
window with the
Ctrl+B accelerator
key in it.

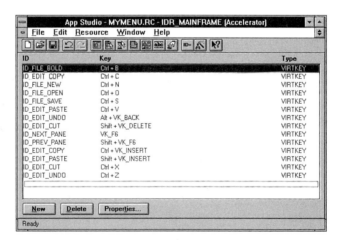

☐ Compile/link and execute the MyMenu application.

As you can see (see Figure 20.17), the text Ctrl+B appears to the right of the Bold menu item.

☐ Select Bold from the File menu.

MyMenu responds by displaying a message box telling you that you did indeed select the Bold item.

630

Figure 20.17.
The Bold Menu
item with its
accelerator key.

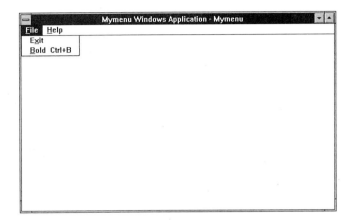

☐ Click the OK button in the message box and then press Ctrl+B.

> *MyMenu responds in the same manner as it did when you selected Bold from*
> *the File menu.*

☐ Select Exit from the File menu to terminate the MyMenu application.

NOTE

As you can see in Figure 20.16, Visual C++ implemented several accelerator keys for you. For example, Ctrl+O is the accelerator key of the File menu's Open item (`ID_FILE_OPEN`). Even though you removed the Open item from the File menu, the accelerator key is functional.

> Execute the MyMenu application and press Ctrl+O.
>
> > MyMenu responds by displaying the Open dialog box.

This isn't desirable, because MyMenu doesn't have an Open menu item. So, you have to go over the accelerator keys and remove the ones that aren't used by your program.

To delete the accelerator key of the `ID_FILE_OPEN` menu item:

> Use App Studio to display the accelerator key table.
>
> Select `ID_FILE_OPEN` and then click the Delete button.

You can repeat the preceding steps to delete the other accelerator keys that aren't used by your programs. In particular, make sure to delete the accelerator keys for the `ID_FILE_NEW` and `ID_FILE_SAVE` menu items.

Implementing Submenus

Typically, you'll implement the Bold menu in a menu heading such as Format, not in the File menu. Thus, the menu of the MyMenu application should look as follows:

```
File                    Format                      Help
```

The Format menu should contain items that are related to the process of formatting highlighted text. A typical Format menu may look as follows:

```
Format
        Size
        Italic
        Underline
```

Suppose your Format menu contains an application within which the user selects different widths for a line in a drawing program. One (bad) way of implementing this Format menu is as follows:

```
Format
        Size 1 point
        Size 2 points
        Size 3 points
        Size 4 points
        Size 5 points
        Size 6 points
        Size 7 points
        Size 8 points
        Size 9 points
        Size 10 points
        Italic
        Underline
```

This implementation isn't recommended, because there are too many items in the Format menu. In fact, there are so many Size options in the menu that the user might not notice the Italic and Underline items.

The recommended implementation is to create the basic Format menu as follows:

```
Format
        Size
        Italic
        Underline
```

Then, when the user selects the Size item, another menu should pop up:

```
Size 1 point
Size 2 points
Size 3 points
Size 4 points
Size 5 points
Size 6 points
Size 7 points
Size 8 points
Size 9 points
Size 10 points
```

Also, the Bold item should be removed from the File menu and placed in the Format menu. However, in this tutorial you're just learning the topic, so leave the Bold item in the File menu.

Here's how you implement a submenu:

☐ Start App Studio.

☐ Display the menu in its design mode.

☐ Implement the Format menu per Table 20.2.

Table 20.2. The MyMenu application's menu, after adding the Format menu. *Figure relating to menu: 20.18*

Menu Item
&File
E&xit
&Bold
Fo&rmat
&Size
&Italic
&Underline
&Help
&About MyMenu...

Figure 20.18.
Implementing the
Format menu.

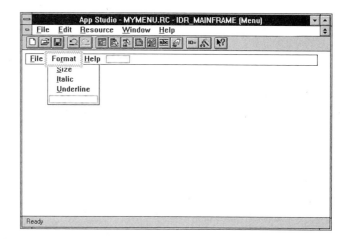

☐ Double-click the Size menu item.

App Studio responds by displaying the Properties window of the Size menu item.

☐ Place a check mark in the Popup check box (see Figure 20.19).

Note that once you place a check mark in the Popup check box, App Studio displays a submenu to the right of the Size menu item (see Figure 20.20) and it removes the ID of the Size item (see Figure 20.19).

☐ Double-click Size's submenu item and type `Size point &1` in the Caption box of its Properties window.

App Studio responds by adding Size point 1 to Size's submenu (see Figure 20.21).

Keep adding items to the submenu until it looks as shown in Figure 20.22.

Figure 20.19.
Making the Size
item a popup menu.

Figure 20.20.
The submenu of the
Size item.

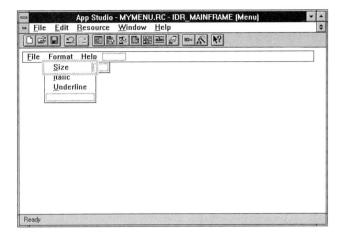

Figure 20.21.
Adding items to the
submenu of the Size
item.

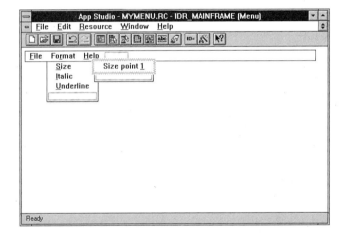

Figure 20.22.
The complete
submenu of Size.

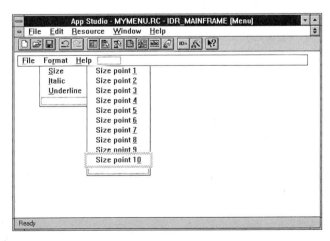

To save your work:

☐ Select Save from the File menu of App Studio.

Now you'll add code to the first two items of the Size submenu. (In practice, you'll add code to all 10 items of the submenu, but for the sake of illustrating the concept it's sufficient to add code to only two items.)

☐ Use ClassWizard to add a function for the event:

Class Name:	CMymenuView
Object ID:	ID_FORMAT_SIZE_SIZEPOINT1
Message:	COMMAND
Function Name:	OnFormatSizeSizepoint1()

Make sure that you add the function to the CMymenuView class (see Figure 20.23).

> **NOTE**
>
> As shown in Figure 20.23, you can add a function to either the COMMAND message or the UPDATE_COMMAND_UI message. The UPDATE_COMMAND_UI message is discussed later in this chapter. Also note that you attach a function to a submenu item in the same way you'd attach a function to a regular menu item.

Figure 20.23.
Adding the
OnFormatSize
Sizepoint1()
function.

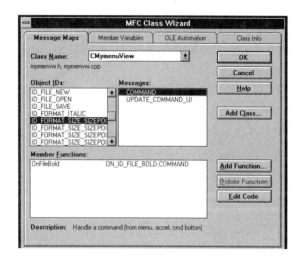

☐ Edit the `OnFormatSizeSizepoint1()` function that you added to the MYMENVW.CPP file. After you edit the `OnFormatSizeSizepoint1()` function, it looks as follows:

```
void CMymenuView::OnFormatSizeSizepoint1()
{
    // TODO: Add your command handler code here


    /////////////////////////
    // MY CODE STARTS HERE
    /////////////////////////

    CString sMessage;

    sMessage = "I'm inside Format->Size-> Point 1";

    MessageBox ( sMessage );

    ///////////////////////
    // MY CODE ENDS HERE
    ///////////////////////

}
```

The code you typed will be executed whenever the user selects Format->Size->Size Point 1. This code will display a message box indicating that this function is executed.

Use ClassWizard to add a function for the event:

Class Name:	CMymenuView
Object ID:	ID_FORMAT_SIZE_SIZEPOINT2
Message:	COMMAND
Function Name:	OnFormatSizeSizepoint2()

NOTE: Make sure you're adding the function to the CMymenuView class.

NOTE

Due to the long IDs that ClassWizard assigns to the menu items, you have to make sure you're adding the function to the proper menu item. Note that ClassWizard displays the IDs in alphabetical order, as follows:

```
ID_FORMAT_SIZE_SIZEPOINT1
ID_FORMAT_SIZE_SIZEPOINT10
ID_FORMAT_SIZE_SIZEPOINT2
ID_FORMAT_SIZE_SIZEPOINT3
ID_FORMAT_SIZE_SIZEPOINT4
ID_FORMAT_SIZE_SIZEPOINT5
ID_FORMAT_SIZE_SIZEPOINT6
ID_FORMAT_SIZE_SIZEPOINT7
ID_FORMAT_SIZE_SIZEPOINT8
ID_FORMAT_SIZE_SIZEPOINT9
```

NOTE: Make sure you're attaching code to ID_FORMAT_SIZE_FORMATPOINT2 (which is the third item in the list, not the second item).

After you click the Add Function button, make sure that the function name suggested by ClassWizard corresponds to the menu item to which you wish to attach the code.

☐ Edit the OnFormatSizeSizepoint2() function that you added to the MYMENVW.CPP file. After you edit the OnFormatSizeSizepoint2() function, it looks as follows:

```
void CMymenuView::OnFormatSizeSizepoint2()
{
    // TODO: Add your command handler code here

    /////////////////////////
    // MY CODE STARTS HERE
    /////////////////////////

    CString sMessage;

    sMessage = "I'm inside Format->Size->Point 2";

    MessageBox ( sMessage );

    /////////////////////////
    // MY CODE ENDS HERE
    /////////////////////////

}
```

☐ Compile/link and execute the MyMenu application.

☐ Select the Format menu.

*MyMenu responds by displaying the Format menu, as shown in Figure 20.3.
Note the arrow icon that's located to the right of the Size menu item. This
arrow icon (placed automatically by App Studio) indicates that when the user
selects this menu item, another menu will pop up.*

☐ Select the Size menu item.

MyMenu responds by displaying Size's submenu.

☐ Select Size point 1 from the submenu.

MyMenu responds by displaying a message box that indicates your selection.

Experiment with the MyMenu application and then select Exit from the File menu
to terminate the application.

Placing a Check Mark in a Menu Item

Suppose the user selects Size from the Format menu, which displays the menu shown
in Figure 20.22. At this point the user may select a different point size from the
submenu. To make the application easier to use, you can place a check mark to the
left of the selected submenu item. The next time the user opens the menu, the
submenu item that was selected last time will have a check mark.

You can place a check mark in a menu item (or remove it) at design time and at
runtime. Here's how to place a check mark at design time:

☐ Use App Studio to display the menu at its design mode.

☐ Double-click the Size point 2 item and place a check mark in the Checked
box that appears in the Properties window.

*App Studio responds by placing a check mark to the left of the Point Size 2
menu item.*

☐ Compile/link and execute the MyMenu application.

Note that when you select Format and then Size, Size's submenu contains the menu
item Size point 2 with a check mark by it (see Figure 20.5). The check mark indicates that the size is currently set to 2.

☐ Terminate the application by selecting Exit from the File menu.

Now you'll modify the MyMenu application so that when the user selects Size point 1
from the submenu, the check mark is moved from Size point 2 to Size point 1.

NOTE

If you have a large number of IDs in your application, you may sometimes want to see a list of them. You can do so as follows:

Select Symbols from App Studio's Edit menu.

App Studio responds by displaying the Symbol Browser dialog box (see Figure 20.24).

After you review the list of IDs, you can close the Symbol Browser dialog box by clicking the Close button.

Figure 20.24.
The Symbol
Browser dialog box.

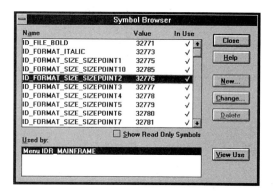

Modify the OnFormatSizeSizepoint1() function in the MYMENVW.CPP file. After the modification, the function looks as follows:

```
void CMymenuView::OnFormatSizeSizepoint1()
{
    // TODO: Add your command handler code here

    ///////////////////////
    // MY CODE STARTS HERE
    ///////////////////////

    // Extract the pointer of the parent window.
    CWnd* pParent = GetParent();

    // Extract the pointer of the menu
    CMenu* pMenu = pParent->GetMenu();
```

```
        // Remove the check mark from the Size point 2 item
        pMenu->CheckMenuItem( ID_FORMAT_SIZE_SIZEPOINT2,
                              MF_UNCHECKED );


        // Place a check mark to the left of
        // the Size point 1 item
        pMenu->CheckMenuItem( ID_FORMAT_SIZE_SIZEPOINT1,
                              MF_CHECKED );


        // Display a message box
        CString sMessage;
        sMessage = "I'm inside Format->Size->Point 1";
        MessageBox ( sMessage );

        /////////////////////
        // MY CODE ENDS HERE
        /////////////////////
}
```

The code you typed removes the check mark from the Size point 2 menu item and places it in the Size point 1 menu item. This is accomplished with the `CheckMenuItem()` member function. For example, if the pointer to the menu is `pMenu`, you would use the following statement to remove the check mark from the Size point 2 menu item:

```
pMenu->CheckMenuItem( ID_FORMAT_SIZE_SIZEPOINT2,
                      MF_UNCHECKED );
```

In the preceding statement, the first parameter is `ID_FORMAT_SIZE_SIZEPOINT2`, which is the ID of the menu item on which you're operating. The second parameter of the `CheckMenuItem()` function is `MF_UNCHECKED`, which tells `CheckMenuItem()` to remove the check mark.

In a similar manner, to place a check mark to the left of the Size point 1 menu item, you use this statement:

```
pMenu->CheckMenuItem( ID_FORMAT_SIZE_SIZEPOINT1,
                      MF_CHECKED );
```

This statement supplies `ID_FORMAT_SIZE_SIZEPOINT1` as the first parameter (the ID of the menu item), and the second parameter tells the `CheckMenuItem()` function to place a check mark.

As you can see, there is a need to extract the pointer of the menu. In the preceding statements, you indicated that `pMenu` is the pointer of the menu.

Here's how you extract the pointer of the menu:

First extract pParent, the pointer of the parent window of the window (the window where the menu is located):

```
CWnd* pParent = GetParent();
```

Once you've extracted pParent, you can extract pMenu, the pointer of the menu:

```
CMenu* pMenu = pParent->GetMenu();
```

Now you'll add code that will be executed whenever the user selects Point size 2 from the Size menu:

Modify the OnFormatSizeSizepoint2() function in the MYMENVW.CPP file. After the modification, the function looks as follows:

```
void CMymenuView::OnFormatSizeSizepoint2()
{
    // TODO: Add your command handler code here

    ////////////////////////
    // MY CODE STARTS HERE
    ////////////////////////


    // Extract the pointer of the parent window.
    CWnd* pParent = GetParent();

    // Extract the pointer of the menu
    CMenu* pMenu = pParent->GetMenu();

    // Remove the check mark from the Size point 1 item
    pMenu->CheckMenuItem( ID_FORMAT_SIZE_SIZEPOINT1,
                          MF_UNCHECKED );


    // Place a check mark to the left of the
    //Size point 2 item
    pMenu->CheckMenuItem( ID_FORMAT_SIZE_SIZEPOINT2,
                          MF_CHECKED );

    // Display a message box
    CString sMessage;
    sMessage = "I'm inside Format->Size->Point 2";
    MessageBox ( sMessage );

    ////////////////////////
    // MY CODE ENDS HERE
    ////////////////////////

}
```

This code is similar to the code you typed in the `OnFormatSizeSizepoint1()` function. However, now you're unchecking Size point 1 and checking Size point 2.

☐ Compile/link and execute the MyMenu application.

☐ Select Size from the Format menu.

> *MyMenu responds by displaying the menu with the Size point 2 item checked (because you checked the check box in this item's Properties window in App Studio).*

☐ Select Size point 1 from the menu and then click the OK button of the message box that appears.

☐ Select Size from the Format menu.

> *Now Size point 1 has a check mark to its left, and there's no check mark to the left of the Size point 2 menu item.*

Experiment with the MyMenu application and verify that the check mark appears next to the menu item that was last selected.

Disabling a Menu Item

It's possible to disable a menu item at design time as well as at execution time. At design time, you can disable a menu item by double-clicking it in App Studio and placing a check mark in the Grayed box in the item's Properties window. (The term *Grayed* is used because a disabled menu is gray.)

☐ From App Studio, display the menu in its design mode and double-click the Size menu item.

> *App Studio responds by displaying the Properties window of the Size menu item.*

☐ Place a check mark in the Grayed check box.

> *App Studio responds by showing the menu item grayed (disabled).*

☐ Select Save from the File menu of App Studio.

☐ Compile/link the MyMenu application and then execute it.

> *The main window of MyMenu appears with the Size menu grayed.*

NOTE

The Italic and Underline items are also gray, even though their Grayed boxes aren't checked. This is because you didn't attach any code to them. Visual C++ displays a menu item as gray if there's no code attached to it.

☐ Select Exit from the File menu to terminate the MyMenu application.

To enable a menu item during execution, you have to use the EnableMenuItem() function. Here's how you enable the Size menu item at runtime:

☐ Modify the OnFileBold() function in the MYMENVW.CPP file. After the modification, your OnFileBold() function looks as follows:

```
void CMymenuView::OnFileBold()
{
    // TODO: Add your command handler code here

    /////////////////////////
    // MY CODE STARTS HERE
    /////////////////////////

    // Extract the pointer of the parent window.
    CWnd* pParent = GetParent();

    // Extract the pointer of the menu
    CMenu* pMenu = pParent->GetMenu();


    // Extract the pointer of the Format menu
    CMenu* pMenuFormatItem = pMenu->GetSubMenu(1);


    // Enable the Size menu
    pMenuFormatItem->EnableMenuItem (0,
                MF_BYPOSITION | MF_ENABLED );

    // Display a message box
    CString sMessage;
     sMessage = "I'm inside OnFileBold() ";
    MessageBox ( sMessage );

    /////////////////////////
    // MY CODE ENDS HERE
    /////////////////////////

}
```

The code you typed enables the Size menu whenever the user clicks the Bold item in the File menu. Of course, in a real application the Bold item would make highlighted text bold, but it's used here to illustrate the topic.

The `OnFileBold()` function starts by extracting `pParent`, the pointer of the parent window:

```
CWnd* pParent = GetParent();
```

Once you've extracted pParent, you can extract `pMenu`, the pointer of the menu:

```
CMenu* pMenu = pParent->GetMenu();
```

The next statement uses the `GetSubMenu()` function to extract the pointer of the Format menu:

```
CMenu* pMenuFormatItem = pMenu->GetSubMenu(1);
```

In the preceding statement, the `GetSubMenu()` function operates on `pMenu`, which you extracted already. pMenu is the pointer of the menu. This means that `GetSubMenu(0)` extracts the pointer of the File menu, because File is the leftmost item on the menu. Similarly, `GetSubMenu(1)` extracts the pointer of the Format menu and `GetSubMenu(2)` extracts the pointer of the Help menu. You used `GetSubMenu(1)` because you are interested in the pointer of the Format menu.

Once you've extracted `pMenuFormatItem` (the pointer of the Format menu), you can access any of its items. The Size item is considered to be item 0 of the Format menu, Italic is item 1, and Underline is item 2.

To enable the Size item, you use this statement:

```
pMenuFormatItem->EnableMenuItem (0,
                MF_BYPOSITION ¦ MF_ENABLED );
```

The first parameter in the previous statement is `0`, because you're enabling the first item in the Format menu. How would the `EnableMenuItem()` function know that the first parameter is the menu item's position and not its ID? Because you supply `MF_BYPOSITION` as its second parameter.

As you can see, the second parameter of `EnableMenuItem()` is

```
MF_BYPOSITION ¦ MF_ENABLED );
```

which tells the `EnableMenuItem()` function that

> The first parameter of `EnableMenuItem()` is supplied as a position (`MF_BYPOSITION`).
> The menu item mentioned in the first parameter should be enabled (`MF_ENABLED`).

MF_BYPOSITION and MF_ENABLED are ORed together by using the OR bitwise operator (¦).

> **NOTE**
>
> If you supply MF_BYCOMMAND as the second parameter of the EnableMenuItem() function, it considers the first parameter to be the ID of the menu item.
>
> If you don't mention MF_BYPOSITION or MF_BYCOMMAND as the second parameter of EnableMenuItem(), EnabledMenuItem() considers the first parameter to be the ID of the menu item.

> **NOTE**
>
> In the OnFileBold() function, you supplied MF_ENABLED as the second parameter of the EnableMenuItem() function. You can also supply MF_GRAYED as the second parameter of the EnableMenuItem() function to make a menu item gray. In addition, you also can supply MF_DISABLED as the second parameter of EnableMenuItem(). MF_DISABLED causes the menu item to be disabled, but it still won't be grayed.

☐ Compile/link and execute the MyMenu application.

☐ Select Format from the menu.

MyMenu responds by displaying the Format menu. The Size menu item is gray because you grayed it during design time, and the Italic and Underline items are gray because you didn't attach any code to them.

☐ Select Bold from the File menu and then select the Format menu again.

MyMenu responds by displaying the Format menu with the Size item enabled. This is because the code that you typed in the OnFileBold() function was executed.

☐ Select Exit from the File menu to terminate the application.

Using the *UPDATE_COMMAND_UI* Message

So far, you've been instructed to attach code to menu items with the COMMAND event. As you've probably noticed, you can attach menu code with either the COMMAND message or the UPDATE_COMMAND_UI message (see Figure 20.23).

The function that you attach to the UPDATE_COMMAND_UI message of a menu item is executed whenever the menu item is just about to be displayed. For example, if the user clicks the File menu, Windows displays the items in the File menu. However, before these items are displayed, the code that you attach to the UPDATE_COMMAND_UI message in each of the File menu's items is executed.

> ### NOTE
>
> Note the difference between the COMMAND message and the UPDATE_COMMAND_UI message. If you attach code to the Bold menu item with the COMMAND message, the code is executed after the user clicks the Bold item. That is, when the OnFileBold() function is called, the Bold menu item has already been drawn.
>
> On the other hand, if you attach code to the Bold item with the UPDATE_COMMAND_UI message, the code is executed after the user clicks the File menu, but before Windows displays the Bold item. The important thing to note is that the function you attach with the UPDATE_COMMAND_UI message is executed *before* the Bold item is drawn.

To see the UPDATE_COMMAND_UI message in action, try attaching code that's executed whenever Windows is about to draw the Italic item. This means that Windows will execute the code whenever the user clicks the Format menu.

The code that you'll attach will determine whether the Italic menu item will be grayed or not based on the value of a variable called m_Italic. If m_Italic is equal to 0, the Italic item will be gray. However, if m_Italic is equal to 1, the Italic menu item will not be gray.

☐ Use ClassWizard to add a function for the event:

Class Name:	CMymenuView
Object ID:	ID_FORMAT_ITALIC
Message:	COMMAND
Function Name:	OnFormatItalic()

NOTE: Make sure that you add the function to the CMymenuView class.

☐ Add code to the `OnFormatItalic()` function in the `MYMENVW.CPP` file. After you add the code, the function looks as follows:

```
void CMymenuView::OnFormatItalic()
{
    // TODO: Add your command handler code here


    /////////////////////////
    // MY CODE STARTS HERE
    /////////////////////////

    MessageBox ("Format->Italic was selected");

    /////////////////////////
    // MY CODE ENDS HERE
    /////////////////////////

}
```

The code that you added will display a message box whenever the user selects Italic from the Format menu.

☐ Open the file `MYMENVW.H` and add the data member `m_Italic` to the declaration of the `CMymenuView` class. After you add this variable, the `CMymenuView` class declaration looks as follows:

```
class CMymenuView : public CView
{
protected: // create from serialization only
    CMymenuView();
    DECLARE_DYNCREATE(CMymenuView)

// Attributes
public:
    CMymenuDoc* GetDocument();

    /////////////////////////
    // MY CODE STARTS HERE
    /////////////////////////

    // This data member is used to determine whether
    // the Italic menu will be gray.
    int m_Italic;
```

```
/////////////////////
// MY CODE ENDS HERE
/////////////////////
```

```
......
......
......
```

```
};
```

Next, initialize the data member `m_Italic` to 1. (You don't want the Italic item to initially be gray.)

☐ Open the file `MYMENVW.CPP` and initialize the data member `m_Italic` to 1 in the constructor function of the `CMymenuView` class. After you add the initialization code, the constructor function looks as follows:

```
CMymenuView::CMymenuView()
{
 // TODO: add construction code here

    /////////////////////
    // MY CODE STARTS HERE
    /////////////////////

    // Initialize the data member to 1.
    m_Italic = 1;

    /////////////////////
    // MY CODE ENDS HERE
    /////////////////////

}
```

The time to determine whether the Italic menu item should be gray or not is just before Windows draws it. As discussed, the `UPDATE_COMMAND_UI` message was invented for this purpose.

☐ Use ClassWizard to add a function for the event:

Class Name:	CMymenuView
Object ID:	ID_FORMAT_ITALIC
Message:	UPDATE_COMMAND_UI
Function Name:	OnUpdateFormatItalic()

NOTE: Make sure that you're adding the function to the `CMymenuView` class.

☐ Add code to the `OnUpdateFormatItalic()` function in the `MYMENVW.CPP` file. After you add the code, the function looks as follows:

```
void CMymenuView::OnUpdateFormatItalic(CCmdUI* pCmdUI)
{
    // TODO: Add your command update UI handler code here

    /////////////////////////
    // MY CODE STARTS HERE
    /////////////////////////

    if ( m_Italic == 0 )
        pCmdUI->Enable(FALSE);
    else
        pCmdUI->Enable(TRUE);

    /////////////////////////
    // MY CODE ENDS HERE
    /////////////////////////

}
```

The code you typed uses `if...else` statements to determine whether the Italic menu item should be drawn as gray. If `m_Italic` is equal to 0, the menu is made gray with this statement:

```
pCmdUI->Enable(FALSE);
```

And if the value of `m_Italic` isn't equal to 0, the Italic menu item isn't made gray.

Note that the `OnUpdateFormatItalic()` function has the parameter `pCmdUI`. This is the pointer to the Italic menu item given by Visual C++, so that you don't have to use the `GetParent()` and `GetMenu()` functions as you did earlier in this chapter.

To prove that `m_Italic` determines the status of the Italic menu item, try using Bold from the File menu to toggle the value of `m_Italic`.

☐ Open the file `MYMENVW.CPP` and modify the `OnFileBold()` function. After the modification, the function looks as follows:

```
void CMymenuView::OnFileBold()
{
    // TODO: Add your command handler code here

    /////////////////////////
    // MY CODE STARTS HERE
    /////////////////////////
```

```
    // Extract the pointer of the parent window.
    CWnd* pParent = GetParent();

    // Extract the pointer of the menu
    CMenu* pMenu = pParent->GetMenu();


    // Extract the pointer of the Format menu
    CMenu* pMenuFormatItem = pMenu->GetSubMenu(1);


    // Enable the Size menu
    pMenuFormatItem->EnableMenuItem (0,
                        MF_BYPOSITION ¦ MF_ENABLED );

    // Display a message box
    CString sMessage;
     sMessage = "I'm inside OnFileBold() ";
    MessageBox ( sMessage );

    // Invert the value of m_Italic
    if ( m_Italic == 0 )
         m_Italic = 1;
    else
         m_Italic = 0;

    /////////////////////
    // MY CODE ENDS HERE
    /////////////////////

}
```

The code that you added to the OnFileBold() function checks the value of m_Italic
and inverts it:

```
if ( m_Italic == 0 )
     m_Italic = 1;
else
     m_Italic = 0;
```

So whenever the user selects Bold from the File menu, the value of m_Italic changes.

☐ Compile/link the MyMenu application and execute it.

☐ Select the Format menu.

> *MyMenu responds by displaying the Format menu. Because you initialized
> m_Italic to 1, the Italic item is not gray. (That is, even if you set the Grayed
> check box in App Studio, it wouldn't be gray.)*

651

☐ Select Bold from the File menu.

> *The* OnFileBold() *function is executed, and the value of* m_Italic *is changed to 0.*

☐ Select the Format menu.

> *MyMenu responds by displaying the Format menu. Because* m_Italic *is now equal to 0, the Italic item is now gray.*

Experiment with the MyMenu application and then select Exit from the File menu.

The GROW Application

Sometimes you need to add items to the menu during the execution of an application. The GROW application demonstrates how this can be accomplished.

Before you start writing the GROW application yourself, execute the copy of it that resides in your C:\VCPROG\ORIGINAL\CH20\GROW directory.

To execute the MyMenu application:

☐ Use Run from the Program Manager's File menu to execute
C:\VCPROG\ORIGINAL\CH20\GROW\Grow.EXE.

> *Windows responds by executing the Grow application. The main window of* Grow.EXE *appears, as shown in Figure 20.25.*

The GROW application has three popup menus: File, Growing, and Help. These popup menus are shown in Figures 20.26, 20.27, and 20.28.

Figure 20.25.
The GROW
application's main
window.

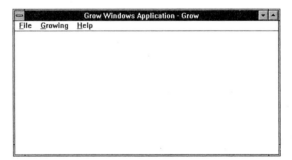

Figure 20.26.
The GROW
application's File
menu.

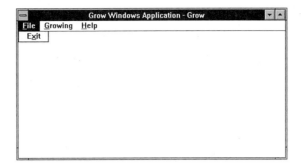

Figure 20.27.
The GROW
application's
Growing menu.

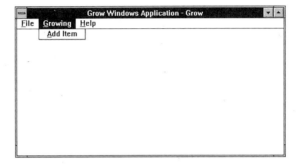

Figure 20.28.
The GROW
application's Help
menu.

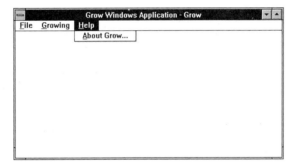

With the GROW application you can add items to the Growing menu at runtime (during the execution of the program). To see this in action:

☐ Select Add Item from the Growing menu.

>   *The GROW application responds by adding an item to the Growing menu.*
>   *You can verify this as follows:*

☐ Select the Growing menu.

> *The GROW application responds by displaying the Growing menu with an added item, as shown in Figure 20.29.*

Figure 20.29.
Adding a menu
item to the
Growing menu.

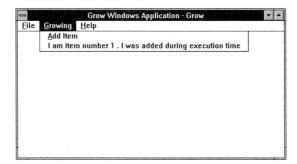

☐ Repeat the preceding steps to add additional menu items to the Growing menu. GROW you can add a maximum of five items to the Growing menu. Figure 20.30 shows the Growing menu with five added items in it.

Experiment with the GROW application and then select Exit from the File menu to terminate this application.

Now that you know what the GROW application does, you can write it.

Creating the Project of the GROW Application

To create the project of the GROW application:

☐ Select AppWizard from the Project menu.

> *Visual C++ responds by running AppWizard.*

☐ Use the Directory list box to select the directory C:\VCCPROG\PRACTICE\CH20.

☐ Type grow in the Project Name box.

Your AppWizard dialog box should now look as shown in Figure 20.31.

☐ Click the Options button and set the options as shown in Figure 20.32 (that is, uncheck all the check boxes except the Generate Source Comments check box).

Figure 20.30.
Adding five items to
the Growing menu.

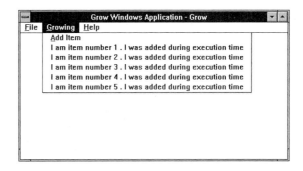

Figure 20.31.
The AppWizard
dialog box for the
GROW applica-
tion.

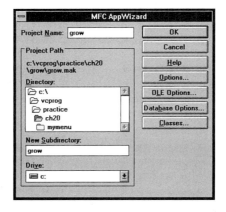

Figure 20.32.
Setting the options
for the GROW
application.

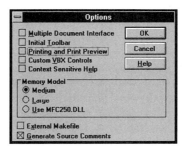

☐ Click the OK button of the Options dialog box and then click the OK
button of the AppWizard dialog box and finally click the Create button of
the New Application Information dialog box.

AppWizard responds by creating the GROW project and all the skeleton files
of the GROW application.

To remove the debug options of the project (so you'll have a small EXE file):

☐ Select Project from Visual C++'s Options menu, click the Release radio button, and then click the OK button of the dialog box.

The Visual Design of the Menu

Now you'll visually design the menu of the GROW application.

☐ Use App Studio to implement the menu of the GROW application per Table 20.3.

Table 20.3. The GROW application's menu.

Menu Item
&File
E&xit
&Growing
&Add Item
Item 1
Item 2
Item 3
Item 4
Item 5
&Help
&About Grow...

This menu is shown in Figure 20.33.

To save your work:

☐ Select Save from the File menu of App Studio.

The visual implementation of the GROW application's menu is complete.

NOTE: The GROW application doesn't have a custom dialog box. It has only an About dialog box.

Figure 20.33.
The GROW
application's
Growing menu.

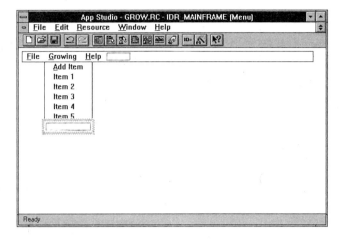

Attaching Code to the Menu Items

Now you'll add functions to Item 1, Item 2, Item 3, Item 4, and Item 5 of the Growing menu.

☐ Use ClassWizard to add a function for the event:

Class Name:	CGrowView
Object ID:	ID_GROWING_ITEM1
Message:	COMMAND
Function Name:	OnGrowingItem1()

NOTE: Make sure that you're adding the function to the CGrowView class.

After you add this function, your OnGrowingItem1() function inside the GROWVIEW.CPP file should look as follows:

```
void CGrowView::OnGrowingItem1()
{
    // TODO: Add your command handler code here

}
```

NOTE: For now, you don't have to add your own code to this function.

☐ Use ClassWizard to add a function for the event:

Class Name:	CGrowView
Object ID:	ID_GROWING_ITEM2
Message:	COMMAND
Function Name:	OnGrowingItem2()

NOTE: Make sure you're adding the function to the `CGrowView` class.

After you add this function, your `OnGrowingItem2()` function in the `GROWVIEW.CPP` file looks as follows:

```
void CGrowView::OnGrowingItem2()
{
    // TODO: Add your command handler code here

}
```

NOTE: For now, you don't have to add your own code to this function.

☐ Use ClassWizard to add a function for the event:

Class Name:	`CGrowView`
Object ID:	`ID_GROWING_ITEM3`
Message:	`COMMAND`
Function Name:	`OnGrowingItem3()`

NOTE: Make sure you're adding the function to the `CGrowView` class.

After you add the `OnGrowingItem3()` function to the `GROWVIEW.CPP` file, the function looks as follows:

```
void CGrowView::OnGrowingItem3()
{
    // TODO: Add your command handler code here

}
```

NOTE: For now, you don't have to add your own code to this function.

☐ Use ClassWizard to add a function for the event:

Class Name:	`CGrowView`
Object ID:	`ID_GROWING_ITEM4`
Message:	`COMMAND`
Function Name:	`OnGrowingItem4()`

NOTE: Make sure you're adding the function to the `CGrowView` class.

After you add the `OnGrowingItem4()` function to the `GROWVIEW.CPP` file, the function looks as follows:

```
void CGrowView::OnGrowingItem4()
{
    // TODO: Add your command handler code here

}
```

☐ Use ClassWizard to add a function for the event:

Class Name:	CGrowView
Object ID:	ID_GROWING_ITEM5
Message:	COMMAND
Function Name:	OnGrowingItem5()

NOTE: Make sure you're adding the function to the CGrowView class.

After you add the OnGrowingItem5() function to the GROWVIEW.CPP file, the function looks as follows:

```
void CGrowView::OnGrowingItem5()
{
    // TODO: Add your command handler code here

}
```

Even though you haven't finished the GROW application, compile/link and execute it to verify that you carried out the operations correctly.

Note that Item 1, Item 2, Item 3, Item 4, and Item 5 in the Growing menu aren't gray. This is because you attached functions to these menu items. (It doesn't matter that you didn't type any of your own code in the functions.)

Removing the Items from the Growing Menu

Now you'll write code that's executed automatically when the application begins. This code removes Item 1, Item 2, Item 3, Item 4, and Item 5 from the Growing menu. Why? Because Add Item is all you want in the Growing menu when the application begins. The other menu items will be added when the user selects Add Item.

Now you'll attach code to the WM_CREATE event of the CMainFrame class.

☐ Use ClassWizard to add a function for the event:

Class Name:	CMainFrame
Object ID:	CMainFrame
Message:	WM_CREATE
Function Name:	OnCreate()

NOTE: Make sure you're adding the function to the CMainFrame class.

> ## WARNING
>
> So far in this book, most of the functions you've added were added to the view class and document class. Note that the preceding instructs you to add a function to the `CMainFrame` class! The ClassWizard dialog box should look as shown in Figure 20.34.

*Figure 20.34.
Adding a function
to the `WM_CREATE`
message of the
`CMainFrame`
class.*

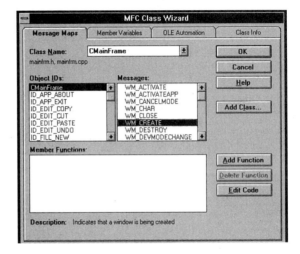

After you add the `OnCreate()` function to the `MAINFRM.CPP` file, the function looks as follows:

```
int CMainFrame::OnCreate(LPCREATESTRUCT lpCreateStruct)
{
    if (CFrameWnd::OnCreate(lpCreateStruct) == -1)
        return -1;

    // TODO: Add your specialized creation code here

    /////////////////////////
    // MY CODE STARTS HERE
    /////////////////////////

    // Extract the pointer of the menu
    CMenu* pMenu = GetMenu();

    // Extract the pointer of the Growing menu
    CMenu* pGrowingMenu = pMenu->GetSubMenu(1);
```

```
    // Delete the current items in the Growing menu
    pGrowingMenu->DeleteMenu(5, MF_BYPOSITION);
    pGrowingMenu->DeleteMenu(4, MF_BYPOSITION);
    pGrowingMenu->DeleteMenu(3, MF_BYPOSITION);
    pGrowingMenu->DeleteMenu(2, MF_BYPOSITION);
    pGrowingMenu->DeleteMenu(1, MF_BYPOSITION);

    ////////////////////////
    // MY CODE ENDS HERE
    ////////////////////////

    return 0;
}
```

Let's go over the code you typed. To begin with, the OnCreate() function is automatically executed whenever the form of the application is created. You need to use this event because the five menu items must be deleted from the Growing menu when the application is started.

The code you typed in the OnCreate() function starts by extracting pMenu, the pointer of the menu:

```
CMenu* pMenu = GetMenu();
```

and then pGrowingMenu, the pointer of the Growing menu, is extracted with the GetSubMenu(1) function:

```
CMenu* pGrowingMenu = pMenu->GetSubMenu(1);
```

Note that because Growing menu is the second menu from the left, the parameter of GetSubMenu() is 1. (The File menu is menu #0, the Growing menu is menu #1, and the Help menu is menu #2).

Next, the items of the Growing menu (except the Add Item) are deleted with the DeleteMenu() function:

```
pGrowingMenu->DeleteMenu(5, MF_BYPOSITION);
pGrowingMenu->DeleteMenu(4, MF_BYPOSITION);
pGrowingMenu->DeleteMenu(3, MF_BYPOSITION);
pGrowingMenu->DeleteMenu(2, MF_BYPOSITION);
pGrowingMenu->DeleteMenu(1, MF_BYPOSITION);
```

The first parameter of the DeleteMenu() function is the position of the menu item that you want to delete, and the second parameter of the DeleteMenu() function is MF_BYPOSITION. MF_BYPOSITION indicates that the first parameter of DeleteMenu() is supplied by its position, not by its ID. Add Item is at position 0, Item 1 is at position 1, Item 2 is at position 2, and so on.

> **NOTE**
>
> The order in which the menu items are deleted is important. Suppose that you start by deleting the first item in the menu. Once you delete this menu item there will be only four menu items in the menu. This means that the menu item that used to be in position 1 is now in position 0, the menu item that used to be in position 2 is now in position 1, and so on. In other words, there is no such thing as an item at position 5, because the last item is now at position 4.

Even though you haven't finished writing the GROW application, compile/link and execute it to verify that you carried out the operations correctly.

☐ Select the Growing menu.

> *GROW responds by displaying the Growing menu. As shown in Figure 20.35, Add Item is the only item in the menu.*

As you know, during the visual implementation of the menu, you assigned five items to the Growing menu. Four of these menu items were deleted by the OnCreate() function when the application was started.

Figure 20.35.
The Growing menu
at the start of the
GROW applica-
tion.

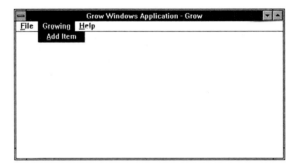

☐ Select Exit from the File menu to terminate the GROW application.

Attaching Code to the Add Item Menu

Now you'll attach code to the Growing menu's Add Item. This code will add an item to the Growing menu whenever the user clicks the Add Item menu.

☐ Use ClassWizard to add a function for the event:

Class Name:	CGrowView
Object ID:	ID_GROWING_ADDITEM
Message:	COMMAND
Function Name:	OnGrowingAdditem()

NOTE: Make sure you're adding the function to the CGrowView class.

After you add this function, your OnGrowingAdditem() function in the GROWVIEW.CPP file looks as follows:

```
void CGrowView::OnGrowingAdditem()
{
    // TODO: Add your command handler code here

    /////////////////////////
    // MY CODE STARTS HERE
    /////////////////////////

    // Extract the pointer of the parent pointer
    CWnd* pParent = GetParent();

    // Extract the pointer of the menu bar
    CMenu* pMenuBar = pParent->GetMenu();

    // Extract the pointer of the Growing menu
    CMenu* pMenuGrowing = pMenuBar->GetSubMenu(1);

    // Append an item to the Growing menu
    pMenuGrowing->AppendMenu ( MF_STRING ¦ MF_ENABLED,
                               ID_GROWING_ITEM1,
"I am item number 1. I was added during execution time" );

    /////////////////////////
    // MY CODE ENDS HERE
    /////////////////////////

}
```

The code you typed uses GetParent() to extract the pointer of the Parent window:

```
CWnd* pParent = GetParent();
```

And then the GetMenu() function is used to extract the pointer of the menu:

```
CMenu* pMenuBar = pParent->GetMenu();
```

Now that you have the pointer of the menu, you can use the `GetSubMenu()` function to extract the pointer of the Growing menu:

```
CMenu* pMenuGrowing = pMenuBar->GetSubMenu(1);
```

The parameter of `GetSubMenu()` is 1, because Growing is the second menu from the left on the menu.

The last statement you typed uses the `AppendMenu()` function on `pMenuGrowing`, the pointer of the Growing menu:

```
    pMenuGrowing->AppendMenu ( MF_STRING | MF_ENABLED,
                               ID_GROWING_ITEM1,
"I am item number 1. I was added during execution time" );
```

The `AppendMenu()` function uses `ID_GROWING_ITEM1` as its second parameter. The third parameter of `AppendMenu()` contains the text that will appear in the appended menu item.

To summarize, the `AppendMenu()` function appends a menu item to the Growing menu.

Even though you haven't finished writing the GROW application, compile/link and execute it to see what the code you typed accomplishes.

☐ Select Add Item from the Growing menu and then select the Growing menu again.

   GROW responds by displaying the Growing menu with the item you added.

Terminate the GROW application by selecting Exit from the File menu.

Adding Five Items at Runtime

Now that you understand how to add items to a menu at runtime, you can modify the code in the `OnGrowingAdditem()` function so that it will add five items to the Growing menu.

The variable that will keep track of how many items have been added to the menu is `m_CurrentAddedItem`.

☐ Add the `m_CurrentAddedItem` variable as a data member of the `CGrowView` class. After you add this data member, the `CGrowView` class declaration in the `GROWVIEW.H file` looks as follows:

```
class CGrowView : public CView
{
protected: // create from serialization only
    CGrowView();
    DECLARE_DYNCREATE(CGrowView)

// Attributes
public:
    CGrowDoc* GetDocument();

    ///////////////////////
    // MY CODE STARTS HERE
    ///////////////////////

    int m_CurrentAddedItem;

    ///////////////////////
    // MY CODE ENDS HERE
    ///////////////////////
...
...
...
};
```

Initially, there are no added items in the Growing menu. This means that you have to initialize the m_CurrentAddedItem variable to 0:

☐ Modify the constructor function of the CGrowView class. After the modification, the constructor function in the GROWVIEW.CPP file looks as follows:

```
CGrowView::CGrowView()
{
    // TODO: add construction code here

    ///////////////////////
    // MY CODE STARTS HERE
    ///////////////////////

    m_CurrentAddedItem = 0;

    ///////////////////////
    // MY CODE ENDS HERE
    ///////////////////////


}
```

☐ Modify the OnGrowingAddItem() function in the GROWVIEW.CPP file. After the modification, the function looks as follows:

```
void CGrowView::OnGrowingAdditem()
{
    // TODO: Add your command handler code here

    ///////////////////////
    // MY CODE STARTS HERE
    ///////////////////////

    // Extract the pointer or the parent pointer
    CWnd* pParent = GetParent();

    // Extract the pointer of the menu bar
    CMenu* pMenuBar = pParent->GetMenu();

    // Extract the pointer of the Growing menu
    CMenu* pMenuGrowing = pMenuBar->GetSubMenu(1);

    CString Message;
    char sCurrentAddedItem[10];


    if (m_CurrentAddedItem == 5 )
        {
        // Display a message to the user
        MessageBox ("Sorry, no more items can be added");
        return;
        }
    else
        {
        // Construct the Message variable
        itoa(m_CurrentAddedItem+1, sCurrentAddedItem, 10);
        Message = "I am item number " +
                    (CString)sCurrentAddedItem +
                    " . I was added during execution time";

        // Append an item to the menu
    pMenuGrowing->AppendMenu ( MF_STRING | MF_ENABLED,
                                (UINT)ID_GROWING_ITEM1 +
                                (UINT)m_CurrentAddedItem,
                                (LPCSTR)Message );
        // Update m_CurrentAddedItem for the next time
        m_CurrentAddedItem++;
        }

    ///////////////////////
    // MY CODE ENDS HERE
    ///////////////////////

}
```

The code you added defines two local variables:

```
CString Message;
char sCurrentAddedItem[10];
```

Then an `if` statement is used to determine whether there are five added items in the Growing menu.

If there are already five items in the menu, a message is displayed telling the user that no more items can be added:

```
if (m_CurrentAddedItem == 5 )
   {
   // Display a message to the user
   MessageBox ("Sorry, no more items can be added");
   return;
   }
```

If there are less than five added items in the Growing menu, the statements in the `else` block are executed:

```
 else
    {
    // Construct the Message variable
    itoa(m_CurrentAddedItem+1, sCurrentAddedItem, 10);
    Message = "I am item number " +
              (CString)sCurrentAddedItem +
              " . I was added during execution time";

    // Append an item to the menu
pMenuGrowing->AppendMenu ( MF_STRING ¦ MF_ENABLED,
                           (UINT)ID_GROWING_ITEM1 +
                           (UINT)m_CurrentAddedItem,
                           (LPCSTR)Message );

    // Update m_CurrentAddedItem for the next time
    m_CurrentAddedItem++;
    return;
    }
```

The statements in the `else` block construct the caption of the added menu item (Message), and then the `AppendMenu()` function is executed to add the item to the menu:

```
pMenuGrowing->AppendMenu ( MF_STRING ¦ MF_ENABLED,
                           (UINT)ID_GROWING_ITEM1 +
                           (UINT)m_CurrentAddedItem,
                           (LPCSTR)Message );
```

The first parameter of `AppendMenu()` tells the `AppendMenu()` function that the added item (whose caption is mentioned as the third parameter) is a string and that the menu item should be enabled.

The second parameter of `AppendMenu()` is

```
(UINT)ID_GROWING_ITEM1 +
(UINT)m_CurrentAddedItem
```

For example, if currently `m_CurrentAddedItem` is equal to 0, the second parameter is equal to

```
(UINT)ID_GROWING_ITEM1 +
        0
```

So in this case, the second parameter is equal to the ID of Item 1 (as assigned by App Studio).

Similarly, depending on the current value of `m_CurrentAddedItem`, the second parameter of `AppendMenu()` can be the ID of any of the added items in the Growing menu. Note that this code assumes that you created the menu items in App Studio in a sequential manner (one after the other) so that App Studio assigned sequential ID numbers to these menu items.

☐ Compile/link and then execute the GROW application.

☐ Add items to the Growing menu by selecting Add Item from the Growing menu.

As you can see, the maximum number of items that you can add to the Growing menu is five.

Deleting and Inserting Items

In a similar manner, you can use the `RemoveMenu()` member function to remove an item from a menu, and you can use the `InsertMenu()` member function to insert an item at any particular position in the menu.

Attaching Code to the Added Menu Items

Now you'll add code that is executed whenever the user selects an added item.

☐ Use ClassWizard to modify the `OnGrowingItem1()` function in the `GROWVIEW.CPP` file. After the modification, your `OnGrowingItem1()` looks as follows:

```
void CGrowView::OnGrowingItem1()
{
    // TODO: Add your command handler code here

    /////////////////////
    // MY CODE STARTS HERE
    /////////////////////

    MessageBox ("I'm now inside OnGrowingItem1()");

    /////////////////////
    // MY CODE ENDS HERE
    /////////////////////

}
```

☐ Now modify the rest of the functions (in the GROWVIEW.CPP file) of the added items of the Growing menu.

After the modifications, these functions should look as follows:

```
void CGrowView::OnGrowingItem2()
{
    // TODO: Add your command handler code here

    /////////////////////
    // MY CODE STARTS HERE
    /////////////////////

    MessageBox ("I'm now inside OnGrowingItem2()");

    /////////////////////
    // MY CODE ENDS HERE
    /////////////////////



}

void CGrowView::OnGrowingItem3()
{
    // TODO: Add your command handler code here

    /////////////////////
    // MY CODE STARTS HERE
    /////////////////////

    MessageBox ("I'm now inside OnGrowingItem3()");
```

```
//////////////////////
// MY CODE ENDS HERE
//////////////////////

}

void CGrowView::OnGrowingItem4()
{
    // TODO: Add your command handler code here

    //////////////////////
    // MY CODE STARTS HERE
    //////////////////////

    MessageBox ("I'm now inside OnGrowingItem4()");

    //////////////////////
    // MY CODE ENDS HERE
    //////////////////////

}

void CGrowView::OnGrowingItem5()
{
    // TODO: Add your command handler code here

    //////////////////////
    // MY CODE STARTS HERE
    //////////////////////

    MessageBox ("I'm now inside OnGrowingItem5()");

    //////////////////////
    // MY CODE ENDS HERE
    //////////////////////

}
```

☐ Compile/link and execute the GROW application.

☐ Add items to the Growing menu and then select the added items to verify that the appropriate function is executed.

The PicMenu Application

Sometimes it's more appropriate for items in a menu to be represented by pictures. The PicMenu (*Picture Menu*) application demonstrates how you can accomplish this.

Before you start writing the PicMenu application yourself, execute the copy of the PicMenu application that resides in your `C:\VCPROG\ORIGINAL\CH20\PicMenu` directory.

To execute the MyMenu application:

☐ Use Run from the Program Manager's File menu to execute
`C:\VCPROG\ORIGINAL\CH20\PICMENU\PicMenu.EXE`.

> *Windows responds by executing the PicMenu application. The main window of `PicMenu.EXE` appears, as shown in Figure 20.36.*

The PicMenu application has three popup menus: File, Picture Menu, and Help. These popup menus are shown in Figures 20.37, 20.38, and 20.39.

Figure 20.36.
The PicMenu application's main window.

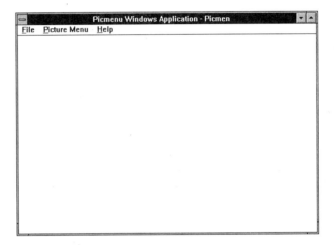

Figure 20.37.
The PicMenu application's File menu.

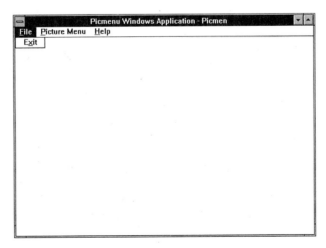

*Figure 20.38.
The PicMenu
application's
Picture Menu.*

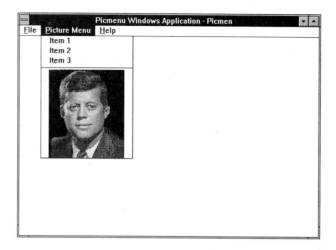

*Figure 20.39.
The PicMenu
application's Help
menu.*

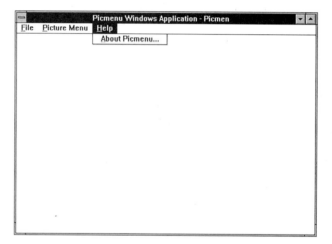

☐ Experiment with the PicMenu application by selecting the various items of the Picture menu.

☐ Select Exit from the File menu to terminate the PicMenu application.

Creating the Project of the PicMenu Application

To create the project of the PicMenu application:

☐ Select AppWizard from the Project menu.

> *Visual C++ responds by running AppWizard.*

☐ Use the Directory list box to select the directory C:\VCCPROG\PRACTICE\CH20.

☐ Type picmenu in the Project Name box.

Now your AppWizard dialog box looks as shown in Figure 20.40.

☐ Click the Options button and set the options as shown in Figure 20.41 (that is, uncheck all the check boxes except the Generate Source Comments check box).

Figure 20.40.
The AppWizard
dialog box for the
PicMenu
application.

Figure 20.41.
Setting the options
for the PicMenu
application.

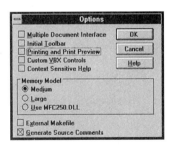

☐ Click the OK button of the Options dialog box and then click the OK button of the AppWizard dialog box and finally click the Create button of the New Application Information dialog box.

AppWizard responds by creating the PicMenu project and all the skeleton files of the PicMenu application.

To remove the debug options of the project (so you'll have a small EXE file):

☐ Select Project from the Options menu of Visual C++, click the Release radio button, and then click the OK button of the dialog box.

The Visual Design of the Menu

Now you'll visually design the menu of the PicMenu application.

Use App Studio to implement the PicMenu application's menu per Table 20.4. If you compare Table 20.4 with Figure 20.38, you'll see that Table 20.4 doesn't represent the final version of the menu. Later you'll write code that will make the menu look as shown in Figure 20.38.

Table 20.4. The PicMenu application's menu.

Menu Item
&File
E&xit
&Picture Menu
Item 1
Item 2
Item 3
Item 4
Item 5
&Help
&About PicMenu...

To save your work:

☐ Select Save from the File menu of App Studio.

The visual implementation of the PicMenu application's menu is complete. At this point, your menu should look as shown in Figure 20.42.

NOTE: The PicMenu application doesn't have a custom dialog box. It has only an About dialog box.

Figure 20.42.
The menu of the
PicMenu
application.

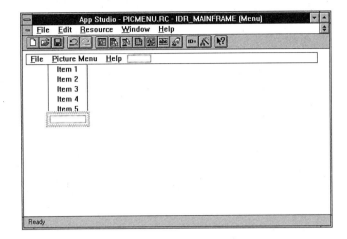

Attaching Code to the Items in the Picture Menu

Now you'll add functions that will be executed whenever the user selects Item 1, Item 2, Item 3, Item 4, or Item 5 from the Picture Menu.

☐ Use ClassWizard to add a function for the event:

Class Name:	CPicmenuView
Object ID:	ID_PICTUREMENU_ITEM1
Message:	COMMAND
Function Name:	OnPicturemenuItem1()

NOTE: Make sure you're adding the function to the CPicmenuView class.

After you add the OnPicturemenuItem1() function to the PICMEVW.CPP file, the function looks as follows:

```
void CPicmenuView::OnPicturemenuItem1()
{
    // TODO: Add your command handler code here

    /////////////////////////
    // MY CODE STARTS HERE
    /////////////////////////

    MessageBox ("You selected the first item");

    /////////////////////////
    // MY CODE ENDS HERE
    /////////////////////////

}
```

☐ Use ClassWizard to add a function for the event:

Class Name:	`CPicmenuView`
Object ID:	`ID_PICTUREMENU_ITEM2`
Message:	`COMMAND`
Function Name:	`OnPicturemenuItem2()`

NOTE: Make sure you're adding the function to the `CPicmenuView` class.

After you add the `OnPicturemenuItem2()` function to the `PICMEVW.CPP` file, the function looks as follows:

```
{
    // TODO: Add your command handler code here

    //////////////////////
    // MY CODE STARTS HERE
    //////////////////////

    MessageBox ("You selected the second item");

    //////////////////////
    // MY CODE ENDS HERE
    //////////////////////

}
```

☐ Use ClassWizard to add a function for the event:

Class Name:	`CPicmenuView`
Object ID:	`ID_PICTUREMENU_ITEM3`
Message:	`COMMAND`
Function Name:	`OnPicturemenuItem3()`

NOTE: Make sure you're adding the function to the `CPicmenuView` class.

After you add the `OnPicturemenuItem3()` function to the `PICMEVW.CPP` file, the function looks as follows:

```
void CPicmenuView::OnPicturemenuItem3()
{
    // TODO: Add your command handler code here

    //////////////////////
    // MY CODE STARTS HERE
    //////////////////////

    MessageBox ("You selected the third item");
```

```
//////////////////////
// MY CODE ENDS HERE
//////////////////////
```

}

☐ Use ClassWizard to add a function for the event:

Class Name:	CPicmenuView
Object ID:	ID_PICTUREMENU_ITEM4
Message:	COMMAND
Function Name:	OnPicturemenuItem4()

NOTE: Make sure you're adding the function to the CPicmenuView class.

After you add the OnPicturemenuItem4() function to the PICMEVW.CPP file, the function looks as follows:

```
void CPicmenuView::OnPicturemenuItem4()
{
        // TODO: Add your command handler code here

        //////////////////////
        // MY CODE STARTS HERE
        //////////////////////

        MessageBox ("You selected the 4th item");

        //////////////////////
        // MY CODE ENDS HERE
        //////////////////////

}
```

☐ Use ClassWizard to add a function for the event:

Class Name:	CPicmenuView
Object ID:	ID_PICTUREMENU_ITEM5
Message:	COMMAND
Function Name:	OnPicturemenuItem5()

NOTE: Make sure you're adding the function to the CPicmenuView class.

After you add the OnPicturemenuItem5() function to the PICMEVW.CPP file, the function looks as follows:

```
void CPicmenuView::OnPicturemenuItem5()
{
        // TODO: Add your command handler code here
```

```
/////////////////////
// MY CODE STARTS HERE
/////////////////////

MessageBox ("You selected the 5th item");

/////////////////////
// MY CODE ENDS HERE
/////////////////////
```

}

☐ Even though you haven't finished writing the PicMenu application, compile/link and execute it to verify that you typed the code correctly.

☐ Experiment with the PicMenu application and verify that it operates as it should.

☐ Select Exit from the File menu to terminate the PicMenu application.

> **NOTE**
>
> At this point you're probably asking yourself, "Am I reading the code for the correct application? Where's the promised bitmap?" Well, don't worry! You'll get to it soon enough. The bitmap that you'll use as one of the items of the Picture Menu is `C:\vcPROG\BMP\Kennedy.BMP`. This bitmap file is shown in Figure 20.43.

Figure 20.43.
The
`Kennedy.BMP`
file.

Using the *WM_CREATE* Message

Now you'll attach code to the WM_CREATE event of the CPicmenuFrame class.

☐ Use ClassWizard to add a function for the event:

Class Name:	CMainFrame
Object ID:	CMainFrame
Message:	WM_CREATE
Function Name:	OnCreate()

NOTE: Make sure you're adding the function to the CMainFrame class.

WARNING

So far in this book, most of the functions you've added have been added to the view and document classes. Note that the preceding instructs you to add a function to the CMainFrame class! The ClassWizard dialog box should look as shown in Figure 20.44.

Figure 20.44.
Adding a function to the WM_CREATE
message of the
CMainFrame
class.

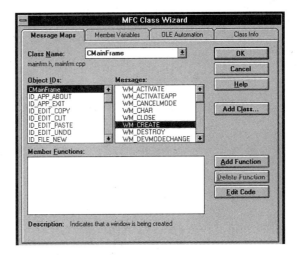

After you add the OnCreate() function to the MAINFRM.CPP file, the function looks as follows:

```
int CMainFrame::OnCreate(LPCREATESTRUCT lpCreateStruct)
{
    if (CFrameWnd::OnCreate(lpCreateStruct) == -1)
        return -1;

    /////////////////////////
    // MY CODE STARTS HERE
    /////////////////////////

    // Extract the pointer of the menu
    CMenu* pMenu = GetMenu();

    // Extract the pointer of the Picture Menu menu
    CMenu* pPictureMenu = pMenu->GetSubMenu(1);

    // Delete the current items in the Picture Menu menu
    pPictureMenu->DeleteMenu(4, MF_BYPOSITION);
    pPictureMenu->DeleteMenu(3, MF_BYPOSITION);
    pPictureMenu->DeleteMenu(2, MF_BYPOSITION);
    pPictureMenu->DeleteMenu(1, MF_BYPOSITION);
    pPictureMenu->DeleteMenu(0, MF_BYPOSITION);

    // Append regular text items to the Picture Menu menu
    pPictureMenu->AppendMenu ( MF_ENABLED | MF_STRING,
                               ID_PICTUREMENU_ITEM1,
            "I am the 1st item, Can you see me?");
    pPictureMenu->AppendMenu ( MF_ENABLED | MF_STRING,
                               ID_PICTUREMENU_ITEM2,
            "I am the 2nd item, Can you see me?");
    pPictureMenu->AppendMenu ( MF_ENABLED | MF_STRING,
                               ID_PICTUREMENU_ITEM3,
            "I am the 3rd item, Can you see me?");
    pPictureMenu->AppendMenu ( MF_ENABLED | MF_STRING,
                               ID_PICTUREMENU_ITEM4,
            "I am the 4th item, Can you see me?");

    pPictureMenu->AppendMenu ( MF_ENABLED | MF_STRING,
                               ID_PICTUREMENU_ITEM5,
            "I am the 5th item, Can you see me?");

    /////////////////////////
    // MY CODE ENDS HERE
    /////////////////////////

    // TODO: Add your specialized creation code here

    return 0;
}
```

Reviewing the code you typed, the `OnCreate()` function is automatically executed whenever the form of the application is created. You need to use this event because there is a need to change the Picture menu that you designed with App Studio.

The `OnCreate()` function starts by extracting pMenu, the pointer of the menu:

```
CMenu* pMenu = GetMenu();
```

and then pPictureMenu, the pointer of the Picture menu is extracted with the `GetSubMenu(1)` function:

```
CMenu* pPictureMenu = pMenu->GetSubMenu(1);
```

Note that because Picture Menu is the second menu from the left, the parameter of `GetSubMenu()` is 1.

Next, the current items of the Picture menu are deleted with the `DeleteMenu()` function:

```
pPictureMenu->DeleteMenu(4, MF_BYPOSITION);
pPictureMenu->DeleteMenu(3, MF_BYPOSITION);
pPictureMenu->DeleteMenu(2, MF_BYPOSITION);
pPictureMenu->DeleteMenu(1, MF_BYPOSITION);
pPictureMenu->DeleteMenu(0, MF_BYPOSITION);
```

The first parameter of the `DeleteMenu()` function is the position of the menu item that you want to delete. The second parameter of the `DeleteMenu()` function, `MF_BYPOSITION`, indicates that the first parameter of `DeleteMenu()` is supplied by its position, not by its ID.

NOTE

The order in which items are deleted from the menu is important. Suppose that you start by deleting the very first item in the menu. Once you delete this menu item, there will be only four menu items in the menu. This means that the menu item which used to be in position 1 is now in position 0, the menu item that used to be in position 2 is now in position 1, and so on. In other words, there is no such thing as an item at position 4, because that item is now at position 3.

The rest of the statements in the `OnCreate()` function append five items to the menu:

```
pPictureMenu->AppendMenu ( MF_ENABLED ¦ MF_STRING,
                           ID_PICTUREMENU_ITEM1,
         "I am the 1st item, Can you see me?");

pPictureMenu->AppendMenu ( MF_ENABLED ¦ MF_STRING,
                           ID_PICTUREMENU_ITEM2,
         "I am the 2nd item, Can you see me?");
 pPictureMenu->AppendMenu ( MF_ENABLED ¦ MF_STRING,
                           ID_PICTUREMENU_ITEM3,
         "I am the 3rd item, Can you see me?");
 pPictureMenu->AppendMenu ( MF_ENABLED ¦ MF_STRING,
                           ID_PICTUREMENU_ITEM4,
         "I am the 4th item, Can you see me?");

pPictureMenu->AppendMenu ( MF_ENABLED ¦ MF_STRING,
                           ID_PICTUREMENU_ITEM5,
         "I am the 5th item, Can you see me?");
```

Note that in the preceding statements, the IDs of the menu items are the IDs as assigned by App Studio.

Even though you haven't finished writing the PicMenu application, compile/link and execute it to verify that you carried out the operations correctly.

☐ Select the Picture menu.

> *PicMenu responds by displaying the Picture menu, as shown in Figure 20.45. The items of the Picture menu aren't the ones that you placed in App Studio; they're the ones that you appended to the* OnCreate() *function of the* CMainFrame *class (in the* MainFRM.CPP *file).*

Figure 20.45.
The PicMenu
application's
Picture menu.

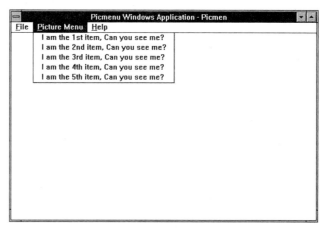

☐ Select Exit from the File menu to terminate the PicMenu application.

Creating a Bitmap with App Studio

And now for the fun part of the PicMenu application. Because the PicMenu application displays a bitmap in its menu, you must first create this bitmap:

☐ Run App Studio from Visual C++'s Tools menu.

☐ Click the New button at the bottom of App Studio's `PICMENU.RC` window.

App Studio responds by displaying the New Resource dialog box (see Figure 20.46).

Figure 20.46.
Creating a new bitmap.

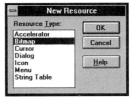

Figure 20.47.
The empty bitmap window that App Studio displays.

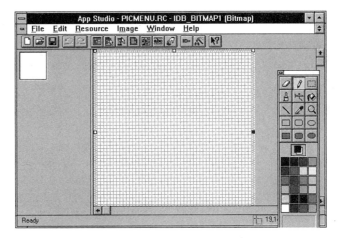

☐ Select Bitmap in the New Resource dialog box (because you're now preparing a bitmap resource for the Picture menu) and then click the OK button of the New Resource dialog box.

App Studio responds by displaying the window shown in Figure 20.47. As shown, App Studio expects you to draw the bitmap in this window. Note that App Studio refers to this new bitmap as `IDB_BITMAP1`.

At this point you may choose to draw the bitmap yourself or use an existing BMP file.

Use an existing BMP file:

☐ Select Open from the File menu, select the file C:\vcProg\Kennedy.BMP, and then click the OK button (see Figure 20.48).

App studio responds by displaying the Kennedy.BMP *file (see Figure 20.49).*

Figure 20.48.
Opening the
C:\vcProg\BMP\
Kennedy.BMP *file.*

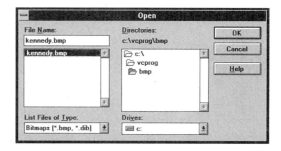

Figure 20.49.
Displaying
Kennedy.BMP
with App Studio.

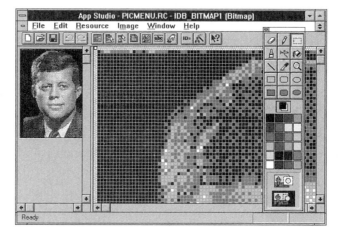

☐ Copy Kennedy.BMP to the Clipboard. First click in a free area on the left side of the window and then select Copy from the Edit menu.

☐ Select IDB_BITMAP1 from App Studio's Window menu.

App Studio responds by displaying the empty IDB_BITMAP1 *window.*

☐ Select Paste from the Edit Menu of App Studio.

App Studio responds by displaying a message box telling you that the empty bitmap is smaller than the bitmap that currently exists in the Clipboard.

☐ Click the Yes button to tell App Studio to enlarge the size of the bitmap that you're currently constructing.

☐ Select Save from App Studio's File menu.

☐ Select `PICMENU.RC` from the Window menu of App Studio.

> *App Studio responds by displaying the pictorial representation of the* `PICMENU.RC` *file. As shown in Figure 20.50, the RC file now contains* `IDB_BITMAP1`.

Figure 20.50.
The `PICMENU.RC`
file with
`IDB_BITMAP1`
shown.

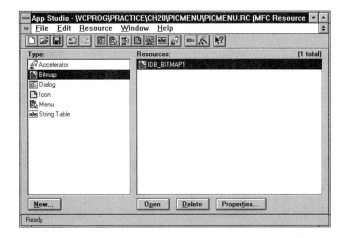

You can verify that `IDB_BITMAP1` is the `Kennedy.BMP` file as follows:

☐ Make sure that `IDB_BITMAP1` is highlighted and then click the Properties button.

> *App Studio responds by displaying the Properties window of* `IDB_BITMAP1` *(see Figure 20.51).*

Figure 20.51.
The Properties
window of
`IDB_BITMAP1`.

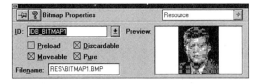

Now you've completed drawing and incorporating a bitmap in the `PICMENU.RC` file.

To save your work:

☐ Select Save from the File menu of App Studio.

Attaching the Bitmaps to the Picture Menu

Now that you've completed preparing the bitmap, you can attach it to the Picture Menu. Here's how you do that:

☐ Open the MAINFRM.CPP file and modify the OnCreate() function. After the modification, the OnCreate() function looks as follows:

```
int CMainFrame::OnCreate(LPCREATESTRUCT lpCreateStruct)
{
    if (CFrameWnd::OnCreate(lpCreateStruct) == -1)
        return -1;

    /////////////////////////
    // MY CODE STARTS HERE
    /////////////////////////

    // Extract the pointer of the menu
    CMenu* pMenu = GetMenu();

    // Extract the pointer of the Picture Menu menu
    CMenu* pPictureMenu = pMenu->GetSubMenu(1);

    // Delete the current items in the Picture Menu menu
    pPictureMenu->DeleteMenu(4, MF_BYPOSITION);
    pPictureMenu->DeleteMenu(3, MF_BYPOSITION);
    //pPictureMenu->DeleteMenu(2, MF_BYPOSITION);
    //pPictureMenu->DeleteMenu(1, MF_BYPOSITION);
    //pPictureMenu->DeleteMenu(0, MF_BYPOSITION);


    // Create the object of the bitmap.
    CBitmap* pBit;


    // Load the bitmap
    pBit->LoadBitmap(IDB_BITMAP1);


     // Append a separator item to the Picture Menu menu
      pPictureMenu->AppendMenu ( MF_SEPARATOR,
                                 ID_PICTUREMENU_ITEM4 );

     // Append a bitmap item to the Picture Menu menu
       pPictureMenu->AppendMenu ( MF_ENABLED,
                                  ID_PICTUREMENU_ITEM1,
                                  pBit);
```

```
/////////////////////
// MY CODE ENDS HERE
/////////////////////

    // TODO: Add your specialized creation code here

    return 0;
}
```

The code in the OnCreate() function starts by extracting the pointer of the menu:

```
CMenu* pMenu = GetMenu();
```

Then, the pointer of the Picture menu is extracted:

```
CMenu* pPictureMenu = pMenu->GetSubMenu(1);
```

The next group of statements delete the fourth and fifth menu items:

```
// Delete the current items in the Picture Menu menu
pPictureMenu->DeleteMenu(4, MF_BYPOSITION);
pPictureMenu->DeleteMenu(3, MF_BYPOSITION);
//pPictureMenu->DeleteMenu(2, MF_BYPOSITION);
//pPictureMenu->DeleteMenu(1, MF_BYPOSITION);
//pPictureMenu->DeleteMenu(0, MF_BYPOSITION);
```

In the preceding statements, you commented (//) the statements that delete the first, second, and third items. In other words, you're going to replace the fourth and fifth items of the menu, but the first, second, and third items should remain the same as you designed them in App Studio.

The next statement creates an object of class CBitmap:

```
CBitmap* pBit;
```

Once the pBit object is created, you can use the LoadBitmap() member function to load the bitmap:

```
pBit->LoadBitmap(IDB_BITMAP1);
```

The parameter of LoadBitmap() is IDB_BITMAP1, the bitmap that you designed in App Studio.

At this point the Picture menu has three items in it (because you deleted the fourth and fifth items with the DeleteMenu() function). So the next two statements add the fourth and fifth items to the menu. Here the fourth menu item is added:

```
pPictureMenu->AppendMenu ( MF_SEPARATOR,
                           ID_PICTUREMENU_ITEM4);
```

687

That is, you supply MF_SEPARATOR as the first parameter of the AppendMenu() function and the ID of the fourth item as its second parameter. It doesn't matter what ID you supply as the second parameter, because the separator can't be selected.

The last statement uses the AppendMenu() function to add the fifth menu item:

```
pPictureMenu->AppendMenu ( MF_ENABLED,
                           ID_PICTUREMENU_ITEM1,
                           pBit);
```

The second parameter is the ID of the first menu item. This means that whenever the user selects this menu item, the function that will be executed is the same function that is executed whenever the first menu item is selected.

> **NOTE**
>
> It's important to understand that by supplying ID_PICTUREMENU_ITEM1 as the second parameter of the AppendMenu() function, you associate the appended menu item with the function whose ID is ID_PICTUREMENU_ITEM1. Usually, you would append menu items so that each appended item caused the execution of a different function. However, to illustrate that two menu items can cause the execution of the same function, you supplied the ID of Item 1 as the ID of the fifth menu item (the bitmap menu item). Thus, during the execution of the application, selecting Item 1 from the menu produces the same result as selecting the bitmap menu item.

The third parameter is pBit, the pointer to the IDB_BITMAP1 you designed in App Studio.

But wait a minute! The first AppendMenu() function (the one that adds the separator) has two parameters, and the other AppendMenu() functions have three parameters! This is, of course, possible, because C++ functions can have default parameters.

☐ Highlight "AppendMenu" in the MAINFRM.CPP file and press F1 for Help.

   App Studio responds by displaying the Help window for this function. As shown in Figure 20.52, the third parameter of the AppendMenu() function is LPCSTR lpszNewItem = NULL.

This means that the default value for the third parameter is NULL. So if you don't supply a third parameter for the AppendMenu() function, it uses the value NULL. Indeed, when adding a separator, the third parameter of AppendMenu() should be NULL.

Figure 20.52.
The Help window
of
AppendMenu().

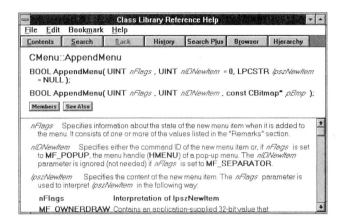

Also note that in Figure 20.52, there are actually two AppendMenu() functions. The top AppendMenu() function is the one you use to append text menu items and separator bars. The bottom one is used to add bitmap menu items. Of course, it's legal in C++ to have two different functions with identical names and different parameters. That's called overloading functions.

☐ Compile/link and execute the PicMenu application to verify its operation. In particular, note that selecting the first item of the Picture Menu produces the same result as selecting the Kennedy bitmap menu item. The same function is executed in both cases.

Synchronizing Sound and Speech

The last enhancement that you'll make to the PicMenu is to synchronize Kennedy's speech with the display of the speech's text.

Because the speech will be played through the PC speaker, you need to use the IM-PORTS statements in the PICMENU.DEF file.

☐ Open the PICMENU.DEF file and modify it. After the modification, your PICMENU.DEF file looks as follows:

```
; picmenu.def : Declares the module parameters for the application.

NAME            PICMENU
DESCRIPTION     'PICMENU Windows Application'
EXETYPE         WINDOWS

CODE            PRELOAD MOVEABLE DISCARDABLE
DATA            PRELOAD MOVEABLE MULTIPLE
```

```
HEAPSIZE      1024    ; initial heap size
; Stack size is passed as argument to linker's /STACK option


;;;;;;;;;;;;;;;;;;;;;;;;;
; MY CODE STARTS HERE
;;;;;;;;;;;;;;;;;;;;;;;;;


;;;;;;;;;;;;;;;;;;;;;;;;;;;;;;;;;;;;;;;;;;;;;;;;;
; sp_ functions from the TegoSND.DLL library
;;;;;;;;;;;;;;;;;;;;;;;;;;;;;;;;;;;;;;;;;;;;;;;;;

IMPORTS
TegoSND.sp_OpenSession
TegoSND.sp_PlaySnd
TegoSND.sp_MouseOn
TegoSND.sp_MouseOff
TegoSND.sp_CloseSession


;;;;;;;;;;;;;;;;;;;;;;;;;
; MY CODE ENDS HERE
;;;;;;;;;;;;;;;;;;;;;;;;;
```

☐ Open the PicMenu.H file and add the #include file of the TegoSND.DLL file.
   After you add this #include statement, the beginning of your PicMenu.H file
   looks as follows:

```
// picmenu.h : main header file for the PICMENU application
//

#ifndef __AFXWIN_H__
    #error include 'stdafx.h' before including this file for PCH
#endif

#include "resource.h"        // main symbols

/////////////////////////
// MY CODE STARTS HERE
/////////////////////////

#include "\vcProg\DLL\TegoSND.H"


/////////////////////////
// MY CODE ENDS HERE
/////////////////////////

.....
.....
.....
```

☐ Add a data member variable (m_KennedySession) to the class declaration of the CPicmenuView class that resides in the PICMEVW.H file. After you add the m_KennedySession variable, the class declaration looks as follows:

```
class CPicmenuView : public CView
{
protected: // create from serialization only
    CPicmenuView();
    DECLARE_DYNCREATE(CPicmenuView)

// Attributes
public:
    CPicmenuDoc* GetDocument();


    /////////////////////////
    // MY CODE STARTS HERE
    /////////////////////////

    int m_KennedySession;

    /////////////////////
    // MY CODE ENDS HERE
    /////////////////////


// Operations
public:

// Implementation
public:
    virtual ~CPicmenuView();
    virtual void OnDraw(CDC* pDC);
// overridden to draw this view
#ifdef _DEBUG
    virtual void AssertValid() const;
    virtual void Dump(CDumpContext& dc) const;
#endif

protected:

// Generated message map functions
protected:
    //{{AFX_MSG(CPicmenuView)
    afx_msg void OnPicturemenuItem1();
    afx_msg void OnPicturemenuItem2();
    afx_msg void OnPicturemenuItem3();
    afx_msg void OnPicturemenuItem4();
    afx_msg void OnPicturemenuItem5();
    //}}AFX_MSG
    DECLARE_MESSAGE_MAP()
};
```

691

Now you have to open a sound session for the 8Kenned3.WAV file:

☐ Open the PICMEVW.CPP file and add code to the constructor function of the CPicmenuView class. This code opens a WAV session for the 8Kenned3.WAV file. After you add the code, the constructor function looks as follows:

```
CPicmenuView::CPicmenuView()
{
    // TODO: add construction code here


    /////////////////////////
    // MY CODE STARTS HERE
    /////////////////////////

    char FileToOpen[255];


    // Open the Kennedy WAV session
    strcpy ( FileToOpen, "\\vcProg\\WAV\\8Kenned3.WAV" );
    m_KennedySession = sp_OpenSession ( FileToOpen );


    // If WAV session can not be opened, display message box.
    if ( m_KennedySession < 0 )
        {
        CString Message, Caption;
        Message = "Can't open the file: ";
        Message = Message + FileToOpen;
        Caption = "Error";
        MessageBox ( Message, Caption );
        }

    /////////////////////////
    // MY CODE ENDS HERE
    /////////////////////////
}
```

☐ Close the WAV session by adding code to the destructor function of the View class that resides in the PICMEVW.CPP file. After you add the code, the destructor function looks as follows:

```
CPicmenuView::~CPicmenuView()
{

    /////////////////////////
    // MY CODE STARTS HERE
    /////////////////////////
```

```
sp_CloseSession ( m_KennedySession );


//////////////////////,
// MY CODE ENDS HERE
```

}

Now the PicMenu application has all the code that it needs to play Kennedy's speech.

Synchronizing the Audio Playback with the Display of Text

Now you'll display the speech on the screen in synchronization with the playback of the speech. You can use any WAV editor to figure out the byte locations of the various audio sections. For example, you can use the Sound Recorder and Media Player programs that come with Windows. With these programs you can examine any particular audio section of a WAV file. However, these programs display the time coordinates. To convert time coordinates to byte coordinates, use this formula:

```
[Byte location] = [Sampling Rate]/[Time location]
```

For example, the formula for the byte location that corresponds to a time location of 1000 milliseconds (1 second) in a WAV file that was recorded at 11 KHz is

```
[Byte location] = [11,025]/[1] = 11,025
```

Similarly, the formula for the byte location that corresponds to time location 500 milliseconds (0.5 second) of a WAV file recorded at 11,025 hertz is

```
[Byte location[ = [11,025]/[0.5] = 5,512
```

> **NOTE**
>
> The preceding formula for calculating the byte location for a given sampling rate and time coordinate is valid provided the following:
>
> The WAV file was recorded as a mono (not stereo) file
>
> The WAV file is an 8-bit file, not a 16-bit file
>
> In the previous calculations, you used the value 11,025 for a WAV file that was recorded at 11 KHz! This is because in WAV jargon, saying that a WAV file was recorded at 11 KHz actually means that the WAV file was recorded at 11,025 hertz.

After examining the various audio sections of the 8Kenned3.WAV file, Table 20.5 was constructed.

Table 20.5. The Kennedy speech.

From	*To*	*Audio Section*
0	25980	So my fellow Americans
25980	54680	Ask not
54680	84092	What your country can do for you
84092	107619	Ask what you can do for your country.
107619	end	(People Cheering)

Now you'll write code in the OnPicturemenuItem1() function. Recall that this function is executed whenever you select Item 1 or the Kennedy bitmap item from the Picture Menu.

☐ Modify the OnPicturemenuItem1() function that resides in the PICMEVW.CPP file. After the modification, the OnPicturemenuItem1() function looks as follows:

```
void CPicmenuView::OnPicturemenuItem1()
{
     // TODO: Add your command handler code here

     /////////////////////////
     // MY CODE STARTS HERE
     /////////////////////////

     // Cause a WM_PAINT message
     Invalidate();

     CString Message;

     CClientDC dc(this);


     // So my fellow Americans
     Message = "So my fellows Americans";
     dc.TextOut ( 10,                       // X coordinate
                  20,                        // Y coordinate
                  Message,                   // The text
                  Message.GetLength() );     // Length of text
```

```
    sp_PlaySnd ( m_KennedySession,
              0,
              25980 );

  // Ask not
Message = "Ask not";
dc.TextOut ( 10,                          // X coordinate
              40,                         // Y coordinate
              Message,                    // The text
              Message.GetLength() );   // Length of text

    sp_PlaySnd ( m_KennedySession,
              25980,
              54680 );

  // What your country can do for you
Message = "What your country can do for you";
dc.TextOut ( 10,                          // X coordinate
              60,                         // Y coordinate
              Message,                    // The text
              Message.GetLength() );   // Length of text

    sp_PlaySnd ( m_KennedySession,
              54680,
              84090 );

  // ask what you can do for your country
Message = "ask what you can do for your country";
dc.TextOut ( 10,                          // X coordinate
              80,                         // Y coordinate
              Message,                    // The text
              Message.GetLength() );   // Length of text

    sp_PlaySnd ( m_KennedySession,
              84090,
              107619 );

  // People cheering
  sp_PlaySnd ( m_KennedySession,
              107619,
              SP_END_OF_FILE );

//////////////////////
// MY CODE ENDS HERE
//////////////////////

}
```

The code you typed starts by executing the `Invalidate()` member function:

```
Invalidate();
```

This function tells Windows that the window needs to be repainted. Windows responds by sending the message WM_PAINT, and as a result the function that corresponds to the WM_PAINT message is executed. Note that you weren't instructed to add any code to this function. For example, if you minimize the PicMenu window and then maximize it again, Windows automatically sends the WM_PAINT message to PicMenu. Because you didn't write any of your own code in the function that is executed when the WM_PAINT message is received, the window is redrawn. Thus, a good trick to erase whatever is in the window is to cause Windows to send the WM_PAINT message. It's important to note that when you execute the Invalidate() function, Windows knows that it should send a WM_PAINT message to PicMenu. However, PicMenu is currently busy executing the OnPicturemenuItem1() function. When PicMenu isn't busy anymore, Windows will control the CPU, and at that time it will send the WM_PAINT message to PicMenu. PicMenu will respond by repainting the window. To summarize, the Invalidate() function causes Windows to send the WM_PAINT message at a later time.

The rest of the statements in the OnPicturemenuItem1() function play and display the speech. When the OnPicturemenuItem1() is terminated, Windows will control the CPU again, and at that time the WM_PAINT message will be sent to PicMenu. This is the reason why the window is erased after the OnPicturemenuItem1() function is terminated. You need to erase the window after the speech is over because you'll want the window to be clean for the next selection of the Kennedy bitmap (or Item 1) from the Picture Menu.

As stated, the rest of the statements in OnPicturemenuItem1() display and play the speech. A local variable is declared:

```
CString Message;
```

A dc object is created:

```
CClientDC dc(this);
```

The first line of the speech is prepared:

```
Message = "So my fellow Americans";
```

Then the TextOut() function is executed to display the first line of the speech:

```
dc.TextOut ( 10,                    // X coordinate
             20,                    // Y coordinate
             Message,               // The text
             Message.GetLength() ); // Length of text
```

After the text is displayed, the `sp_PlaySnd()` function is executed to play the audio section that corresponds to the first line:

```
sp_PlaySnd ( m_KennedySession,
             0,
             25980 );
```

This process of using the `TextOut()` function and the `sp_PlaySnd()` function is repeated for the rest of the speech.

☐ Compile/link and execute the PicMenu application and verify its operation.

21

The Toolbar and Status Bar

In this chapter you'll learn how to implement a *toolbar*. Take a look at Figure 21.1. It shows the window for the Microsoft Word for Windows program. As shown, the window contains a toolbar below the menu bar. The toolbar serves as a pictorial menu. That is, instead of selecting Save from the File menu, the user can click the diskette icon that appears on the toolbar.

Figure 21.1 also shows the status bar (below the horizontal scroll bar). The status bar serves as a placeholder for various types of messages to the user during the execution of the program. For example, the status bar can inform the user about the status of the Num Lock key. The status bar also serves as a place to display messages that correspond to the currently selected menu item. This helps the user to decide which menu items should be selected for performing certain tasks.

Figure 21.1.
The toolbar and
status bar of Word
for Windows.

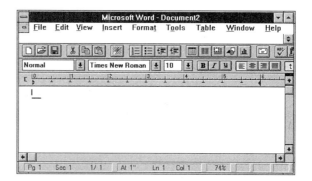

The MyTool Application

The MyTool application demonstrates how to incorporate and design a toolbar.

Before you start writing the MyTool application, execute the copy of it that resides in your C:\VCPROG\ORIGINAL\CH21\MyTool directory.

To execute the MyTool application:

☐ Use Run from Program Manager's File menu to execute
  C:\VCPROG\ORIGINAL\CH21\MYTOOL\MyTool.EXE.

  Windows responds by executing the MyTool application. The main window
  of MyTool.EXE is shown in Figure 21.2.

The MyTool application has four popup menus: File, Try It, View, and Help. These popup menus are shown in Figures 21.3, 21.4, 21.5, and 21.6.

Figure 21.2.
The MyTool
application's main
window.

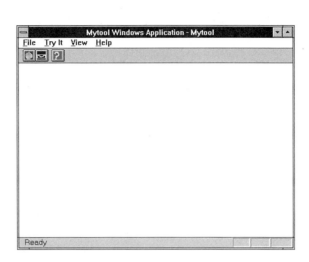

Figure 21.3.
The MyTool
application's File
menu.

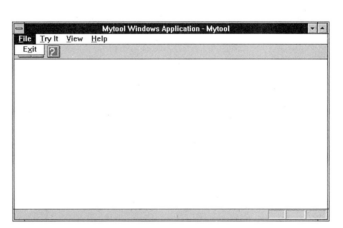

Figure 21.4.
The MyTool
application's Try It
menu.

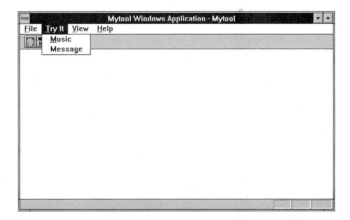

Figure 21.5.
The MyTool
application's View
menu.

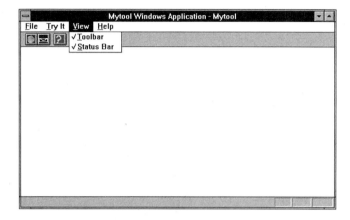

Figure 21.6.
The MyTool
application's Help
menu.

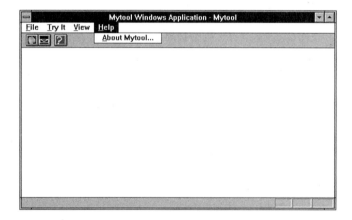

☐ Select Message from the Try It menu.

> *MyTool responds by displaying a message telling you which menu item you selected.*

☐ Click the OK button of the message box to close it.

☐ Select Music from the Try It menu.

> *MyTool responds by playing music through the PC speaker.*

The MyTool application contains a toolbar. The leftmost icon on the toolbar is a picture of a speaker grill.

☐ Click the leftmost icon on the toolbar.

> *MyTool responds in the same way as when you select the Music item from the Try It menu.*

☐ Click the middle icon on the toolbar.

> *MyTool responds in the same way as when you select the Message item from the Try It menu.*

☐ Click the rightmost icon on the toolbar.

> *MyTool responds in the same way as when you select the About item from the Help menu.*

☐ Terminate the MyTool application by selecting Exit from the File menu.

Now that you know what the MyTool application should do, you're ready to write it.

Creating the Project of the MyTool Application

To create the project of the MyTool application:

☐ Select AppWizard from the Project menu.

> *Visual C++ responds by running AppWizard.*

☐ Use the Directory list box to select the C:\VCPROG\PRACTICE\CH21 directory.

☐ Type mytool in the Project Name box.

Now your AppWizard dialog box looks as shown in Figure 21.7.

Figure 21.7.
The AppWizard dialog box for the MyTool application.

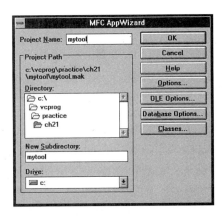

☐ Click the Options button and set the options as shown in Figure 21.8. Note that, unlike in previous applications, you now have to set the Initial Toolbar check box inside the Options dialog box.

> **NOTE**
>
> When you design an application that contains a toolbar and a status bar, let ClassWizard do the work for you. By setting the Initial Toolbar check box as shown in Figure 21.8, you're telling Visual C++ to insert all the necessary code that supports a toolbar and a status bar.

Figure 21.8.
Setting the options
for the MyTool
application.

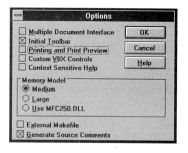

☐ Click the OK button of the Options dialog box and then click the OK button of the AppWizard dialog box and finally click the Create button of the New Application Information dialog box.

> *AppWizard responds by creating the MyTool project and all the skeleton files of the MyTool application.*

To remove the debug options of the project (so you'll have a small EXE file):

☐ Select Project from the Options menu of Visual C++, click the Release radio button, and then click the OK button of the dialog box.

The Visual Design of the Menu

Now you'll visually design the menu of the MyTool application.

☐ Use App Studio to implement the menu of the MyTool application per Table 21.1.

Table 21.1. The MyTool application's menu.
Figures relating to menu: 21.3, 21.4, 21.5, 21.6

Menu Item
&File
E&xit
&Try It
&Music
Messa&ge
&View
&Toolbar
&Status Bar
&Help
&About Mytool...

Figure 21.9.
The View menu.

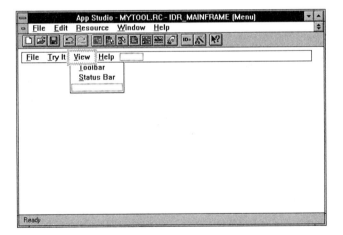

> **NOTE**
>
> Note that you did not have to design the View popup menu! AppWizard designed it for you because you checked the Initial Toolbar option when you created the project (see Figure 21.8).

Figure 21.10.
The Try It menu.

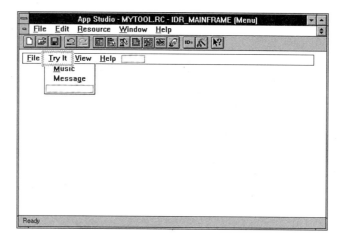

Don't forget to delete the accelerator keys of the menu items that you removed:

☐ Select MYTOOL.RC [MFC-Resource Script] from the Window menu of App
Studio, select Accelerator in the Type list, and then double-click
IDR_MAINFRAME in the Resources list.

☐ Delete the accelerator keys that aren't used by the application. In particular,
delete the accelerator keys of the ID_FILE_NEW, ID_FILE_OPEN, and
ID_FILE_SAVE menu items.

If you don't delete these accelerator keys, they will be active during runtime. If the
user presses Ctrl+N, for example, the application will respond as if the user selected
New from the File menu (even though you removed it from the menu).

To save your work:

☐ Select Save from App Studio's File menu.

The visual implementation of the MyTool application's menu is completed.

> **NOTE**
>
> The MyTool application doesn't have a custom dialog box. It only has an
> About dialog box.

Note that at this point, you haven't written a single line of code! Nevertheless, the
MyTool application already has some powerful features. To see these features in
action:

☐ Compile/link the MyTool application and then execute it.

The main window of MyTool appears. As shown in Figure 21.11, the main window has a toolbar and a status bar.

Figure 21.11.
The MyTool
application's main
window.

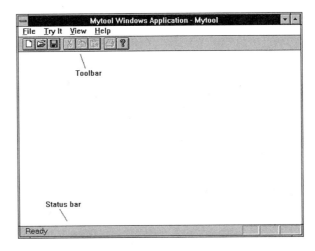

The Music and Message menu items of the Try It menu are dimmed because you haven't attached any code to them. However, the items of the View menu are available and operational. Now you can see them in action.

Currently, the toolbar and the status bar are visible. To hide the status bar:

☐ Select Status Bar from the View menu.

MyTool responds by removing the check mark to the Status Bar menu item and hiding the status bar.

☐ Select Status Bar from the View menu again.

MyTool responds by adding a check mark to the Status Bar menu item and displaying the status bar.

In a similar manner, you can show or hide the toolbar. That is, select the Toolbar menu item from the View menu to show or hide the toolbar. (For now, don't click any of the toolbar's icons.)

☐ Display the status bar and then press the Caps Lock key several times.

MyTool responds by displaying the status of the Caps Lock key on the status bar.

☐ Press the Scroll Lock key several times.

MyTool responds by displaying the status of the Scroll Lock key on the status bar.

☐ Press the Alt key and then use the arrow keys to move from menu to menu.

MyTool responds by displaying a message on the status bar telling you the purpose of the highlighted menu item. (Later in this chapter, you'll design the status bar messages of the Try It menu.)

☐ Select Exit from the File menu to terminate the MyTool application.

As you can see, MyTool includes a sophisticated toolbar and status bar (a gift from Visual C++). All you have to do is customize the toolbar and the status bar according to your application.

Attaching Code to the Menu Items

Now you'll attach code to the Music and Message menu items of the Try It menu.

☐ Use ClassWizard to add a function for the event:

Class Name:	CMytoolView
Object ID:	ID_TRYIT_MESSAGE
Message:	COMMAND
Function Name:	OnTryitMessage()

☐ Add code to the OnTryitMessage() function that resides in the MYTOOVW.CPP file. After you add the code, the function looks as follows:

```
void CMytoolView::OnTryitMessage()
{
    // TODO: Add your command handler code here


    /////////////////////////
    // MY CODE STARTS HERE
    /////////////////////////

    MessageBox ("Try It -> Message was selected");


    /////////////////////////
    // MY CODE ENDS HERE
    /////////////////////////

}
```

The code you typed displays a message whenever the user selects Message from the Try It menu.

☐ Use ClassWizard to add a function for the event:

Class Name:	CMytoolView
Object ID:	ID_TRYIT_MUSIC
Message:	COMMAND
Function Name:	OnTryitMusic()

☐ Add code to the OnTryitMusic() function that resides in the MYTOOVW.CPP file. After you add the code, the function looks as follows:

```
void CMytoolView::OnTryitMusic()
{
    // TODO: Add your command handler code here

    /////////////////////////
    // MY CODE STARTS HERE
    /////////////////////////

    // Play the music
    sp_PlaySnd( m_MusicSession,
                SP_START_OF_FILE,
                SP_END_OF_FILE );



    /////////////////////////
    // MY CODE ENDS HERE
    /////////////////////////

}
```

The code you typed plays music through the PC speaker. The handler of the WAV session that is played is m_MusicSession.

Of course, in order to use the sp_PlaySnd() function, you must

Use the IMPORTS statements in MYTOOL.DEF.
Add an #include statement for the prototypes of the TegoSND.DLL functions in MyTool.H.
Declare the variable m_MusicSession as a data member of the view class in MYTOOVW.H.
Open a WAV session in the constructor function of the view class in MYTOOVW.CPP.
Close the WAV session in the destructor function of the view class in MYTOOVW.CPP.

To do the preceding:

☐ Open the MYTOOL.DEF file and add the IMPORTS statements for the TegoSND.DLL functions. After you add the IMPORTS statements, the MYTOOL.DEF file looks as follows:

```
; mytool.def : Declares the module parameters for the application.

NAME            MYTOOL
DESCRIPTION     'MYTOOL Windows Application'
EXETYPE         WINDOWS

CODE            PRELOAD MOVEABLE DISCARDABLE
DATA            PRELOAD MOVEABLE MULTIPLE

HEAPSIZE        1024    ; initial heap size
; Stack size is passed as argument to linker's /STACK option


;;;;;;;;;;;;;;;;;;;;;;;;;;
; MY CODE STARTS HERE
;;;;;;;;;;;;;;;;;;;;;;;;;;

;;;;;;;;;;;;;;;;;;;;;;;;;;;;;;;;;;;;;;;;;;;;;;;;
; sp_ functions from the TegoSND.DLL library
;;;;;;;;;;;;;;;;;;;;;;;;;;;;;;;;;;;;;;;;;;;;;;;;

IMPORTS
TegoSND.sp_OpenSession
TegoSND.sp_PlaySnd
TegoSND.sp_MouseOn
TegoSND.sp_MouseOff
TegoSND.sp_CloseSession


;;;;;;;;;;;;;;;;;;;;;;;;;;
; MY CODE ENDS HERE
;;;;;;;;;;;;;;;;;;;;;;;;;;
```

☐ Add an #include statement for the prototypes of the TegoSND.DLL function in MyTool.H. After you #include the statement, the beginning of your MYTOOL.H file should look as follows:

```
// mytool.h : main header file for the MYTOOL application
//

#ifndef __AFXWIN_H__
#error include 'stdafx.h' before including this file for PCH
#endif

#include "resource.h"       // main symbols
```

```
/////////////////////
// MY CODE STARTS HERE
/////////////////////

#include "\vcProg\DLL\TegoSND.H"

/////////////////////
// MY CODE ENDS HERE
/////////////////////
.....
.....
.....
```

☐ Open the MYTOOVW.H file and add the data member m_MusicSession to the declaration of the view class. After you add this data member, the class declaration looks as follows:

```
class CMytoolView : public CView
{
protected: // create from serialization only
    CMytoolView();
    DECLARE_DYNCREATE(CMytoolView)

// Attributes
public:
    CMytoolDoc* GetDocument();

    /////////////////////
    // MY CODE STARTS HERE
    /////////////////////

    int m_MusicSession;

    /////////////////////
    // MY CODE ENDS HERE
    /////////////////////

    ....
    ....
    ....
};
```

☐ Open the MYTOOVW.CPP file and open a WAV session in the constructor function of the view class. After you add this code, the constructor function looks as follows:

```
CMytoolView::CMytoolView()
{
    // TODO: add construction code here
```

```
/////////////////////
// MY CODE STARTS HERE
/////////////////////

char FileToOpen[255];


// Open the Kennedy WAV session
strcpy ( FileToOpen, "\\vcProg\\WAV\\LastC1M0.WAV" );
m_MusicSession = sp_OpenSession ( FileToOpen );


// If WAV session can not be opened,
// display message box.
if ( m_MusicSession < 0 )
    {
    CString Message, Caption;
    Message = "Can't open the file: ";
    Message = Message + FileToOpen;
    Caption = "Error";
    MessageBox ( Message, Caption );
    }

/////////////////////
// MY CODE ENDS HERE
/////////////////////
```

}

☐ Open the MYTOOVW.CPP file and close the WAV session in the destructor
function of the view class. After you add this code, the destructor function
should look as follows:

```
CMytoolView::~CMytoolView()
{

    /////////////////////
    // MY CODE STARTS HERE
    /////////////////////

    // Close the WAV session
    sp_CloseSession ( m_MusicSession );

    /////////////////////,
    // MY CODE ENDS HERE
    /////////////////////

}
```

☐ Compile/link the MyTool application and execute it.

☐ Select the Message item from the Try It menu.

MyTool responds by displaying a message stating that you selected Message from the Try It menu.

Select Music from the Try It menu.

MyTool responds by playing music through the PC speaker.

☐ Experiment with the MyTool application and then select Exit from the File menu to terminate the application.

But What About the Toolbar?

So far, the MyTool application displays the default toolbar that was automatically created when you set the Initial Toolbar in the Options dialog box, as shown in Figure 21.8.

Now you'll learn how to modify the default toolbar so that it will be appropriate to your application. The important thing to remember is that when you click the icon on the toolbar, it produces the same result as selecting the corresponding item from the menu. In other words, the toolbar is just another way of executing a menu item. (You can design an icon on the toolbar that doesn't have a corresponding menu item, but usually Windows applications have a menu item for each icon in the toolbar.)

Figure 21.12 shows the icons on the default toolbar. (The figure has been enlarged so that you can take a better look at these icons.)

Figure 21.12.
The icons on the
default toolbar.

The file MAINFRM.CPP contains code (which Visual C++ wrote for you) that declares an array, buttons[]. This array corresponds to the buttons (icons) on the toolbar. To look at this code:

☐ Open the MAINFRM.CPP file and search for the declaration of the buttons[] array.

Currently, the declaration of the buttons[] array looks as follows:

```
// toolbar buttons - IDs are command buttons
static UINT BASED_CODE buttons[] =
{
```

```
        // same order as in the bitmap 'toolbar.bmp'
        ID_FILE_NEW,
        ID_FILE_OPEN,
        ID_FILE_SAVE,
            ID_SEPARATOR,
        ID_EDIT_CUT,
        ID_EDIT_COPY,
        ID_EDIT_PASTE,
            ID_SEPARATOR,
        ID_FILE_PRINT,
        ID_APP_ABOUT,
};
```

In the case of the MyTool application, you need only three icons on the toolbar:

> The Music icon
> The Message icon
> The Help icon

And for cosmetic reasons, it would be nice if there were a separator between the Message icon and the Help icon.

☐ Modify the declaration of the buttons[] array (in the MAINFRM.CPP file). After the modification, the declaration of the buttons[] array looks as follows:

```
/////////////////////////////////////////////////////
// arrays of IDs used to initialize control bars

// toolbar buttons - IDs are command buttons
static UINT BASED_CODE buttons[] =
{
    // same order as in the bitmap 'toolbar.bmp'

    ///////////////////////
    // MY CODE STARTS HERE
    ///////////////////////

    ID_TRYIT_MUSIC,
    ID_TRYIT_MESSAGE,
        ID_SEPARATOR,
    ID_APP_ABOUT,
```

```
///////////////////
// MY CODE ENDS HERE
///////////////////
```

```
};
```

The code you typed defines the first icon on the tool bar as corresponding to the menu item ID_TRYIT_MUSIC, defines the second icon as corresponding to the ID_TRYIT_MESSAGE menu item, and defines the third icon as corresponding to the ID_APP_ABOUT menu item. An ID_SEPARATOR is inserted between ID_TRYIT_MESSAGE and ID_APP_ABOUT. ID_SEPARATOR represents a separator (space) between the icons.

Save the MAINFRM.CPP file:

☐ Select Save from Visual C++'s File menu.

Even though you haven't finished writing the MyTool application, compile/link and execute it to see the effect of changing the buttons[] array:

☐ Compile/link and execute the MyTool application.

MyTool's main window appears. As shown in Figure 21.13, MyTool's toolbar contains only three icons. However, these are the wrong icons! That is, the icons are operational, but the pictures on the icons have nothing to do with the particular tasks that are executed when the icons are clicked.

☐ Click the leftmost icon.

MyTool responds in the same manner that it does when you select Music from the Try It menu.

☐ Click the middle icon.

MyTool responds in the same manner that it does when you select Message from the Try It menu.

☐ Click the rightmost icon.

MyTool responds in the same manner that it does when you select About from the Help menu.

☐ Select Exit from the File menu to terminate the MyTool application.

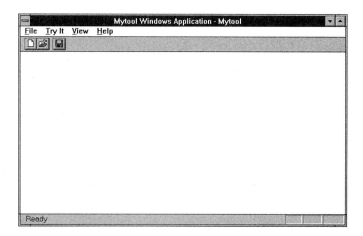

Figure 21.13.
The MyTool
application's main
window with three
inappropriate icons.

Replacing the Icons on the Toolbar

Now you'll replace the icons on the toolbar with more appropriate icons.

☐ Select App Studio from Visual C++'s Tools menu.

☐ Highlight the Bitmap item in the Type list and then double-click IDR_MAINFRAME in the Resource list (see Figure 21.14).

App Studio responds by displaying the IDR_MAINFRAME toolbar, ready for you to edit (see Figure 21.15).

☐ Select Clear from the Edit menu.

App Studio responds by clearing the bitmap (see Figure 21.16).

Note that in Figure 21.15, only three icons are shown. This is because the right edge of the bitmap has been dragged to the left so that only the three leftmost icons are exposed.

The bitmap that you're now drawing includes three toolbar icons. Each icon on the toolbar is 15 pixels tall and 16 pixels wide. Because there are three icons on the toolbar, the bitmap that you're now drawing should be 15 pixels tall and 48 pixels (16×3=48) wide. Don't worry about the separator between the icons, because Visual C++ will insert it automatically. (Recall that you specified a separator when you declared the buttons[] array.)

Figure 21.14.
Opening the
toolbar.

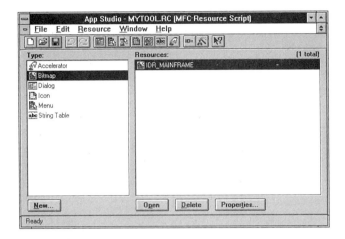

Figure 21.15.
The toolbar, ready
to be edited.

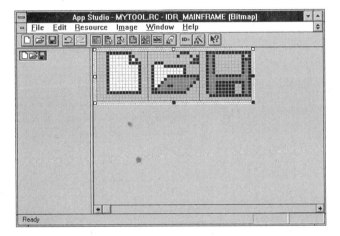

Figure 21.16.
Erasing the contents
of the bitmap.

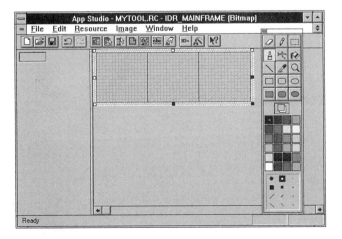

Now you'll use the drawing tools to draw icons that are more appropriate to the particular tasks that are performed when the icons are clicked. Recall that the leftmost button serves as the Music item on the Try It menu, the middle icon serves as the Message item on the Try It menu, and the rightmost icon serves as the About item on the Help menu.

☐ If the Tool window is not currently displayed, select Show Graphics Palette from App Studio's Window menu to display it.

☐ Apply your artistic talent to draw the icons. (If you don't have much patience or artistic talent, select the color black and use the Pencil tool to draw a musical note in the leftmost icon, the character M in the middle icon, and the ? character in the rightmost icon.)

If you put a little effort into the drawings, you can draw something like Figure 21.18. The leftmost icon shows a picture of a speaker grill, the middle icon shows a picture of an envelope, and the rightmost icon shows a picture of a question mark.

When you draw the icons, remember that the left icon should fit within the first 16 pixels, the middle icon should fit within the next 16 pixels, and the right icon should fit within the last 16 pixels.

Figure 21.17.
The icons on the
toolbar (lazy
version).

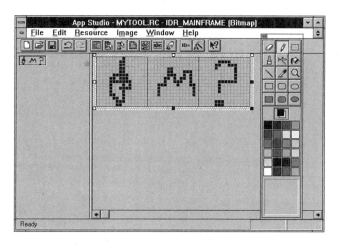

☐ Select Save from the File menu to save your work.

☐ Switch back to Visual C++ and compile/link the MyTool application.

☐ Execute the MyTool application.

Figure 21.18.
The icons on the
toolbar (non-lazy
version).

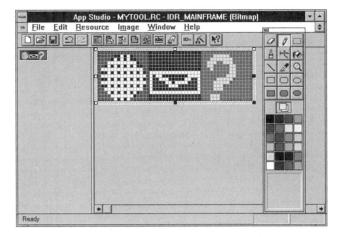

The MyTool window appears. As shown in Figure 21.19, the toolbar contains the icons that you designed in App Studio.

Figure 21.19.
The MyTool
window with the
three custom-made
icons.

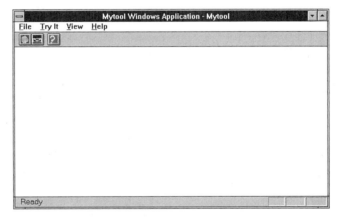

Note that there is a space between the middle icon and rightmost icon on the toolbar. (Recall that you inserted ID_SEPARATOR between these icons in the definition of the buttons[] array.)

Customizing the Status Bar for Menu Prompts

Take a look at Figure 21.20. It shows that the prompt on the status bar when the Toolbar menu item is highlighted is, "Show or hide the toolbar."

Similarly, Figure 20.21 shows the status bar when the Status Bar menu item is highlighted. In this case, the status bar displays the message, "Show or hide the status bar."

719

Figure 21.20.
The status bar
when the Toolbar
menu item is
highlighted.

Figure 21.21.
The status bar
when the Status
Bar menu item is
highlighted.

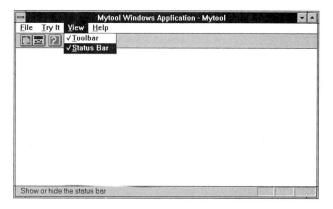

However, when you highlight the Music or Message menu items on the Try It menu, the status bar doesn't display a message. Why? Because you didn't set the prompt of the status bar for these menu items. Here's how you set the prompt of the status bar:

☐ Use App Studio to display the menu in its design mode.

☐ Double-click the Music menu item.

> *App Studio responds by displaying the properties of the Music menu item (see Figure 21.22).*

As shown in Figure 21.22, the Prompt box is empty. This means that when the user highlights the Music menu item, the status bar will not display any message.

☐ Type `Play music through the PC speaker` in the Prompt box (see Figure 21.23).

Figure 21.22.
The Properties
window of the
Music menu item
(without a status
bar prompt).

Figure 21.23.
Assigning a message
prompt to the
Music menu item.

☐ Double-click the Message menu item and type `Display a message` in the Prompt box of its Properties window.

☐ Select Save from App Studio's File menu.

☐ Compile/link the MyTool application and then execute it.

☐ Press the Alt key and then use the arrow keys to highlight the Music menu item.

As shown in Figure 21.24, MyTool displays the message "Play music through the PC speaker" in the status bar.

Figure 21.24.
The prompt on the
status bar when the
Music menu item is
highlighted.

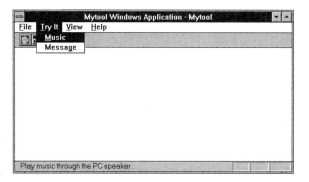

NOTE

As discussed previously, the toolbar is merely a pictorial representation of the menu. As such, the status bar displays the menu prompts when you push the corresponding icons on the toolbar. For example, push the left mouse button on the leftmost icon of the tool bar, which is equivalent to selecting Music from the Try It menu. While the mouse button is still pushed down, the status bar displays the message that corresponds to the prompt for the Music menu item.

22

Multimedia: Playing and Recording WAV Files

In this chapter you'll write an
application that uses the
TegoMM.VBX multimedia control
to play and record a WAV file
through a Windows-compatible
sound card. You'll learn what the
TegoMM.VBX control is and
how to use it to play and
record WAV files.

In this chapter you'll also learn how to use the TegoMM.VBX control to play sound through the PC speaker.

> **NOTE**
>
> The application you'll write in this chapter requires a Windows-compatible sound card. However, even if you don't have a sound card, you'll still be able to play the WAV files through your PC speaker.

What Is the TegoMM.VBX Multimedia Control?

The TegoMM.VBX control is a file that enables you to write multimedia programs easily. You can use it to play multimedia files, such as WAV files and MIDI files, through a Windows-compatible sound card. You can also use the TegoMM.VBX control to control multimedia devices such as audio CD drives. The TegoMM.VBX control can also be used to play WAV files through the PC speaker. That is, if your end user doesn't have a sound card, you can use the TegoMM.VBX control to play WAV files through the PC's internal speaker.

The TegoMM.VBX control was designed to work with Microsoft Visual Basic for Windows and Microsoft Visual C++. In this chapter you'll learn how to use the TegoMM.VBX control from within your Visual C++ programs to play and record WAV files with a sound card.

The most common uses of the TegoMM.VBX control are

    Playing and recording WAV sound files with a sound card
    Playing MIDI files
    Playing CD audio
    Playing video files
    Playing WAV files through the PC speaker (without a sound card)

> **NOTE**
>
> The TegoMM.VBX file included with the book's CD is the limited version of the TegoMM.VBX multimedia control. The full version of the control has more

features. The price of the full version TegoMM.VBX control is $29.95 (plus $5.00 for shipping and handling).

You can order the full version of the TegoMM.VBX control directly from

TegoSoft, Inc.
Box 389
Bellmore, NY 11710
ATTN: TegoMM.VBX for Visual C++
Phone: (516) 783-4824

NOTE

If an application that uses the TegoMM.VBX control is going to work, the TegoMM.VBX file must reside in any of the following directories:

> The \WINDOWS\SYSTEM directory
> Any directory that is within the DOS PATH
> The directory where the application resides

Typically, you copy the TegoMM.VBX file into the \WINDOWS\SYSTEM directory so that other applications can also use the TegoMM.VBX file and so your program doesn't have to depend on the current setting of the user's DOS PATH.

When you installed the book's CD, the TegoMM.VBX file was copied into your \WINDOWS\SYSTEM directory.

The WAVE Application

You'll now write the WAVE application. It is an example of a multimedia application that enables the user to play and record a wave file. Wave files are standard Windows sound files that have the extension .WAV (for example, MySong.WAV or MySpeech.WAV).

Before you start writing the WAVE application, execute the copy of it in your C:\VCPROG\ORIGINAL\CH22\WAVE directory.

> **NOTE**
>
> The WAVE.EXE application uses the TegoMM.VBX control to play a WAV file through a sound card. When you installed the book's CD, the file `TegoMM.VBX` was copied to your `\WINDOWS\SYSTEM` directory. If for some reason this file doesn't exist in your `\WINDOWS\SYSTEM` directory, you won't be able to run the WAVE application.
>
> If you don't see the `TegoMM.VBX` file in your `\WINDOWS\SYSTEM` directory, copy this file from the CD to your `\WINDOWS\SYSTEM` directory.

To execute the WAVE application:

☐ Use the Run item from the Program Manager's File menu to run
`C:\VCPROG\ORIGINAL\CH22\WAVE\WAVE.EXE`.

Windows responds by executing the WAVE application. The WAVE application first displays a limited version message box from the TegoMM.VBX multimedia control.

☐ Click the OK button of the message box.

The main window of WAVE.EXE appears, as shown in Figure 22.1.

Figure 22.1.
The WAVE
application's
main window.

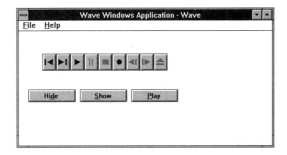

As you can see, the main window of the application contains a multimedia control and three regular buttons (Hide, Show, and Play).

The multimedia control itself is made up of nine buttons: Previous, Next, Play, Pause, Stop, Record, Back, Step, and Eject (see Figure 22.2).

Figure 22.2.
The multimedia
control.

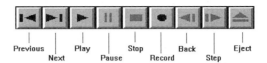

| Previous | | Play | | Stop | | Back | | Eject |
| Next | | Pause | | Record | | Step | |

NOTE

Note that the Eject button of the multimedia control is dimmed (that is, not available). That's because the WAVE application uses the multimedia control to play WAV files, and it makes no sense to "eject" a WAV file. However, if a certain application uses the multimedia control to play audio CDs and the user's CD player supports the Eject feature, the Eject button will appear as available (not dimmed).

The status of the multimedia control buttons also depends on the current playback status. For example, because currently there is no playback in progress, the Stop button is dimmed. Once you start the playback, the Stop button will become available.

To start the playback of a WAV file:

☐ Click the Play button (the third button from the left) of the multimedia control. (See Figure 22.2.)

The WAVE application responds by playing the WAV file ItsBeen1.WAV.

This WAV file was copied to your \VCPROG\WAV directory when you installed the book's CD. If for some reason this file doesn't exist in your \VCPROG\WAV directory, all of the multimedia control's buttons will be dimmed (not available), and you won't be able to start the playback.

NOTE

If you don't have a sound card, you can play the WAV file through the PC speaker. However, you'll need to change a single statement in the source code of the WAVE application. You'll have a chance to do so later in this chapter when you write the WAVE application's code. So if the multimedia control is currently dimmed because you don't have a sound card, don't worry. You'll take care of this later.

To record something:

☐ Click the Previous button, the leftmost button on the multimedia control. (See Figure 22.2.)

   The WAVE application responds by changing the playback position to the beginning of the WAV file.

☐ Prepare yourself to record and then click the Record button, the second button from the right on the multimedia control. (See Figure 22.2.)

☐ Speak into your sound card's microphone. When you're done, click the Stop button on the multimedia control. (See Figure 22.2 for its location.)

To hear your recording:

☐ Click the Previous button, and then click the Play button.

   The WAVE application responds by playing your recording, followed by the playback of the original ItsBeen1.WAV *file.*

☐ Experiment with the other buttons on the multimedia control. Note that during the playback of the WAV file, the Stop and Pause buttons are available, and you can use them to stop or pause the playback.

Experiment with the Hide, Show, and Play buttons that are located below the multimedia control:

☐ Click the Hide button.

   The WAVE application responds by hiding the multimedia control.

☐ Click the Play button.

   The WAVE application responds by playing the WAV file.

☐ Click the Show button.

   The WAVE application responds by redisplaying the multimedia control.

As you have just seen and heard, the WAVE application can play the WAV file even when the multimedia control is hidden.

The WAVE application has two popup menus: File and Help. These popup menus are shown in Figures 22.3 and 22.4.

Figure 22.3.
The WAVE
application's File
popup menu.

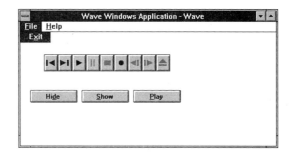

Figure 22.4.
The WAVE
application's Help
popup menu.

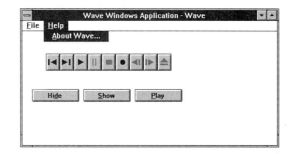

To exit from the WAVE application:

☐ Select Exit from the File menu.

You may think that because the WAVE application supports such powerful multimedia features, you'll have to write a lot of code. However, this isn't the case! All the multimedia features that you saw and heard are built into the TegoMM.VBX control. All you have to do is write code that uses the MCI.VBX control. As you will soon see, using the TegoMM.VBX control from within your Visual C++ application is easy and requires a small amount of code-writing.

Now that you know what the WAVE application should do, you can start writing it.

Creating the Project of the WAVE Application

To create the project of the WAVE application:

☐ Select AppWizard from the Project menu.

Visual C++ responds by running AppWizard.

☐ Use the Directory list box to select the directory C:\VCPROG\PRACTICE\CH22.

☐ Type wave in the Project Name box.

Now your AppWizard dialog box looks as shown in Figure 22.5.

Figure 22.5.
The WAVE
application's
AppWizard dialog
box.

☐ Click the Options button and set the options as shown in Figure 22.6.

WARNING

Because you want the WAVE application to support a VBX control (namely the TegoMM.VBX control), the Custom VBX Controls option should be checked. As you can see from Figure 22.6, the Custom VBX Controls check box is indeed checked.

Figure 22.6.
Setting the options
for the WAVE
application.

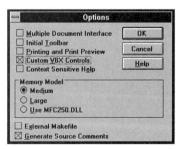

☐ Click the OK button of the Options dialog box, click the OK button of the AppWizard dialog box, and finally click the Create button of the New Application Information dialog box.

730

AppWizard responds by creating the WAVE project and all the skeleton files of the WAVE application.

To remove the debug options of the project (so you'll have a small EXE file):

☐ Select Project from Visual C++'s Options menu, click the Release radio button, and then click the OK button of the dialog box.

NOTE

In your future projects, if you ever forget to set the Custom VBX Controls option in AppWizard's Options dialog box, you can still make your application support VBX files without starting AppWizard all over again. You do that by adding the statement

```
EnableVBX();
```

in the `InitInstance()` function of the main application source file of the application.

When you set the Custom VBX Controls option in AppWizard, this statement is automatically added to the `InitInstance()` function. You can verify this as follows:

Open the main application file of the WAVE application (`WAVE.CPP`).

Look for the `EnableVBX()` statement in the `InitInstance()` function.

Creating the Form of the Application

As shown in Figure 22.1, the main window of the WAVE application should contain a multimedia control and three regular buttons.

To implement this form, you'll replace the current view class of the application with a new view class derived from the `CFormView` class.

Follow these steps to create the form of the application:

☐ Use the Windows File Manager (or DOS Shell) to delete the two view class files of the WAVE application:

Delete `C:\VCPROG\PRACTICE\CH22\WAVE\WAVEVIEW.CPP`.

Delete `C:\VCPROG\PRACTICE\CH22\WAVE\WAVEVIEW.H`.

☐ Select ClassWizard from Visual C++'s Browse menu.

> *ClassWizard responds by displaying a dialog box telling you that the view class files don't exist.*

☐ Click the OK button of the dialog box.

☐ Click the Remove button of the Repair Class Information dialog box.

☐ Click the OK button of ClassWizard's dialog box.

You have just finished removing the view class of the WAVE application.

In the following steps you'll create a dialog box, you'll create a CFormView type class for this dialog box, and you'll make this class the new view class of the application:

☐ Select App Studio from Visual C++'s Tools menu.

☐ Create a new dialog box with App Studio.

☐ Double-click in a free area of the new dialog box.

☐ Select Styles from the drop-down list box at the upper-right corner of the Properties window.

Set the Styles properties of the dialog box as follows:

☐ Select Child from the Style box.

☐ Select None from the Border box.

☐ Uncheck the Visible property (that is, remove the check mark from the Visible check box).

☐ Select General from the drop-down list box at the upper-right corner of the Properties window and make sure that the Caption box is empty.

Now, connect the dialog box to a class derived from CFormView:

☐ Select ClassWizard from App Studio's Resource menu.

> *ClassWizard responds by displaying the Add Class dialog box.*

☐ Type CWaveView in the Class Name box.

☐ Set the Class Type to CFormView.

☐ Make sure the header filename is waveview.h and the implementation filename is waveview.cpp.

☐ Click the Create Class button.

☐ Click ClassWizard's OK button to go back to App Studio.

You have finished creating the new view class of the application. This view class is a derived class from the MFC CFormView class and is connected to the dialog box you created. Thus, the main dialog box of the application will be the dialog box you created.

The Visual Implementation of the Dialog Box

One of the controls you have to place in the WAVE application's dialog box is the multimedia control (see Figure 22.1). Before you can place the multimedia control in a dialog box, you must first install the multimedia control (TegoMM.VBX) in App Studio's Tools window. After you do this, you can place the control in a dialog box just as you would place any other control (a push button, an edit box, and so on).

Follow these steps to install the TegoMM.VBX control in App Studio's Tools window:

☐ Select Install Controls from App Studio's File menu.

> *App Studio responds by displaying the Install Controls dialog box (see Figure 22.7).*

Figure 22.7.
The App Studio's
Install Controls
dialog box.

As you can see from Figure 22.7, App Studio lists all the VBX files that reside in your \WINDOWS\SYSTEM directory. The Installed Files list contains all the VBX files that are currently installed in App Studio. In Figure 22.7, the Installed Files list is empty because no VBX files have been installed yet.

To install the `TegoMM.VBX` file:

☐ Select the file `TegoMM.VBX` and then click the Install button.

> *App Studio responds by adding* `TegoMM.VBX` *to the Installed Files list (see Figure 22.8).*

Figure 22.8.
Installing the
TegoMM. VBX
control in App
Studio.

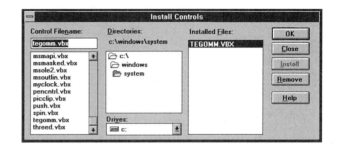

☐ Click the Close button of the Install Controls dialog box.

The TegoMM.VBX control is now installed in App Studio's Tools window! (See Figure 22.9.) You can now place the multimedia control in the dialog box, just as you would place any other control.

Figure 22.9.
The MCI.VBX
(MCI multimedia)
control.

The TegoMM.VBX multimedia control

Implement the WAVE application's dialog box per Table 22.1.

Table 22.1. The WAVE application's dialog box.

Class Name:	`CWaveView`	
Figure:	22.10	
OK button:	No	
Cancel button:	No	

Object	*Property*	*Setting*
Dialog Box	ID	`IDD_DIALOG1`
Multimedia Control	ID	`IDC_TEGOMM_WAV`
	Variable	`m_wav` (Type: `CVBControl *`)
Button	ID	`IDC_BUTTON_HIDE`
	Caption	`Hi&de`
Button	ID	`IDC_BUTTON_SHOW`
	Caption	`&Show`
Button	ID	`IDC_BUTTON_PLAY`
	Caption	`&Play`

NOTE

Table 22.1 specifies that the ID of the multimedia control should be `IDC_TEGOMM_WAV`. Of course, you can give the multimedia control any ID you wish; however, it's a good idea to give it an ID that describes the function of the control. In the WAVE application, the multimedia control will be used to play WAV files; thus, you name it `IDC_TEGOMM_WAV`. As you will see later in the book, it's possible to use the multimedia control with other types of multimedia files and devices (for example, MIDI files, video files, the PC speaker, and so on). For example, if a certain application needs to play both WAV files and MIDI files, you can include two multimedia controls—name one control `IDC_TEGOMM_WAV` and the other control `IDC_TEGOMM_MID`.

> **NOTE**
>
> Table 22.1 specifies that the Caption property of the Hide button should be
> set to Hi&de. The reason for prefixing the d character with & and not H is that
> the Help menu already uses the H character as a hot key. As you can see from
> Figure 22.1, the hot key of the Help menu is H, and the hot key of the Hide
> button is d. Thus, pressing Alt+H will open the Help menu, and pressing
> Alt+D will produce the same effect as clicking the Hide button.

Now your dialog box looks as shown in Figure 22.10.

*Figure 22.10.
The WAVE
application's
dialog box.*

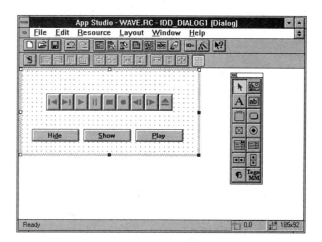

Table 22.1 instructed you to attach a variable called m_wav of type CVBControl * to
the multimedia control. As you will see when you write the WAVE application's code
later in the chapter, the m_wav variable is used to send commands to the multimedia
control. Note that CVBControl is an MFC class. Thus, by making m_wav a variable of
type CVBControl *, you are actually making m_wav a pointer to an object of class
CVBControl. The MFC class CVBControl was specifically designed to work with VBX
controls.

The multimedia control that you placed in the dialog box has several properties. To
see these properties:

☐ Double-click the multimedia control.

> *App Studio responds by displaying the General properties of the multimedia
> control.*

☐ Select Styles from the drop-down list box at the upper-right corner of the Properties window.

App Studio responds by displaying the Styles Properties window of the multimedia control (see Figure 22.11).

Figure 22.11.
The multimedia
control's Styles
Properties window.

As you can see from Figure 22.11, the multimedia control has several properties. (Note that, depending on your particular version of the TegoMM.VBX control, you may see more properties in your Styles Properties window.) Although you can set these properties during design time (now), it is a better programming habit to set them from within your code during runtime. This way, your code is easier to follow and understand. Someone else can see how you set the multimedia control's properties by reading the application's code instead of running App Studio. So don't change any of the multimedia control's properties. You'll set these properties when you write the application's code. Note that in addition to the properties shown in Figure 22.11, the TegoMM.VBX control has additional properties that are available only during runtime.

Save your work:

☐ Select Save from App Studio's File menu.

You've finished designing the dialog box! This dialog box will appear in the main window of the application.

The Visual Implementation of the Menu

The WAVE application should have a menu with two popup menus, as shown in Figures 22.3 and 22.4.

☐ Use App Studio to implement the WAVE application's menu according to Table 22.2.

Table 22.2. The WAVE application's menu.
Figures relating to menu: 22.3, 22.4

Menu Item
&File
E&xit
&Help
&About Wave...

Don't forget to delete the accelerator keys of the menu items that you removed:

☐ Select `WAVE.RC [MFC-Resource Script]` from App Studio's Window menu, select Accelerator from the Type list, and then double-click `IDR_MAINFRAME` in the Resources list.

☐ Delete the accelerator keys that aren't used by the WAVE application. In particular, delete the accelerator keys of the `ID_FILE_NEW`, `ID_FILE_OPEN`, and `ID_FILE_SAVE` menu items.

If you don't delete these accelerator keys, they'll be active during runtime. For example, if the user presses Ctrl+N, it will be as if the user selected New from the File menu (even though you removed that item).

Save your work:

☐ Select Save from App Studio's File menu.

The visual implementation of the WAVE application's menu is completed.

Executing the WAVE Application

Even though you haven't written a single line of code for the WAVE application, execute it to see your visual design in action:

☐ Select Rebuild All WAVE.EXE from Visual C++'s Project menu.

☐ Select Execute WAVE.EXE from the Project menu.

Visual C++ responds by executing the WAVE application. The main window of the application appears with the form that you designed in it (one multimedia control and three regular buttons).

Note that the multimedia control is dimmed (not available). In order to bring the multimedia control to life, you need to write code that sets its properties. You'll do that in the following sections.

To exit the WAVE application:

☐ Select Exit from the File menu.

Initializing the Properties of the Multimedia Control

You must write the code that initializes the multimedia control's properties in the `OnInitialUpdate()` member function of the view class. This way, when the application starts, the multimedia control will come to life.

Recall from previous chapters that Visual C++ didn't write the declaration and skeleton of the `OnInitialUpdate()` function. You have to declare this function and write its skeleton. Here's how you do that:

☐ Open the file `WAVEVIEW.H` and add code to it that defines `OnInitialUpdate()` as a member function of the `CWaveView` class. After you write this code, the `CWaveView` class declaration looks as follows:

```
class CWaveView : public CFormView
{
    DECLARE_DYNCREATE(CWaveView)
protected:
    CWaveView();

    /////////////////////////
    // MY CODE STARTS HERE
    /////////////////////////

    virtual void OnInitialUpdate();

    /////////////////////////
    // MY CODE ENDS HERE
    /////////////////////////

// Form Data
public:
    //{{AFX_DATA(CWaveView)
    enum { IDD = IDD_DIALOG1 };
    CVBControl*    m_wav;
    //}}AFX_DATA

// Attributes
public:
```

739

```
// Operations
public:

// Implementation
protected:
virtual ~CWaveView();
virtual void DoDataExchange(CDataExchange* pDX);
// Generated message map functions
//{{AFX_MSG(CWaveView)
// NOTE - ClassWizard will add/remove member functions here.
//}}AFX_MSG
DECLARE_MESSAGE_MAP()
};
```

Now write the `OnInitialUpdate()` function's code:

☐ Open the file `WAVEVIEW.CPP` and add the `OnInitialUpdate()` function to the end of the file, as follows:

```
/////////////////////////////////////////////////////
// CWaveView message handlers

/////////////////////////
// MY CODE STARTS HERE
/////////////////////////

void CWaveView::OnInitialUpdate()
{

  // Call the base class function.
  CFormView::OnInitialUpdate();

  // Set the device type for playback of WAV files.
  m_wav->SetStrProperty("DeviceType","WaveAudio");

  // To play through the PC speaker, simply set the DeviceType
  // to "PCSpeaker" as follows:
  // m_wav->SetStrProperty("DeviceType","PCSpeaker");


  // Set the WAV file name.
  m_wav->SetStrProperty("FileName",
                        "\\VCPROG\\WAV\\ITSBEEN1.WAV" );

  // Open the Wave device.
  m_wav->SetStrProperty("Command", "Open");

}

/////////////////////////
// MY CODE ENDS HERE
/////////////////////////
```

To review the `OnInitialUpdate()` function's code:

The first statement,

```
CFormView::OnInitialUpdate();
```

calls the `OnInitialUpdate()` member function of the base class. You have to call the base class `OnInitialUpdate()` function. If you don't, the multimedia control is dimmed (unavailable).

The next statement is

```
m_wav->SetStrProperty("DeviceType","WaveAudio");
```

This statement uses the `SetStrProperty()` function to set the `DeviceType` property of the multimedia control to `"WaveAudio"`. The `DeviceType` property specifies the type of device to be opened. `"WaveAudio"` is the device type that you have to specify when you want to use the multimedia control to play WAV files through a sound card.

If you don't have a sound card, specify `"PCSpeaker"` as the `DeviceType` instead of `"WaveAudio"`. In that case, the statement that sets the `DeviceType` property looks as follows:

```
m_wav->SetStrProperty("DeviceType","PCSpeaker");
```

> **NOTE**
>
> The `SetStrProperty()` function is a member function of the MFC class `CVBControl`. Recall that during the visual implementation of the dialog box, you attached the variable `m_wav` to the multimedia control and you declared `m_wav` as type `CVBControl *` (that is, a pointer to an object of class `CVBControl`).
>
> The `Str` in `SetStrProperty()` signifies that this function is used to set a string property. The first parameter of the `SetStrProperty()` function is the name of the property to be changed. The second parameter is the string value that you want to assign to the property. For example, the statement
>
> ```
> m_wav->SetStrProperty("DeviceType","WaveAudio");
> ```
>
> assigns the string `"WaveAudio"` to the `DeviceType` property of the `m_wav` multimedia control.

The next statement in the `OnInitialUpdate()` function is

```
m_wav->SetStrProperty("FileName",
                      "\\VCPROG\\WAV\\ITSBEEN1.WAV" );
```

This statement uses the `SetStrProperty()` function to set the `FileName` property of the `m_wav` multimedia control to

```
"\\VCPROG\\WAV\\ITSBEEN1.WAV"
```

You do this because you want to play the `ITSBEEN1.WAV` sound file.

The last statement in the `OnInitialUpdate()` function is

```
m_wav->SetStrProperty("Command", "Open");
```

This statement issues the Open command to the multimedia control. Note that this statement also uses the `SetStrProperty()` function; it sets the `Command` property of the `m_wav` multimedia control to `"Open"`. After this statement is executed, the multimedia control is ready to be used (that is, the user can click the multimedia control's buttons and hear the WAV file playing).

To summarize what the code you wrote in `OnInitialUpdate()` does:

> It calls the `OnIntialUpdate()` function of the base class.
> It sets the `DeviceType` property of the multimedia control to `"WaveAudio"` (because you want to use the multimedia control to play a WAV file).
> It sets the `FileName` property of the multimedia control to `"\\VCPROG\\WAV\\ITSBEEN1.WAV"` (because this is the WAV file that you want to play).
> It issues the Open command to the multimedia control by setting the `Command` property of the multimedia control to `"Open"`.

Don't forget to save your work:

☐ Select Save from the File menu.

Executing the WAVE Application

You have finished writing the code that brings the multimedia control to life. To see and hear your code in action:

☐ Select Build WAVE.EXE from Visual C++'s Project menu.

☐ When Visual C++ finishes building the application, select Execute WAVE.EXE from the Project menu.

> *Visual C++ responds by executing the WAVE application. As you can see, now the multimedia control is enabled (see Figure 22.1).*

☐ Click the Play button (the third button from the left) of the multimedia control (see Figure 22.2).

> *The WAVE application responds by playing the* ITSBEEN1.WAV *sound file.*

☐ Click the multimedia control's Play button again.

This time nothing happens! Why? Because now the playback position is at the end of the WAV file. To play the WAV file again:

☐ Click the Previous button (the leftmost button) and then click the Play button.

> *The WAVE application responds by playing the WAV file.*

In the following section you'll enhance the WAVE application so that when the playback reaches the end of the WAV file, the multimedia control will automatically rewind itself without the user having to click the Previous button.

☐ Terminate the WAVE application by selecting Exit from the File menu.

Rewinding the Multimedia Control Automatically

As you have just seen, when the multimedia control finishes playing the WAV file, the position of the playback is at the end of the file. In order for the user to hear the WAV file again, the user needs to click the Previous button before clicking the Play button.

You will now add code to the WAVE application so that when the playback position reaches the end of the WAV file, the multimedia control will automatically rewind itself to the beginning of the WAV file, thus relieving the user from the task of clicking the Previous button. To add this code, do the following:

☐ Use ClassWizard to add a function for the event:

Class Name:	CWaveView
Object ID:	IDC_TEGOMM_WAV
Message:	VBN_DONE
Function Name:	OnDoneTegommWav()

> **NOTE**
>
> The message VBN_DONE corresponds to the event
>
> ```
> Playback (or recording) is done
> ```
>
> Thus, whenever playback (or recording) is done (terminated), the OnDoneTegommWav() function is executed automatically. The playback can be terminated by the user clicking the Stop button or by the playback reaching the end of the WAV file.

☐ Edit the OnDoneTegommWav() function that you added to the WAVEVIEW.CPP file, as follows:

```
void CWaveView::OnDoneTegommWav(UINT, int, CWnd*, LPVOID)
{
// TODO: Add your VBX event notification handler code here


}
```

To review the code that you just typed:

```
/////////////////////
//MY CODE STARTS HERE
/////////////////////

//Get current position.
long position=m_wav->GetNumProperty("Position");

//Get total length
long length=m_wav->GetNumProperty("Length");

//If current position is end position, rewind the tape.
if (position == length)
   m_wav->SetStrProperty("Command","Prev");

   /////////////////////
   // MY CODE ENDS HERE
   /////////////////////

}
```

The first statement,

```
long position = m_wav->GetNumProperty("Position");
```

uses the `GetNumProperty()` function to extract the current value of the `Position` property of the `m_wav` multimedia control. The `Position` property is the current playback position. The previous statement assigns the current playback position to the `long` variable `position`.

> **NOTE**
>
> As implied by its name, the `GetNumproperty()` member function of the `CVBControl` class returns the current value of a numeric property of a VBX control. For example, the statement
>
> ```
> long position = m_wav->GetNumProperty("Position");
> ```
>
> assigns the current value of the `m_wav` multimedia control's `Position` property to the `position` variable.

The next statement in the function is

```
long length = m_wav->GetNumProperty("Length");
```

This statement uses the `GetNumProperty()` function to assign the value of the `m_wav` multimedia control's `Length` property to the variable `length`. The `Length` property holds the total length of the WAV file.

At this point, the variable `position` holds the current playback position and the variable `length` holds the total playback length of the WAV file.

The last statement in the function is an `if` statement that checks whether `position` is equal to `length`:

```
if (position == length)
   m_wav->SetStrProperty("Command", "Prev");
```

If `position` is equal to `length`, it means that the current playback position is the end of the file. If this is the case, the `if` condition is satisfied and the statement

```
m_wav->SetStrProperty("Command", "Prev");
```

is executed. This statement sets the `Command` property of the `m_wav` multimedia control to `"Prev"`, which is equivalent to clicking the Previous button.

To summarize how the `OnDoneWavMmcontrol()` automatically rewinds the WAV file:

Whenever the playback or recording stops (for example, when the user clicks the Stop button or when the playback reaches the end of the WAV file), the `OnDoneTegommWav()` function is automatically executed.

The code that you wrote in the `OnDoneTegommWav()` function checks to see whether the `Position` and `Length` properties of the multimedia control are equal. If they are equal (that is, if the playback stopped because it reached the end of the WAV file), the `OnDoneTegommWav()` function's code rewinds the multimedia control by setting the `Command` property of the multimedia control to `"Prev"`.

Save your work:

☐ Select Save from the File menu.

Executing the WAVE Application

To see your automatic rewinding code in action:

☐ Select Build WAVE.EXE from Visual C++'s Project menu.

☐ When Visual C++ finishes building the application, select Execute WAVE.EXE from the Project menu.

☐ Click the multimedia control's Play button.

> *The WAVE application responds by playing the* ITSBEEN1.WAV *sound file.*

☐ Once the playback is done, click the multimedia control's Play button again.

> *As you can hear, the WAVE application responds by playing the WAV file again. You didn't have to click the Previous button before clicking the Play button. The code that you wrote automatically rewinds the multimedia control whenever the playback reaches the end of the WAV file.*

In the following sections, you'll attach code to the three regular buttons of the WAVE application (Hide, Show, and Play).

☐ Terminate the WAVE application by selecting Exit from the File menu.

Attaching Code to the Hide Button

When the user clicks the Hide button, the WAVE application should hide the multimedia control from view.

Follow these steps to attach code to the Hide button:

☐ Use ClassWizard to add a function for the event:

> Class Name: `CWaveView`
> Object ID: `IDC_BUTTON_HIDE`
> Message: `BN_CLICKED`
> Function Name: `OnButtonHide()`

☐ Edit the `OnButtonHide()` function that you added to the `WAVEVIEW.CPP` file, as follows:

```
void CWaveView::OnButtonHide()
{
// TODO: Add your control notification handler code here

//////////////////////
// MY CODE STARTS HERE
//////////////////////

// Hide the multimedia control.
m_wav->SetNumProperty("Visible", FALSE);

//////////////////////
// MY CODE ENDS HERE
//////////////////////

}
```

The code that you typed in the `OnButtonHide()` function is made up of one statement:

```
m_wav->SetNumProperty("Visible", FALSE);
```

This statement uses the `SetNumProperty()` function to set the Visible property of the `m_wav` multimedia control to `FALSE`. This hides the multimedia control from view.

NOTE

As implied by its name, the `SetNumProperty()` member function of the `CVBControl` class sets the current value of a numeric property of a VBX control. For example, the statement

```
m_wav->SetNumProperty("Visible", FALSE);
```

sets the `Visible` property of the `m_wav` multimedia control to `FALSE`. Note that properties that hold logical values (`TRUE` or `FALSE`) are considered numeric properties.

Attaching Code to the Show Button

When the user clicks the Show button, the WAVE application should make the multimedia control visible.

Follow these steps to attach code to the Show button:

☐ Use ClassWizard to add a function for the event:

Class Name:	CWaveView
Object ID:	IDC_BUTTON_SHOW
Message:	BN_CLICKED
Function Name:	OnButtonShow()

☐ Edit the OnButtonShow() function that you added to the WAVEVIEW.CPP file, as follows:

```
void CWaveView::OnButtonShow()
{
// TODO: Add your control notification handler code here

    /////////////////////////
    // MY CODE STARTS HERE
    /////////////////////////

    // Show the multimedia control.
    m_wav->SetNumProperty("Visible", TRUE);

    /////////////////////////
    // MY CODE ENDS HERE
    /////////////////////////

}
```

The OnButtonShow() function's code is similar to the OnButtonHide() function's code. The only difference is that now the Visible property of the multimedia control is set to TRUE:

```
m_wav->SetNumProperty("Visible", TRUE);
```

Setting the Visible property of the multimedia control to TRUE makes the multimedia control visible.

Attaching Code to the Play Button

When the user clicks the Play button, the WAVE application should start playing the WAV file.

Follow these steps to attach code to the Play button:

☐ Use ClassWizard to add a function for the event:

Class Name:	`CWaveView`
Object ID:	`IDC_BUTTON_PLAY`
Message:	`BN_CLICKED`
Function Name:	`OnButtonPlay()`

☐ Edit the `OnButtonPlay()` function that you added to the `WAVEVIEW.CPP` file, as follows:

```
void CWaveView::OnButtonPlay()
{
// TODO: Add your control notification handler code here

    /////////////////////////
    // MY CODE STARTS HERE
    /////////////////////////

    // Play the WAV file.
    m_wav->SetStrProperty("Command", "Play");

    /////////////////////////
    // MY CODE ENDS HERE
    /////////////////////////

}
```

The code you just typed in the `OnPlayButton()` is made up of one statement:

```
m_wav->SetStrProperty("Command", "Play");
```

This statement uses the `SetStrProperty()` function to set the `m_wav` multimedia control's `Command` property to `"Play"`. This has the same effect as clicking the Play button of the multimedia control. That is, after you set the `Command` property to `"Play"`, the multimedia control will start playing the WAV file.

Don't forget to save your work:

☐ Select Save from the File menu.

Executing the Final Version of the WAVE Application

You've finished writing the WAVE application's code. To see the code that you attached to the Hide, Show, and Play buttons in action:

☐ Select Build WAVE.EXE from the Project menu.

☐ Execute the WAVE.EXE application and experiment with the Hide, Show, and Play buttons.

As you can hear, clicking the regular Play button has the same effect as clicking the multimedia control's Play button. Note that the regular Play button works even when the multimedia control is hidden. This demonstrates that you can write programs that play WAV files through the sound card without displaying the multimedia control. That is, at the beginning of the program (in the `OnInitialUpdate()` function of the view class), you can hide the multimedia control by setting its `Visible` property to `FALSE`, and later in the program you can issue the Play command by setting the multimedia control's `Command` property to `"Play"`.

Saving the User's Recording in the WAV File

As you have seen and heard, the WAVE application uses the multimedia control to open the WAV file `ITSBEEN1.WAV`. The user can then play the WAV file by clicking the Play button and can record sound into the sound file by clicking the Record button. However, the sound that the user records isn't saved to the disk. Once the user exits the application, the recording is gone.

To save the WAV file to the disk, you need to issue a Save command to the multimedia control. You can do this by adding a Save button to the application's dialog box and then attaching code to the Save button. The code that you need to attach to the Save button involves only one statement:

```
m_wav->SetStrProperty("Command", "Save");
```

This statement sets the `Command` property of the `m_wav` multimedia control to `"Save"`. In other words, it issues a Save command to the multimedia control. As stated earlier, when you issue a Save command to the multimedia control, the WAV file is saved to the disk.

Using the TegoMM.VBX Multimedia Control to Play Sounds Through the PC Speaker

It's easy to use the TegoMM.VBX control with other devices. For example, to play a WAV file through the PC's internal speaker, all you have to do is set the `DeviceType` property to `"PCSpeaker"`.

☐ Open the `WAVEVIEW.CPP` file and modify the statement that sets the `DeviceType` property in the `OnInitialUpdate()` function. In other words, comment out the statement

```
// m_wav->SetStrProperty("DeviceType","WaveAudio");
```

☐ and instead type the following statement:

```
m_wav->SetStrProperty("DeviceType","PCSpeaker");
```

☐ After making this modification, your `OnInitialUpdate()` function looks as follows:

```
/////////////////////////
// MY CODE STARTS HERE
/////////////////////////

void CWaveView::OnInitialUpdate()
{

    // Call the base class function.
    CFormView::OnInitialUpdate();

    // Set the device type for playback of WAV files.
    //   m_wav->SetStrProperty("DeviceType","WaveAudio");

    // To play through the PC speaker, simply set the DeviceType
    // to PCSpeaker as follows:
    m_wav->SetStrProperty("DeviceType","PCSpeaker");

    // Set the WAV file name.
    m_wav->SetStrProperty("FileName",
                          "\\VCPROG\\WAV\\ITSBEEN1.WAV" );

    // Open the Wave device.
    m_wav->SetStrProperty("Command", "Open");

}

/////////////////////////
// MY CODE ENDS HERE
/////////////////////////
```

☐ Compile/link and execute the WAVE application to verify that now the sound is played through the PC speaker.

Typically, your application will check whether the user owns a sound card and set the DeviceType property to either `"WaveAudio"` or `"PCSpeaker"` accordingly.

This book's appendix explains how to use the TegoMM.VBX control to determine whether the user has a sound card installed. In addition, the appendix shows how to create a multitasking application, where a Visual C++ application plays through the PC speaker and the user can switch to other applications while the playback is still going on (background playback). This multitasking feature emulates a sound card.

751

23

Multimedia: Playing MIDI Files

In this chapter you will write an
application that uses the
TegoMM.VBX control to play a
MIDI file. The application that
you'll write will also illustrate how
you can play a MIDI file and
a WAV file simultaneously.

The MIX Application

Now you'll write the MIX application, which enables the user to play a MIDI file. MIDI files are standard music files that store a series of instructions telling the sound card how to play a piece of music. Unlike WAV files, which can play any sound (for example, music or a human voice), MIDI files are used only for playing music. MIDI files have a .MID extension (for example, MyMusic.MID).

The MIX application illustrates two programming techniques:

> How to use the TegoMM.VBX control to play a MIDI file.

> How to incorporate two multimedia controls into one application. One multimedia control is used to play a WAV file, and the other multimedia control is used to play a MIDI file. The user can play the WAV file and the MIDI file simultaneously by using the two multimedia controls.

As you'll soon see, the code you'll need to write to play a MIDI file is almost identical to the code you wrote in the previous chapter for playing a WAV file.

Before you start writing the MIX application, execute the copy of it that resides in your `C:\VCPROG\ORIGINAL\CH23\MIX` directory.

To execute the MIX.EXE application:

☐ Use Run from the Program Manager's File menu to run
  `C:\VCPROG\ORIGINAL\CH23\MIX\MIX.EXE`.

> *Windows responds by executing the MIX application. The MIX application first displays a limited version message box from the TegoMM.VBX multimedia control.*

☐ Click the OK button of the message box.

> *The main window of* `MIX.EXE` *appears, as shown in Figure 23.1.*

Figure 23.1.
The MIX application's main window.

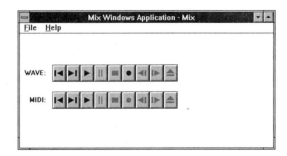

As you can see, the main window of the application contains two multimedia controls. One multimedia control is used to play WAV files and the other is used to play MIDI files.

To start the playback of the WAV file:

☐ Click the Play button of the WAV multimedia control.

> *The MIX application responds by playing the WAV file* 8KENNED3.WAV. *As you can hear, this WAV file contains a portion of a famous speech given by President Kennedy. The* 8KENNED3.WAV *file was copied to your* \VCPROG\WAV *directory when you installed the book's CD. Note that if for some reason this file doesn't exist in your* \VCPROG\WAV *directory, all the buttons on the multimedia control will be dimmed (that is, not available) and you won't be able to start the playback.*

☐ Now click the MIDI multimedia control's Play button.

> *The MIX application responds by playing the MIDI file* BOURBON6.MID. *This MIDI file was copied to your* \VCPROG\MIDI *directory when you installed the book's CD. Again, if for some reason this file doesn't exist in your* \VCPROG\MIDI *directory, all the buttons on the multimedia control will be dimmed (that is, not available) and you won't be able to start the playback.*

You can play the WAV file and the MIDI file simultaneously:

☐ Click the MIDI multimedia control's Play button and click the WAV multimedia control's Play button while the music is being played.

As you can hear, the MIX application plays the MIDI file and the WAV file simultaneously. That is, President Kennedy's speech is played with background MIDI music.

The MIX application has two popup menus, File and Help. These popup menus are shown in Figures 23.2 and 23.3.

To exit from the MIX application:

☐ Select Exit from the File menu.

Now that you know what the MIX application should do, you can begin writing it.

Figure 23.2.
The MIX
application's
File popup
menu.

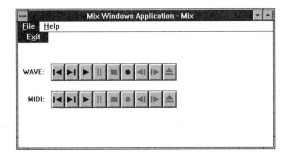

Figure 23.3.
The MIX
application's
Help popup
menu.

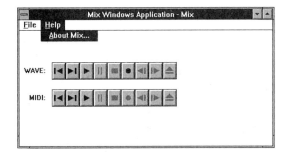

Creating the Project of the MIX Application

To create the project of the MIX application:

Select AppWizard from the Project menu.

>*Visual C++ responds by running AppWizard.*

☐ Use the Directory list box to select the C:\VCPROG\PRACTICE\CH23 directory.

☐ Type mix in the Project Name box.

Now your AppWizard dialog box looks as shown in Figure 23.4.

Click the Options button and set the options as shown in Figure 23.5.

NOTE

As in the previous chapter, you need to check the Custom VBX Controls option in the Options dialog box (see Figure 23.5). This is necessary because the MIX application also uses the TegoMM.VBX control.

Figure 23.4.
The MIX
application's
AppWizard
dialog box.

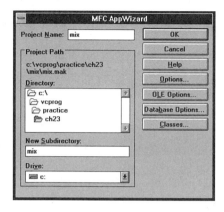

Figure 23.5.
Setting the options
for the MIX
application.

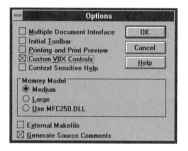

☐ Click the OK button of the Options dialog box and then click the OK button of the AppWizard dialog box and finally click the Create button of the New Application Information dialog box.

> *AppWizard responds by creating the MIX project and all the skeleton files of the MIX application.*

To remove the debug options of the project (so you'll have a small EXE file):

☐ Select Project from Visual C++'s Options menu, click the Release radio button, and then click the OK button of the dialog box.

Creating the Form of the Application

As shown in Figure 23.1, the main window of the MIX application should contain two multimedia controls.

To implement this form you'll replace the current view class of the application with a new view class derived from the CFormView class.

Follow these steps to create the form of the application:

☐ Use the Windows File Manager (or DOS Shell) to delete the two view class files of the MIX application:

> Delete `C:\VCPROG\PRACTICE\CH23\MIX\MIXVIEW.CPP`.
> Delete `C:\VCPROG\PRACTICE\CH23\MIX\MIXVIEW.H`.

☐ Select ClassWizard from Visual C++'s Browse menu.

> *ClassWizard responds by displaying a dialog box telling you that the view class files don't exist.*

☐ Click the OK button of the dialog box.

☐ Click the Remove button of the Repair Class Information dialog box.

☐ Click ClassWizard's OK button.

You've just finished removing the view class of the MIX application.

In the following steps you'll create a dialog box, you'll create a `CFormView` type class for this dialog box, and you'll make this class the new view class of the application:

☐ Select App Studio from Visual C++'s Tools menu.

☐ Create a new dialog box with App Studio.

☐ Double-click in a free area of the new dialog box.

☐ Select Styles from the drop-down list box at the upper-right corner of the Properties window.

Set the Styles properties of the dialog box as follows:

☐ Select Child from the Style box.

☐ Select None from the Border box.

☐ Uncheck the Visible property (that is, remove the check mark from the Visible check box).

☐ Select General from the drop-down list box at the upper-right corner of the Properties window and make sure the Caption box is empty.

Now connect the dialog box to a class derived from `CFormView`:

☐ Select ClassWizard from App Studio's Resource menu.

> *ClassWizard responds by displaying the Add Class dialog box.*

☐ Type `CMixView` in the Class Name box.

☐ Set the Class Type to `CFormView`.

☐ Make sure that the header filename is `mixview.h` and that the implementation filename is `mixview.cpp`.

☐ Click the Create Class button.

☐ Click ClassWizard's OK button to go back to App Studio.

You've finished creating the new view class of the application. This view class is derived from the MFC `CFormView` class and is connected to the dialog box that you created. Thus, the main dialog box of the application will be the dialog box you created.

The Visual Implementation of the Dialog Box

☐ Implement the dialog box of the MIX application according to Table 23.1.

Table 23.1. The MIX application's dialog box.

Class Name:	`CMixView`
Figure:	23.6
OK button:	No
Cancel button:	No

Object	Property	Setting
Dialog Box	ID	`IDD_DIALOG1`
Label	ID	`IDC_STATIC`
	Caption	`WAVE:`
Multimedia Control	ID	`IDC_TEGOMM_WAV`
	Variable	`m_wav` (Type: `CVBControl *`)
Label	ID	`IDC_STATIC`
	Caption	`MIDI:`
Multimedia Control	ID	`IDC_TEGOMM_MIDI`
	Variable	`m_midi` (Type: `CVBControl *`)

NOTE

Table 23.1 instructs you to place two multimedia controls in the dialog box. In order to place a multimedia control in the dialog box, the TegoMM.VBX control must be installed in your App Studio Tools window. In the previous chapter you were instructed to install the TegoMM.VBX control by following a set of step-by-step instructions. If you have not done so, you need to refer back to Chapter 22, "Multimedia: Playing and Recording WAV Files," and install the TegoMM.VBX control.

Now your dialog box looks as shown in Figure 23.6.

Figure 23.6.
The MIX
application's
dialog box.

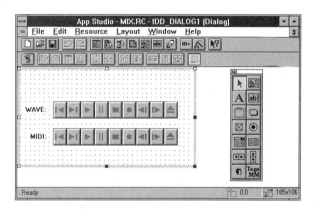

Table 23.1 instructed you to attach the variable m_wav to the IDC_TEGOMM_WAV multimedia control and to attach the variable m_midi to the IDC_TEGOMM_MIDI multimedia control. Both m_wav and m_midi are variables of type CVBControl * (pointers to objects of class CVBControl).

As you'll see later in this chapter, when you write the application's code, you'll use the m_wav multimedia control for playing WAV files, and you'll use the m_midi multimedia control for playing MIDI files.

Don't forget to save your work:

☐ Select Save from App Studio's File menu.

You've finished designing the dialog box! This dialog box will appear in the main window of the application.

The Visual Implementation of the Menu

The MIX application should have a menu with two popup menus, as shown in Figures 23.2 and 23.3. To implement this menu:

☐ Use App Studio to implement the menu of the MIX application according to Table 23.2.

Table 23.2. The MIX application's menu.
Figures relating to menu: 23.2, 23.3

Menu Item
&File
E&xit
&Help
&About Mix...

Don't forget to delete the accelerator keys of the menu items that you removed:

☐ Select `MIX.RC [MFC-Resource Script]` from App Studio's Window menu, select Accelerator from the Type list, and then double-click `IDR_MAINFRAME` in the Resources list.

☐ Delete the accelerator keys that aren't used by the MIX application. In particular, delete the accelerator keys of the `ID_FILE_NEW`, `ID_FILE_OPEN`, and `ID_FILE_SAVE` menu items.

If you don't delete these accelerator keys, they'll be active during runtime. For example, if the user presses Ctrl+N, it will be as if the user selected New from the File menu (even though you removed that item).

To save your work:

☐ Select Save from App Studio's File menu.

The visual implementation of the MIX application's menu is complete.

Executing the MIX Application

Even though you haven't written a single line of code for the MIX application, execute it to see your visual design in action:

☐ Select Build All MIX.EXE from the Visual C++'s Project menu.

☐ Select Execute MIX.EXE from the Project menu.

> *Visual C++ responds by executing the MIX application. The main window of the application appears with the form that you designed in it (two labels and two multimedia controls).*

Note that the two multimedia controls are dimmed (that is, their buttons are not available). In order to bring the two multimedia controls to life, you need to write code that sets their properties. You'll do this in the following sections.

To exit the MIX application:

☐ Select Exit from the File menu.

Initializing the Properties of the Two Multimedia Controls

Recall from the previous chapter that you write the code that initializes the properties of the multimedia control in the `OnInitialUpdate()` member function of the view class. This way, when the application is started, the two multimedia controls will come to life.

Because Visual C++ did not write the declaration and skeleton of the `OnInitialUpdate()` function, you have to declare this function and write its skeleton. Here's how you do that:

☐ Open the file MIXVIEW.H and add code to it that defines the function `OnInitialUpdate()` as a member function of the `CMixView` class. After you write this code, the `CMixView` class declaration looks as follows:

```
class CMixView : public CFormView
{
    DECLARE_DYNCREATE(CMixView)
protected:
    CMixView(); // protected constructor used by dynamic creation

    /////////////////////////
    // MY CODE STARTS HERE
    /////////////////////////
```

```
        virtual void OnInitialUpdate();

        //////////////////////
        // MY CODE ENDS HERE
        //////////////////////

// Form Data
public:
     //{{AFX_DATA(CMixView)
     enum { IDD = IDD_DIALOG1 };
     CVBControl*     m_midi;
     CVBControl*     m_wav;
     //}}AFX_DATA

// Attributes
public:

// Operations
public:

// Implementation
protected:
virtual ~CMixView();
virtual void DoDataExchange(CDataExchange* pDX);
// Generated message map functions
//{{AFX_MSG(CMixView)
    // NOTE - ClassWizard will add/remove member functions here.
//}}AFX_MSG
DECLARE_MESSAGE_MAP()
};
```

Now write the `OnInitialUpdate()` function's code:

☐ Open the file `MIXVIEW.CPP` and add the `OnInitialUpdate()` function to the end of the file. After you write this function, the end of the `MIXVIEW.CPP` file looks as follows:

```
/////////////////////////////////////////////
// CMixView message handlers

//////////////////////
// MY CODE STARTS HERE
//////////////////////

void CMixView::OnInitialUpdate()
{

    // Call the base class function.
    CFormView::OnInitialUpdate();
```

```
    // Open the 8KENNED3.WAV file.
    m_wav->SetStrProperty("DeviceType","WaveAudio");
    m_wav->SetStrProperty("FileName",
                          "\\VCPROG\\WAV\\8KENNED3.WAV" );
    m_wav->SetStrProperty("Command", "Open");


    // Open the BOURBON6.MID file.
    m_midi->SetStrProperty("DeviceType","Sequencer");
    m_midi->SetStrProperty("FileName",
                           "\\VCPROG\\MIDI\\BOURBON6.MID" );
    m_midi->SetStrProperty("Command", "Open");

}

///////////////////////
// MY CODE ENDS HERE
///////////////////////
```

To review the OnInitialUpdate() function's code:

The first statement,

```
CFormView::OnInitialUpdate();
```

calls the OnInitialUpdate() member function of the base class. Recall from the previous chapter that you have to call the base class OnInitialUpdate() function. If you don't, the multimedia control will be dimmed (that is, unavailable).

The next three statements are

```
m_wav->SetStrProperty("DeviceType","WaveAudio");
m_wav->SetStrProperty("FileName",
                      "\\VCPROG\\WAV\\8KENNED3.WAV" );
m_wav->SetStrProperty("Command", "Open");
```

The first statement,

```
m_wav->SetStrProperty("DeviceType","WaveAudio");
```

sets the DeviceType property of the m_wav multimedia control to "WaveAudio". You do this because you want to use the m_wav multimedia control to play a WAV file.

The second statement,

```
m_wav->SetStrProperty("FileName",
                      "\\VCPROG\\WAV\\8KENNED3.WAV" );
```

sets the FileName property of the m_wav multimedia control to "\\VCPROG\\WAV\\8KENNED3.WAV". This is done because you want to play the 8KENNED3.WAV sound file.

The third statement,

```
m_wav->SetStrProperty("Command", "Open");
```

sets the `Command` property of the `m_wav` multimedia control to `"Open"`. After this statement is executed, the `m_wav` multimedia control is ready to be played (that is, the user can click the multimedia control's buttons and hear the WAV file playing).

The last three statements in the `OnInitialUpdate()` function are

```
m_midi->SetStrProperty("DeviceType","Sequencer");
m_midi->SetStrProperty("FileName",
                        "\\VCPROG\\MIDI\\BOURBON6.MID" );
m_midi->SetStrProperty("Command", "Open");
```

The first statement,

```
m_midi->SetStrProperty("DeviceType","Sequencer");
```

sets the `DeviceType` property of the `m_midi` multimedia control to `"Sequencer"`. This is done because you want to use the `m_midi` multimedia control to play a MIDI file.

> **NOTE**
>
> When you want to use a multimedia control to play a MIDI file, you need to set the `DeviceType` property of the multimedia control to `"Sequencer"`. For example, to set the `m_midi` multimedia control so that it can be used to play MIDI files, use the statement,
>
> ```
> m_midi->SetStrProperty("DeviceType","Sequencer");
> ```

The second statement,

```
m_midi->SetStrProperty("FileName",
                        "\\VCPROG\\MIDI\\BOURBON6.MID" );
```

sets the `FileName` property of the `m_midi` multimedia control to `"\\VCPROG\\MIDI\\BOURBON6.MID"`. This is done because you want to play the `BOURBON6.MID` MIDI file.

The third statement,

```
m_midi->SetStrProperty("Command", "Open");
```

sets the `Command` property of the `m_midi` multimedia control to `"Open"`. After this statement is executed, the `m_midi` multimedia control is ready to be used (that is, the user can click the multimedia control's buttons and hear the MIDI file playing).

To summarize what the code you wrote in `OnInitialUpdate()` does:

It calls the `OnIntialUpdate()` function of the base class.

It sets the `DeviceType` property of the `m_wav` multimedia control to `"WaveAudio"` (because you want to use the `m_wav` multimedia control to play a WAV file).

It sets the `FileName` property of the `m_wav` multimedia control to `"\\VCPROG\\WAV\\8KENNED3.WAV"` (because this is the WAV file that you want to play).

It issues the Open command to the `m_wav` multimedia control.

It sets the `DeviceType` property of the `m_midi` multimedia control to `"Sequencer"` (because you want to use the `m_midi` multimedia control to play a MIDI file).

It sets the `FileName` property of the `m_midi` multimedia control to `"\\VCPROG\\MIDI\\BOURBON6.MID"` (because this is the MIDI file that you want to play).

It issues the Open command to the `m_midi` multimedia control.

Don't forget to save your work:

☐ Select Save from the File menu.

Executing the MIX Application

You've finished writing the code that brings the two multimedia controls to life. To see your code in action:

☐ Select Build MIX.EXE from Visual C++'s Project menu.

☐ When Visual C++ finishes building the application, select Execute MIX.EXE from the Project menu.

Visual C++ responds by executing the MIX application. As you can see, now the two multimedia controls are enabled (see Figure 23.1).

☐ Experiment with the two multimedia controls and notice that you can play the MIDI file and the WAV file simultaneously.

Note that when the playback of the MIDI file (or the WAV file) reaches the end, the multimedia control doesn't automatically rewind itself. In other words, before you can play the file again, you must first click the Previous button (the leftmost button).

766

In the following sections you'll enhance the MIX application so that when the play-back of the MIDI file (or WAV file) reaches the end, the multimedia control will automatically rewind itself without the user having to click the Previous button.

☐ Terminate the MIX application by selecting Exit from the File menu.

Rewinding the Multimedia Controls Automatically

Recall from the previous chapter that to make the multimedia control automatically rewind itself, you need to attach code to the multimedia control's VBN_DONE event. You will now attach code to the VBN_DONE event of both the m_wav multimedia control and the m_midi multimedia control.

To attach code to the VBN_DONE event of the m_wav multimedia control:

☐ Use ClassWizard to add a function for the event:

Class Name:	CMixView
Object ID:	IDC_TEGOMM_WAV
Message:	VBN_DONE
Function Name:	OnDoneTegommWav()

☐ Edit the OnDoneTegommWav() function that you added to the MIXVIEW.CPP file. After you edit the OnDoneTegommWav() function, it looks as follows:

```
void CMixView::OnDoneTegommWav(UINT, int, CWnd*, LPVOID)
{
// TODO: Add your VBX event notification handler code here

    //////////////////////////
    // MY CODE STARTS HERE
    //////////////////////////

    // Get current position.
    long position = m_wav->GetNumProperty("Position");

    // Get total length.
    long length = m_wav->GetNumProperty("Length");

    // If current position is end position, rewind the tape.
    if (position == length)
      m_wav->SetStrProperty("Command", "Prev");
```

```
/////////////////////
// MY CODE ENDS HERE
/////////////////////
```

}

As you can see, this code is the same as the code you wrote in the WAVE application in the previous chapter.

To attach code to the `VBN_DONE` event of the `m_midi` multimedia control:

☐ Use ClassWizard to add a function for the event:

Class Name:	`CMixView`
Object ID:	`IDC_TEGOMM_MIDI`
Message:	`VBN_DONE`
Function Name:	`OnDoneTegommMidi()`

☐ Edit the `OnDoneTegommMidi()` function that you added to the `MIXVIEW.CPP` file. After you edit the `OnDoneTegommMidi()` function, it looks as follows:

```
void CMixView::OnDoneTegommMidi(UINT, int, CWnd*, LPVOID)
{
// TODO: Add your VBX event notification handler code here

    /////////////////////////
    // MY CODE STARTS HERE
    /////////////////////////

    // Get current position.
    long position = m_midi->GetNumProperty("Position");

    // Get total length.
    long length = m_midi->GetNumProperty("Length");

    // If current position is end position, rewind the tape.
    if (position == length)
       m_midi->SetStrProperty("Command", "Prev");

    /////////////////////
    // MY CODE ENDS HERE
    /////////////////////

}
```

As you can see, this code is similar to the code that you wrote in the `OnDoneTegommWav()` function. The only difference is that now you are rewinding the `m_midi` multimedia control.

Executing the Final Version of the MIX Application

To see your automatic rewinding code in action:

☐ Select Build MIX.EXE from Visual C++'s Project menu.

☐ When Visual C++ finishes building the application, select Execute MIX.EXE from the Project menu.

Play the MIDI file and WAV file and note that when the playback ends, each control automatically rewinds itself. That is, to hear the playback again, you can click the Play button without first clicking the Previous button.

24

Multimedia: Video for Windows

In this chapter you'll write an application that uses the TegoMM.VBX control to play a Windows-compatible video file (AVI file). You'll also learn how to write code that sets the default size of the application's window to any desired size.

Playing Video Files

Video files contain real movies. A video file includes the video (that is, the pictures) as well as the soundtrack of a movie. When you play a video file on your PC, the pictures are displayed on your PC's monitor and the sound is played through your sound card.

If you don't have a sound card, you can still see the video portion of the movie. As you will soon see, playing a video file on your PC is quite impressive, even if you don't have a sound card.

Before You Can Play Video Files on Your PC...

Before you can play video files on your PC, you have to install special software drivers that enable your Windows system to play video files.

To see whether your Windows system currently has the necessary software drivers for playing video files:

☐ Start the Media Player program in Windows (see Figure 24.1). The Media Player program is usually in the Accessories group of programs.

   Windows responds by running the Media Player program (see Figure 24.2).

> **NOTE**
>
> Media Player, usually found in the Accessories group, enables you to play various multimedia files.
>
> To start the Media Player program:
>
>   Double-click the Media Player icon (see Figure 24.1).

If your Windows system has the software drivers needed to play video files, your Media Player program can play them.

To see if your Media Player program can play video files:

☐ Open Media Player's Device menu (see Figure 24.3).

Figure 24.1.
The Media Player
program's icon.

Figure 24.2.
The Media Player
program.

Figure 24.3.
Media Player's
Device menu.

As you can see from Figure 24.3, one of the items in the Device menu is Video for Windows. If your Media Player's Device menu doesn't include this item, your Windows system currently doesn't have the software drivers necessary to play video files.

The following section describes how to install the necessary software drivers for playing video files.

Installing the Video for Windows Software Drivers

As discussed previously, if your Media Player's Device menu doesn't include the Video for Windows option, your Windows system doesn't have the necessary software drivers for playing video files.

To install the Video for Windows software drivers, you need to run a special Setup program that includes all the necessary video drivers. After you run this Setup program, you'll be able to play video files in Windows. This Setup program is included with the book's CD.

To install the Video for Windows software drivers using the Setup program included with book's CD, follow these steps:

☐ Insert the book's CD into your CD-ROM drive.

☐ Select Run from the File menu in the Windows Program Manager.

Windows responds by displaying the Run dialog box (see Figure 24.4).

Figure 24.4.
The Run dialog
box.

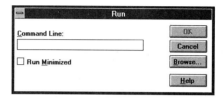

☐ Type X:\VCPROG\VIDEO\SETUP on the Command Line of the Run dialog box.

NOTE

In the preceding step, X represents the letter that corresponds to your CD drive. For example, if your CD drive is D, you should type D:\VCPROG\VIDEO\SETUP.

In some systems, the SETUP program must reside on your a: or b: drive. If you experience difficulties running the SETUP program from your CD-ROM drive, follow these steps:

Copy all the files that reside in the \VCPROG\VIDEO directory of the CD to the root directory of an empty diskette.

Select Run from the Program Manager's File menu to execute the SETUP.EXE program that resides on the diskette you prepared.

☐ Click the OK button of the Run dialog box.

Windows responds by running the SETUP program. The SETUP program initializes itself (see Figure 24.5) and after a while it displays a Welcome dialog box (see Figure 24.6).

Figure 24.5.
The SETUP
program initializ-
ing itself.

Figure 24.6.
The SETUP
program's Welcome
dialog box.

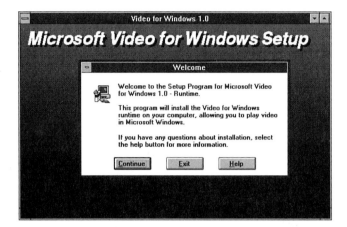

☐ Click the Continue button of the Welcome dialog box.

> *The SETUP program responds by installing all the necessary video software*
> *drivers in your Windows system. When the installation is complete, the*
> *SETUP program displays a Setup Successful dialog box (see Figure 24.7).*

Figure 24.7.
The SETUP
program's Setup
Successful dialog
box.

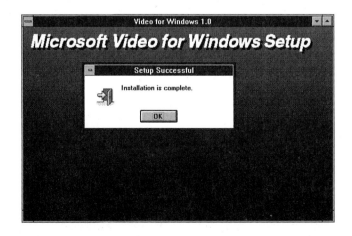

□ Click the OK button of the Setup Successful dialog box.

Now that you've completed installing the Video for Windows software drivers, you can start playing video files.

The following section describes how to play a video file with the Windows Media Player. Later in the chapter, you'll write your own program (a Visual C++ application) that plays a video file.

Playing a Video File with Media Player

Windows-compatible video files have an AVI file extension (for example, MyMovie.AVI). Just as WAV files are used in Windows to play sound, AVI files are used to play movies.

In the following steps, you'll use Media Player to play an AVI file that was copied to your hard drive when you installed the book's CD. This AVI file is called MOVIE.AVI.

To play the MOVIE.AVI video file with Media Player:

□ Double-click the Media Player icon (see Figure 24.1).

> *Windows responds by running the Media Player program (see Figure 24.2).*

□ Select Video for Windows from the Media Player's Device menu (see Figure 24.3).

> *Media Player responds by displaying an Open File dialog box (see Figure 24.8).*

Figure 24.8.
The Media Player's
Open File dialog
box.

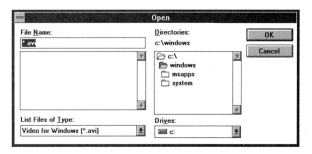

□ Select the file C:\VCPROG\AVI\MOVIE.AVI.

> *Media Player responds by opening the MOVIE.AVI video file and displaying the first frame (picture) of the movie.*

To start playing the movie:

☐ Click the Play button (the leftmost button) of Media Player.

> *Media Player responds by playing the* MOVIE.AVI *video file.*

To stop the playback of the file:

☐ Click the Stop button (the second button from the left).

You can use Media Player's horizontal scroll bar to move to a particular frame in the movie. For example, to start the playback from the middle of the movie, drag the thumb on the horizontal scroll bar to the middle of the scroll bar and then click the Play button.

To terminate the Media Player program:

☐ Select Exit from Media Player's File menu.

Creating Your Own Video Files

To create a video file, you need the following hardware and software:

> A video device, such as a VCR or a camcorder
> A video capture card
> A video capture program

You create the video file by connecting the video device (the VCR or camcorder) to the video card with cables. The video capture program processes the video received from the video device and creates the video file (see Figure 24.9).

Figure 24.9.
Creating your own
video file.

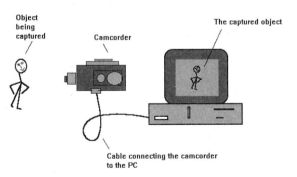

Object being captured

Camcorder

The captured object

Cable connecting the camcorder to the PC

The AVI Application

Now you'll write the AVI application. The AVI application is an example of a multimedia application that enables the user to play an AVI file.

As you'll soon see, the code you need to write to play an AVI file is similar to the code you wrote in the previous two chapters to play a WAV file and a MIDI file.

Before you start writing the AVI application, execute the copy of it that resides in your `C:\VCPROG\ORIGINAL\CH24\AVI` directory.

To execute the AVI.EXE application:

☐ Use Run from Program Manager's File menu to run
`C:\VCPROG\ORIGINAL\CH24\AVI\AVI.EXE`.

Windows responds by executing the AVI application. The AVI application first displays a limited version message box from the TegoMM.VBX multimedia control.

☐ Click the OK button of the message box.

The main window of AVI.EXE appears, as shown in Figure 24.10.

Figure 24.10.
The AVI application's main window.

As you can see, the main window of the application contains a multimedia control and two check boxes, Auto Repeat and Silent.

Note that when the application starts, the main window of the application always appears as shown in Figure 24.10. That is, the AVI application includes code that sets the default size of the application's window to the size shown in Figure 24.10.

To start the playback of the AVI file:

☐ Click the Play button of the multimedia control.

> *The AVI application responds by playing the video file* MOVIE.AVI. *The frames of the video are displayed in the application's main window (see Figure 24.11), and the soundtrack of the video is played through the sound card. As mentioned earlier, the file* MOVIE.AVI *was copied to your hard drive* \VCPROG\AVI *directory when you installed the book's CD. If for some reason* MOVIE.AVI *doesn't exist in your* \VCPROG\AVI *directory, all the buttons on the multimedia control will be dimmed (not available) and you won't be able to start the playback.*

Figure 24.11.
Playing a video file in the AVI application's main window.

☐ Experiment with the other buttons of the multimedia control. In particular, experiment with the Back button (the third button from the right) and the Step button (the second button from the right). These buttons enable you to step through the movie (backward and forward) frame by frame.

☐ Experiment with the Auto Repeat check box. This check box enables you to play the movie in an endless loop.

☐ Experiment with the Silent check box. If you check this check box, the video is played without sound.

The AVI application has two popup menus, File and Help. These popup menus are shown in Figures 24.12 and 24.13.

Figure 24.12.
The AVI
application's File
popup menu.

Figure 24.13.
The AVI
application's Help
popup menu.

To exit from the AVI application:

☐ Select Exit from the File menu.

Now that you know what the AVI application should do, you can start writing it.

Creating the Project of the AVI Application

To create the project of the AVI application:

☐ Select AppWizard from the Project menu.

    Visual C++ responds by running AppWizard.

☐ Use the Directory list box to select the C:\VCPROG\PRACTICE\CH24 directory.

☐ Type avi in the Project Name box.

Now your AppWizard dialog box looks as shown in Figure 24.14.

Figure 24.14.
The AppWizard
dialog box for the
AVI application.

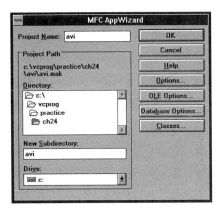

☐ Click the Options button and set the options as shown in Figure 24.15.

> **NOTE**
>
> As in the previous two chapters, you need to check the Custom VBX Controls option in the Options dialog box (see Figure 24.15). This is necessary because the AVI application uses the TegoMM.VBX control.

Figure 24.15.
Setting the AVI
application's
options.

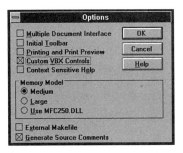

☐ Click the OK button of the Options dialog box and then click the OK button of the AppWizard dialog box and finally click the Create button of the New Application Information dialog box.

> *AppWizard responds by creating the AVI project and all the skeleton files of the AVI application.*

To remove the debug options of the project (so you'll have a small EXE file):

☐ Select Project from the Options menu of Visual C++, click the Release radio button, and then click the OK button of the dialog box.

Creating the Form of the Application

As shown in Figure 24.10, the main window of the AVI application should contain a multimedia control and two check boxes.

To implement this form, you must replace the current view class of the application with a new view class derived from the `CFormView` class.

Follow these steps to create the form of the application:

☐ Use the Windows File Manager (or DOS Shell) to delete the two view class files of the AVI application:

> Delete C:\VCPROG\PRACTICE\CH24\AVI\AVIVIEW.CPP.
> Delete C:\VCPROG\PRACTICE\CH24\AVI\AVIVIEW.H.

☐ Select ClassWizard from Visual C++'s Browse menu.

> *ClassWizard responds by displaying a dialog box telling you that the view class files don't exist.*

☐ Click the OK button of the dialog box.

☐ Click the Remove button of the Repair Class Information dialog box.

☐ Click the OK button of ClassWizard's dialog box.

You have just finished removing the view class of the AVI application.

In the following steps you'll create a dialog box, you'll create a `CFormView` type class for this dialog box, and you'll make this class the new view class of the application:

☐ Select App Studio from Visual C++'s Tools menu.

☐ Create a new dialog box with App Studio.

☐ Double-click in a free area of the new dialog box.

☐ Select Styles from the drop-down list box at the upper-right corner of the Properties window.

Set the Styles properties of the dialog box as follows:

☐ Select Child from the Style box.

☐ Select None from the Border box.

☐ Uncheck the Visible property (that is, remove the check mark from the Visible check box).

☐ Select General from the drop-down list box at the upper-right corner of the Properties window and make sure that the Caption box is empty.

Now connect the dialog box to a class derived from `CFormView`:

☐ Select ClassWizard from App Studio's Resource menu.

    ClassWizard responds by displaying the Add Class dialog box.

☐ Type `CAviView` in the Class Name box.

☐ Set the Class Type to `CFormView`.

☐ Make sure that the header filename is `aviview.h` and that the implementation filename is `aviview.cpp`.

☐ Click the Create Class button.

☐ Click ClassWizard's OK button to go back to App Studio.

You have finished creating the new view class of the application. This view class is derived from the MFC `CFormView` class and is connected to the dialog box that you created. Thus, the main dialog box of the application will be the dialog box that you created.

The Visual Implementation of the Dialog Box

☐ Implement the dialog box of the AVI application according to Table 24.1.

Table 24.1. The AVI application's dialog box.

Class Name:	`CAviView`
Figure:	24.16
OK button:	No
Cancel button:	No

Object	Property	Setting
Dialog Box	ID	`IDD_DIALOG1`
Multimedia Control	ID	`IDC_TEGOMM_AVI`
	Variable	`m_avi` (Type: `CVBControl *`)

continues

Table 24.1. continued

Object	Property	Setting
Check Box	ID	IDC_AUTO_REPEAT
	Caption	&Auto Repeat
	Variable	m_AutoRepeat
Check Box	ID	IDC_SILENT
	Caption	&Silent
	Variable	m_Silent

NOTE

Table 24.1 instructs you on how to place a multimedia control in the dialog box. To do this, the TegoMM.VBX control must be installed in your App Studio Tools window. In Chapter 22, "Multimedia: Playing and Recording WAV Files," you were instructed to install the TegoMM.VBX control by following a set of step-by-step instructions. If you haven't done so, you need to refer to Chapter 22 and install the TegoMM.VBX control.

Now your dialog box looks as shown in Figure 24.16.

Figure 24.16.
The AVI
application's dialog
box.

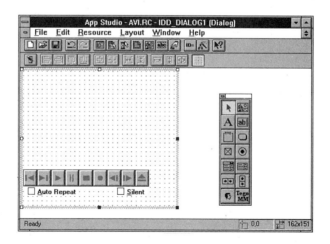

The exact location of the multimedia control and the two check boxes is important, because the movie will be displayed in the main window of the application (see Figure 24.11) and it shouldn't overlap the controls. Thus, you need to place the controls exactly as shown in Figure 24.16. Here's how you do that:

☐ Drag the multimedia control until its position is X=0, Y=110.

> **NOTE**
>
> In the preceding step you were instructed to drag the multimedia control to position X=0, Y=110. Here is how you do that:
>
> > App Studio's status bar displays two pairs of numbers. One pair is the X,Y position of the currently selected control, and the other pair is its width and height.
> >
> > For example, in Figure 24.17 the currently selected item is the multimedia control. Its position is X=15, Y=40, and its size is Width=135, Height=18.
> >
> > So to place the multimedia control at position X=0, Y=110, all you have to do is drag the multimedia control until you see that the status bar displays the position 0,110. (Note that if the dialog box isn't large enough for position Y=110, you'll have to first enlarge the dialog box by dragging its bottom edge downward.)
> >
> > Note that if your App Studio window doesn't have a status bar, you have to select Status Bar from App Studio's Window menu.

Figure 24.17.
App Studio's
status bar.

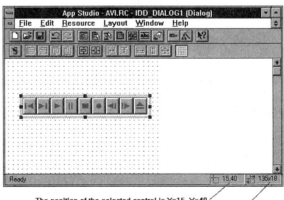

The position of the selected control is X=15, Y=40
The size of the selected control is Width = 135, Height = 18

☐ Drag the Auto Repeat check box until its position is X=5, Y=130.

☐ Drag the Silent check box until its position is X=100, Y=130.

You have finished designing the dialog box of the AVI application!

Don't forget to save your work:

☐ Select Save from App Studio's File menu.

NOTE

In the preceding steps, you were instructed to place the controls of the AVI application at various X,Y positions. What are the units of these X,Y positions? These units are dialog box units (DLUs). A DLU is proportional to the size of the dialog box font. A horizontal DLU is the average width of the dialog box font divided by four. A vertical DLU is the average height of the font divided by eight.

The default font of a dialog box is 8-point MS Sans Serif. To change the default font of a dialog box, you need to double-click any free area in the dialog box and then click the Font button in the Properties window of the dialog box.

Do not change the default font of the AVI application's dialog box! In the preceding steps, when you set the X, Y positions of the controls, it was assumed that the font of the dialog box is the default font (8-point MS Sans Serif).

The Visual Implementation of the Menu

The AVI application should have a menu with two popup menus, as shown in Figures 24.12 and 24.13. To implement this menu:

☐ Use App Studio to implement the AVI application's menu according to Table 24.2.

Table 24.2. The AVI application's menu.
Figures relating to menu: 24.12, 24.13

Menu Item
&File
E&xit
&Help
&About Avi...

Don't forget to delete the accelerator keys of the menu items that you removed:

☐ Select `AVI.RC [MFC-Resource Script]` from the App Studio's Window menu, select Accelerator from the Type list, and then double-click `IDR_MAINFRAME` in the Resources list.

☐ Delete the accelerator keys that aren't used by the AVI application. In particular, delete the accelerator keys of the `ID_FILE_NEW`, `ID_FILE_OPEN`, and `ID_FILE_SAVE` menu items.

If you don't delete these accelerator keys, they will be active during runtime. If the user presses Ctrl+N, for example, it will be as if the user selected New from the File menu (even though you removed that item).

To save your work:

☐ Select Save from App Studio's File menu.

The visual implementation of the AVI application's menu is complete.

Executing the AVI Application

Even though you haven't written any code yet, you can execute the AVI application and see your visual design in action:

☐ Select Build All AVI.EXE from the Visual C++ Project menu.

☐ Select Execute AVI.EXE from the Project menu.

> *Visual C++ responds by executing the AVI application. The main window of the application appears with the form that you designed in it (a multimedia control and two check boxes).*

In the following sections you'll write code that makes the multimedia control and the two check boxes functional. You'll also write code that makes the main window's default size small (as shown in Figure 24.10).

To exit the AVI application:

☐ Select Exit from the File menu.

Initializing the Properties of the Multimedia Control

Recall from the previous chapters that you have to write the code that initializes the properties of the multimedia control in the OnInitialUpdate() member function of the view class. This way, when the application is started, the multimedia control will come to life.

Because Visual C++ did not write the declaration and skeleton of the OnInitialUpdate() function, you have to declare this function and write its skeleton. Here's how you do that:

☐ Open the file AVIVIEW.H and add code to it that defines the function OnInitialUpdate() as a member function of the CAviView class. After you write this code, the CAviView class declaration looks as follows:

```
class CAviView : public CFormView
{
     DECLARE_DYNCREATE(CAviView)
protected:
    CAviView();  // protected constructor used by dynamic creation

    /////////////////////////
    // MY CODE STARTS HERE
    /////////////////////////

    virtual void OnInitialUpdate();

    /////////////////////////
    // MY CODE ENDS HERE
    /////////////////////////

// Form Data
public:
    //{{AFX_DATA(CAviView)
    enum { IDD = IDD_DIALOG1 };
    CVBControl*  m_avi;
    BOOL  m_AutoRepeat;
    BOOL  m_Silent;
```

```
          //}}AFX_DATA

// Attributes
public:

// Operations
public:

// Implementation
protected:
virtual ~CAviView();
virtual void DoDataExchange(CDataExchange* pDX);
// Generated message map functions
//{{AFX_MSG(CAviView)
// NOTE - ClassWizard will add/remove functions here.
//}}AFX_MSG
DECLARE_MESSAGE_MAP()
};
```

Now write the `OnInitialUpdate()` function's code:

☐ Open the file AVIVIEW.CPP and add the `OnInitialUpdate()` function to the
end of the file. After you write this function, the end of the AVIVIEW.CPP file
looks as follows:

```
/////////////////////////
// MY CODE STARTS HERE
/////////////////////////

void CAviView::OnInitialUpdate()
{

    // Call the base class function.
    CFormView::OnInitialUpdate();

    // Open the MOVIE.AVI file.
    m_avi->SetStrProperty("DeviceType","AVIVideo");
    m_avi->SetStrProperty("FileName",
                          "\\VCPROG\\AVI\\MOVIE.AVI" );
    m_avi->SetStrProperty("Command", "Open");

    // Movie should play inside application's window.
    m_avi->SetNumProperty("hWndDisplay",(int)m_hWnd);

}

/////////////////////////
// MY CODE ENDS HERE
/////////////////////////
```

789

To review the `OnInitialUpdate()` function's code:

The first statement,

```
CFormView::OnInitialUpdate();
```

calls the `OnInitialUpdate()` member function of the base class. Recall from the previous chapters that you have to call the base class `OnInitialUpdate()` function. If you don't, the multimedia control will be dimmed (unavailable).

The next three statements are

```
m_avi->SetStrProperty("DeviceType","AVIVideo");
m_avi->SetStrProperty("FileName",
                      "\\VCPROG\\AVI\\MOVIE.AVI" );
m_avi->SetStrProperty("Command", "Open");
```

The first statement,

```
m_avi->SetStrProperty("DeviceType","AVIVideo");
```

sets the `DeviceType` property of the `m_avi` multimedia control to `"AVIVideo"`. You do this because you want to use the `m_avi` multimedia control to play a video file. (Recall that `m_avi` is the name of the variable that you attached to the multimedia control during the visual design.)

> **NOTE**
>
> When you want to use a multimedia control to play a video (AVI) file, you need to set the `DeviceType` property of the multimedia control to `"AVIVideo"`. For example, to set the `m_avi` multimedia control so that it can be used to play AVI files, use the statement
>
> ```
> m_avi->SetStrProperty("DeviceType","AVIVideo");
> ```

The next statement,

```
m_avi->SetStrProperty("FileName",
                      "\\VCPROG\\AVI\\MOVIE.AVI" );
```

sets the `FileName` property of the `m_avi` multimedia control to `"\\VCPROG\\AVI\\MOVIE.AVI"`. This is done because you want to play the `MOVIE.AVI` video file.

The next statement,

```
m_avi->SetStrProperty("Command", "Open");
```

sets the Command property of the m_avi multimedia control to "Open". After this statement is executed, the m_avi multimedia control is ready to be used (that is, the user can click the buttons of the multimedia control and see and hear the AVI file playing).

The last statement in the OnInitialUpdate() function is

```
m_avi->SetNumProperty("hWndDisplay",(int)m_hWnd);
```

This statement sets the hWndDisplay property of the m_avi multimedia control to the m_hWnd data member of the view class. Setting the hWndDisplay property to m_hWnd tells the multimedia control that you want to play the video file in the application's window. That is, when the user clicks the multimedia control's Play button, the movie will start playing in the application's window. If you set the hWndDisplay property to 0, the movie won't be played in the application's window. Rather, it will be played in a separate window.

NOTE

In the preceding code, you set the hWndDisplay property of the m_avi multimedia control to m_hwnd. As a result, the movie will be displayed in the application's window. If instead of setting the hWndDisplay property to m_hwnd, you set it to 0, as in

```
m_avi->SetNumProperty("hWndDisplay", 0);
```

the movie will be played in a separate window. (This separate window is called the *stage* window.) Note that 0 is the default value of the hWndDisplay property. Thus, if you do not set the hWndDisplay property to any value, the movie will appear in a separate window.

To summarize what the code that you wrote in OnInitialUpdate() does:

It calls the OnIntialUpdate() function of the base class.
It sets the DeviceType property of the m_avi multimedia control to AVIVideo (because you want to use the m_avi multimedia control to play an AVI file).
It sets the FileName property of the m_avi multimedia control to \\VCPROG\\AVI\\MOVIE.AVI (because this is the AVI file that you want to play).

It issues the Open command to the `m_avi` multimedia control.

It sets the `hWndDisplay` property of the `m_avi` multimedia control to the `m_hWnd` data member of the view class (because you want to play the AVI file in the application's window).

Don't forget to save your work:

☐ Select Save from the File menu.

Executing the AVI Application

You've finished writing the code that brings the multimedia control to life. To see your code in action:

☐ Select Build AVI.EXE from Visual C++'s Project menu.

☐ Select Execute AVI.EXE from the Project menu.

Visual C++ responds by executing the AVI application. As you can see, now the multimedia control is enabled.

☐ Click the multimedia control's Play button.

The AVI application responds by playing the MOVIE.AVI *video file in the AVI application's window.*

☐ Experiment with the other buttons of the multimedia control.

Note that when the playback of the AVI file reaches the end, the multimedia control doesn't automatically rewind itself (in other words, before you can play the file again you must first click the Previous button).

In the following sections you'll enhance the AVI application by

Adding code that makes the default size of the application's window small (as shown in Figure 24.10).

Writing the code that automatically rewinds the multimedia control when the playback is over and repeats the playback if the Auto Repeat check box is checked.

Writing the code that instructs the multimedia control to play the video file with no sound whenever the Silent check box is checked.

Terminate the AVI application.

☐ Select Exit from the File menu.

Setting the Default Size of the Application's Window

Recall that when the application starts, the default size of the application's window should be as shown in Figure 24.10. You want the window to appear that way for cosmetic reasons. The movie is displayed on a small area of the screen, so the application's window should be sized accordingly.

You need to write the code that sets the default size of the application's window in the `PreCreateWindow()` member function of the `CMainFrame` class. The header file of the `CMainFrame` class is `MAINFRM.H` and the implementation file is `MAINFRM.CPP`.

☐ Open the file `MAINFRM.H` and add code to it that defines the function `PreCreateWindow()` as a member function of the `CMainFrame` class. After you write this code, the `CMainFrame` class declaration looks as follows:

```
class CMainFrame : public CFrameWnd
{
protected: // create from serialization only
    CMainFrame();
    DECLARE_DYNCREATE(CMainFrame)

    //////////////////////
    // MY CODE STARTS HERE
    //////////////////////

    BOOL PreCreateWindow(CREATESTRUCT& cs);

    //////////////////////
    // MY CODE ENDS HERE
    //////////////////////
...
...
...
```

Now write the `PreCreateWindow()` function's code:

☐ Open the file `MAINFRM.CPP` and add the `PreCreateWindow()` function to the end of the file. After you write this function, the end of the `MAINFRM.CPP` file looks as follows:

```
//////////////////////
// MY CODE STARTS HERE
//////////////////////

BOOL CMainFrame::PreCreateWindow(CREATESTRUCT& cs)
{
```

```
    // Call the base class function.
    CFrameWnd::PreCreateWindow( cs );

    // Set the width of the window to 260.
    cs.cx = 260;

    // Set the height of the window to 290.
    cs.cy = 290;

    return TRUE;
}

////////////////////////
// MY CODE ENDS HERE
////////////////////////
```

As its name implies, the PreCreateWindow() function is automatically executed prior to the creation of the window. You can use this function to override the default characteristics of the window. The parameter of PreCreateWindow(), cs, is a structure of type CREATESTRUCT. You set the characteristics of the window by setting the members of the cs structure.

To review the code that you typed in the PreCreateWindow() function:

The first statement,

```
CFrameWnd::PreCreateWindow( cs );
```

calls the PreCreateWindow() base class. This is necessary because the base class performs various initialization tasks.

The next statement is

```
cs.cx = 260;
```

This statement sets the value of the cs structure's cx member to 260. The cx member specifies the width of the window. Thus, the width of the window will be 260.

The next statement is

```
cs.cy = 290;
```

This statement sets the value of the cs structure's cy to 290. The cy member specifies the height of the window. Thus, the height of the window will be 290.

The last statement in the PreCreateWindow() function is

```
return TRUE;
```

When `PreCreateWindow()` returns `TRUE`, it indicates that the window creation should continue. If `PreCreateWindow()` returns `FALSE`, the window won't be created.

Note that the `cs` `CREATESTRUCT` structure has other members in addition to the `cx` and `cy` members. In the preceding code you set only the values of `cx` and `cy`, because these were the only characteristics that you wanted to modify.

Don't forget to save your work:

☐ Select Save from the File menu.

To see in action the code you typed in the `PreCreateWindow()` function:

☐ Select Build AVI.EXE from Visual C++'s Project menu.

☐ Select Execute AVI.EXE from the Project menu.

> *Visual C++ responds by executing the AVI application. As you can see, now the main window of the application appears as you set it! (See Figure 14.10.)*

☐ Terminate the AVI application.

Automatic Rewinding and Repeat of Playback

Whenever the multimedia control plays the AVI video file completely, the multimedia control should automatically rewind itself. Also, if the Auto Repeat check box is checked, the playback should automatically start over again when it reaches the end.

Now you'll attach code to the `VBN_DONE` event of the multimedia control to implement these features. (Recall from the previous two chapters that the `VBN_DONE` event occurs whenever the playback stops.)

☐ Use ClassWizard to add a function for the event:

Class Name:	`CAviView`
Object ID:	`IDC_TEGOMM_AVI`
Message:	`VBN_DONE`
Function Name:	`OnDoneTegommAvi()`

☐ Edit the `OnDoneTegommAvi()` function that you added to the `AVIVIEW.CPP` file. After you edit the function, your `OnDoneTegommAvi()` function looks as follows:

```
void CAviView::OnDoneTegommAvi(UINT, int, CWnd*, LPVOID)
{
// TODO: Add your VBX event notification handler code here
```

```
/////////////////////////
// MY CODE STARTS HERE
/////////////////////////

// Update the variable m_AutoRepeat.
UpdateData(TRUE);

// Get current position.
long position = m_avi->GetNumProperty("Position");

// Get total length.
long length = m_avi->GetNumProperty("Length");

// If current position is end position, rewind the tape.
   if (position == length)
      {
      m_avi->SetStrProperty("Command", "Prev");

      // If Auto Repeat check box is checked, play again.
      if (m_AutoRepeat == TRUE )
         {
         m_avi->SetStrProperty("Command", "Play");
         }

      }

/////////////////////////
// MY CODE ENDS HERE
/////////////////////////

}
```

To review the OnDoneTegommAvi() function's code:

The first statement is

```
UpdateData(TRUE);
```

This statement updates the variables attached to the controls with the current status of controls. This is necessary because subsequent statements in the OnDoneTegommAvi() function make use of the m_AutoRepeat variable (the variable of the Auto Repeat check box).

The next two statements are

```
long position = m_avi->GetNumProperty("Position");
long length   = m_avi->GetNumProperty("Length");
```

These statements update the position variable with the current playback position and the length variable with the total playback length.

Then an `if` statement is used to see whether the playback has reached the end of the file:

```
if (position == length)
    {
    m_avi->SetStrProperty("Command", "Prev");

    // If Auto Repeat check box is checked, play again.
    if (m_AutoRepeat == TRUE )
        {
        m_avi->SetStrProperty("Command", "Play");
        }
    }
```

If the playback has reached the end of the file (that is, if the condition `position==length` is satisfied), the code within the `if` statement is executed.

The first statement in the `if` statement rewinds the multimedia control by issuing a `Prev` command:

```
m_avi->SetStrProperty("Command", "Prev");
```

The second statement in the `if` statement is another `if` statement that checks whether the Auto Repeat check box is currently checked:

```
if (m_AutoRepeat == TRUE )
    {
    m_avi->SetStrProperty("Command", "Play");
    }
```

If the Auto Repeat check box is currently checked (that is, if `m_AutoRepeat == TRUE`), a Play command is issued to the multimedia control so that the video file will start playing again.

To see the code you typed in the `OnDoneTegommAvi()` function in action:

☐ Select Build AVI.EXE from Visual C++'s Project menu.

☐ Select Execute AVI.EXE from the Project menu.

Verify that the automatic rewinding feature you implemented is working:

☐ Click the Play button and wait until the playback of the movie is done. Then click the Play button again.

As you can see, you don't have to click the Previous button prior to playing the movie again. When the multimedia control reaches the end of the file, the code that you wrote automatically rewinds the multimedia control.

Verify that the automatic playback feature you implemented is working:

☐ Place a check mark in the Auto Repeat check box and then click the Play button.

Because you checked the Auto Repeat check box, the playback will automatically repeat when it reaches the end of the file.

☐ Terminate the AVI application.

Attaching Code to the Silent Check Box

Whenever the Silent check box is checked, the AVI application should play the video file without sound.

To implement this feature, you need to attach code to Silent check box:

☐ Use ClassWizard to add a function for the event.

Class Name:	CAviView
Object ID:	IDC_SILENT
Message:	BN_CLICKED
Function Name:	OnSilent()

☐ Edit the OnSilent() function that you added to the AVIVIEW.CPP file. After you edit the function, your OnSilent() function looks as follows:

```
void CAviView::OnSilent()
{
// TODO: Add your control notification handler code here

    ////////////////////////
    // MY CODE STARTS HERE
    ////////////////////////

    // Update the m_Silent variable.
    UpdateData(TRUE);

    // Set the Silent property.
    m_avi->SetNumProperty("Silent", m_Silent);

    ////////////////////////
    // MY CODE ENDS HERE
    ////////////////////////

}
```

This code is made of two statements. The first statement,

```
UpdateData(TRUE);
```

updates the variables of the controls with the current status of the controls. Thus, after this statement is executed, the variable of the Silent check box (m_Silent) is updated with the current status of the Silent check box. If the Silent check box is checked, m_Silent is equal to TRUE. If it isn't checked, m_Silent is equal to FALSE.

The second statement in the OnSilent() function is

```
m_avi->SetNumProperty("Silent", m_Silent);
```

This statement sets the Silent property of the m_avi multimedia control with the current value of the Silent check box (m_Silent). When the Silent property of the m_avi multimedia control is set to TRUE, the multimedia control will play the movie without sound. Thus, whenever the user checks the Silent check box, the movie will be played without sound.

Executing the Final Version of the AVI Application

To see the code you attached to the Silent check box in action:

☐ Select Build AVI.EXE from Visual C++'s Project menu.

☐ Execute the AVI.EXE application.

☐ Click the multimedia control's Play button.

☐ While the movie is playing, experiment with the Silent check box.

As you can see and hear, whenever the Silent check box isn't checked, the movie is played with sound. Whenever the Silent check box is checked, the movie is played without sound.

Experimenting with Other Video Files

The AVI application's code plays the video file MOVIE.AVI. The book's CD includes other video (AVI) files that you can experiment with. These AVI files reside in the \VCPROG\AVI directory of the book's CD.

You can experiment with these AVI files as follows:

☐ Copy an AVI file from the `\VCPROG\AVI` directory of the book's CD to your `\VCPROG\AVI` hard drive directory.

☐ Change the statement that sets the `FileName` property of the `m_avi` multimedia control so that it specifies the appropriate AVI filename. (The statement that sets the `FileName` property is in the function `OnInitialUpdate()` in the file `AVIVIEW.CPP`.)

25

Multimedia: CD Audio

In this chapter you'll write an

application that uses the

TegoMM.VBX control to play an

audio CD.

> **NOTE**
>
> In this chapter you'll write an application that plays an audio CD. Thus, you'll need a Windows-compatible CD-ROM drive that supports playback of audio CDs. If your system doesn't have such a CD-ROM drive, you may skip this chapter or just browse through it.

Playing an Audio CD with Media Player

 Before you start writing an application that plays an audio CD, verify that your system is capable of playing audio CDs.

☐ Start the Windows Media Player (see Figure 25.1). Media Player usually resides in the Accessories group.

> *Windows responds by running the Media Player program (see Figure 25.2).*

> **NOTE**
>
> Media Player enables you to play various multimedia files, as well as control various multimedia devices (for example, a CD-ROM drive that supports audio CDs).
>
> The Media Player program usually resides in the Accessories group.
>
> To start the Media Player program:
>
> > Double-click the Media Player icon (see Figure 25.1).

Figure 25.1
The Media Player
program's icon.

Figure 25.2.
The Media Player
program.

If your system has the hardware and software needed to play audio CDs, your Media Player program can play them.

To see whether your Media Player program can play audio CDs:

☐ Open the Media Player's Device menu (see Figure 25.3).

Figure 25.3.
The Media Player's
Device menu.

As you can see from Figure 25.3, one of the items in the Device menu is CD Audio. If your Device menu doesn't include this item, it means that your system currently doesn't have the necessary hardware and/or software to play audio CDs. In order to make your system support playback of audio CDs, you need to install the software that comes with your CD-ROM drive.

In the following steps, you'll use Media Player to play an audio CD. If you're already familiar with Media Player's capability of playing audio CDs, you may skip these steps and start reading the next section, which shows you how to write a Visual C++ application that plays audio CDs.

☐ Insert an audio CD into your CD-ROM drive.

NOTE

There are two types of CDs, data CDs and audio CDs.

Data CDs are used to store regular files. For example, the CD that comes with this book is a data CD. Data CDs may contain any type of file (for example, EXE, CPP, WAV, MIDI, BMP).

Audio CDs do not store files. They contain audio only. Typically, an audio CD is purchased in a record store.

☐ Select CD Audio from Media Player's Device menu (see Figure 25.3).

Media Player responds by making its buttons available and changing its title to "Media Player - CD Audio [stopped]" (see Figure 25.4).

Figure 25.4.
Media Player, after
you select CD
Audio from the
Device menu.

To start the playback of the audio CD:

☐ Click the Play button (the leftmost button) in Media Player.

Media Player responds by playing the first track of the audio CD.

> **NOTE**
>
> Some CD-ROM drives must be connected to earphones or external speakers before you can hear an audio CD playing. (There's usually a socket in the front panel of the CD-ROM drive for this purpose.) Other types of CD-ROM drives are internally connected to your sound card's speakers.

To stop the playback:

☐ Click the Stop button (the second button from the left).

Experiment with the other buttons of Media Player.

To terminate the Media Player program:

☐ Select Exit from the Media Player's File menu.

The CD Application

Now you'll write the CD application, which enables the user to play an audio CD.

As you will see soon, the code you'll need to write to play an audio CD is similar to the code you wrote in previous chapters to play a WAV file, a MIDI file, and a video file.

Before you start writing the CD application, execute the copy of it that resides in your C:\VCPROG\ORIGINAL\CH25\CD directory.

To execute the CD.EXE application:

☐ Use Run from Program Manager's File menu to run
`C:\VCPROG\ORIGINAL\CH25\CD\CD.EXE`.

> *Windows responds by executing the CD application. The CD application first displays a limited version message box from the TegoMM.VBX multimedia control.*

☐ Click the OK button of the message box.

> *The main window of* `CD.EXE` *appears, as shown in Figure 25.5.*

Figure 25.5.
The CD application's main window.

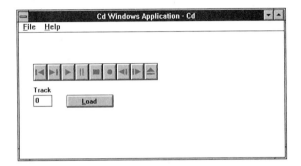

As you can see, the main window of the application contains a multimedia control, a push button (Load), and an edit box that displays the current track number of the audio CD. Note that all of the multimedia control's buttons are currently dimmed, and the number that's displayed in the Track text box is 0.

☐ Insert an audio CD into your CD-ROM drive.

☐ Click the Load button.

> *The CD application responds by making the multimedia control available and displaying the number 1 in the Track text box (see Figure 25.6).*

Figure 25.6.
The CD application after clicking the Load button.

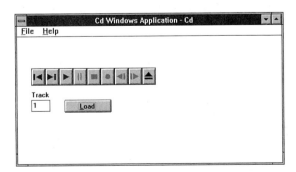

☐ Click the multimedia control's Play button (the third button from the left).

The CD application responds by playing the first track of the audio CD.

To stop the playback:

☐ Click the Stop button (the fifth button from the left).

Experiment with the Previous and Next buttons. The Previous button (the leftmost button) is used to move back to the previous track, and the Next button (the second button from the left) is used to move forward to the next track.

The CD application has two popup menus, File and Help. These popup menus are shown in Figures 25.7 and 25.8.

Figure 25.7.
The CD application's File menu.

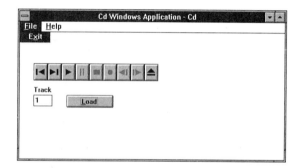

Figure 25.8.
The CD application's Help menu.

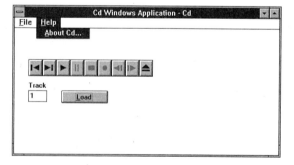

To exit from the CD application:

☐ Select Exit from the File menu.

Now that you know what the CD application should do, you can start writing it.

Creating the Project of the CD Application

To create the project of the CD application:

☐ Select AppWizard from the Project menu.

    Visual C++ responds by running AppWizard.

☐ Use the Directory list box to select the directory `C:\VCPROG\PRACTICE\CH25`.

☐ Type `cd` in the Project Name box.

Now your AppWizard dialog box looks as shown in Figure 25.9.

Figure 25.9.
The CD
application's
AppWizard dialog.

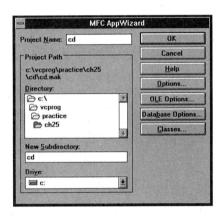

☐ Click the Options button and set the options as shown in Figure 25.10.

NOTE

Just as in the previous three chapters, you need to check the Custom VBX Controls option in the Options dialog box (see Figure 25.10). This is necessary because the CD application uses the TegoMM.VBX control.

☐ Click the OK button of the Options dialog box and then click the OK button of the AppWizard dialog box and finally click the Create button of the New Application Information dialog box.

    AppWizard responds by creating the CD project and all the skeleton files of the CD application.

Figure 25.10.
Setting the options
for the CD
application.

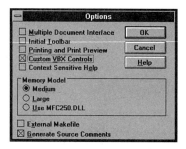

To remove the debug options of the project (so you'll have a small EXE file):

☐ Select Project from Visual C++'s Options menu, click the Release radio button, and then click the OK button of the dialog box.

Creating the Form of the Application

As shown in Figure 25.5, the main window of the CD application should contain a multimedia control, a push button, a label, and an edit box.

To implement this form, you must replace the current view class of the application with a new view class derived from the CFormView class.

Follow these steps to create the form of the application:

☐ Use the Windows File Manager (or DOS Shell) to delete the two view class files of the CD application:

Delete C:\VCPROG\PRACTICE\CH25\CD\CDVIEW.CPP.
Delete C:\VCPROG\PRACTICE\CH25\CD\CDVIEW.H.

☐ Select ClassWizard from Visual C++'s Browse menu.

ClassWizard responds by displaying a dialog box telling you that the view class files don't exist.

☐ Click the OK button of the dialog box.

☐ Click the Remove button of the Repair Class Information dialog box.

☐ Click ClassWizard's OK button.

You've just finished removing the view class of the CD application.

In the following steps you'll create a dialog box, you'll create a `CFormView` type class for this dialog box, and you'll make this class the new view class of the application:

☐ Select App Studio from Visual C++'s Tools menu.

☐ Create a new dialog box with App Studio.

☐ Double-click in a free area of the new dialog box.

☐ Select Styles from the drop-down list box at the upper-right corner of the Properties window.

Set the Styles properties of the dialog box as follows:

☐ Select Child from the Style box.

☐ Select None from the Border box.

☐ Uncheck the Visible property (that is, remove the check mark from the Visible check box).

☐ Select General from the drop-down list box at the upper-right corner of the Properties window, and make sure that the Caption box is empty.

Now connect the dialog box to a class derived from `CFormView`:

☐ Select ClassWizard from App Studio's Resource menu.

ClassWizard responds by displaying the Add Class dialog box.

☐ Type `CCdView` in the Class Name box.

☐ Set the Class Type to `CFormView`.

☐ Make sure that the header filename is `cdview.h` and that the implementation filename is `cdview.cpp`.

☐ Click the Create Class button.

☐ Click ClassWizard's OK button to go back to App Studio.

You've finished creating the new view class of the application. This view class is a derived class from the MFC `CFormView` class and is connected to the dialog box that you created. Thus, the main dialog box of the application will be the dialog box you created.

The Visual Implementation of the Dialog Box

☐ Implement the dialog box of the CD application per Table 25.1.

Table 25.1. The CD application's dialog box.

Class Name:	CCdView
Figure:	25.11
OK button:	No
Cancel button:	No

Object	Property	Setting
Dialog Box	ID	IDD DIALOG1
Multimedia Control	ID	IDC TEGOMM CD
	Variable	m cd (Type: CVBControl *)
Label	ID	IDC STATIC
	Caption	Track
Edit Box	ID	IDC CURRENT TRACK
	Variable	m CurrentTrack (Type: BYTE)
	Disabled	Yes
Push Button	ID	IDC_BUTTON_LOAD
	Caption	&Load

NOTE

Table 25.1 instructs you to place a multimedia control in the dialog box. In order to do this, the TegoMM.VBX control must be installed in your App Studio Tools window. In Chapter 22, "Multimedia: Playing and Recording WAV Files," you were instructed to install the TegoMM.VBX control by following a set of step-by-step instructions. If you haven't done so, you need to refer back to Chapter 22 and install the TegoMM.VBX control.

NOTE

Table 25.1 instructs you to attach the variable m_cd (of type CVBControl *) to the multimedia control. As in previous chapters, the variable that you attach to the multimedia control is later used by the application's code to communicate with the multimedia control.

NOTE

Table 25.1 instructs you to set the `Disabled` property of the
`IDC_CURRENT_TRACK` edit box. This is necessary because the
`IDC_CURRENT_TRACK` edit box should be read-only. In other words, the user
isn't allowed to type in this edit box.

Note also that Table 25.1 instructs you to attach the variable `m_CurrentTrack`
of type `BYTE` to the `IDC_CURRENT_TRACK` edit box. This is necessary because, as
you will see later, the current track number of the CD is stored as a `BYTE`.

Now your dialog box looks as shown in Figure 25.11.

*Figure 25.11.
The CD
application's dialog
box.*

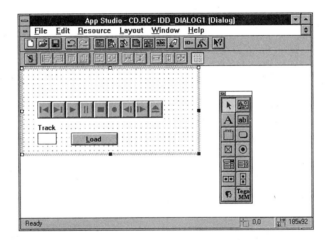

The Visual Implementation of the Menu

The CD application should have a menu with two popup menus, as shown in Figures 25.7 and 25.8.

☐ Use App Studio to implement the menu of the CD application per
Table 25.2.

Table 25.2. The CD application's menu.
Figures relating to menu: 25.7, 25.8

Menu Item
&File
E&xit
&Help
&About Cd...

Don't forget to delete the accelerator keys of the menu items that you removed:

☐ Select `CD.RC [MFC-Resource Script]` from App Studio's Window menu, select Accelerator from the Type list, and then double-click `IDR_MAINFRAME` in the Resources list.

☐ Delete the accelerator keys that aren't used by the CD application. In particular, delete the accelerator keys of the `ID_FILE_NEW`, `ID_FILE_OPEN`, and `ID_FILE_SAVE` menu items.

If you don't delete these accelerator keys, they'll be active during runtime. If the user presses Ctrl+N, for example, it's as if the user selected New from the File menu (even though you removed that item).

Save your work:

☐ Select Save from App Studio's File menu.

The visual implementation of the CD application's menu is complete.

Executing the CD Application

Even though you haven't written any code, execute the CD application and see in action your visual design:

☐ Select Build All CD.EXE from Visual C++'s Project menu.

☐ Select Execute CD.EXE from the Project menu.

Visual C++ responds by executing the CD application. The main window of the application appears with the form that you designed (a multimedia control, a push button, a label, and a disabled edit box).

In the following sections you'll write code that makes the multimedia control and Load button functional.

To exit the CD application:

☐ Select Exit from the File menu.

Initializing the Properties of the Multimedia Control

Recall from the previous chapters that you write the code that initializes the properties of the multimedia control in the OnInitialUpdate() member function of the view class. This way, when the application is started, the multimedia control comes to life.

Because Visual C++ did not write the declaration and skeleton of the OnInitialUpdate() function, you have to declare this function and write its skeleton. Here's how you do that:

☐ Open the file CDVIEW.H and add code to it that defines the function OnInitialUpdate() as a member function of the CCdView class. After you write this code, the CCdView class declaration looks as follows:

```
class CCdView : public CFormView
{
     DECLARE_DYNCREATE(CCdView)
protected:
 CCdView();  // protected constructor dynamic creation


     /////////////////////////
     // MY CODE STARTS HERE
     /////////////////////////

     virtual void OnInitialUpdate();

     /////////////////////////
     // MY CODE ENDS HERE
     /////////////////////////

// Form Data
public:
     //{{AFX_DATA(CCdView)
     enum { IDD = IDD_DIALOG1 };
     CVBControl*  m_cd;
     BYTE   m_CurrentTrack;
     //}}AFX_DATA
 . . .
 . . .
 . . .
```

Now write the `OnInitialUpdate()` function's code:

☐ Open the file `CDVIEW.CPP` and add the `OnInitialUpdate()` function to the end of the file. After you write this function, the end of the `CDVIEW.CPP` file looks as follows:

```
/////////////////////////
// MY CODE STARTS HERE
/////////////////////////

void CCdView::OnInitialUpdate()
{

    // Call the base class function.
    CFormView::OnInitialUpdate();

    // Set the DeviceType property to "CDAudio".
    m_cd->SetStrProperty("DeviceType","CDAudio");

    // Set the UpdateInterval property to 250 milliseconds.
    m_cd->SetNumProperty("UpdateInterval",250);

}

/////////////////////////
// MY CODE ENDS HERE
/////////////////////////
```

To review the `OnInitialUpdate()` function's code:

The first statement,

```
CFormView::OnInitialUpdate();
```

calls the `OnInitialUpdate()` member function of the base class. Recall from the previous chapters that you have to call the base class `OnInitialUpdate()` function. If you don't, the multimedia control will be dimmed (unavailable).

The next statement,

```
m_cd->SetStrProperty("DeviceType","CDAudio");
```

sets the `DeviceType` property of the `m_cd` multimedia control to `"CDAudio"`. This is necessary because you want to use the `m_cd` multimedia control to play an audio CD. (Recall that `m_cd` is the name of the variable that you attached to the multimedia control during the visual design.)

> **NOTE**
>
> When you want to use a multimedia control to play an audio CD, you need to set the `DeviceType` property of the multimedia control to `CDAudio`. For example, to set the `m_cd` multimedia control so that it can be used to play audio CDs, use the statement
>
> ```
> m_cd->SetStrProperty("DeviceType","CDAudio");
> ```

The last statement in the `OnInitialUpdate()` function is

```
m_cd->SetNumProperty("UpdateInterval",250);
```

This statement sets the `UpdateInterval` property of the `m_cd` multimedia control to 250 milliseconds. What is the `UpdateInterval` property of the multimedia control? The following section explains it.

The *UpdateInterval* Property of the Multimedia Control

The multimedia control, like other controls, has events that are associated with it. In the previous three chapters you attached code to one of these events: the `VBN_DONE` event.

Another important event that's associated with the multimedia control is the `VBN_STATUSUPDATE` event. This event occurs every X milliseconds, where X is the current value of the multimedia control's `UpdateInterval` property.

The last statement that you typed in the `OnInitialUpdate()` function is

```
m_cd->SetNumProperty("UpdateInterval",250);
```

This statement sets the `UpdateInterval` property of the `m_cd` multimedia control to 250 milliseconds. This means that the `VBN_STATUSUPDATE` event will be executed every 250 milliseconds, and so will the code you'll attach to it. You'll attach code to the `VBN_STATUSUPDATE` event later in this chapter.

Attaching Code to the Load Button

The code that you wrote in the `OnInitialUpdate()` function sets the `DeviceType` property of the multimedia control to `CDAudio`, and it sets the `UpdateInterval` property of the multimedia control to 250 milliseconds. But this code does not issue an

Open command to the multimedia control. Why not? Because in the CD application, there's no point in issuing an Open command before the user places a CD in the CD-ROM drive.

Thus, the code that issues the Open command should be attached to the Load push button. This way, the user is given an opportunity to place an audio CD in the CD-ROM drive. Once the CD is safely secured in the CD-ROM drive, the user can click the Load button.

Follow these steps to attach code to the Load push button:

☐ Use ClassWizard to add a function for the event:

Class Name:	CCdView
Object ID:	IDC_LOAD_BUTTON
Message:	BN_CLICKED
Function Name:	OnButtonLoad()

☐ Edit the OnButtonLoad() function that you added to the CDVIEW.CPP file. After you edit the OnButtonLoad() function, it looks as follows:

```
void CCdView::OnButtonLoad()
{
// TODO: Add your control notification handler code here

    /////////////////////////
    // MY CODE STARTS HERE
    /////////////////////////

    // Issue an Open command to the multimedia control.
    m_cd->SetStrProperty("Command", "Open");

    /////////////////////
    // MY CODE ENDS HERE
    /////////////////////

}
```

The code that you just typed in the OnButtonLoad() function is made up of one statement:

```
// Issue an Open command to the multimedia control.
m_cd->SetStrProperty("Command", "Open");
```

This statement issues an Open command to the m_cd multimedia control. Thus, whenever the user clicks the Load button, an Open command is issued to the multimedia control.

Don't forget to save your work:

☐ Select Save from the File menu.

Executing the CD Application

You've finished writing the code that brings the multimedia control to life. To see your code in action:

☐ Select Build CD.EXE from Visual C++'s Project menu.

☐ Select Execute CD.EXE from the Project menu.

> *Visual C++ responds by executing the CD application. The multimedia control is dimmed because an Open command has not yet been issued to the multimedia control.*

☐ Insert an audio CD into your CD-ROM drive.

☐ Click the Load button.

> *The CD application responds by issuing an Open command to the multimedia control. The multimedia control is now available.*

☐ Click the Play button.

> *The CD application responds by playing the first track of the CD.*

To stop the playback:

☐ Click the Stop button.

☐ Experiment with the Previous and Next buttons. The Previous button (the leftmost button) is used to move back to the previous track, and the Next button (the second button from the left) is used to move forward to the next track.

Note that the Track edit box always displays the number 0. In the following section you'll add code to the CD application so that the Track edit box will display the current track number.

Terminate the CD application:

☐ Select Exit from the File menu.

Updating the Track Edit Box

At any given time, the Track edit box should display the number of the track currently being played. You will attach the code that updates the Track edit box to the VBN_STATUSUPDATE event.

As stated earlier, the VBN_STATUSUPDATE event is executed every X milliseconds, where X is the current value of the multimedia control's UpdateInterval property.

Recall that in the OnInitialUpdate() function you set the m_cd multimedia control's UpdateInterval property to 250 milliseconds. Thus, the code that you'll attach to the VBN_STATUSUPDATE event will be executed every 250 milliseconds.

☐ Use ClassWizard to add a function for the event:

Class Name:	CCdView
Object ID:	IDC_TEGOMM_CD
Message:	VBN_STATUSUPDATE
Function Name:	OnStatusupdateTegommCd()

☐ Edit the OnStatusupdateTegommCd() function that you added to the CDVIEW.CPP file. After you edit this function, it looks as follows:

```
void CCdView::OnStatusupdateTegommCd(UINT, int, CWnd*, LPVOID)
{
// TODO: Add your VBX event notification handler code here

///////////////////////
// MY CODE STARTS HERE
///////////////////////

// Set the TimeFormat property to "tmsf".
// (TimeFormat = "tmsf" = Tracks, Minutes, Seconds, Frames)
m_cd->SetStrProperty("TimeFormat","tmsf");

// Get the current track.
m_CurrentTrack =  (BYTE)m_cd->GetNumProperty("Position");

// Update the screen with the new value of m_CurrentTrack
UpdateData(FALSE);

///////////////////////
// MY CODE ENDS HERE
///////////////////////

}
```

To review the `OnStatusupdateTegommCd()` function's code:

The first statement is

```
m_cd->SetStrProperty("TimeFormat","tmsf");
```

This statement sets the `TimeFormat` property of the `m_cd` multimedia control to `tmsf`. This causes the `Position` property of the multimedia control to store the current playback position in four bytes (Tracks, Minutes, Seconds, and Frames). The least significant byte (Tracks) stores the current track number.

The next statement is

```
m_CurrentTrack = (BYTE)m_cd->GetNumProperty("Position");
```

This statement updates the `m_CurrentTrack` variable (the variable of the `IDC_CURRENT_TRACK` edit box) with the `m_cd` multimedia control's `Position` property. Note that in this statement the cast `(BYTE)` is used, because the `Position` property is a 4-byte number. However, you're interested only in the least significant byte. As discussed previously, because you set the `TimeFormat` property to `tmsf`, the least significant byte of the `Position` property is the current track number.

The last statement in the `OnStatusupdateTegommCd()` function is

```
UpdateData(FALSE);
```

This statement updates the screen (the `IDC_CURRENT_TRACK` edit box) with the new value of `m_CurrentTrack`.

Executing the Final Version of the CD Application

To see the code that you attached to the `VBN_STATUSUPDATE` event in action:

☐ Select Build CD.EXE from Visual C++'s Project menu.

☐ Execute the CD.EXE application.

☐ Insert an audio CD into your CD-ROM drive.

☐ Click the Load button.

> *The CD application responds by issuing an Open command to the multimedia control. The multimedia control is now available.*

☐ Experiment with the Previous and Next buttons.

As you can see, as you move from one track to another, the Track edit box is updated accordingly. As expected, the code that you attached to the VBN_STATUSUPDATE event is executed every 250 milliseconds, and the Track edit box is updated with the current track number.

26

The Timer

In this chapter you'll learn how to utilize a Windows timer. You will learn what a Windows timer is and how to install and utilize one from within your Visual C++ applications.

You'll also learn how to change the default characteristics of the application's main window.

The MyTimer Application

The MyTimer application is an example of a Visual C++ application that installs and uses a Windows timer.

Before you start writing the MyTimer application, execute the copy of it that resides in your `C:\VCPROG\ORIGINAL\CH27\MyTimer` directory.

To execute the MyTimer application:

☐ Use Run from Program Manager's File menu to execute
   `C:\VCPROG\ORIGINAL\CH26\MyTimer\MyTimer.EXE`.

> *Windows responds by executing the MyTimer application. The main window of* `MyTimer.EXE` *appears, as shown in Figure 26.1.*

Figure 26.1.
The MyTimer
application's main
window.

As you can see, the main window of the application displays the current time, and the application keeps updating the displayed time.

Note that the MyTimer application has two special characteristics:

> Whenever the application is started, the application's window appears with the size shown in Figure 26.1.
> The application's window always appears on the top of the desktop.

To prove that the application's main window is always on top of the desktop:

☐ While the MyTimer application is running, switch to any other Windows application.

As you can see, the window of the MyTimer application always remains on the top of the desktop, even when another application's window is active. Figure 26.2 shows the Window of the MyTimer application when the Paintbrush application's window is active.

The MyTimer application has two popup menus: File and Help. These popup menus are shown in Figures 26.3 and 26.4.

*Figure 26.2.
The MyTimer
window while
Paintbrush is
active.*

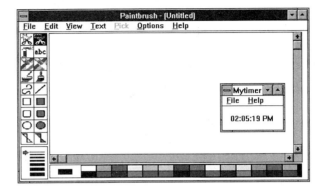

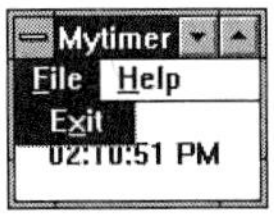

*Figure 26.3.
The MyTimer
application's File
popup menu.*

*Figure 26.4.
The MyTimer
application's Help
popup menu.*

To exit from the MyTimer application:

☐ Select Exit from the File menu.

Now that you know what the MyTimer application does, you can start writing it.

Creating the Project of the MyTimer Application

To create the project of the MyTimer application:

☐ Select AppWizard from the Project menu.

> *Visual C++ responds by running AppWizard.*

☐ Use the Directory list box to select the directory C:\VCPROG\PRACTICE\CH26.

☐ Type mytimer in the Project Name box.

Now your AppWizard dialog box looks as shown in Figure 26.5.

Figure 26.5.
The MyTime
application's
AppWizard dialog
box.

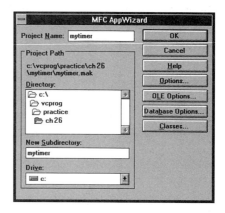

☐ Click the Options button and set the options as shown in Figure 26.6 (that is, uncheck all the check boxes except the Generate Source Comments check box).

Figure 26.6.
Setting the options
for the MyTimer
application.

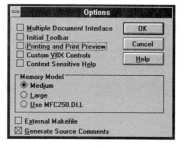

☐ Click the OK button of the Options dialog box and then click the OK button of the AppWizard dialog box and finally click the Create button of the New Application Information dialog box.

> *AppWizard responds by creating the MyTimer project and all the skeleton files of the MyTimer application.*

To remove the debug options of the project (so that you'll have a small EXE file):

☐ Select Project from the Options menu of Visual C++, click the Release radio button, and then click the OK button of the dialog box.

The Visual Implementation of the Menu

The MyTimer application has a menu with two popup menus as shown in Figures 26.3 and 26.4. To implement this menu:

☐ Use App Studio to implement the menu of the MyTimer application per Table 26.1.

Table 26.1. The menu of the MyTimer application.
Figures relating to menu: 26.3, 26.4

Menu Item
&File
E&xit
&Help
&About Mytimer...

Don't forget to delete the accelerator keys of the menu items that you removed:

☐ Select MYTIMER.RC [MFC-Resource Script] from the Window menu of App Studio, select Accelerator in the Type list, and then double-click IDR_MAINFRAME in the Resources list.

☐ Delete the accelerator keys that aren't used by the application. In particular, delete the accelerator keys of the ID_FILE_NEW, ID_FILE_OPEN, and ID_FILE_SAVE menu items.

If you don't delete these accelerator keys, they'll be active during runtime. If the user presses Ctrl+N, for example, it will be like selecting New from the File menu, even though you deleted that menu item.

Save your work:

☐ Select Save from the File menu of App Studio.

The visual implementation of the MyTimer application's menu is complete.

Installing a Timer in the MyTimer Application

The MyTimer application installs and utilizes a Windows timer. What does it mean to install a Windows timer? After you install a Windows timer, a WM_TIMER event will occur at regular intervals (for example, every 500 milliseconds). You can then attach code to the WM_TIMER event, and this code will be executed automatically at regular intervals (for example, every 500 milliseconds).

Now you will write the code that installs a Windows timer in the MyTimer application. You will write this code in the OnCreate() member function of the view class, because you want the timer to be installed when the application is started.

☐ Use ClassWizard to add a function for the event:

Class Name:	CMytimerView
Object ID:	CMytimerView
Message:	WM_CREATE
Function Name:	OnCreate()

☐ Edit the OnCreate() function that you added to the MYTIMVW.CPP file. After you edit this function, it looks as follows:

```
int CMytimerView::OnCreate(LPCREATESTRUCT lpCreateStruct)
{
    if (CView::OnCreate(lpCreateStruct) == -1)
        return -1;

    // TODO: Add your specialized creation code here


    /////////////////////////
    // MY CODE STARTS HERE
    /////////////////////////

    // Install a system timer with 500 milliseconds interval.
    if ( SetTimer (1, 500, NULL) == 0 )
        MessageBox ("Cannot install timer!!!");

    /////////////////////////
    // MY CODE ENDS HERE
    /////////////////////////


    return 0;

}
```

The code that you typed is made of a single `if` statement:

```
if ( SetTimer (1, 500, NULL) == 0 )
   MessageBox ("Cannot install timer!!!");
```

This `if` statement uses the `SetTimer()` function to install a timer. If the `SetTimer()` function fails, it returns 0, in which case this `if` condition is satisfied and the user is prompted with an error message:

```
MessageBox ("Error: Cannot install timer!!!");
```

> **NOTE**
>
> The returned value of the `SetTimer()` function indicates whether `SetTimer()` was successful in installing a timer. If the returned value of `SetTimer()` is 0, it means that `SetTimer()` wasn't able to install a timer. Windows (Version 3.1) allows a total of 32 timers to be active at one time. Thus, if all 32 timers are in use by other applications, you won't be able to install a timer, and `SetTimer()` will return 0.

The `SetTimer()` function takes three parameters. The first parameter is the ID that you're assigning to the timer. In this code, the first parameter is 1. Thus, the ID of the timer will be 1.

The second parameter of the `SetTimer()` function is the interval time of the timer (in milliseconds). The interval time specifies how often a `WM_TIMER` event should occur for this timer. For example, in this code, the second parameter is 500 milliseconds (1/2 second), thus a `WM_TIMER` event will be generated every 500 milliseconds.

The third parameter of the `SetTimer()` function is the address of the function that should be executed whenever a `WM_TIMER` event occurs for the timer. If this parameter is `NULL` (as it is in the previous code), the function that's executed whenever a `WM_TIMER` event occurs is the function attached to the `WM_TIMER` event of the application. You will write this function in the following section.

Attaching Code to the *WM_TIMER* Event

The code that you wrote in the `OnCreate()` function of the view class installed a timer with a 500-millisecond interval. This means that a `WM_TIMER` event will occur every 500 milliseconds. You'll now attach code to the `WM_TIMER` event. Thus, this code will be executed every 500 milliseconds.

☐ Use ClassWizard to add a function for the event:

Class Name:	CMytimerView
Object ID:	CMytimerView
Message:	WM_TIMER
Function Name:	OnTimer()

☐ Edit the OnTimer() function that you added to the MYTIMVW.CPP file. After you edit this function, it looks as follows:

```
void CMytimerView::OnTimer(UINT nIDEvent)
{
// TODO: Add your message handler code
// here and/or call default


    /////////////////////////
    // MY CODE STARTS HERE
    /////////////////////////

    MessageBeep(-1);

    /////////////////////////
    // MY CODE ENDS HERE
    /////////////////////////



    CView::OnTimer(nIDEvent);
}
```

The code that you just typed in the OnTimer() function calls the MessageBeep() function to beep:

```
MessageBeep(-1);
```

Later you'll change this code so that instead of just beeping, the code of OnTimer() will display the current time in the application window. For now, the MessageBeep() function illustrates the timer concept.

To summarize what you've done so far:

You wrote code in the OnCreate() function of the view class that installs a timer with a 500-millisecond interval. Thus, a WM_TIMER event will occur every 500 milliseconds.

You attached code to the WM_TIMER event. This code uses the MessageBeep() function to generate a beep. Thus, when you run the MyTimer application you hear the PC speaker beep every 500 milliseconds.

NOTE

Note that the OnTimer() function has one parameter, nIDEvent. This parameter specifies the ID of the timer for which the WM_TIMER event occurred. In the MyTimer application, you didn't have to use this parameter because you installed only one timer. However, in applications where you install more than one timer, you need to use this parameter to check for which timer the WM_TIMER event has occurred. You can use a series of if statements or a switch statement to check the value of nIDEvent and then execute the appropriate code.

Don't forget to save your work:

☐ Select Save from the File menu.

Executing the MyTimer Application

Try executing the MyTimer application and hear in action the code that you attached to the WM_TIMER event:

☐ Select Rebuild MYTIMER.EXE from the Project menu of Visual C++.

☐ Select Execute MYTIMER.EXE from the Project menu.

Visual C++ responds by executing the MyTimer application. As you can hear, the MyTimer application beeps every 500 milliseconds.

☐ Switch to another Windows application.

The MyTimer application keeps on beeping every 500 milliseconds, even when the window of another Windows application is active!

☐ Switch back to the MyTimer application and terminate it.

In the following sections, you'll enhance the MyTimer application as follows:

You'll change the code in OnTimer() so that instead of beeping every 500 milliseconds, it displays the current time in the application's main window. You'll change the default characteristics of the application main window so that

When the application is started, the size of the window will be as shown in Figure 26.1.

The application's main window will always be on top of the desktop (even when another application is active).

Displaying the Current Time in the Application's Window

Now you'll modify the OnTimer() function so that instead of beeping every 500 milliseconds, it displays the current time in the application's window.

☐ Modify the OnTimer() function in the MYTIMVW.CPP file until it looks as follows:

```
void CMytimerView::OnTimer(UINT nIDEvent)
{
// TODO: Add your message handler code here
// and/or call default

    /////////////////////////
    // MY CODE STARTS HERE
    /////////////////////////

    //MessageBeep(-1);

    // Create an object of class CTime.
    CTime tNow;

    // Update tNow with the current time.
    tNow =  CTime::GetCurrentTime();

    // Format the current time.
    CString sNow = tNow.Format("%I:%M:%S %p");

    // Display the current time.
    CClientDC dc(this);
    dc.TextOut(15,15,sNow);

    /////////////////////////
    // MY CODE ENDS HERE
    /////////////////////////

    CView::OnTimer(nIDEvent);
}
```

In the modification that you just made to the OnTimer() function, you commented out (//) the MessageBeep(-1) statement, and you added the statements that display the current time in the application's window.

The first statement,

```
CTime tNow;
```

creates an object `tNow` of class `CTime`.

The next statement,

```
tNow =  CTime::GetCurrentTime();
```

uses the `GetCurrentTime()` member function of the `CTime` class to update the `tNow` object with the current time.

The next statement is

```
CString sNow = tNow.Format("%I:%M:%S %p");
```

This statement creates a `CString` object (`sNow`) and fills this object with a string that corresponds to the time stored in `tNow`. In the previous statement, `tNow` is converted to a string (`sNow`) by using the `Format()` member function of the `CTime` class. The parameter that is passed to the `Format()` function is

```
"%I:%M:%S %p"
```

The `%I` represents the Hour portion of the time in 12-hour format (01 through 12), the `%M` represents the Minutes portion (00 through 59), the `%S` represents the Seconds portion (00 through 59), and the `%p` represents the AM/PM portion. For example, if the value of `tNow` is 23:30:45 (11:30:45 PM) currently, the statement

```
CString sNow = tNow.Format("%I:%M:%S %p");
```

updates `sNow` with the string "11:30:45 PM".

The last two statements in `OnTimer()` display the `sNow` string:

```
CClientDC dc(this);
dc.TextOut(15,15,sNow);
```

Execute the MyTimer application and see the code that you just entered in action:

☐ Select Build MYTIMER.EXE from the Project menu of Visual C++.

☐ Select Execute MYTIMER.EXE from the Project menu.

Visual C++ responds by executing the MyTimer application. As you can see, the MyTimer application displays the current time in the application's window. The code that you wrote in `OnTimer()` *updates the displayed time every 500 milliseconds.*

In the following sections, you'll add code that changes the default characteristics of the application's main window:

> When the application is started, the size of the window will be as shown in Figure 26.1.
>
> The application's main window will always be on top of the desktop (even when another application is active).

Changing the Default Characteristics of the Application's Main Window

Recall that when the application starts, the default size of the application's window is as shown in Figure 26.1. The window should appear that way for cosmetic reasons. That is, because the area that's needed to display the current time is small, the application's window should be sized accordingly. In addition, the main window of the application should always be on the top of the desktop. That is, even when the window of another application is active, the window of the MyTimer application should remain on top.

You need to write the code that sets the default characteristics of the application window in the PreCreateWindow() member function of the CMainFrame class. The header file of the CMainFrame class is MAINFRM.H and the implementation file of the CmainFrame class is MAINFRM.CPP.

☐ Open the file MAINFRM.H, and add code to it that defines the function PreCreateWindow() as a member function of the CMainFrame class. After you write this code, the CMainFrame class declaration looks as follows:

```
class CMainFrame : public CFrameWnd
{
protected: // create from serialization only
    CMainFrame();
    DECLARE_DYNCREATE(CMainFrame)


    /////////////////////////
    // MY CODE STARTS HERE
    /////////////////////////

    BOOL PreCreateWindow(CREATESTRUCT& cs);

    /////////////////////////
    // MY CODE ENDS HERE
    /////////////////////////
```

```
// Attributes
public:

// Operations
public:

// Implementation
public:
     virtual ~CMainFrame();
#ifdef _DEBUG
     virtual void AssertValid() const;
     virtual void Dump(CDumpContext& dc) const;
#endif

// Generated message map functions
protected:
//{{AFX_MSG(CMainFrame)
// NOTE - the ClassWizard will add and remove
// member functions here.
//    DO NOT EDIT what you see in these blocks of
//    generated code!
    //}}AFX_MSG
    DECLARE_MESSAGE_MAP()
};
```

Now write the code of the `PreCreateWindow()` function:

☐ Open the file `MAINFRM.CPP` and add to it (at the end of the file) the `PreCreateWindow()` function. After you write this function, the end of the `MAINFRM.CPP` file looks as follows:

```
/////////////////////////
// MY CODE STARTS HERE
/////////////////////////

BOOL CMainFrame::PreCreateWindow(CREATESTRUCT& cs)
{

    // Call the base class function.
    CFrameWnd::PreCreateWindow( cs );

    // Set the width of the window to 122.
    cs.cx = 122;

    // Set the height of the window to 90.
    cs.cy = 90;

    // Make the window a topmost window.
    cs.dwExStyle = WS_EX_TOPMOST;
```

```
    return TRUE;
}

///////////////////////
// MY CODE ENDS HERE
///////////////////////
```

As its name implies, the PreCreateWindow() function is automatically executed prior to the creation of the window. You can use this function to override the default characteristics of the window. The parameter of PreCreateWindow(), cs, is a structure of type CREATESTRUCT. You set the characteristics of the window by setting the members of the cs structure.

Review the code you typed in the PreCreateWindow() function.

The first statement,

```
CFrameWnd::PreCreateWindow( cs );
```

calls the PreCreateWindow() base class. This is necessary because the base class performs various initialization tasks.

The next statement is

```
cs.cx = 122;
```

This statement sets the value of the cx member of the cs structure to 122. The cx member specifies the width of the window. Thus, the width of the window will be 122.

The next statement is

```
cs.cy = 90;
```

This statement sets the value of the cy member of the cs structure to 90. The cy member specifies the height of the window. Thus, the height of the window will be 90.

The next statement is

```
// Make the window a topmost window.
cs.dwExStyle = WS_EX_TOPMOST;
```

This statement sets the value of the dwExStyle member of the cs structure to the constant WS_EX_TOPMOST. The dwExStyle member specifies the extended style of the window. When dwExStyle is set to WS_EX_TOPMOST, the window is created as a topmost window. That is, the window will always remain on the top of the desktop (even when another window is active).

The last statement in the `PreCreateWindow()` function is

```
return TRUE;
```

When `PreCreateWindow()` returns `TRUE`, it's an indication that the window creation should continue. If `PreCreateWindow()` returns `FALSE`, the window won't be created.

Don't forget to save your work:

☐ Select Save from the File menu.

Executing the Final Version of the MyTimer Application

To see the code that you attached to the `PreCreateWindow()` function in action:

☐ Select Build MYTIMER.EXE from the Project menu of Visual C++.

☐ Select Execute MYTIMER.EXE from the Project menu.

> *Visual C++ responds by executing the MyTimer application. As you can see, the window of the MyTimer application appears as you specified in the* `PreCreateWindow()` *function (see Figure 26.1).*

Now you can verify that the window of the MyTimer application is the topmost window (as you specified in the `PreCreateWindow()` function):

☐ Switch to another application.

As you can see, the window of the MyTimer application remains on the top of the desktop, even when you switch to another application.

Killing the Timer

In the MyTimer application you didn't have to kill (that is, remove) the timer, because MyTimer needs the timer throughout the lifetime of the application. Once the application is terminated, the timer is killed automatically.

However, in some applications, you'll need to kill the timer during runtime (from within your code). To do this, you need to use the `KillTimer()` function. The `KillTimer()` function takes one parameter: the ID of the timer to be killed. Recall that when you install a timer with the `SetTimer()` function, you specify the ID of the timer. For example, in the MyTimer application you called the `SetTimer()` function as follows:

```
SetTimer (1, 500, NULL)
```

This statement defines the ID of the timer as 1 (the first parameter). Thus, if later in the program you want to kill this timer, you need to call `KillTimer()` as follows:

```
KillTimer(1)
```

Note that both `SetTimer()` and `KillTimer()` are member functions of the `CWnd` class. You can call these functions from the view class of the application, because the view class (`CView`) is derived from `CWnd`.

27

Animation

In this chapter you'll learn how to
write Visual C++ applications that
perform animation.

The BALL Application

Animation is the process of displaying pictures one after the other, thereby creating the illusion that the objects shown in the pictures are moving.

Now you'll write the BALL application, a Visual C++ application that displays an animation show. The BALL application's animation show is silent. Later in this chapter, you'll write other Visual C++ animation applications that include sound.

Before you start writing the BALL application, execute the copy of it that resides in your `C:\VCPROG\ORIGINAL\CH27\BALL` directory.

To execute the BALL application:

☐ Use Run from Program's Manager File menu to execute
`C:\VCPROG\ORIGINAL\CH27\BALL\Ball.EXE`.

> *Windows responds by executing the Ball application. The main window of* `Ball.EXE` *appears, as shown in Figure 27.1.*

*Figure 27.1.
The BALL
application's
main window.*

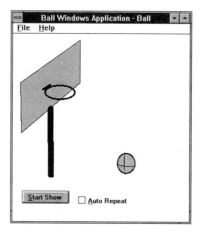

As you can see, the application's main window contains a picture of a basketball and a basket, a push button (Start Show), and a check box (Auto Repeat).

To start the animation show:

☐ Click the Start Show button.

> *The BALL application responds by displaying an animation show. The animation show creates the illusion that the basketball is thrown into the basket and then falls down.*

To make the animation show automatically repeat itself:

☐ Check the Auto Repeat box and then click the Start Show button.

> *The BALL application now displays the animation show continuously; when the animation show ends, it starts all over again automatically.*

The animation show takes place even when another Windows application is active. To verify this fact:

☐ While the animation show is running with the Auto Repeat check box checked, switch to another Windows application (Paintbrush, for example).

☐ Place the other application's window so that you can see both applications at the same time.

> *As you can see, the animation show in the BALL application's window runs even when the other application's window is active. Figure 27.2 shows a snapshot of the BALL application's animation while the Paintbrush window is active.*

Figure 27.2.
The show must go on (even when the Paintbrush window is active).

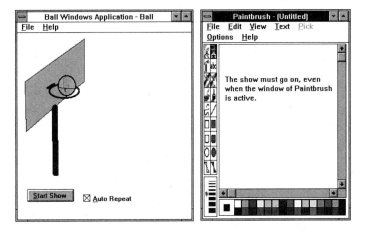

You can also run several instances of the BALL application and view several animation shows simultaneously! To see this:

☐ Terminate the BALL application by selecting Exit from its File menu.

☐ Switch to the Program Manager.

☐ Select Run from Program Manager's File menu and execute
`C:\VCPROG\ORIGINAL\CH27\BALL.EXE`.

☐ Repeat this step to run another copy of the BALL application.

You now have two instances of the BALL application running.

☐ Arrange the two BALL windows so that you can see both of them, check the Auto Repeat check box in each of the two windows and then click the Start Show button.

You now have two animation shows! Figure 27.3 shows a snapshot of the two animation shows.

Figure 27.3.
Running two
animation shows
simultaneously.

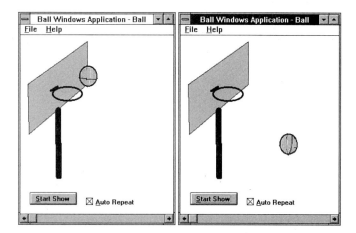

The BALL application has two popup menus, File and Help. These popup menus are shown in Figures 27.4 and 27.5.

Figure 27.4.
The BALL
application's File
popup menu.

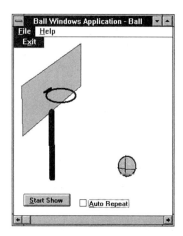

Figure 27.5.
The BALL
application's Help
popup menu.

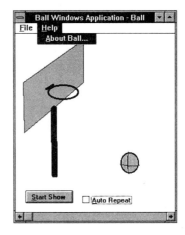

Terminate the two instances of the BALL application that you started earlier:

☐ Select Exit from the File menu of each BALL application.

Now that you know what the BALL application does, you can start writing it.

Creating the Project of the BALL Application

To create the project of the BALL application:

☐ Select AppWizard from the Project menu.

Visual C++ responds by running AppWizard.

☐ Use the Directory list box to select the directory C:\VCPROG\PRACTICE\CH27.

☐ Type ball in the Project Name box.

Now your AppWizard dialog box looks as shown in Figure 27.6.

Figure 27.6.
The BALL
application's
AppWizard dialog
box.

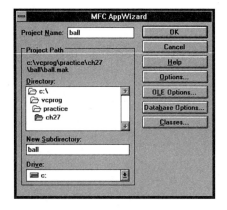

□ Click the Options button and set the options as shown in Figure 27.7.

Figure 27.7.
Setting the options
for the BALL
application.

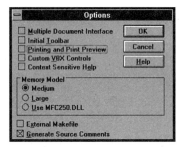

□ Click the OK button of the Options dialog box and then click the OK button of the AppWizard dialog box and finally click the Create button of the New Application Information dialog box.

AppWizard responds by creating the BALL project and all the skeleton files of the BALL application.

To remove the debug options of the project (so you'll have a small EXE file):

□ Select Project from Visual C++'s Options menu, click the Release radio button, and then click the OK button of the dialog box.

Creating the Form of the Application

As shown in Figure 27.1, the BALL application's main window should contain a push button (Start Show) and a check box (Auto Repeat).

To implement this form, you must replace the current view class of the application with a new view class derived from the CFormView class.

Follow these steps to create the form of the application:

☐ Use the Windows File Manager (or DOS Shell) to delete the two view class files of the BALL application:

> Delete C:\VCPROG\PRACTICE\CH27\BALL\BALLVIEW.CPP.
> Delete C:\VCPROG\PRACTICE\CH27\BALL\BALLVIEW.H.

☐ Select ClassWizard from Visual C++'s Browse menu.

> *ClassWizard responds by displaying a dialog box telling you that the view class files don't exist.*

☐ Click the OK button in the dialog box.

☐ Click the Remove button in the Repair Class Information dialog box.

☐ Click ClassWizard's OK button.

You have just finished removing the view class of the BALL application.

In the following steps you'll create a dialog box, you'll create a CFormView type class for this dialog box, and you'll make this class the new view class of the application.

☐ Select App Studio from Visual C++'s Tools menu.

☐ Create a new dialog box with App Studio.

☐ Double-click a free area of the new dialog box.

☐ Select Styles from the drop-down list box at the upper-right corner of the Properties window.

Set the Styles properties of the dialog box as follows:

☐ Select Child from the Style box.

☐ Select None from the Border box.

☐ Uncheck the Visible property (that is, remove the check mark from the Visible check box).

☐ Select General from the drop-down list box at the upper-right corner of the Properties window and make sure that the Caption box is empty.

Now connect the dialog box to a class derived from CFormView:

☐ Select ClassWizard from App Studio's Resource menu.

ClassWizard responds by displaying the Add Class dialog box.

☐ Type CBallView in the Class Name box.

☐ Set the Class Type to CFormView.

☐ Make sure the header filename is ballview.h and the implementation filename is ballview.cpp.

☐ Click the Create Class button.

☐ Click ClassWizard's OK button to go back to App Studio.

You've finished creating the new view class of the application. This view class is a derived class from the MFC CFormView class and is connected to the dialog box that you created. Thus, the main dialog box of the application is the dialog box that you created.

The Visual Implementation of the Dialog Box

☐ Implement the dialog box of the BALL application per Table 27.1.

Table 27.1. The BALL application's dialog box.

Class Name:	CBallView
Figure:	27.8
OK button:	No
Cancel button:	No

Object	Property	Setting
Dialog Box	ID	IDD_DIALOG1
Push Button	ID	IDC_START_BUTTON
	Caption	&Start Show
Check Box	ID	IDC_AUTO_REPEAT
	Caption	&Auto Repeat
	Variable	m_AutoRepeat (Type: BOOL)

Now your dialog box looks as shown in Figure 27.8.

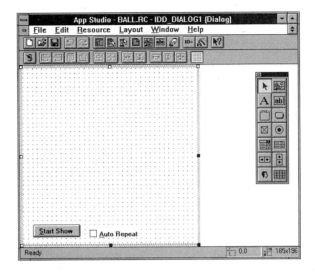

Figure 27.8.
The BALL
application's dialog
box.

The exact locations of the IDC_START_BUTTON push button and the IDC_AUTO_REPEAT check box are important, because the animation show is displayed in the application's main window (see Figure 27.1), and the show shouldn't overlap the controls. Thus, you need to place the controls exactly as shown in Figure 27.8. Here's how you do that:

☐ Drag IDC_START_BUTTON until its position is X=10, Y=175.

NOTE

In the preceding step you were instructed to drag the IDC_START_BUTTON push button to position X=10, Y=175. Here's how you do that:

The status bar of the dialog box displays two pairs of numbers: one pair is the X,Y position of the currently selected control, and the other pair is its width and height.

In Figure 27.9, the currently selected control is a push button. Its position is X=60, Y=70 and its size is Width=75, Height=20.

To place the IDC_START_BUTTON push button at position X=10, Y=175, all you have to do is drag it until you see that the status bar displays the position 10,175. (Note that if the dialog box is not large enough for position Y=175, you'll have to enlarge it by dragging its bottom edge downward.)

*Figure 27.9.
Determining the
position and size of
the selected control
with the status bar.*

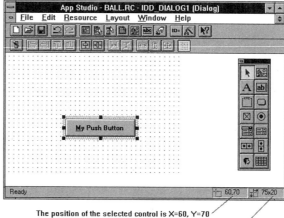

The position of the selected control is X=60, Y=70
The size of the selected control is Width = 75, Height = 20

☐ Drag the Auto Repeat check box until its position is X=70, Y=180.

You've finished designing the dialog box of the BALL application!

Don't forget to save your work:

☐ Select Save from the App Studio's File menu.

NOTE

In the preceding steps, you were instructed to place the BALL application's controls at various X,Y positions. What are the units of these X,Y positions? They're dialog box units (DLUs). A DLU is proportional to the size of the dialog box font. A horizontal DLU is the average width of the dialog box font divided by four. A vertical DLU is the average height of the font divided by eight.

The default font for dialog boxes is 8-point MS Sans Serif. To change the default font, you double-click any free area in the dialog box and click the Font button in the dialog box's Properties window.

Do not change the default font of the BALL application's dialog box. When you set the X,Y positions of the controls, you assumed that the font of the dialog box was the default.

The Visual Implementation of the Menu

The BALL application should have a menu with two popup menus, as shown in Figures 27.4 and 27.5. Use App Studio to implement the BALL application's menu per Table 27.2.

Table 27.2. The BALL application's menu.
Figures relating to menu: 27.4, 27.5

Menu Item
&File
E&xit
&Help
&About Ball...

Don't forget to delete the accelerator keys of the menu items that you removed:

☐ Select BALL.RC [MFC-Resource Script] from App Studio's Window menu, select Accelerator from the Type list, and then double-click IDR_MAINFRAME in the Resources list.

☐ Delete the accelerator keys that are not used by the BALL application. In particular, delete the accelerator keys of the ID_FILE_NEW, ID_FILE_OPEN, and ID_FILE_SAVE menu items.

If you don't delete these accelerator keys, they'll be active during runtime. If the user presses Ctrl+N, for example, it's like selecting New from the File menu, even though you deleted that item.

Save your work:

☐ Select Save from App Studio's File menu.

The visual implementation of the BALL application's menu is completed.

Adding Bitmap Files to the BALL Application

The BALL application uses 11 bitmap (BMP) files for the animation. As you'll see later, the BALL application's code displays these bitmaps one after the other to create the illusion that the object shown in these bitmaps (a basketball) is moving. (See Figures 27.10–27.20.)

The 11 bitmaps of the BALL application are

    `BALL1.BMP` (Figure 27.10)
    `BALL2.BMP` (Figure 27.11)
    `BALL3.BMP` (Figure 27.12)
    `BALL4.BMP` (Figure 27.13)
    `BALL5.BMP` (Figure 27.14)
    `BALL6.BMP` (Figure 27.15)
    `BALL7.BMP` (Figure 27.16)
    `BALL8.BMP` (Figure 27.17)
    `BALL9.BMP` (Figure 27.18)
    `BALL10.BMP` (Figure 27.19)
    `BALL11.BMP` (Figure 27.20)

Figure 27.10.
The `BALL1.BMP`
bitmap file.

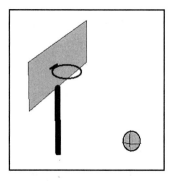

Figure 27.11.
The `BALL2.BMP`
bitmap file.

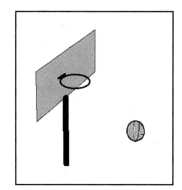

Figure 27.12.
The BALL3.BMP
bitmap file.

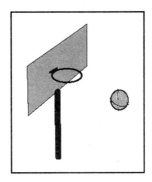

Figure 27.13.
The BALL4.BMP
bitmap file.

Figure 27.14.
The BALL5.BMP
bitmap file.

Figure 27.15.
The BALL6.BMP
bitmap file.

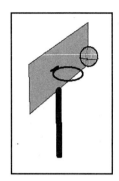

Figure 27.16.
The BALL7.BMP
bitmap file.

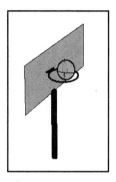

Figure 27.17.
The BALL8.BMP
bitmap file.

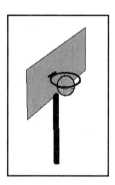

Figure 27.18.
The BALL9.BMP
bitmap file.

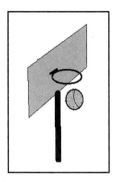

Figure 27.19.
The BALL10.BMP
bitmap file.

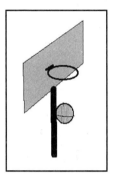

Figure 27.20.
The BALL11.BMP
bitmap file.

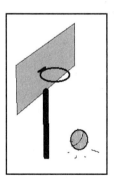

To add these 11 bitmaps to the BALL application, follow these steps:

☐ Select Import from App Studio's Resource menu.

> *App Studio responds by displaying the Import Resource dialog box*
> *(see Figure 27.21).*

851

Figure 27.21.
The Import
Resource dialog box.

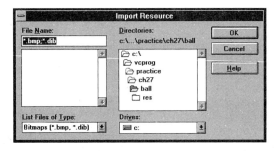

☐ Use the Import Resource dialog box to select the file
C:\VCPROG\BMP\BALL1.BMP. App Studio responds by importing the bitmap
BALL1.BMP into the BALL application and displaying the bitmap (see Figure 27.22).

Figure 27.22.
Importing the
BALL1.BMP
bitmap into the
BALL application.

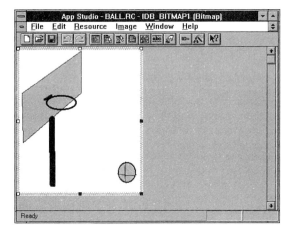

Note that the ID App Studio assigned to the BALL1.BMP bitmap is IDB_BITMAP1 (see Figure 27.22).

☐ Repeat the preceding steps to import the rest of the BMP files:

Import C:\VCPROG\BMP\BALL2.BMP.
Import C:\VCPROG\BMP\BALL3.BMP.
Import C:\VCPROG\BMP\BALL4.BMP.
Import C:\VCPROG\BMP\BALL5.BMP.
Import C:\VCPROG\BMP\BALL6.BMP.
Import C:\VCPROG\BMP\BALL7.BMP.
Import C:\VCPROG\BMP\BALL8.BMP.

Import C:\VCPROG\BMP\BALL9.BMP.
Import C:\VCPROG\BMP\BALL10.BMP.
Import C:\VCPROG\BMP\BALL11.BMP.

NOTE

In the preceding steps, you were instructed to import 11 BMP files into the BALL application. The order in which you import the BMP files is important (first BALL1.BMP and then BALL2.BMP and then BALL3.BMP and so on), because as you import them, App Studio assigns to them the constant names IDB_BITMAP1, IDB_BITMAP2, IDB_BITMAP3, and so on. When you write the BALL application's code, you'll assume that IDB_BITMAP1 corresponds to BALL1.BMP, IDB_BITMAP2 corresponds to BALL2.BMP, IDB_BITMAP3 corresponds to BALL3.BMP, and so on.

You've finished importing 11 bitmaps into the BALL application. Verify that you imported the bitmaps properly:

☐ Select BALL.RC [MFC Resource Script] from App Studio's Window menu.

☐ Select Bitmap from the Type list in the BALL.RC window.

App Studio responds by listing all of the BALL application's bitmaps in the Resources list (see Figure 27.23).

Figure 27.23.
The BALL
application's
bitmaps.

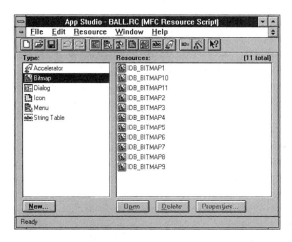

As you can see from Figure 27.23, the IDs that App Studio assigned to the 11 bitmaps you imported are IDB_BITMAP1, IDB_BITMAP2, IDB_BITMAP3, and so on.

To inspect the properties of the IDB_BITMAP1 bitmap:

☐ Highlight the IDB_BITMAP1 item in the Resource list and then click the Properties button (below the Resource list).

App Studio responds by displaying the Properties window of the IDB_BITMAP1 bitmap (see Figure 27.24).

Figure 27.24.
The
IDB_BITMAP1
bitmap's Properties
window.

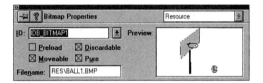

As shown in Figure 27.24, the Properties window displays the IDB_BITMAP1 bitmap as well as its filename, RES\BALL1.BMP. When you imported the file C:\VCPROG\BMP\BALL1.BMP into the BALL application, App Studio copied this file into the application's RES directory. (The RES directory of the BALL application is C:\VCPROG\PRACTICE\CH27\BALL\RES.)

In a similar manner, you can now inspect the other bitmaps that you imported into the BALL application.

NOTE

When you import bitmaps into your application and compile/link them, they become an integral part of the application's EXE file. Thus, the more bitmaps you import into your application, the larger your EXE file becomes!

Don't forget to save your work:

☐ Select Save from App Studio's File menu.

Executing the BALL Application

Even though you haven't written any code yet, execute the BALL application to see your visual design in action.

☐ Select Build All BALL.EXE from Visual C++'s Project menu.

☐ Select Execute BALL.EXE from the Project menu.

Visual C++ responds by executing the BALL application.

The application's main window appears with the form that you designed in it (a push button and a check box). Of course, none of the bitmaps that you imported into the BALL application are displayed yet, because you haven't written any code to accomplish that. In the following sections, you'll write code that brings the BMP files to life.

To exit the BALL application:

☐ Select Exit from the File menu.

Declaring Variables for the Animation Show

Now you'll write code to declare variables that are used by the animation show. You'll declare these variables as data members of the view class, because these variables need to be visible in several member functions of the view class.

☐ Open the file BALLVIEW.H and add code to it that declares two data members in the CBallView class. After you add this code, the CBallView class declaration looks as follows:

```
class CBallView : public CFormView
{
    DECLARE_DYNCREATE(CBallView)
protected:
    CBallView();
// protected constructor used by dynamic creation

// Form Data
public:
    //{{AFX_DATA(CBallView)
    enum { IDD = IDD_DIALOG1 };
    BOOL    m_AutoRepeat;
    //}}AFX_DATA

// Attributes
public:


    /////////////////////////
    // MY CODE STARTS HERE
    /////////////////////////
```

```
     // The current frame number.
     int m_CurrentFrame;

     // An array for the 11 bitmaps.
     CBitmap* m_pB[11];

     ////////////////////////
     // MY CODE ENDS HERE
     ////////////////////////

// Operations
public:

// Implementation
protected:
     virtual ~CBallView();
     virtual void DoDataExchange(CDataExchange* pDX);
// DDX/DDV support
     // Generated message map functions
     //{{AFX_MSG(CBallView)
// NOTE - the ClassWizard will add and
// remove member functions here.
     //}}AFX_MSG
     DECLARE_MESSAGE_MAP()
};
```

In the previous code, you declared two data members for the view class. You declared the first data member as

```
int m_CurrentFrame;
```

m_CurrentFrame is an integer that is used to maintain the current frame number (bitmap) that is being displayed. During the animation show, the application displays the bitmaps one after the other. m_CurrentFrame indicates which bitmap is currently displayed. For example, when m_CurrentFrame is 0, the program should display the first bitmap (IDB_BITMAP1), when m_CurrentFrame is 1, the program should display the second bitmap (IDB_BITMAP2), and so on. As the animation show progresses, the code you wrote increments the m_CurrentFrame variable.

You declared the second data member as

```
CBitmap* m_pB[11];
```

m_pB[] is an array with 11 elements that is used to store pointers to objects of class CBitmap. CBitmap is an MFC class that was specifically designed to work with bitmaps. As you'll see in the next section, the m_pB[] array is used to load the 11 bitmaps of the animation show. m_pB[0] is used for the first bitmap (IDB_BITMAP1), m_pB[1] is used for the second bitmap (IDB_BITMAP2), m_pB[2] is used for the third bitmap (IDB_BITMAP3), and so on.

Don't forget to save your work:

☐ Select Save from Visual C++'s File menu.

Loading the Bitmaps

Before you can display the bitmaps, you need to load them. The code that loads the bitmaps should go in the OnInitialUpdate() function, because you want to load the bitmaps when the application is started. Loading the bitmaps takes time, and if they're loaded during the animation show, it will affect the performance of the animation. When you use OnInitialUpdate(), the code that performs the animation show doesn't need to load the bitmaps, and the animation is performed more smoothly.

Because Visual C++ didn't write the declaration and skeleton of the OnInitialUpdate() function, you have to declare this function and write its skeleton. Here's how you do that:

☐ Open the file BALLVIEW.H and add code to it that defines the function OnInitialUpdate() as a member function of the CBallView class. After you add this code, the CBallView class declaration looks as follows:

```
class CBallView : public CFormView
{
    DECLARE_DYNCREATE(CBallView)
protected:
    CBallView();
// protected constructor used by dynamic creation


    /////////////////////////
    // MY CODE STARTS HERE
    /////////////////////////

    virtual void OnInitialUpdate();

    /////////////////////////
    // MY CODE ENDS HERE
    /////////////////////////

// Form Data
public:
    //{{AFX_DATA(CBallView)
    enum { IDD = IDD_DIALOG1 };
    BOOL    m_AutoRepeat;
    //}}AFX_DATA
```

```
// Attributes
public:


    /////////////////////////
    // MY CODE STARTS HERE
    /////////////////////////

    // The current frame number.
    int m_CurrentFrame;

    // An array for the 11 bitmaps.
    CBitmap* m_pB[11];

    /////////////////////////
    // MY CODE ENDS HERE
    /////////////////////////


// Operations
public:

// Implementation
protected:
    virtual ~CBallView();
    virtual void DoDataExchange(CDataExchange* pDX);
// DDX/DDV support
// Generated message map functions
//{{AFX_MSG(CBallView)
// NOTE - the ClassWizard will add and remove
// member functions here.
//}}AFX_MSG
DECLARE_MESSAGE_MAP()
};
```

Now write the `OnInitialUpdate()` function's code:

☐ Open the file BALLVIEW.CPP and add the `OnInitialUpdate()` function to the end of the file. After you add this function, the end of the BALLVIEW.CPP file looks as follows:

```
/////////////////////////
// MY CODE STARTS HERE
/////////////////////////

void CBallView::OnInitialUpdate()
{

    // Load IDB_BITMAP1
    m_pB[0] = new CBitmap;
    m_pB[0]->LoadBitmap(IDB_BITMAP1);
```

```
    // Load IDB_BITMAP2
    m_pB[1] = new CBitmap;
    m_pB[1]->LoadBitmap(IDB_BITMAP2);

    // Load IDB_BITMAP3
    m_pB[2] = new CBitmap;
    m_pB[2]->LoadBitmap(IDB_BITMAP3);

    // Load IDB_BITMAP4
    m_pB[3] = new CBitmap;
    m_pB[3]->LoadBitmap(IDB_BITMAP4);

    // Load IDB_BITMAP5
    m_pB[4] = new CBitmap;
    m_pB[4]->LoadBitmap(IDB_BITMAP5);

    // Load IDB_BITMAP6
    m_pB[5] = new CBitmap;
    m_pB[5]->LoadBitmap(IDB_BITMAP6);

    // Load IDB_BITMAP7
    m_pB[6] = new CBitmap;
    m_pB[6]->LoadBitmap(IDB_BITMAP7);

    // Load IDB_BITMAP8
    m_pB[7] = new CBitmap;
    m_pB[7]->LoadBitmap(IDB_BITMAP8);

    // Load IDB_BITMAP9
    m_pB[8] = new CBitmap;
    m_pB[8]->LoadBitmap(IDB_BITMAP9);

    // Load IDB_BITMAP10
    m_pB[9] = new CBitmap;
    m_pB[9]->LoadBitmap(IDB_BITMAP10);

    // Load IDB_BITMAP11
    m_pB[10] = new CBitmap;
    m_pB[10]->LoadBitmap(IDB_BITMAP11);

}

/////////////////////
// MY CODE ENDS HERE
/////////////////////
```

To review the OnInitialUpdate() function's code:

The first statement is

```
m_pB[0] = new CBitmap;
```

This statement creates an object of class CBitmap and fills the first element of the m_pB[ ] array (m_pB[0]) with the address of this object. So now, m_pB[0] points to an object of class CBitmap.

The next statement,

```
m_pB[0]->LoadBitmap(IDB_BITMAP1);
```

uses the LoadBitmap() member function of the CBitmap class to load the first bitmap of the animation show (IDB_BITMAP1). So now, for all intents and purposes, m_pB[0] points to the first bitmap of the animation show.

In a similar manner, the rest of the OnInitialUpdate() function's statements load the other bitmaps of the animation show. That is, after OnInitialupdate() is executed, m_pB[0] points to the first bitmap (IDB_BITMAP1), m_pB[1] points to the second bitmap (IDB_BITMAP2), m_pB[2] points to the third bitmap (IDB_BITMAP3), and so on.

> **NOTE**
>
> As stated earlier, the BMP files that you imported into the application with App Studio become an integral part of the EXE file. When you use the LoadBitmap() function, the bitmaps are loaded from the application's EXE file.

Don't forget to save your work:

☐ Select Save from Visual C++'s File menu.

Displaying the First Frame of the Show

Okay, you've written the code that loads the show's 11 bitmaps. Now you can write the code that displays the first bitmap of the show.

When the application starts, the first bitmap of the show should be displayed (see Figure 27.1). To do this, you must attach code to the OnDraw() member function of the view class. The OnDraw() function is automatically executed whenever there's a need to repaint the view window. For example, if the user minimizes the window and then maximizes it again, the OnDraw() function will be executed automatically. It's also executed when the application is started.

Recall that during the visual implementation of the BALL application, you replaced the regular view of the application with a form view (a CFormView class). Visual C++ doesn't write the declaration and skeleton of the OnDraw() function when the view is a form view, so you have to do it. Here's how:

☐ Open the file BALLVIEW.H and add code to it that defines the function OnDraw() as a public member function of the CBallView class. After you add this code, the CBallView class declaration looks as follows:

```
class CBallView : public CFormView
{
     DECLARE_DYNCREATE(CBallView)
protected:
     CBallView();
// protected constructor used by dynamic creation


     ////////////////////////
     // MY CODE STARTS HERE
     ////////////////////////

     virtual void OnInitialUpdate();

     ////////////////////////
     // MY CODE ENDS HERE
     ////////////////////////

// Form Data
public:
     //{{AFX_DATA(CBallView)
     enum { IDD = IDD_DIALOG1 };
     BOOL      m_AutoRepeat;
     //}}AFX_DATA

// Attributes
public:


     ////////////////////////
     // MY CODE STARTS HERE
     ////////////////////////

     // The current frame number.
     int m_CurrentFrame;

     // An array for the 11 bitmaps.
     CBitmap* m_pB[11];
```

```
///////////////////////
// MY CODE ENDS HERE
///////////////////////


// Operations
public:

    ///////////////////////
    // MY CODE STARTS HERE
    ///////////////////////

    virtual void OnDraw(CDC* pDC);

    ///////////////////////
    // MY CODE ENDS HERE
    ///////////////////////

// Implementation
protected:
    virtual ~CBallView();
    virtual void DoDataExchange(CDataExchange* pDX);
// DDX/DDV support
// Generated message map functions
//{{AFX_MSG(CBallView)
// NOTE - the ClassWizard will add and
// remove member functions here.
    //}}AFX_MSG
    DECLARE_MESSAGE_MAP()
};
```

Now write the OnDraw() function's code:

☐ Open the file BALLVIEW.CPP and add the OnDraw() function to the end of the file. After you add this function, the end of the BALLVIEW.CPP file looks as follows:

```
///////////////////////
// MY CODE STARTS HERE
///////////////////////

void CBallView::OnDraw(CDC* pDC)
{

// Create a memory DC.
CDC* pMemDC = new CDC;
pMemDC->CreateCompatibleDC(pDC);

// Select the bitmap into the memory DC.
pMemDC->SelectObject( m_pB[0] );
```

```
// Copy the bitmap from the memory DC into the screen DC.
pDC->BitBlt(10,10,500,500,pMemDC,0,0,SRCCOPY);

// Delete the memory DC.
delete pMemDC;

}
```

```
////////////////////////
// MY CODE ENDS HERE
////////////////////////
```

As stated previously, the OnDraw() function is automatically executed whenever there is a need to paint the window (for example, when the application is started). The parameter of the OnDraw() function (pDC) is the *device context* (DC for short) that corresponds to the window. You draw in the window by calling data members of the CDC class (pDC is a pointer to an object of class CDC).

The code you just typed in the OnDraw() function places the first bitmap of the show in the application's window. Now review this code:

The first two statements that you typed are

```
CDC* pMemDC = new CDC;
pMemDC->CreateCompatibleDC(pDC);
```

These statements create a memory DC called pMemDC. You need a memory DC because you can't place a bitmap directly into the screen DC. You must first place the bitmap into a memory DC and then copy the bitmap from the memory DC to the screen DC.

The next statement is

```
pMemDC->SelectObject( m_pB[0] );
```

This statement places the m_pB[0] bitmap into the memory DC. Recall that m_pB[0] points to the first bitmap of the animation show (IDB_BITMAP1). So at this point, the memory DC p_MemDC contains the first bitmap of the show.

The next statement uses the BitBlt() function to copy the bitmap from the memory DC (pMemDC) to the screen DC (dc). So after this statement is executed, the screen DC (the application's window) contains the first bitmap of the animation show. Recall that the screen DC is pDC (the parameter of OnDraw()).

Now take a close look at the `BitBlt()` statement:

```
pDC->BitBlt(10,10,500,500,pMemDC,0,0,SRCCOPY);
```

As stated previously, this statement copies the bitmap from the `pMemDC` DC (the fifth parameter) into the `pDC` DC (that is, into the screen DC).

The first parameter (10) specifies the X coordinate of the destination bitmap's upper-left corner. The second parameter (also 10) specifies the Y coordinate of the destination bitmap's upper-left corner. Thus, the upper-left corner of the bitmap is at coordinate X=10, Y=10.

The third parameter (500) specifies the width of the bitmap, and the fourth parameter (also 500) specifies the height of the bitmap.

The fifth parameter (`pMemDC`) specifies the DC from which the bitmap is copied. That is, you're copying the bitmap from the memory DC `pMemDC`.

The sixth parameter (0) specifies the X coordinate of the source bitmap's upper-left corner. The seventh parameter (also 0) specifies the Y coordinate of the source bitmap's upper-left corner. Thus, the upper-left corner of the source bitmap is X=0, Y=0.

The eighth parameter is a constant that specifies the operation to be performed. When the constant `SRCCOPY` is supplied as the eighth parameter, the operation to be performed is copying the source bitmap into the destination bitmap.

The last statement that you typed in the `OnDraw()` function is

```
delete pMemDC;
```

This statement deletes the memory DC.

To summarize what the code that you typed in the `OnDraw()` function does:

It creates a memory DC.
It places the first bitmap of the animation show into the memory DC.
It copies the bitmap from the memory DC to the screen DC by using the `BitBlt()` function.
It deletes the memory DC.

Overall, the code that you typed in the `OnDraw()` function places the first bitmap of the animation show in the screen DC. Thus, when the application starts and when there's a need to repaint the application's window, the first bitmap is displayed in the application's window (see Figure 27.1).

Don't forget to save your work:

☐ Select Save from Visual C++'s File menu.

Deleting the Bitmaps

In the `OninitialUpdate()` function, you wrote code that creates 11 `CBitmap` objects:

```
void CBallView::OnInitialUpdate()
{

   // Load IDB_BITMAP1
   m_pB[0] = new CBitmap;
   m_pB[0]->LoadBitmap(IDB_BITMAP1);

   // Load IDB_BITMAP2
   m_pB[1] = new CBitmap;
   m_pB[1]->LoadBitmap(IDB_BITMAP2);

...
...
...

   // Load IDB_BITMAP10
   m_pB[10] = new CBitmap;
   m_pB[10]->LoadBitmap(IDB_BITMAP10);

}
```

You need to write code that deletes these objects when the application terminates. If you don't do this, the memory occupied by these objects won't be released, and the available memory of the user's system will be decreased every time the user executes your application.

Now you'll write the code that deletes the 11 bitmaps from the destructor function of the view class. Here's how you do that:

☐ Open the file BALLVIEW.CPP and add code to the destructor function `~CBallView()` so that it looks as follows:

```
CBallView::~CBallView()
{

   /////////////////////////
   // MY CODE STARTS HERE
   /////////////////////////

   // Delete the 11 bitmaps.
   for (int i=0; i<11; i++)
      delete m_pB[i];
```

```
/////////////////////
// MY CODE ENDS HERE
/////////////////////
```

```
}
```

The code you just typed uses a `for` loop to delete the 11 bitmaps:

```
for (int i=0; i<11; i++)
    delete m_pB[i];
```

Thus, when the application is terminated, the memory occupied by these bitmaps is freed.

Executing the BALL Application

Execute the BALL application and see the code you typed in the `OnDraw()` function in action:

☐ Select Build BALL.EXE from Visual C++'s Project menu.

☐ Select Execute BALL.EXE from the Project menu.

> *As you can see, now the application's main window appears with the first bitmap of the animation show. Try to minimize the window and then maximize it. Again, the application's window appears with the first bitmap of the animation show in it. That is, whenever there is a need to redraw the window (for example, when the application is started), the code you wrote in the* `OnDraw()` *function is executed automatically, and this code displays the* `IDB_BITMAP1` *bitmap (* `pB[0]` *) in the window.*

To terminate the BALL application:

☐ Select Exit from the File menu.

Starting the Animation Show

Now you'll write the code that starts the animation show. The animation show should start running when the user clicks the Start Show button. Thus, you'll attach the code that starts the animation show to the Start Show push button:

☐ Use ClassWizard to add a function for the event:

Class Name:	CBallView
Object ID:	IDC_START_BUTTON

Message:	BN_CLICKED
Function Name:	OnStartButton()

☐ Edit the OnStartButton() function that you added to the BALLVIEW.CPP file. After you edit the OnStartButton() function, it looks as follows:

```
void CBallView::OnStartButton()
{
// TODO: Add your control notification handler code here


//////////////////////////
// MY CODE STARTS HERE
//////////////////////////

// Initialize the current frame number to 0.
m_CurrentFrame = 0;

// Install a system timer.
if ( SetTimer (1, 200, NULL) == 0 )
   MessageBox ("Cannot install timer!!!");

//////////////////////////
// MY CODE ENDS HERE
//////////////////////////


}
```

The code you just typed is made up of two statements. The first statement is

```
m_CurrentFrame = 0;
```

This statement initializes the m_CurrentFrame variable to 0. As stated earlier, the m_CurrentFrame variable is used to store the index number of the current bitmap. When the animation starts, the first bitmap is displayed. Thus, in the previous statement m_CurrentFrame is set to 0.

The next statement is

```
if ( SetTimer (1, 200, NULL) == 0 )
   MessageBox ("Cannot install timer!!!");
```

This statement starts the animation! Recall from the previous chapter that the SetTimer() function installs a timer. In this statement, the second parameter of SetTimer() is 200. Thus, from now on, a WM_TIMER event will occur every 200 milliseconds. In the following section you'll attach code to the WM_TIMER event.

The Animation Show

The code that you attached to the Start Show push button installed a timer with an interval of 200 milliseconds. Now you'll attach code to the WM_TIMER event. This code will be automatically executed every 200 milliseconds.

Here's how you attach code to the WM_TIMER event:

☐ Use ClassWizard to add a function for the event:

Class Name:	CBallView
Object ID:	CBallView
Message:	WM_TIMER
Function Name:	OnTimer()

☐ Edit the OnTimer() function that you added to the BALLVIEW.CPP file. After you edit the OnTimer() function, it looks as follows:

```
void CBallView::OnTimer(UINT nIDEvent)
{
// TODO: Add your message handler code
// here and/or call default

/////////////////////////
// MY CODE STARTS HERE
/////////////////////////

// Increment the current frame number.
m_CurrentFrame++;

// Is it the end of the show?
if (m_CurrentFrame==11)
    {

    // Reset the frame number.
    m_CurrentFrame=0;

    // If Auto Repeat not requested, kill the timer.
    UpdateData(TRUE);
    if (m_AutoRepeat == FALSE)
       KillTimer(1);

    }

// Get a dc for the screen.
CClientDC dc(this);
```

```
// Create a memory DC.
CDC* pMemDC = new CDC;
pMemDC->CreateCompatibleDC(&dc);

// Select the bitmap into the memory DC.
pMemDC->SelectObject( m_pB[m_CurrentFrame] );

// Copy the bitmap from the memory DC into the screen DC.
dc.BitBlt(10,10,550,500,pMemDC,0,0,SRCCOPY);

// Delete the memory DC.
delete pMemDC;

////////////////////
// MY CODE ENDS HERE
////////////////////


    CFormView::OnTimer(nIDEvent);
}
```

The purpose of the code you just typed in the OnTimer() function is to display the next bitmap of the animation show. Every 200 milliseconds the OnTimer() function is executed automatically and the next bitmap of the show is displayed. This creates the illusion that the object in the bitmaps (the basketball) is moving.

The first statement you typed in the OnTimer() function is

```
m_CurrentFrame++;
```

This statement increments the m_CurrentFrame variable because you want to display the next bitmap. For example, if m_CurrentBitmap is currently 0, it means that the m_pB[0] bitmap is displayed. Thus, you increment m_CurrentFrame by 1 because the next bitmap you want to display is m_pB[1].

The next statement is an if statement that checks whether the final bitmap of the show has been displayed:

```
if (m_CurrentFrame==11)
   {

   // Reset the frame number.
   m_CurrentFrame=0;

   // If Auto Repeat not requested, kill the timer.
   UpdateData(TRUE);
   if (m_AutoRepeat == FALSE)
      KillTimer(1);

   }
```

If m_CurrentFrame is 11, it means that the final bitmap of the animation show has been displayed and the show is over. If this is the case, the code under the `if` statement is executed. The first statement in the `if` statement,

```
m_CurrentFrame=0;
```

resets m_CurrentFrame back to 0 because the final bitmap of the show has been displayed and you now want to display the first bitmap.

The next two statements in the `if` statement are

```
UpdateData(TRUE);
if (m_AutoRepeat == FALSE)
   KillTimer(1);
```

These statements determine the current status of the Auto Repeat check box. If it's not checked, the condition m_AutoRepeat==FALSE is satisfied and the KillTimer() function kills the timer. After the timer is killed, the animation show stops, because the OnTimer() function is no longer executed every 200 milliseconds. Note that the parameter that's passed to the KillTimer() function is 1. That's because when you wrote the code that installs the timer in OnStartButton(), you made 1 the ID of the timer.

The next statement in the OnTimer() function is

```
CClientDC dc(this);
```

This statement creates a DC called dc for the view window.

The remaining code in the OnTimer() function is like the code you wrote in the OnDraw() function. It displays the bitmap that's specified by m_CurrentFrame in the application's window.

The first two statements create a memory DC (pMemDC):

```
CDC* pMemDC = new CDC;
pMemDC->CreateCompatibleDC(&dc);
```

Then the bitmap specified by m_CurrentFrame is placed into the memory DC:

```
pMemDC->SelectObject( m_pB[m_CurrentFrame] );
```

For example, if m_CurrentFrame is currently 3, this statement places the bitmap m_pB[3] into the memory DC.

Then, the bitmap from the memory DC (pMemDC) is copied to the screen DC:

```
dc.BitBlt(10,10,550,500,pMemDC,0,0,SRCCOPY);
```

Finally, the memory DC is deleted:

```
delete pMemDC;
```

Executing the BALL Application

You've finished writing the code that performs the animation. To see this code in action:

☐ Build the BALL application and then execute it.

☐ Experiment with the Start Show button and Auto Repeat check box.

As expected, the animation code that you wrote performs the animation.

In the following section, you'll add code to the BALL application that sets the default size of the application's window as shown in Figure 27.1.

☐ Terminate the BALL application by selecting Exit from the File menu.

Setting the Default Size of the Application's Window

When the application starts, the application's window should be the default size, as shown in Figure 27.1. You want the window to appear like this for cosmetic reasons. The animation show is displayed on a small area of the screen, so the application's window should be sized accordingly.

The code that sets the default size of the application's window goes in the PreCreateWindow() member function of the CMainFrame class. The header file of the CMainFrame class is MAINFRM.H and the implementation file is MAINFRM.CPP.

☐ Open the file MAINFRM.H and add code to it that defines the function PreCreateWindow() as a member function of the CMainFrame class. After you add this code, the CMainFrame class declaration looks as follows:

```
class CMainFrame : public CFrameWnd
{
protected: // create from serialization only
    CMainFrame();
    DECLARE_DYNCREATE(CMainFrame)

    /////////////////////////
    // MY CODE STARTS HERE
    /////////////////////////
```

```
      BOOL PreCreateWindow(CREATESTRUCT& cs);

      /////////////////////
      // MY CODE ENDS HERE
      /////////////////////
```

```
// Attributes
public:

// Operations
public:

// Implementation
public:
      virtual ~CMainFrame();
#ifdef _DEBUG
      virtual void AssertValid() const;
      virtual void Dump(CDumpContext& dc) const;
#endif

// Generated message map functions
protected:
      //{{AFX_MSG(CMainFrame)
// NOTE - the ClassWizard will add and remove
// member functions here.
//      DO NOT EDIT what you see in these blocks
// of generated code!
      //}}AFX_MSG
      DECLARE_MESSAGE_MAP()
};
```

Now write the PreCreateWindow() function's code:

☐ Open the file MAINFRM.CPP and add the PreCreateWindow() function to the end of the file. After you add this function, the end of the MAINFRM.CPP file looks as follows:

```
/////////////////////
// MY CODE STARTS HERE
/////////////////////

BOOL CMainFrame::PreCreateWindow(CREATESTRUCT& cs)
{

    // Call the base class function.
    CFrameWnd::PreCreateWindow( cs );

    // Set the width of the window to 335.
    cs.cx = 335;
```

```
    // Set the height of the window to 385.
    cs.cy = 385;

    return TRUE;
}

///////////////////////
// MY CODE ENDS HERE
///////////////////////
```

Recall from previous chapters that the PreCreateWindow() function is automatically executed prior to the creation of the window. You can use this function to override the default characteristics of the window. The parameter of PreCreateWindow(), cs, is a structure of type CREATESTRUCT. You set the characteristics of the window by setting the members of the cs structure.

To review the code that you typed in the PreCreateWindow() function:

The first statement,

```
CFrameWnd::PreCreateWindow( cs );
```

calls the PreCreateWindow() base class. This is necessary because the base class performs various initialization tasks.

The next statement is

```
cs.cx = 335;
```

This statement sets the value of the cs structure's cx member to 335. The cx member specifies the width of the window. Thus, the width of the window is 335.

The next statement is

```
cs.cy = 385;
```

This statement sets the value of the cs structure's cy member to 385. The cy member specifies the height of the window. Thus, the height of the window is 385.

The last statement in the PreCreateWindow() function is

```
return TRUE;
```

When PreCreateWindow() returns TRUE, it indicates that the window should be created. If PreCreateWindow() returns FALSE, the window won't be created.

Don't forget to save your work:

☐ Select Save from the File menu.

To see the code you attached to the `PreCreateWindow()` function in action:

☐ Compile/link and execute the BALL application.

As you can see, now the application's main window is the size shown in Figure 27.1.

The DANCE Application—Animation with Sound

The code you wrote in the BALL application performs animation without sound. Now you'll write another Visual C++ application: the DANCE application. The DANCE application performs animation with music in the background.

> **NOTE**
>
> The DANCE application requires a Windows-compatible sound card. If you don't have a sound card, you may skip this section or just browse through it. Chapter 29, "Advanced PC Speaker Topics," includes an application that performs animation with background music that is played through the built-in PC speaker.

Before you start writing the DANCE application, execute the copy of it that resides in your `C:\VCPROG\ORIGINAL\CH27\DANCE` directory.

To execute the DANCE application:

☐ Use Run from the Program Manager's File menu to execute
`C:\VCPROG\ORIGINAL\CH27\DANCE\Dance.EXE`.

Windows responds by executing the Dance application. The main window of `Dance.EXE` appears, as shown in Figure 27.25.

Figure 27.25
The DANCE
application's main
window.

As you can see, the application's main window contains a picture of a man and a woman, a Start Show button, and a Stop button.

To start the animation show:

☐ Click the Start Show button.

> *The DANCE application responds by playing an animation show with background music. The animation show creates the illusion that the couple is dancing to the music.*

To stop the animation show:

☐ Click the Stop button.

The DANCE application stops the playback of the music and displays the couple standing up (see Figure 27.25).

The DANCE application has two popup menus, File and Help. These popup menus are shown in Figures 27.26 and 27.27.

Figure 27.26.
The DANCE
application's File
popup menu.

Figure 27.27.
The DANCE
application's Help
popup menu.

☐ Terminate the DANCE application by selecting Exit from its File menu.

Now that you know what the DANCE application does, you can start writing it.

Creating the Project of the DANCE Application

To create the project of the DANCE application:

☐ Select AppWizard from the Project menu.

> *Visual C++ responds by running AppWizard.*

☐ Use the Directory list box to select the directory C:\VCPROG\PRACTICE\CH27.

☐ Type dance in the Project Name box.

Now your AppWizard dialog box looks as shown in Figure 27.28.

Figure 27.28.
The DANCE
application's
AppWizard
dialog box.

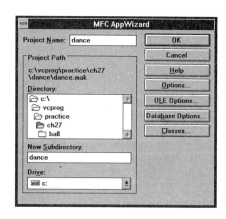

☐ Click the Options button and set the options as shown in Figure 27.29.

Figure 27.29.
Setting the options
for the DANCE
application.

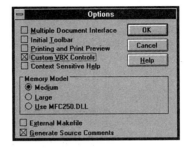

> **NOTE**
>
> The DANCE application uses the TegoMM.VBX control. Thus, as shown in Figure 27.29, you need to check the Custom VBX Controls check box in AppWizard's Options dialog box.

☐ Click the OK button of the Options dialog box and then click the OK button of the AppWizard dialog box and finally click the Create button of the New Application Information dialog box.

> *AppWizard responds by creating the DANCE project and all the skeleton files of the DANCE application.*

To remove the debug options of the project (so you'll have a small EXE file):

☐ Select Project from Visual C++'s Options menu, click the Release radio button, and then click the OK button of the dialog box.

Creating the Form of the Application

As shown in Figure 27.25, the main window of the DANCE application should contain two push buttons, Start Show and Stop. The application's window should also include a multimedia control, but as you'll see later, the application's code makes the multimedia control invisible.

To implement this form you must replace the current view class of the application with a new view class derived from the CFormView class. Follow these steps to create the form of the application:

☐ Use the Windows File Manager (or DOS Shell) to delete the two view class files of the DANCE application:

> Delete `C:\VCPROG\PRACTICE\CH27\DANCE\DANCEVW.CPP`.
> Delete `C:\VCPROG\PRACTICE\CH27\DANCE\DANCEVW.H`.

☐ Select ClassWizard from Visual C++'s Browse menu.

> *ClassWizard responds by displaying a dialog box telling you that the view class files don't exist.*

☐ Click the dialog box's OK button.

☐ Click the Remove button of the Repair Class Information dialog box.

☐ Click ClassWizard's OK button.

You've just finished removing the view class of the DANCE application.

In the following steps you'll create a dialog box, you'll create a `CFormView` type class for this dialog box, and you'll make this class the new view class of the application:

☐ Select App Studio from Visual C++'s Tools menu.

☐ Create a new dialog box with App Studio.

☐ Double-click in a free area of the new dialog box.

☐ Select Styles from the drop-down list box at the upper-right corner of the Properties window.

Set the Styles properties of the dialog box as follows:

☐ Select Child from the Style box.

☐ Select None from the Border box.

☐ Uncheck the Visible property (that is, remove the check mark from the Visible check box).

☐ Select General from the drop-down list box at the upper-right corner of the Properties window and make sure that the Caption box is empty.

Now connect the dialog box to a class derived from `CFormView`:

☐ Select ClassWizard from App Studio's Resource menu.

> *ClassWizard responds by displaying the Add Class dialog box.*

☐ Type CDanceView in the Class Name box.

☐ Set the Class Type to CFormView.

☐ Type dancevw.h in the Header File box.

☐ Type dancevw.cpp in the Implementation File box.

☐ Click the Create Class button.

☐ Click ClassWizard's OK button to go back to App Studio.

You've finished creating the new view class of the application. This view class is a derived class from the MFC CFormView class and is connected to the dialog box that you created. Thus, the main dialog box of the application is the dialog box that you created.

The Visual Implementation of the Dialog Box

☐ Implement the dialog box of the DANCE application per Table 27.3.

Table 27.3. The DANCE application's dialog box.

Class Name:	CDanceView
Figure:	27.30
OK button:	No
Cancel button:	No

Object	Property	Setting
Dialog Box	ID	IDD_DIALOG1
Multimedia Control	ID	IDC_TEGOMM1
	Variable	m_midi (Type: CVBControl *)
Push Button	ID	IDC_START_BUTTON
	Caption	&Start Show
Push Button	ID	IDC_STOP_BUTTON
	Caption	&Stop

Now your dialog box looks as shown in Figure 27.30.

Figure 27.30.
The DANCE
application's dialog
box.

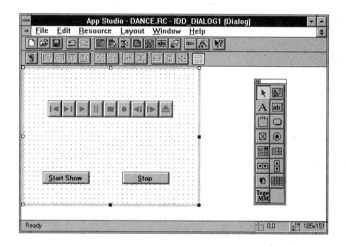

The exact locations of the IDC_START_BUTTON and the IDC_STOP_BUTTON push buttons are important. This is because the animation show is displayed in the application's main window (see Figure 27.25), and the animation shouldn't overlap the controls. Thus, you need to place the controls exactly as shown in Figure 27.30. Here's how you do that:

☐ Drag the IDC_START_BUTTON push button until its position is X=20, Y=105.

NOTE

To drag an object to a particular X,Y coordinate, you need to use the status bar of the dialog box (refer back to Figure 27.9).

☐ Drag the IDC_STOP_BUTTON push button until its position is X=110, Y=105.

These X,Y coordinates assume that the dialog box font is the default font (8-point MS Sans Serif), so do not change the default font of the dialog box.

Note that the exact location of the multimedia control is not important. That's because you're going to make the multimedia control invisible, as you'll see later when you write the DANCE application's code.

You've finished designing the DANCE application's dialog box!

Don't forget to save your work:

☐ Select Save from App Studio's File menu.

The Visual Implementation of the Menu

The DANCE application should have a menu with two popup menus, as shown in Figures 27.26 and 27.27. Use App Studio to implement the DANCE application's menu per Table 27.4.

Table 27.4. The DANCE application's menu.
Figures relating to menu: 27.26, 27.27

Menu Item
&File
E&xit
&Help
&About Dance...

Don't forget to delete the accelerator keys of the menu items that you removed:

☐ Select DANCE.RC [MFC-Resource Script] from App Studio's Window menu, select Accelerator from the Type list and then double-click IDR_MAINFRAME in the Resources list.

☐ Delete the accelerator keys that are not used by the DANCE application. In particular, delete the accelerator keys of the ID_FILE_NEW, ID_FILE_OPEN, and ID_FILE_SAVE menu items.

Save your work:

☐ Select Save from App Studio's File menu.

The visual implementation of the DANCE application's menu is completed.

Adding Bitmap Files to the DANCE Application

The DANCE application uses four bitmap (BMP) files for the animation. The DANCE application's code displays these bitmaps one after the other to create the illusion that the objects in these bitmaps (a couple) are moving.

The four bitmaps of the DANCE application are

DANCE1.BMP (Figure 27.31)
DANCE2.BMP (Figure 27.32)
DANCE3.BMP (Figure 27.33)
DANCE4.BMP (Figure 27.34)

Figure 27.31.
The DANCE1.BMP
bitmap file.

Figure 27.32.
The DANCE2.BMP
bitmap file.

Figure 27.33.
The DANCE3.BMP
bitmap file.

To add these four bitmaps to the DANCE application, follow these steps:

☐ Select Import from App Studio's Resource menu.

App Studio responds by displaying the Import Resource dialog box.

☐ Use the Import Resource dialog box to select the file
C:\VCPROG\BMP\DANCE1.BMP.

App Studio responds by importing the bitmap DANCE1.BMP *into the DANCE application and displaying the bitmap (see Figure 27.35).*

Figure 27.34.
Importing the
DANCE1.BMP
bitmap into the
DANCE
application.

Figure 27.35.
The DANCE4.BMP
bitmap file.

Note that the ID that App Studio assigned to the DANCE1.BMP bitmap is IDB_BITMAP1 (see Figure 27.35).

Repeat these steps to import the three other BMP files:

> Import C:\VCPROG\BMP\DANCE2.BMP.
> Import C:\VCPROG\BMP\DANCE3.BMP.
> Import C:\VCPROG\BMP\DANCE4.BMP.

You've finished importing four bitmaps into the DANCE application. To verify that you imported the bitmaps properly:

☐ Select `DANCE.RC [MFC Resource Script]` from App Studio's Window menu.

☐ Select Bitmap from the Type list in the DANCE.RC window.

> *App Studio responds by listing all of the DANCE application's bitmaps in the Resources list (see Figure 27.36).*

Figure 27.36.
The DANCE
application's
bitmaps.

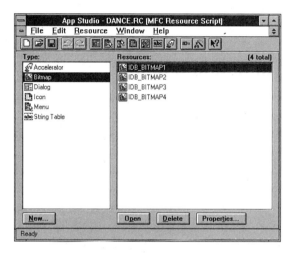

As you can see from Figure 27.36, the IDs that App Studio assigned to the four bitmaps you imported are `IDB_BITMAP1`, `IDB_BITMAP2`, `IDB_BITMAP3`, and `IDB_BITMAP4`.

To inspect the properties of the `IDB_BITMAP1` bitmap:

☐ Highlight the `IDB_BITMAP1` item in the Resource list and then click the Properties button (below the Resource list).

> *App Studio responds by displaying the Properties window of the* `IDB_BITMAP1` *bitmap (see Figure 27.37).*

Figure 27.37.
The
IDB_BITMAP1
bitmap's Properties
window.

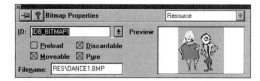

As you can see from Figure 27.37, the Properties window displays the `IDB_BITMAP1` bitmap as well as its filename, `RES\DANCE1.BMP`. When you imported the file `C:\VCPROG\BMP\DANCE1.BMP` into the DANCE application, App Studio copied this file into the application's `RES` directory. (The `RES` directory of the DANCE application is `C:\VCPROG\PRACTICE\CH27\DANCE\RES`.)

In a similar manner, you can now inspect the other bitmaps you imported to the DANCE application.

Don't forget to save your work:

☐ Select Save from App Studio's File menu.

Executing the DANCE Application

Even though you haven't written any code yet, execute the DANCE application to see in action your visual design:

☐ Select Build All DANCE.EXE from Visual C++'s Project menu.

☐ Select Execute DANCE.EXE from the Project menu.

> *Visual C++ responds by executing the DANCE application.*

The application's main window appears with the form that you designed in it (a multimedia control and two push buttons). Of course, none of the bitmaps you imported into the DANCE application is displayed yet, because you haven't written any code to accomplish that. In the following sections, you'll write code that displays the BMP files.

☐ Exit the DANCE application by selecting Exit from the File menu.

Declaring Variables for the Animation Show

Now you'll write code that declares variables that are used by the animation show. You'll declare these variables as data members of the view class, because these variables need to be visible in several member functions of the view class.

☐ Open the file `DANCEVW.H` and add code to it that declares two data members to the `CDanceView` class declaration. After you add this code, the `CDanceView` class declaration looks as follows:

```
class CDanceView : public CFormView
{
        DECLARE_DYNCREATE(CDanceView)
```

```
protected:
    CDanceView();
// protected constructor used by dynamic creation

// Form Data
public:
    //{{AFX_DATA(CDanceView)
    enum { IDD = IDD_DIALOG1 };
    CVBControl*     m_midi;
    //}}AFX_DATA

    ////////////////////////
    // MY CODE STARTS HERE
    ////////////////////////

    // The current frame number.
    int m_CurrentFrame;

    // An array for the 4 bitmaps.
    CBitmap* m_pB[4];

    ///////////////////////
    // MY CODE ENDS HERE
    ///////////////////////

// Attributes
public:

// Operations
public:

// Implementation
protected:
    virtual ~CDanceView();
    virtual void DoDataExchange(CDataExchange* pDX);
// DDX/DDV support
    // Generated message map functions
    //{{AFX_MSG(CDanceView)
// NOTE - the ClassWizard will add and
// remove member functions here.
    //}}AFX_MSG
    DECLARE_MESSAGE_MAP()
};
```

As you can see, these data members are the same as the data members that you declared in the BALL application. The first data member, m_CurrentFrame, is an integer that is used to maintain the current frame number (bitmap) that's being displayed.

For example, when m_CurrentFrame is 0, the program should display the first bitmap (IDB_BITMAP1); when m_CurrentFrame is 1, the program should display the second frame (IDB_BITMAP2); and so on. As the animation show progresses, your code increments the m_CurrentFrame variable.

You declared the second data member as

```
CBitmap* m_pB[4];
```

m_pB[] is an array with four elements that is used to store pointers to objects of class CBitmap. m_pB[0] is used for the first bitmap (IDB_BITMAP1), m_pB[1] is used for the second bitmap (IDB_BITMAP2), m_pB[2] is used for the third bitmap (IDB_BITMAP3), and m_pB[3] is used for the fourth bitmap (IDB_BITMAP4).

Don't forget to save your work:

☐ Select Save from Visual C++'s File menu.

Loading the Bitmaps and Initializing the Multimedia Control

Now you'll add code to the OnInitialUpdate() function that initializes the multimedia control and loads the bitmaps. This way, the multimedia control and the bitmaps become available when the application starts.

Because Visual C++ didn't write the declaration and skeleton of the OnInitialUpdate() function, you have to declare this function and write its skeleton. Here's how you do that:

☐ Open the file DANCEVW.H and add code to it that defines the function OnInitialUpdate() as a member function of the CDanceView class. After you add this code, the CDanceView class declaration looks as follows:

```
class CDanceView : public CFormView
{
    DECLARE_DYNCREATE(CDanceView)
protected:
  CDanceView();
// protected constructor used by dynamic creation

  /////////////////////////
  // MY CODE STARTS HERE
  /////////////////////////

  virtual void OnInitialUpdate();
```

```
///////////////////
// MY CODE ENDS HERE
///////////////////


// Form Data
public:
    //{{AFX_DATA(CDanceView)
    enum { IDD = IDD_DIALOG1 };
    CVBControl*    m_midi;
    //}}AFX_DATA

    /////////////////////
    // MY CODE STARTS HERE
    /////////////////////

    // The current frame number.
    int m_CurrentFrame;

    // An array for the 4 bitmaps.
    CBitmap* m_pB[4];

    ///////////////////
    // MY CODE ENDS HERE
    ///////////////////


// Attributes
public:

// Operations
public:

// Implementation
protected:
    virtual ~CDanceView();
    virtual void DoDataExchange(CDataExchange* pDX);
// DDX/DDV support
// Generated message map functions
//{{AFX_MSG(CDanceView)
// NOTE - the ClassWizard will add and remove
// member functions here.
    //}}AFX_MSG
    DECLARE_MESSAGE_MAP()
};
```

Now write the `OnInitialUpdate()` function's code:

☐ Open the file `DANCEVW.CPP` and add the `OnInitialUpdate()` function to the end of the file. After you add this function, the end of the `DANCEVW.CPP` file looks as follows:

889

```
/////////////////////
// MY CODE STARTS HERE
/////////////////////

void CDanceView::OnInitialUpdate()
{

 // Call the base class function.
 CFormView::OnInitialUpdate();

 // Set the multimedia control for playback of MIDI files.
 m_midi->SetStrProperty("DeviceType","Sequencer");

 // Disable the timer of the multimedia control.
 m_midi->SetNumProperty("UpdateInterval",0);

 // Set the FileName property.
 m_midi->SetStrProperty("FileName",
                        "\\VCPROG\\MIDI\\BOURBON6.MID");

 // Make the multimedia control invisible.
 m_midi->SetNumProperty("Visible", FALSE);

 // Issue an Open command to the multimedia control.
 m_midi->SetStrProperty("Command","Open");

 // Load IDB_BITMAP1
 m_pB[0] = new CBitmap;
 m_pB[0]->LoadBitmap(IDB_BITMAP1);

 // Load IDB_BITMAP2
 m_pB[1] = new CBitmap;
 m_pB[1]->LoadBitmap(IDB_BITMAP2);

 // Load IDB_BITMAP3
 m_pB[2] = new CBitmap;
 m_pB[2]->LoadBitmap(IDB_BITMAP3);

 // Load IDB_BITMAP4
 m_pB[3] = new CBitmap;
 m_pB[3]->LoadBitmap(IDB_BITMAP4);

}

/////////////////////
// MY CODE ENDS HERE
/////////////////////
```

To review the `OnInitialUpdate()` function's code:

The first statement,

```
CFormView::OnInitialUpdate();
```

calls the `OnInitialUpdate()` member function of the base class. Recall from previous chapters that you have to call the base class `OnInitialUpdate()` function. If you don't, the multimedia control won't be available.

The next statement,

```
m_midi->SetStrProperty("DeviceType","Sequencer");
```

sets the `DeviceType` property of the multimedia control to `"Sequencer"`. Recall from previous chapters that setting the `DeviceType` property to `"Sequencer"` sets the multimedia control for playback of MIDI files.

The next statement is

```
m_midi->SetNumProperty("UpdateInterval",0);
```

This statement sets the `UpdateInterval` property of the multimedia control to 0. What is the `UpdateInterval` property? It affects an important event that's associated with the multimedia control: the `VBN_STATUSUPDATE` event. This event occurs every X milliseconds, where X is the current value of the multimedia control's `UpdateInterval` property. For example, if you set the `UpdateInterval` property to 250, the code you attach to the `VBN_STATUSUPDATE` event will be executed every 250 milliseconds. Thus, you can think of the `VBN_STATUSUPDATE` event as a timer event. As you'll see later, the code that performs the animation show goes in the `VBN_STATUSUPDATE` event. In the preceding statement, you set the `UpdateInterval` property of the multimedia control to 0 because there should be no animation when the application starts. By setting the `UpdateInterval` property to 0, you're disabling the timer of the multimedia control, and the code that is attached to the `VBN_STATUSUPDATE` event isn't executed.

The next statement in the `OnInitialUpdate()` function,

```
m_midi->SetStrProperty("FileName",
                       "\\VCPROG\\MIDI\\BOURBON6.MID");
```

sets the multimedia control `FileName` property to `"\\VCPROG\\MIDI\\BOURBON6.MID"`. You do this because `BOURBON6.MID` is the MIDI file you want to play during the animation show.

The next statement,

```
m_midi->SetNumProperty("Visible", FALSE);
```

sets the `Visible` property of the multimedia control to `FALSE`. This makes the multimedia control invisible.

The next statement,

```
m_midi->SetStrProperty("Command","Open");
```

issues an `Open` command to the multimedia control.

The remaining statements in the `OnInitialUpdate()` function load the four bitmaps of the animation show. For example, the first bitmap (`IDB_BITMAP1`) is loaded by two statements. The first statement,

```
m_pB[0] = new CBitmap;
```

creates an object of class `CBitmap` and fills the first element of the `m_pB[]` array (`m_pB[0]`) with the address of this object. So now `m_pB[0]` points to an object of class `CBitmap`.

The second statement,

```
m_pB[0]->LoadBitmap(IDB_BITMAP1);
```

uses the `LoadBitmap()` member function of the `CBitmap` class to load the first bitmap of the animation show (`IDB_BITMAP1`). So now `m_pB[0]` points to the first bitmap of the animation show.

In a similar manner, the rest of the statements in the `OnInitialUpdate()` function load the other bitmaps of the animation show. That is, after the `OnInitialupdate()` code is executed, `m_pB[0]` points to the first bitmap (`IDB_BITMAP1`), `m_pB[1]` points to the second bitmap (`IDB_BITMAP2`), `m_pB[2]` points to the third bitmap (`IDB_BITMAP3`), and `m_pB[3]` points to the fourth bitmap (`IDB_BITMAP4`).

Don't forget to save your work:

☐ Select Save from Visual C++'s File menu.

Displaying the First Frame of the Show

So far, you've written the code that initializes the multimedia control and loads the four bitmaps of the animation show. Now you can write the code that displays the first bitmap of the show.

When the application begins, the first bitmap of the show should be displayed (see Figure 27.25). Now you'll attach code that displays the first bitmap (`IDB_BITMAP1`) to the `OnDraw()` member function of the view class. Here's how you do that:

☐ Open the file DANCEVW.H and add code to it that defines the OnDraw() function as a public member function of the CDanceView class. After you add this code, the CDanceView class declaration looks as follows:

```
class CDanccView : public CFormView
{
      DECLARE_DYNCREATE(CDanceView)
protected:
     CDanceView();
// protected constructor used by dynamic creation

     /////////////////////////
     // MY CODE STARTS HERE
     /////////////////////////

     virtual void OnInitialUpdate();

     /////////////////////////
     // MY CODE ENDS HERE
     /////////////////////////


// Form Data
public:
     //{{AFX_DATA(CDanceView)
     enum { IDD = IDD_DIALOG1 };
     CVBControl*     m_midi;
     //}}AFX_DATA

     /////////////////////////
     // MY CODE STARTS HERE
     /////////////////////////

     // The current frame number.
     int m_CurrentFrame;

     // An array for the 4 bitmaps.
     CBitmap* m_pB[4];

     /////////////////////////
     // MY CODE ENDS HERE
     /////////////////////////


// Attributes
public:

// Operations
public:
```

```
////////////////////////
// MY CODE STARTS HERE
////////////////////////

virtual void OnDraw(CDC* pDC);

////////////////////////
// MY CODE ENDS HERE
////////////////////////


// Implementation
protected:
    virtual ~CDanceView();
    virtual void DoDataExchange(CDataExchange* pDX);
// DDX/DDV support
// Generated message map functions
//{{AFX_MSG(CDanceView)
// NOTE - the ClassWizard will add and remove
// member functions here.
//}}AFX_MSG
    DECLARE_MESSAGE_MAP()
};
```

Now write the `OnDraw()` function's code:

☐ Open the file DANCEVW.CPP and add the `OnDraw()` function to the end of the
file. After you add this function, the end of the DANCEVW.CPP file looks as
follows:

```
////////////////////////
// MY CODE STARTS HERE
////////////////////////

void CDanceView::OnDraw(CDC* pDC)
{

 // Create a memory DC.
 CDC* pMemDC = new CDC;
 pMemDC->CreateCompatibleDC(pDC);

 // Select the bitmap into the memory DC.
 pMemDC->SelectObject( m_pB[0] );

 // Copy the bitmap from the memory DC into the screen DC.
 pDC->BitBlt(100,10,500,500,pMemDC,0,0,SRCCOPY);

 // Delete the memory DC.
 delete pMemDC;

}
```

```
///////////////////
// MY CODE ENDS HERE
///////////////////
```

As you can see, the OnDraw() function of the DANCE application does the same things as the OnDraw() function of the BALL application:

> It creates a memory DC.
> It places the first bitmap of the animation show into the memory DC.
> It copies the bitmap from the memory DC to the screen DC by using the BitBlt() function.
> It deletes the memory DC.

Overall, the code you typed in the OnDraw() function places the first bitmap of the animation show in the screen DC. Thus, when the application begins, and whenever there is a need to repaint the application's window (that is, whenever OnDraw() is executed), the first bitmap of the animation show is displayed in the application's window (see Figure 27.25).

Don't forget to save your work:

☐ Select Save from Visual C++'s File menu.

Deleting the Bitmaps

☐ You wrote code in the OninitialUpdate() function that creates four CBitmap objects:

```
void CDanceView::OnInitialUpdate()
{

 ...
 ...
 ...

// Load IDB_BITMAP1
 m_pB[0] = new CBitmap;
 m_pB[0]->LoadBitmap(IDB_BITMAP1);

 // Load IDB_BITMAP2
 m_pB[1] = new CBitmap;
 m_pB[1]->LoadBitmap(IDB_BITMAP2);

 // Load IDB_BITMAP3
 m_pB[2] = new CBitmap;
 m_pB[2]->LoadBitmap(IDB_BITMAP3);
```

```
// Load IDB_BITMAP4
m_pB[3] = new CBitmap;
m_pB[3]->LoadBitmap(IDB_BITMAP4);
```

}

When the application terminates, your code should delete these objects. If you don't write this code, the memory occupied by these objects won't be released, and the available memory of the user's system will be decreased every time your application is executed.

The code that deletes the four bitmaps goes in the destructor function of the view class, just as in the BALL application.

☐ Open the file DANCEVW.CPP and add code to the destructor function
~CDanceView() so that it looks as follows:

```
CDanceView::~CDanceView()
{

    //////////////////////////
    // MY CODE STARTS HERE
    //////////////////////////

    // Delete the 4 bitmaps.
    for (int i=0; i<4; i++)
        delete m_pB[i];

    //////////////////////////
    // MY CODE ENDS HERE
    //////////////////////////

}
```

The code that you just typed uses a for loop to delete the four bitmaps:

```
for (int i=0; i<4; i++)
    delete m_pB[i];
```

Thus, when the application terminates, the memory occupied by the four bitmaps is freed.

Executing the DANCE Application

Now execute the DANCE application and see the code that you typed in the OnDraw() function in action:

☐ Compile/link and execute the DANCE.EXE application.

As you can see, now the application's main window appears with the first bitmap of the animation show. Minimize the window and then maximize it. Again, the application's window appears with the first bitmap of the animation show in it. Whenever there's a need to repaint the window (for example, when the application starts), the code you wrote in the OnDraw() function is executed automatically, and this code displays the IDB_BITMAP1 bitmap (pB[0]) in the window.

☐ Terminate the DANCE application by selecting Exit from the File menu.

Starting the Animation Show

Now you'll write the code that starts the animation show. The animation show should start running when the user clicks the Start Show button. Thus, you'll attach the code that starts the animation show to the Start Show push button.

Here's how you attach code to the Start Show push button:

☐ Use ClassWizard to add a function for the event:

Class Name:	CDanceView
Object ID:	IDC_START_BUTTON
Message:	BN_CLICKED
Function Name:	OnStartButton()

☐ Edit the OnStartButton() function that you added to the DANCEVW.CPP file. After you edit the function, it looks as follows:

```
void CDanceView::OnStartButton()
{
// TODO: Add your control notification handler code here

    ////////////////////////
    // MY CODE STARTS HERE
    ////////////////////////

    // Disable the Start push button.
    GetDlgItem(IDC_START_BUTTON)->EnableWindow(FALSE);

    // Initialize the current frame number to 0.
    m_CurrentFrame = 0;
```

```
// Rewind the multimedia control.
m_midi->SetStrProperty("Command","Prev");

// Start playing the MIDI file.
m_midi->SetStrProperty("Command","Play");

// Set the interval of the multimedia control timer.
m_midi->SetNumProperty("UpdateInterval",350);

////////////////////////
// MY CODE ENDS HERE
////////////////////////

}
```

To review the OnStartButton() function:

The first statement disables the Start Show push button,

```
GetDlgItem(IDC_START_BUTTON)->EnableWindow(FALSE);
```

You disable the Start Show push button because you don't want the user to click it while the animation show is in progress.

The next statement is

```
m_CurrentFrame = 0;
```

This statement initializes the m_CurrentFrame variable to 0. As stated earlier, the m_CurrentFrame variable is used to store the index number of the currently displayed bitmap. When the animation starts the first bitmap is displayed, so in the preceding statement m_CurrentFrame is set to 0.

The next two statements start the playback of the MIDI file. The first statement,

```
m_midi->SetStrProperty("Command","Prev");
```

rewinds the multimedia control so that the playback starts from the beginning of the MIDI file.

The second statement,

```
m_midi->SetStrProperty("Command","Play");
```

issues a Play command to the multimedia control.

The last statement in the OnStartButton() function is

```
// Set the interval of the multimedia control timer.
m_midi->SetNumProperty("UpdateInterval",350);
```

This statement starts the animation! As stated earlier, the `UpdateInterval` property determines the interval of the multimedia control's timer. The preceding statement sets the `UpdateInterval` property to 350. This means that from now on, the `VBN_STATUSUPDATE` event (the timer event of the multimedia control) will be automatically executed every 350 milliseconds. The code that you'll attach to the multimedia control's `VBN_STATUSUPDATE` event is the code that performs the animation. You'll write this code in the following section.

The Animation Show

The code that you attached to the Start Show push button sets the interval of the multimedia control to 350 milliseconds. Now you'll attach code to the multimedia control's `VBN_STATUSUPDATE` event. This code will be automatically executed every 350 milliseconds.

☐ Use ClassWizard to add a function for the event:

Class Name:	CDanceView
Object ID:	IDC_TEGOMM1
Message:	VBN_STATUSUPDATE
Function Name	OnStatusupdateTegomm1()

☐ Edit the `OnStatusupdateTegomm1()` function that you added to the `DANCEVW.CPP` file. After you edit the function, it looks as follows:

```
void CDanceView::OnStatusupdateTegomm1(UINT, int,
                            CWnd*, LPVOID)
{
// TODO: Add your VBX event notification handler code here

///////////////////////
// MY CODE STARTS HERE
///////////////////////

// Increment the current frame number.
m_CurrentFrame++;

// Was the last frame of the dance displayed?
if (m_CurrentFrame==4)
   m_CurrentFrame=1;

// Get a DC for the screen.
CClientDC dc(this);

// Create a memory DC.
CDC* pMemDC = new CDC;
pMemDC->CreateCompatibleDC(&dc);
```

```
// Select the bitmap into the memory DC.
pMemDC->SelectObject( m_pB[m_CurrentFrame] );

// Copy the bitmap from the memory DC into the screen DC.
dc.BitBlt(100,10,500,500,pMemDC,0,0,SRCCOPY);

// Delete the memory DC.
delete pMemDC;

/////////////////////
// MY CODE ENDS HERE
/////////////////////
```

}

The purpose of the code you just attached to the VBN_STATUSUPDATE event is to display the next bitmap of the animation show. Every 350 milliseconds, the code will be executed automatically and the next bitmap of the show will be displayed. This creates the illusion that the objects in the bitmaps (the couple) are moving.

The first statement you typed in the function is

```
m_CurrentFrame++;
```

This statement increments the m_CurrentFrame variable because you want to display the next bitmap. For example, if m_CurrentBitmap is currently 0, the m_pB[0] bitmap is displayed. Thus, you increment m_CurrentFrame by 1 because the next bitmap you want to display is the m_pB[1] bitmap.

The next statement is an if statement that checks whether the final bitmap of the animation has been displayed:

```
if (m_CurrentFrame==4)
   m_CurrentFrame=1;
```

If m_CurrentFrame is 4, the final bitmap of the animation has been displayed, the if condition is satisfied, and the m_CurrentFrame variable is reset to 1. In other words, m_CurrentFrame is incremented every 350 milliseconds, and once its value reaches 4 it is reset to 1. Thus, the cycle of values that m_CurrentFrame goes through is 1->2->3->4->1->2->3->4->1->2->3->4...

The next statement in the function is

```
CClientDC dc(this);
```

This statement creates a DC called dc for the application's window.

The remaining code in the function is similar to the code you wrote in the OnDraw() function. It displays the bitmap specified by m_CurrentFrame in the application's window.

The first two statements create a memory DC (pMemDC):

```
CDC* pMemDC = new CDC;
pMemDC->CreateCompatibleDC(&dc);
```

Then the bitmap specified by m_CurrentFrame is placed into the memory DC:

```
pMemDC->SelectObject( m_pB[m_CurrentFrame] );
```

For example, if m_CurrentFrame is currently 2, this statement places the bitmap m_pB[2] into the memory DC.

Then the bitmap from the memory DC (pMemDC) is copied into the screen DC:

```
dc.BitBlt(100,10,500,500,pMemDC,0,0,SRCCOPY);
```

Finally, the memory DC is deleted:

```
delete pMemDC;
```

Putting it all together, every 350 milliseconds this code is executed, and a different bitmap of the animation show is displayed in each iteration. This creates the illusion that the cartoon characters in the bitmaps are dancing.

Stopping the Animation Show

The code that you attached to the Start Show button starts the playback of the MIDI file and starts the animation show. Now you'll attach code to the multimedia control's VBN_DONE event. Recall from previous chapters that the VBN_DONE event occurs when the playback is over. The code you'll attach to the VBN_DONE event will stop the animation show and display the bitmap that shows the dancers standing up (see Figure 27.25).

Follow these steps to attach code to the multimedia control's VBN_DONE event:

☐ Use ClassWizard to add a function for the event:

Class Name:	CDanceView
Object ID:	IDC_TEGOMM1
Message:	VBN_DONE
Function Name:	OnDoneTegomm1()

☐ Edit the OnDoneTegomm1() function that you added to the DANCEVW.CPP file. After you edit the function, it looks as follows:

```
void CDanceView::OnDoneTegomm1(UINT, int, CWnd*, LPVOID)
{
// TODO: Add your VBX event notification handler code here

    /////////////////////////
    // MY CODE STARTS HERE
    /////////////////////////

    // Disable the multimedia control timer.
    m_midi->SetNumProperty("UpdateInterval",0);

    // Enable the Start push button.
    GetDlgItem(IDC_START_BUTTON)->EnableWindow(TRUE);

    // Trigger a call to the OnDraw() function.
    Invalidate();

    /////////////////////////
    // MY CODE ENDS HERE
    /////////////////////////


}
```

This code is made up of three statements. The first statement,

```
m_midi->SetNumProperty("UpdateInterval",0);
```

sets the UpdateInterval property of the multimedia control to 0. Recall that this disables the timer event of the multimedia control. Thus, the code you attached to the VBN_STATUSUPDATE event won't be executed anymore, and as a result the animation show will stop.

The second statement,

```
GetDlgItem(IDC_START_BUTTON)->EnableWindow(TRUE);
```

enables the Start Show push button. Recall that you disabled the Start Show push button in the OnStartButton() function because the user shouldn't be able to click this button while the animation is in progress. However, now you re-enable the Start Show push button because the show is over and the user should be able to start the show again.

The third statement,

```
Invalidate();
```

triggers a call to the OnDraw() function that you wrote earlier. That is, when you call the Invalidate() function, you cause a later call to the OnDraw() function. Recall that the code you wrote in the OnDraw() function displays the bitmap of the two dancers standing up.

Putting it all together, when the multimedia control finishes playing the MIDI file, the VBN_DONE event occurs and the code that you attached to the VBN_DONE event:

> Stops the animation show by setting the multimedia control's UpdateInterval property to 0.
> Enables the Start Show button so that the user can start the show all over again.
> Displays the bitmap of the two dancers standing up by calling the Invalidate() function, which causes a later call to the OnDraw() function.

Attaching Code to the Stop Button

The code that you attached to the VBN_DONE event terminates the animation show when the multimedia control completes the playback of the MIDI file. But what if the user wants to stop the animation and playback before they're done? To allow the user to stop the playback and animation at any time, you must attach code to the Stop push button:

☐ Use ClassWizard to add a function for the event:

Class Name:	CDanceView
Object ID:	IDC_STOP_BUTTON
Message:	BN_CLICKED
Function Name:	OnStopButton()

☐ Edit the OnStopButton() function that you added to the DANCEVW.CPP file. After you edit the function, it looks as follows:

```
void CDanceView::OnStopButton()
{
// TODO: Add your control notification handler code here

    /////////////////////////
    // MY CODE STARTS HERE
    /////////////////////////

    // Stop the playback.
    m_midi->SetStrProperty("Command","Stop");
```

```
/////////////////////
// MY CODE ENDS HERE
/////////////////////
```

}

The code you just typed in the OnStopButton() function is made up of one statement:

```
m_midi->SetStrProperty("Command","Stop");
```

This statement issues the Stop command to the multimedia control, which stops the playback of the MIDI file. But what about stopping the animation show? Well, once the multimedia control stops playing the MIDI file, a VBN_DONE event occurs, and the code that you attached to the VBN_DONE event earlier stops the animation show.

Executing the DANCE Application

You've finished writing the code that plays the MIDI file and performs the animation. To see the animation and hear the playback of the MIDI file:

☐ Build the DANCE application and then execute it.

☐ Experiment with the Start Show and Stop buttons.

As expected, the animation code you wrote performs the animation while the MIDI file plays in the background.

In the following section you'll add code to the DANCE application that makes the default size of the application's window small (as shown in Figure 27.25).

☐ Terminate the DANCE application by selecting Exit from the File menu.

Setting the Default Size of the Application's Window

When the application begins, the default size of the application's window looks as shown in Figure 27.25.

Now you'll add the code that sets the default size of the application's window to the PreCreateWindow() member function of the CMainFrame class, just as you did in the BALL application.

☐ Open the file MAINFRM.H and add code to it that defines the function
PreCreateWindow() as a member function of the CMainFrame class. After you
add this code, the CMainFrame class declaration looks as follows:

```
class CMainFrame : public CFrameWnd
{
protected: // create from serialization only
    CMainFrame();
    DECLARE_DYNCREATE(CMainFrame)

    /////////////////////////
    // MY CODE STARTS HERE
    /////////////////////////

    BOOL PreCreateWindow(CREATESTRUCT& cs);

    /////////////////////
    // MY CODE ENDS HERE
    /////////////////////


// Attributes
public:

// Operations
public:

// Implementation
public:
    virtual ~CMainFrame();
#ifdef _DEBUG
    virtual void AssertValid() const;
    virtual void Dump(CDumpContext& dc) const;
#endif

// Generated message map functions
protected:
//{{AFX_MSG(CMainFrame)
// NOTE - the ClassWizard will add and remove
// member functions here.
//    DO NOT EDIT what you see in these blocks
// of generated code!
    //}}AFX_MSG
    DECLARE_MESSAGE_MAP()
};
```

Now write the `PreCreateWindow()` function's code:

☐ Open the file `MAINFRM.CPP` and add the `PreCreateWindow()` function to the end of the file. After you add this function, the end of the `MAINFRM.CPP` file looks as follows:

```
/////////////////////////
// MY CODE STARTS HERE
/////////////////////////

BOOL CMainFrame::PreCreateWindow(CREATESTRUCT& cs)
{

    // Call the base class function.
    CFrameWnd::PreCreateWindow( cs );

    // Set the width of the window to 335.
    cs.cx = 335;

    // Set the height of the window to 275.
    cs.cy = 275;

    return TRUE;
}

/////////////////////////
// MY CODE ENDS HERE
/////////////////////////
```

As you can see, this code sets the width of the application's window to 335 and the height to 275.

Don't forget to save your work:

☐ Select Save from the File menu.

To see the code that you attached to the `PreCreateWindow()` function in action:

☐ Compile/link and execute the DANCE application.

As you can see, now the default size of the application's main window is as shown in Figure 27.25.

Synchronizing Sound and Animation—
The KENNEDY Application

The DANCE application that you just wrote is an example of an application that creates an animation show with background sound. However, the animation show is not synchronized with the sound. Every 350 milliseconds a different bitmap of the animation show is displayed but without regard to the current playback position. Such an animation show works well in cases where the sound being played is music and the displayed bitmaps don't have to match a specific playback position. However, in cases where the background sound is speech, you need to write code that synchronizes the background speech with the displayed bitmaps.

The KENNEDY application synchronizes the background sound (a speech by President Kennedy) with the displayed bitmaps. Before you start writing the KENNEDY application, first execute the copy of the application that resides in your `C:\VCPROG\ORIGINAL\CH27\KENNEDY` directory.

☐ Use Run from the Program Manager's File menu to execute
   `C:\VCPROG\ORIGINAL\CH27\KENNEDY\Kennedy.EXE`.

   Windows responds by executing the KENNEDY application. The main window of KENNEDY appears, as shown in Figure 27.38.

Figure 27.38.
The KENNEDY application's main window.

As you can see, the application's main window contains a picture of President Kennedy and a Start button.

To start the animation:

☐ Click the Start button.

   The KENNEDY application responds by playing a portion of a famous speech by President Kennedy through the sound card and displaying bitmaps with text that corresponds to the current playback position of the speech. That is, the bitmaps that display the text of the speech are synchronized with the audio of the speech.

The KENNEDY application has two popup menus, File and Help. These popup menus are shown in Figures 27.39 and 27.40.

Figure 27.39.
The KENNEDY application's File popup menu.

Figure 27.40.
The KENNEDY application's Help popup menu.

☐ Terminate the KENNEDY application by selecting Exit from the File menu.

Now that you know what the KENNEDY application does, you can start writing it.

Creating the Project of the Application

To create the project of the KENNEDY application:

☐ Select AppWizard from the Project menu.

Visual C++ responds by running AppWizard.

☐ Use the Directory list box to select the directory C:\VCPROG\PRACTICE\CH27.

☐ Type kennedy in the Project Name box.

Now your AppWizard dialog box looks as shown in Figure 27.41.

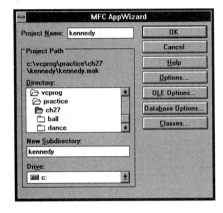

Figure 27.41.
The KENNEDY
application's
AppWizard dialog
box.

☐ Click the Options button and set the options as shown in Figure 27.42.

NOTE

The KENNEDY application uses the TegoMM.VBX control. Thus, as shown in Figure 27.42, you need to check the Custom VBX Controls check box of AppWizard's Options dialog box.

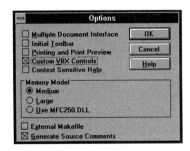

Figure 27.42.
Setting the options
for the KENNEDY
application.

☐ Click the OK button of the Options dialog box and click the OK button of the AppWizard dialog box and finally click the Create button of the New Application Information dialog box.

> *AppWizard responds by creating the KENNEDY project and all the skeleton files of the KENNEDY application.*

To remove the debug options of the project (so you'll have a small EXE file):

☐ Select Project from Visual C++'s Options menu, click the Release radio button, and then click the OK button of the dialog box.

Creating the Form of the Application

As shown in Figure 27.38, the main window of the KENNEDY application should contain a Start push button. The application's window should also include a multimedia control, but as you'll see later, the application's code makes the multimedia control invisible.

To implement the form of the KENNEDY application, you must replace the current view class of the application with a new view class derived from the `CFormView` class.

Follow these steps to create the form of the application:

☐ Use the Windows File Manager (or DOS Shell) to delete the two view class files of the KENNEDY application:

> Delete `C:\VCPROG\PRACTICE\CH27\KENNEDY\KENNEVW.CPP`.
> Delete `C:\VCPROG\PRACTICE\CH27\KENNEDY\KENNEVW.H`.

☐ Select ClassWizard from Visual C++'s Browse menu.

> *ClassWizard responds by displaying a dialog box telling you that the view class files don't exist.*

☐ Click the OK button of the dialog box.

☐ Click the Remove button of the Repair Class Information dialog box.

☐ Click ClassWizard's OK button.

You've just finished removing the view class of the KENNEDY application.

In the following steps you'll create a dialog box, you'll create a `CFormView` type class for this dialog box, and you'll make this class the new view class of the application:

☐ Select App Studio from Visual C++'s Tools menu.

☐ Create a new dialog box with App Studio.

☐ Double-click in a free area of the new dialog box.

☐ Select Styles from the drop-down list box at the upper-right corner of the Properties window.

Set the Styles properties of the dialog box as follows:

☐ Select Child from the Style box.

☐ Select None from the Border box.

☐ Uncheck the Visible property (that is, remove the check mark from the Visible check box).

☐ Select General from the drop-down list box at the upper-right corner of the Properties window and make sure that the Caption box is empty.

Now connect the dialog box to a class derived from CFormView:

☐ Select ClassWizard from App Studio's Resource menu.

> *ClassWizard responds by displaying the Add Class dialog box.*

☐ Type CKennedyView in the Class Name box.

☐ Set the Class Type to CFormView.

☐ Type kennevw.h in the Header File box.

☐ Type kennevw.cpp in the Implementation File box.

☐ Click the Create Class button.

☐ Click ClassWizard's OK button to go back to App Studio.

You've finished creating the new view class of the application. This view class is a derived class from the MFC CFormView class, and it's connected to the dialog box that you created. Thus, the main dialog box of the application is the dialog box that you created.

The Visual Implementation of the Dialog Box

☐ Implement the dialog box of the KENNEDY application per Table 27.5.

Table 27.5. The KENNEDY application's dialog box.

Class Name:	CKennedyView
Figure:	27.43
OK button:	No
Cancel button:	No

Object	Property	Setting
Dialog Box	ID	IDD_DIALOG1
Multimedia Control	ID	IDC_TEGOMM1
	Variable	m_wav
	Type:	CVBControl *
Push Button	ID	IDC_START_BUTTON
	Caption	&Start

Now your dialog box looks as shown in Figure 27.43.

Figure 27.43.
The KENNEDY
application's dialog
box.

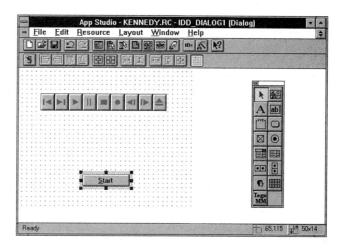

The exact location of the `IDC_START_BUTTON` push button is important. This is because the animation show is displayed in the application's main window (see Figure 27.38), and the animation shouldn't overlap the controls. Thus, you need to place the `IDC_START_BUTTON` push button exactly as shown in Figure 27.43. Here's how you do that:

☐ Drag the `IDC_START_BUTTON` push button until its position is X=65, Y=115.

> **NOTE**
>
> To drag an object to a particular X,Y coordinate, you need to use the status bar of the dialog box (refer to Figure 27.9).

The preceding X,Y coordinates assume that the font of the dialog box is the default font (8-point MS Sans Serif), so do not change the default font of the dialog box.

Note that the exact location of the multimedia control is not important. That's because you're going to make it invisible, as you'll see when you write the KENNEDY application's code.

You've finished designing the dialog box of the KENNEDY application!

Don't forget to save your work:

☐ Select Save from App Studio's File menu.

The Visual Implementation of the Menu

The KENNEDY application should have a menu with two popup menus, as shown in Figures 27.39 and 27.40. Use App Studio to implement the KENNEDY application's menu per Table 27.6.

Table 27.6. The KENNEDY application's menu.
Figures relating to menu: 27.39, 27.40

Menu Item
&File
E&xit
&Help

Don't forget to delete the accelerator keys of the menu items that you removed:

☐ Select `KENNEDY.RC [MFC-Resource Script]` from App Studio's Window menu, select Accelerator from the Type list, and then double-click `IDR_MAINFRAME` in the Resources list.

☐ Delete the accelerator keys that are not used by the KENNEDY application. In particular, delete the accelerator keys of the `ID_FILE_NEW`, `ID_FILE_OPEN`, and `ID_FILE_SAVE` menu items.

Save your work:

☐ Select Save from App Studio's File menu.

The visual implementation of the KENNEDY application's menu is completed.

Adding Bitmap Files to the KENNEDY Application

The KENNEDY application uses four bitmap (BMP) files for the animation.

☐ The four bitmaps of the KENNEDY application are

    `KENNEDY.BMP` (Figure 27.44)
    `KEN1.BMP` (Figure 27.45)
    `KEN2.BMP` (Figure 27.46)
    `KEN3.BMP` (Figure 27.47)

Figure 27.44.
The
KENNEDY.BMP
bitmap file.

Figure 27.45.
The KEN1.BMP
bitmap file.

SO MY

FELLOW

AMERICANS

Figure 27.46.
The KEN2.BMP
bitmap file.

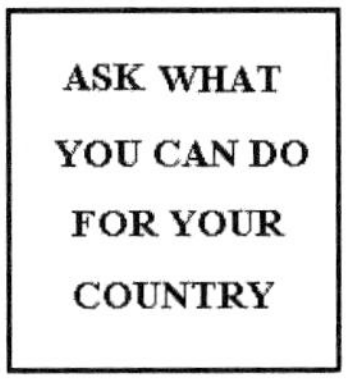

> ASK NOT
> WHAT YOUR
> COUNTRY
> CAN DO FOR
> YOU

Figure 27.47.
The KEN3.BMP
bitmap file.

> ASK WHAT
> YOU CAN DO
> FOR YOUR
> COUNTRY

To add these four bitmaps to the KENNEDY application, follow these steps:

☐ Select Import from App Studio's Resource menu and then select the file
C:\VCPROG\BMP\KENNEDY.BMP.

> *App Studio responds by importing the bitmap KENNEDY.BMP into the application and displaying the BMP bitmap. Note that the ID that App Studio assigned to the KENNEDY.BMP bitmap is IDB_BITMAP1.*

Repeat these steps to import the other three BMP files:

> Import C:\VCPROG\BMP\KEN1.BMP.
> Import C:\VCPROG\BMP\KEN2.BMP.
> Import C:\VCPROG\BMP\KEN3.BMP.

You've finished importing four bitmaps into the KENNEDY application. Don't forget to save your work:

☐ Select Save from App Studio's File menu.

Executing the KENNEDY Application

Even though you haven't written any code yet, execute the application to see your visual design in action:

☐ Select Build All KENNEDY.EXE from Visual C++'s Project menu.

☐ Select Execute KENNEDY.EXE from the Project menu.

915

The application's main window appears with the form that you designed in it (a multimedia control and a push button). Of course, none of the bitmaps you imported into the application are displayed yet, because you haven't written any code to accomplish that. In the following sections, you'll write code that brings the BMP files to life.

☐ Terminate the application by selecting Exit from the File menu.

Declaring Variables for the Animation Show

Now you'll write the code that declares variables that are used by the animation show. You'll declare these variables as data members of the view class, because these variables need to be visible in several member functions of the view class.

☐ Open the file KENNEVW.H and write code in the CKennedyView class declaration that declares two data members. When you finish writing this code, the CKennedyView class declaration looks as follows:

```
class CKennedyView : public CFormView
{
    DECLARE_DYNCREATE(CKennedyView)
protected:
    CKennedyView();
// protected constructor used by dynamic creation

// Form Data
public:
    //{{AFX_DATA(CKennedyView)
    enum { IDD = IDD_DIALOG1 };
    CVBControl*     m_wav;
    //}}AFX_DATA

// Attributes
public:

    /////////////////////////
    // MY CODE STARTS HERE
    /////////////////////////

    // The current frame number.
    int m_CurrentFrame;

    // An array for the 4 bitmaps.
    CBitmap* m_pB[4];
```

```
//////////////////
// MY CODE ENDS HERE
//////////////////

// Operations
public:

// Implementation
protected:
    virtual ~CKennedyView();
    virtual void DoDataExchange(CDataExchange* pDX);
// DDX/DDV support
// Generated message map functions
//{{AFX_MSG(CKennedyView)
// NOTE - the ClassWizard will add and
// remove member functions here.
    //}}AFX_MSG
    DECLARE_MESSAGE_MAP()
};
```

As you can see, these data members are the same as the data members you declared in the DANCE application. The first data member, m_CurrentFrame, is an integer that is used to maintain the current frame number (bitmap) that is being displayed. The array m_pB[4] is used for the four bitmaps that are used by the application.

Don't forget to save your work:

☐ Select Save from Visual C++'s File menu.

Loading the Bitmaps and Initializing the Multimedia Control

Now you'll add code to the OnInitialUpdate() function that initializes the multi-media control and loads the bitmaps, just as you did in the DANCE application.

☐ Open the file KENNEVW.H and add code to it that defines the function OnInitialUpdate() as a member function of the CKennedyView class. After you add this code, the CKennedyView class declaration looks as follows:

```
class CKennedyView : public CFormView
{
    DECLARE_DYNCREATE(CKennedyView)
protected:
    CKennedyView();
// protected constructor used by dynamic creation
```

```
///////////////////////
// MY CODE STARTS HERE
///////////////////////

virtual void OnInitialUpdate();

///////////////////////
// MY CODE ENDS HERE
///////////////////////

// Form Data
public:
    //{{AFX_DATA(CKennedyView)
    enum { IDD = IDD_DIALOG1 };
    CVBControl*    m_wav;
    //}}AFX_DATA

// Attributes
public:

    ///////////////////////
    // MY CODE STARTS HERE
    ///////////////////////

    // The current frame number.
    int m_CurrentFrame;

    // An array for the 4 bitmaps.
    CBitmap* m_pB[4];

    ///////////////////////
    // MY CODE ENDS HERE
    ///////////////////////


// Operations
public:

// Implementation
protected:
    virtual ~CKennedyView();
    virtual void DoDataExchange(CDataExchange* pDX);
// DDX/DDV support
    // Generated message map functions
    //{{AFX_MSG(CKennedyView)
// NOTE - the ClassWizard will add and
// remove member functions here.
    //}}AFX_MSG
    DECLARE_MESSAGE_MAP()
};
```

Now write the OnInitialUpdate() function's code:

☐ Open the file KENNEVW.CPP and add the OnInitialUpdate() function to the end of the file. After you add this function, the end of the KENNEVW.CPP file looks as follows:

```
/////////////////////////
// MY CODE STARTS HERE
/////////////////////////

void CKennedyView::OnInitialUpdate()
{

// Call the base class function.
CFormView::OnInitialUpdate();

// Set the DeviceType property for playback of WAV files.
m_wav->SetStrProperty("DeviceType","WaveAudio");

// Disable the timer of the multimedia control.
m_wav->SetNumProperty("UpdateInterval",0);

// Set the FileName property.
m_wav->SetStrProperty("FileName",
                      "\\VCPROG\\WAV\\8KENNED3.WAV");

// Make the multimedia control invisible.
m_wav->SetNumProperty("Visible", FALSE);

// Issue an Open command to the multimedia control.
m_wav->SetStrProperty("Command","Open");

// Load IDB_BITMAP1
m_pB[0] = new CBitmap;
m_pB[0]->LoadBitmap(IDB_BITMAP1);

// Load IDB_BITMAP2
m_pB[1] = new CBitmap;
m_pB[1]->LoadBitmap(IDB_BITMAP2);

// Load IDB_BITMAP3
m_pB[2] = new CBitmap;
m_pB[2]->LoadBitmap(IDB_BITMAP3);

// Load IDB_BITMAP4
m_pB[3] = new CBitmap;
m_pB[3]->LoadBitmap(IDB_BITMAP4);

}
```

```
/////////////////////
// MY CODE ENDS HERE
/////////////////////
```

The code you just typed is almost identical to the code you typed in the DANCE application's `OnInitialUpdate()` function. The only difference is that now, instead of initializing the multimedia control for playing a MIDI file, it's initialized for playing a WAV file (`8KENNED3.WAV`).

Don't forget to save your work:

☐ Select Save from Visual C++'s File menu.

Displaying the First Frame of the Show

So far, you've written the code that initializes the multimedia control and loads the four bitmaps of the animation show. Now you can write the code that displays the first bitmap of the show.

When the application begins, the first bitmap of the show should be displayed (see Figure 27.38). Now you'll attach code to the `OnDraw()` member function of the view class that displays the first bitmap (`IDB_BITMAP1`) in the application's window. Here's how you do that:

☐ Open the file `KENNEVW.H` and add code to it that defines the function `OnDraw()` as a public member function of the `CKennedyView` class. After you add this code, the `CKennedyView` class declaration looks as follows:

```
class CKennedyView : public CFormView
{
    DECLARE_DYNCREATE(CKennedyView)
protected:
    CKennedyView();
// protected constructor used by dynamic creation

    /////////////////////////
    // MY CODE STARTS HERE
    /////////////////////////

    virtual void OnInitialUpdate();

    /////////////////////
    // MY CODE ENDS HERE
    /////////////////////

// Form Data
public:
```

```
        //{{AFX_DATA(CKennedyView)
        enum { IDD = IDD_DIALOG1 };
        CVBControl*     m_wav;
        //}}AFX_DATA

// Attributes
public:

    /////////////////////////
    // MY CODE STARTS HERE
    /////////////////////////

    // The current frame number.
    int m_CurrentFrame;

    // An array for the 4 bitmaps.
    CBitmap* m_pB[4];

    /////////////////////////
    // MY CODE ENDS HERE
    /////////////////////////


// Operations
public:

    /////////////////////////
    // MY CODE STARTS HERE
    /////////////////////////

    virtual void OnDraw(CDC* pDC);

    /////////////////////////
    // MY CODE ENDS HERE
    /////////////////////////


// Implementation
protected:
    virtual ~CKennedyView();
    virtual void DoDataExchange(CDataExchange* pDX);
// DDX/DDV support
    // Generated message map functions
    //{{AFX_MSG(CKennedyView)
// NOTE - the ClassWizard will add
// and remove member functions here.
    //}}AFX_MSG
    DECLARE_MESSAGE_MAP()
};
```

Now write the `OnDraw()` function's code:

☐ Open the file KENNEVW.CPP and add the `OnDraw()` function to the end of the file. After you add this function, the end of the KENNEVW.CPP file looks as follows:

```
////////////////////////
// MY CODE STARTS HERE
////////////////////////

void CKennedyView::OnDraw(CDC* pDC)
{

    // Create a memory DC.
    CDC* pMemDC = new CDC;
    pMemDC->CreateCompatibleDC(pDC);

    // Select the bitmap into the memory DC.
    pMemDC->SelectObject( m_pB[0] );

    // Copy the bitmap from the memory DC into the screen DC.
    pDC->BitBlt(90,10,500,500,pMemDC,0,0,SRCCOPY);

    // Delete the memory DC.
    delete pMemDC;

}

////////////////////////
// MY CODE ENDS HERE
////////////////////////
```

The code you just typed is identical to the code you typed in the DANCE application's `OnDraw()` function. It does four things:

> It creates a memory DC.
> It places the first bitmap of the animation show into the memory DC.
> It copies the bitmap from the memory DC into the screen DC by using the `BitBlt()` function.
> It deletes the memory DC.

In other words, the code you just typed in the `OnDraw()` function places the first bitmap of the animation show into the screen DC. Thus, when the application begins, and whenever there is a need to repaint the window of the application (that is, whenever `OnDraw()` is executed), the first bitmap of the animation show is displayed in the application's window (see Figure 27.38).

Don't forget to save your work:

☐ Select Save from Visual C++'s File menu.

Deleting the Bitmaps

Now you'll add code that deletes the four bitmaps to the view class destructor function, just as you did in the DANCE application. Here's how you do that:

☐ Open the file KENNEVW.CPP and add code to the destructor function ~CKennedyView() so that it looks as follows:

```
CKennedyView::~CKennedyView()
{

    /////////////////////////
    // MY CODE STARTS HERE
    /////////////////////////

    // Delete the 4 bitmaps.
    for (int i=0; i<4; i++)
        delete m_pB[i];

    /////////////////////////
    // MY CODE ENDS HERE
    /////////////////////////


}
```

This code is identical to the code you added to the destructor of the DANCE application's view class. It uses a for loop to delete the four bitmaps. Thus, when the application ends, the memory occupied by these bitmaps is freed.

Executing the KENNEDY Application

Now execute the KENNEDY application and see the code you typed in the OnDraw() function in action:

☐ Select Build KENNEDY.EXE from Visual C++'s Project menu.

☐ Select Execute KENNEDY.EXE from the Project menu.

Now the application's main window appears with the first bitmap of the animation show.

☐ Terminate the KENNEDY application by selecting Exit from the File menu.

Starting the Animation Show

Now you'll write the code that starts the animation show. The animation show should start running when the user clicks the Start Show button. Thus, you'll attach the code that starts the animation show to the Start Show push button.

☐ Use ClassWizard to add a function for the event:

Class Name:	CKennedyView
Object ID:	IDC_START_BUTTON
Message:	BN_CLICKED
Function Name:	OnStartButton()

☐ Edit the OnStartButton() function that you added to the KENNEVW.CPP file. After you edit the OnStartButton() function, it looks as follows:

```
void CKennedyView::OnStartButton()
{
// TODO: Add your control notification handler code here

    /////////////////////////
    // MY CODE STARTS HERE
    /////////////////////////

    // Disable the Start button.
    GetDlgItem(IDC_START_BUTTON)->EnableWindow(FALSE);

    // Initialize the current frame number to 0.
    m_CurrentFrame = 0;

    // Rewind the multimedia control.
    m_wav->SetStrProperty("Command","Prev");

    // Start playing the WAV file.
    m_wav->SetStrProperty("Command","Play");

    // Set the interval of the multimedia control timer.
    m_wav->SetNumProperty("UpdateInterval",350);

    /////////////////////////
    // MY CODE ENDS HERE
    /////////////////////////

}
```

This code is the same as the code you typed in the DANCE application's `OnStartButton()` function. It does the following:

It disables the Start button so the user can't click it while the animation show is in progress.

It initializes the `m_CurrentFrame` variable to 0, because initially the first bitmap (`m_pB[0]`) is displayed.

It rewinds the multimedia control.

It starts the playback of the WAV file.

It sets the timer interval of the multimedia control to 350 milliseconds. This means that from now on, the `VBN_STATUSUPDATE` event (the timer event of the multimedia control) will be automatically executed every 350 milliseconds. The code that you attach to the `VBN_STATUSUPDATE` event is the code that performs the animation. You'll write this code in the following section.

The Synchronized Animation Show

The code you attached to the Start Show push button sets the interval of the multimedia control to 350 milliseconds. Now you'll attach code to the multimedia control's `VBN_STATUSUPDATE` event. Because you set the interval of the multimedia timer to 350 milliseconds, that's how often this code will be executed. The code displays the animation show's bitmaps in synchronization with the current position of the playback.

Here's how you attach code to the multimedia control's `VBN_STATUSUPDATE` event:

☐ Use ClassWizard to add a function for the event:

Class Name:	CKennedyView
Object ID:	IDC_TEGOMM1
Message:	VBN_STATUSUPDATE
Function Name:	OnStatusupdateTegomm1()

☐ Edit the `OnStatusupdateTegomm1()` function you added to the KENNEVW.CPP file. After you edit the function, it looks as follows:

```
void CKennedyView::OnStatusupdateTegomm1(UINT, int,
                                    CWnd*, LPVOID)
{
// TODO: Add your VBX event notification
// handler code here
```

```
/////////////////////////
// MY CODE STARTS HERE
/////////////////////////

// Get the current position.
long position = m_wav->GetNumProperty("Position");

// Set the frame number in accordance with the current
// playback position.
if (position<3000)
   m_CurrentFrame = 1;
if (position>3000 && position<7000)
   m_CurrentFrame = 2;
if (position>7000)
   m_CurrentFrame = 3;

// Get a DC for the screen.
CClientDC dc(this);

// Create a memory DC.
CDC* pMemDC = new CDC;
pMemDC->CreateCompatibleDC(&dc);

// Select the bitmap into the memory DC.
pMemDC->SelectObject( m_pB[m_CurrentFrame] );

// Copy the bitmap from the memory DC into the screen DC.
dc.BitBlt(90,10,500,500,pMemDC,0,0,SRCCOPY);

// Delete the memory DC.
delete pMemDC;

////////////////////////
// MY CODE ENDS HERE
////////////////////////

}
```

The purpose of the code you just attached to the VBN_STATUSUPDATE event is to display the appropriate bitmap in accordance with the current playback position.

The WAV file that the multimedia control is playing (8KENNED3.WAV) contains the audio phrase, "So my fellow Americans, ask not what your country can do for you, ask what you can do for your country."

The KENNEDY application's animation show uses three BMP files to display this audio phrase. Each of these BMP files displays a different section of the phrase:

KEN1.BMP—SO MY FELLOW AMERICANS (Figure 27.45)

`KEN2.BMP`—ASK NOT WHAT YOUR COUNTRY CAN DO FOR YOU (Figure 27.46)

`KEN3.BMP`—ASK WHAT YOU CAN DO FOR YOUR COUNTRY (Figure 27.47)

The corresponding audio sections within the WAV file are

Bitmap	*Audio section (in milliseconds)*
`KEN1.BMP`	0 through 3,000
`KEN2.BMP`	3,000 through 7,000
`KEN3.BMP`	7,000 through end of file

To determine which bitmap should be displayed, the code you typed earlier first retrieves the current playback position:

```
// Get the current position.
long position = m_wav->GetNumProperty("Position");
```

Then a series of three `if` statements is used to determine which bitmap should be displayed:

```
if (position<3000)
   m_CurrentFrame = 1;
if (position>3000 && position<7000)
   m_CurrentFrame = 2;
if (position>7000)
   m_CurrentFrame = 3;
```

For example, if the playback position is currently 4,000 milliseconds, the second `if` statement is satisfied and `m_CurrentFrame` is set to 2.

The next statement in the function is

```
CClientDC dc(this);
```

This statement creates a DC called `dc` for the application's window.

The remaining code in the function displays the bitmap specified by `m_CurrentFrame` in the application's window.

The first two statements create a memory DC (`pMemDC`):

```
CDC* pMemDC = new CDC;
pMemDC->CreateCompatibleDC(&dc);
```

Then the bitmap specified by `m_CurrentFrame` is placed into the memory DC:

```
pMemDC->SelectObject( m_pB[m_CurrentFrame] );
```

For example, if m_CurrentFrame is currently 2, this statement places the bitmap m_pB[2] into the memory DC.

Then the bitmap from the memory DC (pMemDC) is copied into the screen DC:

```
dc.BitBlt(90,10,500,500,pMemDC,0,0,SRCCOPY);
```

Finally, the memory DC is deleted:

```
delete pMemDC;
```

Putting it all together, the preceding code is executed every 350 milliseconds, and in each iteration a different bitmap is displayed corresponding to the current playback position. Thus, the speech and the bitmaps are synchronized.

Stopping the Animation Show

The code you attached to the Start Show button starts the playback of the WAV file and starts the animation show. Now you'll attach code to the multimedia control's VBN_DONE event. Recall that the VBN_DONE event occurs when the playback is over. The code that you'll attach to the VBN_DONE event stops the animation show and displays a bitmap with a picture of President Kennedy (see Figure 27.38).

Follow these steps to attach code to the VBN_DONE event of the multimedia control:

☐ Use ClassWizard to add a function for the event:

Class Name:	CKennedyView
Object ID:	IDC_TEGOMM1
Message:	VBN_DONE
Function Name:	OnDoneTegomm1()

☐ Edit the OnDoneTegomm1() function that you added to the KENNEVIEW.CPP file. After you edit the function, it looks as follows:

```
void CKennedyView::OnDoneTegomm1(UINT, int, CWnd*, LPVOID)
{
// TODO: Add your VBX event notification
// handler code here

    /////////////////////////
    // MY CODE STARTS HERE
    /////////////////////////

    // Disable the multimedia control timer.
    m_wav->SetNumProperty("UpdateInterval",0);
```

```
// Enable the Start button.
GetDlgItem(IDC_START_BUTTON)->EnableWindow(TRUE);

// Trigger a call to the OnDraw() function.
Invalidate();

//////////////////////
// MY CODE ENDS HERE
//////////////////////
```

}

The code you just typed is made up of three statements. These statements do the following:

Disable the multimedia control's timer by setting the UpdateInterval property to 0. Thus, the code you attached to the VBN_STATUSUPDATE event won't be executed any more, and the animation show will stop.

Enable the Start push button. Recall that in the OnStartButton() function you disabled the Start push button, because the user shouldn't be able to click the Start button while the animation is in progress. However, now the show is over and the user should be able to start the show again.

Trigger a call to the OnDraw() function by calling the Invalidate() function. That is, when you call the Invalidate() function, you cause a later call to the OnDraw() function. Recall that the code you wrote in the OnDraw() function displays the bitmap of President Kennedy.

Executing the KENNEDY Application

You've finished writing the code that plays the WAV file and displays the bitmaps in synchronization with the sound. To see the bitmaps and hear the playback of the WAV file:

☐ Build the KENNEDY application and then execute it.

☐ Click the Start button.

As expected, the code you wrote plays the WAV file and displays the bitmaps in accordance with the playback position.

In the following section you'll add code to the KENNEDY application that makes the default size of the application's window small (as shown in Figure 27.38).

☐ Terminate the KENNEDY application by selecting Exit from the File menu.

Setting the Default Size of the Application's Window

Now you'll add code that sets the default size of the application's window to the PreCreateWindow() member function of the CMainFrame class, just as you did in the BALL and DANCE applications.

☐ Open the file MAINFRM.H and add code to it that defines the function PreCreateWindow() as a member function of the CMainFrame class. After you add this code, the CMainFrame class declaration looks as follows:

```
class CMainFrame : public CFrameWnd
{
protected: // create from serialization only
    CMainFrame();
    DECLARE_DYNCREATE(CMainFrame)

    /////////////////////////
    // MY CODE STARTS HERE
    /////////////////////////

    BOOL PreCreateWindow(CREATESTRUCT& cs);

    /////////////////////////
    // MY CODE ENDS HERE
    /////////////////////////

// Attributes
public:

// Operations
public:

// Implementation
public:
    virtual ~CMainFrame();
#ifdef _DEBUG
    virtual void AssertValid() const;
    virtual void Dump(CDumpContext& dc) const;
#endif

// Generated message map functions
protected:
    //{{AFX_MSG(CMainFrame)
// NOTE - the ClassWizard will add and
```

```
// remove member functions here.
// DO NOT EDIT what you see in these blocks
// of generated code!
    //}}AFX_MSG
    DECLARE_MESSAGE_MAP()
};
```

Now write the PreCreateWindow() function's code:

☐ Open the file MAINFRM.CPP and add the PreCreateWindow() function to the end of the file. After you add this function, the end of the MAINFRM.CPP file looks as follows:

```
///////////////////////
// MY CODE STARTS HERE
///////////////////////

BOOL CMainFrame::PreCreateWindow(CREATESTRUCT& cs)
{

    // Call the base class function.
    CFrameWnd::PreCreateWindow( cs );

    // Set the width of the window to 335.
    cs.cx = 335;

    // Set the height of the window to 275.
    cs.cy = 275;

    return TRUE;
}

///////////////////////
// MY CODE ENDS HERE
///////////////////////
```

As you can see, this code sets the width of the application's window to 335 and the height to 275.

Don't forget to save your work:

☐ Select Save from the File menu.

To see the code you attached to the PreCreateWindow() function in action:

☐ Compile/link and execute the KENNEDY application.

As you can see, the default size of the application's main window is as shown in Figure 27.38.

28

The **OnIdle()** *Function*

In this chapter you will learn about the OnIdle() member function of the CWinApp class. You'll learn when this function is executed and how you can utilize this function in your Visual C++ applications.

What Is the *OnIdle()* Function?

Whenever an event occurs, Windows sends a message to the application that is associated with that event. The message informs the application of the event. For example, if your application has a dialog box with a button with an ID in it of IDC_MY_BUTTON, and the user clicks this button, Windows sends a BN_CLICKED message to your application telling it that the IDC_MY_BUTTON button was clicked. Your application then executes the code you attached to the BN_CLICKED event of the IDC_MY_BUTTON button.

When no events are occurring in your application (that is, when your application is *idle*), the OnIdle() member function of the CWinApp class is automatically executed. You can write code in the OnIdle() function, and this code will be executed whenever your application is idle.

Note that the OnIdle() function is not executed

> When other applications aren't idle. That is, if another application is currently processing messages that Windows sent it, the OnIdle() function of your application won't be executed. Once all other applications are idle, the OnIdle() function of your application will be executed automatically.

> When your application's menu (or your application's system menu) is active. That is, if the user clicks the minus icon (on the upper-left corner) of your application window or if the user opens any of the popup menus of your application, the OnIdle() function of your application won't be executed.

> When the user opens a modal dialog box in your application. That is, if the user opens any modal dialog box in your application, your application's OnIdle() function won't be executed.

To summarize, the OnIdle() function of your application is automatically executed whenever all applications (including your applications) are idle.

The ANNOUNCE application is an example of a Visual C++ application that utilizes the OnIdle() function.

The ANNOUNCE Application

Before you start writing the ANNOUNCE application, execute the copy of it that resides in your C:\VCPROG\ORIGINAL\CH28\ANNOUNCE directory.

To execute the Announce.EXE application:

☐ Use Run from the Program Manager's File menu to execute
C:\VCPROG\ORIGINAL\CH28\ANNOUNCE\Announce.EXE.

> *Windows responds by executing the Announce application. An hourglass icon is displayed for a while and then the main window of* ANNOUNCE.EXE *appears, as shown in Figure 28.1.*

Figure 28.1.
The ANNOUNCE application's main window.

As you can see, the main window of the application instructs the user to leave the ANNOUNCE application running and then to try to exit Windows.

☐ Try to exit Windows. That is, switch to the Program Manager and then select Exit from the Program Manager's File menu.

> *The ANNOUNCE application detects that you are trying to exit Windows, and it plays an audio prompt that says, "It's been fun working with you."*

As you have just heard, the ANNOUNCE application continuously monitors the Windows session, and when it discovers that you are trying to quit Windows, it plays an audio prompt through the PC speaker.

The ANNOUNCE application has two popup menus: File and Help. These popup menus are shown in Figures 28.2 and 28.3.

Figure 28.2.
The ANNOUNCE application's File popup menu.

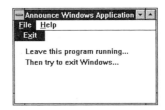

935

Figure 28.3.
The ANNOUNCE
application's Help
popup menu.

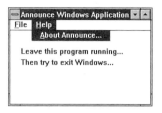

To exit from the ANNOUNCE application:

☐ Select Exit from the File menu.

Now that you know what the ANNOUNCE application does, you can start writing it.

Creating the Project of the ANNOUNCE Application

To create the project of the ANNOUNCE application:

☐ Select AppWizard from the Project menu.

Visual C++ responds by running AppWizard.

☐ Use the Directory list box to select the directory C:\VCPROG\PRACTICE\CH28.

☐ Type announce in the Project Name box.

Now your AppWizard dialog box looks as shown in Figure 28.4.

Figure 28.4.
The ANNOUNCE
application's
AppWizard dialog
box.

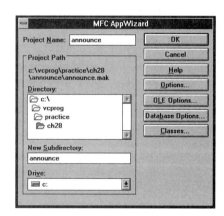

☐ Click the Options button and set the options as shown in Figure 28.5 (that is, uncheck all the check boxes except the Generate Source Comments check box).

Figure 28.5.
Setting the options
for the AN-
NOUNCE
application.

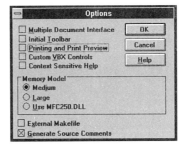

☐ Click the Options dialog box's OK button and then click the OK button of the AppWizard dialog box and finally click the Create button of the New Application Information dialog box.

AppWizard responds by creating the ANNOUNCE project and all the skeleton files of the ANNOUNCE application.

To remove the debug options of the project (so that you'll have a small EXE file):

☐ Select Project from Visual C++'s Options menu, click the Release radio button, and then click the OK button of the dialog box.

The Visual Implementation of the Menu

The ANNOUNCE application has a menu with two popup menus, as shown in Figures 28.2 and 28.3. Implement this menu:

Use App Studio to implement the menu of the ANNOUNCE application per Table 28.1.

Table 28.1. The ANNOUNCE application's menu.
  Figures relating to menu: 28.2, 28.3

Menu Item
&File
E&xit
&Help
&About Announce...

Don't forget to delete the accelerator keys of the menu items that you removed:

☐ Select `ANNOUNCE.RC [MFC-Resource Script]` from App Studio's Window menu, select Accelerator from the Type list, and then double-click `IDR_MAINFRAME` in the Resources list.

☐ Delete the accelerator keys that aren't used by the application. In particular, delete the accelerator keys of the `ID_FILE_NEW`, `ID_FILE_OPEN`, and `ID_FILE_SAVE` menu items.

If you don't delete these accelerator keys, they will be active during runtime. If the user presses Ctrl+N, for example, it will be like selecting New from the File menu, even though you deleted that menu item.

Save your work:

☐ Select Save from App Studio's File menu.

The visual implementation of the ANNOUNCE application's menu is completed.

Writing Code in the ANNOUNCE Application's *OnIdle()* Function

As stated earlier, whenever the ANNOUNCE application is idle the `OnIdle()` member function of the `CWinApp` class is automatically executed. The ANNOUNCE application's code (code that Visual C++ wrote for you) declares a class called `CAnnounceApp` that is derived from `CWinApp`. The header file of the `CAnnounceApp` class is `ANNOUNCE.H`, and the implementation file is `ANNOUNCE.CPP`.

Now you'll write the `OnIdle()` function. Because Visual C++ didn't write the declaration and skeleton of the `OnIdle()` function, you have to declare this function and write its skeleton. Here is how you do that:

☐ Open the file `ANNOUNCE.H` and add code to it that defines the function `OnIdle()` as a member function of the `CAnnounceApp` class. After you write this code, the `CAnnounceApp` class declaration looks as follows:

```
class CAnnounceApp : public CWinApp
{
public:
    CAnnounceApp();

// Overrides
    virtual BOOL InitInstance();
```

```
/////////////////////
// MY CODE STARTS HERE
/////////////////////

    virtual BOOL OnIdle(LONG lCount);

/////////////////////
// MY CODE ENDS HERE
/////////////////////


// Implementation

    //{{AFX_MSG(CAnnounceApp)
    afx_msg void OnAppAbout();
// NOTE - the ClassWizard will add and remove
// member functions here.
//    DO NOT EDIT what you see in these blocks
// of generated code !
    //}}AFX_MSG
    DECLARE_MESSAGE_MAP()
};
```

Now write the code of the OnIdle() function:

☐ Open the file ANNOUNCE.CPP and add the OnIdle() function to the end of the file. After you write this function, the end of the ANNOUNCE.CPP file looks as follows:

```
/////////////////////
// MY CODE STARTS HERE
/////////////////////

BOOL CAnnounceApp::OnIdle(LONG lCount)
{

    // Call the base class function.
    CWinApp::OnIdle(lCount);

    // Beep.
    MessageBeep(-1);

    return TRUE;

}

/////////////////////
// MY CODE ENDS HERE
/////////////////////
```

The first statement that you typed in OnIdle() is

```
CWinApp::OnIdle(lCount);
```

This statement calls the OnIdle() function of the base class. This is necessary because the OnIdle() function of the base class performs various initialization tasks. For example, it updates the menu items and tool bar items (if any) of the application.

The next statement calls the MessageBeep() function to beep:

```
MessageBeep(-1);
```

Later you'll change this code so that instead of just beeping, the code of OnIdle() will monitor the Windows session and will check whether the user is trying to exit Windows. If the user is trying to exit Windows, the code will play an appropriate audio message through the PC speaker. For now, the MessageBeep() function just illustrates the OnIdle() concept.

The last statement that you typed in the OnIdle() function returns TRUE:

```
return TRUE;
```

When OnIdle() returns TRUE, it serves as an indication (to Windows) that OnIdle() should be called again. That is, when OnIdle() returns TRUE, OnIdle() will be called continuously for as long as the application is idle. If OnIdle() returns FALSE, OnIdle() will be executed only the first time the application is idle.

Don't forget to save your work:

☐ Select Save from the File menu.

Executing the ANNOUNCE Application

Now execute the ANNOUNCE application and hear the code that you wrote in the OnIdle() function in action:

☐ Select Build All ANNOUNCE.EXE from Visual C++'s Project menu.

☐ Select Execute ANNOUNCE.EXE from the Project menu.

Visual C++ responds by executing the ANNOUNCE application.

As you can hear, the ANNOUNCE application sounds a continuous beep through the PC speaker. That is, whenever the ANNOUNCE application is idle, the `OnIdle()` function that you wrote is executed. Because the `OnIdle()` function that you typed returns TRUE, the `OnIdle()` function is executed many times and each time a beep is played. This results in a continuous beep.

The `OnIdle()` function is executed even when the window of another application is active. To verify this:

☐ Leave the ANNOUNCE application running and start any other Windows application.

As you can hear, the ANNOUNCE application keeps on beeping. That is, even though the window of another application is active, the `OnIdle()` *function of the ANNOUNCE application keeps on executing.*

As stated earlier, the `OnIdle()` function is not executed:

When other applications aren't idle
When your application's menu (or system menu) is active
When the user opens a modal dialog box in your application

To verify this:

☐ While the ANNOUNCE application is still running, start the Paintbrush program.

☐ Use the Paintbrush's pencil tool to draw something.

Note that as you're drawing (that is, when Paintbrush isn't idle), the PC speaker stops beeping. That is, for as long as Paintbrush isn't idle, the ANNOUNCE application's `OnIdle()` *function is not executed.*

☐ Terminate the Paintbrush application and switch back to the ANNOUNCE application.

☐ Now, try to open any of the menus of the ANNOUNCE application.

As you can hear (or rather, not hear), when you open a menu (a regular menu or the system menu), the PC speaker doesn't beep. That is, when a menu is open, the `OnIdle()` *function isn't executed.*

☐ Now select About from the ANNOUNCE application's Help menu.

Again, as long as the About dialog box is active, the ANNOUNCE application stops beeping. That is, because the ANNOUNCE application's About dialog box is a modal dialog box and while it is active, the OnIdle() *function is not executed. However, if you open another application's menu or modal dialog box, the ANNOUNCE application's* OnIdle() *function will be executed.*

In the following sections, you'll enhance the ANNOUNCE application as follows:

You'll change the code in OnIdle() so that instead of just beeping, it will monitor the Windows session and play an audio recording through the PC speaker whenever the user tries to quit Windows.

You'll write code that displays text in the main window of the application as shown in Figure 28.1.

You'll write code so that when the application is started the default size of the application window will be as shown in Figure 28.1.

Declaring the Functions of the TegoSND.DLL Library

Later you'll modify the OnIdle() function so that instead of beeping, it will monitor the Windows session and play an audio recording whenever the user tries to quit Windows. Because this code will play sound through the PC speaker with the TegoSND.DLL functions, you need to declare the functions of the TegoSND.DLL in ANNOUNCE.DEF, and you need to #include the TegoSND.H header file in ANNOUNCE.H.

☐ Open the file ANNOUNCE.DEF and modify it until it looks as follows:

```
; announce.def : Declares the module parameters
; for the application.

NAME          ANNOUNCE
DESCRIPTION   'ANNOUNCE Windows Application'
EXETYPE       WINDOWS

CODE          PRELOAD MOVEABLE DISCARDABLE
DATA          PRELOAD MOVEABLE MULTIPLE

HEAPSIZE      1024   ; initial heap size
; Stack size is passed as argument to
; linker's /STACK option


;;;;;;;;;;;;;;;;;;;;;;;;;;;;
; MY CODE STARTS HERE
;;;;;;;;;;;;;;;;;;;;;;;;;;;;
```

```
;;;;;;;;;;;;;;;;;;;;;;;;;;;;;;;;;;;;;;;;;;;;
; sp_ functions from the TegoSND.DLL library
;;;;;;;;;;;;;;;;;;;;;;;;;;;;;;;;;;;;;;;;;;;;

IMPORTS
TegoSND.sp_OpenSession
TegoSND.sp_PlaySnd
TegoSND.sp_MouseOn
TegoSND.sp_MouseOff
TegoSND.sp_CloseSession

;;;;;;;;;;;;;;;;;;;;;;;;;
; MY CODE ENDS HERE
;;;;;;;;;;;;;;;;;;;;;;;;;
```

☐ Open the file ANNOUNCE.H and add the #include "TegoSND.h" statement
at the beginning of the file. After you add this statement, the beginning
of ANNOUNCE.H looks as follows:

```
// announce.h : main header file for
// the ANNOUNCE application
//

#ifndef __AFXWIN_H__
#error include 'stdafx.h' before including this file for PCH
#endif

#include "resource.h"        // main symbols

///////////////////////
// MY CODE STARTS HERE
///////////////////////

#include "\vcProg\DLL\TegoSND.h"

///////////////////////
// MY CODE ENDS HERE
///////////////////////

.....
.....
.....
```

Opening the Sound Session

The ANNOUNCE application uses the WAV file ITSBEEN1.WAV. This WAV file contains the audio prompt, "It's been fun working with you." Now you'll declare the variable that is used to store the session number of the ITSBEEN1.WAV sound file:

☐ Open the file ANNOUNCE.H, and add code to the CAnnounceApp class declaration that defines the int variable m_ItsBeenFunSession as a data member. After you write this code, the CAnnounceApp class declaration looks as follows:

```
class CAnnounceApp : public CWinApp
{
public:
     CAnnounceApp();

     /////////////////////////
     // MY CODE STARTS HERE
     /////////////////////////

     int m_ItsBeenFunSession;

     /////////////////////////
     // MY CODE ENDS HERE
     /////////////////////////

// Overrides
     virtual BOOL InitInstance();

     /////////////////////////
     // MY CODE STARTS HERE
     /////////////////////////

     virtual BOOL OnIdle(LONG lCount);

     /////////////////////////
     // MY CODE ENDS HERE
     /////////////////////////


// Implementation

     //{{AFX_MSG(CAnnounceApp)
     afx_msg void OnAppAbout();
// NOTE - the ClassWizard will add and
// remove member functions here.
//    DO NOT EDIT what you see in these blocks
// of generated code !
     //}}AFX_MSG
     DECLARE_MESSAGE_MAP()
};
```

Now that you have the m_ItsBeenFunSession data member, you can write the code that opens the WAV sessions for the ITSBEEN1.WAV sound file:

☐ Open the file ANNOUNCE.CPP and add code to the constructor function of the CAnnounceApp class. After adding this code, the constructor of the CAnnounceApp class looks as follows:

```
CAnnounceApp::CAnnounceApp()
{
// TODO: add construction code here,
// Place all significant initialization in InitInstance

    ////////////////////////
    // MY CODE STARTS HERE
    ////////////////////////

    // Open a sound session with the ITSBEEN1.WAV file.
    m_ItsBeenFunSession =
        sp_OpenSession ("\\VCPROG\\WAV\\ITSBEEN1.WAV");

    ///////////////////////
    // MY CODE ENDS HERE
    ///////////////////////

}
```

Monitoring the Windows Session

Now you'll modify the OnIdle() function so that instead of beeping, it will monitor the Windows session and play the ITSBEEN1.WAV file whenever the user quits Windows.

☐ Open the ANNOUNCE.CPP file and modify the OnIdle() function until it looks as follows:

```
////////////////////////
// MY CODE STARTS HERE
////////////////////////

BOOL CAnnounceApp::OnIdle(LONG lCount)
{

    // Call the base class.
    CWinApp::OnIdle(lCount);

    // Beep.
    ////MessageBeep(-1);

    // Is the Exit Windows window on the desktop?
    HWND hWindow = FindWindow (NULL, "Exit Windows" );
    if (hWindow)
        {
```

```
    sp_PlaySnd (m_ItsBeenFunSession,
                SP_START_OF_FILE,
                SP_END_OF_FILE);
    }

return TRUE;

}
```

```
//////////////////////
// MY CODE ENDS HERE
//////////////////////
```

In the modification you just made to the OnIdle() function, you commented out (//) the MessageBeep(-1) statement, and you added the statements that monitor the Windows session.

The purpose of the code that you wrote in OnIdle() is to detect whether the user is trying to quit Windows, and if this is the case, play the audio prompt "It's been fun working with you" through the PC speaker.

The code checks whether the user is quitting Windows by using the FindWindow() function:

```
// Is the Exit Windows window on the desktop?
HWND hWindow = FindWindow (NULL, "Exit Windows" );
if (hWindow)
    {
    sp_PlaySnd (m_ItsBeenFunSession,
                SP_START_OF_FILE,
                SP_END_OF_FILE);
    }
```

The statement

```
HWND hWindow = FindWindow (NULL, "Exit Windows" );
```

updates the variable hWindow with a number that indicates whether the window whose title is Exit Windows is present on the desktop. Recall that when the user quits Windows, the Exit Windows window is displayed on the desktop (see Figure 28.6).

Figure 28.6.
The Exit Windows
window.

If the Exit Windows window is present on the desktop, the statement

```
HWND hWindow = FindWindow (NULL, "Exit Windows" );
```

will update the hWindow variable with a non-zero number. If, however, the Exit Windows window isn't present on the desktop, the previous statement will update hWindow with 0.

The if statement,

```
if (hWindow)
   {
   sp_PlaySnd (m_ItsBeenFunSession,
               SP_START_OF_FILE,
               SP_END_OF_FILE);
   }
```

evaluates the value of hWindow. If hWindow isn't zero (that is, if the Exit Windows window is present on the desktop), the if condition is satisfied and the WAV file ITSBEEN1.WAV is played through the PC speaker.

Closing the Sound Session

When the user terminates the application, you need to close the sound session of the ITSBEEN1.WAV sound file. You'll write the code that closes the sound session in the ExitInstance() member function of the CAnnounceApp class.

Visual C++ didn't write the declaration and skeleton of the ExitInstance() function, so you have to declare this function and write its skeleton. Here's how you do that:

☐ Open the file ANNOUNCE.H and add code to it that defines the function ExitInstance() as a member function of the CAnnounceApp class. After you write this code, the CAnnounceApp class declaration looks as follows:

```
class CAnnounceApp : public CWinApp
{
public:
    CAnnounceApp();
```

```
/////////////////////
// MY CODE STARTS HERE
/////////////////////

    int m_ItsBeenFunSession;

/////////////////////
// MY CODE ENDS HERE
/////////////////////

// Overrides
    virtual BOOL InitInstance();


    /////////////////////
    // MY CODE STARTS HERE
    /////////////////////

    virtual BOOL OnIdle(LONG lCount);

    virtual int ExitInstance();

    /////////////////////
    // MY CODE ENDS HERE
    /////////////////////


// Implementation

    //{{AFX_MSG(CAnnounceApp)
    afx_msg void OnAppAbout();
// NOTE - the ClassWizard will add and
/ remove member functions here.
//    DO NOT EDIT what you see in these
// blocks of generated code !
    //}}AFX_MSG
    DECLARE_MESSAGE_MAP()
};
```

Now write the code of the ExitInstance() function:

☐ Open the file ANNOUNCE.CPP, and add to it (at the end of the file) the ExitInstatnce() function. After you write this function, the end of the ANNOUNCE.CPP file looks as follows:

```
/////////////////////
// MY CODE STARTS HERE
/////////////////////
```

```
int CAnnounceApp::ExitInstance()
{

// Close the sound session.
sp_CloseSession(m_ItsBeenFunSession);

return CWinApp::ExitInstance();

}

/////////////////////
// MY CODE ENDS HERE
/////////////////////
```

Don't forget to save your work:

☐ Select Save from the File menu.

To see the code that you wrote in the OnIdle() function in action:

☐ Compile/link, and execute the ANNOUNCE application.

☐ Now, try to exit from Windows.

> *As you can hear, the ANNOUNCE application responds by playing the audio prompt, "It's been fun working with you."*

Displaying Text in the Main Window of the Application

The main window of the application contains text, as shown in Figure 28.1. To display this text, you need to attach code to the WM_PAINT event of the view class. Here's how you do that:

☐ Use ClassWizard to add a function for the event:

Class Name:	CAnnounceView
Object ID:	CAnnounceView
Message:	WM_PAINT
Function Name:	OnPaint()

☐ Edit the OnPaint() function that you added to the ANNOUNCE.CPP file. After you edit the function, your OnPaint() function looks as follows:

```
void CAnnounceView::OnPaint()
{
CPaintDC dc(this); // device context for painting

// TODO: Add your message handler code here

    /////////////////////////
    // MY CODE STARTS HERE
    /////////////////////////

    // Display instructions inside the application window.
    dc.TextOut(20,30,"Leave this program running...");
    dc.TextOut(20,50,"Then try to exit Windows...");

    /////////////////////////
    // MY CODE ENDS HERE
    /////////////////////////

// Do not call CView::OnPaint() for painting messages
}
```

Save your work.

Changing the Default Size of the Application Main Window

Recall that when the application begins, the default size of the application window looks as shown in Figure 28.1.

You need to write the code that sets the default characteristics of the application's window in the PreCreateWindow() member function of the CMainFrame class. The header file of the CMainFrame class is MAINFRM.H and the implementation file of the CMainFrame class is MAINFRM.CPP.

☐ Open the file MAINFRM.H and add code to it that defines the function PreCreateWindow() as a member function of the CMainFrame class. After you write this code, the CMainFrame class declaration looks as follows:

```
class CMainFrame : public CFrameWnd
{
protected: // create from serialization only
    CMainFrame();
    DECLARE_DYNCREATE(CMainFrame)
```

```
/////////////////////
// MY CODE STARTS HERE
/////////////////////

    BOOL PreCreateWindow(CREATESTRUCT& cs);

/////////////////////
// MY CODE ENDS HERE
/////////////////////


// Attributes
public:

// Operations
public:

// Implementation
public:
    virtual ~CMainFrame();
#ifdef _DEBUG
    virtual void AssertValid() const;
    virtual void Dump(CDumpContext& dc) const;
#endif

// Generated message map functions
protected:
    //{{AFX_MSG(CMainFrame)
// NOTE - the ClassWizard will add and
// remove member functions here.
//    DO NOT EDIT what you see in these
// blocks of generated code!
    //}}AFX_MSG
    DECLARE_MESSAGE_MAP()
};
```

Now write the code of the `PreCreateWindow()` function:

☐ Open the file `MAINFRM.CPP` and add to it (at the end of the file) the
 `PreCreateWindow()` function. After writing this function, the end of the
 `MAINFRM.CPP` file looks as follows:

```
/////////////////////
// MY CODE STARTS HERE
/////////////////////

BOOL CMainFrame::PreCreateWindow(CREATESTRUCT& cs)
{

    // Call the base class function.
    CFrameWnd::PreCreateWindow( cs );
```

```
// Set the width of the window to 270.
cs.cx = 270;

// Set the height of the window to 180.
cs.cy = 180;

return TRUE;
}

//////////////////////
// MY CODE ENDS HERE
//////////////////////
```

Recall from previous chapters that the `PreCreateWindow()` function is automatically executed prior to the creation of the window. You can use this function to override the default characteristics of the window. The parameter of `PreCreateWindow()`, `cs`, is a structure of type `CREATESTRUCT`. You set the characteristics of the window by setting the members of the `cs` structure.

To review the code you typed in the `PreCreateWindow()` function.

The first statement,

```
CFrameWnd::PreCreateWindow( cs );
```

calls the `PreCreateWindow()` base class. This is necessary because the base class performs various initialization tasks.

The next statement is

```
cs.cx = 270;
```

This statement sets the value of the `cx` member of the `cs` structure to 270. The `cx` member specifies the width of the window. Thus, the width of the window will be 270.

The next statement is

```
cs.cy = 180;
```

This statement sets the value of the `cy` member of the `cs` structure to 180. The `cy` member specifies the height of the window. Thus, the height of the window will be 180.

The last statement in the `PreCreateWindow()` function is

```
return TRUE;
```

When `PreCreateWindow()` returns `TRUE`, it serves as an indication that the window creation continues. If `PreCreateWindow()` returns `FALSE`, the window won't be created.

Don't forget to save your work:

☐ Select Save from the File menu.

To see the code you attached to the `OnPaint()` and `PreCreateWindow()` functions in action:

☐ Compile, link, and execute the ANNOUNCE application.

As you can see, now the main window of the application appears as shown in Figure 28.1.

29

Advanced PC Speaker Topics

In this chapter you'll write applications that play sound through the PC speaker. The first application illustrates how you can play background sound through the PC speaker while other applications are running! The second application illustrates how you can perform animation together with playback of sound through the PC speaker.

> **NOTE**
>
> In this chapter you'll learn how to use a DLL for the playback of sound. In this book's appendix, you'll learn how to use the TegoMM.VBX control for the playback.

Playing Background Sound Through the PC Speaker While Other Applications Are Running

Playing background sound through an installed sound card while other applications are running is easy. That's because once your application issues a Play command to the sound card, the sound card takes care of the playback, and the PC processor is free to perform other tasks (that is, run other applications).

However, playing background sound through the PC speaker (while other applications are running) is a different story. When you play background sound through the PC speaker, the PC processor is the one that performs the playback, not a sound card. Thus, to play background sound through the PC speaker while other applications are running, you need to utilize the OnIdle() function that was discussed in the previous chapter. The PLAY application illustrates how this is done.

The PLAY Application

Before you start writing the Play application, first execute the copy of it that resides in your C:\VCPROG\ORIGINAL\CH29\PLAY directory.

To execute the PLAY application:

Use Run from Program Manager's File menu to execute
  C:\VCPROG\ORIGINAL\CH29\PLAY\PLAY.EXE.

The PLAY.EXE file uses the REGGA2M3.WAV file. During the installation of the book's CD, the REGGA2M3.WAV file was copied from the CD to your C:\VCPROG\WAV directory.

☐ Select Execute PLAY.EXE from the Project menu.

  Visual C++ responds by executing the PLAY application. An hourglass icon is displayed for a while, and then the main window of PLAY.EXE *appears as shown in Figure 29.1. The PLAY application plays the* REGGA2M3.WAV *file through the PC speaker. You can switch to other Windows applications, and the PC will keep playing the WAV file in the background.*

☐ While the WAV file is playing, switch to another Windows application (for example, a word processing program or Paintbrush).

As you can hear, the PLAY application keeps playing the WAV file.

Figure 29.1.
The main window
of the PLAY
application.

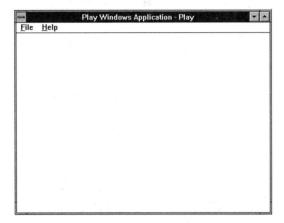

The PLAY application has two popup menus: File and Help. These popup menus are shown in Figures 29.2 and 29.3.

Figure 29.2.
The PLAY
application's File
popup menu.

Figure 29.3.
The PLAY
application's Help
popup menu.

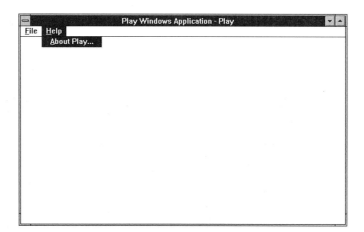

To exit from the PLAY application:

☐ Select Exit from the File menu.

Now that you know what the PLAY application should do, you can start writing it.

Creating the Project of the PLAY Application

To create the project of the PLAY application:

☐ Select AppWizard from the Project menu.

Visual C++ responds by running AppWizard.

☐ Use the Directory list box to select the directory C:\VCPROG\PRACTICE\CH29.

☐ Type play in the Project Name box.

Now your AppWizard dialog box should look as shown in Figure 29.4.

☐ Click the Options button and set the options as shown in Figure 29.5 (that is, uncheck all the check boxes except the Generate Source Comments check box).

Figure 29.4.
The AppWizard
dialog box for the
PLAY application.

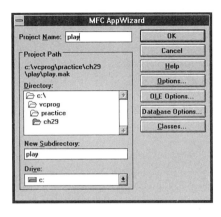

Figure 29.5.
Setting the options
for the PLAY
application.

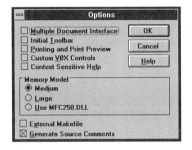

☐ Click the OK button of the Options dialog box and then click the OK
button of the AppWizard dialog box and finally click the Create button of
the New Application Information dialog box.

*AppWizard responds by creating the PLAY project and all the skeleton files of
the PLAY application.*

To remove the debug options of the project (so that you'll have a small EXE file):

☐ Select Project from the Options menu of Visual C++, click the Release radio
button, and then click the OK button of the dialog box.

The Visual Implementation of the PLAY Application's Menu

☐ The PLAY application should have a menu with two popup menus, as
shown in Figures 29.2 and 29.3. Use App Studio to implement the menu of
the PLAY application per Table 29.1.

Table 29.1. The menu bar of the PLAY application.
Figures relating to menu: 29.2, 29.3

Menu Item
&File
E&xit
&Help
&About Play...

Don't forget to delete the accelerator keys of the menu items that you removed:

☐ Select `PLAY.RC [MFC-Resource Script]` from the Window menu of App Studio, select Accelerator in the Type list and then double-click `IDR_MAINFRAME` in the Resources list.

☐ Delete the accelerator keys that aren't used by the application. In particular, delete the accelerator keys of the `ID_FILE_NEW`, `ID_FILE_OPEN`, and `ID_FILE_SAVE` menu items.

If you don't delete these accelerator keys, they will be active during runtime. If, for example, the user presses Ctrl+N, it's as if he or she selected New from the File menu (even though you removed the New item from the File menu).

Save your work:

☐ Select Save from the File menu of App Studio.

The visual implementation of the PLAY application's menu bar is completed.

Opening a WAV Session

Because the PLAY application plays a WAV file through the PC speaker, you have to add the `IMPORT` statement in the `PLAY.DEF` file.

☐ Open the `PLAY.DEF` file and add the `IMPORT` statement. After you add the `IMPORT` statement, the `PLAY.DEF` file looks as follows:

```
; play.def : Declares the module parameters
; for the application.

NAME          PLAY
DESCRIPTION   'PLAY Windows Application'
EXETYPE       WINDOWS
```

```
CODE          PRELOAD MOVEABLE DISCARDABLE
DATA          PRELOAD MOVEABLE MULTIPLE

HEAPSIZE    1024    ; initial heap size
; Stack size is passed as argument to
; linker's /STACK option


;;;;;;;;;;;;;;;;;;;;;;;;
; MY CODE STARTS HERE
;;;;;;;;;;;;;;;;;;;;;;;;


;;;;;;;;;;;;;;;;;;;;;;;;;;;;;;;;;;;;;;;;;;;;;;;;
; sp_ functions from the TegoSND.DLL library
;;;;;;;;;;;;;;;;;;;;;;;;;;;;;;;;;;;;;;;;;;;;;;;;

IMPORTS
TegoSND.sp_OpenSession
TegoSND.sp_PlaySnd
TegoSND.sp_MouseOn
TegoSND.sp_MouseOff
TegoSND.sp_CloseSession


;;;;;;;;;;;;;;;;;;;;;;;;
; MY CODE ENDS HERE
;;;;;;;;;;;;;;;;;;;;;;;;
```

Now that the DEF file includes the IMPORT statement for the sp_ functions from the TegoSND.DLL, your code can execute sp_ functions.

Now you'll open a WAV session. You'll open the WAV session in the constructor function of the CPlayApp class:

☐ Open the PLAY.CPP file and add code to the CPlayApp() constructor function. After you add the code, the CPlayApp() constructor function looks as follows:

```
CPlayApp::CPlayApp()
{
// TODO: add construction code here,
// Place all significant initialization in InitInstance

    /////////////////////////
    // MY CODE STARTS HERE
    /////////////////////////

    // Open a sound session.
    char FileToPlay[255];

    strcpy( FileToPlay, "\\VCPROG\\WAV\\regga2m3.WAV" );
    m_MusicSession = sp_OpenSession ( FileToPlay );
```

961

```
// If WAV session cannot be opened, display message box.
   if ( m_MusicSession < 0 )
      {
      char Message[255], Caption[255];
      strcpy ( Message, "Can't open the file: ");
      strcat ( Message,  FileToPlay );
      strcpy ( Caption, "Error" );
      MessageBox ( NULL,
                   Message,
                   Caption,
                   MB_OK ¦ MB_ICONHAND);
      }

   // Mouse should be available during playback.
   sp_MouseON(m_MusicSession);

   // Initialize the playback position.
   m_PlayPosition = 0;

   ///////////////////////
   // MY CODE ENDS HERE
   ///////////////////////

}
```

The code you typed in the CPlayApp() constructor function opens a WAV session for the WAV file \VCPROG\\WAV\\regga2m3.WAV. The reason for opening the WAV file in the constructor function of the CPlayApp class is that you're going to play from within the OnIdle() function. This means that OnIdle() needs to know the value of m_MusicSession. By opening the WAV session in the constructor function of CPlayApp, you are able to update m_MusicSession, a data member of CPlayApp. OnIdle() will be able to access m_MusicSession, because OnIdle() is a member function of CPlayApp.

If the WAV file can't be opened, a message is displayed with the MessageBox() function.

The code you typed also executes the sp_MouseON() function:

```
sp_MouseON(m_MusicSession);
```

The sp_MouseOn() function makes the mouse available during the playback of the WAV file.

The code you typed also initializes the `m_PlayPosition` data member:

```
// Initialize the playback position.
m_PlayPosition = 0;
```

As you'll soon see, `m_PlayPosition` holds the current position of the playback.

Note that the `MessageBox()` function you used is a regular Windows API function. It isn't a member function of any class. We didn't use the `MessageBox()` member function because the `CPlayApp` class doesn't have a `MessageBox()` member function.

You can verify this as follows:

☐ Select Foundation Classes from the Help menu.

Visual C++ responds by displaying the Class Library Reference Help window (see Figure 29.6).

Figure 29.6.
The Class Library Reference Help window.

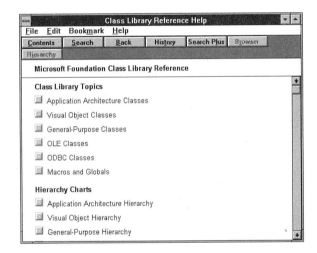

☐ Click the Search button and type `MessageBox` in the edit box (see Figure 29.7).

☐ Click the Show Topics button.

Visual C++ responds by listing the `CWnd::MessageBox` item (see Figure 29.8).

Figure 29.7.
Searching for help
about the
MessageBox( )
function.

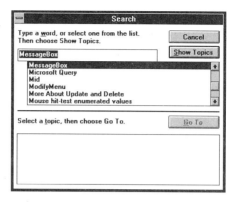

Figure 29.8.
Visual C++
finds the topic
CWnd::MessageBox.

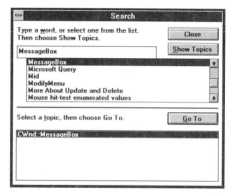

☐ Click the Go To button.

> *Visual C++ responds by displaying the Help window for* CWnd::MessageBox
> *(see Figure 29.9).*

As shown in Figure 29.9, MessageBox() is a member function of the CWnd class. The text CWnd:: that precedes the name of the function indicates that MessageBox() is a member function of the CWnd class.

The question now is, can you use MessageBox() from within the CPlayApp() constructor function? The answer is, no. To see why you can't use MessageBox() from within the CPlayApp() constructor function:

☐ Click the Help window's Contents button.

> *Visual C++ responds by displaying the Class Library Reference Help window*
> *(see Figure 29.6).*

☐ Click the Application Architecture Hierarchy item that appears under the Hierarchy Charts heading (see Figure 29.6).

Visual C++ responds by displaying the class hierarchy (see Figure 29.10).

Figure 29.9.
The Help
window of
CWnd::MessageBox.

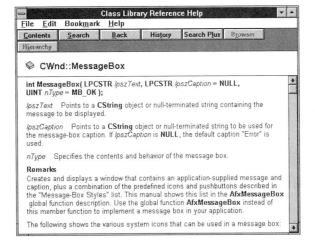

Figure 29.10.
The Class
Hierarchy.

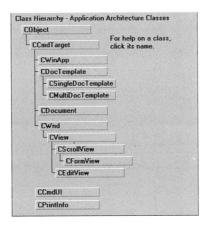

You can see from Figure 29.10 that you can use the MessageBox() member function from within the member functions of the CView class, because CView is derived from CWnd. For example, you can use the MessageBox() member function from within the constructor function of the CPlayView class. This is because MessageBox() is a member function of the CWnd class, CView is a derived class from CWnd, and CPlayView is a derived class from CView. However, CPlayApp is derived from CWinApp, and CWinApp is not derived from CWnd.

Okay, you can't use the MessageBox() member function of CWnd from within CPlayApp(). However, you can use the regular Windows MessageBox() function. Windows API functions are regular C functions that Windows supports. (Because C++ is a superset of C, you can use the regular API functions of Windows.)

Here is how you get help about the Windows API MessageBox() function:

☐ Close the Class Library Reference Help window.

☐ Select Windows 3.1 SDK from the Help menu of Visual C++.

> *Visual C++ responds by displaying the Windows 3.1 SDK Help window (see Figure 29.11).*

Figure 29.11.
The Windows 3.1
SDK Help window.

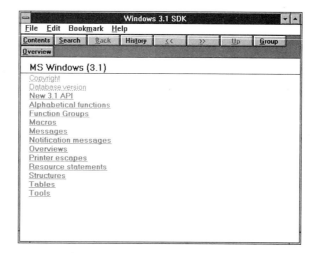

☐ Click the Search button and type MessageBox in the edit box (see Figure 29.12).

> *Visual C++ responds by listing the MessageBox function item (see Figure 29.13).*

☐ Click the Go To button.

> *Visual C++ responds by displaying the Help window of the MessageBox() function of the Windows 3.1 SDK (see Figure 29.14).*

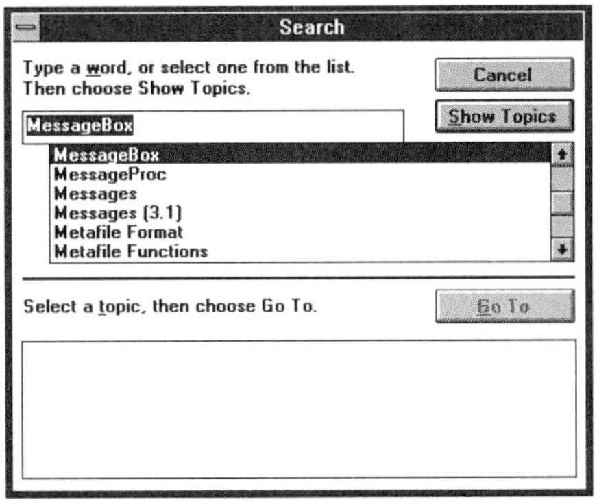

Figure 29.12.
Searching for the
`MessageBox( )`
of the Windows 3.1
SDK.

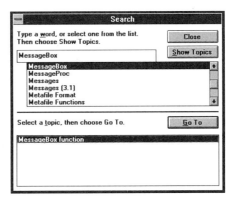

Figure 29.13.
Visual C++
finds the topic
`MessageBox`
function.

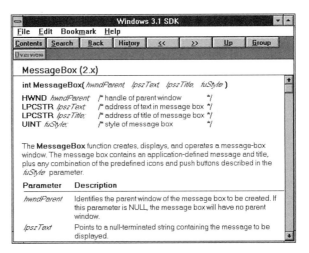

Figure 29.14.
The Help window
of the Windows 3.1
SDK
`MessageBox( )`
function.

967

As shown in Figure 29.14, the `MessageBox()` function of the Windows SDK takes four parameters. This is the reason for typing the `MessageBox()` function in `CPlayApp()` as follows:

```
MessageBox ( NULL,
             Message,
             Caption,
             MB_OK ¦ MB_ICONHAND);
```

If your `\VCPROG\WAV` directory doesn't contain the `REGGA2M3.WAV` file, the `sp_OpenSession()` function will return a negative number, the `if` statement will be satisfied, and the message box of Figure 29.15 will be displayed.

Figure 29.15.
The Error
message box.

Declaring the Data Members

The code you typed utilizes two data members, `m_MusicSession` and `m_PlayPosition`. Thus, you must include these data members in the declaration of the `CPlayApp` class.

☐ Open the `PLAY.H` file and add the data members `m_MusicSession` and `m_PlayPosition` in the declaration of the `CPlayApp` class. After you add these data members, the `CPlayApp` class declaration should look as follows:

```
class CPlayApp : public CWinApp
{
public:
     CPlayApp();

     ///////////////////////////
     // MY CODE STARTS HERE
     ///////////////////////////

     int m_MusicSession;
     long m_PlayPosition;

     ///////////////////////////
     // MY CODE ENDS HERE
     ///////////////////////////

// Overrides
     virtual BOOL InitInstance();
```

```
// Implementation

    //{{AFX_MSG(CPlayApp)
    afx_msg void OnAppAbout();
// NOTE - the ClassWizard will add and remove
// member functions here.
//    DO NOT EDIT what you see in these blocks
//    of generated code !
    //}}AFX_MSG
    DECLARE_MESSAGE_MAP()
};
```

Including the *TegoSND.H* File

Of course, in order to be able to use the sp_ functions, you must #include the TegoSND.h file:

☐ Open the PLAY.CPP file and add an #include statement that includes the TegoSND.h file. After including this statement, the beginning of the PLAY.CPP file should look as follows:

```
// play.cpp : Defines the class behaviors for
// the application.
//

#include "stdafx.h"
#include "play.h"

/////////////////////
// MY CODE STARTS HERE
/////////////////////

#include "\vcprog\dll\TegoSND.h"

/////////////////////
// MY CODE ENDS HERE
/////////////////////

#include "mainfrm.h"
#include "playdoc.h"
#include "playview.h"

#ifdef _DEBUG
#undef THIS_FILE
static char BASED_CODE THIS_FILE[] = __FILE__;
#endif
....
....
....
```

969

Writing Code in the *OnIdle()* Function of the PLAY Application

Whenever the PLAY application is idle, the `OnIdle()` member function of the `CWinApp` class is automatically executed. The code of the PLAY application (that part of the code that Visual C++ wrote for you) declares a class called `CPlayApp` that is derived from `CWinApp`. The header file of the `CPlayApp` class is `PLAY.H`, and the implementation file is `PLAY.CPP`.

Now you'll write the `OnIdle()` function. Because Visual C++ didn't write the declaration and skeleton of the `OnIdle()` function, you have to declare this function, and write the skeleton of this function. Here is how you do that:

☐ Open the `PLAY.H` file and add code to it that defines the function `OnIdle()` as a member function of the `CPlayApp` class. After you write this code, the `CPlayApp` class declaration looks as follows:

```
class CPlayApp : public CWinApp
{
public:
    CPlayApp();

    /////////////////////////
    // MY CODE STARTS HERE
    /////////////////////////

    int m_MusicSession;
    long m_PlayPosition;

    /////////////////////////
    // MY CODE ENDS HERE
    /////////////////////////

// Overrides
    virtual BOOL InitInstance();

    /////////////////////////
    // MY CODE STARTS HERE
    /////////////////////////

    virtual BOOL OnIdle(LONG lCount);

    /////////////////////////
    // MY CODE ENDS HERE
    /////////////////////////

// Implementation
```

```
    //{{AFX_MSG(CPlayApp)
    afx_msg void OnAppAbout();
// NOTE - the ClassWizard will add and remove
// member functions here.
//    DO NOT EDIT what you see in these blocks
//    of generated code !
    //}}AFX_MSG
    DECLARE_MESSAGE_MAP()
};
```

The code you typed declares the prototype of the OnIdle() function. Now write the code of the OnIdle() function:

☐ Open the file PLAY.CPP and add (at the end of the file) the OnIdle() function. After you write this function, the end of the PLAY.CPP file looks as follows:

```
/////////////////////////
// MY CODE STARTS HERE
/////////////////////////

BOOL CPlayApp::OnIdle(LONG lCount)
{

    // Call the base class function.
    CWinApp::OnIdle(lCount);


    m_PlayPosition =
            sp_PlaySnd ( m_MusicSession,
                         m_PlayPosition,
                         m_PlayPosition + 10000 );


    return TRUE;

}

/////////////////////////
// MY CODE ENDS HERE
/////////////////////////
```

The first statement that you typed in OnIdle() is

```
CWinApp::OnIdle(lCount);
```

This statement calls the OnIdle() function of the base class, which is necessary because the OnIdle() function of the base class performs various initialization tasks. For example, it updates the menu items and toolbar items (if any) of the application.

The next statement uses the sp_PlaySnd() function to play 10,000 bytes from the WAV file:

```
m_PlayPosition =
        sp_PlaySnd ( m_MusicSession,
                     m_PlayPosition,
                     m_PlayPosition + 10000 );
```

The first parameter is m_MusicSession. This is the value returned from the sp_OpenSession() function that you used in the CPlayApp() constructor function when you opened the WAV session.

The second parameter of sp_PlaySnd() is the data member m_PlayPosition. Thus, if m_PlayPosition is 0, the sp_PlaySnd() function will play the WAV file starting at byte 0.

The third parameter of sp_PlaySnd() is m_PlayPosition+10000.

For example, when m_PlayPosition is equal to 0, the sp_PlaySnd() function plays from byte 0 to byte 10,000.

The returned value of sp_PlaySnd() is assigned to m_PlayPosition. The returned value from sp_PlaySnd() is the last byte played. So if, for example, m_PlayPosition is equal to 0, the sp_PlaySnd() function will play from byte location 0 to byte location 10,000, and then m_PlayPosition is updated with 10,000. When the OnIdle() function is executed again, the sp_PlaySnd() function will play from byte location 10,000 to byte location 20,000, and m_PlayPosition will be updated with the value 20,000. On the next execution of OnIdle(), the sp_PlaySnd() will play from byte location 20,000 to 30,000. This process of playing 10,000 bytes at a time continues until the end of the WAV file is played, and then sp_PlaySnd() returns 0. Thus, on the next execution of the OnIdle() function, the sp_PlaySnd() function will play from byte 0 to byte 10,000.

The last statement that you typed in the OnIdle() function returns TRUE:

```
return TRUE;
```

When OnIdle() returns TRUE, OnIdle() should be called again. That is, when OnIdle() returns TRUE, OnIdle() will be called continuously for as long as the application is idle. If OnIdle() returns FALSE, OnIdle() will be executed only at the first time the application is idle.

Don't forget to save your work:

☐ Select Save from the File menu.

Closing the Sound Session

When the user terminates the application, you need to close the sound session of the
Regga2m3.WAV sound file. You'll write the code that closes the sound session inside
the ExitInstance() member function of the CPlayApp class.

Visual C++ did not write the declaration and skeleton of the ExitInstance() function. You have to declare this function and write the skeleton of this function. Here
is how you do that:

☐ Open the file PLAY.H and add code to it that defines the function
ExitInstance() as a member function of the CPlayApp class. After you write
this code, the CPlayApp class declaration looks as follows:

```
class CPlayApp : public CWinApp
{
public:
     CPlayApp();

     /////////////////////////
     // MY CODE STARTS HERE
     /////////////////////////

     int m_MusicSession;
     long m_PlayPosition;

     /////////////////////////
     // MY CODE ENDS HERE
     /////////////////////////

// Overrides
     virtual BOOL InitInstance();

     /////////////////////////
     // MY CODE STARTS HERE
     /////////////////////////

     virtual BOOL OnIdle(LONG lCount);
     virtual int ExitInstance();

     /////////////////////////
     // MY CODE ENDS HERE
     /////////////////////////

// Implementation

     //{{AFX_MSG(CPlayApp)
     afx_msg void OnAppAbout();
```

```
// NOTE - the ClassWizard will add and remove
//   member functions here.
//     DO NOT EDIT what you see in these blocks
//     of generated code !
    //}}AFX_MSG
    DECLARE_MESSAGE_MAP()
};
```

Now write the code of the `ExitInstance()` function:

☐ Open the file `PLAY.CPP` and add to it (at the end of the file) the `ExitInstance()` function. After you write this function, the end of the `PLAY.CPP` file looks as follows:

```
//////////////////////////
// MY CODE STARTS HERE
//////////////////////////

int CPlayApp::ExitInstance()
{

// Close the sound session.
sp_CloseSession(m_MusicSession);

return CWinApp::ExitInstance();

}

//////////////////////////
// MY CODE ENDS HERE
//////////////////////////
```

Don't forget to save your work:

☐ Select Save from the File menu.

Executing the PLAY Application

Now execute the PLAY application and hear the code you wrote in the `OnIdle()` function in action:

☐ Select Build All PLAY.EXE from Visual C++'s Project menu.

☐ Select Execute PLAY.EXE from the Project menu.

> *Visual C++ responds by executing the PLAY application. As you can hear, the PLAY application plays the REGGA2M3.WAV file in a continuous loop. That is, whenever the PLAY application is idle, the OnIdle() function that you wrote is executed.*

The `OnIdle()` function is executed even when another application's window is active. To verify this:

☐ Leave the PLAY application running and start any other Windows application.

> *As you can hear, the PLAY application keeps on playing. That is, even though the window of another application is active, the* `OnIdle()` *function of the PLAY application keeps on executing.*

As stated in the previous chapter, the `OnIdle()` function isn't executed:

> When other applications aren't idle.
> When the menu of your application (or the system menu of your application) is active.
> When the user opens a modal dialog box in your application.

To verify this:

☐ While the PLAY application is still running, start the Paintbrush program.

☐ Use the pencil tool of Paintbrush to draw something.

> *Note that as you are drawing (when Paintbrush isn't idle), the PC speaker stops playing. That is, for as long as Paintbrush isn't idle, the* `OnIdle()` *function of the PLAY application is not executed.*

☐ Terminate the Paintbrush application and then switch back to the PLAY application.

☐ Now, try to open any of the PLAY application's menus.

> *As you can see, when you open a menu (a regular menu or the system menu), the PC speaker doesn't play. That is, when a menu is open, the* `OnIdle()` *function isn't executed.*

The MUSIC Application

The MUSIC application is similar to the PLAY application. However, the MUSIC application also displays animation simultaneously with the playback of a WAV file through the PC speaker.

The animation of the MUSIC application is composed of seven BMP files. These BMP files are called d1.BMP, d2.BMP, d3.BMP, d4.BMP, d5.BMP, d6.BMP and d7.BMP. The BMP files reside in your C:\VCPROG\BMP directory. Figures 29.16 through 29.22 show these BMP files.

Figure 29.16.
The d1.BMP *file.*

Figure 29.17.
The d2.BMP *file.*

Figure 29.18.
The d3.BMP *file.*

Figure 29.19.
The d4.BMP *file.*

Figure 29.20.
The d5.BMP *file.*

Figure 29.21.
The d6.BMP *file.*

Figure 29.22.
The d7.BMP file.

Before you start writing the MUSIC application, execute a copy of it. A copy of this application resides in your \VCPROG\ORIGINAL\CH29\MUSIC directory.

To execute the MUSIC.EXE application:

☐ Select Run from the File Manager of Windows and execute the C:\VCPROG\ORIGINAL\CH29\MUSIC\MUSIC.EXE file.

> *Windows responds by executing the MUSIC application. An hourglass icon is displayed for a while, and then the main window of* MUSIC.EXE *appears as shown in Figure 29.23. The MUSIC application plays the* regga2m3.WAV *file through the PC speaker simultaneously with the display of animation.*

Figure 29.23.
The window
of the MUSIC
application.

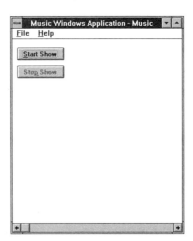

The MUSIC application has two popup menus: File and Help. These popup menus are shown in Figures 29.24 and 29.25.

Figure 29.24.
The MUSIC
application's File
popup menu.

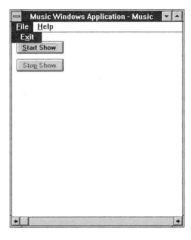

Figure 29.25.
The MUSIC
application's Help
popup menu.

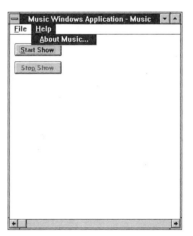

☐ Click the Start Show button.

> *The MUSIC application plays music through the PC speaker simultaneously with the display of animation.*

Experiment with the Start Show and Stop Show buttons.

To exit from the MUSIC application:

☐ Select Exit from the File menu.

Now that you know what the MUSIC application should do, you can start writing it.

Creating the Project of the MUSIC Application

To create the project of the MUSIC application:

☐ Select AppWizard from the Project menu.

> *Visual C++ responds by running AppWizard.*

☐ Use the Directory list box to select the directory C:\VCPROG\PRACTICE\CH29. Type music in the Project Name box.

Your AppWizard dialog box should now look as shown in Figure 29.26.

Figure 29.26.
The AppWizard
dialog box for
the MUSIC
application.

☐ Click the Options button and set the options as shown in Figure 29.27 (that is, uncheck all the check boxes except the Generate Source Comments check box).

Figure 29.27.
Setting the options
for the MUSIC
application.

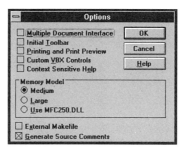

☐ Click the OK button of the Options dialog box and then click the OK button of the AppWizard dialog box and finally click the Create button of the New Application Information dialog box.

> *AppWizard responds by creating the MUSIC project and all the skeleton files of the MUSIC application.*

To remove the debug options of the project (so that you'll have a small EXE file):

☐ Select Project from Visual C++'s Options menu, click the Release radio button, and then click the OK button of the dialog box.

The Visual Implementation of the MUSIC Application's Menu

The MUSIC application should have a menu with two popup menus, as shown in Figures 29.24 and 29.25. To implement this menu:

☐ Use App Studio to implement the menu of the PLAY application per Table 29.2.

Table 29.2. The menu of the MUSIC application.
Figures relating to menu: 29.24, 29.25

Menu Item
&File
E&xit
&Help
&About Music...

Don't forget to delete the accelerator keys of the menu items that you removed:

☐ Select MUSIC.RC [MFC-Resource Script] from App Studio's Window menu, select Accelerator in the Type list, and then double-click IDR_MAINFRAME in the Resources list.

☐ Delete the accelerator keys that aren't used by the application. In particular, delete the accelerator keys of the ID_FILE_NEW, ID_FILE_OPEN, and ID_FILE_SAVE menu items.

Save your work:

☐ Select Save from App Studio's File menu.

The visual implementation of the MUSIC application's menu is completed.

Creating the Form of the MUSIC Application

The main window of the MUSIC application should contain the Start Show and Stop Show push buttons (see Figure 29.23).

To implement this form you'll replace the current view class of the application with a new view class derived from the CFormView class.

Follow these steps to create the form of the application:

☐ Use the Windows File Manager (or DOS Shell) to delete the two view class files of the MUSIC application:

☐ Delete C:\VCPROG\PRACTICE\CH29\MUSIC\MUSICVW.CPP.

☐ Delete C:\VCPROG\PRACTICE\CH29\MUSIC\MUSICVW.H.

☐ Select ClassWizard from Visual C++'s Browse menu.

ClassWizard responds by displaying a dialog box telling you that the view class files don't exist.

☐ Click the dialog box's OK button.

☐ Click the Remove button of the Repair Class Information dialog box.

☐ Click the OK button of ClassWizard's dialog box.

You have just finished removing the view class of the MUSIC application.

In the following steps you'll create a dialog box, you'll create a CFormView type class for this dialog box, and you'll make this class the new view class of the application:

☐ Select App Studio from Visual C++'s Tools menu.

☐ Create a new dialog box with App Studio.

☐ Double-click in a free area of the new dialog box.

☐ Select Styles from the drop-down list box at the upper-right corner of the Properties window.

Set the Styles properties of the dialog box as follows:

☐ Select Child in the Style box.

☐ Select None in the Border box.

☐ Uncheck the Visible property (that is, remove the check mark from the Visible check box).

☐ Select General from the drop-down list box at the upper-right corner of the Properties window and make sure that the Caption box is empty.

Now connect the dialog box to a class derived from CFormView:

☐ Select ClassWizard from App Studio's Resource menu.

ClassWizard responds by displaying the Add Class dialog box.

☐ Type CMusicView in the Class Name box

☐ Set the Class Type to CFormView

☐ Make sure that the header filename is musicvw.h and that the implementation filename is musicvw.cpp.

☐ Click the Create Class button.

☐ Click the OK button of ClassWizard's window to go back to App Studio.

You've finished creating the new view class of the application. This view class is a derived class from the MFC CFormView class, and it is connected to the dialog box that you created. Thus, the main dialog box of the application will be the dialog box that you created.

The Visual Implementation of the MUSIC Application's Dialog Box

☐ Implement the dialog box of the MUSIC application per Table 29.3.

Table 29.3. The MUSIC application's dialog box.

Class Name:	CMusicView
Figure:	29.28
OK button:	No
Cancel button:	No

Object	Property	Setting
Dialog box	ID	IDD_DIALOG1
Push button	ID	IDC_START_BUTTON
	Caption	&Start Show
Push button	ID	IDC_STOP_BUTTON
	Caption	Sto&p Show

Now your dialog box looks like the one shown in Figure 29.28.

Figure 29.28. The dialog box of the MUSIC application.

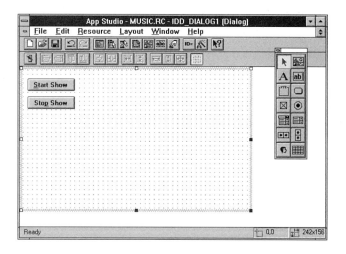

Save your work:

☐ Select Save from App Studio's File menu.

Adding Bitmap Files to the MUSIC Application

The MUSIC application uses seven bitmap files (BMP files) for the animation. As you will see later (when you write the application's code), the code of the MUSIC application will display these bitmaps one after the other to create the illusion that the cartoon character shown in these bitmaps (a dancer) is dancing.

To add the seven bitmaps to the MUSIC application, follow these steps:

☐ Select Import from App Studio's Resource menu.

   App Studio responds by displaying the Import Resource dialog box.

☐ Use the Import Resource dialog box to select the file `C:\VCPROG\BMP\D1.BMP`.

   App Studio responds by importing the bitmap `D1.BMP` into the MUSIC application and by displaying the `D1.BMP` bitmap (see Figure 29.29).

Figure 29.29.
Importing the
`D1.BMP` *bitmap*
into the MUSIC
application.

Note that the ID App Studio assigned to the `D1.BMP` bitmap is `IDB_BITMAP1` (see Figure 29.29).

Repeat the preceding steps to import the rest of the BMP files:

☐ Import `C:\VCPROG\BMP\D2.BMP`.

☐ Import `C:\VCPROG\BMP\D3.BMP`.

985

☐ Import `C:\VCPROG\BMP\D4.BMP`.

☐ Import `C:\VCPROG\BMP\D5.BMP`.

☐ Import `C:\VCPROG\BMP\D6.BMP`.

☐ Import `C:\VCPROG\BMP\D7.BMP`.

NOTE

In the preceding steps you were instructed to import seven BMP files into the MUSIC application. The order in which you imported the BMP files is important (that is, first `D1.BMP` and then `D2.BMP` and then `D3.BMP` and so on). The order is important because as you import the BMP files, App Studio assigns to the BMP files the constant names `IDB_BITMAP1`, `IDB_BITMAP2`, `IDB_BITMAP3`, and so on. Later, when you write the code of the MUSIC application, we assume that `IDB_BITMAP1` corresponds to `D1.BMP`, `IDB_BITMAP2` corresponds to `D2.BMP`, `IDB_BITMAP3` corresponds to `D3.BMP`, and so on.

You've finished importing seven bitmaps into the MUSIC application. To verify that you imported the bitmaps properly:

☐ Select `MUSIC.RC [MFC Resource Script]` from App Studio's Window menu.

☐ Select Bitmap from the `MUSIC.RC` window's Type list.

App Studio responds by listing all the bitmaps of the MUSIC application in the Resources list (see Figure 29.30).

As you can see from Figure 29.30, the IDs that App Studio assigned to the seven bitmaps that you imported are `IDB_BITMAP1`, `IDB_BITMAP2`, `IDB_BITMAP3`, and so on.

To inspect the properties of the `IDB_BITMAP1` bitmap:

☐ Highlight the `IDB_BITMAP1` item in the Resource list and then click the Properties button. (This button is below the Resource list.)

App Studio responds by displaying the Properties window of the `IDB_BITMAP1` bitmap (see Figure 29.31).

Figure 29.30.
The bitmaps of
the MUSIC
application.

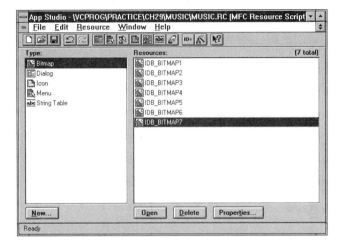

Figure 29.31.
The Properties
window of the
IDB_BITMAP1
bitmap.

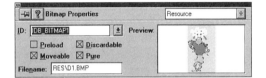

As shown in Figure 29.31, the properties window displays the picture of the IDB_BITMAP1 bitmap as well as the filename of the bitmap. Note that the filename is RES\D1.BMP. When you imported the file C:\VCPROG\BMP\D1.BMP into the MUSIC application, App Studio copied this file into the RES directory of the application. (The RES directory of the MUSIC application is C:\VCPROG\PRACTICE\CH29\MUSIC\RES.)

In a similar manner you can now inspect the other bitmaps that you imported into the MUSIC application.

NOTE

When you import bitmaps to your application (as you did previously), the bitmaps become an integral part of the application's EXE file. That is, after you compile/link your application, these bitmap files will be part of the EXE file.

Don't forget to save your work:

☐ Select Save from App Studio's File menu.

The visual implementation of the MUSIC application is completed.

Opening a WAV Session

Because the MUSIC application plays a WAV file through the PC speaker, you have to add the IMPORT statement to the MUSIC.DEF file.

☐ Open the MUSIC.DEF file and add the IMPORT statement. After you add the IMPORT statement, the MUSIC.DEF file looks as follows:

```
; music.def : Declares the module parameters for the application.

NAME           MUSIC
DESCRIPTION    'MUSIC Windows Application'
EXETYPE        WINDOWS

CODE           PRELOAD MOVEABLE DISCARDABLE
DATA           PRELOAD MOVEABLE MULTIPLE

HEAPSIZE       1024    ; initial heap size
; Stack size is passed as argument to linker's /STACK option


;;;;;;;;;;;;;;;;;;;;;;;;;;
; MY CODE STARTS HERE
;;;;;;;;;;;;;;;;;;;;;;;;;;

;;;;;;;;;;;;;;;;;;;;;;;;;;;;;;;;;;;;;;;;;;;;;;;;;
; sp_ functions from the TegoSND.DLL library
;;;;;;;;;;;;;;;;;;;;;;;;;;;;;;;;;;;;;;;;;;;;;;;;;

IMPORTS
TegoSND.sp_OpenSession
TegoSND.sp_PlaySnd
TegoSND.sp_MouseOn
TegoSND.sp_MouseOff
TegoSND.sp_CloseSession

;;;;;;;;;;;;;;;;;;;;;;;;;;
; MY CODE ENDS HERE
;;;;;;;;;;;;;;;;;;;;;;;;;;
```

Now that the DEF file includes the IMPORT statement for the sp_ functions from the TegoSND.DLL, your code can execute sp_ functions.

Now you'll open a WAV session in the constructor function of the `CPlayApp` class:

☐ Open the `MUSIC.CPP` file and add code to the `CMusicApp()` constructor function. After you add the code, the `CMusicApp()` constructor function looks as follows:

```
CMusicApp::CMusicApp()
{
// TODO: add construction code here,
// Place all significant initialization in InitInstance


    //////////////////////////
    // MY CODE STARTS HERE
    //////////////////////////

    // Open a sound session.
    char FileToPlay[255];

    strcpy( FileToPlay, "\\VCPROG\\WAV\\regga2m3.WAV" );
    m_MusicSession = sp_OpenSession ( FileToPlay );


// If WAV session cannot be opened, display message box.
    if ( m_MusicSession < 0 )
        {
        char Message[255], Caption[255];
        strcpy ( Message, "Can't open the file: ");
        strcat ( Message,  FileToPlay );
        strcpy ( Caption, "Error" );
        MessageBox ( NULL,
                     Message,
                     Caption,
                     MB_OK | MB_ICONHAND);
        }


    // Mouse should be available during playback.
    sp_MouseON(m_MusicSession);

    // Initialize the playback position.
    m_PlayPosition = 0;

    //////////////////////////
    // MY CODE ENDS HERE
    //////////////////////////

}
```

The code you typed inside the `CMusicApp()` constructor function opens a WAV session for the WAV file `\VCPROG\\WAV\\regga2m3.WAV`.

If the WAV file can't be opened, a message is displayed with the `MessageBox()` function.

The code you typed also executes the `sp_MouseON()` function:

```
sp_MouseON(m_MusicSession);
```

The `sp_MouseOn()` function makes the mouse available during the playback of the WAV file.

The code you typed also initializes the `m_PlayPosition` data member:

```
// Initialize the playback position.
m_PlayPosition = 0;
```

`m_PlayPosition` holds the current position of the playback.

Note that the `MessageBox()` function you used is a regular Windows SDK API function. It isn't a member function of any class. We didn't use the `MessageBox()` member function because the `CMusicApp` class doesn't have one.

Declaring the Data Members

The code you typed utilizes two data members, `m_MusicSession` and `m_PlayPosition`. Thus, you must include these data members in the declaration of the `CMusicApp` class.

☐ Open the `MUSIC.H` file and add the data members `m_MusicSession` and `m_PlayPosition` in the declaration of the `CMusicApp` class. After you add these data members, the `CMusicApp` class declaration should look as follows:

```
class CMusicApp : public CWinApp
{
public:
    CMusicApp();

    //////////////////////////
    // MY CODE STARTS HERE
    //////////////////////////

    int m_MusicSession;
    long m_PlayPosition;

    //////////////////////////
    // MY CODE ENDS HERE
    //////////////////////////

// Overrides
    virtual BOOL InitInstance();
```

```
// Implementation

    //{{AFX_MSG(CMusicApp)
    afx_msg void OnAppAbout();
// NOTE - the ClassWizard will add and remove member
// functions here.
//    DO NOT EDIT what you see in these blocks
//    of generated code !
    //}}AFX_MSG
    DECLARE_MESSAGE_MAP()
};
```

Including the *TegoSND.H* File

To be able to use the sp_ functions, you must #include the TegoSND.h file:

☐ Open the MUSIC.CPP file and add an #include statement that includes the TegoSND.h file. After including this statement, the beginning of the MUSIC.CPP file should look as follows:

```
// music.cpp : Defines the class behaviors for
// the application.
//

#include "stdafx.h"
#include "music.h"

/////////////////////
// MY CODE STARTS HERE
/////////////////////

#include "\vcprog\dll\TegoSND.h"

/////////////////////
// MY CODE ENDS HERE
/////////////////////


#include "mainfrm.h"
#include "musicdoc.h"
#include "musicvw.h"

#ifdef _DEBUG
#undef THIS_FILE
static char BASED_CODE THIS_FILE[] = __FILE__;
#endif
....
....
....
```

Writing Code in the *OnIdle()* Function of the MUSIC Application

The OnIdle() member function of the CWinApp class is automatically executed whenever the MUSIC application is idle.

Now you'll write the OnIdle() function. Because Visual C++ didn't write the declaration and skeleton of the OnIdle() function, you have to declare this function and write its skeleton. Here is how you do that:

☐ Open the file MUSIC.H and add code to it that defines the function OnIdle() as a member function of the CMusicApp class. After you write this code, the CMusicApp class declaration looks as follows:

```
class CMusicApp : public CWinApp
{
public:
    CMusicApp();

    ///////////////////////
    // MY CODE STARTS HERE
    ///////////////////////

    int m_MusicSession;
    long m_PlayPosition;

    ///////////////////////
    // MY CODE ENDS HERE
    ///////////////////////

// Overrides
    virtual BOOL InitInstance();

    ///////////////////////
    // MY CODE STARTS HERE
    ///////////////////////

    virtual BOOL OnIdle(LONG lCount);

    ///////////////////////
    // MY CODE ENDS HERE
    ///////////////////////

// Implementation

    //{{AFX_MSG(CMusicApp)
    afx_msg void OnAppAbout();
```

```
// NOTE - the ClassWizard will add and remove member
// functions here.
//     DO NOT EDIT what you see in these blocks
//     of generated code !
     //}}AFX_MSG
     DECLARE_MESSAGE_MAP()
};
```

The code you typed declares the prototype of the OnIdle() function. Now write the
OnIdle() function's code:

☐ Open the file MUSIC.CPP and add to it (at the end of the file) the OnIdle()
function. After you write this function, the end of the MUSIC.CPP file looks
as follows:

```
/////////////////////////
// MY CODE STARTS HERE
/////////////////////////

BOOL CMusicApp::OnIdle(LONG lCount)
{

    // Call the base class function.
    CWinApp::OnIdle(lCount);


    m_PlayPosition =
            sp_PlaySnd ( m_MusicSession,
                         m_PlayPosition,
                         m_PlayPosition + 10000 );


    return TRUE;


}

/////////////////////////
// MY CODE ENDS HERE
/////////////////////////
```

The first statement that you typed inside OnIdle() is

```
CWinApp::OnIdle(lCount);
```

This statement calls the OnIdle() function of the base class, which is necessary
because the OnIdle() function of the base class performs various initialization tasks.
For example, it updates the menu items and toolbar items (if any) of the application.

The next statement uses the sp_PlaySnd() function to play 10,000 bytes from the WAV file:

```
m_PlayPosition =
          sp_PlaySnd ( m_MusicSession,
                       m_PlayPosition,
                       m_PlayPosition + 10000 );
```

Just as was done in the PLAY application discussed earlier in this chapter, the preceding sp_PlaySnd() statement plays 10,000 bytes whenever the OnIdle() function is executed.

The last statement that you typed in the OnIdle() function returns TRUE:

```
return TRUE;
```

When OnIdle() returns TRUE, it indicates that OnIdle() should be called again.

Don't forget to save your work:

☐ Select Save from the File menu.

Closing the Sound Session

When the user terminates the application, you need to close the sound session of the Regga2m3.WAV sound file. You'll write the code that closes the sound session inside the ExitInstance() member function of the CMusicApp class.

Visual C++ didn't write the declaration and skeleton of the ExitInstance() function. You have to declare this function and write its skeleton. Here is how you do that:

☐ Open the file MUSIC.H and add code to it that defines the function ExitInstance() as a member function of the CMusicApp class. After you write this code, the CMusicApp class declaration should look as follows:

```
class CMusicApp : public CWinApp
{
public:
     CMusicApp();

     /////////////////////////
     // MY CODE STARTS HERE
     /////////////////////////

     int m_MusicSession;
     long m_PlayPosition;
```

```
     ////////////////////
     // MY CODE ENDS HERE
     ////////////////////

// Overrides
     virtual BOOL InitInstance();

     /////////////////////////
     // MY CODE STARTS HERE
     /////////////////////////

     virtual BOOL OnIdle(LONG lCount);
     virtual int ExitInstance();

     ////////////////////
     // MY CODE ENDS HERE
     ////////////////////

// Implementation

     //{{AFX_MSG(CMusicApp)
     afx_msg void OnAppAbout();
// NOTE - the ClassWizard will add and remove
// member functions here.
//    DO NOT EDIT what you see in these blocks
//    of generated code !
     //}}AFX_MSG
     DECLARE_MESSAGE_MAP()
};
```

Now write the code of the `ExitInstance()` function:

☐ Open the file MUSIC.CPP and add to the end of the file the `ExitInstance()`
   function. After you write this function, the end of the MUSIC.CPP file looks
   as follows:

```
/////////////////////////
// MY CODE STARTS HERE
/////////////////////////

int CMusicApp::ExitInstance()
{

// Close the sound session.
sp_CloseSession(m_MusicSession);

return CWinApp::ExitInstance();

}
```

```
/////////////////////
// MY CODE ENDS HERE
/////////////////////
```

Don't forget to save your work:

☐ Select Save from the File menu.

You didn't complete writing the MUSIC application. However, this is a good time to compile/link and execute the application so that you can verify that the code you typed was entered without any errors.

☐ Compile/link the MUSIC application.

☐ Select Execute MUSIC.EXE from the Project menu.

The main window of the MUSIC application appears as shown in Figure 29.32, and the `Regga2m3.WAV` is played through the PC speaker in an endless loop. Of course, clicking the Stop Show button doesn't stop the playback, because you haven't attached any code to that button.

☐ Select Exit from the File menu to terminate the MUSIC application.

Figure 29.32.
The window of the
MUSIC applica-
tion with its two
buttons.

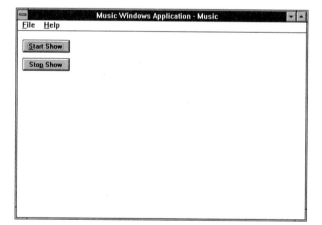

Attaching Code to the Buttons That Start and Stop the Show

Now you'll attach code that starts the show when the user clicks the Start Show button and stops it when the Stop Show button is clicked. The technique you'll use is as follows:

You'll declare a data member called m_ShowStatus, which will hold the current status of the show. When m_ShowStatus is equal to 0, there is no show currently in progress; when m_ShowStatus is equal to 1, the show is currently in progress. However, the question is, should m_ShowStatus be a data member of the CMusicApp class or a data member of the CMusicView class? Declare m_ShowStatus as a data member of the CMusicApp class:

☐ Open the MUSIC.H file and add m_ShowStatus as a data member of the CMusicApp class. After you add this data member to the CMusicApp class declaration, it looks as follows:

```
class CMusicApp : public CWinApp
{
public:
     CMusicApp();

     /////////////////////
     // MY CODE STARTS HERE
     /////////////////////

     int m_MusicSession;
     long m_PlayPosition;
     int m_ShowStatus;

     /////////////////////
     // MY CODE ENDS HERE
     /////////////////////

// Overrides
     virtual BOOL InitInstance();

     /////////////////////
     // MY CODE STARTS HERE
     /////////////////////

     virtual BOOL OnIdle(LONG lCount);
     virtual int ExitInstance();

     /////////////////////
     // MY CODE ENDS HERE
     /////////////////////


// Implementation

     //{{AFX_MSG(CMusicApp)
     afx_msg void OnAppAbout();
```

```
// NOTE - the ClassWizard will add and remove
// member functions here.
//     DO NOT EDIT what you see in these
//     blocks of generated code !
    //}}AFX_MSG
    DECLARE_MESSAGE_MAP()
};
```

☐ Initially, you don't want the show to be in progress, so in the constructor
function of the CMusicApp class (in the MUSIC.CPP file), set m_ShowStatus to
0:

```
CMusicApp::CMusicApp()
{
// TODO: add construction code here,
// Place all significant initialization in InitInstance


    ////////////////////////
    // MY CODE STARTS HERE
    ////////////////////////

    // Open a sound session.
    char FileToPlay[255];

    strcpy( FileToPlay, "\\VCPROG\\WAV\\regga2m3.WAV" );
    m_MusicSession = sp_OpenSession ( FileToPlay );


// If WAV session cannot be opened, display message box.
    if ( m_MusicSession < 0 )
        {
        char Message[255], Caption[255];
        strcpy ( Message, "Can't open the file: ");
        strcat ( Message,  FileToPlay );
        strcpy ( Caption, "Error" );
        MessageBox ( NULL,
                    Message,
                    Caption,
                    MB_OK | MB_ICONHAND);
        }


    // Mouse should be available during playback.
    sp_MouseON(m_MusicSession);

    // Initialize the playback position.
    m_PlayPosition = 0;
```

```
// Initially, the show will not be in progress
m_ShowStatus = 0;


/////////////////////
// MY CODE ENDS HERE
/////////////////////
```

}

You can now add code to the Start Show and Stop Show buttons. When the Start Show button is clicked, the m_ShowStatus data member of the CMusicApp class should be set to 1, and when the Stop Show button is clicked, the m_ShowStatus data member of the CMusicApp class should be set to 0.

☐ Use ClassWizard to add a function for the event:

Class Name:	CMusicView
Object ID:	IDC_STOP_BUTTON
Message:	BN_CLICKED
Function Name:	OnStopButton()

☐ Edit the OnStopButton() function that you added to the MUSICVW.CPP file. After you edit the OnStopButton() function, it looks as follows:

```
void CMusicView::OnStopButton()
{
// TODO: Add your control notification handler code here


    /////////////////////
    // MY CODE STARTS HERE
    /////////////////////

  // Get a pointer to the CMusicApp object
  CMusicApp* pApp = (CMusicApp*) AfxGetApp();

  // Update the data member of the CMusicApp class
  pApp->m_ShowStatus = 0;

    /////////////////////
    // MY CODE ENDS HERE
    /////////////////////
```

}

The code you typed sets the m_ShowStatus data member of the CMusicApp class to 0. To accomplish this, you used the AfxGetApp() function to extract the pointer of the CMusicApp class:

```
CMusicApp* pApp = (CMusicApp*) AfxGetApp();
```

Now that you've extracted pApp, the pointer of CMusicApp, you can access its data members:

```
pApp->m_ShowStatus = 0;
```

In a similar way, you can now attach code to the Start Show button. This code will set m_ShowStatus of the CMusicApp class to 1.

Use ClassWizard to add a function for the event:

Class Name:	CMusicView
Object ID:	IDC_START_BUTTON
Message:	BN_CLICKED
Function Name:	OnStartButton()

☐ Edit the OnStartButtont() function that you added to the MUSICVW.CPP file. After you edit the OnStartButton() function, it looks as follows:

```
void CMusicView::OnStartButton()
{
    // TODO: Add your control notification handler code here

    /////////////////////////
    // MY CODE STARTS HERE
    /////////////////////////

    // Get a pointer to the CMusicApp object
    CMusicApp* pApp = (CMusicApp*) AfxGetApp();

    // Update the data member of the CMusicApp class
    pApp->m_ShowStatus = 1;

    /////////////////////////
    // MY CODE ENDS HERE
    /////////////////////////

}
```

The code you typed is similar to the code you typed in the OnStopButton() function. However, in the OnStopButton() function, you set m_ShowStatus to 0, but in the OnStartButton() function, you set m_ShowStatus to 1.

Of course, setting m_ShowStatus to either 0 or 1 isn't enough to stop or start the show. You have to do something with the value of this data member.

Starting and Stopping the Show

The place to start and stop the show is inside the OnIdle() function.

☐ Open the MUSIC.CPP file and modify the OnIdle() function. After modifying the code, the OnIdle() function looks as follows:

```
////////////////////////
// MY CODE STARTS HERE
////////////////////////

BOOL CMusicApp::OnIdle(LONG lCount)
{

    // Call the base class function.
    CWinApp::OnIdle(lCount);


    if ( m_ShowStatus == 1 )
       {
        m_PlayPosition =
               sp_PlaySnd ( m_MusicSession,
                            m_PlayPosition,
                            m_PlayPosition + 10000 );
       }

    return TRUE;

}

////////////////////////
// MY CODE ENDS HERE
////////////////////////
```

The code you typed uses an if() statement to determine whether the value of m_ShowStatus is 1. If it is 1, the sp_PlaySnd() function is executed, and if it isn't equal to 1, the sp_PlaySnd() function isn't executed.

☐ Compile/link and execute the MUSIC application.

The Start Show button starts the playback, and the Stop Show button stops it.

Experiment with the MUSIC application and then select Exit from the File menu to terminate the MUSIC application.

NOTE

The m_ShowStart variable is declared as a data member of the CMusicApp class.

Thus, the OnIdle() function can access this data member directly, because OnIdle() is a member function of the CWinApp class, and CMusicApp is a derived class from the CWinApp class.

The code you typed in the OnStartButton() and OnStopButton() functions cannot access the m_ShowStatus data member directly, because these functions are member functions of the CMusicView class that was derived from the CFormView class.

To access m_ShowStart from within the functions of the view class, you have to use the AfxGetApp() function:

```
CMusicApp* pApp = (CMusicApp*) AfxGetApp();
```

and only then can you access the data member as follows:

```
pApp->m_ShowStatus = 1;
```

Adding Animation

Now that the MUSIC application's main code is written, you can easily add the animation code to the application.

Recall that during the visual implementation, you added seven bitmaps. These bitmaps are used for the animation.

For the animation, you'll need two additional data members,

m_pB[] and m_CurrentFrame.

☐ Open the MUSIC.H file and add the m_pB[] and m_CurrentFrame data members to the CMusicApp. After you add these two data members, the CMusicApp class declaration looks as follows:

```
class CMusicApp : public CWinApp
{
public:
    CMusicApp();
```

```
///////////////////////
// MY CODE STARTS HERE
///////////////////////

    int m_MusicSession;
    long m_PlayPosition;
    int m_ShowStatus;


    // The current frame number.
    int m_CurrentFrame;

    // An array for the 7 bitmaps.
    CBitmap* m_pB[7];

    ///////////////////////
    // MY CODE ENDS HERE
    ///////////////////////

// Overrides
    virtual BOOL InitInstance();

    ///////////////////////
    // MY CODE STARTS HERE
    ///////////////////////

    virtual BOOL OnIdle(LONG lCount);
    virtual int ExitInstance();

    ///////////////////////
    // MY CODE ENDS HERE
    ///////////////////////


// Implementation

    //{{AFX_MSG(CMusicApp)
    afx_msg void OnAppAbout();
// NOTE - the ClassWizard will add and remove
// member functions here.
//    DO NOT EDIT what you see in these
// blocks of generated code !
    //}}AFX_MSG
    DECLARE_MESSAGE_MAP()
};
```

The m_CurrentFrame data member that you added will hold the number of the currently displayed bitmap. Because there are seven bitmaps, m_CurrentFrame can have a value between 0 and 6.

The m_pB[7] data that you added to the CMusicApp class declaration is an array that will hold the bitmaps. This is the reason for declaring this array with seven elements.

Now you'll add code to the constructor function of the CMusicApp class. The code that you'll add sets the initial value of m_CurrentFrame to 0.

☐ Open the MUSIC.CPP file and add a statement to it that sets m_CurrentFrame to 0. After you add the statement, the constructor function of the CMusicApp class looks as follows:

```
CMusicApp::CMusicApp()
{
// TODO: add construction code here,
// Place all significant initialization in InitInstance

    /////////////////////////
    // MY CODE STARTS HERE
    /////////////////////////

    // Open a sound session.
    char FileToPlay[255];

    strcpy( FileToPlay, "\\VCPROG\\WAV\\regga2m3.WAV" );
    m_MusicSession = sp_OpenSession ( FileToPlay );


// If WAV session cannot be opened, display message box.
    if ( m_MusicSession < 0 )
        {
        char Message[255], Caption[255];
        strcpy ( Message, "Can't open the file: ");
        strcat ( Message,  FileToPlay );
        strcpy ( Caption, "Error" );
        MessageBox ( NULL,
                     Message,
                     Caption,
                     MB_OK | MB_ICONHAND);
        }


    // Mouse should be available during playback.
    sp_MouseON(m_MusicSession);

    // Initialize the playback position.
    m_PlayPosition = 0;


    // Initially, the show will not be in progress
    m_ShowStatus = 0;
```

```
// Set the current frame number to 0
m_CurrentFrame = 0;


//////////////////////
// MY CODE ENDS HERE
//////////////////////

}
```

Now you'll load the seven bitmaps. This loading should be performed in the InitInstance() member function of the CMusicApp class (because we want to load the bitmaps when the application is started).

☐ Open the MUSIC.CPP file and add code to the InitInstance() function. After you add the code, the InitInstance() function looks as follows:

```
BOOL CMusicApp::InitInstance()
{
// Standard initialization
// If you are not using these features and
// wish to reduce the size
// of your final executable, you should
// remove from the following
// the specific initialization routines you
// do not need.

SetDialogBkColor();
// Set dialog background color to gray

LoadStdProfileSettings();
// Load standard INI file options (including MRU)

// Register the application's document templates.
// Document templates
// serve as the connection between documents,
// frame windows and views.

    CSingleDocTemplate* pDocTemplate;
    pDocTemplate = new CSingleDocTemplate(
        IDR_MAINFRAME,
        RUNTIME_CLASS(CMusicDoc),
        RUNTIME_CLASS(CMainFrame),
        // main SDI frame window
        RUNTIME_CLASS(CMusicView));
    AddDocTemplate(pDocTemplate);

    // create a new (empty) document
    OnFileNew();
```

```
        if (m_lpCmdLine[0] != '\0')
        {
            // TODO: add command line processing here
        }


//////////////////////////
// MY CODE STARTS HERE
//////////////////////////

    // Load IDB_BITMAP1
    m_pB[0] = new CBitmap;
    m_pB[0]->LoadBitmap(IDB_BITMAP1);


    // Load IDB_BITMAP2
    m_pB[1] = new CBitmap;
    m_pB[1]->LoadBitmap(IDB_BITMAP2);

    // Load IDB_BITMAP3
    m_pB[2] = new CBitmap;
    m_pB[2]->LoadBitmap(IDB_BITMAP3);


    // Load IDB_BITMAP4
    m_pB[3] = new CBitmap;
    m_pB[3]->LoadBitmap(IDB_BITMAP4);

    // Load IDB_BITMAP5
    m_pB[4] = new CBitmap;
    m_pB[4]->LoadBitmap(IDB_BITMAP5);

    // Load IDB_BITMAP6
    m_pB[5] = new CBitmap;
    m_pB[5]->LoadBitmap(IDB_BITMAP6);

    // Load IDB_BITMAP7
    m_pB[6] = new CBitmap;
    m_pB[6]->LoadBitmap(IDB_BITMAP7);


//////////////////////////
// MY CODE ENDS HERE
//////////////////////////

        return TRUE;
    }
```

The first statement in code that you added creates a new object of class CBitmap, and
the address of the new object is assigned to the pointer m_pB[0],

```
m_pB[0] = new CBitmap;
```

and then the `LoadBitmap()` function is used to load the bitmap into the object that you created:

```
m_pB[0]->LoadBitmap(IDB_BITMAP1);
```

So putting it all together, the first element of the array, `m_pB[0]`, is filled with the first bitmap. Recall that during the visual implementation of the MUSIC application you imported the file `D1.BMP`, and App Studio assigned the ID `IDB_BITMAP1` to this bitmap.

In a similar manner, the remaining code that you typed loads the other bitmaps into the other elements of the `m_pB[]` array.

Deleting the Bitmaps

☐ Because you used the `new` operator to create the elements of the `m_pB[]` object, you must use the `delete` operator to free the memory that is occupied by these objects.

> ### NOTE
>
> Recall that whenever you use the `new` operator to create an object (or a variable), you must use the `delete` operator to free the memory.
>
> For example, the statement
>
> ```
> m_pB[0] = new CBitmap;
> ```
>
> creates an object of class `CBitmap` with the new operator. The address of this object is assigned to `m_pB[0]`. When the application terminates, the memory occupied by `m_pB[0]` is freed automatically. However, the memory that is pointed to by `m_pB[0]` is not freed! To free this memory, you need to use the delete operator as in
>
> ```
> delete m_pB[0];
> ```

☐ Open the `MUSIC.CPP` file and add code to the `ExitInstance()` function. After you add the code, the `ExitInstance()` function looks as follows:

```
/////////////////////
// MY CODE STARTS HERE
/////////////////////

int CMusicApp::ExitInstance()
{

// Close the sound session.
sp_CloseSession(m_MusicSession);


// Delete the 7 bitmaps.
for (int i=0; i<7; i++)
    delete m_pB[i];


return CWinApp::ExitInstance();

}

/////////////////////
// MY CODE ENDS HERE
/////////////////////
```

The code you added to the ExitInstance() function uses a for() loop to delete the seven bitmaps.

Displaying the Bitmaps

You are now ready to display the bitmaps.

☐ Open the MUSIC.CPP file and add code to and modify the OnIdle() function. After you add and modify the code, the OnIdle() function looks as follows:

```
/////////////////////
// MY CODE STARTS HERE
/////////////////////

BOOL CMusicApp::OnIdle(LONG lCount)
{

    // Call the base class function.
    CWinApp::OnIdle(lCount);


    if ( m_ShowStatus == 0 )
       return TRUE;
```

```
        m_PlayPosition =
              sp_PlaySnd ( m_MusicSession,
                           m_PlayPosition,
                           m_PlayPosition + 10000 );




        // Increment the current frame number.
        m_CurrentFrame++;

        // Is it the last frame?
        if ( m_CurrentFrame == 7 )
            m_CurrentFrame=0;


        // Get a dc for the screen.
        CClientDC dc(m_pMainWnd);

        // Create a memory DC.
        CDC* pMemDC = new CDC;
        pMemDC->CreateCompatibleDC(&dc);

        // Select the bitmap into the memory DC.
        pMemDC->SelectObject( m_pB[m_CurrentFrame] );

        // Copy the bitmap from the memory DC into
        // the screen DC.
        dc.BitBlt( 150,
                   40,
                   150+149,
                   40+249,
                   pMemDC,
                   0,
                   0,
                   SRCCOPY);
        // Delete the memory DC.
        delete pMemDC;


        return TRUE;

}

///////////////////////
// MY CODE ENDS HERE
///////////////////////
```

The code inside the OnIdle() function uses an if() statement to check the value of
m_ShowStatus:

```
if ( m_ShowStatus == 0 )
    return TRUE;
```

If the value of m_ShowStatus is equal to 0, the return TRUE statement is executed. Thus, nothing will happen; there won't be any playback, and there won't be any bitmap displayed.

If the value of m_ShowStatus isn't equal to 0, the rest of the code in OnIdle() is executed.

This means that the sp_PlaySnd() function is executed to play another 10,000 bytes:

```
m_PlayPosition =
        sp_PlaySnd ( m_MusicSession,
                     m_PlayPosition,
                     m_PlayPosition + 10000 );
```

The next statements in the OnIdle() function display the current bitmap. Because the frame that will be displayed is the next bitmap in the series of seven bitmaps, the m_CurrentFrame is increased by 1:

```
m_CurrentFrame++;
```

And then an if() statement is used to determine whether m_CurrentFrame is equal to 7:

```
if ( m_CurrentFrame == 7 )
    m_CurrentFrame=0;
```

If the preceding if condition is satisfied, m_CurrentFrame is set to 0 so that the next frame will be the first bitmap in the series of seven bitmaps.

The next statement in OnIdle() creates a dc object:

```
CClientDC dc(m_pMainWnd);
```

Note that the parameter is m_pMainWnd. This is the pointer that you should use when creating a dc from within the CMusicApp class.

NOTE

When creating a dc object from within a class derived from the CWinApp class, use the m_pMainWnd pointer as the parameter of the constructor function of the CClientDC class as in

```
CClientDC dc(m_pMainWnd);
```

Then a memory DC is created:

```
CDC* pMemDC = new CDC;
pMemDC->CreateCompatibleDC(&dc);
```

Now that the memory DC has been created, you can use the SelectObject() function to select the bitmap that corresponds to the current value of m_CurrentFrame:

```
pMemDC->SelectObject( m_pB[m_CurrentFrame] );
```

And finally, the BitBlt() function is executed to copy the memory dc (pMemDC) into the screen DC (dc) (to actually display the bitmap):

```
dc.BitBlt( 150,
           40,
           150+149,
           40+249,
           pMemDC,
           0,
           0,
           SRCCOPY);
```

Now that the bitmap is displayed on the screen you can delete the pMemDC pointer with the delete operator:

```
delete pMemDC;
```

It is necessary to delete pMemDC because it was created with the new operator.

Fixing the Size of the Window

To fix the size of the application's window, you need to write code that sets the default size of the application's window in the PreCreateWindow() member function of the CMainFrame class. The header file of the CMainFrame class is MAINFRM.H and the implementation file of the CMainFrame class is MAINFRM.CPP.

☐ Open the file MAINFRM.H and add code to it that defines the function PreCreateWindow() as a member function of the CMainFrame class. After you write this code, the CMainFrame class declaration looks as follows:

```
class CMainFrame : public CFrameWnd
{
protected: // create from serialization only
    CMainFrame();
    DECLARE_DYNCREATE(CMainFrame)
```

```
/////////////////////
// MY CODE STARTS HERE
/////////////////////

BOOL PreCreateWindow(CREATESTRUCT& cs);

/////////////////////
// MY CODE ENDS HERE
/////////////////////


// Attributes
public:

// Operations
public:

....
....
....

};
```

Now write the code of the `PreCreateWindow()` function:

☐ Open the file MAINFRM.CPP and add to it (at the end of the file) the
`PreCreateWindow()` function. After you write this function, the end of the
MAINFRM.CPP file looks as follows:

```
/////////////////////
// MY CODE STARTS HERE
/////////////////////

BOOL CMainFrame::PreCreateWindow(CREATESTRUCT& cs)
{

    // Call the base class function.
    CFrameWnd::PreCreateWindow( cs );

    // Set the width of the window.
    cs.cx = 325;

    // Set the height of the window.
    cs.cy = 400;

    return TRUE;
}

/////////////////////
// MY CODE ENDS HERE
/////////////////////
```

Don't forget to save your work:

☐ Select Save from the File menu.

To see in action the code you typed:

☐ Compile/link and execute the MUSIC application.

> *As you can see, now the size of the application's main window is fixed, and when the Start Show button is clicked, the MUSIC application plays the WAV file through the PC speaker simultaneously with the display of the animation.*

Experiment with the MUSIC application and then select Exit from the File menu to terminate the application.

Disabling the Buttons During Runtime

Currently, the Start Show and Stop Show buttons are enabled at all times. Thus, you can click the Start Show button and then click it again, although clicking it again doesn't have any effect (because the show is already in progress).

For cosmetic reasons, it would be nice if you make only one button available at any given time. Thus, when the application is started, the Stop Show button should be disabled, and the Start Show button should be enabled. And once the Start Show button is clicked, the Start Show button should be disabled and the Stop Show button should be enabled.

Here's how you accomplish the preceding:

☐ Open the MUSICVW.CPP file, and add code to the OnStopButton() function. After adding the code, the OnStopButton() function looks as follows:

```
void CMusicView::OnStopButton()
{
// TODO: Add your control notification handler code here


        ////////////////////////
        // MY CODE STARTS HERE
        ////////////////////////

    // Get a pointer to the CMusicApp object
    CMusicApp* pApp = (CMusicApp*) AfxGetApp();
```

```
        // Update the data member of the CMusicApp class
        pApp->m_ShowStatus = 0;


        // Disable the Stop Show button
        GetDlgItem(IDC_STOP_BUTTON)->EnableWindow(FALSE);


        // Enable the Start Show button
        GetDlgItem(IDC_START_BUTTON)->EnableWindow(TRUE);

        /////////////////////////
        // MY CODE ENDS HERE
        /////////////////////////

}
```

☐ Open the MUSICVW.CPP file and add code to the OnStartButton() function. After you add the code, the OnStartButton() function looks as follows:

```
void CMusicView::OnStartButton()
{
        // TODO: Add your control notification handler code here


        /////////////////////////
        // MY CODE STARTS HERE
        /////////////////////////

    // Get a pointer to the CMusicApp object
     CMusicApp* pApp = (CMusicApp*) AfxGetApp();

        // Update the data member of the CMusicApp class
        pApp->m_ShowStatus = 1;


        // Disable the Start Show button
        GetDlgItem(IDC_START_BUTTON)->EnableWindow(FALSE);


        // Enable the Stop Show button
        GetDlgItem(IDC_STOP_BUTTON)->EnableWindow(TRUE);
        /////////////////////////
        // MY CODE ENDS HERE
        /////////////////////////

}
```

The code you added extracts the pointer of the button with the `GetDlgItem()` function, and the button is enabled or disabled with the `EnableWindow()` function. For example, to disable the Start Show button, the following statement is executed:

```
GetDlgItem(IDC_START_BUTTON)->EnableWindow(FALSE);
```

and to enable the Start Show button, the following statement is executed:

```
GetDlgItem(IDC_START_BUTTON)->EnableWindow(TRUE)
```

☐ Compile/link and execute the MUSIC application.

> *As you can see, when you click the Start Show button, the show starts, the Start Show button becomes disabled, and the Stop Show button becomes enabled. And when you click the Stop Show button, the show stops, the Stop Show button becomes disabled, and the Start Show button becomes enabled.*

Experiment with the MUSIC application and then select Exit from the File menu to terminate the application.

Disabling the Stop Show Button When the Program Begins

In the preceding version of the MUSIC application, both the Start Show and Stop Show buttons appear enabled when the application is started. Because the Stop Show button should be disabled when the application is started, you have to disable it.

☐ Start App Studio.

☐ Double-click the Stop Show button and check its Disabled property.

☐ Select Save from App Studio's File menu.

☐ Compile/link the MUSIC application and verify that the Stop Show button appears disabled when the application is started.

Note that while the show is running, the Start Show button is disabled (see Figure 29.33).

Figure 29.33.
The MUSIC
application with its
Start Show button
disabled.

30

The Grid Control

In this chapter you'll write an application that displays data in a tabular (grid) format by using the GRID.VBX control. You'll learn what the GRID.VBX control is and how to use it to display data.

What Is the GRID.VBX Control?

The GRID.VBX control is a file that enables you to write spreadsheet-like programs easily. You use the GRID.VBX control to display data in a tabular format.

The GRID.VBX control was designed to work with the Microsoft Visual Basic for Windows package as well as with the Microsoft Visual C++ package. In this chapter you'll learn how to use the GRID.VBX control from within your Visual C++ applications.

NOTE

In order for an application that uses the GRID.VBX control to work, the `GRID.VBX` file must reside in any of the following directories:

The `\WINDOWS\SYSTEM` directory

Any directory that's within the DOS PATH

The directory where the application resides

Typically, you copy the `GRID.VBX` file into the `\WINDOWS\SYSTEM` directory, because that way other applications can also use this `GRID.VBX` file, and your program doesn't depend on the current setting of the user's DOS PATH.

NOTE

Usually, a spreadsheet is used to enter and display data in a tabular format. However, the GRID control was designed to display data only. You have to write your own code so that your user can enter data into the spreadsheet.

The MyGrid Application

Now you'll write the MyGrid application. This application utilizes the GRID control to display data in a tabular format.

Before you start writing the MyGrid application, execute the copy of it that resides in your `C:\VCPROG\ORIGINAL\CH30\MYGRID` directory.

To execute the MyGrid application:

☐ Use Run from the Program Manager's File menu to execute
`C:\VCPROG\ORIGINAL\CH30\MYGRID\MyGrid.EXE`.

> *Windows responds by executing the MyGrid application. The main window of MyGrid is shown in Figure 30.1.*

*Figure 30.1.
The MyGrid
application's main
window.*

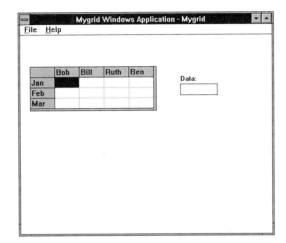

As you can see, the main window of the application contains an empty Grid control and an edit box.

The MyGrid application has two popup menus, File and Help. These popup menus are shown in Figures 30.2 and 30.3.

The GRID control was designed to save designing time. For example, the GRID shown in Figure 30.1 is supposed to contain the number of software packages sold by a company's salespersons during January, February, and March. You can design such a table by using lines, edit boxes, and labels; however, thanks to the GRID control, incorporating such a table into your program is easy.

Figure 30.2.
The MyGrid
application's File
popup menu.

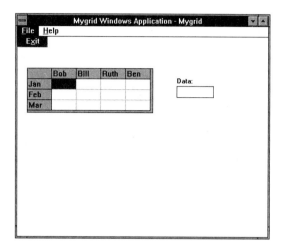

Figure 30.3.
The MyGrid
application's Help
popup menu.

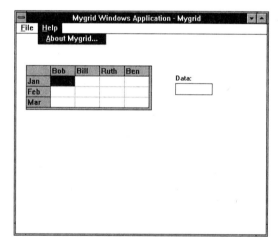

To enter data into the GRID:

☐ Click in the Data box and type a number (see Figure 30.4).

☐ Click the mouse in any of the GRID's cells.

> *MyGrid responds by transferring the data from the edit box into the cell that you clicked (see Figure 30.5).*

Figure 30.4.
Entering data into
the Data box.

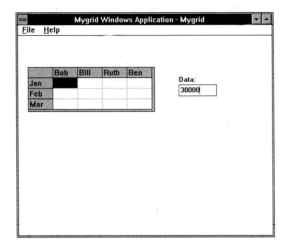

Figure 30.5.
Filling a cell in the
GRID control.

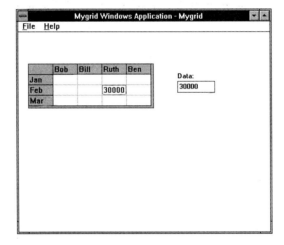

Figure 30.6 shows the GRID control after its cells have been filled with data.

Experiment with the MyGrid application and then select exit from the File menu to terminate the application.

Now that you know what the MyGrid application should do, you can start writing it.

Figure 30.6.
The GRID control
after its cells have
been filled.

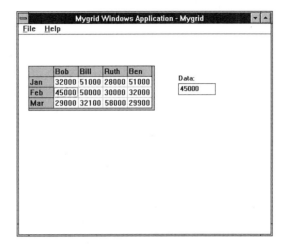

Creating the Project of the MyGrid Application

To create the project of the MyGrid application:

☐ Select AppWizard from the Project menu.

Visual C++ responds by running AppWizard.

☐ Use the Directory list box to select the directory C:\VCPROG\PRACTICE\CH30.

☐ Type mygrid in the Project Name box.

Now your AppWizard dialog box looks as shown in Figure 30.7.

☐ Click the Options button and set the options as shown in Figure 30.8.

WARNING

Because you want the MyGrid application to support a VBX control (namely, the GRID.VBX control), the Custom VBX Controls option should be checked, as shown in Figure 30.8.

---

*Figure 30.7.
The MyGrid
application's
AppWizard
dialog box.*

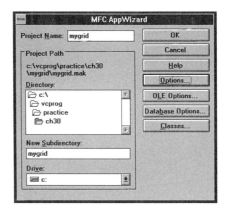

*Figure 30.8.
Setting the options
for the MyGrid
application.*

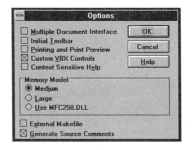

☐ Click the OK button of the Options dialog box and then click the OK
button of the AppWizard dialog box and finally click the Create button of
the New Application Information dialog box.

> *AppWizard responds by creating the MyGrid project and all the skeleton files
> of the MyGrid application.*

To remove the debug options of the project (so you'll have a small EXE file):

☐ Select Project from Visual C++'s Options menu, click the Release radio
button, and then click the OK button of the dialog box.

> **NOTE**
>
> In your future projects, if you ever forget to set the Custom VBX Controls option in AppWizard's Options dialog box, you can still make your application support VBX files without starting AppWizard all over again. You do that by adding the statement
>
> ```
> EnableVBX();
> ```
>
> to the `InitInstance()` function of the main application source file.
>
> When you set the Custom VBX Controls option in AppWizard, this statement is automatically added to the `InitInstance()` function. You can verify this as follows:
>
> Open the main application file of the MyGrid application (`MyGrid.CPP`).
>
> Look for the `EnableVBX()` statement in the `InitInstance()` function.

Creating the Form of the Application

As shown in Figure 30.1, the main window of the MyGrid application should contain a Grid control and an edit box.

To implement this form you must replace the current view class of the application with a new view class derived from the `CFormView` class.

Follow these steps to create the form of the application:

☐ Use the Windows File Manager (or DOS Shell) to delete the two view class files of the MyGrid application:

> Delete `C:\VCPROG\PRACTICE\CH30\MYGRID\MYGRIVW.CPP`.
> Delete `C:\VCPROG\PRACTICE\CH30\MYGRID\MYGRIVW.H`.

☐ Select ClassWizard from Visual C++'s Browse menu.

> *ClassWizard responds by displaying a dialog box telling you that the view class files don't exist.*

☐ Click the OK button of the dialog box.

☐ Click the Remove button of the Repair Class Information dialog box.

☐ Click ClassWizard's OK button.

You have just finished removing the view class of the MyGrid application.

In the following steps you'll create a dialog box, you'll create a `CFormView` type class for this dialog box, and you'll make this class the new view class of the application:

☐ Select App Studio from Visual C++'s Tools menu.

☐ Create a new dialog box with App Studio.

☐ Double-click in a free area of the new dialog box.

☐ Select Styles from the drop-down list box at the upper-right corner of the Properties window.

Set the Styles properties of the dialog box as follows:

☐ Select Child from the Style box.

☐ Select None from the Border box.

☐ Uncheck the Visible property (that is, remove the check mark from the Visible check box).

☐ Select General from the drop-down list box at the upper-right corner of the Properties window and make sure that the Caption box is empty.

Now connect the dialog box to a class derived from `CFormView`:

☐ Select ClassWizard from App Studio's Resource menu.

> *ClassWizard responds by displaying the Add Class dialog box.*

☐ Type `CMygridView` in the Class Name box.

☐ Set the Class Type to `CFormView`.

☐ Set the header filename to `mygrivw.h` and the implementation filename to `mygrivw.cpp`.

☐ Click the Create Class button.

☐ Click ClassWizard's OK button to go back to App Studio.

You've finished creating the new view class of the application. This view class is a derived class from the MFC CFormView class and is connected to the dialog box that you created. Thus, the main dialog box of the application will be the dialog box that you created.

The Visual Implementation of the Dialog Box

One of the controls that you have to place in the MyGrid application's dialog box is the GRID.VBX (see Figure 30.1). Before you can place the GRID control in a dialog box, you must first install the GRID.VBX control in App Studio's Tools window. You can then place the GRID control in a dialog box just as you would place any other control (for example, a push button or an edit box).

If your Tools window currently doesn't contain the GRID.VBX control, follow these steps to install the GRID.VBX control in App Studio's Tools window:

☐ Select Install Controls from App Studio's File menu.

> *App Studio responds by displaying the Install Controls dialog box (see Figure 30.9).*

Figure 30.9.
App Studio's Install Controls dialog box.

As you can see from Figure 30.9, App Studio lists all the VBX files that reside in your \WINDOWS\SYSTEM directory. The Installed Files list shows all the VBX files currently installed in App Studio. In Figure 30.9, the Installed Files list is empty because no VBX files have been installed yet.

To install the GRID.VBX file:

☐ Select the file GRID.VBX and then click the Install button.

App Studio responds by adding GRID.VBX *to the Installed Files list.*

☐ Click the Close button of the Install Controls dialog box.

The GRID.VBX control is now installed in App Studio's Tools window (see Figure 30.10). Now you can place the GRID.VBX control in the dialog box just as you would place any other control.

Figure 30.10.
The GRID.VBX
control.

———— Grid Control

☐ Implement the MyGrid application's dialog box per Table 30.1.

Table 30.1. MyGrid application's dialog box.

Class Name:	CMygridView	
Figure:	30.11	
OK Button:	No	
Cancel Button:	No	

Object	Property	Setting
Dialog Box	ID	IDD_DIALOG1
Grid Control	ID	IDC_GRID1
	Variable	m_grid (Type: CVBControl*)

continues

Table 30.1. continued

Object	Property	Setting
	Size:	Drag the handlers of the GRID control horizontally and vertically to make it wider and longer
Label	ID	`IDC_STATIC`
	Caption	`Data:`
Edit Box	ID	`IDC_FOR_DATA`
	Variable	`m_ForData` (Type: `CString`)

Now your dialog box looks as shown in Figure 30.11.

Figure 30.11.
The MyGrid
application's
dialog box.

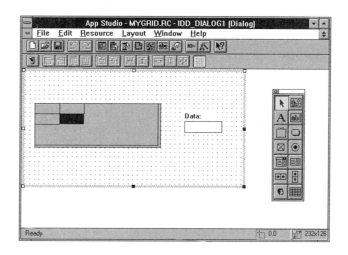

Table 30.1 instructed you to attach a variable called `m_grid`, of type `CVBControl *`, to the GRID. As you'll see when you write the MyGrid application's code, you use the `m_grid` variable to send commands to the GRID control. Note that `CVBControl` is an MFC class. Thus, by making `m_grid` a variable of type `CVBControl*`, you're actually making `m_grid` a pointer to an object of class `CVBControl`. The MFC class `CVBControl` was specifically designed to work with VBX controls.

The GRID control that you placed in the dialog box has many properties. To see these properties:

☐ From App Studio, display the dialog box in its design mode and then double-click the GRID control.

> *App Studio responds by displaying the Properties window of the GRID control.*

☐ Select Styles from the drop-down list box at the upper-right corner of the Properties window.

> *App Studio responds by displaying the Styles Properties window of the GRID control (see Figure 30.12).*

Figure 30.12.
The GRID control's
Styles Properties
window.

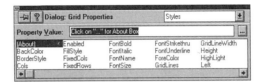

As you can see from Figure 30.12, the GRID control has many properties. For now, don't change any of them.

Save your work:

☐ Select Save from App Studio's File menu.

You've finished designing the dialog box. This dialog box will appear in the main window of the application.

The Visual Implementation of the Menu

The MyGrid application should have a menu with two popup menus, as shown in Figures 30.2 and 30.3. To implement this menu:

Use App Studio to implement the MyGrid application's menu per Table 30.2.

Table 30.2. The MyGrid application's menu.
Figures relating to menu: 30.2, 30.3

Menu Item
&File
E&xit
&Help
&About MyGrid...

Don't forget to delete the accelerator keys of the menu items that you removed:

☐ Select `MYGRID.RC [MFC-Resource Script]` from App Studio's Window menu, select Accelerator from the Type list, and then double-click `IDR_MAINFRAME` in the Resources list.

☐ Delete the accelerator keys that aren't used by the MyGrid application. In particular, delete the accelerator keys of the `ID_FILE_NEW`, `ID_FILE_OPEN`, and `ID_FILE_SAVE` menu items.

If you don't delete these accelerator keys, they'll be active during runtime. If the user presses Ctrl+N, for example, it will be like selecting New from the File menu, even though you deleted that menu item.

Save your work:

☐ Select Save from App Studio's File menu.

The visual implementation of the MyGrid application's menu is completed.

Executing the MyGrid Application

Even though you haven't written any code for the MyGrid application, execute it to see your visual design in action:

☐ Select Build All MYGRID.EXE from Visual C++'s Project menu.

☐ Select Execute MYGRID.EXE from the Project menu.

> *Visual C++ responds by executing the MyGrid application. The main window of the application appears with the form that you designed in it. Note that the GRID control currently has a single column and a single row (see Figure 30.13), creating one cell. This cell of the GRID doesn't contain any data at this point, and you can't enter any.*

To exit the MyGrid application:

☐ Select Exit from the File menu.

Figure 30.13.
*The GRID
control with a
single column
and a single row.*

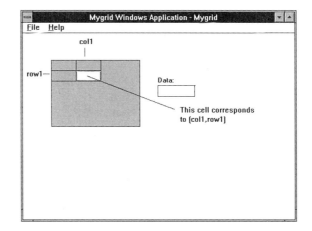

Initializing the Properties of the GRID Control

As shown in Figure 30.13, currently the GRID control has a single cell. To change the number of rows and columns in the GRID:

☐ In App Studio, display the dialog box in its design mode and then double-click the GRID control.

> *App Studio responds by displaying the Properties window of the GRID control.*

☐ Select Styles from the drop-down list box at the upper-right corner of the Properties window.

☐ Change the Rows property to 4 (see Figure 30.14).

☐ Change the Cols property to 5 (see Figure 30.15).

Figure 30.14.
*Changing the
number of rows
to 4.*

Figure 30.15.
Changing the
number of columns
to 5.

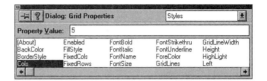

☐ Resize and move the controls until the dialog box looks as shown in Figure 30.16.

Figure 30.16.
The GRID with
five columns and
four rows.

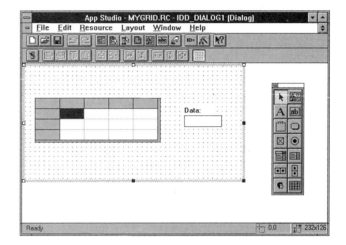

NOTE

The GRID control has properties called `Cols` and `Rows`, and it also has properties called `Col` and `Row`. Don't confuse the `Col` and `Row` properties with the `Cols` and `Rows` properties.

The `Cols` and `Rows` properties are used to set the number of columns and rows in the GRID control. As you'll see later, the `Col` and `Row` properties are used to select the current cell. `Col` and `Row` can be set during runtime only.

Setting the Row and Column Headings of the GRID

Now you'll write code that initializes the properties of the GRID control in the OnInitialUpdate() member function of the view class. This way, when the application begins, the GRID control will be updated with some initial values.

Recall from previous chapters that Visual C++ did not write the declaration and skeleton of the OnInitialUpdate() function. You have to declare this function and write its skeleton. Here's how you do that:

☐ Open the file MYGRIVW.H and add code to it that defines the function OnInitialUpdate() as a member function of the CMygridView class. After you write this code, the CMygridView class declaration looks as follows:

```
class CMygridView : public CFormView
{
     DECLARE_DYNCREATE(CMygridView)
protected:
CMygridView(); // protected constructor used
               // by dynamic creation


     /////////////////////////
     // MY CODE STARTS HERE
     /////////////////////////

     virtual void OnInitialUpdate();

     /////////////////////////
     // MY CODE ENDS HERE
     /////////////////////////


// Form Data
public:
     //{{AFX_DATA(CMygridView)
     enum { IDD = IDD_DIALOG1 };
     CVBControl*     m_grid;
     CString     m_ForData;
     //}}AFX_DATA

// Attributes
```

```
public:

// Operations
public:

// Implementation
protected:
    virtual ~CMygridView();
    virtual void DoDataExchange(CDataExchange* pDX);
// DDX/DDV support
    // Generated message map functions
    //{{AFX_MSG(CMygridView)
// NOTE - the ClassWizard will add and remove
// member functions here.
    //}}AFX_MSG
    DECLARE_MESSAGE_MAP()
};
```

Now write the `OnInitialUpdate()` function's code:

☐ Open the file MYGRIVW.CPP and add the `OnInitialUpdate()` function to the end of the file. After you write this function, the end of the MYGRIVW.CPP file looks as follows:

```
/////////////////////////
// MY CODE STARTS HERE
/////////////////////////

void CMygridView::OnInitialUpdate()
{

    // Call the base class function.
    CFormView::OnInitialUpdate();


    // Set the current row to row 0.
    m_grid->SetNumProperty("Row",0);

    // Set the current col to 1.
    m_grid->SetNumProperty("Col",1);

    // Fill the cell (Row = 0, Col = 1)
    m_grid->SetStrProperty ("Text", "Bob");

 }

/////////////////////////
// MY CODE ENDS HERE
/////////////////////////
```

The code that you typed first calls the base class:

```
CFormView::OnInitialUpdate();
```

Then the current row is set to 0:

```
m_grid->SetNumProperty("Row",0);
```

and the current column is set to 1:

```
m_grid->SetNumProperty("Col",1);
```

The preceding two statements set the cell in row 0, col 1 as the current cell of the GRID.

Now that the current cell is set, you can fill its contents:

```
m_grid->SetStrProperty ("Text", "Bob");
```

To see the code that you typed in action:

☐ Compile/link and execute the MyGrid application.

The MyGrid's main window appears as shown in Figure 30.17. As shown, the text Bob is displayed in the cell at row 0, col 1.

Figure 30.17.
Displaying the text
"Bob" in the cell at
row 0, col 1.

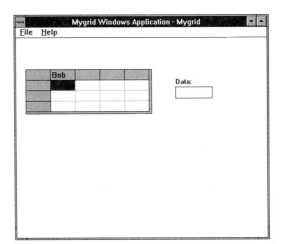

Filling the Rest of the Column and Row Headings

☐ Modify the OnInitialUpdate() function in MYGRIVW.CPP so that it fills the rest of the column and row headings of the GRID control. After the modification, the OnInitialUpdate() function looks as follows:

```
//////////////////////////
// MY CODE STARTS HERE
//////////////////////////

void CMygridView::OnInitialUpdate()
{

    // Call the base class function.
    CFormView::OnInitialUpdate();


    // Set the current row to row 0.
    m_grid->SetNumProperty("Row",0);
    // Set the current col to 1.
    m_grid->SetNumProperty("Col",1);
    // Fill the cell (Row = 0, Col = 1)
    m_grid->SetStrProperty ("Text", "Bob");


    // Fill the cell (Row = 0, Col = 2)
    m_grid->SetNumProperty("Col",2);
    m_grid->SetStrProperty ("Text", "Bill");

    // Fill the cell (Row = 0, Col = 3)
    m_grid->SetNumProperty("Col",3);
    m_grid->SetStrProperty ("Text", "Ruth");

    // Fill the cell (Row = 0, Col = 4)
    m_grid->SetNumProperty("Col",4);
    m_grid->SetStrProperty ("Text", "Ben");


    // Set the current col to 0.
    m_grid->SetNumProperty("Col",0);

    // Fill the cell (Row = 1, Col = 0)
    m_grid->SetNumProperty("Row",1);
    m_grid->SetStrProperty ("Text", "Jan");

    // Fill the cell (Row = 2, Col = 0)
```

```
        m_grid->SetNumProperty("Row",2);
        m_grid->SetStrProperty ("Text", "Feb");

        // Fill the cell (Row = 3, Col = 0)
        m_grid->SetNumProperty("Row",3);
        m_grid->SetStrProperty ("Text", "Mar");
    }

/////////////////////
// MY CODE ENDS HERE
/////////////////////
```

The code you typed fills the rest of the row and column headings. For example, to fill the second column heading, the following statements are executed:

```
m_grid->SetNumProperty("Col",2);
m_grid->SetStrProperty ("Text", "Bill");
```

That is, the `Col` property is set to 2 and the `Text` property is set to `Bill`. Recall that the `Row` property is already set to 0. Thus, the text `"Bill"` will be displayed in the cell at row 0, col 2.

In a similar manner, the row headings are set to

```
    Jan
    Feb
    Mar
```

This is accomplished by first setting the `Col` property to 0:

```
m_grid->SetNumProperty("Col",0);
```

and then filling the cells in this column. For example, to fill the cell at row 1, col 0 with `Jan`, the following statements are used:

```
m_grid->SetNumProperty("Row",1);
m_grid->SetStrProperty ("Text", "Jan");
```

To see in action the code that you typed:

☐ Compile/link and execute the MyGrid application.

The main window of MyGrid appears, as shown in Figure 30.1.

Filling the Data Cells of the GRID

The GRID shown in Figure 30.1 is ready. The inner cells will contain the data, such as the total number of software packages sold each month by various salespersons.

However, the question is, how will the user type the data in the data cells? As previously stated, the GRID control enables the user to fill cells only from within the code. In other words, the cells don't act like edit boxes.

One solution is for the user to enter data into an edit box. Then the code transfers that data into a cell. For example, the user could type data in an edit box and then click one of the cells to fill it with the contents of the edit box.

At first glance, the code required to accomplish this task looks complicated. However, it's actually quite simple, thanks to the fact that once a cell is clicked, the Row and Col properties are automatically updated. For example, if you click in the cell at row 2, col 3, the Row property is automatically updated with the number 2, and the Col property is automatically updated with the number 3.

☐ Use ClassWizard to add a function for the event:

Class Name:	CMygridView
Object ID:	IDC_GRID1
Message:	VBN_CLICK
Function Name:	OnClickGrid1()

NOTE: Make sure you're adding the function to the CMygridView class.

NOTE

Depending on your particular version of Visual C++, the ClassWizard window may or may not display the IDC_GRID1 control's messages. If it doesn't, you won't be able to attach the OnClickGrid1() function. If this happens, you need to remove the GRID control and then reinstall it. Microsoft is expected to fix this problem in future versions of the package.

☐ Edit the OnClickGrid1() function that you added to the MYGRIVW.CPP file. After you edit the OnClickGrid1() function, it looks as follows:

```
void CMygridView::OnClickGrid1(UINT, int, CWnd*, LPVOID)
{
// TODO: Add your VBX event notification handler code here
```

```
/////////////////////
// MY CODE STARTS HERE
/////////////////////

// Update the m_ForData with Current contents of
// the edit box.
UpdateData(TRUE);


 m_grid->SetStrProperty ("Text", m_ForData);

/////////////////////
// MY CODE ENDS HERE
/////////////////////
```

}

The `OnClickGrid1()` function is executed whenever any of the cells of the GRID control are clicked.

The code that you typed transfers the contents of the Data edit box to the `m_ForData` variable:

`UpdateData(TRUE);`

and then the cell that was clicked is updated with the value of `m_ForData`:

`m_grid->SetStrProperty ("Text", m_ForData);`

The `Row` and `Col` properties are automatically updated. This is why the `SetStrProperty()` function places the text in `m_ForData` into the cell that was clicked.

☐ Compile/link and execute the MyGrid application and verify its operation.

31

Displaying and Printing Graphs

In this chapter you will write an application that displays and prints data in a graph format by using the GRAPH.VBX control. You'll learn what the GRAPH.VBX control is, and how to use it to display and print data.

What Is the GRAPH.VBX Control?

The GRAPH.VBX control is a file that enables you to easily display and print data as graphs.

The GRAPH.VBX control was designed to work with Microsoft Visual Basic for Windows, as well as with Microsoft Visual C++. In this chapter you'll learn how to use the GRAPH.VBX control from within your Visual C++ programs.

NOTE

In order for an application that uses the GRAPH.VBX control to work, the files `GRAPH.VBX`, `GSWDLL.DLL`, and `GSW.EXE` must reside in any of the following directories:

The `\WINDOWS\SYSTEM` directory

Any directory that's within the DOS PATH

The directory where the application resides

Typically, you copy these files into the `\WINDOWS\SYSTEM` directory so that other applications can also use these files, and so that your program doesn't depend on the current setting of the user's DOS PATH.

The MyGraph Application

Now you'll write the MyGraph application, which utilizes the GRAPH.VBX control to display and print data in a graph format.

Before you start writing the MyGraph application, execute the copy of it that resides in your `C:\VCPROG\ORIGINAL\CH31\MYGRAPH` directory.

To execute the MyGraph application:

☐ Use Run from the Program Manager's File menu to execute
`C:\VCPROG\ORIGINAL\CH31\MYGRAPH\MyGraph.EXE`.

Windows responds by executing the MyGraph application. The main window of `MyGraph.EXE` *appears, as shown in Figure 31.1.*

Figure 31.1.
The MyGraph
application's main
window.

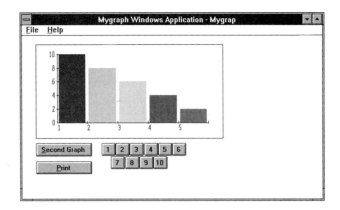

As you can see, the main window of the application contains several buttons and a graph.

The MYGRAPH application has two popup menus, File and Help. These popup menus are shown in Figures 31.2 and 31.3.

Figure 31.2.
The MyGraph
application's File
popup menu.

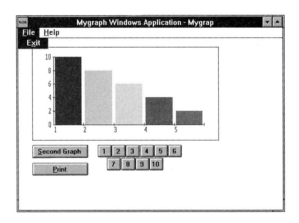

Figure 31.3.
The MyGraph
application's Help
popup menu.

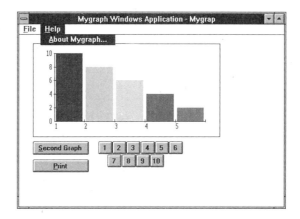

The GRAPH control is capable of displaying more than one graph. To display a second graph:

☐ Click the Second Graph button.

MyGraph responds by displaying a second graph (see Figure 31.4).

Figure 31.4.
Displaying two
graphs.

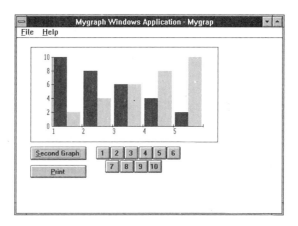

The small numbered buttons in MyGraph let you display the information found in one type of graph within a different type of graph.

☐ Click any of the small buttons.

Figure 31.5 shows the graph that results from clicking the 1 button, and Figure 31.6 shows the graph that results from clicking the 2 button.

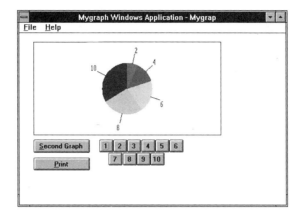

Figure 31.5.
The graph after
clicking the
1 button.

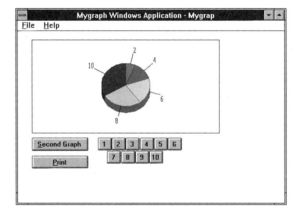

Figure 31.6.
The graph after
clicking the
2 button.

☐ To print a graph, click the Print button.

☐ To clear the graph, click anywhere in the graph.

☐ Experiment with the MyGraph application and then select exit from the File menu to terminate the application.

Now that you know what the MyGraph application should do, you can start writing it.

Creating the Project of the MyGraph Application

To create the project of the MyGraph application:

☐ Select AppWizard from the Project menu.

> *Visual C++ responds by running AppWizard.*

☐ Use the Directory list box to select the directory C:\VCPROG\PRACTICE\CH31.

☐ Type mygraph in the Project Name box.

Your AppWizard dialog box looks as shown in Figure 31.7.

Figure 31.7.
The MyGraph
application's
AppWizard
dialog box.

☐ Click the Options button and set the options as shown in Figure 31.8.

WARNING

Because you want the MyGraph application to support a VBX control (namely, the GRAPH.VBX control), the Custom VBX Controls option should be checked, as shown in Figure 31.8.

☐ Click the OK button of the Options dialog box and then click the OK button of the AppWizard dialog box and finally click the Create button of the New Application Information dialog box.

> *AppWizard responds by creating the MyGraph project and all the skeleton files of the MyGraph application.*

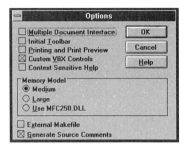

Figure 31.8.
Setting the options
for the MyGraph
application.

To remove the debug options of the project (so you'll have a small EXE file):

☐ Select Project from Visual C++'s Options menu, click the Release radio button, and then click the OK button of the dialog box.

NOTE

In your future projects, if you ever forget to set the Custom VBX Controls option in AppWizard's Options dialog box, you can still make your application support VBX files without starting AppWizard all over again. You do this by adding the statement

```
EnableVBX();
```

to the `InitInstance()` function of the main application source file.

When you set the Custom VBX Controls option in AppWizard, this statement is automatically added to the `InitInstance()` function. You can verify this as follows:

> Open the main application file of the MyGraph application (`MYGRAPH.CPP`).

> Look for the `EnableVBX()` statement in the `InitInstance()` function.

Creating the Form of the Application

As shown in Figure 31.1, the MyGraph application's main window should contain a GRAPH.VBX control and several buttons.

To implement this form, you will replace the current view class of the application with a new view class derived from the `CFormView` class.

Follow these steps to create the form of the application:

☐ Use the Windows File Manager (or DOS Shell) to delete the two view class files of the MyGraph application:
Delete `C:\VCPROG\PRACTICE\CH31\MYGRAPH\MYGRAVW.CPP`.
Delete `C:\VCPROG\PRACTICE\CH31\MYGRAPH\MYGRAVW.H`.

☐ Select ClassWizard from Visual C++'s Browse menu.

> *ClassWizard responds by displaying a dialog box telling you that the view class files don't exist.*

☐ Click the OK button of the dialog box.

☐ Click the Remove button of the Repair Class Information dialog box.

☐ Click ClassWizard's OK button.

You have just finished removing the view class of the MyGraph application.

In the following steps you'll create a dialog box, you'll create a `CFormView` type class for this dialog box, and you'll make this class the new view class of the application:

☐ Select App Studio from Visual C++'s Tools menu.

☐ Create a new dialog box with App Studio.

☐ Double-click in a free area of the new dialog box.

☐ Select Styles from the drop-down list box at the upper-right corner of the Properties window.

Set the Styles properties of the dialog box as follows:

☐ Select Child from the Style box.

☐ Select None from the Border box.

☐ Uncheck the Visible property (that is, remove the check mark from the Visible check box).

☐ Select General from the drop-down list box at the upper-right corner of the Properties window, and make sure that the Caption box is empty.

Now, connect the dialog box to a class derived from `CFormView`:

☐ Select ClassWizard from App Studio's Resource menu.

> *ClassWizard responds by displaying the Add Class dialog box.*

☐ Type `CMygraphView` in the Class Name box.

☐ Set the Class Type to `CFormView`.

☐ Change the header filename to `mygravw.h` and the implementation filename to `mygravw.cpp`.

☐ Click the Create Class button.

☐ Click ClassWizard's OK button to go back to App Studio.

You've finished creating the new view class of the application. This view class is a derived class from the MFC `CFormView` class and is connected to the dialog box that you created. Thus, the main dialog box of the application will be the dialog box that you created.

The Visual Implementation of the Dialog Box

One of the controls that you have to place in the MyGraph application's dialog box is the GRAPH.VBX control (see Figure 31.1). Before you can place the GRAPH.VBX control in a dialog box, you must first install it in App Studio's Tools window. You can then place it in a dialog box just as you would place any other control (for example, a push button or an edit box).

If your Tools window currently doesn't contain the GRAPH.VBX control, follow these steps to install it in App Studio's Tools window:

☐ Select Install Controls from App Studio's File menu.

> *App Studio responds by displaying the Install Controls dialog box (see Figure 31.9).*

Figure 31.9.
App Studio's Install Controls dialog box.

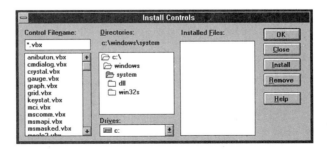

As you can see from Figure 31.9, App Studio lists all the VBX files that reside in your `\WINDOWS\SYSTEM` directory. The Installed Files list contains all the VBX files that are currently installed in App Studio. In Figure 31.9, the Installed Files list is empty because no VBX files have been installed yet.

To install the GRAPH.VBX file:

☐ Select the file GRAPH.VBX and then click the Install button.

App Studio responds by adding GRAPH.VBX *to the Installed Files list.*

☐ Click the Close button of the Install Controls dialog box.

The GRAPH.VBX control is now installed in App Studio's Tools window (see Figure 31.10). You can now place the GRAPH.VBX control in the dialog box just as you would place any other control.

Figure 31.10.
The GRAPH.VBX
control.

Graph Control —

☐ Implement the MyGraph application's dialog box per Table 31.1.

Table 31.1. The MyGraph application's dialog box.

Class Name:	CMygraphView
Figure:	31.11
OK button:	No
Cancel button:	No

Object	Property	Setting
Dialog Box	ID	IDD_DIALOG1
	Size	Drag the handles of the dialog box horizontally and vertically to make it wider and longer
GRAPH.VBX	ID	IDC_GRAPH1
	Variable	m_graph (Type: CVBControl *)
	Size	Drag the handles of the GRAPH control horizontally and vertically to make it wider and longer

Now your dialog box looks as shown in Figure 31.11.

Figure 31.11.
The MyGraph
application's
dialog box.

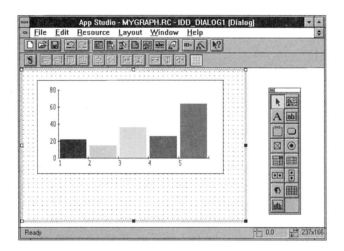

Table 31.1 instructed you to attach a variable called m_graph of type CVBControl * to the GRAPH.VBX control. As you'll see when you write the MyGraph application's code, you use the m_graph variable to send commands to the GRAPH.VBX control. Note that CVBControl is an MFC class. Thus, by making m_graph a variable of type CVBControl* you're actually making m_graph a pointer to an object of class CVBControl. The MFC class CVBControl was specifically designed to work with VBX controls.

The GRAPH.VBX control that you placed in the dialog box has many properties. To see these properties:

☐ Double-click the GRAPH control that you placed in the dialog box.

App Studio responds by displaying the General properties of the GRAPH control.

☐ Select Styles from the drop-down list box at the upper-right corner of the Properties window.

App Studio responds by displaying the Styles Properties window of the GRAPH control (see Figure 31.12).

Figure 31.12.
The GRAPH control's Styles Properties window.

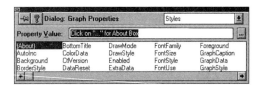

As you can see from Figure 31.12, the GRAPH control has many properties.

Save your work:

☐ Select Save from App Studio's File menu.

You've finished designing the dialog box. This dialog box will appear in the main window of the application.

The Visual Implementation of the Menu

The MyGraph application should have a menu with two popup menus as shown in Figures 31.2 and 31.3. Use App Studio to implement the MyGraph application's menu per Table 31.2.

Table 31.2. The MyGraph application's menu.
Figures relating to menu: 31.2, 31.3

Menu Item
&File
E&xit
&Help
&About MyGraph...

Don't forget to delete the accelerator keys of the menu items that you removed:

☐ Select MYGRAPH.RC [MFC-Resource Script] from App Studio's Window menu, select Accelerator from the Type list and then double-click IDR_MAINFRAME in the Resources list.

☐ Delete the accelerator keys that aren't used by the MYGRAPH application. In particular, delete the accelerator keys of the ID_FILE_NEW, ID_FILE_OPEN, and ID_FILE_SAVE menu items.

If you don't delete these accelerator keys, they'll be active during runtime. If the user presses Ctrl+N, for example, it will be like selecting New from the File menu, even though you deleted that menu item.

Save your work:

☐ Select Save from App Studio's File menu.

The visual implementation of the MyGraph application's menu is complete.

Executing the MyGraph Application

Even though you haven't written a single line of code for the MyGraph application, execute it to see your visual design in action.

☐ Select Rebuild All MYGRAPH.EXE from Visual C++'s Project menu.

☐ Select Execute MYGRAPH.EXE from the Project menu.

> *Visual C++ responds by executing the MyGraph application. The main window of the application appears with the form that you designed in it (see Figure 31.13).*

Figure 31.13.
The GRAPH control in the MyGraph window.

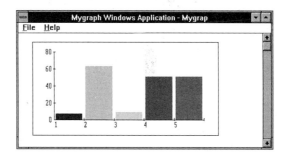

To exit the MyGraph application:

☐ Select Exit from the File menu.

Initializing the Properties of the GRAPH Control

As shown in Figure 31.13, the GRAPH control currently displays a graph. A graph of what? Well, the GRAPH.VBX wants you to see how the graph looks, so it generates some random data for the sake of illustration.

Naturally, the graph in Figure 31.13 is useless because it displays random data. Now you'll learn how to set the graph (from within App Studio) so that it will display your own data. (Later in this chapter, you'll learn how to set the graph's data from within your code.)

Suppose, for example, that you want to plot a graph in accordance with the set of points shown in Table 31.3.

Table 31.3. The points on the graph.

Horizontal	Vertical
1	2
2	4
3	6
4	8
5	10

☐ Use App Studio to display the dialog box in its design mode.

☐ Double-click the GRAPH control.

  App Studio responds by displaying the Properties window of the GRAPH control.

☐ Select Styles from the drop-down list in the upper-right corner of the Properties window and then select the ThisPoint property.

Make sure that the ThisPoint property is set to 1, as shown in Figure 31.14.

Figure 31.14.
Setting the
`ThisPoint`
property.

The `ThisPoint` property represents the horizontal coordinate. Per Table 31.3, the vertical coordinate that corresponds to `ThisPoint` = 1 is 2. The vertical coordinate is represented by the `GraphData` property, so you have to set GraphData to 2:

☐ Set the `GraphData` property to 2 (see Figure 31.15).

So far, you set `ThisPoint` to 1 and `GraphData` to 2, which corresponds to the first point in Table 31.3.

☐ Make sure that `ThisPoint` is set to 2 and then set `GraphData` to 4. This takes care of the second point in Table 31.3.

☐ In a similar manner, set the other points per Table 31.3.

After setting the five points from Table 31.3, the graph looks as shown in Figure 31.16.

Figure 31.15.
Setting the
`GraphData`
property.

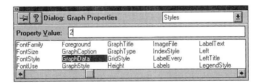

Figure 31.16.
Setting the five
points of the graph.

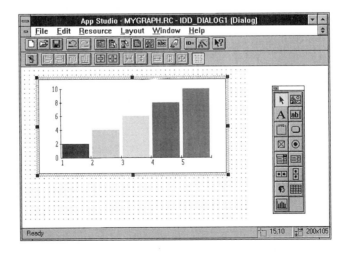

> **NOTE**
>
> You might have noticed that as you entered the five points of the graph, the `ThisPoint` property was incremented automatically. For example, once you set the first point (`ThisPoint=1`, `GraphData=2`), when you examined the `ThisPoint` property again, it was automatically set to 2. This is because the `AutoInc` property was set to 1 (see Figure 31.17). So if you want to enter data into `GraphData` point after point without the need to set the `ThisPoint` property, set the `AutoInc` property to 1.
>
> If you made a mistake and want to enter a different `GraphData`, make sure that `ThisPoint` is set to the proper point.

Figure 31.17.
The `AutoInc`
property.

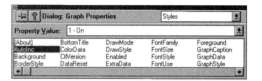

Another important property is the `NumPoints` property (see Figure 31.18). As shown in Figure 31.18, the `NumPoints` property is currently set to 5 (because there are 5 points in the graph). As you'll soon see, it's also possible to set the points of the graph from in your code instead of from App Studio. The `NumPoints` property determines the maximum number of points in the graph. You can set this property at design time (in App Studio), as well as from in your code.

Figure 31.18.
The `NumPoints`
property.

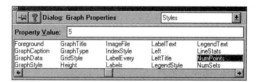

☐ Even though you haven't written a single line of code, compile/link and execute the MyGraph application to see your visual design in action.

☐ Compile/link and execute the MyGraph application.

> *The MyGraph window appears. As shown in Figure 31.19, the graph corresponds to the points that you set during the App Studio session.*

Figure 31.19.
The graph with five points, as set during the App Studio session.

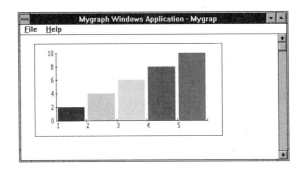

☐ Select Exit from the File menu to terminate the MyGraph application.

Setting the Points of a Graph at Runtime

So far, you've set the points of the graph at design time. Now you'll learn how to set the points of the graph from within your code. You'll write code that initializes the properties of the GRAPH control in the `OnInitialUpdate()` member function of the view class. This way, when the application starts, the GRAPH control is updated with some initial values.

Recall from previous chapters that Visual C++ did not write the declaration and skeleton of the `OnInitialUpdate()` function. You have to declare this function and write its skeleton. Here's how you do that:

☐ Open the file MYGRAVW.H and add code to it that defines the function `OnInitialUpdate()` as a member function of the `CMygraphView` class. After you write this code, the `CMygraphView` class declaration looks as follows:

```
class CMygraphView : public CFormView
{
    DECLARE_DYNCREATE(CMygraphView)
protected:
    CMygraphView();
// protected constructor used by dynamic creation

    /////////////////////////
    // MY CODE STARTS HERE
    /////////////////////////

    virtual void OnInitialUpdate();

    /////////////////////////
    // MY CODE ENDS HERE
    /////////////////////////
```

```
// Form Data
public:
    //{{AFX_DATA(CMygraphView)
    enum { IDD = IDD_DIALOG1 };
    CVBControl*    m_graph;
    //}}AFX_DATA

// Attributes
public:

// Operations
public:

// Implementation
protected:
    virtual ~CMygraphView();
    virtual void DoDataExchange(CDataExchange* pDX);
// DDX/DDV support
// Generated message map functions
//{{AFX_MSG(CMygraphView)
// NOTE - the ClassWizard will add and remove
// member functions here.
    //}}AFX_MSG
    DECLARE_MESSAGE_MAP()
};
```

Now write the `OnInitialUpdate()` function's code:

☐ Open the file MYGRAVW.CPP and add the `OnInitialUpdate()` function to the end of the file. After you write this function, the end of the MYGRAVW.CPP file looks as follows:

```
////////////////////////
// MY CODE STARTS HERE
////////////////////////

void CMygraphView::OnInitialUpdate()
{

        // Call the base class function.
        CFormView::OnInitialUpdate();


    // Set the current point to 1
     m_graph->SetNumProperty("ThisPoint",1);
    // Set the current data to 10.
     m_graph->SetFloatProperty("GraphData",10);


    // Set the current point to 2
     m_graph->SetNumProperty("ThisPoint",2);
```

```
    // Set the current data to 8.
     m_graph->SetFloatProperty("GraphData",8);


    // Set the current point to 3
     m_graph->SetNumProperty("ThisPoint",3);
    // Set the current data to 6.
     m_graph->SetFloatProperty("GraphData",6);


    // Set the current point to 4
     m_graph->SetNumProperty("ThisPoint",4);
    // Set the current data to 4.
     m_graph->SetFloatProperty("GraphData",4);


    // Set the current point to 5
     m_graph->SetNumProperty("ThisPoint",5);
    // Set the current data to 2.
     m_graph->SetFloatProperty("GraphData",2);

}

/////////////////////
// MY CODE ENDS HERE
/////////////////////
```

The code you typed executes the base class:

```
CFormView::OnInitialUpdate();
```

Then the `ThisPoint` property is set to 1:

```
m_graph->SetNumProperty("ThisPoint",1);
```

And the data that corresponds to this point is set to 10:

```
m_graph->SetFloatProperty("GraphData",10);
```

The rest of the code sets the other points of the graph. At this point the graph looks as indicated by the set of points shown in Table 31.4.

Table 31.4. The new set of points for the graph.

Horizontal	Vertical
1	10
2	8

continues

1059

Table 31.4. continued

Horizontal	Vertical
3	6
4	4
5	2

To see the new graph in action:

☐ Compile/link and execute the MyGraph application.

> *The graph appears as shown in Figure 31.20.*

☐ Select Exit from the File menu to terminate the application.

Figure 31.20.
The graph per
Table 31.4.

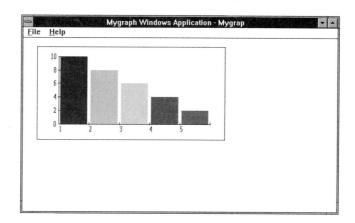

Displaying Two Sets of Points

So far, you've learned how to use the GRAPH control to display one set of points. However, the GRAPH.VBX control can be used to display two sets of points on a graph. For example, it's possible to display the set of points in Table 31.3 on the same graph with the set of points in Table 31.4.

☐ Start App Studio and display the dialog box in its design mode.

☐ Add a button to the dialog box. The button should have the following properties:

ID:	IDC_SECOND_BUTTON
Caption:	&Second Graph

When you've added the button, the dialog box looks as shown in Figure 31.21.

Figure 31.21.
Adding the Second
Graph button to the
dialog box.

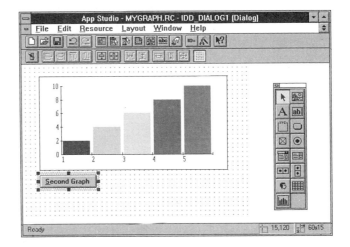

☐ Use ClassWizard to add a function for the event:

Class Name:	CMygraphView
Object ID:	IDC_SECOND_BUTTON
Message:	BN_CLICK
Function Name:	OnSecondButton()

NOTE: Make sure you're adding the function to the CMygraphView class.

☐ Edit the OnSecondButton() function that you added to the MYGRAVW.CPP file.
After you edit the OnSecondButton() function, it looks as follows:

```
void CMygraphView::OnSecondButton()
{
// TODO: Add your control notification handler code here

    //////////////////////
    // MY CODE STARTS HERE
    //////////////////////

    // Set the NumSets property to 2
     m_graph->SetNumProperty("NumSets",2);

    // Set the ThisSet property to 2
     m_graph->SetNumProperty("ThisSet",2);

    // Set the NumPoints property to 5
     m_graph->SetNumProperty("NumPoints",5);
```

```
    // Set the current point to 1
     m_graph->SetNumProperty("ThisPoint",1);
    // Set the current data to 2.
     m_graph->SetFloatProperty("GraphData",2);


    // Set the current point to 2
     m_graph->SetNumProperty("ThisPoint",2);
    // Set the current data to 4.
     m_graph->SetFloatProperty("GraphData",4);


    // Set the current point to 3
     m_graph->SetNumProperty("ThisPoint",3);
    // Set the current data to 6.
     m_graph->SetFloatProperty("GraphData",6);


    // Set the current point to 4
     m_graph->SetNumProperty("ThisPoint",4);
    // Set the current data to 8.
     m_graph->SetFloatProperty("GraphData",8);


    // Set the current point to 5
     m_graph->SetNumProperty("ThisPoint",5);
    // Set the current data to 10.
     m_graph->SetFloatProperty("GraphData",10);


    // Draw it
     m_graph->SetNumProperty("DrawMode",2);

    //////////////////////
    // MY CODE ENDS HERE
    //////////////////////

}
```

The code you typed sets the NumsSets property to 2:

```
m_graph->SetNumProperty("NumSets",2);
```

This means that the graph will hold two separate sets of points.

Before you enter the second set of points, you must tell the GRAPH control that the current set is set number 2. You do this by setting the ThisSet property to 2:

```
m_graph->SetNumProperty("ThisSet",2);
```

Next, you have to tell the graph that there are a total of five points in the set. You do this by setting the `NumPoints` property to 5:

```
m_graph->SetNumProperty("NumPoints",5);
```

Note that the GRAPH control knows that you mean five points in the second set (not the first), because `ThisSet` is currently equal to 2.

The next statements set the points on the graph per Table 31.3. For example, the first point in the second set of points is set as follows:

```
m_graph->SetNumProperty("ThisPoint",1);
m_graph->SetFloatProperty("GraphData",2);
```

Again, the GRAPH control knows that you mean to place the point in the second set, because `ThisSet` is currently equal to 2.

The last statement in this function tells the GRAPH control to draw the new graph. This is accomplished by setting the value of `DrawMode` to 2:

```
m_graph->SetNumProperty("DrawMode",2);
```

> **NOTE**
>
> When you set the properties of a VBX, you have to make sure that you don't have any syntax errors. For example, if you type `DrwMode` instead of `DrawMode` as the first parameter of `SetNumProperty()`, the compiler won't complain. However, the VBX won't know what to do with `DrwMode`, and as a result, the graph won't be redrawn.

To see in action the code that you typed:

☐ Compile/link and execute the MyGraph application.

> *The main window of MyGraph appears. As shown in Figure 31.20, the graph displays only one set of points (per Table 31.4).*

To display the two sets (Table 31.3 and Table 31.4):

☐ Click the Second Graph button.

> *MyGraph responds by displaying the two sets as shown in Figure 31.22.*

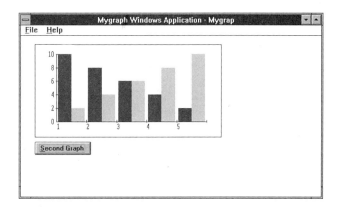

Figure 31.22.
Displaying the two
sets of points.

Printing the Graph

Printing the graph is easy. Next you'll write code that sends the graph to the printer.

☐ Start App Studio and display the dialog box in its design mode.

☐ Add a button to the dialog box. The button should have the following properties:

ID:	IDC_PRINT_BUTTON
Caption:	&Print

When you've added the button, the dialog box looks as shown in Figure 31.23.

Figure 31.23.
Adding the Print
button to the dialog
box.

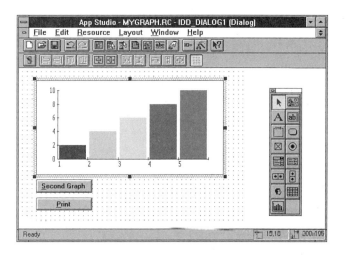

☐ Use ClassWizard to add a function for the event:

Class Name:	CMygraphView
Object ID:	IDC_PRINT_BUTTON
Message:	BN_CLICK
Function Name:	OnPrintButton()

NOTE: Make sure that you're adding the function to the CMygraphView class.

☐ Edit the OnPrintButton() function that you added to the MYGRAVW.CPP file. After you edit the OnPrintButton() function, it looks as follows:

```
void CMygraphView::OnPrintButton()
{
// TODO: Add your control notification
// handler code here


    /////////////////////////
    // MY CODE STARTS HERE
    /////////////////////////

    m_graph->SetNumProperty("DrawMode",5);

    /////////////////////////
    // MY CODE ENDS HERE
    /////////////////////////

}
```

The code that you typed sets the DrawMode property to 5:

```
m_graph->SetNumProperty("DrawMode",5);
```

This causes the GRAPH control to be sent to the printer. To see that this is indeed the case:

☐ Compile/link and execute the MyGraph application.

☐ Click the Print button.

> *MyGraph responds by sending the graph (with one set of points on it) to the printer.*

☐ Click the Second Graph button.

> *MyGraph responds by adding a second set of points to the graph.*

☐ Click the Print button.

    MyGraph responds by sending the graph (with two sets of points in it) to the printer.

☐ Select Exit from the File menu to terminate the MyGraph application.

Setting Other Properties of the GRAPH Control

You now have the know-how to set the properties of the GRAPH control from within App Studio and from within your code. Due to the large number of properties GRAPH has, we can't cover all of them here. However, you should know that you can set the appearance of a graph in many ways. For example, you can attach label titles to a graph.

> **NOTE**
>
> For complete documentation on the GRAPH control, you should read the *Professional Features Book 1* manual that comes with the Microsoft Visual Basic 3.0 package.

The *GraphType* Property

We can't resist showing you the GraphType property of the GRAPH.VBX control in action.

☐ Use App Studio to attach 10 buttons to the MyGraph window, as shown in Figure 31.24. The captions of the buttons should be 1—10. The IDs of the buttons should be IDC_BUTTON_1—IDC_BUTTON_10.

    The dialog box, after adding the 10 buttons, is shown in Figure 31.24.

☐ Use ClassWizard to add a function for the event:

Class Name:	CMygraphView
Object ID:	IDC_BUTTON_1
Message:	BN_CLICK
Function Name:	OnButton1()

NOTE: Make sure that you're adding the function to the CMygraphView class.

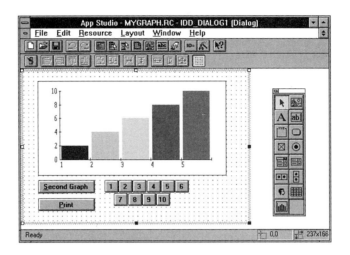

Figure 31.24.
Adding 10 buttons
to the dialog box.

☐ Edit the OnButton1() function that you added to the MYGRAVW.CPP file. After you edit the OnButton1() function, it looks as follows:

```
void CMygraphView::OnButton1()
{
// TODO: Add your control notification
// handler code here

    ///////////////////////
    // MY CODE STARTS HERE
    ///////////////////////

    m_graph->SetNumProperty("GraphType",1);

    // Draw it
    m_graph->SetNumProperty("DrawMode",2);

    ///////////////////////
    // MY CODE ENDS HERE
    ///////////////////////

}
```

The code you typed sets GraphType to 1:

```
m_graph->SetNumProperty("GraphType",1);
```

Setting the GraphType to 1 makes the graph a 2D pie graph. However, just changing the GraphType doesn't cause the graph to be redrawn. The graph is redrawn by this statement:

```
m_graph->SetNumProperty("DrawMode",2);
```

1067

To summarize, when the user clicks the 1 button the graph will be redrawn as a 2D pie graph.

☐ Use ClassWizard to add functions for the rest of the nine buttons:

Class Name:	CMygraphView
Object ID:	IDC_BUTTON_?
Message:	BN_CLICK
Function Name:	OnButton?()

☐ After you add these nine functions to the MYGRAVW.CPP file, they look as follows:

```
void CMygraphView::OnButton2()
{
// TODO: Add your control notification handler code here

        ////////////////////////
        // MY CODE STARTS HERE
        ////////////////////////

        m_graph->SetNumProperty("GraphType",2);

        // Draw it
        m_graph->SetNumProperty("DrawMode",2);


        ////////////////////////
        // MY CODE ENDS HERE
        ////////////////////////

}

void CMygraphView::OnButton3()
{
// TODO: Add your control notification handler code here

        ////////////////////////
        // MY CODE STARTS HERE
        ////////////////////////

        m_graph->SetNumProperty("GraphType",3);

        // Draw it
        m_graph->SetNumProperty("DrawMode",2);


        ////////////////////////
        // MY CODE ENDS HERE
        ////////////////////////
```

```
}
void CMygraphView::OnButton4()
{
// TODO: Add your control notification handler code here

        /////////////////////
        // MY CODE STARTS HERE
        /////////////////////

        m_graph->SetNumProperty("GraphType",4);

    // Draw it
        m_graph->SetNumProperty("DrawMode",2);


        /////////////////////
        // MY CODE ENDS HERE
        /////////////////////


}
void CMygraphView::OnButton5()
{
// TODO: Add your control notification handler code here


        /////////////////////
        // MY CODE STARTS HERE
        /////////////////////

        m_graph->SetNumProperty("GraphType",5);

        // Draw it
        m_graph->SetNumProperty("DrawMode",2);


        /////////////////////
        // MY CODE ENDS HERE
        /////////////////////

}
void CMygraphView::OnButton6()
{
// TODO: Add your control notification handler code here


        /////////////////////
        // MY CODE STARTS HERE
        /////////////////////
```

```
        m_graph->SetNumProperty("GraphType",6);

        // Draw it
        m_graph->SetNumProperty("DrawMode",2);


        ////////////////////
        // MY CODE ENDS HERE
        ////////////////////

}
void CMygraphView::OnButton7()
{
// TODO: Add your control notification handler code here


        ////////////////////
        // MY CODE STARTS HERE
        ////////////////////

        m_graph->SetNumProperty("GraphType",7);

      // Draw it
        m_graph->SetNumProperty("DrawMode",2);


        ////////////////////
        // MY CODE ENDS HERE
        ////////////////////

}
void CMygraphView::OnButton8()
{
// TODO: Add your control notification handler code here


        ////////////////////
        // MY CODE STARTS HERE
        ////////////////////

        m_graph->SetNumProperty("GraphType",8);

        // Draw it
        m_graph->SetNumProperty("DrawMode",2);


        ////////////////////
        // MY CODE ENDS HERE
        ////////////////////
```

```
}
void CMygraphView::OnButton9()
{
// TODO: Add your control notification handler code here

        //////////////////////
        // MY CODE STARTS HERE
        //////////////////////

        m_graph->SetNumProperty("GraphType",9);

        // Draw it
        m_graph->SetNumProperty("DrawMode",2);


        //////////////////////
        // MY CODE ENDS HERE
        //////////////////////

}

void CMygraphView::OnButton10()
{
// TODO: Add your control notification handler code here

        //////////////////////
        // MY CODE STARTS HERE
        //////////////////////

        m_graph->SetNumProperty("GraphType",10);

        // Draw it
        m_graph->SetNumProperty("DrawMode",2);


        //////////////////////
        // MY CODE ENDS HERE
        //////////////////////

}
```

☐ The code that you typed sets the GraphType property in accordance with the button that was clicked, and then the DrawMode property is set to 2 to redraw the graph. For example, when the 2 button is clicked, GraphType is set to 2; when the 3 button is clicked, GraphType is set to 3; and so on.

☐ Compile/link and execute the MyGraph application.

☐ Click the Second Graph button.

☐ Click button 1 and notice that the graph appears as a 2D pie graph.

☐ Click the other buttons and notice that the graph appears as shown in Figures 31.25 through 31.34.

Figure 31.25.
2D pie graph
(button 1).

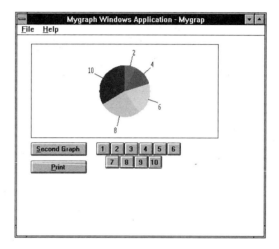

Figure 31.26.
3D pie graph
(button 2).

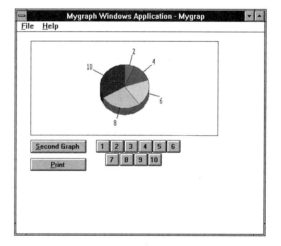

*Figure 31.27.
2D bar graph
(button 3). The
default graph.*

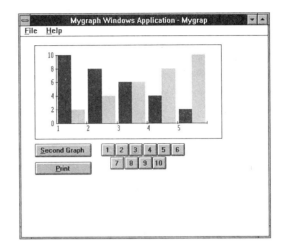

*Figure 31.28.
3D bar graph
(button 4).*

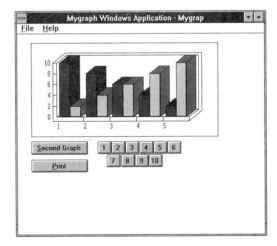

Figure 31.29.
Gantt graph
(button 5).

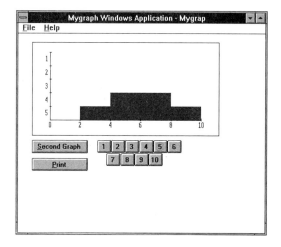

Figure 31.30.
Line graph
(button 6).

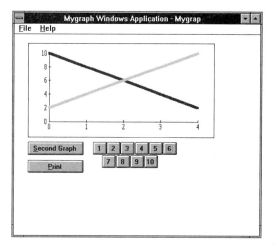

Figure 31.31.
Log graph
(button 7).

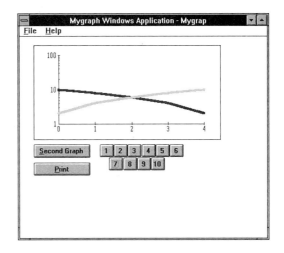

Figure 31.32.
Area graph
(button 8).

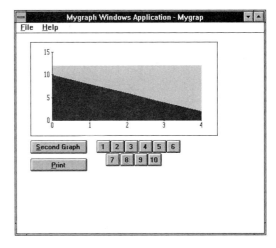

Figure 31.33.
Scatter graph
(button 9).

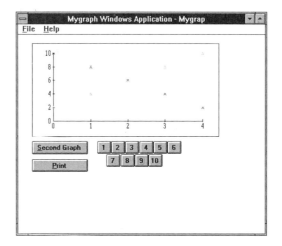

Figure 31.34.
Polar graph
(button 10).

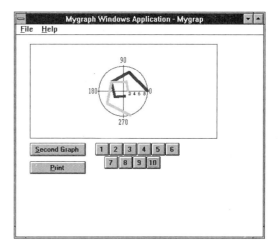

Attaching Code to the GRAPH Control

The GRAPH control has events associated with it, just like any other control (for example, a push button). To see the message events of the GRAPH control:

☐ Select ClassWizard from Visual C++'s Browse menu, select `CMygraphView` as the Class Name and then select `IDC_GRAPH1` as the Object ID.

The resulting ClassWizard dialog box is shown in Figure 31.35.

Figure 31.35.
IDC_GRAPH1's
messages.

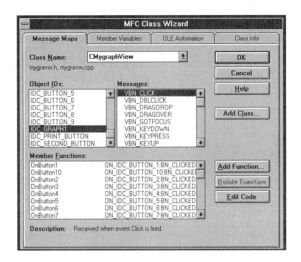

☐ Use ClassWizard to add a function for the event:

Class Name:	CMygraphView
Object ID:	IDC_GRAPH1
Message:	BN_CLICK
Function Name:	OnClickGraph1()

NOTE: Make sure that you're adding the function to the CMygraphView class.

☐ Edit the OnClickGraph1() function that you added to the MYGRAVW.CPP file.
   After you edit the OnClickGraph1() function, it looks as follows:

```
void CMygraphView::OnClickGraph1(UINT, int, CWnd*, LPVOID)
{
// TODO: Add your VBX event notification handler code here

    ///////////////////////
    // MY CODE STARTS HERE
    ///////////////////////


    // Clear the graph
    m_graph->SetNumProperty("DrawMode",1);


    ///////////////////////
    // MY CODE ENDS HERE
    ///////////////////////

}
```

The code you typed sets the DrawMode property to 1. This causes the graph to clear.

☐ Compile/link and execute the MyGraph application.

☐ Click the Second Graph button.

　　MyGraph responds by displaying the two sets of points.

☐ Click in the graph area.

　　MyGraph responds by clearing the graph.

☐ Experiment with the MyGraph application and then select Exit from the File menu to terminate the application.

NOTE

Depending on your particular version of Visual C++, the ClassWizard window may or may not display the GRAPH control's messages. If not, you won't be able to attach the OnClickGraph1() function. If this happens, you need to remove the GRAPH.VBX control and then reinstall it. Microsoft is expected to fix this problem in future versions of the package.

To remove a VBX control:

　　Remove the control from the dialog box (you can't use App Studio to remove a control if that control is used in the dialog box).

　　Select Install Controls from the File menu, highlight the control that you want to remove from App Studio, and then click the Remove button.

　　Click the Close button in the Install Controls dialog box.

32

3D Controls: Push Buttons

In this chapter you'll learn
how to incorporate three-
dimensional (3D) button
controls into your Visual
C++ programs.

Why should you use a 3D button control and not the regular 2D button control? For cosmetic reasons: an application that contains 3D controls is prettier and more pleasant to work with. One of the most exciting features of a 3D button is the fact that you can display a bitmap in it with great ease. You'll have a chance to see such a button in this chapter.

What Is the THREED.VBX Control?

The THREED.VBX control is a file that enables you to easily incorporate 3D controls into your applications.

The THREED.VBX control was designed to work with the Microsoft Visual Basic for Windows package as well as with the Microsoft Visual C++ package. In this chapter you will learn how to use the THREED.VBX control from within your Visual C++ programs.

NOTE

In order for an application that uses the THREED.VBX control to work, the `THREED.VBX` file must reside in any of the following directories:

The `\WINDOWS\SYSTEM` directory.

Any directory that's within the DOS PATH.

The directory where the application resides.

Typically, you copy this file to the `\WINDOWS\SYSTEM` directory because this way other applications can also use the file, and your program doesn't depend on the current setting of the user's DOS PATH.

The My3D Application

Now you'll write the My3D application. The My3D application utilizes the THREED control to create 3D controls in your Visual C++ applications.

Before you start writing the My3D application, execute the copy of it that resides in your `C:\VCPROG\ORIGINAL\CH32\MY3D` directory.

To execute the My3D application:

☐ Use Run from the Program Manager's File menu to execute
`C:\VCPROG\ORIGINAL\CH32\MY3D\My3D.EXE`.

Windows responds by executing the My3D application. The main window of My3D.EXE appears, as shown in Figure 32.1.

*Figure 32.1.
The My3D
application's main
window.*

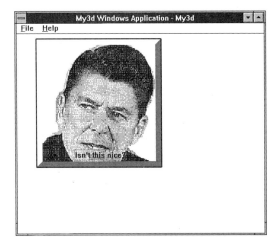

As you can see, the main window of the application contains a 3D button with a picture of President Reagan.

The My3D application has two popup menus: File and Help. These popup menus are shown in Figures 32.2 and 32.3.

*Figure 32.2.
The My3D
application's File
popup menu.*

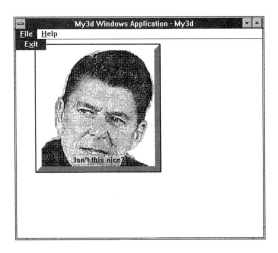

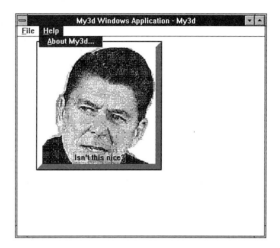

*Figure 32.3.
The My3D
application's Help
popup menu.*

☐ Click the button of the My3D application (the button has a picture of President Reagan on it).

  My3D responds by playing through the PC speaker one of Reagan's speeches.

☐ Experiment with the My3D application and then select exit from the File menu to terminate the application.

Now that you know what the My3D application does, you can start writing it.

Creating the Project of the My3D Application

To create the project of the My3D application:

☐ Select AppWizard from the Project menu.

  Visual C++ responds by running AppWizard.

☐ Use the Directory list box to select the directory C:\VCPROG\PRACTICE\CH32.

☐ Type my3d in the Project Name box.

Now your AppWizard dialog box looks as shown in Figure 32.4.

Figure 32.4.
The My3D
application's
AppWizard dialog
box.

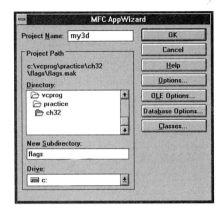

☐ Click the Options button and set the options as shown in Figure 32.5.

WARNING

Because you want the My3D application to support a VBX control (namely, the THREED.VBX control), the Custom VBX Controls option should be checked. As you can see from Figure 32.5, the Custom VBX Controls check box is indeed checked.

Figure 32.5.
Setting the options
for the My3D
application.

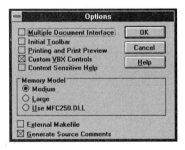

☐ Click the Options dialog box's OK button, click the OK button of the AppWizard dialog box, and finally click the Create button of the New Application Information dialog box.

> *AppWizard responds by creating the My3D project and all the skeleton files of the My3D application.*

To remove the debug options of the project (so that you'll have a small EXE file):

☐ Select Project from Visual C++'s Options menu, click the Release radio button, and then click the OK button of the dialog box.

> **NOTE**
>
> In your future projects, if you ever forget to set the Custom VBX Controls option in AppWizard's Options dialog box, you can still make your application support VBX files without starting AppWizard all over again. You do that by adding the statement: `EnableVBX();` in the `InitInstance()` function of the main application's source file.
>
> When you set the Custom VBX Controls option in AppWizard, this statement is automatically added to the `InitInstance()` function. You can verify this as follows:
>
> Open the main application file of the My3D application (`MY3D.CPP`).
>
> Look for the `EnableVBX()` statement in the `InitInstance()` function.

Creating the Form of the Application

As shown in Figure 32.1, the main window of the My3D application contains a 3D push button control.

To implement this form you'll replace the current view class of the application with a new view class derived from the `CFormView` class.

Follow these steps to create the form of the application:

☐ Use the Windows File Manager (or DOS Shell) to delete the two view class files of the My3D application:

> Delete `C:\VCPROG\PRACTICE\CH32\MY3D\MY3DVIEW.CPP`.
> Delete `C:\VCPROG\PRACTICE\CH32\MY3D\MY3DVIEW.H`.

☐ Select ClassWizard from Visual C++'s Browse menu.

> *ClassWizard responds by displaying a dialog box telling you that the view class files don't exist.*

☐ Click the dialog box's OK button.

☐ Click the Remove button of the Repair Class Information dialog box.

☐ Click the OK button of ClassWizard's dialog box.

You've just finished removing the view class of the My3D application.

In the following steps you'll create a dialog box, you'll create a CFormView type class for this dialog box, and you'll make this class the new view class of the application.

☐ Select App Studio from Visual C++'s Tools menu.

☐ Create a new dialog box with App Studio.

☐ Double-click in a free area of the new dialog box.

☐ Select Styles from the drop-down list box at the upper-right corner of the Properties window.

☐ Set the Styles properties of the dialog box as follows:

☐ Select Child in the Style box.

☐ Select None in the Border box.

☐ Uncheck the Visible property (that is, remove the check mark from the Visible check box).

☐ Select General from the drop-down list box at the upper-right corner of the Properties window and make sure the Caption box is empty.

Now, connect the dialog box to a class derived from CFormView:

☐ Select ClassWizard from the Resource menu of App Studio.

ClassWizard responds by displaying the Add Class dialog box.

☐ Type CMy3dView in the Class Name box.

☐ Set the Class Type to CFormView.

☐ Make sure the header filename is my3dview.h and that the implementation filename is my3d.

☐ Click the Create Class button.

☐ Click the OK button of ClassWizard's window to go back to App Studio.

You've finished creating the new view class of the application. This view class is a derived class from the MFC CFormView class, and it's connected to the dialog box that you created. Thus, the main dialog box of the application will be the dialog box that you created.

The Visual Implementation of the My3D Dialog Box

The control you have to place in of the My3D application dialog box is the THREED.VBX control. Before you can place the 3D control in a dialog box, you must install the THREED.VBX control in App Studio's Tools window. After you install the THREED.VBX control, several 3D controls will appear in App Studio's Tools window. Then you can place these tools in a dialog box just as you would place any other control (for example, a 2D push button or an edit box).

☐ Select Install Controls from App Studio's File menu.

> *App Studio responds by displaying the Install Controls dialog box (see Figure 32.6).*

Figure 32.6.
App Studio's Install Controls dialog box.

As you can see from Figure 32.6, App Studio lists all the VBX files that reside in your \WINDOWS\SYSTEM directory. The Installed Files list displays the names of all the VBX files currently installed in App Studio. In Figure 32.6, the Installed Files list is empty because no VBX files have been installed yet.

To install the THREED.VBX file:

☐ Select the file THREED.VBX, and then click the Install button.

> *App Studio responds by adding THREED.VBX to the Installed Files list.*

☐ Click the Close button of the Install Controls dialog box.

The THREED.VBX controls are now installed in App Studio's Tools window (see Figure 32.7). You can now place the THREED.VBX controls in the dialog box, just as you place any other control.

NOTE

After you install the `THREED.VBX` file, the Tools window appears with six additional 3D controls.

3D check box
3D option button
3D panel
3D frame
3D button

Figure 32.7.
The
THREED.VBX
controls.

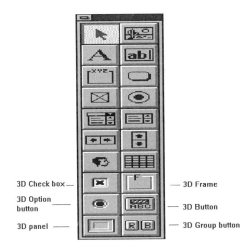

□ Implement the dialog box of the My3d application per Table 32.1.

Table 32.1. The My3d application's dialog box.

Class Name:	`CMy3DView`
Figure:	32.8
OK button:	No
Cancel button:	No

continues

Table 32.1. continued

Object	Property	Setting
Dialog Box	ID	IDD_DIALOG1
	Size	Drag the handles of the dialog box in the horizontal and vertical directions to make it wider and longer.
3D Button	ID	IDC_COMMAND3D1
	Size	Drag the handles of the control in the horizontal and vertical directions to make it wider and longer.

Now your dialog box looks as shown in Figure 32.8.

*Figure 32.8.
The My3D
application's dialog
box.*

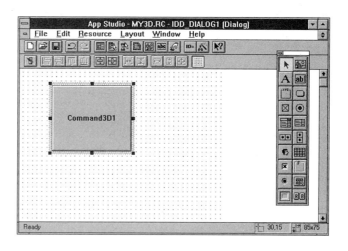

The 3D button control that you placed in the dialog box has many properties. To see these properties:

☐ Double-click the 3D button control that you placed in the dialog box.

App Studio responds by displaying the General properties of the 3D control.

☐ Select Styles from the drop-down list box at the upper-right corner of the Properties window.

App Studio responds by displaying the Styles Properties window of the 3D button control (see Figure 32.9).

Figure 32.9.
The 3D control's
Styles Properties
window.

As you can see from Figure 32.9, the 3D button control has many properties. (You'll have a chance to change the properties of the 3D button later in this chapter. For now, don't change any of its properties, not even its Caption property.)

To appreciate the 3D button, you have to see it with a regular 2D button.

☐ Place a regular 2D button in the dialog box as shown in Figure 32.10. (Don't worry about the ID of the 2D button, because you're going to delete it soon enough.)

Figure 32.10.
Placing a 3D and a
2D control in the
dialog box.

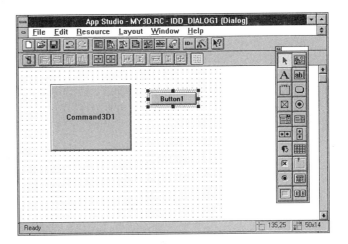

Save your work:

☐ Select Save from App Studio's File menu.

The Visual Implementation of the Menu

☐ The My3D application has a menu with two popup menus as shown in Figures 32.2 and 32.3. Use App Studio to implement the My3D application menu per Table 32.2.

Table 32.2. The My3D application's menu.
Figures relating to menu: 32.2, 32.3

Menu Item
&File
E&xit
&Help
&About My3d...

Don't forget to delete the accelerator keys of the menu items you removed:

☐ Select `MY3D.RC [MFC-Resource Script]` from App Studio's Window menu, select Accelerator from the Type list, and then double-click `IDR_MAINFRAME` in the Resources list.

☐ Delete the accelerator keys that aren't used by the MY3D application. In particular, delete the accelerator keys of the `ID_FILE_NEW`, `ID_FILE_OPEN`, and `ID_FILE_SAVE` menu items.

If you don't delete these accelerator keys, they'll be active during runtime. If the user presses Ctrl+N, for example, it will be like selecting New from the File menu, even though you deleted that menu item.

Save your work:

☐ Select Save from App Studio's File menu.

The visual implementation of the My3D application's menu is complete.

Executing the My3D Application

Although you haven't written a single line of code for the My3D application, execute it to see your visual design in action.

☐ Select Build All MY3D.EXE from Visual C++'s Project menu.

☐ Select Execute MY3D.EXE from the Project menu.

> *Visual C++ responds by executing the My3D application. The main window of the application appears with the form that you designed in it (see Figure 32.11).*

☐ Click the 2D and 3D buttons.

Of course, nothing happens when you click these buttons, because you didn't attach any code to them. Also, it doesn't look as if the 3D button is any different than the 2D button!

☐ Select Exit from the File menu to terminate the My3D application.

Figure 32.11.
The My3D
application with a
2D button and a
3D button in its
main window.

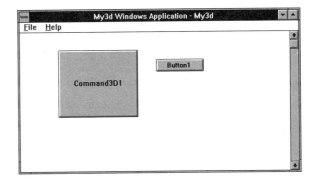

Initializing the Properties of the 3D Button Control

As shown in Figure 32.11, both buttons are currently two-dimensional.

☐ Use App Studio to display the dialog box in its design mode.

☐ Double-click the 3D button control.

App Studio responds by displaying the Properties window of the 3D button control.

☐ Select Styles from the drop-down list in the upper-right corner of the Properties window and then select the BevelWidth property.

☐ Set the BevelWidth property to 10, as shown in Figure 32.12.

Figure 32.12.
Setting the
BevelWidth
property.

The BevelWidth property represents the thickness of the button (see Figure 32.13). The higher the number, the "thicker" the button.

Figure 32.13.
The dialog box (in design mode) after the BevelWidth property is set to 10.

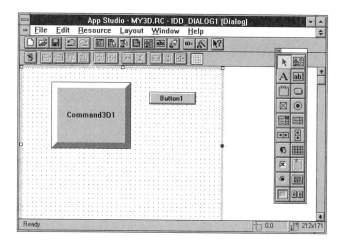

NOTE

One of the advantages of using Visual C++ is the fact that you can see your visual design in action without the need to compile/link the program. To see how your visual design looks without linking the application:

Select Test from App Studio's Resource menu.

App Studio responds by displaying the dialog box as it will look during execution time.

To exit from the Test:

Press the Esc key.

Now that you know that the 3D button is indeed a three-dimensional button, you can delete the 2D button.

Setting the Caption Property of the 3D Button

Now you'll set the Caption property of the 3D button:

☐ Set the Caption property of the 3D button to `Isn't this nice?`

You can now set the font of the 3D button to bold by setting the FontBold property to True. In a similar manner, you can change the font of the caption by setting the FontItalic property to True, as well as all the other properties that start with the characters *Font.*

An interesting property of the 3D button is the Font3D property. To see this property in action:

☐ Select the Font3D property and then click the down-arrow icon that appears on the right side of the Property Value box.

App Studio responds by dropping down a list of 3D font options (see Figure 32.14).

Figure 32.14.
Setting the Font3D
property.

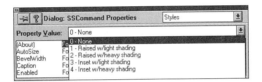

☐ Select the 2-Raised w/heavy shading option for the Font3D property, and then select Test from the Resource menu to see your visual design in action.

App Studio responds by displaying the dialog box, as shown in Figure 32.15.

NOTE: In Figure 32.15, the button's caption doesn't look raised with heavy shading; however, on your monitor this 3D font will be more noticeable.

NOTE

Don't fall into the trap of assigning a too-fancy font to the caption of the button. By selecting the FontSize property, you can assign to the button's caption any font that your version of Windows supports. App Studio will respond by displaying a dialog box in which you select the font and the size. For example, Figure 32.16 shows the 3D button after the Dom Casual font was assigned. However, not all PCs support this font. This means that when the application is executed on a PC that doesn't support this font, Windows will automatically substitute the font that is closest to the Dom Casual font. This may confuse your users if you display a picture of the button in your manual (with the Dom Casual font), because they'll see a different font on their monitors. So be safe and use only popular fonts that most people own. (For example, the system font is always available.)

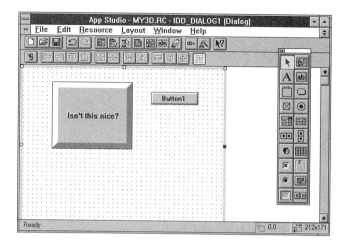

*Figure 32.15.
The 3D button's
caption after the
Font3D property is
set to the "Raised w/
heavy shading"
option.*

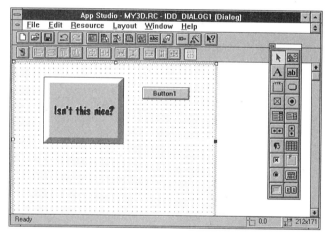

*Figure 32.16.
Using the FontSize
property to assign
the Dom Casual
font to the 3D
button's caption.*

☐ Compile/link and execute the My3D application.

The My3D application responds by displaying the 3D button as you designed it in App Studio.

☐ Select Exit from the File menu to terminate the My3D application.

Using Bitmaps for the 3D Button

So far, you've assigned text to the button's caption. Is it possible to assign a picture to the 3D button? Yes. Next you'll assign a picture of President Reagan (shown in Figure 32.17) to the 3D button.

Figure 32.17.
President Reagan's
picture used as the
bitmap for the 3D
button.

Here's how you assign bitmaps to the 3D button:

☐ Double-click the 3D button control to display its Properties window and
select the Picture property.

> *App Studio responds by displaying* (none) *in the Property Value box (see*
> *Figure 32.18).*

Figure 32.18.
Assigning a value to
the 3D button's
Picture property.

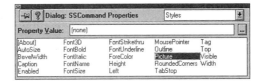

☐ Click the three dots that appear to the right of the Property Value.

> *App Studio responds by displaying the Open dialog box (see Figure 32.19).*

☐ Select the file C:\VCPROG\BMP\REAGAN1.BMP and then click the OK button in
the Open dialog box.

Figure 32.19.
Selecting the
C:\VCPROG\BMP
\REAGAN1.BMP
· file.

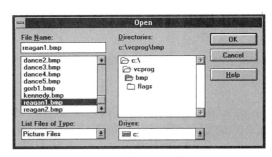

App Studio responds by placing the bitmap in the 3D button (see Figure 32.20).

Figure 32.20.
Placing the
Reagan1.BMP
picture in the 3D
button.

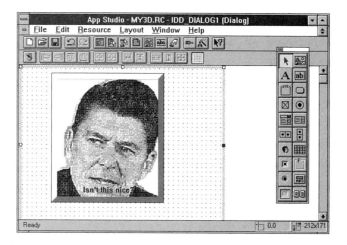

☐ Enlarge the 3D button so that it will fit around the picture, as shown in Figure 32.20.

☐ Save your work (select Save from App Studio's File menu).

☐ Compile/link the My3D application, and then execute it.

The main window of the My3D application appears, as shown in Figure 32.21.

Figure 32.21.
The My3D
application window
with a button
containing
President Reagan's
picture.

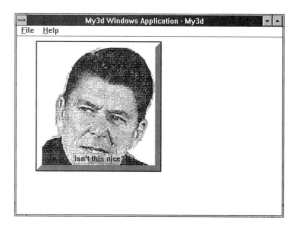

Attaching Code to the 3D Button

As stated at the beginning of this chapter, the 3D controls are provided for cosmetic reasons only. You attach code to these controls in much the same way you attach code to regular 2D controls.

Now you can attach code to the 3D button. When you click the 3D button, the code that you'll attach will play through the PC speaker one of President Reagan's speeches.

Because the speech will be played through the PC speaker, you need to use the IMPORTS statements in the MY3D.DEF file.

☐ Open the MY3D.DEF file and modify it. After the modification, your MY3D.DEF file looks as follows:

```
; my3d.def : Declares the module parameters for the application.

NAME        MY3D
DESCRIPTION 'MY3D Windows Application'
EXETYPE     WINDOWS

CODE        PRELOAD MOVEABLE DISCARDABLE
DATA        PRELOAD MOVEABLE MULTIPLE

HEAPSIZE    1024   ; initial heap size
; Stack size is passed as argument to linker's /STACK option


;;;;;;;;;;;;;;;;;;;;;;;;;;
; MY CODE STARTS HERE
;;;;;;;;;;;;;;;;;;;;;;;;;;

;;;;;;;;;;;;;;;;;;;;;;;;;;;;;;;;;;;;;;;;;;;;;;;;;
; sp_ functions from the TegoSND.DLL library
;;;;;;;;;;;;;;;;;;;;;;;;;;;;;;;;;;;;;;;;;;;;;;;;;

IMPORTS
TegoSND.sp_OpenSession
TegoSND.sp_PlaySnd
TegoSND.sp_MouseOn
TegoSND.sp_MouseOff
TegoSND.sp_CloseSession


;;;;;;;;;;;;;;;;;;;;;;;;;;
; MY CODE ENDS HERE
;;;;;;;;;;;;;;;;;;;;;;;;;;
```

☐ Open the MY3D.H file and add the #include TegoSND.H statement of the TegoSND.DLL. After you add this #include statement, the beginning of your MY3D.H file looks as follows:

```
// my3d.h : main header file for the MY3D application
//

#ifndef __AFXWIN_H__
#error include 'stdafx.h' before including this file for PCH
#endif

#include "resource.h"        // main symbols

////////////////////////
// MY CODE STARTS HERE
////////////////////////

#include "\vcProg\DLL\TegoSND.H"

////////////////////////
// MY CODE ENDS HERE
////////////////////////

. . . . .
. . . . .
. . . . .
```

☐ Add a data member variable (m_ReaganSession) to the class declaration of the CMy3dView class that resides in the MY3DVIEW.H file. After you add the m_ReaganSession variable, the class declaration looks as follows:

```
class CMy3dView : public CFormView
{
    DECLARE_DYNCREATE(CMy3dView)
protected:
    CMy3dView();
// protected constructor used by dynamic creation

// Form Data
public:
    //{{AFX_DATA(CMy3dView)
    enum { IDD = IDD_DIALOG1 };
        // Note: the ClassWizard will add data members here
    //}}AFX_DATA

// Attributes
public:
```

```
///////////////////////
// MY CODE STARTS HERE
///////////////////////

int m_ReaganSession;

///////////////////////
// MY CODE ENDS HERE
///////////////////////

// Operations
public:

// Implementation
protected:
    virtual ~CMy3dView();
    virtual void DoDataExchange(CDataExchange* pDX);
// DDX/DDV support
    // Generated message map functions
    //{{AFX_MSG(CMy3dView)
// NOTE - the ClassWizard will add and remove
// member functions here.
    //}}AFX_MSG
    DECLARE_MESSAGE_MAP()
};
```

You now have to open a sound session for the 8Reagan.WAV file:

☐ Open the MY3DVIEW.CPP file and add code to the constructor function of the View class that opens a WAV session for the 8Reagan.WAV file. After you add the code, the constructor function looks as follows:

```
CMy3dView::CMy3dView()
     : CFormView(CMy3dView::IDD)
{
//{{AFX_DATA_INIT(CMy3dView)
// Note: the ClassWizard will add member initialization here
//}}AFX_DATA_INIT

    ///////////////////////
    // MY CODE STARTS HERE
    ///////////////////////

    char FileToOpen[255];


    // Open the 8Reagan WAV session
    strcpy ( FileToOpen, "\\vcProg\\WAV\\8Reagan.WAV" );
    m_ReaganSession = sp_OpenSession ( FileToOpen );
```

```
    // If WAV session cannot be opened, display message box.
    if ( m_ReaganSession < 0 )
        {
         CString Message, Caption;
         Message = "Can't open the file: ";
         Message = Message + FileToOpen;
         Caption = "Error";
         MessageBox ( Message, Caption );
        }

 ///////////////////////
 // MY CODE ENDS HERE
 ///////////////////////

}
```

☐ Close the WAV session by adding code to the destructor function of the View class that resides in the My3D.CPP file. After you add the code, the destructor function looks as follows:

```
CMy3dView::~CMy3dView()
{

    ///////////////////////
    // MY CODE STARTS HERE
    ///////////////////////

    sp CloseSession ( m_ReaganSession );

    ///////////////////////,
    // MY CODE ENDS HERE
    ///////////////////////

}
```

The My3D application now has all the code that it needs to play President Reagan's speech.

Use ClassWizard to add a function for the event:

Class Name:	CMy3DView
Object ID:	IDC_COMMAND3D1
Message:	VBN_CLICK
Function Name:	OnClickCommand3D1()

NOTE: Make sure you're adding the function to the CMy3dView class (see Figure 32.22).

Figure 32.22.
Attaching code to
the 3D button's
VBN_CLICK
event.

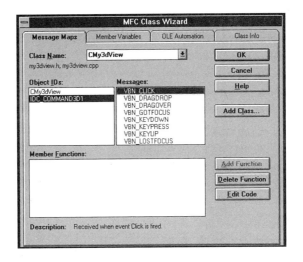

☐ Edit the OnClickCommand3d1() function that you added to the MY3DVIEW.CPP file. After you edit the function, it looks as follows:

```
void CMy3dView::OnClickCommand3d1(UINT, int, CWnd*, LPVOID)
{
// TODO: Add your VBX event notification handler code here

        /////////////////////////
        // MY CODE STARTS HERE
        /////////////////////////

        // Play the Reagan speech
        sp_PlaySnd ( m_ReaganSession,
                    SP_START_OF_FILE,
                    SP_END_OF_FILE);

        ////////////////////////
        // MY CODE ENDS HERE
        ////////////////////////

}
```

☐ Compile/link and execute the My3D application.

The main window of My3D appears with the picture of President Reagan as the 3D button's bitmap.

☐ Click the 3D button.

My3D responds by playing through the PC speaker a speech made by President Reagan.

☐ Select Exit from the File menu to terminate the application.

The Flags Application

The Flags application illustrates how to use 3D controls to create an encyclopedia-type application.

> **NOTE**
>
> The Flags application plays MIDI files. Thus, to execute the Flags application, your PC must have a sound card that is capable of playing MIDI files.
>
> If your PC doesn't have a sound card, just browse through the rest of this chapter.

Before you start writing the Flags application, execute the copy of it that resides in your `C:\VCPROG\ORIGINAL\CH32\FLAGS` directory.

To execute the Flags application:

☐ Use Run from Program Manager's File menu to execute
`C:\VCPROG\ORIGINAL\CH32\FLAGS\Flags.EXE`.

Windows responds by executing the Flags application. The main window of
`Flags.EXE` *appears, as shown in Figure 32.23.*

Figure 32.23.
The Flags
application's main
window.

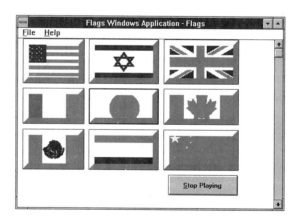

As you can see, the main window of the application contains 3D buttons with flags from several countries.

The Flags application has two popup menus: File and Help. These popup menus are shown in Figures 32.24 and 32.25.

*Figure 32.24.
The Flags
application's File
popup menu.*

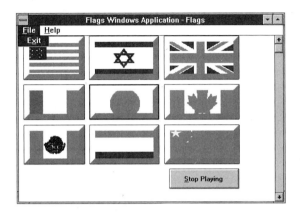

*Figure 32.25.
The Flags
application's Help
popup menu.*

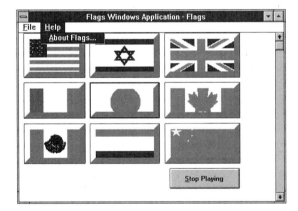

☐ Click the Flags application's 3D buttons.

> *Flags responds by playing the national anthem of the country whose flag you clicked.*

Experiment with the Flags application and then select exit from File menu to terminate the application.

Now that you know what the Flags application does, you can start writing it.

Creating the Project of the Flags Application

To create the project of the Flags application:

☐ Select AppWizard from the Project menu.

    Visual C++ responds by running AppWizard.

☐ Use the Directory list box to select the directory `C:\VCPROG\PRACTICE\CH32`.

☐ Type `flags` in the Project Name box.

Now your AppWizard dialog box looks as shown in Figure 32.26.

Figure 32.26.
The Flags application's AppWizard dialog box.

☐ Click the Options button and set the options as shown in Figure 32.27.

Figure 32.27.
Setting the options for the Flags application.

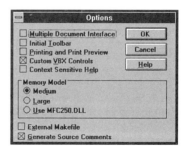

WARNING

Because you want the Flags application to support a VBX control (namely, the THREED.VBX control), the Custom VBX Controls option should be checked. As you can see from Figure 32.27, the Custom VBX Controls check box is checked.

☐ Click the Options dialog box's OK button, click the OK button of the AppWizard dialog box, and finally click the Create button of the New Application Information dialog box.

> *AppWizard responds by creating the Flags project and all the skeleton files of the Flags application.*

To remove the debug options of the project (so that you'll have a small EXE file):

☐ Select Project from Visual C++'s Options menu, click the Release radio button, and then click the OK button of the dialog box.

Creating the Form of the Application

As shown in Figure 32.23, the main window of the Flags application contains 3D push button controls.

To implement this form you'll replace the current view class of the application with a new view class derived from the `CFormView` class.

Follow these steps to create the form of the application:

☐ Use the Windows File Manager (or DOS Shell) to delete the view class file of the Flags application:

> Delete `C:\VCPROG\PRACTICE\CH32\FLAGS\FLAGSVW.CPP`.

☐ Select ClassWizard from Visual C++'s Browse menu.

> *ClassWizard responds by displaying a dialog box telling you that the view class files don't exist.*

☐ Click the dialog box's OK button.

☐ Click the Remove button of the Repair Class Information dialog box.

☐ Click the OK button of ClassWizard's dialog box.

You've just finished removing the view class of the Flags application.

1105

In the following steps you'll create a dialog box, you'll create a CFormView type class for this dialog box, and you'll make this class the new view class of the application:

☐ Select App Studio from Visual C++'s Tools menu.

☐ Create a new dialog box with App Studio.

☐ Double-click in a free area of the new dialog box.

☐ Select Styles from the drop-down list box at the upper-right corner of the Properties window.

Set the Styles properties of the dialog box as follows:

☐ Select Child in the Style box.

☐ Select None in the Border box.

☐ Uncheck the Visible property (that is, remove the check mark from the Visible check box).

☐ Select General from the drop-down list box at the upper-right corner of the Properties window and make sure that the Caption box is empty.

Now, connect the dialog box to a class derived from CFormView:

☐ Select ClassWizard from App Studio's Resource menu.

   ClassWizard responds by displaying the Add Class dialog box.

☐ Type CFlagsView in the Class Name box.

☐ Set the Class Type to CFormView.

☐ Type in the Header File edit box flagsvw.h.

☐ Type in the Implementation File edit box flagsvw.cpp.

☐ Click the Create Class button.

☐ Click the OK button of ClassWizard's window to go back to App Studio.

You've finished creating the new view class of the application. This view class is a derived class from the MFC CFormView class, and it's connected to the dialog box that you created. Thus, the main dialog box of the application will be the dialog box that you created.

The Visual Implementation of the Flags Dialog Box

The visual implementation of the dialog box requires that your App Studio Tool window includes the TegoMM.VBX control and the 3D button control (THREED.VBX). You installed the THREED.VBX file at the beginning of this chapter. (See Figure 32.28.)

Figure 32.28.
The Tools window
with the
TegoMM.VBX and
THREED.VBX
controls.

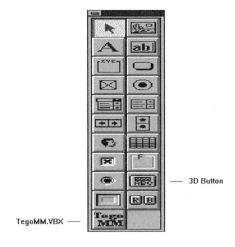

— 3D Button

TegoMM.VBX —

☐ Implement the dialog box of the Flags application per Table 32.3.

Table 32.3. The Flags application's dialog box.

Class Name:	CFlagsView
Figure:	32.29
OK button:	No
Cancel button:	No

Object	Property	Setting
Dialog Box	ID	IDD_DIALOG1
	Size	Drag the dialog box's handles horizontally and vertically so that all the flags fit in the dialog box.

continues

Table 32.3. continued

Object	Property	Setting
3D Button	ID	IDC_COMMAND3D_USA
	Picture	C:\VCPROG\BMP\FLAGS\USA.BMP
	Caption	None (No caption)
	Size	Drag the button's handles horizontally and vertically so that the flag fits in the button.
3D Button	ID	IDC_COMMAND3D_ISRAEL
	Picture	C:\VCPROG\BMP\FLAGS\ISRAEL.BMP
	Caption	None (No caption)
	Size	Drag the button's handles horizontally and vertically so that the flag fits in the button.
3D Button	ID	IDC_COMMAND3D_ENGLAND
	Picture	C:\VCPROG\BMP\FLAGS\ENGLAND.BMP
	Caption	None (No caption)
	Size	Drag the button's handles horizontally and vertically so that the flag fits in the button.
3D Button	ID	IDC_COMMAND3D_FRANCE
	Picture	C:\VCPROG\BMP\FLAGS\FRANCE.BMP
	Caption	None (No caption)
	Size	Drag the button's handles horizontally and vertically so that the flag fits in the button.
3D Button	ID	IDC_COMMAND3D_JAPAN
	Picture	C:\VCPROG\BMP\FLAGS\JAPAN.BMP
	Caption	None (No caption)
	Size	Drag the button's handles horizontally and vertically so that the flag fits in the button.
3D Button	ID	IDC_COMMAND3D_CANADA
	Picture	C:\VCPROG\BMP\FLAGS\CANADA.BMP
	Caption	None (No caption)
	Size	Drag the button's handles horizontally and vertically so that the flag fits in the button.

Object	Property	Setting
3D Button	ID	`IDC_COMMAND3D_MEXICO`
	Picture	`C:\VCPROG\BMP\FLAGS\MEXICO.BMP`
	Caption	None (No caption)
	Size	Drag the button's handles horizontally and vertically so that the flag fits in the button.
3D Button	ID	`IDC_COMMAND3D_NETHERLANDS`
	Picture	`C:\VCPROG\BMP\FLAGS\NETHERLA.BMP`
	Caption	None (No caption)
	Size	Drag the button's handles horizontally and vertically so that the flag fits in the button.
3D Button	ID	`IDC_COMMAND3D_CHINA`
	Picture	`C:\VCPROG\BMP\FLAGS\CHINA.BMP`
	Caption	None (No caption)
	Size	Drag the button's handles horizontally and vertically so that the flag fits in the button.
2D Button	ID	`IDC_STOP_BUTTON`
	Caption	`&Stop Playing`
TegoMM.VBX	ID	`IDC_TEGOMM1`
	Variable	`m_midi` (Type: `CVBControl *`)

Now your dialog box looks as shown in Figure 32.29.

Table 32.3 instructed you to attach the variable `m_midi` to the `IDC_TEGOMM1` multimedia control. `m_midi` is a variable of type `CVBControl *` (pointer to object of class `CVBControl`). As you'll see later in the chapter, when you write the application's code you'll use `m_midi` to manage the multimedia control for playing a MIDI file.

Save your work:

☐ Select Save from App Studio's File menu.

Figure 30.29.
The Flags
application's
dialog box.

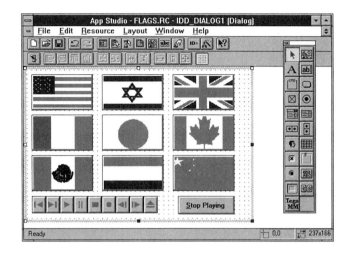

The Visual Implementation of the Flags Menu

The Flags application has a menu with two popup menus, as shown in Figures 32.24 and 32.25. To implement this menu:

☐ Use App Studio to implement the Flags application menu per Table 32.4.

Table 32.4. The Flags application's menu.
Figures relating to menu: 32.24, 32.25

Menu Item
&File
E&xit
&Help
&About Flags...

Don't forget to delete the accelerator keys of the menu items that you removed:

☐ Select FLAGS.RC [MFC-Resource Script] from App Studio's Window menu, select Accelerator from the Type list and then double-click IDR_MAINFRAME in the Resources list.

☐ Delete the accelerator keys that aren't used by the Flags application. In particular, delete the accelerator keys of the ID_FILE_NEW, ID_FILE_OPEN, and ID_FILE_SAVE menu items.

Save your work:

☐ Select Save from App Studio's File menu.

The visual implementation of the Flags application's menu is complete.

Executing the Flags Application

Although you haven't written a single line of code for the Flags application, execute it to see your visual design in action:

☐ Select Build All FLAGS.EXE from Visual C++'s Project menu.

☐ Select Execute FLAGS.EXE from the Project menu.

> *Visual C++ responds by executing the FLAGS application. The main window of the application appears with the form that you designed in it (see Figure 32.30).*

Figure 32.30.
The Flags main window.

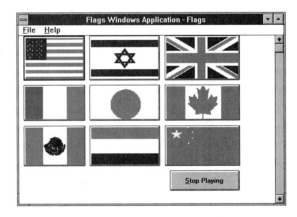

☐ Click the Flag buttons.

Of course, nothing happens when you click these buttons because you haven't attached any code to them.

☐ Select Exit from the File menu to terminate the Flags application.

Initializing the Properties of the Multimedia Control

Recall from Chapter 23, "Multimedia: Playing MIDI Files," that you write the code that initializes the properties of the multimedia control in the `OnInitialUpdate()` member function of the view class. This way, when the application starts, the multimedia control comes to life.

Because Visual C++ did not write the declaration and skeleton of the `OnInitialUpdate()` function, you have to declare it and write its skeleton. Here's how you do that:

☐ Open the file `FLAGSVW.H` and add code to it that defines the function `OnInitialUpdate()` as a member function of the `CFlagsView` class. After you write this code, the `CFlagsView` class declaration looks as follows:

```
class CFlagsView : public CFormView
{
     DECLARE_DYNCREATE(CFlagsView)
protected:
     CFlagsView();
// protected constructor used by dynamic creation


     ////////////////////////
     // MY CODE STARTS HERE
     ////////////////////////

     virtual void OnInitialUpdate();

     ////////////////////////
     // MY CODE ENDS HERE
     ////////////////////////


// Form Data
public:
     //{{AFX_DATA(CFlagsView)
     enum { IDD = IDD_DIALOG1 };
     CVBControl*     m_midi;
     //}}AFX_DATA

// Attributes
public:

// Operations
public:
```

```
// Implementation
protected:
    virtual ~CFlagsView();
    virtual void DoDataExchange(CDataExchange* pDX);
// DDX/DDV support
    // Generated message map functions
//{{AFX_MSG(CFlagsView)
// NOTE - the ClassWizard will add and remove
// member functions here.
//}}AFX_MSG
    DECLARE_MESSAGE_MAP()
};
```

Now write the code of the `OnInitialUpdate()` function:

☐ Open the file `FLAGS.CPP` and add (at the end of the file) the
`OnInitialUpdate()` function. After you write this function, the end of the
`FLAGS.CPP` file looks as follows:

```
/////////////////////
// MY CODE STARTS HERE
/////////////////////

void CFlagsView::OnInitialUpdate()
{

    // Call the base class function.
    CFormView::OnInitialUpdate();

    // Set the MCI control for playback of MIDI files.
    m_midi->SetStrProperty("DeviceType","Sequencer");

    // Make the MCI control invisible.
    m_midi->SetNumProperty("Visible",FALSE);
}

/////////////////////
// MY CODE ENDS HERE
/////////////////////
```

To review the `OnInitialUpdate()` function:

The first statement,

```
CFormView::OnInitialUpdate();
```

calls the `OnInitialUpdate()` member function of the base class. Recall that you have
to call the base class `OnInitialUpdate()` function. If you don't, the multimedia control won't be available.

The next statement sets the `DeviceType` property to `"Sequencer"`:

```
m_midi->SetStrProperty("DeviceType","Sequencer");
```

This means that the multimedia control is set to play MIDI files.

The next statement makes the multimedia control invisible by setting the `Visible` property to `FALSE`:

```
m_midi->SetNumProperty("Visible",FALSE);
```

Attaching Code to the USA Flag Button

Now you'll write code that will be executed whenever the user clicks the USA flag:

☐ Use ClassWizard to add a function for the event:

Class Name:	`CFlagsView`
Object ID:	`IDC_COMMAND3D_USA`
Message:	`VBN_CLICK`
Function Name:	`OnClickCommand3DUsa()`

NOTE: Make sure you're adding the function to the `CFlagsView` class.

☐ Edit the `OnClickCommand3dUsa()` function that you added to the `FLAGSVW.CPP` file. After you edit the `OnClickCommand3dUsa()` function, it looks as follows:

```
void CFlagsView::OnClickCommand3dUsa(UINT, int, CWnd*, LPVOID)
{
// TODO: Add your VBX event notification handler code here

    ///////////////////////////
    // MY CODE STARTS HERE
    ///////////////////////////

    // Close the MIDI device
    m_midi->SetStrProperty("Command", "Close");

    // Set the name of the MIDI file
    m_midi->SetStrProperty("FileName",
                     "\\VCPROG\\MIDI\\ANTHEMS\\USA.MID" );
    // Open the MIDI file
    m_midi->SetStrProperty("Command", "Open");

    // Rewind the MIDI file
    m_midi->SetStrProperty("Command", "Prev");
```

```
// Play the MIDI file
m_midi->SetStrProperty("Command", "Play");

//////////////////////
// MY CODE ENDS HERE
//////////////////////
```

}

The first statement closes the MIDI device:

`m_midi->SetStrProperty("Command", "Close");`

Thus, whenever you click a new flag, the previous anthem (if any) is closed.

The next statement sets the name of the MIDI file:

```
m_midi->SetStrProperty("FileName",
              "\\VCPROG\\MIDI\\ANTHEMS\\USA.MID" );
```

The next statement opens the MIDI file:

`m_midi->SetStrProperty("Command", "Open");`

Because you want to play the MIDI file from its beginning, you have to rewind the file:

`m_midi->SetStrProperty("Command", "Prev");`

And finally, the MIDI file is played:

`m_midi->SetStrProperty("Command", "Play");`

Attaching Code to the Stop Playing Button

Now you'll attach code that will be executed whenever the user clicks the Stop Playing button:

☐ Use ClassWizard to add a function for the event:

Class Name:	CFlagsView
Object ID:	IDC_STOP_COMMAND
Message:	VBN_CLICK
Function Name:	OnStopButton()

NOTE: Make sure that you are adding the function to the CFlagsView class.

☐ Edit the `OnStopButton()` function that you added to the `FLAGSVW.CPP` file. After you edit the `OnStopButton()` function, it looks as follows:

```
void CFlagsView::OnStopButton()
{
// TODO: Add your control notification handler code here

    /////////////////////////
    // MY CODE STARTS HERE
    /////////////////////////

    // Stop the playback
    m_midi->SetStrProperty("Command", "Stop");

    /////////////////////////
    // MY CODE ENDS HERE
    /////////////////////////

}
```

The statement that you typed uses the `SetStrProperty()` function to set the `Command` property to `"Stop"` (that is, to stop the playback).

☐ Compile/link and execute the Flags application.

☐ Click the USA flag button.

Flags responds by playing the national anthem.

☐ Click the Stop Playing button to stop the playback and then select Exit from the File menu to terminate the application.

Attaching Code to the Other Flag Buttons

Now you'll attach code to the other flags of the Flags application.

☐ Use ClassWizard to add a function for the event:

Class Name:	CFlagsView
Object ID:	IDC_COMMAND3D_ISRAEL
Message:	VBN_CLICK
Function Name:	OnClickCommand3DIsrael()

NOTE: Make sure you add the function to the `CFlagsView` class.

☐ Edit the `OnClickCommand3dIsrael()` function that you added to the `FLAGSVW.CPP` file. After you edit the `OnClickCommand3dIsrael()` function, it looks as follows:

```
void CFlagsView::OnClickCommand3dIsrael(UINT, int, CWnd*, LPVOID)
{
    // TODO: Add your VBX event notification handler code here

    /////////////////////////
    // MY CODE STARTS HERE
    /////////////////////////

    // Close the MIDI device
    m_midi->SetStrProperty("Command", "Close");

    // Set the name of the MIDI file
    m_midi->SetStrProperty("FileName",
            "\\VCPROG\\MIDI\\ANTHEMS\\ISRAEL.MID" );

    // Open the MIDI file
    m_midi->SetStrProperty("Command", "Open");

    // Rewind the MIDI file
    m_midi->SetStrProperty("Command", "Prev");


    // Play the MIDI file
    m_midi->SetStrProperty("Command", "Play");


    /////////////////////////
    // MY CODE ENDS HERE
    /////////////////////////

}
```

☐ Use ClassWizard to add a function for the event:

Class Name:	`CFlagsView`
Object ID:	`IDC_COMMAND3D_ENGLAND`
Message:	`VBN_CLICK`
Function Name:	`OnClickCommand3DEngland()`

NOTE: Make sure you add the function to the `CFlagsView` class.

☐ Edit the `OnClickCommand3dEngland()` function that you added to the `FLAGSVW.CPP` file. After you edit the `OnClickCommand3dEngland()` function, it looks as follows:

```
void CFlagsView::OnClickCommand3dEngland(UINT, int, CWnd*, LPVOID)
{
// TODO: Add your VBX event notification handler code here

    ///////////////////////
    // MY CODE STARTS HERE
    ///////////////////////

    // Close the MIDI device
    m_midi->SetStrProperty("Command", "Close");


    // Set the name of the MIDI file
    m_midi->SetStrProperty("FileName",
                   "\\VCPROG\\MIDI\\ANTHEMS\\ENGLAND.MID" );

    // Open the MIDI file
    m_midi->SetStrProperty("Command", "Open");

    // Rewind the MIDI file
    m_midi->SetStrProperty("Command", "Prev");


    // Play the MIDI file
    m_midi->SetStrProperty("Command", "Play");


    ///////////////////////
    // MY CODE ENDS HERE
    ///////////////////////

}
```

☐ Use ClassWizard to add a function for the event:

Class Name:	CFlagsView
Object ID:	IDC_COMMAND3D_FRANCE
Message:	VBN_CLICK
Function Name:	OnClickCommand3DFrance()

NOTE: Make sure you add the function to the CFlagsView class.

☐ Edit the OnClickCommand3dFrance() function that you added to the FLAGSVW.CPP file. After you edit the OnClickCommand3dFrance() function, it looks as follows:

```
void CFlagsView::OnClickCommand3dFrance(UINT, int, CWnd*, LPVOID)
{
// TODO: Add your VBX event notification handler code here
```

```
/////////////////////
// MY CODE STARTS HERE
/////////////////////

// Close the MIDI device
m_midi->SetStrProperty("Command", "Close");


// Set the name of the MIDI file
m_midi->SetStrProperty("FileName",
              "\\VCPROG\\MIDI\\ANTHEMS\\FRANCE.MID" );

// Open the MIDI file
m_midi->SetStrProperty("Command", "Open");

// Rewind the MIDI file
m_midi->SetStrProperty("Command", "Prev");


// Play the MIDI file
m_midi->SetStrProperty("Command", "Play");


/////////////////////
// MY CODE ENDS HERE
/////////////////////

}
```

☐ Use ClassWizard to add a function for the event:

Class Name:	CFlagsView
Object ID:	IDC_COMMAND3D_JAPAN
Message:	VBN_CLICK
Function Name:	OnClickCommand3DJapan()

NOTE: Make sure you add the function to the CFlagsView class.

☐ Edit the OnClickCommand3dJapan() function that you added to the FLAGSVW.CPP file. After you edit the OnClickCommand3dJapan() function, it looks as follows:

```
void CFlagsView::OnClickCommand3dJapan(UINT, int, CWnd*, LPVOID)
{

// TODO: Add your VBX event notification handler code here

/////////////////////
// MY CODE STARTS HERE
/////////////////////
```

```
// Close the MIDI device
m_midi->SetStrProperty("Command", "Close");


// Set the name of the MIDI file
m_midi->SetStrProperty("FileName",
            "\\VCPROG\\MIDI\\ANTHEMS\\JAPAN.MID" );

// Open the MIDI file
m_midi->SetStrProperty("Command", "Open");

// Rewind the MIDI file
m_midi->SetStrProperty("Command", "Prev");


// Play the MIDI file
m_midi->SetStrProperty("Command", "Play");


/////////////////////
// MY CODE ENDS HERE
/////////////////////


}
```

☐ Use ClassWizard to add a function for the event:

Class Name:	CFlagsView
Object ID:	IDC_COMMAND3D_CANADA
Message:	VBN_CLICK
Function Name:	OnClickCommand3DCanada()

NOTE: Make sure you add the function to the CFlagsView class.

☐ Edit the OnClickCommand3DCanada() function that you added to the FLAGSVW.CPP file. After you edit the function, it looks as follows:

```
void CFlagsView::OnClickCommand3dCanada(UINT, int, CWnd*, LPVOID)
{
// TODO: Add your VBX event notification handler code here

    /////////////////////
    // MY CODE STARTS HERE
    /////////////////////

    // Close the MIDI device
    m_midi->SetStrProperty("Command", "Close");
```

```
    // Set the name of the MIDI file
    m_midi->SetStrProperty("FileName",
                "\\VCPROG\\MIDI\\ANTHEMS\\CANADA.MID" );

    // Open the MIDI file
    m_midi->SetStrProperty("Command", "Open");

    // Rewind the MIDI file
    m_midi->SetStrProperty("Command", "Prev");


    // Play the MIDI file
    m_midi->SetStrProperty("Command", "Play");


    /////////////////////
    // MY CODE ENDS HERE
    /////////////////////


}
```

☐ Use ClassWizard to add a function for the event:

Class Name:	CFlagsView
Object ID:	IDC_COMMAND3D_MEXICO
Message:	VBN_CLICK
Function Name:	OnClickCommand3DMexico()

NOTE: Make sure you add the function to the CFlagsView class.

☐ Edit the OnClickCommand3dMexico() function that you added to the FLAGSVW.CPP file. After you edit the OnClickCommand3dMexico() function, it looks as follows:

```
void CFlagsView::OnClickCommand3dMexico(UINT, int, CWnd*, LPVOID)
{
// TODO: Add your VBX event notification handler code here

    /////////////////////
    // MY CODE STARTS HERE
    /////////////////////

    // Close the MIDI device
    m_midi->SetStrProperty("Command", "Close");
```

```
    // Set the name of the MIDI file
    m_midi->SetStrProperty("FileName",
                "\\VCPROG\\MIDI\\ANTHEMS\\MEXICO.MID" );

    // Open the MIDI file
    m_midi->SetStrProperty("Command", "Open");

    // Rewind the MIDI file
    m_midi->SetStrProperty("Command", "Prev");


    // Play the MIDI file
    m_midi->SetStrProperty("Command", "Play");


    //////////////////////
    // MY CODE ENDS HERE
    //////////////////////


}
```

☐ Use ClassWizard to add a function for the event:

Class Name:	CFlagsView
Object ID:	IDC_COMMAND3D_NETHERLANDS
Message:	VBN_CLICK
Function Name:	OnClickCommand3DNetherlands()

NOTE: Make sure you add the function to the CFlagsView class.

☐ Edit the OnClickCommand3DNetherlands() function that you added to the FLAGSVW.CPP file. After you edit the function, it looks as follows:

```
void CFlagsView::OnClickCommand3dNetherlands(UINT, int, CWnd*, LPVOID)
{
// TODO: Add your VBX event notification handler code here

    //////////////////////
    // MY CODE STARTS HERE
    //////////////////////

    // Close the MIDI device
    m_midi->SetStrProperty("Command", "Close");


    // Set the name of the MIDI file
    m_midi->SetStrProperty("FileName",
                "\\VCPROG\\MIDI\\ANTHEMS\\NETHERLA.MID" );
```

```
// Open the MIDI file
m_midi->SetStrProperty("Command", "Open");

// Rewind the MIDI file
m_midi->SetStrProperty("Command", "Prev");


// Play the MIDI file
m_midi->SetStrProperty("Command", "Play");


/////////////////////
// MY CODE ENDS HERE
/////////////////////

}
```

☐ Use ClassWizard to add a function for the event:

Class Name:	CFlagsView
Object ID:	IDC_COMMAND3D_CHINA
Message:	VBN_CLICK
Function Name:	OnClickCommand3DChina()

NOTE: Make sure you add the function to the CFlagsView class.

☐ Edit the OnClickCommand3DChina() function that you added to the
FLAGSVW.CPP file. After you edit the OnClickCommand3dChina() function, it
looks as follows:

```
void CFlagsView::OnClickCommand3dChina(UINT, int, CWnd*, LPVOID)
{
// TODO: Add your VBX event notification handler code here

    /////////////////////
    // MY CODE STARTS HERE
    /////////////////////

    // Close the MIDI device
    m_midi->SetStrProperty("Command", "Close");


    // Set the name of the MIDI file
    m_midi->SetStrProperty("FileName",
                "\\VCPROG\\MIDI\\ANTHEMS\\CHINA.MID" );

    // Open the MIDI file
    m_midi->SetStrProperty("Command", "Open");
```

```
     // Rewind the MIDI file
     m_midi->SetStrProperty("Command", "Prev");


     // Play the MIDI file
     m_midi->SetStrProperty("Command", "Play");


     /////////////////////////
     // MY CODE ENDS HERE
     /////////////////////////

}
```

Changing the Default Size of the Application's Main Window

The last enhancement that you'll make to the Flags application is to set the default size of the application's main window.

You need to write the code that sets the default size of the application window in the PreCreateWindow() member function of the CMainFrame class. The header file of the CMainFrame class is MAINFRM.H and the implementation file of the CMainFrame class is MAINFRM.CPP.

☐ Open the file MAINFRM.H and add code to it that defines the function PreCreateWindow() as a member function of the CMainFrame class. After you write this code, the CMainFrame class declaration looks as follows:

```
class CMainFrame : public CFrameWnd
{
protected: // create from serialization only
     CMainFrame();
     DECLARE_DYNCREATE(CMainFrame)


     /////////////////////////
     // MY CODE STARTS HERE
     /////////////////////////

     BOOL PreCreateWindow(CREATESTRUCT& cs);

     /////////////////////////
     // MY CODE ENDS HERE
     /////////////////////////
```

```
// Attributes
public:

// Operations
public:

// Implementation
public:
     virtual ~CMainFrame();
#ifdef _DEBUG
     virtual void AssertValid() const;
     virtual void Dump(CDumpContext& dc) const;
#endif

// Generated message map functions
protected:
//{{AFX_MSG(CMainFrame)
// NOTE - the ClassWizard will add and remove member
// functions here.
// DO NOT EDIT what you see in these blocks of generated code!
//}}AFX_MSG
     DECLARE_MESSAGE_MAP()
};
```

Now write the code of the `PreCreateWindow()` function:

☐ Open the file MAINFRM.CPP and add (at the end of the file) the
PreCreateWindow() function. After you write this function, the end of the
MAINFRM.CPP file looks as follows:

```
///////////////////////
// MY CODE STARTS HERE
///////////////////////

BOOL CMainFrame::PreCreateWindow(CREATESTRUCT& cs)
{

     // Call the base class function.
     CFrameWnd::PreCreateWindow( cs );

     // Set the width of the window
     cs.cx = 500;

     // Set the height of the window
     cs.cy = 350;

     return TRUE;
}
```

1125

```
/////////////////////
// MY CODE ENDS HERE
/////////////////////
```

☐ Compile/link and execute the Flags application.

☐ Experiment with the Flags application and verify its operation.

The Last Cosmetic Touch

The last cosmetic touch that you'll perform is to give the flags a 3D look:

☐ Use AppStudio to set the BevelWidth property of all the flags to 5.

The resulting dialog box now looks as shown in Figure 32.31.

Figure 32.31.
The dialog box after the flags'
BevelWidth property is set to 5.

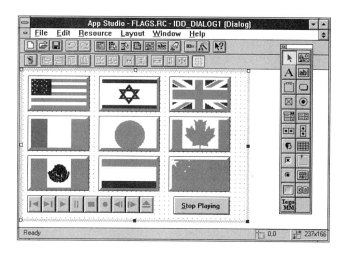

☐ Compile/link and execute the Flags application and verify its operation.

33

3D Controls: 3D Group Buttons

In this chapter you'll learn to incorporate
a three-dimensional (3D) group button
control into your Visual C++ programs.
This control resembles the 3D button
that was discussed
in Chapter 32, "3D Controls: Push
Buttons." However,
as you'll see in this chapter, the 3D group
control has more features to it.

As discussed in Chapter 32, the THREED.VBX control enables you to easily incorporate 3D controls into your applications. This chapter assumes that you've already installed THREED.VBX in App Studio. (If you didn't install the THREED.VBX file, refer back to Chapter 32.)

To understand the capabilities of the 3D group button control, take a look at the toolbar of Microsoft Word for Windows (see Figure 33.1). As shown, one of the icons on the toolbar is the B icon, which serves the same purpose as the Bold menu item. In Figure 33.1, the B icon is shown active. Figure 33.2 shows the B icon when it isn't active. The B icon is similar to the 3D group button because it's capable of displaying two bitmaps. One bitmap represents the icon in its pressed state, and the other bitmap represents the icon in its unpressed state. The toolbar of Word for Windows also contains four icons that represent the alignment of the text. In Figure 33.1, the Align Left icon is active, and in Figure 33.2, the Center icon is active. Of course, the document's text can't be centered and left-aligned simultaneously. Whenever you select one of the adjustment icons, all the other adjustment icons become inactive. Only one adjustment icon can be pressed at a time.

The 3D group button control is similar to the icons on the toolbar in Word for Windows. The 3D group button control has the following main characteristics:

> You can assign more than one bitmap to it (just like the B icon in Word for Windows).

> When you select one button from a group of buttons, the selected button is pushed down, and all the rest of the buttons in the group are not pushed down (just like the alignment icons in Word for Windows).

Of course, unlike the icons in Word for Windows, which are positioned on the toolbar, you can place 3D group buttons in a dialog box.

Figure 33.1.
The Word for Windows toolbar (with the B icon and the Adjust Left icon active).

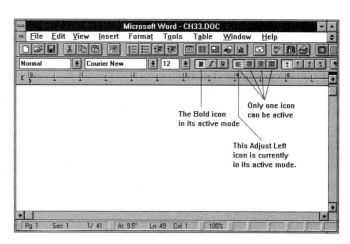

Figure 33.2.
The Word for
Windows toolbar
(with the B icon
and the Center icon
not active).

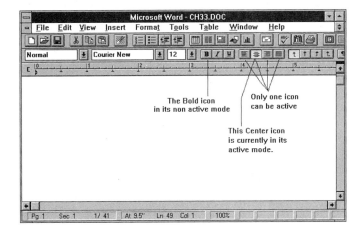

The Bold icon
in its non active mode

Only one icon
can be active

This Center icon
is currently in its
active mode.

The Group Application

The Group application illustrates how to use a 3D group button control from within your Visual C++ application.

Before you start writing the Group application, execute a copy of it. A copy of this application resides in your `C:\VCPROG\ORIGINAL\CH33\GROUP` directory.

To execute the `Group.EXE` application:

☐ Use Run from the Program Manager's File menu to execute
   `C:\VCPROG\ORIGINAL\CH33\GROUP\Group.EXE`.

   Windows responds by executing the Group application. The main window of
   `Group.EXE` *appears, as shown in Figure 33.1.*

Figure 33.3.
The Group
application's main
window.

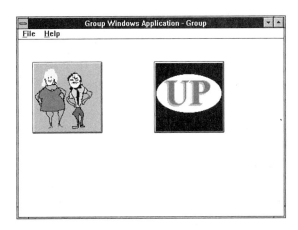

As you can see, the main window of the application contains two 3D buttons. The left button has a picture of a couple standing, and the right button has a picture of the word *UP* in it.

☐ Click the left button.

> *The Group application responds by pushing down the left button and leaving the button in its down state. As you can see, the pressed button has a different picture in it.*

☐ Click the right button.

> *The Group application responds by pushing down the right button and lifting the left button back up. Note that the right button now has a different picture in it.*

The Group application has two popup menus: File and Help. These popup menus are shown in Figures 33.4 and 33.5.

Figure 33.4.
The Group
application's File
popup menu.

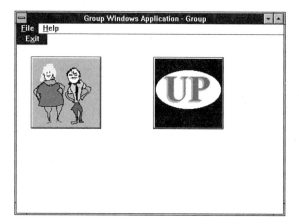

Experiment with the Group application and then select Exit from File menu to terminate it.

Now that you know what the Group application does, you can start writing it.

Figure 33.5.
The Group
application's Help
popup menu.

Creating the Project of the Group Application

To create the project of the Group application:

☐ Select AppWizard from the Project menu.

> *Visual C++ responds by running AppWizard.*

☐ Use the Directory list box to select the directory `C:\VCPROG\PRACTICE\CH33`. Type group in the Project Name box.

Now your AppWizard dialog box looks as shown in Figure 33.6.

Figure 33.6.
The AppWizard
dialog box for the
Group application.

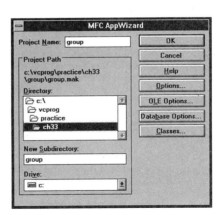

☐ Click the Options button and set the options as shown in Figure 33.7.

WARNING

Because you want the Group application to support a VBX control (namely, the THREED.VBX control), the Custom VBX Controls option should be checked. As you can see from Figure 33.7, the Custom VBX Controls box is checked.

Figure 33.7.
Setting the options
for the Group
application.

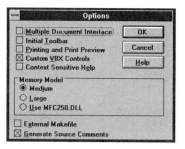

☐ Click the Options dialog box's OK button, click the OK button of the AppWizard dialog box, and finally click the Create button of the New Application Information dialog box.

> *AppWizard responds by creating the Group project and all the skeleton files of the Group application.*

To remove the debug options of the project (so that you'll have a small EXE file):

☐ Select Project from Visual C++'s Options menu, click the Release radio button and then click the OK button of the dialog box.

Creating the Form of the Application

As shown in Figure 33.3, the main window of the Group application contains two buttons.

To implement this form you'll replace the current view class of the application with a new view class derived from the CFormView class.

Follow these steps to create the form of the application:

☐ Use the Windows File Manager (or DOS Shell) to delete the two view class files of the Group application:

> Delete `C:\VCPROG\PRACTICE\CH33\GROUP\GROUPVW.CPP`.
> Delete `C:\VCPROG\PRACTICE\CH33\GROUP\GROUPVW.H`.

☐ Select ClassWizard from Visual C++'s Browse menu.

> *ClassWizard responds by displaying a dialog box telling you that the view class files don't exist.*

☐ Click the dialog box's OK button.

☐ Click the Remove button of the Repair Class Information dialog box.

☐ Click the OK button of ClassWizard's dialog box.

You have just finished removing the view class of the Group application.

In the following steps you'll create a dialog box, you'll create a `CFormView` type class for this dialog box, and you'll make this class the new view class of the application.

☐ Select App Studio from Visual C++'s Tools menu.

☐ Create a new dialog box with App Studio.

☐ Double-click in a free area of the new dialog box.

Select Styles from the drop-down list box in the upper-right corner of the Properties window.

☐ Set the Styles properties of the dialog box as follows:

☐ Select Child in the Style box.

☐ Select None in the Border box.

☐ Uncheck the Visible property (that is, remove the check mark from the Visible check box).

☐ Select General from the drop-down list box in the upper-right corner of the Properties window and make sure that the Caption box is empty.

Now, connect the dialog box to a class derived from `CFormView`:

☐ Select ClassWizard from App Studio's Resource menu.

> *ClassWizard responds by displaying the Add Class dialog box.*

☐ Type `CGroupView` in the Class Name box.

☐ Type `groupvw.h` in the Header File edit box.

☐ Type `groupvw.cpp` in the Implementation File edit box.

☐ Click the Create Class button.

☐ Click the OK button of ClassWizard's window to go back to App Studio.

You've finished creating the new view class of the application. This view class is a derived class from the MFC `CFormView` class, and it's connected to the dialog box that you created. Thus, the main dialog box of the application will be the dialog box that you created.

The Visual Implementation of the Group Dialog Box

☐ Implement the dialog box of the Group application per Table 33.1. In this table, you are instructed to place 3D group buttons in the dialog box. The icon of the 3D group button is shown in Figure 33.8. It will appear in your Tools window, provided that you installed the THREED.VBX file (see Chapter 32).

Figure 33.8.
The Tools window with the THREED.VBX control.

— 3D Group Button

Table 33.1. The Group application's dialog box.

Class Name:		CGroupView
Figure:		33.9
OK button:		No
Cancel button:		No

Object	*Property*	*Setting*
Dialog Box	ID	IDD_DIALOG1
	Size	Drag the dialog box's handles horizontally and vertically to make it wider and longer.
3D Group Button	ID	IDC_GROUPPUSH3D1
	Variable	m_grp1 (Type: CVBControl *)
3D Group Button	ID	IDC_GROUPPUSH3D2
	Variable	m_grp2 (Type: CVBControl *)

Table 33.1 instructed you to attach two variables, called m_grp1 and m_grp2, of type CVBControl * to the two 3D group button controls. As you'll see later in the chapter, when you write the code of the application, you'll use the m_grp1 and m_grp2 variables to send commands to the controls. Note that CVBControl is an MFC class. Thus, by making m_grp1 and m_grp2 variables of type CVBControl *, you're actually making these variables pointers to objects of class CVBControl. The MFC class CVBControl was specifically designed to work with VBX controls.

Your dialog box now looks like the one shown in Figure 33.9.

The 3D group button controls that you placed in the dialog box have many properties. To see these properties:

☐ Double-click either of the 3D group button controls that you placed in the dialog box.

> *App Studio responds by displaying the General properties of the 3D group button control.*

☐ Select Styles from the drop-down list box in the upper-right corner of the Properties window.

> *App Studio responds by displaying the Styles Properties window of the 3D button control (see Figure 33.10).*

1135

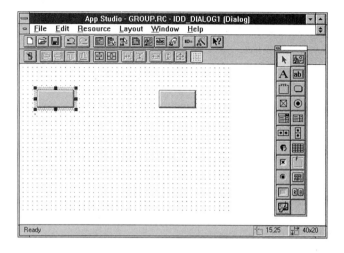

Figure 33.9.
The Group
application's dialog
box after placing
two 3D group
buttons.

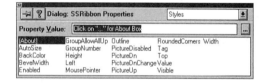

Figure 33.10.
The Styles
Properties window
of the 3D group
button control.

As you can see from Figure 33.10, the 3D group button control has many properties. You'll have a chance to change the properties of the 3D group button later in this chapter. For now, don't change any of its properties.

Save your work:

☐ Select Save from App Studio's File menu.

The Visual Implementation of the Group Menu

The Group application has a menu with two popup menus, as shown in Figures 33.4 and 33.5. Implement this menu:

☐ Use App Studio to implement the menu of the Group application per Table 33.2.

Table 33.2. The Group application's menu.
Figures relating to menu: 33.4, 33.5

Menu Item
&File
E&xit
&Help
&About Group...

Don't forget to delete the accelerator keys of the menu items that you removed:

☐ Select GROUP.RC [MFC-Resource Script] from the Window menu of App Studio, select Accelerator in the Type list, and then double-click IDR_MAINFRAME in the Resources list.

☐ Delete the accelerator keys that aren't used by the Group application. In particular, delete the accelerator keys of the ID_FILE_NEW, ID_FILE_OPEN, and ID_FILE_SAVE menu items.

If you don't delete these accelerator keys, they will be active during runtime. If, for example, the user presses Ctrl+N, it's as if the user selected New from the File menu (even though you removed the New item from the File menu).

Save your work:

☐ Select Save from App Studio's File menu.

The visual implementation of the Group application's menu is complete.

Executing the Group Application

Even though you haven't finished writing the Group application, execute it to see in action your visual design.

☐ Select Rebuild All GROUP.EXE from Visual C++'s Project menu.

☐ Select Execute GROUP.EXE from the Project menu.

Visual C++ responds by executing the Group application. The main window of the application appears with the form that you designed in it.

☐ Click the left button.

☐ Click the right button.

> *The Group application responds by displaying the left button in its unpressed state and displaying the right button in its pressed state.*

Experiment with the left and right buttons and note that at any given time, only one button can be displayed in its pressed state.

☐ Select Exit from the File menu to terminate the Group application.

Attaching Bitmaps to the 3D Group Buttons

Now you'll attach bitmaps to the 3D group buttons.

☐ Use App Studio to display the dialog box in its design mode.

☐ Double-click the left 3D group button control.

> *App Studio responds by displaying the Properties window of the 3D group button control.*

☐ Select Styles from the drop-down list in the upper-right corner of the Properties window.

☐ Select the `AutoSize` property.

☐ Click the down-arrow icon that appears on the right side of the Property Value box.

> *App Studio responds by dropping down a list of possible values for the `AutoSize` property (see Figure 33.11).*

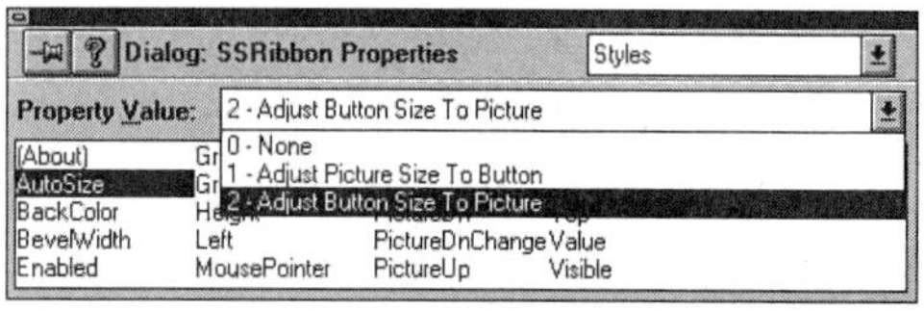

Figure 33.11.
Setting the
AutoSize property.

☐ Select the 2-Adjust Button Size To Picture property.

This means that the size of the button will be automatically adjusted to the size of the bitmap (which you'll place soon).

☐ Select the `PictureUp` property, click the three dots that appear on the right side of the Property Value box, and then select the file
`C:\VCPROG\BMP\DANCE1.BMP`.

> *App Studio responds by displaying the* `DANCE1.BMP` *picture in the button. Note that the button adjusted itself to the size of the bitmap (see Figure 33.12).*

Figure 33.12.
The 3D group
button with the
`DANCE1.BMP`
picture in it.

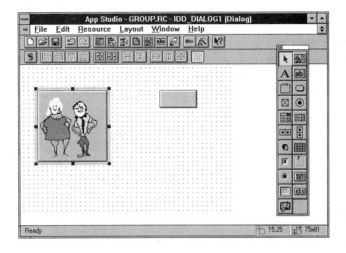

In the preceding step you assigned the `DANCE1.BMP` picture to the `PictureUp` property. This means that this BMP file will be displayed when the button is in its up (unpressed) status.

☐ Select the `PictureDn` property, click the three dots that appears on the right side of the Property Value box, and then select the file
`C:\VCPROG\BMP\DANCE2.BMP`.

In the preceding step you assigned the `DANCE2.BMP` picture to the `PictureDn` property. This means that this BMP file will be displayed when the button is in its down (pressed) status.

☐ Now set the `PictureUp`, `PictureDn`, and `AutoSize` properties of the right button as follows:

AutoSize:	`2-Adjust Button Size To Picture`
PictureDn:	`C:\VCPROG\BMP\DOWN.BMP`
PictureUp:	`C:\VCPROG\BMP\UP.BMP`

To see your visual design in action:

☐ Compile/link and execute the Group application.

> *The Group application displays its main window with the bitmaps in the 3D group buttons that you placed in App Studio.*

Experiment with the Group application and then select Exit to terminate it.

Attaching Code to the 3D Group Button

You attach code to the 3D group button in the same way you attach code to other controls. For example, if you attach a function to the VBN_CLICKED message of the 3D group button, that function will be executed whenever the button is clicked.

> **NOTE**
>
> As shown in Figure 33.10, the 3D group button has many other properties. For the complete description of these properties, see Professional Features Book 1, which comes with Microsoft Visual Basic for Windows Version 3.0.

Setting the Properties of the 3D Group Button from Within Your Code

So far, you've used App Studio to set the properties of the 3D group button control. However, you can also set the properties from within your code.

In this section you'll set the MousePointer property of the left 3D group button. This property determines the shape of the mouse cursor when the mouse is placed on the button.

Before setting the property from within your code, examine this property from App Studio:

☐ From App Studio display the dialog box in its design mode.

☐ Double-click the left 3D group button.

☐ Select Styles from the drop-down list box at the upper-right corner of the Properties window.

☐ Select the MousePointer property.

> *App Studio responds by displaying the possible values for this property.*

Don't change the value of this property, but note that with App Studio you can select a variety of values for this property. For example, you can set the value of this property to 2-Cross. This means that whenever the mouse will be placed over the left 3D group button, the mouse cursor will be displayed as a cross shape.

Initializing the Properties

You write the code that initializes the properties of the 3D group button control in the OnInitialUpdate() member function of the view class. This way, when the application starts, the 3D group button control already has the required properties.

Recall (from previous chapters) that Visual C++ did not write the declaration and skeleton of the OnInitialUpdate() function. You have to declare this function and write its skeleton. Here's how you do that:

☐ Open the file GROUPVW.H and add code to it that defines the function OnInitialUpdate() as a member function of the CGroupView class. After you write this code, the CGroupView class declaration looks as follows:

```
class CGroupView : public CFormView
{
    DECLARE_DYNCREATE(CGroupView)
protected:
    CGroupView();
// protected constructor used by dynamic creation


    /////////////////////////
    // MY CODE STARTS HERE
    /////////////////////////

    virtual void OnInitialUpdate();

    /////////////////////////
    // MY CODE ENDS HERE
    /////////////////////////


// Form Data
public:
    //{{AFX_DATA(CGroupView)
    enum { IDD = IDD_DIALOG1 };
    CVBControl*    m_grp2;
    CVBControl*    m_grp1;
    //}}AFX_DATA
```

```
// Attributes
public:

// Operations
public:

// Implementation
protected:
    virtual ~CGroupView();
    virtual void DoDataExchange(CDataExchange* pDX);
// DDX/DDV support
    // Generated message map functions
    //{{AFX_MSG(CGroupView)
// Note - the ClassWizard will add and remove member
// functions here.
    //}}AFX_MSG
    DECLARE_MESSAGE_MAP()
};
```

Now write the code of the OnInitialUpdate() function:

☐ Open the file GROUPVW.CPP and add to it (at the end of the file) the OnInitialUpdate() function. After writing this function, the end of the GROUPVW.CPP file looks as follows:

```
//////////////////////////
// MY CODE STARTS HERE
//////////////////////////

void CGroupView::OnInitialUpdate()
{

  // Call the base class function.
  CFormView::OnInitialUpdate();

  // Set the MousePointer property of the
  // left button to 2-Cross
  m_grp1->SetNumProperty("MousePointer", 2);

}

//////////////////////////
// MY CODE ENDS HERE
//////////////////////////
```

To review the code you added for the OnInitialUpdate() function:

The first statement,

```
CFormView::OnInitialUpdate();
```

calls the `OnInitialUpdate()` member function of the base class. If you don't call the base class `OnInitialUpdate()` function, the VBX control won't work properly.

The next statement is

```
m_grp1->SetNumProperty("MousePointer", 2);
```

This statement uses the `SetStrProperty()` function to set the `MousePointer` property of the control to 2.

> **NOTE**
>
> The `SetNumProperty()` function is a member function of the MFC class `CVBControl`. Recall that during the visual implementation of the dialog box, you attached the variable `m_grp1` to the left group button control, and you declared `m_grp1` as type `CVBControl *` (that is, a pointer to an object of class `CVBControl`).
>
> The `Num` in the name of the `SetNumProperty()` function signifies that `SetNumProperty()` is used to set a numerical property. The first parameter of the `SetNumProperty()` function is the name of the property to be changed, and the second parameter is the value that you want to assign to the property. For example, the statement
>
> ```
> m_grp1->SetNumProperty("MousePointer", 2);
> ```
>
> assigns the value 2 to the `MousePointer` property of the `m_grp1` control.
>
> Similarly, you can set the properties of the right group button control by executing the `SetNumProperty()` function on the `m_grp2` pointer, as in
>
> ```
> m_grp1->SetNumProperty("MousePointer", 2);
> ```

☐ Compile/link and execute the Group application.

☐ Place the mouse cursor over the left 3D group button and note that the cursor changes to a cross shape.

Experiment with the Group application and then select Exit from the File menu to terminate the application.

> **NOTE**
>
> When using the `SetNumProperty()` function you must be careful when you type the name of the property. For example, if instead of providing `MousePointer` as the first parameter of this function, you type by mistake `MosePointer`, the compiler won't complain. However, when you execute the application, the VBX control won't do what you want it to, because the VBX control doesn't have a property `MosePointer`.

The 3D Frame, 3D Option Button, 3D Check Box, and 3D Panel Controls

The `THREED.VBX` control that comes with the Microsoft Visual Basic for Windows 3.0 package also contains the 3D Frame, 3D option button, 3D check box, and 3D Panel controls. These controls are the same as their 2D counterparts. (The 3D Panel control is used as a label control, only it can appear as a 3D panel and it can display three-dimensional text.) Figures 33.13 through 33.16 show the appearance of these 3D controls.

Figure 33.13.
A 3D Frame
control.

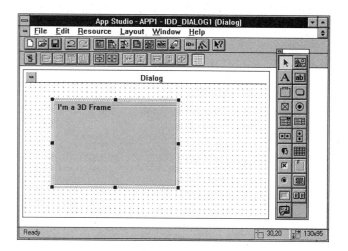

Figure 33.14.
A 3D Option
control.

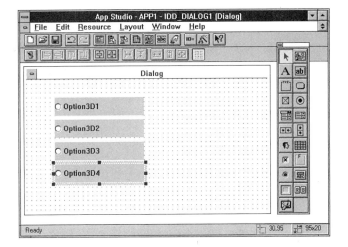

Figure 33.15.
A 3D Check Box
control.

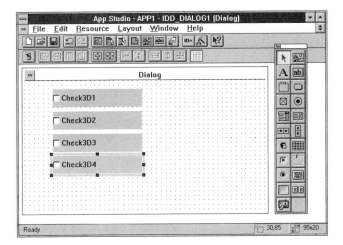

Figure 33.16.
A 3D Panel
control.

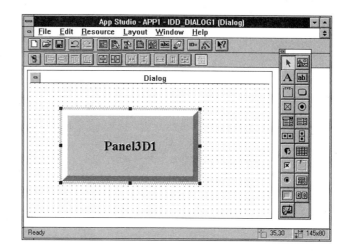

34

Drawing

In this chapter you'll learn about
additional drawing topics in Visual C++.

Drawing from Within Visual C++ Versus Drawing from Within Paintbrush

Drawing from within your Visual C++ programs is similar to drawing with the Paintbrush program that ships with Windows. Recall that in Paintbrush you first click the mouse on a tool (for example, the pencil, circle, or line) and then you move the mouse to the drawing area and draw the shape. As you'll soon see, the same technique is used when drawing from within your Visual C++ programs. The only difference is that instead of selecting the drawing tool with the mouse, you execute a function that selects the tool, and instead of drawing the shape with the mouse, you execute a function that draws the shape.

The Draw Application

Before you start writing the DRAW application yourself, execute the copy of it that resides in your `C:\VCPROG\ORIGINAL\CH34\DRAW` directory.

To execute the Draw.EXE application:

☐ Use Run from the Program Manager's File menu to execute
`C:\VCPROG\ORIGINAL\CH34\DRAW\Draw.EXE`.

Windows responds by executing the Draw application. The main window of `Draw.EXE` *appears as shown in Figure 34.1.*

Figure 34.1.
The DRAW application's main window.

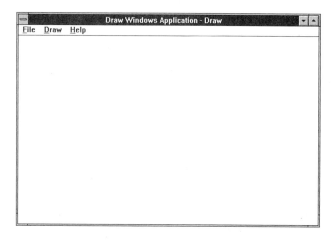

The DRAW application has three popup menus: File, Draw, and Help. These popup menus are shown in Figures 34.2, 34.3, and 34.4.

Figure 34.2.
The DRAW
application's File
menu.

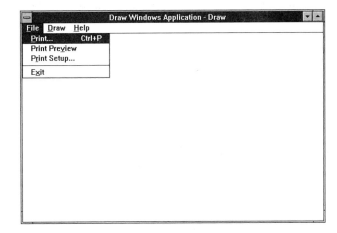

Figure 34.3.
The DRAW
application's Draw
menu.

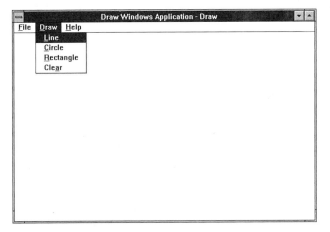

Figure 34.4.
The DRAW
application's Help
menu.

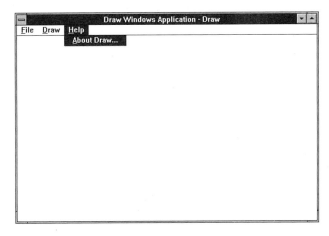

The DRAW application enables you to draw various shapes.

☐ Select Line from the Draw menu.

> *The DRAW application responds by drawing a line composed of two parts. The left part is a thick green line, and the right part is a thin black line.*

☐ Select Clear to clear the window.

☐ Select Circle from the Draw menu.

> *The DRAW application responds by drawing a red circle with thick boundaries.*

☐ Select Rectangle from the Draw menu.

> *The DRAW application responds by drawing a rectangle filled with diagonal lines.*

Draw has the standard Print menu items (see Figure 34.2).

☐ Select Print Preview from the File menu.

> *The DRAW application responds by displaying a window that shows how the printout will look (see Figure 34.5). Note that the mouse pointer looks like a magnifying-glass tool.*

☐ Click the area you want to magnify.

> *The DRAW application responds by magnifying that section of the Print Preview window (see Figure 34.6).*

Figure 34.5.
The Print Preview window.

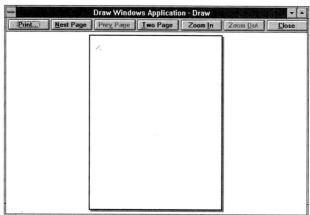

Figure 34.6.
The magnified
section of the Print
Preview window.

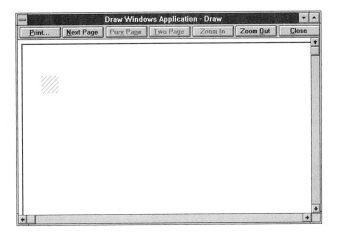

☐ Click the Print Preview window's Close button. The Close button is the rightmost button on the toolbar. If you don't see this button, maximize the window.

The DRAW application responds by returning to its main window.

With the DRAW application you can print the contents of the window:

☐ Select Print from the File menu.

The DRAW application responds by displaying the Print dialog box (see Figure 34.7).

☐ Press the Print dialog box's OK button to send the contents of the window to the printer.

Figure 34.7.
The Print dialog
box.

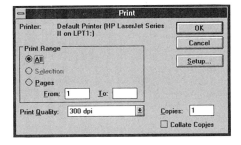

Experiment with the DRAW application and then select Exit from the File menu to terminate it.

Now that you know what DRAW should do, you can write it.

Creating the Project of the DRAW Application

To create the project of the DRAW application:

☐ Select AppWizard from the Project menu.

> *Visual C++ responds by running AppWizard.*

☐ Use the Directory list box to select the directory `C:\VCPROG\PRACTICE\CH34`.

☐ Type `draw` in the Project Name box.

Now your AppWizard dialog box looks as shown in Figure 34.8.

Figure 34.8.
The AppWizard
dialog box for the
DRAW application.

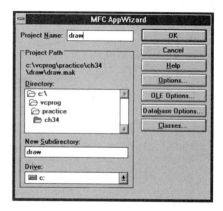

☐ Click the Options button and set the options as shown in Figure 34.9. Note that in Figure 34.9 you are instructed to check the Printing and Print Preview check box.

Figure 34.9.
Setting the options
for the DRAW
application.

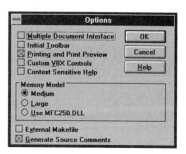

☐ Click the Options dialog box's OK button, click the OK button of the
AppWizard dialog box, and finally click the Create button of the New
Application Information dialog box.

> *AppWizard responds by creating the DRAW project and all the skeleton files
> of the DRAW application.*

To remove the debug options of the project (so you'll have a small EXE file):

☐ Select Project from Visual C++'s Options menu, click the Release radio
button, and then click the dialog box's OK button.

The Visual Design of the Menu

Now you'll visually design the menu of the DRAW application. Use App Studio to
implement the DRAW application's menu per Table 34.1.

Table 34.1. The DRAW application's menu.

Menu Item
&File
&Print...
Print Pre&view
P&rint Setup...
Separator
E&xit
&Draw
&Line
&Circle
&Rectangle
C&lear
&Help
&About Draw...

Figure 34.10 shows the File menu in App Studio.

Figure 34.10.
The File menu
(design mode).

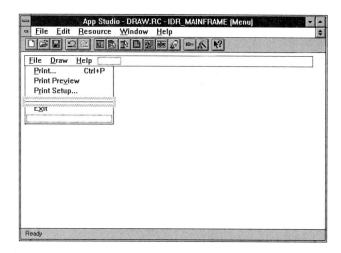

☐ Use App Studio to remove the accelerator keys that aren't used by the application.

To save your work:

☐ Select Save from App Studio's File menu.

The visual implementation of the DRAW application's menu is complete.

NOTE: The DRAW application doesn't have a custom dialog box. It only has an About dialog box.

The *OnDraw()* Function

One of the most important concepts of drawing in Windows with Visual C++ is the OnDraw() function. As you'll soon see, the OnDraw() function is executed automatically whenever there is a need to draw the application's window. Windows or your own code may require that the window be drawn.

As stated, if Windows decides it's time to draw the application's window, the OnDraw() function will be automatically executed. This happens when the application is started, for example. (This makes sense because on starting an application, the window of the application must be drawn.)

Another example where Windows decides to execute the OnDraw() function is when you minimize the application's window and then maximize it. Under these conditions, there is a need to redraw the application's window.

Another example is when you cover the application's window with another application's window and then move the other application's window to expose your application's window.

As you can see, Windows is working hard for you. It constantly monitors your operations, and whenever there's a need to draw the application's window, the OnDraw() function is executed.

As stated, you also can cause the execution of the OnDraw() function. However, in Visual C++ you don't call the OnDraw() function directly. Instead, you call another function, known as the Invalidate() function, which causes the OnDraw() function's execution. You'll have a chance to experiment with the Invalidate() function during the course of this chapter.

Attaching Code to the *OnDraw()* Function

In the previous section you read about the capability of Windows to execute the OnDraw() function. Now you'll prove to yourself that the OnDraw() function is executed automatically under these conditions.

☐ Open the DRAWVIEW.CPP file and modify the OnDraw() function. (Visual C++ wrote the skeleton of the OnDraw() function for you.) After you modify the OnDraw() function, it looks as follows:

```
void CDrawView::OnDraw(CDC* pDC)
{
    CDrawDoc* pDoc = GetDocument();
    ASSERT_VALID(pDoc);

    // TODO: add draw code for native data here

    /////////////////////////
    // MY CODE STARTS HERE
    /////////////////////////

    // Beep (to demonstrate that the OnDraw() function
    // was executed)
    MessageBeep(-1);

    /////////////////////////
    // MY CODE ENDS HERE
    /////////////////////////

}
```

The code that you typed executes the MessageBeep() function. This means that whenever the OnDraw() function is executed, you'll hear a beep.

☐ Compile/link and execute the DRAW application.

When the application displays its window, you hear a beep. This means that the OnDraw() function has been executed.

☐ Minimize the application's window and then maximize it.

When you maximize the window, you'll hear a beep because the OnDraw() function has been executed and the application's window has been redrawn.

☐ Cover application's window with another application's window and then remove the other application's window to expose the DRAW application's window.

The DRAW application responds by beeping, because the moment you exposed its window, the window had to be redrawn, which means that the OnDraw() function had to be executed.

☐ Experiment with the DRAW application and then select Exit from the File menu to terminate it.

NOTE

If you move the application's window by dragging its title, you won't hear the beep (which means that the OnDraw() function hasn't been executed).

OnDraw() isn't executed because Windows is responsible for the redrawing in this case.

Drawing in the Window

Now you'll declare a data member called m_Shape. This variable indicates which shape to draw.

☐ Open the file DRAWVIEW.H and add the data member m_Shape to the class declaration of CDrawView. After you add this data member, the CDrawView class declaration looks as follows:

```
class CDrawView : public CView
{
protected: // create from serialization only
    CDrawView();
    DECLARE_DYNCREATE(CDrawView)

// Attributes
public:
    CDrawDoc* GetDocument();

    /////////////////////////
    // MY CODE STARTS HERE
    /////////////////////////

    int m_Shape;

    /////////////////////////
    // MY CODE ENDS HERE
    /////////////////////////


// Operations
public:

// Implementation
public:
    virtual ~CDrawView();
    virtual void OnDraw(CDC* pDC);
// overridden to draw this view
#ifdef _DEBUG
    virtual void AssertValid() const;
    virtual void Dump(CDumpContext& dc) const;
#endif

protected:

// Printing support
virtual BOOL OnPreparePrinting(CPrintInfo* pInfo);
virtual void OnBeginPrinting(CDC* pDC, CPrintInfo* pInfo);
virtual void OnEndPrinting(CDC* pDC, CPrintInfo* pInfo);

// Generated message map functions
protected:
//{{AFX_MSG(CDrawView)
// NOTE - the ClassWizard will add and remove member
// functions here.
//    DO NOT EDIT what you see in these blocks
// of generated code !
    //}}AFX_MSG
    DECLARE_MESSAGE_MAP()
};
```

The value of the data member m_Shape is set as follows:

When the value of m_Shape is equal to 0, OnDraw() clears the window.
When the value of m_Shape is equal to 1, OnDraw() draws a line.
When the value of m_Shape is equal to 2, OnDraw() draws a circle.
When the value of m_Shape is equal to 3, OnDraw() draws a rectangle.

Initially, set the value of m_Shape is set to 0:

☐ Open the DRAWVIEW.CPP file and initialize the value of m_Shape to 0 in the constructor function of the CDrawView class. After the modification, the constructor function looks as follows:

```
CDrawView::CDrawView()
{
    // TODO: add construction code here

    /////////////////////////
    // MY CODE STARTS HERE
    /////////////////////////

    m_Shape = 0;

    /////////////////////////
    // MY CODE ENDS HERE
    /////////////////////////

}
```

Attaching Code to the Menu Items

Now you'll add code to the Draw menu's Line item.

☐ Use ClassWizard to add a function for the event:

Class Name:	CDrawView
Object ID:	ID_DRAW_LINE
Message:	COMMAND
Function Name:	OnDrawLine()

NOTE: Make sure you're adding the function to the CDrawView class.

☐ Edit the OnDrawLine() function that you added to the DRAWVIEW.CPP file. After you edit the OnDrawLine() function, it looks as follows:

```
void CDrawView::OnDrawLine()
{
    // TODO: Add your command handler code here

    ////////////////////////
    // MY CODE STARTS HERE
    ////////////////////////


    // Set the flag to 1 (Line)
    m_Shape = 1;

    // Trigger a call to OnDraw()
    Invalidate();


    ////////////////////////
    // MY CODE ENDS HERE
    ////////////////////////

}
```

The code you typed sets the value of m_Shape to 1.

The Invalidate() function causes the execution of the OnDraw() function.

To summarize, when the user selects Line from the Draw menu, your code sets the value of m_Shape to 1 and the OnDraw() function is executed.

Now you'll add code to the Draw menu's Circle item.

☐ Use ClassWizard to add a function for the event:

Class Name:	CDrawView
Object ID:	ID_DRAW_CIRCLE
Message:	COMMAND
Function Name:	OnDrawCircle()

NOTE: Make sure that you're adding the function to the CDrawView class.

☐ Edit the OnDrawCircle() function that you added to the DRAWVIEW.CPP file.
   After you edit the OnDrawCircle() function, it looks as follows:

```
void CDrawView::OnDrawCircle()
{
    // TODO: Add your command handler code here
```

```
/////////////////////
// MY CODE STARTS HERE
/////////////////////

// Set the flag to 2 (Circle)
m_Shape = 2;

// Trigger a call to OnDraw()
Invalidate();


/////////////////////
// MY CODE ENDS HERE
/////////////////////

}
```

☐ Use ClassWizard to add a function for the event:

Class Name:	CDrawView
Object ID:	ID_DRAW_RECTANGLE
Message:	COMMAND
Function Name:	OnDrawRectangle()

NOTE: Make sure that you're adding the function to the CDrawView class.

☐ Edit the OnDrawRectangle() function you added to the DRAWVIEW.CPP file. After you edit the OnDrawRectangle() function, it looks as follows:

```
void CDrawView::OnDrawRectangle()
{
    // TODO: Add your command handler code here

    /////////////////////
    // MY CODE STARTS HERE
    /////////////////////

    // Set the flag to 3 (Rectangle)
    m_Shape = 3;

    // Trigger a call to OnDraw()
    Invalidate();


    /////////////////////
    // MY CODE ENDS HERE
    /////////////////////

}
```

☐ Use ClassWizard to add a function for the event:

Class Name:	`CDrawView`
Object ID:	`ID_DRAW_CLEAR`
Message:	`COMMAND`
Function Name:	`OnDrawClear()`

NOTE: Make sure you're adding the function to the `CDrawView` class.

☐ Edit the `OnDrawClear()` function that you added to the `DRAWVIEW.CPP` file. After you edit the `OnDrawClear()` function, it looks as follows:

```
void CDrawView::OnDrawClear()
{
    // TODO: Add your command handler code here

    /////////////////////////
    // MY CODE STARTS HERE
    /////////////////////////

    // Set the flag to 0 (clear)
    m_Shape = 0;

    // Trigger a call to OnDraw()
    Invalidate();


    /////////////////////
    // MY CODE ENDS HERE
    /////////////////////

}
```

Drawing a Line from Within the *OnDraw()* Function

So far, you've attached code to the Line, Circle, Rectangle, and Clear items of the Draw menu. The code you attached sets the value of m_Shape to either 0, 1, 2, or 3, and then the OnDraw() function is executed by calling the Invalidate() function.

Of course, if you compile/link and execute the DRAW application, nothing will be drawn, because the fact that you changed the value of m_Shape doesn't draw anything. To actually draw the shapes, you have to add code to the OnDraw() function that draws a shape in accordance with the value of m_Shape.

☐ Open the DRAWVIEW.CPP file and add the following code to the OnDraw() function. After you add the code, your OnDraw() function looks as follows:

```
void CDrawView::OnDraw(CDC* pDC)
{
    CDrawDoc* pDoc = GetDocument();
    ASSERT_VALID(pDoc);

    // TODO: add draw code for native data here

    ///////////////////////////
    // MY CODE STARTS HERE
    ///////////////////////////

    // Beep (to demonstrate that the OnDraw() function
    // was executed)
    // MessageBeep(-1);

    if ( m_Shape == 1 )
        {
        pDC->MoveTo ( 10, 30 );
        pDC->LineTo ( 50, 30 );
        }

    ///////////////////////
    // MY CODE ENDS HERE
    ///////////////////////

}
```

The code that you typed comments out (//) the MessageBeep() function:

```
// MessageBeep(-1);
```

And then an if statement is used to determine whether the current value of m_Shape is equal to 1:

```
if ( m_Shape == 1 )
    {
    pDC->MoveTo ( 10, 30 );
    pDC->LineTo ( 50, 30 );
    }
```

If m_Shape is equal to 1, the MoveTo() function is executed:

```
pDC->MoveTo ( 10, 30 );
```

Note that pDC is one of the parameters of the OnDraw() function. pDC is a pointer to the *device context* (DC stands for Device Context). The device context represents the screen. The MoveTo() function makes (x=10, y=30) the current position.

The next statement under the `if` statement draws a line from the current position to the position (50,30):

```
pDC->LineTo ( 50, 30 );
```

Putting it all together, a line is drawn from position (10,30) to position (50,30).

To see the code that you typed in action:

☐ Compile/link and execute the DRAW application.

The DRAW application's main window appears without a drawing in it.

☐ Select Line from the Draw menu.

> *The DRAW application responds by drawing a line, as shown in Figure 34.11.*

Figure 34.11.
Drawing a line.

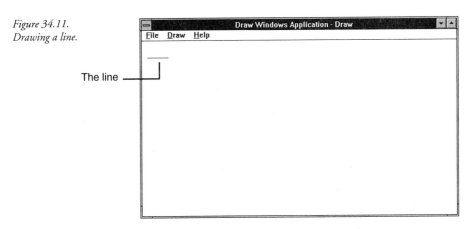

Note that the Print, Print Review, and Print Setup items of the File menu are operational.

☐ Select Print from the File menu.

> *The DRAW application responds by sending the contents of the DRAW window to the printer.*

Experiment with the File menu's items and then select Exit from the File menu to terminate the application.

Changing the Characteristics of the Line

The width of the line that you drew is one pixel (see Figure 34.11). This is the default width of the pen that Windows uses to draw lines. However, just like in Paintbrush, you can change the width of the pen.

☐ Modify the OnDraw() function (inside DRAWVIEW.CPP) so it looks as follows:

```
void CDrawView::OnDraw(CDC* pDC)
{
    CDrawDoc* pDoc = GetDocument();
    ASSERT_VALID(pDoc);

    // TODO: add draw code for native data here

    ////////////////////////
    // MY CODE STARTS HERE
    ////////////////////////

    // Beep (to demonstrate that the OnDraw() function
    // was executed)
    // MessageBeep(-1);

    if ( m_Shape == 1 )
        {

        // Create a new pen
        CPen NewPen (PS_SOLID,          // The Style
                     10,                // The width
                     RGB(0,255,0) );    // The color

        // Set the new pen (and save the original pen)
        CPen* pOriginalPen = pDC->SelectObject ( &NewPen );

        pDC->MoveTo ( 10, 30 );
        pDC->LineTo ( 50, 30 );

        // Restore the original pen
         pDC->SelectObject ( pOriginalPen );


        pDC->MoveTo ( 50, 30 );
        pDC->LineTo ( 80, 30 );


        }
```

```
/////////////////////
// MY CODE ENDS HERE
/////////////////////
```

```
}
```

The code that you typed creates an object called NewPen of class CPen:

```
CPen NewPen (PS_SOLID,         // The Style
             10,               // The width
             RGB(0,255,0) );   // The color
```

The constructor function of CPen takes three parameters. The first parameter is PS_SOLID. This means that the pen will draw a solid line.

The second parameter is the width of the pen. You typed 10 as the second parameter because you want the pen to be 10 logical units wide.

The third parameter is the color of the pen. You supplied the value RGB(0,255,0) because you want the pen to be green.

The next statement executes the SelectObject() function:

```
CPen* pOriginalPen = pDC->SelectObject ( &NewPen );
```

Note that the SelectObject() function "works" on pDC (which was received as the parameter of the OnDraw() function). As implied by its name, the SelectObject() function selects the object that will be used to draw. Think of it as selecting a drawing tool in Paintbrush. The parameter of SelectObject() is the address of the drawing tool. You typed &NewPen as the parameter of SelectObject() because you want the drawing tool to be the NewPen tool you declared in the previous statement (that is, a solid green pen with a width of 10).

Note that the return value of SelectObject() is saved as pOriginalPen. pOriginalPen is the pointer to the current pen. SelectObject() returns this value because, in many cases, you want to change to a different drawing tool, draw something with it, and then return to the original drawing tool.

Now that the pen of your choice has been selected, you can draw the line,

```
pDC->MoveTo ( 10, 30 );
pDC->LineTo ( 50, 30 );
```

To prove that pOriginalPen, which was returned previously from the SelectObject() function, is the original pen, execute the SelectObject() function again with pOriginalPen as its parameter:

1165

```
pDC->SelectObject ( pOriginalPen );
```

Then, continue to draw the line:

```
pDC->MoveTo ( 50, 30 );
pDC->LineTo ( 80, 30 );
```

To summarize, you first draw a thick green line and then continue to draw the line with the original thin black pen.

To see your code in action:

☐ Compile/link and execute the DRAW application.

☐ Select Line from the DRAW menu.

The DRAW application responds by drawing the line shown in Figure 34.12.

Figure 34.12.
A line drawn with
two pens.

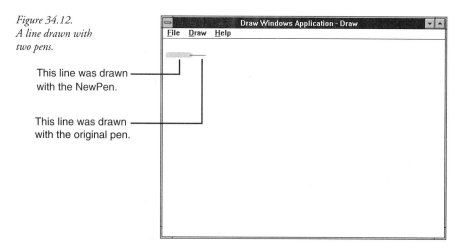

This line was drawn —— with the NewPen.

This line was drawn —— with the original pen.

Experiment with the DRAW application and then select Exit from the File menu to terminate it.

> **NOTE**
>
> The Clear menu item is operational because the `Invalidate()` function executes `OnDraw()`, and when `m_Shape` is equal to 0 the `OnDraw()` function doesn't draw any shape in the window. In other words, the `Invalidate()` function erases the current contents of the window because `OnDraw()` doesn't draw a shape. Putting it all together, a clear-window operation is performed.

You should know, however, that the Invalidate() function has a parameter. The parameter can be TRUE or FALSE. When the parameter of Invalidate() is TRUE, the Invalidate() function erases the contents of the window, and when the parameter of Invalidate() is FALSE, the contents of the window aren't erased. So why did you type Invalidate() instead of Invalidate(TRUE)? Because the default value of the parameter is TRUE. Executing Invalidate() produces the same results as executing Invalidate(TRUE).

Drawing a Circle

Now you'll attach code to the OnDraw() function that draws a circle.

☐ Open the DRAWVIEW.CPP file and add code to the OnDraw() function. After you add the code, your OnDraw() function looks as follows:

```
void CDrawView::OnDraw(CDC* pDC)
{
    CDrawDoc* pDoc = GetDocument();
    ASSERT_VALID(pDoc);

    // TODO: add draw code for native data here

    ////////////////////////
    // MY CODE STARTS HERE
    ////////////////////////

    // Beep (to demonstrate that the OnDraw() function
    // was executed)
    // MessageBeep(-1);


    // Draw the line.
    if ( m_Shape == 1 )
       {
       // Create a new pen
        CPen NewPen (PS_SOLID,           // The Style
                     10,                 // The width
                     RGB(0,255,0) );     // The color

       // Set the new pen (and save the original pen)
       CPen* pOriginalPen = pDC->SelectObject ( &NewPen );
```

```
        pDC->MoveTo ( 10, 30 );
        pDC->LineTo ( 50, 30 );

        // Restore the original pen
         pDC->SelectObject ( pOriginalPen );


        // Draw a line with the original pen
        pDC->MoveTo ( 50, 30 );
        pDC->LineTo ( 80, 30 );

        }


    // Draw the circle
    if ( m_Shape == 2 )
        {

        // Create a new pen
        CPen NewPen (PS_SOLID,          // The Style
                     40,                // The width
                     RGB(255, 0, 0) );  // The color

        // Set the new pen (and save the original pen)
        CPen* pOriginalPen = pDC->SelectObject ( &NewPen );


        // Create a rectangle object
        CRect theRect ( 20, 100, 120, 200 );

        // Draw the Circle
        pDC->Ellipse ( &theRect );

        // Restore the original pen
         pDC->SelectObject ( pOriginalPen );


        }

    ////////////////////////
    // MY CODE ENDS HERE
    ////////////////////////

}
```

The code that you added to the OnDraw( ) function is executed whenever m_Shape is
equal to 2:

```
if ( m_Shape == 2 )
   {
   ....
   // A circle is drawn here
   ....
   }
```

The code starts by creating a new pen:

```
CPen NewPen (PS_SOLID,             // The Style
             40,                   // The width
             RGB(255, 0, 0) );     // The color
```

This pen is called `NewPen`. The pen has the following characteristics:

> It's a solid pen (First parameter).
> Its width is 40 (Second parameter).
> Its color is red (Third parameter).

Next, you put this pen to use by selecting it with the `SelectObject()` function:

```
CPen* pOriginalPen = pDC->SelectObject ( &NewPen );
```

Again, the original pen is returned from the `SelectObject()` function.

The next statement creates an object of type `CRect`:

```
CRect theRect ( 20, 100, 120, 200 );
```

As implied by its name, the `CRect` class defines a rectangle area. The upper-left corner of the rectangle is at point (x=20, y=100), and the lower-right corner of the rectangle is at point (x=100, y=200).

Now you can draw the circle:

```
pDC->Ellipse ( &theRect );
```

Note that the parameter of the `Ellipse()` function is `&theRect`. This means that the ellipse will be bounded by `theRect`. Because you defined `theRect` as a square, the ellipse will be drawn as a circle.

The last statement restores the original pen:

```
pDC->SelectObject ( pOriginalPen );
```

This means that if you draw something now, it will be done with the original pen.

To see your code in action:

☐ Compile/link and execute the DRAW application.

☐ Select the Circle item from the Draw menu.

> *The DRAW application responds by drawing the circle, as shown in Figure 34.13.*

Figure 34.13.
Drawing the circle.

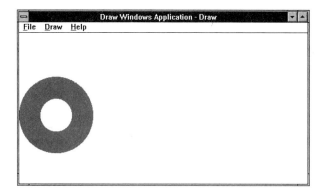

Drawing a Rectangle

Now you'll attach code that draws a rectangle to the OnDraw() function.

☐ Open the DRAWVIEW.CPP file and add code to the OnDraw() function. After you add the code, your OnDraw() function looks as follows:

```
void CDrawView::OnDraw(CDC* pDC)
{
    CDrawDoc* pDoc = GetDocument();
    ASSERT_VALID(pDoc);

// TODO: add draw code for native data here

    ////////////////////////
    // MY CODE STARTS HERE
    ////////////////////////

    // Beep (to demonstrate that the OnDraw() function
    // was executed)
    // MessageBeep(-1);

    // Draw the line.
    if ( m_Shape == 1 )
        {
```

```
    // Create a new pen
     CPen NewPen (PS_SOLID,              // The Style
                 10,                     // The width
                 RGB(0,255,0) );         // The color

    // Set the new pen (and save the original pen)
    CPen* pOriginalPen = pDC->SelectObject ( &NewPen );

    pDC->MoveTo ( 10, 30 );
    pDC->LineTo ( 50, 30 );

    // Restore the original pen
    pDC->SelectObject ( pOriginalPen );


    // Draw a line with the original pen
    pDC->MoveTo ( 50, 30 );
    pDC->LineTo ( 80, 30 );


    }


// Draw the circle
if ( m_Shape == 2 )
    {

    // Create a new pen
    CPen NewPen (PS_SOLID,               // The Style
                40,                      // The width
                RGB(255, 0, 0) );        // The color

    // Set the new pen (and save the original pen)
    CPen* pOriginalPen = pDC->SelectObject ( &NewPen );


    // Create a rectangle object
    CRect theRect ( 20, 100, 120, 200 );

    // Draw the Circle
    pDC->Ellipse ( &theRect );

    // Restore the original pen
    pDC->SelectObject ( pOriginalPen );


    }
```

```
      // Draw the rectangle
      if ( m_Shape == 3 )
          {
          // Create a rectangle object
          CRgn theRgn;
          theRgn.CreateRectRgn ( 50, 100, 150, 200 );

          // Create a new brush
          CBrush MyBrush( HS_BDIAGONAL, RGB(0, 0, 255) );

          // Draw the rectangle
          pDC->FillRgn ( &theRgn, &MyBrush );

          }

      ////////////////////////
      // MY CODE ENDS HERE
      ////////////////////////


      }
```

The code you typed will be executed whenever the user selects Rectangle from the Draw menu:

```
if ( m_Shape == 3 )
    {
    ...
    ...
    ...
    // Draw the rectangle
    ...
    ...
    ...
    }
```

The first statement under the if block creates the object theRgn of class CRgn:

```
CRgn theRgn;
```

Then the region is defined with the CreateRectRgn() member function of CRgn:

```
theRgn.CreateRectRgn ( 50, 100, 150, 200 );
```

The upper-left corner of the rectangle region is (x=50, y=100), and the lower-right corner of the region is (x=150, y=200).

The next statement creates a brush (an object MyBrush of class CBrush):

```
CBrush MyBrush( HS_BDIAGONAL, RGB(0, 0, 255) );
```

The first parameter of the constructor function `MyBrush()` is `HS_BDIAGONAL`. This means that the brush will draw diagonal lines. The second parameter of the constructor function is `RGB(0,0,255)`. This means that the brush is blue.

Now that you've defined the brush and the region, you can execute the `FillRgn()` function:

```
pDC->FillRgn ( &theRgn, &MyBrush );
```

The first parameter of `FillRgn()` is the address of the region that you defined, and the second parameter is the address of the brush that will be used to fill the region.

To see your code in action:

☐ Compile/link and execute the DRAW application.

☐ Select Rectangle from the Draw menu.

> *The DRAW application responds by drawing the rectangle shown in Figure 34.14.*

Figure 34.14.
Drawing the
rectangle.

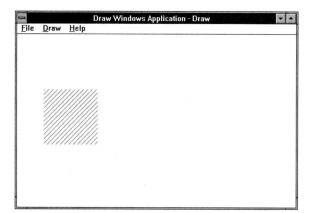

The CircleIt Application

So far in this chapter, you've drawn shapes by taking advantage of the `OnDraw()` function. The `OnDraw()` function is a good function to use for drawing, because it's automatically executed whenever there is a need to redraw the window. If you minimize the window and then maximize it, for example, `OnDraw()` will be executed and everything it drew will be redrawn. As you might guess, this is a great feature because you don't have to write code that detects when the application's window has to be redrawn. Nevertheless, there are occasions where you'll need to draw outside the OnDraw() function. The CircleIt application demonstrates how this is accomplished.

Before you start writing the CircleIt application yourself, execute the copy of it that resides in your C:\VCPROG\ORIGINAL\CH34\CircleIt directory.

To execute the Draw.EXE application:

☐ Use Run from the Program Manager's File menu to execute
C:\VCPROG\ORIGINAL\CH34\CIRCLEIT\CircleIt.EXE.

Windows responds by executing the CircleIt application. CircleIt.EXE*'s main window appears as shown in Figure 34.15.*

Figure 34.15.
The CircleIt
application's main
window.

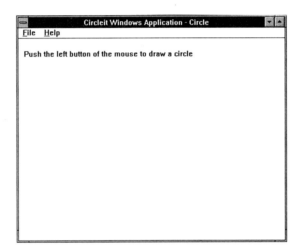

The CIRCLEIT application has two popup menus: File and Help. The File menu contains the standard Print menu items (see Figure 34.16).

☐ Click the left mouse button inside the CircleIt application's window.

The CircleIt application responds by drawing a circle with a thick boundary (see Figure 34.17).

Figure 34.16.
The CircleIt
application's File
menu.

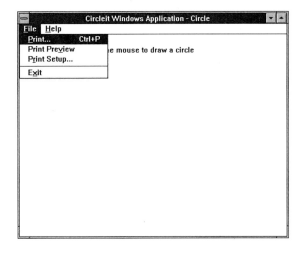

Figure 34.17.
Drawing a circle.

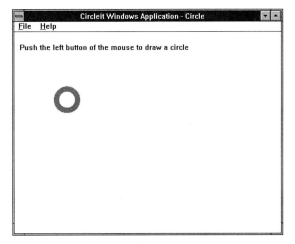

☐ Keep clicking the mouse at various points in the CircleIt application's window.

The CircleIt application responds by drawing a circle for each click (see Figure 34.18).

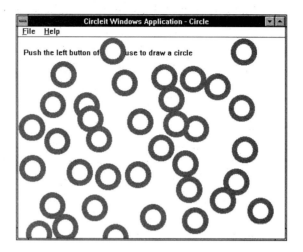

Figure 34.18.
Drawing several
circles with
the CircleIt
application.

☐ Drag the CircleIt window's title bar downward until half of the window is outside the screen.

☐ Drag the title bar upward.

As shown in Figure 34.19, the part of the window that went off the screen isn't re-drawn. This is because the drawing wasn't performed by the OnDraw() function.

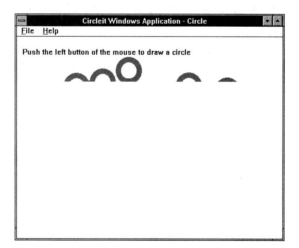

Figure 34.19.
The area that went
off the screen is not
redrawn.

☐ Minimize the CircleIt window and then restore it to its original size.

> *The CircleIt application responds by displaying its window without any circles in it because the original circles weren't drawn from within* OnDraw(). *However, the original text, "Push the left button of the mouse to draw a circle," appears because it's drawn from within* OnDraw().

Experiment with the CircleIt application and then select Exit from the File menu to terminate it.

Now that you know what the CircleIt should do, you can write it.

Creating the Project of the CircleIt Application

To create the project of the CircleIt application:

☐ Select AppWizard from the Project menu.

> *Visual C++ responds by running AppWizard.*

☐ Use the Directory list box to select the directory C:\VCPROG\PRACTICE\CH34.

☐ Type circleit in the Project Name box.

Now your AppWizard dialog box looks as shown in Figure 34.20.

Figure 34.20.
The AppWizard dialog box for the CircleIt application.

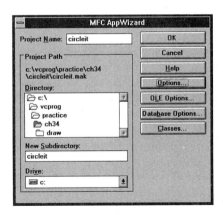

☐ Click the Options button and set the options as shown in Figure 34.21. Note that in Figure 34.21, you're instructed to check the Printing and Print Preview check box.

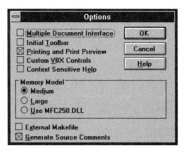

Figure 34.21.
Setting the options
for the CircleIt
application.

☐ Click the Options dialog box's OK button, click the OK button of the
AppWizard dialog box, and finally click the Create button of the New
Application Information dialog box.

> *AppWizard responds by creating the CircleIt project and all the skeleton files*
> *of the CircleIt application.*

To remove the debug options of the project (so you'll have a small EXE file):

☐ Select Project from Visual C++'s Options menu, click the Release radio
button, and then click the OK button of the dialog box.

The Visual Design of CircleIt's Menu

Use App Studio to implement the menu of the CircleIt application per Table 34.2.

Table 34.2. The CircleIt Application's Menu.

Menu Item
&File
&Print...
Print Pre&view
P&rint Setup...
Separator
E&xit
&Help
&About Circleit...

To save your work:

☐ Select Save from App Studio's File menu.

The visual implementation of the CircleIt application's menu is complete.

Adding Code to the *OnDraw()* Function

Before writing "drawing code" outside the OnDraw() function, add code to the OnDraw() function. That way you'll be able to see the difference between drawings that are generated inside the OnDraw() function and those generated outside.

☐ Open the CIRCLVW.CPP file and add the following code to the OnDraw() function. After you add the code, your OnDraw() function looks as follows:

```
void CCircleitView::OnDraw(CDC* pDC)
{
CCircleitDoc* pDoc = GetDocument();
ASSERT_VALID(pDoc);

// TODO: add draw code for native data here


/////////////////////
// MY CODE STARTS HERE
/////////////////////

CString MyString =
   "Push the left button of the mouse to draw a circle";

pDC->TextOut( 10,
              20,
              MyString );



/////////////////////
// MY CODE ENDS HERE
/////////////////////

}
```

The code you typed creates an object MyString of type CString:

```
CString MyString =
   "Push the left button of the mouse to draw a circle";
```

Then the TextOut() function is executed:

```
pDC->TextOut( 10,          // X-coordinate
              20,          // Y-coordinate
              MyString );
```

Note that in the preceding statement, TextOut() "works" on the pDC. pDC was received as the parameter of the OnDraw() function.

NOTE

You can display the Help window in TextOut() as follows:

Highlight the TextOut text and then press F1 for help.

Visual C++ responds by displaying the Help window of the TextOut() function, as shown in Figure 34.22.

As shown, there are two TextOut() functions: one with four parameters and the other with three parameters. In the code you typed in OnDraw(), you used the TextOut() function with three parameters.

It's possible to have more than one function with the same name (and a different number of parameters) in C++; they're called *overloaded functions.*

Figure 34.22.
The Help window
of TextOut().

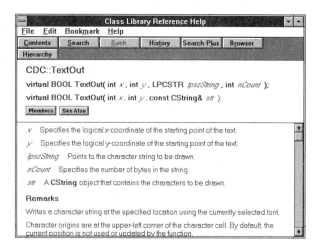

Drawing Outside the *OnDraw()* Function

Now you'll attach code to the CIRCLVW.CPP file that is executed whenever the left mouse button is pressed.

☐ Use ClassWizard to add a function for the event:

Class Name:	CCircleitView
Object ID:	CCircleitView
Message:	WM_LBUTTONDOWN
Function Name:	OnLButtonDown()

NOTE: Make sure you're adding the function to the CCircleitView class.

☐ Edit the OnLButtonDown() function that you added to the CIRCLVW.CPP file.
   After you edit the OnLButtonDown() function, it looks as follows:

```
void CCircleitView::OnLButtonDown(UINT nFlags,
                                  CPoint point)
{
// TODO: Add your message handler code
// here and/or call default


    ////////////////////////
    // MY CODE STARTS HERE
    ////////////////////////

    CDC* pDC = GetDC();

    // Create a new pen
    CPen NewPen (PS_SOLID,            // The Style
               10,                    // The width
               RGB(255, 0, 0) );     // The color

    // Set the new pen (and save the original pen)
    CPen* pOriginalPen = pDC->SelectObject ( &NewPen );


    // Create a rectangle object
    CRect theRect ( point.x-20,
                    point.y-20,
                    point.x+20,
                    point.y+20 );

    // Draw the Circle
    pDC->Ellipse ( &theRect );
```

```
// Restore the original pen
pDC->SelectObject ( pOriginalPen );


ReleaseDC (pDC);

////////////////////
// MY CODE ENDS HERE
////////////////////
```

```
CView::OnLButtonDown(nFlags, point);
}
```

The code that you typed uses the GetDC() member function to get a device context called pDC:

```
CDC* pDC = GetDC();
```

This wasn't necessary when you used the OnDraw() function, because pDC was supplied as the parameter of the OnDraw() function.

The important thing to know is that because you extracted pDC with GetDC(), it's your responsibility to release it with the ReleaseDC() function.

This means that your code must look as follows:

```
CDC* pDC = GetDC();
    ......
    ......
    ......
    // Draw whatever you want to draw
    ......
    ......
    ......
ReleaseDC (pDC);
```

You can write "drawing code" between GetDC() and ReleaseDC(), the same way you write it in the OnDraw() function.

> **NOTE**
>
> As stated, when you use the GetDC() function, it's your responsibility to release the DC with the ReleaseDC() function.
>
> However, when you draw from within OnDraw(), don't use the ReleaseDC() function to release the pDC, because this is done for you automatically.

Now take a look at the code that you typed between `GetDC()` and `ReleaseDC()`:

First, you created a new pen object:

```
CPen NewPen (PS_SOLID,            // The Style
             10,                  // The width
             RGB(255, 0, 0) );    // The color
```

and then you used the `SelectObject()` function to put this new pen to use:

```
CPen* pOriginalPen = pDC->SelectObject ( &NewPen );
```

Note that in the preceding statement the pen that existed before the new pen was created is saved as `pOriginalPen`.

The next statement creates the object `theRect` of class `CRect`:

```
CRect theRect ( point.x-20,
                point.y-20,
                point.x+20,
                point.y+20 );
```

The rectangle is defined in reference to the point where the left mouse button is pushed. Note that the point was received as the parameter of the `OnLButtonDown()` function. Putting it all together, the `theRect` rectangle is defined as shown in Figure 34.23.

Figure 34.23.
Defining
`theRect` *in*
reference to the
`point` *parameter.*

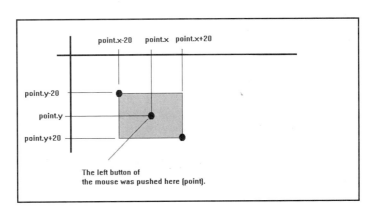

Now that the pen and the rectangle are defined, you can use the `Ellipse()` function to draw the circle:

```
pDC->Ellipse ( &theRect );
```

And finally, the `SelectObject()` function is used to restore the original pen:

```
pDC->SelectObject ( pOriginalPen );
```

NOTE

It's a good programming habit to restore the original pen. Consider, for example, the case of an application that uses Function1() to draw something with a particular pen. Let's say that Function1() draws something and then calls Function2(). Function2() draws something with a different pen, and then Function1() continues drawing.

This process is shown as follows:

```
void Function1(void)
{
// Create a pen,(pen1)
...
...
...


// Draw with pen1
...
...
...


// Execute Function2()
Function2();

// Continue the drawing (with pen1)
...
...
...
}
```

If Function2() uses a different pen but returns the original pen, there's no need for Function1() to create pen1 all over again when it continues the drawing with the current pen (Pen1).

So the rule of thumb is a function that changes the current pen should be responsible for restoring the original pen. This is not a C++ requirement, but it makes programs easier to read and maintain.

To see your code in action:

☐ Compile/link and execute the CircleIt application.

☐ Click in the application's window.

> *The CircleIt application responds by drawing a circle. The center of the circle is at the point where you clicked the mouse.*

☐ Keep clicking the mouse to draw circles at various places.

☐ Drag the application's window (or minimize it and then maximize it).

The CircleIt application displays the text that was drawn in the OnDraw() function, but the circles you drew disappear. This is because the circles weren't drawn in OnDraw().

☐ Select Exit from the File menu to terminate the CircleIt application.

The MyText Application

The MyText application demonstrates how your Visual C++ application can draw text with various fonts.

Before you start writing the MyText application, execute the copy of it that resides in your C:\VCPROG\ORIGINAL\CH34\MYTEXT directory.

To execute the MyText.EXE application:

☐ Use Run from the Program Manager's File menu to execute
C:\VCPROG\ORIGINAL\CH34\MYTEXT\MyText.EXE.

> *Windows responds by executing the MyText application. The main window of* MyText.EXE *appears as shown in Figure 34.24.*

The MyText application has two popup menus, File and Help. The MyText application's File menu contains the standard Print menu items (see Figure 34.25).

Now that you know what the MyText should do, you can write it.

Figure 34.24.
The MyText
application's main
window.

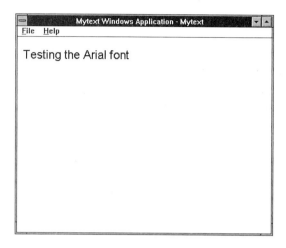

Figure 34.25.
The MyText
application's File
menu.

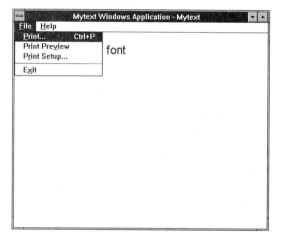

Creating the Project of the MyText Application

To create the project of the MyText application:

☐ Select AppWizard from the Project menu.

> *Visual C++ responds by running AppWizard.*

☐ Use the Directory list box to select the directory C:\VCPROG\PRACTICE\CH34.

☐ Type mytext in the Project Name box.

Now your AppWizard dialog box looks as shown in Figure 34.26.

Figure 34.26.
The AppWizard
dialog box for
the MyText
application.

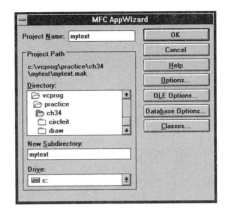

☐ Click the Options button and set the options as shown in Figure 34.27.
   Note that in Figure 34.27, you're instructed to check the Printing and Print
   Preview check box.

Figure 34.27.
Setting the options
for the MyText
application.

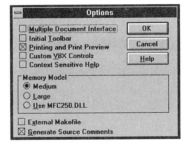

☐ Click the Options dialog box, click the OK button of the AppWizard dialog
   box, and finally click the Create button of the New Application Information
   dialog box.

   AppWizard responds by creating the MyText project and all the skeleton files
   of the MyText application.

To remove the debug options of the project (so you'll have a small EXE file):

☐ Select Project from Visual C++'s Options menu, click the Release radio
   button, and then click the OK button of the dialog box.

The Visual Design of MyText's Menu

☐ Use App Studio to implement the menu of the MyText application per Table 34.3.

Table 34.3. The MyText application's menu.

Menu Item
&File
&Print...
Print Pre&view
P&rint Setup...
Separator
E&xit
&Help
&About Mytext...

☐ Use App Studio to remove the Accelerator keys that are not used by the application.

To save your work:

☐ Select Save from App Studio's File menu.

The visual implementation of the MyText application's menu is complete.

NOTE: The MyText application doesn't have a custom dialog box. It only has an About dialog box.

Displaying Text with Different Fonts

You've already had several opportunities in this book to display text with the TextOut() function. The MyText application demonstrates how to use the TextOut() function to display text with various fonts.

☐ Open the MYTEXVW.CPP file and add code to the OnDraw() function. After you add the code, your OnDraw() function looks as follows:

```
void CMytextView::OnDraw(CDC* pDC)
{
    CMytextDoc* pDoc = GetDocument();
    ASSERT_VALID(pDoc);

    // TODO: add draw code for native data here

    /////////////////////////
    // MY CODE STARTS HERE
    /////////////////////////

    CFont MyFont;

    MyFont.CreateFont   ( 25,
                          0,
                          0,
                          0,
                          400,
                          FALSE,
                          FALSE,
                          0,
                          ANSI_CHARSET,
                          OUT_DEFAULT_PRECIS,
                          CLIP_DEFAULT_PRECIS,
                          DEFAULT_QUALITY,
                          DEFAULT_PITCH|FF_SWISS,
                          "Arial");

    CFont* pOldFont = (CFont*)pDC->SelectObject(&MyFont);

    pDC->TextOut(10,
                 20,
                 "Testing the Arial font");

    /////////////////////////
    // MY CODE ENDS HERE
    /////////////////////////

}
```

The code that you typed creates an object MyFont of class CFont:

```
CFont MyFont;
```

The next statement uses the CreateFont() function to create the font:

```
MyFont.CreateFont   ( 25,
                      0,
                      0,
                      0,
                      400,
```

```
FALSE,
FALSE,
0,
ANSI_CHARSET,
OUT_DEFAULT_PRECIS,
CLIP_DEFAULT_PRECIS,
DEFAULT_QUALITY,
DEFAULT_PITCH|FF_SWISS,
"Arial");
```

As you can see, the `CreateFont()` function has many parameters. To see the purpose of each of the parameters:

☐ Highlight the `CreateFont` text and then press F1 for help.

> *Visual C++ responds by displaying the Help window for the* `CreateFont()` *function (see Figure 34.28).*

Figure 34.28.
The
`CreateFont()`
function's Help
window.

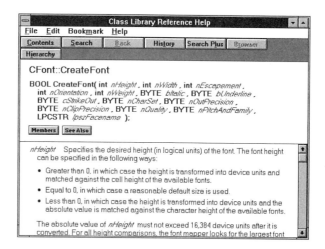

For now, pay attention to the first and last parameters. The first parameter is the height of the text, and the last parameter is the name of the font.

The next statement that you typed actually puts the font to use by using the `SelectObject()` function:

```
CFont* pOldFont = (CFont*)pDC->SelectObject(&MyFont);
```

Note that as usual, the returned value of `SelectObject()` is the pointer of the object that was replaced. So after executing the `SelectObject()` function, `pOldFont` is updated with the pointer of the font that existed before the Arial font was selected with the `SelectObject()`.

Finally, the `TextOut()` function is executed to display text with the font specified in the `CreateFont()` function:

```
pDC->TextOut(10,
            20,
            "Testing the Arial font");
```

☐ Compile/link and execute the MyText application.

The MyText application responds by displaying its main window, as shown in Figure 34.29.

Figure 34.29.
Arial font
(Height: 25).

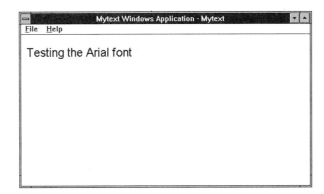

You can now experiment by changing the value of the first parameter of the `CreateFont()` function.

☐ Open the MYTEXVW.CPP file and change the first parameter of the `CreateFont()` function inside the `OnDraw()` function. After you change the value of the first parameter, the `CreateFont()` function looks as follows:

```
MyFont.CreateFont    ( 100,
                     0,
                     0,
                     0,
                     400,
                     FALSE,
                     FALSE,
                     0,
                     ANSI_CHARSET,
                     OUT_DEFAULT_PRECIS,
                     CLIP_DEFAULT_PRECIS,
                     DEFAULT_QUALITY,
                     DEFAULT_PITCH¦FF_SWISS,
                     "Arial");
```

☐ Compile/link and execute the MyText application.

The main window of the MyText application appears as shown in Figure 34.30.

Figure 34.30.
Arial font
(Height: 100).

☐ Experiment with the MyText application by changing its first parameter as well as its last parameter.

For example, Figure 34.31 shows the main window of MyText after the OnDraw() function is modified as follows:

```
void CMytextView::OnDraw(CDC* pDC)
{
    CMytextDoc* pDoc = GetDocument();
    ASSERT_VALID(pDoc);

    // TODO: add draw code for native data here

    /////////////////////////
    // MY CODE STARTS HERE
    /////////////////////////

    CFont MyFont;

    MyFont.CreateFont    ( 25,
                           0,
                           0,
                           0,
                           400,
                           FALSE,
                           FALSE,
                           0,
                           ANSI_CHARSET,
                           OUT_DEFAULT_PRECIS,
                           CLIP_DEFAULT_PRECIS,
```

```
                    DEFAULT_QUALITY,
                    DEFAULT_PITCH¦FF_SWISS,
                    "Courier New");


   CFont* pOldFont = (CFont*)pDC->SelectObject(&MyFont);

   pDC->TextOut(10,
                20,
                "Testing the Courier New font");


   /////////////////////
   // MY CODE ENDS HERE
   /////////////////////


}
```

Figure 34.31.
Displaying text
with the Courier
New font
(Height: 25).

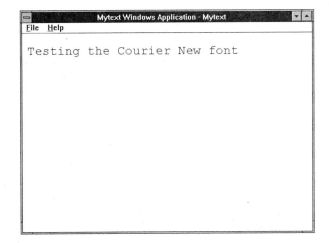

35

Creating Your Own VBX Controls

In this chapter you'll create your own VBX control. Your VBX control can be used by Visual C++ applications as well as by Visual Basic applications. That is, after you finish implementing the VBX control, you can distribute it to Visual C++ programmers as well as to Visual Basic programmers. Then both could use your VBX control in their applications.

The MYCLOCK.VBX Control

The VBX control that you'll create in this chapter is called MYCLOCK.VBX (MyClock). As implied by its name, this VBX control is used to display the current time. As always, before you start writing the code yourself, you'll be instructed to look at a copy of this control in action. That way, you'll have a better understanding of what the control does.

In the following two sections you'll test a copy of the MYCLOCK.VBX control. In the first section you'll test the control with a Visual C++ application, and in the second section you'll test the control with a Visual Basic application. After these two sections, the remainder of the chapter will instruct you step-by-step on how to create the MYCLOCK.VBX control.

Testing the MYCLOCK.VBX Control with Visual C++

Before you can test the MYCLOCK.VBX control, you have to first copy the MYCLOCK.VBX file to your \WINDOWS\SYSTEM directory. A copy of the MYCLOCK.VBX control was copied to your \VCPROG\ORIGINAL\CH35\MYCLOCK directory when you installed the book's CD. Follow these steps to copy the MYCLOCK.VBX file to your \WINDOWS\SYSTEM directory:

☐ Exit to a DOS Shell or switch to the File Manager program.

☐ Copy the file C:\VCPROG\ORIGINAL\CH35\MYCLOCK\MYCLOCK.VBX to your
   C:\WINDOWS\SYSTEM directory.

To test the MYCLOCK.VBX control with Visual C++, you need to have an MFC Visual C++ project that includes a dialog box (you've created many such applications throughout the course of the book). Then you can test the MYCLOCK.VBX control by placing it in the application's dialog box.

To save you time, an application with a dialog box (called TESTVBX) was copied to your hard drive when you installed the book's CD. You will use the TESTVBX application as a benchmark for testing the MYCLOCK.VBX control.

Before you place the MYCLOCK.VBX in the TESTVBX application's dialog box, open the project of the TESTVBX application and execute it:

☐ Select Open from Visual C++'s Project menu and then select the project file
   C:\VCPROG\ORIGINAL\CH35\TESTVBX\TESTVBX.MAK.

   Visual C++ responds by opening the TESTVBX project.

☐ Select Execute TESTVBX.EXE from the Project menu.

> *Visual C++ responds by executing the TESTVBX application. The main window of* TESTVBX.EXE *appears as shown in Figure 35.1.*

Figure 35.1.
The TESTVBX
application's main
window.

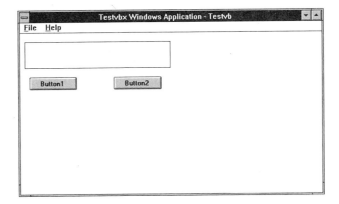

As you can see, the application's main window contains an edit box and two push buttons. These elements don't perform any functions. As stated previously, the only purpose of the TESTVBX application is to test the MYCLOCK.VBX control.

☐ Exit the TESTVBX application by selecting Exit from the File menu.

Now add the MYCLOCK.VBX control to the dialog box of the TESVBX application:

☐ Use App Studio to open the IDD_DIALOG1 dialog box of the TESTVBX application. The IDD_DIALOG1 dialog box is shown in Figure 35.2.

Figure 35.2.
The TESTVBX
application's
IDD_DIALOG1
dialog box.

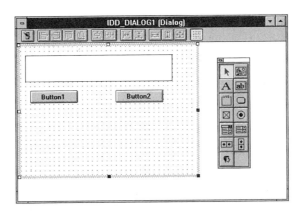

Before you can place the MYCLOCK.VBX control in the dialog box, you must first install it in App Studio's Tools window (just as you did with other VBX controls in previous chapters). Here's how you do that:

☐ Select Install Controls from App Studio's File menu.

App Studio responds by displaying the Install Controls dialog box (see Figure 35.3).

Figure 35.3.
App Studio's Install
Controls dialog box.

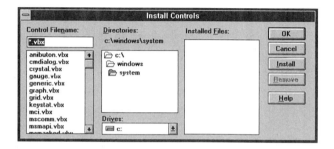

The leftmost list in the Install Controls dialog box displays all the VBX files that reside in your \WINDOWS\SYSTEM directory. The MYCLOCK.VBX file is also listed, because earlier you were instructed to copy the MYCLOCK.VBX file to your WINDOWS\SYSTEM directory.

The Installed Files list (the rightmost list) lists all the VBX files that are currently installed in App Studio. In Figure 35.3, the Installed Files list is empty because no VBX files have been installed yet.

To install the MYCLOCK.VBX file:

☐ Select the file MYCLOCK.VBX and then click the Install button.

App Studio responds by adding MYCLOCK.VBX to the Installed Files list (see Figure 35.4).

Figure 35.4.
Installing the
MYCLOCK.VBX
control in App
Studio.

☐ Click the Close button of the Install Controls dialog box.

The MYCLOCK.VBX control is now installed in App Studio's Tools window. As you can see from Figure 35.5, the MYCLOCK.VBX icon displays a picture of a clock. When you design the MYCLOCK.VBX control later in the chapter, you'll learn how to customize the picture in the VBX icon.

Figure 35.5.
The MYCLOCK.VBX
icon in the Tools
window.

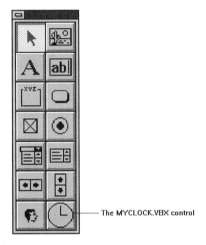

The MYCLOCK.VBX control

You can now place the MYCLOCK.VBX control in the dialog box, just as you would place any other control:

☐ Place the MYCLOCK.VBX control below the push buttons, as shown in Figure 35.6.

Figure 35.6.
Placing the
MYCLOCK.VBX
control in the
dialog box.

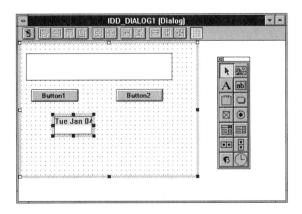

To see the MYCLOCK.VBX working, you need to widen it:

☐ Drag the MYCLOCK.VBX control's handles until it looks as shown in Figure 35.7.

Figure 35.7.
The MYCLOCK.VBX
control after
changing its size.

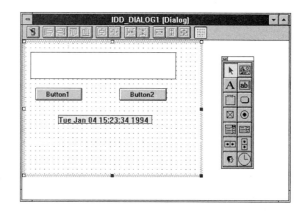

Surprise! Surprise! The MYCLOCK.VBX control is working (that is, it keeps on displaying the current time) even though right now you are in design mode. This is a nice feature of VBX controls. The VBX control's code (code that you'll write later in this chapter) is running even when the control is in design mode (in App Studio).

Just like other VBX controls you've worked with, the MYCLOCK.VBX control has properties. To see these properties:

☐ Double-click the MYCLOCK.VBX icon.

App Studio responds by displaying the MYCLOCK Properties window.

☐ Select Styles from the drop-down list box at the upper-right corner of the Properties window.

App Studio responds by displaying the Styles Properties window of the control (see Figure 35.8).

As you can see from Figure 35.8, the MYCLOCK control has several properties. The Height and Width properties enable you to set the size of the MYCLOCK.VBX control. You can use these properties instead of dragging the control's handles. For example, to set the control to the size shown in Figure 35.7:

☐ Set the Width property to 103.

☐ Set the Height property to 10.

Figure 35.8.
The MYCLOCK.VBX
control's Styles
Properties window.

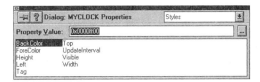

For now, don't change any of the values of the other properties. Later in the chapter you'll have a chance to experiment with these properties.

The MYCLOCK.VBX control also has events associated with it. To see these events:

☐ Select ClassWizard from App Studio's Resource menu.

App Studio responds by displaying the ClassWizard dialog box.

Make sure that the IDC_MYCLOCK1 object is selected in the Object IDs list, and observe the Messages list (see Figure 35.9).

Figure 35.9.
The events
(messages)
associated with the
MYCLOCK.VBX
control.

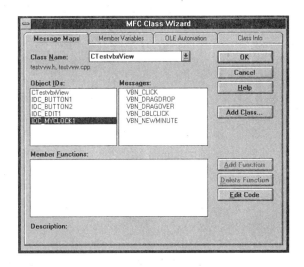

As you can see from Figure 35.9, the MYCLOCK.VBX control has several events (messages) associated with it—VBN_CLICK, VBN_DRAGDROP, VBN_DRAGOVER, VBN_DBLCLICK, and VBN_NEWMINUTE. For now, don't attach code to any of these events. Later in the chapter you'll have a chance to attach code to some of these events.

☐ Click ClassWizard's Cancel button to go back to App Studio.

As you've just seen, the MYCLOCK.VBX control has properties and events like any other VBX control. Another standard VBX feature it has is that it allows you to place several MYCLOCK.VBX objects in the dialog box:

☐ Place several more MYCLOCK.VBX controls inside the dialog box.

Figure 35.10 shows the IDD_DIALOG1 dialog box with five MYCLOCK.VBX controls in it. All of them display the current time.

Figure 35.10.
The
IDD_DIALOG1
dialog box with five
MYCLOCK.VBX
controls in it.

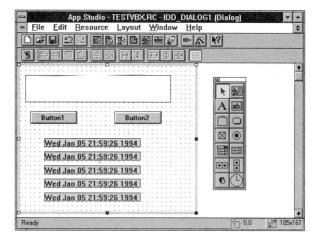

Removing the MYCLOCK.VBX Control from App Studio

Because you'll develop a new version of the MYCLOCK.VBX control later in this chapter, you should remove the current MYCLOCK.VBX control from App Studio's Tools window. This is because after you create your own MYCLOCK.VBX control you'll need to fully test its performance by installing the control, placing it in the dialog box, examining its properties, examining its events, and so on.

Follow these steps to remove the MYCLOCK.VBX control from App Studio's Tools window:

☐ Delete all the MYCLOCK controls from the IDD_DIALOG1 dialog box. You need to do this because you can't use App Studio to remove a VBX control if this control is in the dialog box.

☐ Select Install Controls from App Studio's File menu.

App Studio responds by displaying the Install Controls dialog box. The Installed Files list (the leftmost list) includes the MYCLOCK.VBX control (see Figure 35.4). Your objective is to remove this item.

☐ Highlight the MYCLOCK.VBX item in the Installed Files list and then click the Remove button.

App Studio responds by removing the MYCLOCK.VBX control from the Installed Files list.

☐ Click the Close button of the Install Controls dialog box.

You've finished removing the MYCLOCK.VBX control. App Studio's Tools window doesn't include the MYCLOCK.VBX control anymore.

Testing the MYCLOCK.VBX Control with Visual Basic

As stated earlier, the MYCLOCK.VBX control can be used by both Visual C++ and Visual Basic for Windows applications. Now you'll test the MYCLOCK.VBX control with Visual Basic.

> **NOTE**
>
> The following steps tell you how to test the MYCLOCK.VBX control with Visual Basic for Windows. Of course, you need to have Visual Basic for Windows installed in your PC to do this. Even if you don't, browse through this section anyway. You'll see how easy it is to incorporate VBX controls into Visual Basic. This way, when you develop a VBX control for Visual C++, you'll keep in mind that Visual Basic programmers can also use your VBX control.

Test the MYCLOCK.VBX control from Visual Basic:

☐ Start Visual Basic for Windows.

The main window (actually, several windows) of Visual Basic appears as shown in Figure 35.11. Note that, depending on the particular version and configuration of your Visual Basic package, your screen may look different (for example, there may be more or fewer controls in the Tools window).

Figure 35.11.
Visual Basic's
main window.

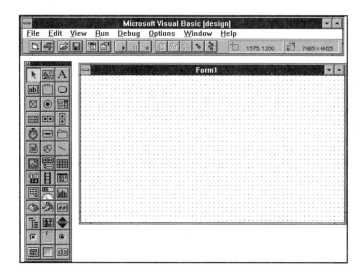

Add the MYCLOCK.VBX control to Visual Basic's Tools window:

☐ Select Add File from Visual Basic's File menu.

> *Visual Basic responds by displaying the Add File dialog box (see Figure 35.12).*

Figure 35.12.
Visual Basic's Add
File dialog box.

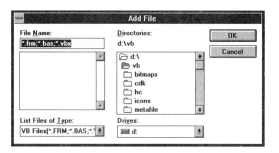

☐ Use the Add File dialog box to select the file MYCLOCK.VBX from your
\WINDOWS\SYSTEM directory and then click the OK button.

> *Visual Basic responds by adding the MYCLOCK.VBX control to the Tools*
> *window (see Figure 35.13).*

Figure 35.13.
Visual Basic's Tools
window after
you add the
MYCLOCK.VBX
control.

The MYCLOCK.VBX control

Place the MYCLOCK.VBX control in the form of the application:

☐ Double-click the MYCLOCK icon in the Tools window.

> *Visual Basic responds by placing the MYCLOCK.VBX control in the*
> *application's form (see Figure 35.14).*

☐ Adjust the size of the MYCLOCK.VBX control until it looks as shown in
Figure 35.15.

Figure 35.14.
Placing the
MYCLOCK.VBX
control in a Visual
Basic form.

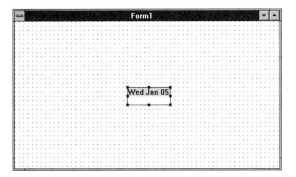

Figure 35.15.
Adjusting the
size of the
MYCLOCK.VBX
control in a Visual
Basic form.

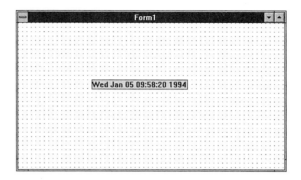

As you can see, the MYCLOCK.VBX control's code is working; it keeps on display-ing the current time.

You can now inspect the properties of the MYCLOCK.VBX control, just as you would inspect any other control:

☐ Make sure that the MYCLOCK object is selected in the form (that is, click it in the form) and then press the F4 key.

   Visual Basic responds by displaying the Properties window for the MYCLOCK object (see Figure 35.16).

Figure 35.16.
Visual Basic's
Properties window
displaying the
properties of the
MYCLOCK object.

The MYCLOCK object also has event procedures associated with it. To see them:

☐ Double-click the MYCLOCK object inside the form.

   Visual Basic responds by opening the Click event procedure of the MYCLOCK object (see Figure 35.17).

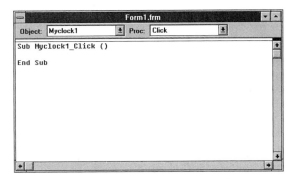

Figure 35.17.
The MYCLOCK
object's Click event
procedure window.

To see a list of all the event procedures of the MYCLOCK object:

☐ Open the drop-down list box at the upper-right corner of the event procedure window (see Figure 35.18).

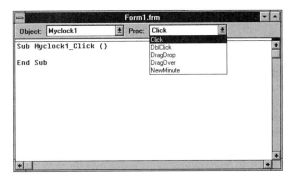

Figure 35.18.
The event
procedures of the
MYCLOCK object.

As you have just seen, the MYCLOCK control is plugged into Visual Basic just like
any other control; it has its own properties and event procedures.

> **NOTE**
>
> If you have no experience with Visual Basic, you can use the following Visual
> Basic for Windows book:
>
> Title: *Teach Yourself Visual Basic 3.0 in 21 Days*
> Authors: Gurewich & Gurewich
> Publisher: Sams Publishing
> ISBN: 0-672-30378-7

Now that you know what the MYCLOCK.VBX control does, you can start designing it from scratch. In the following sections, you'll implement the MYCLOCK.VBX control by following a set of step-by-step instructions.

Before you start developing the MYCLOCK.VBX control, you should first terminate Visual Basic:

☐ Terminate Visual Basic and switch back to Visual C++.

NOTE

In the preceding step you were instructed to terminate Visual Basic. It's very important to do this! Why? Because in subsequent sections of this chapter you'll write code to create your own version of the MYCLOCK.VBX control. After creating your own MYCLOCK.VBX control, you'll need to override the old version of MYCLOCK.VBX. However, if MYCLOCK.VBX is currently being used by any active application, Windows won't let you override the current MYCLOCK.VBX file. Thus, before you start writing the code for MYCLOCK.VBX, you should close all applications that use the MYCLOCK.VBX control.

Developing the MYCLOCK.VBX Control Yourself

Writing a VBX control involves writing a lot of overhead code that is the same for all VBX controls. Thus, to save time, you can use template files that include all the necessary overhead code. You can then copy these template files to your development directory whenever you start a new VBX project.

This book's CD includes such template files. In the following section, you'll use these template files to start the MYCLOCK.VBX project. As you gain more experience in developing VBX files, you can write your own template files for various types of VBX projects.

Using Generic Files to Start Your VBX Project

When you installed the book's CD, the directory \VCPROG\GENVBX was created on your hard drive. This directory contains generic files for developing a VBX control. In the following steps you'll copy these generic files to your development directory and you'll customize these files to fit the VBX control you're currently developing (that is, the MYCLOCK.VBX control).

Begin by creating a development directory for the MYCLOCK.VBX control:

☐ Use the Windows File Manager (or DOS Shell) to create the subdirectory `C:\VCPROG\PRACTICE\CH35\MYCLOCK`.

You already have the directory `\VCPROG\PRACTICE\CH35`, so create the subdirectory `MYCLOCK` in this directory.

☐ Now, copy all the files from `C:\VCPROG\GENVBX\*.*` to `C:\VCPROG\PRACTICE\CH35\MYCLOCK`.

Your MYCLOCK directory now contains the following files:

```
GENERIC.C
GENERIC.H
GENERIC.DEF
GENERIC.RC
DOWN.BMP
UP.BMP
UPEGA.BMP
UPMONO.BMP
```

In addition to the preceding eight files, you need two additional files in your development directory:

```
VBAPI.LIB
VBAPI.H
```

These files are included with Microsoft Visual Basic for Windows, Professional Edition, and you must have them in order to develop VBX controls. Typically, these files reside in your `VB\CDK` directory.

NOTE

The files `VBAPI.LIB` and `VBAPI.H` are not included with the book's CD. These two files are included with Visual Basic for Windows, Professional Edition. You need to have these files in order to develop a VBX control.

☐ Copy the files `VBAPI.LIB` and `VBAPI.H` from your `VB\CDK` directory into your `C:\VCPROG\PRACTICE\CH35\MYCLOCK` directory.

NOTE

Before you read the rest of this chapter, make sure that your development directory (C:\VCPROG\PRACTICE\CH35\MYCLOCK) now has the following 10 files:

GENERIC.C

GENERIC.H

GENERIC.DEF

GENERIC.RC

DOWN.BMP

UP.BMP

UPEGA.BMP

UPMONO.BMP

VBAPI.LIB

VBAPI.H

If you don't have all of these files, you won't be able to perform the steps in the following sections.

Renaming the Files from GENERIC to MYCLOCK

Now that you have all the generic files for developing a VBX control, you can start customizing these files to fit the VBX control that you are developing (MYCLOCK.VBX).

To begin with, you need to rename all the GENERIC.* files in the development directory to MYCLOCK.*:

☐ Use the File Manager in Windows or DOS to rename the files
   C:\VCPROG\PRACTICE\CH35\MYCLOCK\GENERIC.* to
   C:\VCPROG\PRACTICE\CH35\MYCLOCK\MYCLOCK.*.

At this point, your `C:\VCPROG\PRACTICE\CH35\MYCLOCK` directory contains the following files:

```
MYCLOCK.C
MYCLOCK.H
MYCLOCK.DEF
MYCLOCK.RC
DOWN.BMP
UP.BMP
UPEGA.BMP
UPMONO.BMP
VBAPI.LIB
VBAPI.H
```

Replacing All the *GENERIC* References with *MYCLOCK*

The next step in customizing the MYCLOCK VBX project's files is to replace all occurrences of the word `GENERIC` with the word `MYCLOCK` in all of the project's source files. Here's how you do that:

☐ Switch to Visual C++.

☐ Close the current project by selecting Close from the Project menu.

☐ Open the file `MYCLOCK.H` (in the `C:\VCPROG\PRACTICE\CH35\MYCLOCK\MYCLOCK` directory) and perform the following global replacements:

Replace all occurrences of `GENERIC` with `MYCLOCK`
Replace all occurrences of `Generic` with `Myclock`

☐ Save the `MYCLOCK.H` file and close it.

> **NOTE**
>
> The capitalization of the replacements is important! For example, the `GenericCtlProc` is replaced with the word `MyclockCtlProc`, not `MyClockCtlProc`.
>
> A good, systematic way to make the preceding replacements is to use the Edit menu's Replace option twice. First replace all occurrences of `GENERIC` with

MYCLOCK, and then replace all occurrences of Generic with Myclock. If you use this method, make sure that the Match Case check box is checked and that the Match Whole Word Only check box is not checked (see Figure 35.19).

When you make replacements, make them "across the board." That is, replace all occurrences, even inside comments. Although replacements within comments won't affect the code, they will make the code easier to understand.

Figure 35.19.
Replacing
occurrences of
GENERIC with
MYCLOCK.

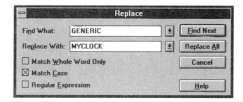

You need to perform the same replacements you made in MYCLOCK.H in the files MYCLOCK.C, MYCLOCK.RC, and MYCLOCK.DEF:

☐ Open the file MYCLOCK.C and perform the following global replacements:

> Replace all occurrences of GENERIC with MYCLOCK
> Replace all occurrences of Generic with Myclock

☐ Save the file MYCLOCK.C and close it.

☐ Open the file MYCLOCK.RC and perform the following global replacements:

> Replace all occurrences of GENERIC with MYCLOCK
> Replace all occurrences of Generic with Myclock

☐ Save the file MYCLOCK.RC and close it.

☐ Open the file MYCLOCK.DEF and perform the following global replacements:

> Replace all occurrences of GENERIC with MYCLOCK
> Replace all occurrences of Generic with Myclock

☐ Save and close the MYCLOCK.DEF file.

Creating the Project of the MYCLOCK.VBX Control

Follow these steps to create the project of the MYCLOCK.VBX control:

☐ Select New from Visual C++'s Project menu.

Visual C++ responds by displaying the New Project dialog box.

☐ Set the Project Type to Visual Basic Custom Control (see Figure 35.20).

Figure 35.20.
Setting the Project
Type to Visual
Basic Custom
Control.

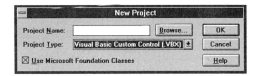

☐ Set the Project Name to `C:\VCPROG\PRACTICE\CH35\MYCLOCK\MYCLOCK.MAK`.

☐ Click the OK button.

Visual C++ responds by displaying the Edit Project dialog box (see Figure 35.21).

Figure 35.21.
The Edit Project
dialog box.

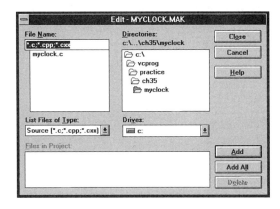

You now need to add the following four files to the MYCLOCK.MAK project:

```
MYCLOCK.C
MYCLOCK.DEF
MYCLOCK.RC
VBAPI.LIB
```

☐ Type `myclock.c` in the File Name box and then click the Add button.

> *Visual C++ responds by adding the MYCLOCK.C file to the Files In Project list.*

☐ Repeat the preceding step to add the files MYCLOCK.DEF, MYCLOCK.RC, and VBAPI.LIB.

Now your Edit Project dialog box looks as shown in Figure 35.22.

☐ Click the Close button of the Edit Project dialog box.

> *Visual C++ responds by creating the MYCLOCK.MAK project.*

Figure 35.22.
The Edit Project
dialog box of the
MYCLOCK.MAK
project.

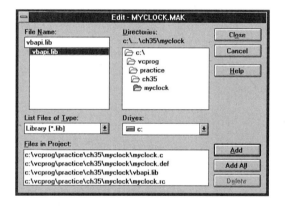

Let's See What You've Accomplished So Far

Believe it or not, even though you haven't written a single line of code, you already have all the code necessary to create the first version of the MYCLOCK.VBX control. The code you borrowed from the GENERIC files produces a working VBX control!

To create the MYCLOCK.VBX file:

☐ Select Rebuild All MYCLOCK.VBX from Visual C++'s Project menu.

> *Visual C++ responds by compiling/linking the files of the MYCLOCK project and creating the file MYCLOCK.VBX.*

To test the MYCLOCK.VBX control that you just created, you first need to copy it to your \WINDOWS\SYSTEM directory:

☐ Switch to the File Manager program (or to DOS) and copy the file C:\VCPROG\PRACTICE\CH35\MYCLOCK.VBX to your C:\WINDOWS\SYSTEM directory.

> **NOTE**
>
> If Windows refuses to overwrite the current MYCLOCK.VBX in your
> WINDOWS\SYSTEM directory, it means that an open application is currently
> using the MYCLOCK.VBX control. If this is the case, you must close the
> application currently using the MYCLOCK.VBX control (for example,
> Visual Basic or App Studio) before you can overwrite the old version of
> MYCLOCK.VBX. If after closing the application Windows won't overwrite
> the old version of MYCLOCK.VBX, you need to quit Windows and
> restart it.

Now that you've copied your MYCLOCK.VBX control to your \WINDOWS\SYSTEM
directory, you can test the MYCLOCK.VBX control with the TESTVBX project:

☐ Open the TESTVBX.MAK project. Note that because you used the
TESTVBX.MAK project earlier, you can easily open it by selecting
TESTVBX.MAK from Visual C++'s Project menu. That is, the MRU (Most
Recently Used) list in the Project menu includes the TESTVBX.MAK
project (see Figure 35.23).

Figure 35.23.
Opening the
TESTVBX.MAK
project.

☐ Start App Studio from Visual C++'s Tools menu and use it to display the
TESTVBX application's IDD_DIALOG1 dialog box in design mode (see Figure
35.24).

Figure 35.24.
The TESTVBX
application's
IDD_DIALOG1
dialog box in design
mode.

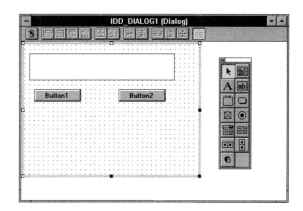

Note that in Figure 35.24, the MYCLOCK icon isn't in App Studio's Tools window. That's because you removed the original version of the MYCLOCK.VBX control.

Now install the MYCLOCK.VBX control you created:

☐ Select Install Controls from App Studio's File menu.

   App Studio responds by displaying the Install Controls dialog box (see Figure 35.3).

☐ Select the file MYCLOCK.VBX and then click the Install button.

   App Studio responds by adding MYCLOCK.VBX to the Installed Files list (see Figure 35.4).

☐ Click the Close button of the Install Controls dialog box.

The MYCLOCK.VBX control that you created is installed in App Studio's Tools window (see Figure 35.25). The MYCLOCK icon contains the letter X. This is what the original Generic files display. Later in the chapter, you'll customize the bitmap files of the MYCLOCK project so that the icon displays a more appropriate picture.

You can now place the MYCLOCK.VBX control inside the dialog box, just as you would place any other control:

☐ Place the MYCLOCK.VBX control below the push buttons, as shown in Figure 35.26.

Figure 35.25.
The
MYCLOCK.VBX
control in the Tools
window.

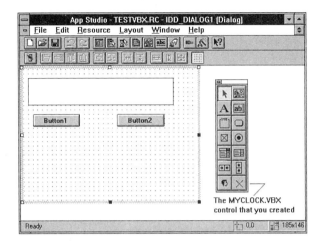

Figure 35.26.
Placing the
MYCLOCK.VBX
control in the
dialog box.

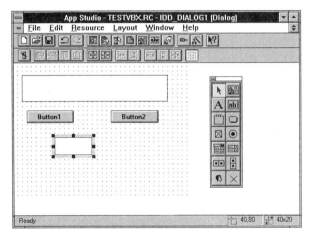

As you can see, the MYCLOCK.VBX control you created is blank. It has a rectangular frame that can be sized like any other control, but there's nothing in it. The code you borrowed from the Generic files produces a blank control. In subsequent sections, you'll add code to the MYCLOCK source files so that the MYCLOCK.VBX control will do what it's supposed to (display the current time).

Even though the MYCLOCK.VBX control displays only an empty frame at this point, it does have properties and events. To see the properties of the control:

☐ Double-click the MYCLOCK control.

App Studio responds by displaying the General properties of the control.

☐ Select Styles from the drop-down list box at the upper-right corner of the Properties window.

App Studio responds by displaying the Styles Properties window of the control (see Figure 35.27).

Figure 35.27.
The Styles
Properties window
of the MYCLOCK
control.

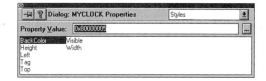

As shown in Figure 35.27, even though you haven't written any code yet, the MYCLOCK control has several properties. The code you borrowed from the Generic files already attached these properties to the control. Later you'll learn how to add your own properties to the MYCLOCK.VBX control by customizing the MYCLOCK project's code.

Experiment with the Height and Width properties of the MYCLOCK control:

☐ Set the Height property to 10.

☐ Set the Width property to 103.

Now your dialog box looks as shown in Figure 35.28.

For now, don't change any of the values of the other properties. You'll have a chance to experiment with these properties later in the chapter.

Figure 35.28.
The MYCLOCK
control, after setting
its Height
property to 10 and
its Width property
to 103.

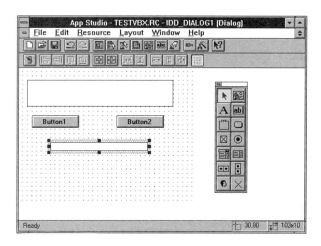

The code that you borrowed from the Generic files also attached events to the control. To see these events:

☐ Select ClassWizard from App Studio's Resource menu.

App Studio responds by displaying the ClassWizard dialog box.

☐ Select the `IDC_MYCLOCK1` object in the Object IDs list and observe the Messages list (see Figure 35.29).

Figure 35.29.
The events
(messages)
associated with the
MYCLOCK.VBX
control.

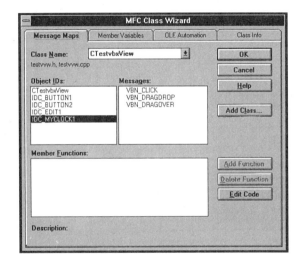

As shown in Figure 35.29, the MYCLOCK.VBX control has several events (messages) associated with it (`VBN_CLICK`, `VBN_DRAGDROP`, and `VBN_DRAGOVER`). Later you'll learn how to add your own events to the MYCLOCK.VBX control by customizing the MYCLOCK project's code.

For now, don't attach code to any of the events of the MYCLOCK control. Later in the chapter you'll have a chance to attach code to some of the MYCLOCK.VBX events.

☐ Click ClassWizard's Cancel button to go back to App Studio.

☐ Select Save from App Studio's File menu to save the `IDD_DIALOG1` dialog box and then terminate App Studio.

As stated earlier, it's important that you terminate App Studio, because each time you enhance the MYCLOCK.VBX control, you'll need to overwrite the older version of the control, and Windows won't let you do this if any active application is currently using the control.

To summarize what you've done so far:

> You copied all the files from the C:\VCPROG\GENVBX directory into your
> development directory (C:\VCPROG\PRACTICE\CH35\MYCLOCK).
>
> You copied two additional files (VBAPI.LIB and VBAPI.H) from your VB\CDK
> directory to your development directory.
>
> You renamed all the GENERIC.* files in the development directory to
> MYCLOCK.*.
>
> You replaced all occurrences of the words GENERIC and Generic with MYCLOCK
> and Myclock in all the MYCLOCK source files (MYCLOCK.H, MYCLOCK.C,
> MYCLOCK.RC and MYCLOCK.DEF).
>
> You created a Visual Basic Custom Control project, you named this project
> MYCLOCK.MAK, and you added the files MYCLOCK.C, MYCLOCK.DEF,
> MYCLOCK.RC, and VBAPI.LIB to this project.
>
> You created the MYCLOCK.VBX file by compiling/linking the
> MYCLOCK.MAK project.
>
> You copied the MYCLOCK.VBX file that you created to your \WINDOWS\SYSTEM
> directory, and then you tested the MYCLOCK.VBX control by experiment-
> ing with it inside the dialog box of the TESTVBX project.

As you have seen, MYCLOCK.VBX is a functional VBX control when created right
out of the Generic files! Of course, it doesn't do what you want it to do yet, because
you haven't customized the MYCLOCK project's code. In the following sections,
you'll write code in the MYCLOCK project files so that the MYCLOCK.VBX control will do what you want it to.

Drawing in the MYCLOCK.VBX Control

Currently, the MYCLOCK.VBX control is blank. Nothing is displayed in it. Now
you'll add code to the MYCLOCK project that will draw text in the MYCLOCK.VBX
control.

☐ Open the MYCLOCK.MAK project. Note that because you used
the MYCLOCK.MAK project earlier, you can easily open it by selecting
MYCLOCK.MAK from Visual C++'s Project menu. The Most Recently
Used (MRU) list at the bottom of the Project menu includes the
MYCLOCK.MAK project (see Figure 35.30).

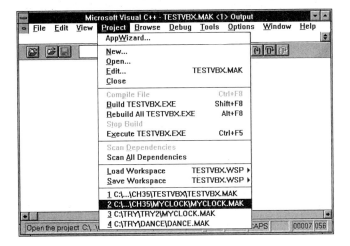

Figure 35.30.
Opening the
MYCLOCK.MAK
project.

☐ Open the file MYCLOCK.C and look for the function MyclockCtlProc(). This is the first function in the MYCLOCK.C file, and it looks as follows:

```
//-------------------------------------------------------
// Myclock Control Procedure
//-------------------------------------------------------
LONG FAR PASCAL _export MyclockCtlProc
(
    HCTL    hctl,
    HWND    hwnd,
    USHORT  msg,
    USHORT  wp,
    LONG    lp
)
{

    // Process messages of the VBX control.
    switch (msg)
        {
        case WM_NCCREATE:

            // TODO: Add initialization code here


            break;
```

```
        case WM_PAINT:

            // Note: Write the control drawing code
            //       inside the function DrawTheControl().

            if (wp)
                DrawTheControl(hctl, hwnd, (HDC)wp);
            else
                {
                PAINTSTRUCT ps;
                BeginPaint(hwnd, &ps);
                DrawTheControl(hctl, hwnd, ps.hdc);
                EndPaint(hwnd, &ps);
                }

            break;


        case VBM_SETPROPERTY:

            // NOTE: wp = Property that was just changed.
            //       lp = New value of the property.

            switch (wp)
                {
                // TODO: Add a case for each custom property

                }

            break;

        case WM_TIMER:
                {
                // TODO: Add timer code here



            break;
                }


        // TODO: Add cases for other events here


        }

    return VBDefControlProc(hctl, hwnd, msg, wp, lp);
    }
```

The `MyclockCtlProc()` function is made up of a switch statement with several cases under it. Each case corresponds to a message that Windows sends to the MYCLOCK.VBX control that pertains to the control. For example, the code under the `WM_NCCREATE` case is executed when the MYCLOCK.VBX control is first created.

The case that you're interested in right now is the `WM_PAINT` case. As you might have guessed, the code under the `WM_PAINT` case is executed whenever there's a need to paint (draw) the control. Whenever there's a need to repaint the control, Windows sends a `WM_PAINT` message to the MYCLOCK.VBX control and the code under the `WM_PAINT` case is executed. This code draws the control. Take a close look at the code under the `WM_PAINT` case:

```
case WM_PAINT:

                // Note: Write the control drawing code
                //       inside the function DrawTheControl().

            if (wp)
                DrawTheControl(hctl, hwnd, (HDC)wp);
            else
                {
                PAINTSTRUCT ps;
                BeginPaint(hwnd, &ps);
                DrawTheControl(hctl, hwnd, ps.hdc);
                EndPaint(hwnd, &ps);
                }

break;
```

The code under the `WM_PAINT` case, code that you borrowed from the `GENERIC.C` file, performs several overhead tasks (if necessary) such as beginning and ending a painting cycle, and it calls the `DrawTheControl()` function.

The bottom line is that the code under the `WM_PAINT` case calls the `DrawTheControl()` function, and the `DrawTheControl()` function is where you'll write your drawing code.

☐ Look for the `DrawTheControl()` function in the `MYCLOCK.C` file (the last function in the file).

Currently, the `DrawTheControl()` function looks as follows:

```
//-------------------------------------------------------
// Draw inside the control.
//-------------------------------------------------------
VOID NEAR DrawTheControl
```

```
(
    HCTL hctl,
    HWND hwnd,
    HDC  hdc
)
{
    // Variables for the brush.
    HBRUSH hbr;
    HBRUSH hbrOld = NULL;

    // TODO: Define your own local variables here (if any)


    // Select new brush, and save old brush.
    hbr = (HBRUSH)SendMessage(GetParent(hwnd),
        WM_CTLCOLOR, hdc, MAKELONG(hwnd,0));
    if (hbr)
        hbrOld = SelectObject(hdc, hbr);


    // TODO: Add your drawing code here


    // Restore the old brush
    if (hbrOld)
        SelectObject(hdc, hbrOld);

}
```

The `DrawTheControl()` function already contains some overhead code (which you borrowed from the GENERIC.C file), and it has two TODO: comment lines, under which you will write your own code. The first TODO: comment line is

```
// TODO: Define your own local variables here (if any)
```

and the second TODO: comment line is

```
// TODO: Add your drawing code here
```

To see the effects of writing code in the `DrawTheControl()` function:

☐ Add code to the `DrawTheControl()` function until it looks as follows:

```
//---------------------------------------------------------
// Draw inside the control.
//---------------------------------------------------------
VOID NEAR DrawTheControl
```

```
(
    HCTL hctl,
    HWND hwnd,
    HDC  hdc
)
{
    // Variables for the brush.
    HBRUSH hbr;
    HBRUSH hbrOld = NULL;

    // TODO: Define your own local variables here (if any)



    // Select new brush, and save old brush.
    hbr = (HBRUSH)SendMessage(GetParent(hwnd),
            WM_CTLCOLOR, hdc, MAKELONG(hwnd,0));
    if (hbr)
        hbrOld = SelectObject(hdc, hbr);


    // TODO: Add your drawing code here

    ///////////////////////////
    // MY CODE STARTS HERE
    ///////////////////////////

    // Display text inside the control.
    TextOut(hdc, 0, 0, "This is my first VBX control", 28);

    ///////////////////////////
    // MY CODE ENDS HERE
    ///////////////////////////

    // Restore the old brush
    if (hbrOld)
        SelectObject(hdc, hbrOld);

}
```

The code you just typed in the DrawTheControl() function is made up of one statement:

```
TextOut(hdc, 0, 0, "This is my first VBX control", 28);
```

This statement uses the TextOut() function to display the text "This is my first VBX control" in the control. The first parameter of the TextOut() function, hdc, is the device context handle of the control (it's one of the parameters of the DrawTheControl() function). The second and third parameters of the TextOut() function are the X,Y coordinates where the text is displayed. The fourth parameter of the

`TextOut()` function is the string to be displayed, and the fifth parameter is the length of the string.

To see the code you typed inside the `DrawTheControl()` function in action:

☐ Select Rebuild All MYCLOCK.VBX from Visual C++'s Project menu.

> *Visual C++ responds by compiling/linking the files of the MYCLOCK project and creating the* `MYCLOCK.VBX` *file.*

☐ Switch to the File Manager program (or to DOS) and copy the file you just created, `C:\VCPROG\PRACTICE\CH35\MYCLOCK.VBX`, into your `C:\WINDOWS\SYSTEM` directory.

Now that you've copied the new version of the MYCLOCK.VBX control to your `\WINDOWS\SYSTEM` directory, you can test it with the TESTVBX project:

☐ Open the TESTVBX.MAK project.

☐ Start App Studio from Visual C++'s Tools menu and use it to display the TESTVBX application's `IDD_DIALOG1` dialog box in design mode (see Figure 35.31).

Figure 35.31.
The
IDD_DIALOG1
dialog box in design
mode.

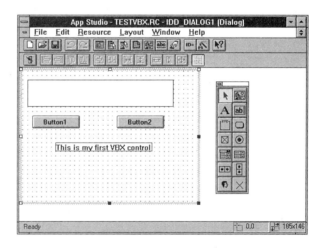

As you can see from Figure 35.31, the MYCLOCK.VBX control that you placed in the dialog box earlier is no longer blank! Now it contains the text `"This is my first VBX control."` The code you typed in `MYCLOCK.C`'s `DrawTheControl()` function is working!

☐ Place several more MYCLOCK controls in the dialog box and set their `Height` properties to 10 and their `Width` properties to 103 (see Figure 35.32).

The code you wrote in the `DrawTheControl()` function is executed for each MYCLOCK control that you place in the dialog box.

☐ Delete all the MYCLOCK controls from the dialog box, select Save from App Studio's File menu, and then terminate App Studio.

Figure 35.32.
The
IDD_DIALOG1
dialog box with
three MYCLOCK
controls in it.

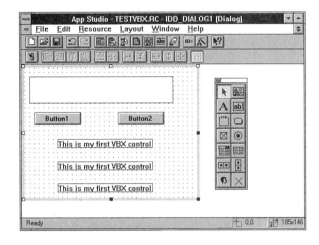

Displaying the Current Time in the MYCLOCK Control

Currently, the MYCLOCK.VBX control's code displays the text "`This is my first VBX control.`" Now you'll change the MYCLOCK control's code so that it displays the current time.

☐ Open the project MYCLOCK.MAK.

☐ Open the file `MYCLOCK.C` and modify the `DrawTheControl()` function until it looks as follows:

```
//-----------------------------------------------------
// Draw inside the control.
//-----------------------------------------------------
VOID NEAR DrawTheControl
(
    HCTL hctl,
    HWND hwnd,
    HDC  hdc
)
{
    // Variables for the brush.
    HBRUSH hbr;
    HBRUSH hbrOld = NULL;
```

1227

```
// TODO: Define your own local variables here (if any)

////////////////////////
// MY CODE STARTS HERE
////////////////////////

char CurrentTime[30];
struct tm *newtime;
long lTime;

////////////////////////
// MY CODE ENDS HERE
////////////////////////


// Select new brush, and save old brush.
hbr = (HBRUSH)SendMessage(GetParent(hwnd),
        WM_CTLCOLOR, hdc, MAKELONG(hwnd,0));
if (hbr)
    hbrOld = SelectObject(hdc, hbr);


// TODO: Add your drawing code here

////////////////////////
// MY CODE STARTS HERE
////////////////////////

// Get the current time
time(&lTime);
newtime=localtime(&lTime);

// Convert the time into a string.
strcpy(CurrentTime, asctime(newtime));

// Pad the string with 5 blanks
CurrentTime[24]=' ';
CurrentTime[25]=' ';
CurrentTime[26]=' ';
CurrentTime[27]=' ';
CurrentTime[28]=' ';

// Display the current time
TextOut(hdc, 0, 0, CurrentTime, 29);

////////////////////////
// MY CODE ENDS HERE
////////////////////////
```

```
    // Restore the old brush
    if (hbrOld)
        SelectObject(hdc, hbrOld);

}
```

The code you typed at the top of the function declares three local variables:

```
char CurrentTime[30];
struct tm *newtime;
long lTime;
```

The rest of the code you typed uses these three variables to get the current time and display it:

```
// Get the current time
time(&lTime);
newtime=localtime(&lTime);

// Convert the time into a string.
strcpy(CurrentTime, asctime(newtime));

// Pad the string with 5 blanks
CurrentTime[24]=' ';
CurrentTime[25]=' ';
CurrentTime[26]=' ';
CurrentTime[27]=' ';
CurrentTime[28]=' ';

// Display the current time
TextOut(hdc, 0, 0, CurrentTime, 29);
```

The first statement,

```
time(&lTime);
```

uses the `time()` function to store the number of seconds that have elapsed since midnight, December 31, 1899, in the variable `lTime`. Of course, this number isn't friendly enough, so use the statement

```
newtime=localtime(&lTime);
```

to convert the number that is stored in `lTime` into a friendlier representation of time. This statement uses the `localtime()` function to convert `lTime` into a structure of type `tm` and assigns the result to the structure `newtime`. So at this point, the fields of the structure `newtime` store the current time.

The next statement is

```
strcpy(CurrentTime, asctime(newtime));
```

This statement uses the asctime() function to convert the current time stored in newtime into a string. The resultant string is assigned to the CurrentTime string. So at this point, CurrentTime contains a string with 24 characters that represents the current time. This string includes the day and date, month, time, and year (see Figure 35.7).

The next five statements,

```
CurrentTime[24]=' ';
CurrentTime[25]=' ';
CurrentTime[26]=' ';
CurrentTime[27]=' ';
CurrentTime[28]=' ';
```

fill the 24th through 28th characters of the CurrentTime string with blanks. This is done to pad the end of the CurrentTime string with five blanks for cosmetic reasons.

Finally, the last statement you typed in DrawTheControl() displays the CurrentTime string:

```
TextOut(hdc, 0, 0, CurrentTime, 26);
```

If you try to compile and link the MYCLOCK project now, you'll get linking errors. Why? Because the code you typed in the DrawTheControl() function uses time functions, but the prototypes of these time functions are not known in the MYCLOCK.C file. Thus, you must include the statement #include <time.h> at the beginning of the MYCLOCK.C file:

☐ Add the #include <time.h> statement at the beginning of the MYCLOCK.C file (immediately after the #include statement of the myclock.h file). After you add this #include statement, the beginning of the MYCLOCK.C file looks as follows:

```
//----------------------------------------------------------
// MYCLOCK.C
//----------------------------------------------------------
// Contains code for Myclock VBX control.
//
// Use the following files as templates for building your
// own VBX control:
//
// - MYCLOCK.C (this file)
// - MYCLOCK.H
// - MYCLOCK.DEF
// - MYCLOCK.RC
//----------------------------------------------------------
```

```
#include <windows.h>
#include "vbapi.h"
#include "MYCLOCK.H"

/////////////////////////
// MY CODE STARTS HERE
/////////////////////////

#include <time.h>

/////////////////////////
// MY CODE ENDS HERE
/////////////////////////
...
...
...
```

To see in action the code you typed in the `DrawTheControl()` function:

☐ Select Rebuild All MYCLOCK.VBX from Visual C++'s Project menu.

> *Visual C++ responds by compiling/linking the files of the MYCLOCK project and creating the `MYCLOCK.VBX` file.*

☐ Switch to the File Manager program (or to DOS) and copy the file that you just created, `C:\VCPROG\PRACTICE\CH35\MYCLOCK.VBX`, into your `C:\WINDOWS\SYSTEM` directory.

☐ Open the TESTVBX.MAK project.

☐ Start App Studio from Visual C++'s Tools menu and use it to display the TESTVBX application's `IDD_DIALOG1` dialog box in design mode.

☐ Use the Tools window to place a MYCLOCK control in the dialog box.

☐ Set the `Height` property of the control to 10 and the `Width` property to 103 (see Figure 35.33).

As you can see, the code you wrote in the `DrawTheControl()` function displays the current time in the control. However, the time isn't updated continuously. In the following section you'll enhance the MYCLOCK project's code so that the control displays the current time continuously.

☐ Delete the MYCLOCK control from the dialog box, select Save from App Studio's File menu and then terminate App Studio.

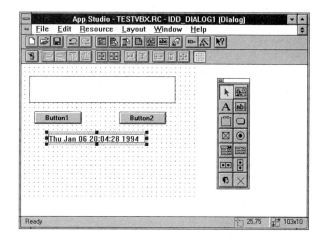

Figure 35.33.
The IDD_DIALOG1
dialog box with a
MYCLOCK control
inside it.

Displaying the Current Time Continuously

In order to display the time continuously, you need to

> Write code that installs a timer for the MYCLOCK control with a 1,000-millisecond interval.
>
> Write code under the WM_TIMER case of the MYCLOCK control.

After you install such a timer, Windows sends a WM_TIMER message every 1,000 milliseconds (that is, every second) to the MYCLOCK.VBX control and the code you'll write under the MYCLOCK control's WM_TIMER case is executed. The code you'll write under the WM_TIMER case will call the DrawTheControl() function. Thus, the current time will be displayed continuously.

Because you want to install the timer when the control is first created, you need to write the code that installs the timer under the WM_NCCREATE case:

☐ Open the project MYCLOCK.MAK.

☐ Open the file MYCLOCK.C and write code under the WM_NCCREATE case (in the function MyclockCtlProc()) until it looks as follows:

```
case WM_NCCREATE:

     // TODO: Add initialization code here

     /////////////////////////
     // MY CODE STARTS HERE
     /////////////////////////

     // Install a timer.
     SetTimer(hwnd,1,1000,NULL);
```

```
/////////////////////
// MY CODE ENDS HERE
/////////////////////

    break;
```

The code you typed under the WM_NCCREATE case is made up of one statement:

```
SetTimer(hwnd,1,1000,NULL);
```

This statement uses the SetTimer() function to install a timer with a 1,000-millisecond interval. From now on, Windows will send a WM_TIMER message to the control every 1,000 milliseconds.

☐ Now you need to write code under the WM_TIMER case:

```
case WM_TIMER:
    {
    // TODO: Add timer code here

    /////////////////////////
    // MY CODE STARTS HERE
    /////////////////////////

    // Draw the control.
    HDC hdc = GetDC(hwnd);
    DrawTheControl(hctl, hwnd, hdc);
    ReleaseDC(hwnd,hdc);

    /////////////////////////
    // MY CODE STARTS HERE
    /////////////////////////

    break;
    }
```

The code you just typed under the WM_TIMER case is made up of three statements. The first statement gets a handle for the device context:

```
HDC hdc = GetDC(hwnd);
```

The second statement calls the DrawTheControl() function:

```
DrawTheControl(hctl, hwnd, hdc);
```

and the third statement releases the device context:

```
ReleaseDC(hwnd,hdc);
```

To see the code you wrote under the WM_TIMER case in action:

☐ Select Rebuild All MYCLOCK.VBX from Visual C++'s Project menu.

Visual C++ responds by compiling/linking the MYCLOCK project's files and creating the MYCLOCK.VBX *file.*

☐ Switch to the File Manager program (or to DOS) and copy the file that you just created, C:\VCPROG\PRACTICE\CH35\MYCLOCK.VBX, into your C:\WINDOWS\SYSTEM directory.

☐ Open the TESTVBX.MAK project.

☐ Start App Studio from Visual C++'s Tools menu and use it to display the TESTVBX application's IDD_DIALOG1 dialog box in design mode.

☐ Use the Tools window to place a MYCLOCK control in the dialog box.

☐ Set the Height property of the control to 10 and the Width property to 103 (see Figure 35.33).

As you can see, now the MYCLOCK control displays the current time continuously. The code you wrote under the WM_NCCREATE case installed a timer with a 1,000-millisecond interval. As a result, the code you wrote under the WM_TIMER case is executed every 1,000 milliseconds, and this code calls the DrawTheControl() function. Thus, every 1,000 milliseconds the DrawTheControl() function is executed and the displayed time is updated.

Note that the default background color of the MYCLOCK control is white. To change the background color of the control:

☐ Double-click the MYCLOCK control in the dialog box and display the Styles Properties window (see Figure 35.27).

☐ Double-click the BackColor property.

App Studio responds by displaying the Color dialog box (see Figure 35.34).

Figure 35.34.
The Color
dialog box.

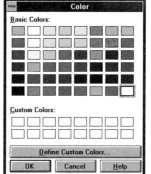

☐ Click the red color box and then click the OK button of the Color dialog box.

The background color of the MYCLOCK control is now red! Note that the value assigned to the BackColor property after you selected red is 0x000000ff in Hex, which is 255 in Decimal (see Figure 35.35).

Figure 35.35.
The BackColor
property with the
value 0x000000ff
(red).

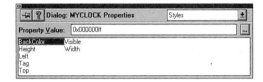

In the following section, you'll write code that sets the default color of the MYCLOCK control to green. When the control is created, the background color will be green.

☐ Delete the MYCLOCK control from the dialog box, select Save from App Studio's File menu, and then terminate App Studio.

Setting a Default Value for the *BackColor* Property

As you have just seen, when the MYCLOCK control is created (that is, when it's placed in the form), its default background color is white. Now you'll add code under the WM_NCCREATE case that sets the BackColor property to green. This way, when the control is first created, its default color will be green.

☐ Open the project MYCLOCK.MAK.

☐ Open the file MYCLOCK.C and add code under the WM_NCCREATE case until it looks as follows:

```
case WM_NCCREATE:

    // TODO: Add initialization code here

    ////////////////////////
    // MY CODE STARTS HERE
    ////////////////////////

    // Install a timer.
    SetTimer(hwnd,1,1000,NULL);
```

```
// Set the BackColor property to 65280 ( Green).
VBSetControlProperty(hctl,
                     IPROP_MYCLOCK_BACKCOLOR,
                     65280L);

/////////////////////
// MY CODE ENDS HERE
/////////////////////

break;
```

The statement you just added to the WM_NCCREATE case,

```
VBSetControlProperty(hctl,
                     IPROP_MYCLOCK_BACKCOLOR,
                     65280L);
```

uses the VBSetControlProperty() function to set the BackColor property of the control to 65280L. The value 65280 (0x0000ff00) is the value for green.

In the preceding statement, you passed three parameters to the VBSetControlProperty() function. The first parameter, hctl, is the control handle. The second parameter, IPROP_MYCLOCK_BACKCOLOR, is the ID of the MYCLOCK control's BackColor property (this ID is defined in the header file MYCLOCK.H). The third parameter, 65280L, is the value you want to assign to the property.

To see the code you just added under the WM_NCCREATE case in action:

☐ Select Rebuild All MYCLOCK.VBX from Visual C++'s Project menu.

  Visual C++ responds by compiling/linking the files of the MYCLOCK project and creating the MYCLOCK.VBX file.

☐ Switch to the File Manager program (or to DOS) and copy the file that you just created, C:\VCPROG\PRACTICE\CH35\MYCLOCK.VBX, into your C:\WINDOWS\SYSTEM directory.

☐ Open the TESTVBX.MAK project.

☐ Start App Studio from Visual C++'s Tools menu and use it to display the TESTVBX application's IDD_DIALOG1 dialog box in design mode.

☐ Use the Tools window to place a MYCLOCK control in the dialog box.

As you can see, the background color of the control is green!

☐ Delete the MYCLOCK control from the dialog box, select Save from App Studio's File menu, and then terminate App Studio.

Adding a Standard Property to the MYCLOCK.VBX Control

Standard properties are properties such as `Height`, `Width`, and `BackColor`. These properties are predefined, and adding them to a VBX control is easy. Table 35.1 lists all the standard properties you can add to a VBX control.

Table 35.1. Standard properties.

Property	Constant
Align	PPROPINFO_STD_ALIGN
BackColor	PPROPINFO_STD_BACKCOLOR
BorderStyle (off)	PPROPINFO_STD_BORDERSTYLEOFF
BorderStyle (on)	PPROPINFO_STD_BORDERSTYLEON
Caption	PPROPINFO_STD_CAPTION
ClipControls	PPROPINFO_STD_CLIPCONTROLS
CtlName	PPROPINFO_STD_CTLNAME
DataChanged	PPROPINFO_STD_DATACHANGED
DataField	PPROPINFO_STD_DATAFIELD
DataSource	PPROPINFO_STD_DATASOURCE
DragIcon	PPROPINFO_STD_DRAGICON
DragMode	PPROPINFO_STD_DRAGMODE
Enabled	PPROPINFO_STD_ENABLED
FontBold	PPROPINFO_STD_FONTBOLD
FontItalic	PPROPINFO_STD_FONTITALIC
FontName	PPROPINFO_STD_FONTNAME
FontSize	PPROPINFO_STD_FONTSIZE
FontStrikethru	PPROPINFO_STD_FONTSTRIKETHRU
FontUnderline	PPROPINFO_STD_FONTUNDERLINE
ForeColor	PPROPINFO_STD_FORECOLOR
Height	PPROPINFO_STD_HEIGHT
HelpContextID	PPROPINFO_STD_HELPCONTEXTID
hWnd	PPROPINFO_STD_HWND

continues

Table 35.1. continued

Property	Constant
ImeMode	PPROPINFO_STD_IMEMODE
Index	PPROPINFO_STD_INDEX
Last	PPROPINFO_STD_LAST
Left	PPROPINFO_STD_LEFT
LeftNoRun	PPROPINFO_STD_LEFTNORUN
LinkItem	PPROPINFO_STD_LINKITEM
LinkMode	PPROPINFO_STD_LINKMODE
LinkTimeOut	PPROPINFO_STD_LINKTIMEOUT
LinkTopic	PPROPINFO_STD_LINKTOPIC
MousePointer	PPROPINFO_STD_MOUSEPOINTER
Name	PPROPINFO_STD_NAME
None	PPROPINFO_STD_NONE
Parent	PPROPINFO_STD_PARENT
TabIndex	PPROPINFO_STD_TABINDEX
TabStop	PPROPINFO_STD_TABSTOP
Tag	PPROPINFO_STD_TAG
Text	PPROPINFO_STD_TEXT
Top	PPROPINFO_STD_TOP
TopNoRun	PPROPINFO_STD_TOPNORUN
Visible	PPROPINFO_STD_VISIBLE
Width	PPROPINFO_STD_WIDTH

If you have some experience with Visual Basic, you're probably familiar with many of the properties listed in Table 35.1. Even if you don't have any experience with Visual Basic, some of the names of these properties are self-explanatory. For example, the Visible property determines whether the control will be visible during runtime.

The MYCLOCK.VBX control already has several properties (see Figure 35.27). The code that defines these properties resides in the header file MYCLOCK.H. You didn't have to write the code that defines these properties, because you borrowed it from the GENERIC.H file.

For practice, add the standard property `ForeColor` to the MYCLOCK.VBX control. The `ForeColor` property determines the foreground color of the control. (Currently, the MYCLOCK.VBX control has a `BackColor` property, but it doesn't have a `ForeColor` property.)

Follow these steps to add the `ForeColor` property to the MYCLOCK.VBX control:

☐ Open the project MYCLOCK.MAK.

☐ Open the header file `MYCLOCK.H` and look for the Property Information Table. Currently, the Property Information Table looks as follows:

```
//-----------------------------------------------------
// Property Information Table
//-----------------------------------------------------
PPROPINFO Myclock_Properties[] =
    {
    PPROPINFO_STD_CTLNAME,
    PPROPINFO_STD_INDEX,
    PPROPINFO_STD_BACKCOLOR,
    PPROPINFO_STD_LEFT,
    PPROPINFO_STD_TOP,
    PPROPINFO_STD_WIDTH,
    PPROPINFO_STD_HEIGHT,
    PPROPINFO_STD_VISIBLE,
    PPROPINFO_STD_PARENT,
    PPROPINFO_STD_DRAGMODE,
    PPROPINFO_STD_DRAGICON,
    PPROPINFO_STD_TAG,
    PPROPINFO_STD_HWND,

    // TODO: Specify addresses of properties structures
    //
    // Example:
    // &Property_MyProperty,     // Custom
    // &Property_HerProperty,    // Custom
    // PPROPINFO_STD_CAPTION,    // Standard


    NULL
    };
```

The Property Information Table lists the addresses of structures that correspond to the properties. That is, each property has a structure that defines it, and you specify the address of each of these structures in the Property Information Table. As you can see, the Property Information Table currently has 13 entries. This means that the MYCLOCK.VBX control currently has 13 properties.

Now, to add the ForeColor property, add the address of the structure that defines the ForeColor property to the Property Information Table. This address is given by one of the constants that points to the structure of the property. As you can see from Table 35.1, the constant that points to the address of the ForeColor property is PPROPINFO_STD_FORECOLOR.

☐ Add the constant PPROPINFO_STD_FORECOLOR to the Property Information Table. After you add this constant, the Property Information Table looks as follows:

```
//------------------------------------------------------
// Property Information Table
//------------------------------------------------------
PPROPINFO Myclock_Properties[] =
    {
    PPROPINFO_STD_CTLNAME,
    PPROPINFO_STD_INDEX,
    PPROPINFO_STD_BACKCOLOR,
    PPROPINFO_STD_LEFT,
    PPROPINFO_STD_TOP,
    PPROPINFO_STD_WIDTH,
    PPROPINFO_STD_HEIGHT,
    PPROPINFO_STD_VISIBLE,
    PPROPINFO_STD_PARENT,
    PPROPINFO_STD_DRAGMODE,
    PPROPINFO_STD_DRAGICON,
    PPROPINFO_STD_TAG,
    PPROPINFO_STD_HWND,

    // TODO: Specify addresses of properties structures
    //
    // Example:
    // &Property_MyProperty,     // Custom
    // &Property_HerProperty,    // Custom
    // PPROPINFO_STD_CAPTION,    // Standard

    /////////////////////////
    // MY CODE STARTS HERE
    /////////////////////////

    PPROPINFO_STD_FORECOLOR,

    /////////////////////////
    // MY CODE ENDS HERE
    /////////////////////////

    NULL
    };
```

NOTE: When you add PPROPINFO_STD_FORECOLOR to the table, don't forget the comma. The comma is needed because the PPROPINFO_STD_FORECOLOR item isn't the last entry in the table. As you can see from the preceding code, the last entry in the table is NULL.

Next, you need to define a constant that corresponds to the property you just added to the Property Information Table:

☐ Look for the Property List Constants section. It is located immediately after the Property Information Table. Currently, the Property List Constants section looks as follows:

```
//-------------------------------------------------------
// Property List Constants
//-------------------------------------------------------
#define IPROP_MYCLOCK_CTLNAME            0
#define IPROP_MYCLOCK_INDEX             1
#define IPROP_MYCLOCK_BACKCOLOR         2
#define IPROP_MYCLOCK_LEFT              3
#define IPROP_MYCLOCK_TOP               4
#define IPROP_MYCLOCK_WIDTH             5
#define IPROP_MYCLOCK_HEIGHT            6
#define IPROP_MYCLOCK_VISIBLE           7
#define IPROP_MYCLOCK_PARENT            8
#define IPROP_MYCLOCK_DRAGMODE          9
#define IPROP_MYCLOCK_DRAGICON          10
#define IPROP_MYCLOCK_TAG               11
#define IPROP_MYCLOCK_HWND              12

// TODO: Define consecutive ID's of more properties
//
// Example:
// #define IPROP_MYCLOCK_MYPROPERTY     13
// #define IPROP_MYCLOCK_HERPROPERTY    14
// #define IPROP_MYCLOCK_CAPTION        15  // Standard
```

As you can see, the Property List Constants section defines a constant for each of the control's properties. Each constant corresponds to a property listed in the Property Information Table. Now you want to add a constant for the ForeColor property. The ForeColor property is property #13 (zero-based) within the Property Information Table, so the constant of the ForeColor property is #defined as 13:

☐ Add the #define statement for the ForeColor property at the end of the Property List Constants section. After adding this statement, the Property List Constants section looks as follows:

```
//-------------------------------------------------------
// Property List Constants
//-------------------------------------------------------
```

```
#define IPROP_MYCLOCK_CTLNAME          0
#define IPROP_MYCLOCK_INDEX            1
#define IPROP_MYCLOCK_BACKCOLOR        2
#define IPROP_MYCLOCK_LEFT             3
#define IPROP_MYCLOCK_TOP              4
#define IPROP_MYCLOCK_WIDTH            5
#define IPROP_MYCLOCK_HEIGHT           6
#define IPROP_MYCLOCK_VISIBLE          7
#define IPROP_MYCLOCK_PARENT           8
#define IPROP_MYCLOCK_DRAGMODE         9
#define IPROP_MYCLOCK_DRAGICON         10
#define IPROP_MYCLOCK_TAG              11
#define IPROP_MYCLOCK_HWND             12

// TODO: Define consecutive ID's of more properties
//
// Example:
// #define IPROP_MYCLOCK_MYPROPERTY    13
// #define IPROP_MYCLOCK_HERPROPERTY   14
// #define IPROP_MYCLOCK_CAPTION       15


///////////////////////
// MY CODE STARTS HERE
///////////////////////

#define IPROP_MYCLOCK_FORECOLOR        13

///////////////////////
// MY CODE ENDS HERE
///////////////////////
```

> **NOTE**
>
> The reason for defining a constant for the property is because later you'll use this constant to refer to the ForeColor property. For example, the statement,
>
> ```
> VBSetControlProperty(hctl,
>                 IPROP_MYCLOCK_FORECOLOR,
>                 255L);
> ```
>
> sets the ForeColor property of the control to 255L.

That's it! You've finished adding the ForeColor property to the MYCLOCK.VBX control.

To summarize what you did:

> You added the address of the ForeColor property structure (PPROPINFO_STD_FORECOLOR) to the Property Information Table.
> You #defined a constant for the ForeColor property that specifies the location of the ForeColor property within the Property Information Table.

Now verify that the ForeColor property is now added to the MYCLOCK.VBX control:

☐ Select Rebuild All MYCLOCK.VBX from Visual C++'s Project menu.

> *Visual C++ responds by compiling/linking the files of the MYCLOCK project and creating the* MYCLOCK.VBX *file.*

☐ Switch to the File Manager program (or to DOS) and copy the file that you just created, C:\VCPROG\PRACTICE\CH35\MYCLOCK.VBX, into your C:\WINDOWS\SYSTEM directory.

☐ Open the TESTVBX.MAK project.

☐ Start App Studio from Visual C++'s Tools window and use it to display the TESTVBX application's IDD_DIALOG1 dialog box in design mode.

☐ Use the Tools window to place a MYCLOCK control in the dialog box.

☐ Double-click the MYCLOCK control.

> *App Studio responds by displaying the General properties of the control.*

☐ Select Styles from the drop-down list box at the upper-right corner of the Properties window.

> *App Studio responds by displaying the Styles Properties window of the control (see Figure 35.36).*

Figure 35.36.
The Styles
Properties
window of the
MYCLOCK.VBX
control (with
the ForeColor
property).

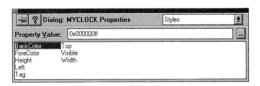

As shown in Figure 35.36, the MYCLOCK control now has the ForeColor property (underneath the BackColor property).

☐ Double-click the ForeColor property, select a color, and see the effect it has on the control.

Whatever color you select as the ForeColor determines the foreground color of the control (that is, the color of the text).

Delete the MYCLOCK control from the dialog box, select Save from App Studio's File menu, and then terminate App Studio.

Adding a Custom Property to the MYCLOCK.VBX Control

In many cases, you'll have to add a property to your VBX control that isn't a standard property. Such a property is called a *custom property* (a property that is custom-made by you).

Now you'll add a custom property to the MYCLOCK.VBX control. The name of this property will be UpdateInterval, and it will be used to store numbers. For now, don't concern yourself with the purpose of the UpdateInterval property. Later you'll make use of this property, but for now just add it to the MYCLOCK.VBX control.

The first thing to do when you add a custom property is to define a variable for the custom property in the control's structure. Here's how you do that:

☐ Open the project MYCLOCK.MAK.

☐ Open the header file MYCLOCK.H and look for the section that defines the structure of the control. Currently, the structure of the control is as follows:

```
//-------------------------------------------------------
// The structure of the control.
//-------------------------------------------------------
typedef struct tagMYCLOCK
    {
    BOOL dummy;

    // TODO: Define variables that correspond to the
    //       custom properties
    //
    // Example:
    // BOOL MyProperty;
    // LONG HerProperty;


} MYCLOCK;
```

As you can see, the control's structure currently has only one element, called dummy. As you might have guessed, the dummy variable isn't used. The only reason it's included is because a compiling error occurs when the structure doesn't include any elements.

Now add a variable to the structure of the control. This variable will be used to store the data of the custom property UpdateInterval, so name this variable UpdateInterval:

☐ Add the variable UpdateInterval (of type SHORT) to the structure of the control. After adding this variable, the structure of the control looks as follows:

```
//---------------------------------------------------
// The structure of the control.
//---------------------------------------------------
typedef struct tagMYCLOCK
    {
    BOOL dummy;

    // TODO: Define variables that correspond to the
    //       custom properties
    //
    // Example:
    // BOOL MyProperty;
    // LONG HerProperty;

    /////////////////////////
    // MY CODE STARTS HERE
    /////////////////////////

    // The UpdateInterval custom property.
    SHORT UpdateInterval;

    /////////////////////////
    // MY CODE ENDS HERE
    /////////////////////////

} MYCLOCK;
```

The next thing you have to do is define the structure of the UpdateInterval property. As stated earlier, each property has a structure that defines it. When you added the ForeColor property you didn't have to define a structure, because the ForeColor property is a standard (predefined) property. However, the property that you're adding now is your own custom property, so you must define a structure for it. Here's how you do that:

☐ Look for the Property Information Structures section in the MYCLOCK.H file. Currently, the Property Information Structures section looks as follows:

```
//----------------------------------------------------------
// Property Information Structures
//----------------------------------------------------------
//
// TODO: Define PROPINFO structure for each custom property
//
// Example:
//
//PROPINFO Property_MyProperty =
//    {
//      "MyProperty",
//      DT_SHORT | PF_fGetData | PF_fSetMsg | PF_fSaveData,
//      OFFSETIN(MYCLOCK, MyProperty),
//      0, 0, NULL, 0
//    };
```

Currently, the Property Information Structures section has only comments. The comments include a declaration of a Property Information (PROPINFO) structure. You can use this example as a template for declaring the structure of the UpdateInterval property:

☐ Declare the structure of the UpdateInterval property by using the commented example as a template. That is, copy/paste the example and then replace the three occurrences of the word MyProperty with the word UpdateInterval. After declaring the structure of the UpdateInterval property, the Property Information Structures section looks as follows:

```
//----------------------------------------------------------
// Property Information Structures
//----------------------------------------------------------
//
// TODO: Define PROPINFO structure for each custom property
//
// Example:
//
//PROPINFO Property_MyProperty =
//    {
//      "MyProperty",
//      DT_SHORT | PF_fGetData | PF_fSetMsg | PF_fSaveData,
//      OFFSETIN(MYCLOCK, MyProperty),
//      0, 0, NULL, 0
//    };

/////////////////////////
// MY CODE STARTS HERE
/////////////////////////
```

```
PROPINFO Property_UpdateInterval =
    {
    "UpdateInterval",
    DT_SHORT ¦ PF_fGetData ¦ PF_fSetMsg ¦ PF_fSaveData,
    OFFSETIN(MYCLOCK, UpdateInterval),
    0, 0, NULL, 0
    };
```

```
/////////////////////
// MY CODE ENDS HERE
/////////////////////
```

> **NOTE**
>
> In your future VBX projects, you can use the preceding step to declare a structure of a custom property. That is, copy and paste the commented example and then replace occurrences of the word MyProperty with the name of the property you're declaring. In addition, you'll also have to change the first flag in the second parameter from DT_SHORT to whatever type the property is. In the case of the UpdateInterval property, you should declare the property as a SHORT type, so leave the first flag of the second parameter as DT_SHORT. However, if you wanted to declare the property as a LONG type, you would have to change DT_SHORT to DT_LONG.
>
> The other flags and fields of the PROPINFO structure are discussed later in this chapter. For now, just note that the way you created the structure of the UpdateInterval property is typical, and you can repeat the preceding step to create other custom properties.

To summarize what you've done so far:

> You declared a variable called UpdateInterval in the structure of the control. You declared a structure (Property_UpdateInterval) for the UpdateInterval property.

Now that you have a structure that defines the UpdateInterval property, you can enter the address of this structure in the Property Information Table:

☐ Look for the Property Information Table in the MYCLOCK.H file and modify it until it looks as follows:

```
//-------------------------------------------------------
// Property Information Table
//-------------------------------------------------------
PPROPINFO Myclock_Properties[] =
    {
    PPROPINFO_STD_CTLNAME,
    PPROPINFO_STD_INDEX,
    PPROPINFO_STD_BACKCOLOR,
    PPROPINFO_STD_LEFT,
    PPROPINFO_STD_TOP,
    PPROPINFO_STD_WIDTH,
    PPROPINFO_STD_HEIGHT,
    PPROPINFO_STD_VISIBLE,
    PPROPINFO_STD_PARENT,
    PPROPINFO_STD_DRAGMODE,
    PPROPINFO_STD_DRAGICON,
    PPROPINFO_STD_TAG,
    PPROPINFO_STD_HWND,

    // TODO: Specify addresses of properties structures
    //
    // Example:
    // &Property_MyProperty,    // Custom
    // &Property_HerProperty,   // Custom
    // PPROPINFO_STD_CAPTION,   // Standard

    /////////////////////////
    // MY CODE STARTS HERE
    /////////////////////////

    PPROPINFO_STD_FORECOLOR,

    &Property_UpdateInterval,

    /////////////////////////
    // MY CODE ENDS HERE
    /////////////////////////

    NULL
};
```

The entry you just added to the table,

```
&Property_UpdateInterval,
```

is the address of the UpdateInterval structure that you defined.

Earlier, when you specified the address of the ForeColor property, you used the constant

```
PPROPINFO_STD_FORECOLOR
```

However, the UpdateInterval property is not a standard property, so it doesn't have a constant that points to its address. Thus, you specify the address of the UpdateInterval property with

```
&Property_UpdateInterval
```

which is the address of the structure that you declared for the UpdateInterval property.

The last thing you have to do is define a constant that corresponds to the UpdateInterval property (just as you did for the ForeColor property):

☐ Look for the Property List Constants section (it's located immediately after the Property Information Table) and modify it until it looks as follows:

```
//-------------------------------------------------------
// Property List Constants
//-------------------------------------------------------
#define IPROP_MYCLOCK_CTLNAME        0
#define IPROP_MYCLOCK_INDEX          1
#define IPROP_MYCLOCK_BACKCOLOR      2
#define IPROP_MYCLOCK_LEFT           3
#define IPROP_MYCLOCK_TOP            4
#define IPROP_MYCLOCK_WIDTH          5
#define IPROP_MYCLOCK_HEIGHT         6
#define IPROP_MYCLOCK_VISIBLE        7
#define IPROP_MYCLOCK_PARENT         8
#define IPROP_MYCLOCK_DRAGMODE       9
#define IPROP_MYCLOCK_DRAGICON       10
#define IPROP_MYCLOCK_TAG            11
#define IPROP_MYCLOCK_HWND           12

// TODO: Define consecutive ID's of more properties
//
// Example:
// #define IPROP_MYCLOCK_MYPROPERTY     13
// #define IPROP_MYCLOCK_HERPROPERTY    14
// #define IPROP_MYCLOCK_CAPTION        15
```

```
///////////////////////
// MY CODE STARTS HERE
///////////////////////

#define IPROP_MYCLOCK_FORECOLOR          13

#define IPROP_MYCLOCK_UPDATEINTERVAL     14

///////////////////////
// MY CODE ENDS HERE
///////////////////////
```

The constant you just defined,

```
#define IPROP_MYCLOCK_UPDATEINTERVAL     14
```

corresponds to the `UpdateInterval` property you added to the Property Information Table. Because the `UpdateInterval` property is property #14 (zero-based) within the Property Information Table, you `#define` the constant as 14.

That's it! You've finished adding the `UpdateInterval` property to the MYCLOCK.VBX control.

To summarize what you did to add the custom property `UpdateInterval` to the MYCLOCK.VBX control:

> You declared a variable called `UpdateInterval` in the structure of the control.
> You declared a structure (`Property_UpdateInterval`) that defines the `UpdateInterval` property.
> You entered the address of the `Property_UpdateInterval` structure in the Property Information Table.
> You `#defined` a constant for the `UpdateInterval` property that specifies the location of the `UpdateInterval` property within the Property Information Table.

Verify that the `UpdateInterval` property is now added to the MYCLOCK.VBX control:

☐ Select Rebuild All MYCLOCK.VBX from Visual C++'s Project menu.

> *Visual C++ responds by compiling/linking the MYCLOCK project's files and creating the* MYCLOCK.VBX *file.*

☐ Switch to the File Manager program (or to DOS) and copy the file that you just created, C:\VCPROG\PRACTICE\CH35\MYCLOCK.VBX, to your C:\WINDOWS\SYSTEM directory.

☐ Open the TESTVBX.MAK project.

☐ Start App Studio from Visual C++'s Tools menu and use it to display the TESTVBX application's `IDD_DIALOG1` dialog box in design mode.

☐ Use the Tools window to place a MYCLOCK control in the dialog box.

☐ Double-click the MYCLOCK control.

> *App Studio responds by displaying the General properties of the control.*

☐ Select Styles from the drop-down list box at the upper-right corner of the Properties window.

> *App Studio responds by displaying the Styles Properties window of the control (see Figure 35.37).*

Figure 35.37.
The Styles Properties window of the MYCLOCK.VBX control (with the `UpdateInterval` property).

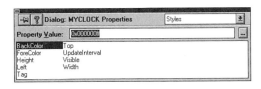

As shown in Figure 35.37, the MYCLOCK control now has the `UpdateInterval` property (underneath the `Top` property). Of course, the `UpdateInterval` property doesn't perform any function yet. That is, if you set the `UpdateInterval` property to a value, it won't have any effect on the control. Later in the chapter, you'll write the code that actually does something to the control when the `UpdateInterval` property is set to a certain value.

☐ Delete the MYCLOCK control from the dialog box, select Save from App Studio's File menu, and then terminate App Studio.

The Structure of the *UpdateInterval* Property

In the preceding steps, you defined the structure of the `UpdateInterval` property as follows:

```
PROPINFO Property_UpdateInterval =
    {
    "UpdateInterval",
    DT_SHORT | PF_fGetData | PF_fSetMsg | PF_fSaveData,
    OFFSETIN(MYCLOCK, UpdateInterval),
    0, 0, NULL, 0
    };
```

1251

You created this structure by copying and pasting a typical example of a property structure. As stated earlier, you can use this example as a template for declaring structures of other custom properties.

Now look at the syntax of the property structure. To begin with, the first line of the structure,

```
PROPINFO Property_UpdateInterval =
```

declares the structure as a `PROPINFO` type structure and names it `Property_UpdateInterval`.

The remaining lines of the structure definition are the structure's fields. The first field of the structure is the string

```
"UpdateInterval"
```

This field specifies the name of the property as it will appear in the Properties window. Indeed, as you can see from Figure 35.37, the name of the property as it appears in the Properties window is `UpdateInterval`.

The second field of the structure is

```
DT_SHORT ¦ PF_fGetData ¦ PF_fSetMsg ¦ PF_fSaveData
```

This field is an OR expression that ORs four property flags:

```
DT_SHORT
PF_fGetData
PF_fSetMsg
PF_fSaveData
```

The first flag, `DT_SHORT`, specifies that the property is a `SHORT` type. That is, the property will be used to hold data of type `SHORT`. If you want the property to hold a different type of data, you need to specify a different `DT_` constant. For example, `DT_LONG` specifies a `LONG` type.

The remaining three property flags are

```
PF_fGetData ¦ PF_fSetMsg ¦ PF_fSaveData
```

These flag settings are typical, and you can use them as shown here when you declare other custom properties. However, in case you have a special property in which you want to change these flag settings, here are the explanations for these flags:

`PF_GetData` specifies what should happen whenever someone tries to *get* (that is, read) the value of the property. If you specify `PF_GetData`, whenever someone tries to get the current value of the property, the value will be read directly from the property's variable. However, if you specify `PF_GetMsg` instead of `PF_GetData`, a VBM_GETPROPERTY message will be generated whenever someone tries to get the value of the property, and the code that you type under the VBM_GETPROPERTY case will be executed. Typically, when someone tries to get the current value of a property, there is no need to perform any action. Thus, in most cases you can use the `PF_GetData` flag.

`PF_SetMsg` specifies what should happen whenever someone tries to *set* the value of the property. If you specify `PF_SetMsg`, whenever someone tries to set the value of the property a VBM_SETPROPERTY message will be generated, and the code that you type under the VBM_SETPROPERTY case will be executed. However, if you specify `PF_SetData` instead of `PF_SetMsg`, whenever someone tries to set the value of the property the new value will be transferred directly to the property's variable without generating a VBM_SETPROPERTY message. Typically, when someone sets the value of the property, you want to perform some action. Thus, you should use the `PF_SetMsg` flag and write code under the VBM_SETPROPERTY case. Writing code under the VBM_SETPROPERTY case is covered later in this chapter.

`PF_SaveData` specifies what should happen whenever someone tries to *save* (or load) the form onto the disk (for example, when someone selects Save from Visual Basic's File menu to save the form). If you specify `PF_SaveData`, the value of the property is saved to the disk directly from the property's variable whenever someone saves the form. However, if you specify `PF_SaveMsg` instead of `PF_SaveData`, a VBM_SAVEPROPERTY message is generated whenever someone saves the form, and a VBM_LOADPROPERTY message is generated whenever someone loads the form from the disk. Typically, when someone saves the form to the disk, there's no need to perform any action. Thus, the `PF_SaveData` flag is typically used.

The third field of the `UpdateInterval` structure is

`OFFSETIN(MYCLOCK, UpdateInterval),`

This field specifies the offset of the property's variable within the structure of the control. To get this offset, use the `OFFSETIN` macro, which is defined in the `MYCLOCK.H` file.

The remaining four fields of the `UpdateInterval` structure aren't used in the MYCLOCK.VBX control, so they are set to 0 and NULL.

Making the *UpdateInterval* **Property Functional**

At this point the MYCLOCK.VBX control has the UpdateInterval property (see Figure 35.37), but this property doesn't do anything. It can hold data of type SHORT, but if someone sets the UpdateInterval property to a value, it has no effect on the control. Now you'll add code to the MYCLOCK.VBX control that makes the UpdateInterval property functional.

What should the UpdateInterval property do? Well, as its name implies, this property determines the interval at which the MYCLOCK.VBX control updates itself. Currently, the MYCLOCK.VBX control updates the displayed time every 1,000 milliseconds (because you installed the control's timer under the WM_NCCREATE case with a 1,000-millisecond interval). Now you'll enhance the MYCLOCK.VBX control so that it will update the displayed time every X milliseconds, where X is the current setting of the UpdateInterval property. Here's how you do that:

☐ Open the project MYCLOCK.MAK.

☐ Open the file MYCLOCK.C and write code under the WM_SETPROPERTY case until it looks as follows:

```
case VBM_SETPROPERTY:

    // NOTE: wp = Property that was just changed.
    //       lp = New value of the property.

    switch (wp)
        {
        // TODO: Add a case for each custom property

        ///////////////////////
        // MY CODE STARTS HERE
        ///////////////////////

        case IPROP_MYCLOCK_UPDATEINTERVAL:

            // Set the UpdateInterval property with
            // the new value.
            pMYCLOCK(hctl)->UpdateInterval = (SHORT)lp;

            // Set the timer with the new value.
            SetTimer(hwnd,
                     1,
                     pMYCLOCK(hctl)->UpdateInterval,
                     NULL);
            return 0;
```

```
/////////////////////
// MY CODE ENDS HERE
/////////////////////

    }
```

```
break;
```

If someone sets one of the properties of the MYCLOCK.VBX control, a VBM_SETPROPERTY message is generated and the code you just typed under the VBM_SETPROPERTY case is executed. The wp parameter determines which property has been set, and the lp parameter holds the value with which the property was set.

For example, if someone uses App Studio to set the UpdateInterval property of the MYCLOCK.VBX control to 2,000, the code under the VBM_SETPROPERTY case will be executed and the values of the parameters wp and lp will be

```
wp =  IPROP_MYCLOCK_UPDATEINTERVAL (the constant of the
      UpdateInterval property)

lp = 2000
```

The code you typed under the VBM_SETPROPERTY case uses a case statement to determine whether the property that was just changed was the UpdateInterval property:

```
case IPROP_MYCLOCK_UPDATEINTERVAL:

    // Set the UpdateInterval property with
    // the new value.
    pMYCLOCK(hctl)->UpdateInterval = (SHORT)lp;

    // Set the timer with the new value.
    SetTimer(hwnd,
             1,
             pMYCLOCK(hctl)->UpdateInterval,
             NULL);

    return 0;
```

If the parameter wp is equal to

```
IPROP_MYCLOCK_UPDATEINTERVAL
```

it means that the UpdateInterval property was just changed, so the three statements under the preceding case are executed. The first statement,

```
pMYCLOCK(hctl)->UpdateInterval = (SHORT)lp;
```

uses the pMYCLOCK macro to set the UpdateInterval property with the value of lp. As stated previously, the lp parameter holds the value with which the property was set.

NOTE

Recall that to set the value of a standard property of the MYCLOCK control (such as the BackColor property), you need to use the VBSetControlProperty() function. For example, to set the BackColor property to 255, use the statement

```
VBSetControlProperty(hctl,
                IPROP_MYCLOCK_BACKCOLOR,
                255L);
```

However, to set the value of a custom property of the MYCLOCK.VBX control (such as the UpdateInterval property), you need to use the pMYCLOCK macro. For example, to set the value of the UpdateInterval property to 3,000, use the following statement:

```
pMYCLOCK(hctl)->UpdateInterval = 3000;
```

The pMYCLOCK macro is defined in the header file MYCLOCK.H. It returns a pointer to the MYCLOCK control structure.

Note that you didn't write the code that declares the pMYCLOCK macro! You borrowed this code from the GENERIC.H file. Originally, the name of this macro was pGENERIC. But when you started the MYCLOCK project, you replaced all occurrences of the word GENERIC with MYCLOCK. Thus, the macro pGENERIC became pMYCLOCK.

The second statement under the IPROP_MYCLOCK_UPDATEINTERVAL case is

```
SetTimer(hwnd,
        1,
        pMYCLOCK(hctl)->UpdateInterval,
        NULL);
```

This statement uses the SetTimer() function to set the interval of the timer with the new value of the UpdateInterval property. Thus, from now on, the code under the WM_TIMER case (the code that displays the current time) will be executed every X milliseconds, where X is the new value of the UpdateInterval property.

The last statement under the IPROP_MYCLOCK_UPDATEINTERVAL case is

```
return 0;
```

Returning 0 indicates that all is OK (that is, the property was set successfully).

To summarize how the code you wrote under the VBM_SETPROPERTY works:

> Whenever the UpdateInterval property is set to a value, a VBM_SETPROPERTY message is generated and the code under the VBM_SETPROPERTY case is executed.
>
> The code you typed under the VBM_SETPROPERTY case determines (by examining the value of the parameter wp) whether the UpdateInterval property is the property that was just set. If so, the UpdateInterval property is assigned the value of the parameter lp, and the interval of the timer is set to the new value of the UpdateInterval property.

The last thing you have to do with the UpdateInterval property is write the code that sets the default value of this property. Recall that a good place to set the default values of properties is under the WM_NCCREATE case:

☐ Add code under the WM_NCCREATE case until it looks as follows:

```
case WM_NCCREATE:

    // TODO: Add initialization code here

    /////////////////////////
    // MY CODE STARTS HERE
    /////////////////////////

    // Install a timer.
    SetTimer(hwnd,1,1000,NULL);

    // Set the BackColor property to 65280 (green).
    VBSetControlProperty(hctl,
                         IPROP_MYCLOCK_BACKCOLOR,
                         65280L);

    // Set the UpdateInterval property to 1000
    pMYCLOCK(hctl)->UpdateInterval = 1000;

    /////////////////////////
    // MY CODE ENDS HERE
    /////////////////////////

break;
```

The statement you just added under the WM_NCCREATE case,

```
pMYCLOCK(hctl)->UpdateInterval = 1000;
```

sets the value of the `UpdateInterval` property to 1,000. Thus, when a MYCLOCK.VBX control is created, the default value of the `UpdateInterval` property will be 1,000.

Verify that the code you wrote under the `VBM_SETPROPERTY` case makes the `UpdateInterval` property operational:

☐ Select Rebuild All MYCLOCK.VBX from Visual C++'s Project menu.

> *Visual C++ responds by compiling/linking the files of the MYCLOCK project and creating the* `MYCLOCK.VBX` *file.*

☐ Switch to the File Manager program (or to DOS) and copy the file you just created, `C:\VCPROG\PRACTICE\CH35\MYCLOCK.VBX`, to your `C:\WINDOWS\SYSTEM` directory.

☐ Open the TESTVBX.MAK project.

☐ Start App Studio from Visual C++'s Tools menu and use App Studio to display TESTVBX application's `IDD_DIALOG1` dialog box in design mode.

☐ Use the Tools window to place a MYCLOCK control in the dialog box.

☐ Set the `Height` property of the MYCLOCK control to 10 and the `Width` property to 103, so you'll be able to see the seconds changing.

As you can see, the seconds of the clock change every 1,000 milliseconds (1 second).

☐ Double-click the MYCLOCK control and inspect the current value of the `UpdateInterval` property (see Figure 35.38).

Figure 35.38.
Inspecting the
`UpdateInterval`
property.

As you can see, the current value of the `UpdateInterval` property is 1,000 milliseconds. That's because you set the value of the `UpdateInterval` property to 1,000 under the `WM_NCCREATE` case.

☐ Change the `UpdateInterval` property to 5,000.

Now observe the MYCLOCK control and notice that the time is updated every 5,000 milliseconds (five seconds).

As soon as you changed the `UpdateInterval` property to 5,000, the code you wrote under the `VBM_SETPROPERTY` case was executed, and this code set the interval period of the timer to the new value of the `UpdateInterval` property.

☐ Delete the MYCLOCK control from the dialog box, select Save from App Studio's File menu, and then terminate App Studio.

Adding a Standard Event to the MYCLOCK.VBX Control

So far you've added a standard property and a custom property to the MYCLOCK.VBX control. Now you'll learn how to add a standard event to the control. As you'll soon see, the steps necessary to add a standard event are similar to the steps you took when you added a standard property.

Standard events are events such as `Click` (mouse click) and `DblClick` (mouse double-click). These events are predefined, and adding them to a VBX control is easy. Table 35.2 lists all the standard events you can add to a VBX control.

Table 35.2. Standard events.

Event	Constant
Click	PEVENTINFO_STD_CLICK
DblClick	PEVENTINFO_STD_DBLCLICK
DragDrop	PEVENTINFO_STD_DRAGDROP
DragOver	PEVENTINFO_STD_DRAGOVER
GotFocus	PEVENTINFO_STD_GOTFOCUS
KeyDown	PEVENTINFO_STD_KEYDOWN
KeyPress	PEVENTINFO_STD_KEYPRESS
KeyUp	PEVENTINFO_STD_KEYUP
Last	PEVENTINFO_STD_LAST
LinkClose	PEVENTINFO_STD_LINKCLOSE
LinkError	PEVENTINFO_STD_LINKERROR
LinkNotify	PEVENTINFO_STD_LINKNOTIFY
LinkOpen	PEVENTINFO_STD_LINKOPEN
LostFocus	PEVENTINFO_STD_LOSTFOCUS
MouseDown	PEVENTINFO_STD_MOUSEDOWN

continues

Table 35.2. continued

Event	Constant
MouseMove	PEVENTINFO_STD_MOUSEMOVE
MouseUp	PEVENTINFO_STD_MOUSEUP
None	PEVENTINFO_STD_NONE

If you have any experience with Visual Basic, you're probably familiar with many of the events listed in Table 35.2. Even if you don't, some of the names of these events are self-explanatory. For example, the MouseMove event occurs when the user moves the mouse over the control.

The MYCLOCK.VBX control already has three standard events (see Figure 35.29). The code that defines these events resides in the header file MYCLOCK.H. You didn't have to write the code that defines these events because you borrowed it from the GENERIC.H file.

Now you'll add the standard event DblClick to the MYCLOCK.VBX control. The DblClick event occurs when the user double-clicks the control. Currently, the MYCLOCK.VBX control has a Click event but not a DblClick event.

Follow these steps to add the DblClick event to the MYCLOCK.VBX control:

☐ Open the project MYCLOCK.MAK.

☐ Open the header file MYCLOCK.H and look for the Event Information Table. Currently, the Event Information Table looks as follows:

```
//-------------------------------------------------------
// Event Information Table
//-------------------------------------------------------
PEVENTINFO Myclock_Events[] =
    {
    PEVENTINFO_STD_CLICK,
    PEVENTINFO_STD_DRAGDROP,
    PEVENTINFO_STD_DRAGOVER,

    // TODO: Specify addresses of events structures
    //
    // Example:
    // &Event_MyEvent,          // Custom
    // &Event_HerEvent,         // Custom
    // PEVENTINFO_STD_DBLCLICK, // Standard


    NULL
    };
```

The Event Information Table lists the addresses of structures that correspond to the events. Each event has a structure that defines it, and you specify each structure's address in the Event Information Table. As you can see, the Event Information Table currently has three entries. This means that the MYCLOCK.VBX control currently has three events.

Now add the DblClick event. You need to add the address of the structure that defines the DblClick event to the Event Information Table. What is this address? It's given by a constant that points to the structure of the event. The constants that point to the standard events are listed in Table 35.2. As you can see, the constant that points to the address of the DblClick event is PEVENTINFO_STD_DBLCLICK.

☐ Add the constant PEVENTINFO_STD_DBLCLICK to the Event Information Table. After you add this constant, the Event Information Table looks as follows:

```
//---------------------------------------------------------
// Event Information Table
//---------------------------------------------------------
PEVENTINFO Myclock_Events[] =
    {
    PEVENTINFO_STD_CLICK,
    PEVENTINFO_STD_DRAGDROP,
    PEVENTINFO_STD_DRAGOVER,

    // TODO: Specify addresses of events structures
    //
    // Example:
    // &Event_MyEvent,           // Custom
    // &Event_HerEvent,          // Custom
    // PEVENTINFO_STD_DBLCLICK,  // Standard

    /////////////////////////
    // MY CODE STARTS HERE
    /////////////////////////

    PEVENTINFO_STD_DBLCLICK,

    /////////////////////////
    // MY CODE ENDS HERE
    /////////////////////////

    NULL
};
```

NOTE: When you add PEVENTINFO_STD_DBLCLICK to the table, don't forget the comma. It's needed because the PEVENTINFO_STD_DBLCLICK item isn't the last entry in the table. As you can see from the preceding code, the last entry in the table is NULL.

Next, you need to define a constant that corresponds to the property you just added to the Event Information Table:

☐ Look for the Event List Constants section. It's located immediately after the Event Information Table. Currently, the Event List Constants section looks as follows:

```
//-----------------------------------------------------
// Event List Constants
//-----------------------------------------------------
#define IEVENT_MYCLOCK_CLICK            0
#define IEVENT_MYCLOCK_DRAGDROP         1
#define IEVENT_MYCLOCK_DRAGOVER         2

// TODO: Define consecutive ID's of more events
//
// Example:
// #define IEVENT_MYCLOCK_MYEVENT       3
// #define IEVENT_MYCLOCK_HEREVENT      4
// #define IEVENT_MYCLOCK_DBLCLICK      5
```

As you can see, the Event List Constants section defines a constant for each of the control's events. Each constant corresponds to an event listed in the Event Information Table. Now you want to add a constant for the DblClick event. The DblClick event is event #3 (zero-based) within the Event Information Table, so the constant of the DblClick event is #defined as 3:

☐ Add the #define statement for the DblClick event to the end of the Event List Constants section. After you add this statement, the Event List Constants section looks as follows:

```
//-----------------------------------------------------
// Event List Constants
//-----------------------------------------------------
#define IEVENT_MYCLOCK_CLICK            0
#define IEVENT_MYCLOCK_DRAGDROP         1
#define IEVENT_MYCLOCK_DRAGOVER         2

// TODO: Define consecutive ID's of more events
//
// Example:
// #define IEVENT_MYCLOCK_MYEVENT       3
// #define IEVENT_MYCLOCK_HEREVENT      4
// #define IEVENT_MYCLOCK_DBLCLICK      5

/////////////////////////
// MY CODE STARTS HERE
/////////////////////////
```

```
#define IEVENT_MYCLOCK_DBLCLICK          3
```

```
/////////////////////
// MY CODE ENDS HERE
/////////////////////
```

That's it! You've finished adding the DblClick event to the MYCLOCK.VBX control.

To summarize what you did:

> You added the address of the DblClick event structure
> (PPROPINFO_STD_FORECOLOR) to the Event Information Table.
> You #defined a constant for the DblClick event that specifies its location within the Event Information Table.

Verify that the DblClick event has been added to the MYCLOCK.VBX control:

☐ Select Rebuild All MYCLOCK.VBX from Visual C++'s Project menu.

> *Visual C++ responds by compiling/linking the MYCLOCK project's files and creating the* MYCLOCK.VBX *file.*

☐ Switch to the File Manager program (or to DOS) and copy the file you just created, C:\VCPROG\PRACTICE\CH35\MYCLOCK.VBX, to your C:\WINDOWS\SYSTEM directory.

☐ Open the TESTVBX.MAK project.

☐ Start App Studio from Visual C++'s Tools menu and use it to display the TESTVBX application's IDD_DIALOG1 dialog box in design mode.

> **NOTE**
>
> In the following step, you'll be instructed to remove the MYCLOCK.VBX control from App Studio's Tools window and then reinstall it. Why? Because when you add a new event to a VBX control that has already been installed in App Studio, the new event isn't recognized by App Studio unless you first remove and then reinstall the control.

☐ Remove the MYCLOCK.VBX control from App Studio's Tools window. That is, select Install Controls from App Studio's File menu, highlight MYCLOCK.VBX in the Installed Files list, click the Remove button, and click the Close button.

The MYCLOCK.VBX is now removed from App Studio's Tools window.

☐ Now reinstall the MYCLOCK.VBX control. That is, select Install Controls from App Studio's File menu, highlight MYCLOCK.VBX in the leftmost File list, click the Install button, and click the OK button.

Now the MYCLOCK.VBX control is reinstalled in App Studio's Tools window.

☐ Use the Tools window to place a MYCLOCK control in the dialog box.

☐ Set the Height property of the MYCLOCK control to 10 and the Width property to 103.

Select ClassWizard from App Studio's Resource menu.

App Studio responds by displaying the ClassWizard dialog box.

☐ Make sure that the IDC_MYCLOCK1 object is selected in the Object IDs list and observe the Messages list (see Figure 35.39).

Figure 35.39.
The events
(messages)
associated with the
MYCLOCK.VBX
control.

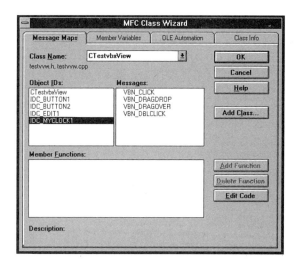

As shown in Figure 35.39, the DblClick event you added to the MYCLOCK.VBX control is now listed in the messages list; it's called VBN_DBLCLICK.

Attach code to the VBN_DBLCLICK event:

☐ Use the ClassWizard dialog box to add a function for the `VBN_DBLCLICK` event:

Class Name:	CTestvbxView
Object ID:	IDC_MYCLOCK1
Message:	VBN_DBLCLICK
Function Name:	OnDblclickMyclock1()

☐ Edit the `OnDblclickMyclock1()` function that you added to the `TESTVVW.CPP` file. After you edit the `OnDblclickMyclock1()` function, it looks as follows:

```
void CTestvbxView::OnDblclickMyclock1(UINT, int, CWnd*, LPVOID)
{
// TODO: Add your VBX event notification handler code here

/////////////////////////
// MY CODE STARTS HERE
/////////////////////////

MessageBox("You double clicked the MYCLOCK control!");

/////////////////////////
// MY CODE ENDS HERE
/////////////////////////

}
```

The code you just attached to the `DblClick` event of the MYCLOCK control is made up of one statement:

```
MessageBox("You double clicked the MYCLOCK control!");
```

Thus, whenever the `DblClick` event occurs (that is, whenever the user double-clicks the MYCLOCK control), the message "You double-clicked the MYCLOCK control" will be displayed.

To see the code you attached to the DblClick event in action:

☐ Select Build TESTVBX.EXE from Visual C++'s Project menu and then execute the TESTVBX.EXE application.

The main window of the TESTVBX.EXE application appears as shown in Figure 35.40.

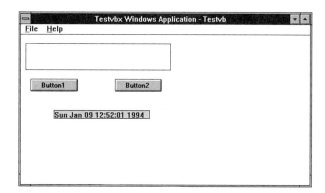

Figure 35.40.
The
TESTVBX.EXE
application with
the MYCLOCK
control inside it.

☐ Double-click the MYCLOCK control.

The TESTVBX application displays a message box, as shown in Figure 35.41.

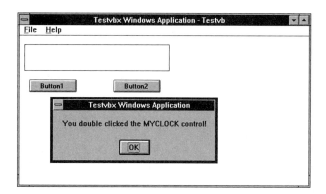

Figure 35.41.
The
TESTVBX.EXE
application after
double-clicking the
MYCLOCK
control.

☐ Quit the TESTVBX.EXE application.

Okay, you've added a standard event to the MYCLOCK.VBX control and tested this event. In the following section, you'll add a custom event to the MYCLOCK.VBX control.

Before you go to the next section, you need to terminate App Studio, because you won't be able to overwrite the current version of the MYCLOCK.VBX control if any open application is currently using the control.

☐ Switch back to App Studio and select Exit from the File menu.

Adding a Custom Event to the MYCLOCK.VBX Control

In many cases, you'll have to add an event to your VBX control that isn't a standard event. Such an event, an event custom-made by you, is called a *custom event*.

Now you'll add a custom event to the MYCLOCK.VBX control. You'll name this event NewMinute. For now, don't concern yourself with the purpose of the NewMinute event. Later you'll make use of this event, but now all you want to do is add it to the MYCLOCK.VBX control.

The first thing to do when you add a custom event is to declare the structure of the event. Each event must have a structure that defines it. When you added the DblClick event you didn't have to define a structure, because it's a standard (predefined) event. However, the property that you're adding now is your own custom property, so you must define a structure for it. Here's how you do that:

☐ Open the project MYCLOCK.MAK.

☐ Open the header file MYCLOCK.H and look for the Event Information Structures section. Currently, the Event Information Structures section looks as follows:

```
//------------------------------------------------------
// Event Information Structures
//------------------------------------------------------
//
// TODO: Define EVENTINFO structure for each custom event
//
// Example:
//
// EVENTINFO Event_MyEvent =
//         {
//         "MyEvent",
//         0,
//         0,
//         NULL,
//         NULL
//         };
```

As you can see, the Event Information Structures section has only comments. The comments include the declaration of an Event Information (EVENTINFO) structure. You can use this example as a template for declaring the structure of the NewMinute event:

☐ Declare the structure of the NewMinute event by using the commented example as a template. That is, copy and paste the example and replace the

1267

two occurrences of the word `MyProperty` with the word `NewMinute`. After declaring the structure of the `NewMinute` event, the Event Information Structures section looks as follows:

```
//------------------------------------------------------
// Event Information Structures
//------------------------------------------------------
//
// TODO: Define EVENTINFO structure for each custom event
//
// Example:
//
// EVENTINFO Event_MyEvent =
//      {
//      "MyEvent",
//      0,
//      0,
//      NULL,
//      NULL
//      };

////////////////////////
// MY CODE STARTS HERE
////////////////////////

EVENTINFO Event_NewMinute =
    {
    "NewMinute",
    0,
    0,
    NULL,
    NULL
    };

////////////////////////
// MY CODE ENDS HERE
////////////////////////
```

The structure declaration of the `NewMinute` event is simple. The first line,

```
EVENTINFO Event_NewMinute =
```

declares the structure as an `EVENTINFO` type structure and names it `Event_NewMinute`.

The remaining lines of the structure definition are the fields of the structure.

The first field of the structure is the string

```
"NewMinute"
```

This field specifies the name of the event.

The remaining four fields of the structure aren't used for the `NewMinute` event, so they're set to `0` and `NULL`.

> **NOTE**
>
> The last four fields of the `NewMinute` event's structure aren't used, so they're set to `0` and `NULL`. These parameters are used when you want the event procedure to have parameters. The event procedure is the procedure (in Visual Basic) or the function (in Visual C++) that is executed when the event occurs. In most cases there's no need to pass parameters to the event procedure, because the control can communicate with the event procedure through properties. Consider a case where you want to pass the current time to the event procedure. One way to "tell" the event procedure the current time is to pass to it a parameter that specifies the current time. However, a way to do this without using a parameter is to add a custom property to the control that specifies the current time.

Now that you have a structure that defines the `NewMinute` event, you can add the address of this structure to the Event Information Table:

☐ Look for the Event Information Table in the `MYCLOCK.H` file and modify it until it looks as follows:

```
//-------------------------------------------------------
// Event Information Table
//-------------------------------------------------------
PEVENTINFO Myclock_Events[] =
    {
    PEVENTINFO_STD_CLICK,
    PEVENTINFO_STD_DRAGDROP,
    PEVENTINFO_STD_DRAGOVER,

    // TODO: Specify addresses of events structures
    //
    // Example:
    // &Event_MyEvent,          // Custom
    // &Event_HerEvent,         // Custom
    // PEVENTINFO_STD_DBLCLICK, // Standard

    /////////////////////////
    // MY CODE STARTS HERE
    /////////////////////////

    PEVENTINFO_STD_DBLCLICK,
```

```
        &Event_NewMinute,

        ////////////////////
        // MY CODE ENDS HERE
        ////////////////////

        NULL
};
```

The entry that you just added to the table,

```
&Event_NewMinute,
```

is the address of the `NewMinute` structure you defined.

> **NOTE**
>
> Earlier, when you specified the address of the `DblClick` event, you used the constant
>
> ```
> PEVENTINFO_STD_DBLCLICK
> ```
>
> However, the `NewMinute` event isn't a standard event, so it doesn't have a constant that points to its address. Thus, you specify the address of the `NewMinute` event with
>
> ```
> &Event_NewMinute
> ```
>
> which is the address of the structure you declared for the `NewMinute` event.

The last thing you have to do is define a constant that corresponds to the `NewMinute` event (just as you did for the `DblClick` event):

☐ Look for the Event List Constants section (it's located immediately after the Event Information Table) and modify it until it looks as follows:

```
//-------------------------------------------------------
// Event List Constants
//-------------------------------------------------------
#define IEVENT_MYCLOCK_CLICK          0
#define IEVENT_MYCLOCK_DRAGDROP       1
#define IEVENT_MYCLOCK_DRAGOVER       2

// TODO: Define consecutive ID's of more events
//
// Example:
// #define IEVENT_MYCLOCK_MYEVENT      3
// #define IEVENT_MYCLOCK_HEREVENT     4
```

```
// #define IEVENT_MYCLOCK_DBLCLICK        5
```

```
/////////////////////////
// MY CODE STARTS HERE
/////////////////////////
```

```
#define IEVENT_MYCLOCK_DBLCLICK          3
```

```
#define IEVENT_MYCLOCK_NEWMINUTE         4
```

```
/////////////////////
// MY CODE ENDS HERE
/////////////////////
```

The constant you just defined,

```
#define IEVENT_MYCLOCK_NEWMINUTE         4
```

corresponds to the NewMinute event you added to the Event Information Table. Because the NewMinute event is event #4 (zero-based) within the Event Information Table, you #define the constant as 4.

That's it! You've finished adding the NewMinute custom event to the MYCLOCK.VBX control.

To summarize what you did to add the custom event NewMinute to the MYCLOCK.VBX control:

> You declared a structure (Event_NewMinute) that defines the NewMinute event.
> You entered the address of the Event_NewMinute structure inside the Event Information Table.
> You #defined a constant for the NewMinute event that specifies the location of the NewMinute event within the Event Information Table.

Verify that the NewMinute event is now added to the MYCLOCK.VBX control:

☐ Select Rebuild All MYCLOCK.VBX from Visual C++'s Project menu.

> *Visual C++ responds by compiling/linking the files of the MYCLOCK project and creating the MYCLOCK.VBX file.*

☐ Switch to the File Manager program (or to DOS) and copy the file you just created, C:\VCPROG\PRACTICE\CH35\MYCLOCK.VBX, to your C:\WINDOWS\SYSTEM directory.

☐ Open the TESTVBX.MAK project.

1271

☐ Start App Studio from Visual C++'s Tools menu and use it to display the
TESTVBX application's `IDD_DIALOG1` dialog box in design mode.

As before, because you added a new event to the MYCLOCK.VBX control, you need
to remove the MYCLOCK.VBX control from App Studio's Tools window and then
reinstall it so App Studio will recognize the new event.

☐ Remove the MYCLOCK object from the dialog box. You need to do this
because you can't use App Studio to remove the MYCLOCK.VBX control
from the Tools window if the dialog box has a MYCLOCK object in it.

☐ Remove the MYCLOCK.VBX control from App Studio's Tools window.
That is, select Install Controls from App Studio's File menu, highlight
MYCLOCK.VBX in the Installed Files list, click the Remove button, and
click the Close button.

Now the MYCLOCK.VBX control is removed from App Studio's Tools window.

☐ Now reinstall the MYCLOCK.VBX control. That is, select Install Controls
from App Studio's File menu, highlight MYCLOCK.VBX in the leftmost
File list, click the Install button, and click the OK button.

Now the MYCLOCK.VBX control is reinstalled in App Studio's Tools window.

☐ Use the Tools window to place a MYCLOCK control in the dialog box.

☐ Set the `Height` property of the MYCLOCK control to 10 and set the `Width`
property to 103.

☐ Select ClassWizard from App Studio's Resource menu.

App Studio responds by displaying the ClassWizard dialog box.

☐ Make sure that the `IDC_MYCLOCK1` object is selected in the Object IDs list,
and observe the Messages list (see Figure 35.42).

As you can see from Figure 35.42, the `NewMinute` event you added to the
MYCLOCK.VBX control is now listed in the messages list—it's called `VBN_NEWMINUTE`.

For now, don't attach code to the `VBN_NEWMINUTE` event. You'll have a chance to do
this later.

☐ Click ClassWizard's Cancel button to go back to App Studio.

☐ Select Save from App Studio's File menu and then terminate App Studio.

Figure 35.42.
The events
(messages)
associated with the
MYCLOCK.VBX
control.

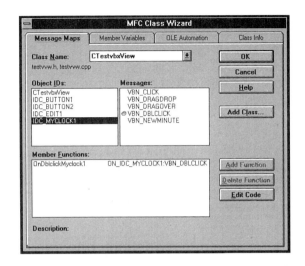

Firing the NewMinute Event

At this point, the MYCLOCK.VBX control has the `NewMinute` event that you added to it, but this event never happens. To make the `NewMinute` event happen, you need to write some code.

> **NOTE**
>
> When you add a standard event to a VBX control, such as the `DblClick` event that you added earlier, you don't need to write any code to make the event happen. That is, a standard event already has built-in code that makes the event happen. In the case of the `DblClick` event, the event occurs automatically whenever the user double-clicks the VBX control.
>
> However, when you add a custom event to a VBX control, you need to write code that makes the event happen. Your code needs to recognize that the event has occurred and then use the function `VBFireEvent()` to fire the event (that is, to make the event happen).

The question is, when does the `NewMinute` event occur? Well, as its name implies, it occurs whenever a new minute begins. Follow these steps to write the code that fires the `NewMinute` event:

☐ Open the project MYCLOCK.MAK.

❑ Open the file MYCLOCK.C and add code to the DrawTheControl() function until it looks as follows:

```
//------------------------------------------------------
// Draw inside the control.
//------------------------------------------------------
VOID NEAR DrawTheControl
(
    HCTL hctl,
    HWND hwnd,
    HDC  hdc
)
{
    // Variables for the brush.
    HBRUSH hbr;
    HBRUSH hbrOld = NULL;

    // TODO: Define your own local variables here (if any)

    /////////////////////////
    // MY CODE STARTS HERE
    /////////////////////////

    char CurrentTime[30];
    struct tm *newtime;
    long lTime;

    /////////////////////////
    // MY CODE ENDS HERE
    /////////////////////////

    // Select new brush, and save old brush.
    hbr = (HBRUSH)SendMessage(GetParent(hwnd),
            WM_CTLCOLOR, hdc, MAKELONG(hwnd,0));
    if (hbr)
       hbrOld = SelectObject(hdc, hbr);


    // TODO: Add your drawing code here

    /////////////////////////
    // MY CODE STARTS HERE
    /////////////////////////

    // Get the current time
    time(&lTime);
    newtime=localtime(&lTime);

    // Convert the time into a string.
    strcpy(CurrentTime, asctime(newtime));
```

```
// Pad the string with 5 blanks
CurrentTime[24]=' ';
CurrentTime[25]=' ';
CurrentTime[26]=' ';
CurrentTime[27]=' ';
CurrentTime[28]=' ';

// Display the current time
TextOut(hdc, 0, 0, CurrentTime, 29);

// If new minute has just begun, fire a NEWMINUTE event.
if (newtime->tm_sec==0)
   VBFireEvent(hctl, IEVENT_MYCLOCK_NEWMINUTE, NULL);

///////////////////////
// MY CODE ENDS HERE
///////////////////////

// Restore the old brush
if (hbrOld)
   SelectObject(hdc, hbrOld);

}
```

The code you just added to the `DrawTheControl()` function is made up of one `if` statement:

```
if (newtime->tm_sec==0)
   VBFireEvent(hctl, IEVENT_MYCLOCK_NEWMINUTE, NULL);
```

This `if` statement determines whether the `tm_sec` field of the `newtime` structure is currently `0`. If it is, a new minute has just begun, and the `VBFireEvent()` function is executed to fire the `NewTime` event:

```
VBFireEvent(hctl, IEVENT_MYCLOCK_NEWMINUTE, NULL);
```

The first parameter of the `VBFireEvent()` function, `hctl`, is the handle of the control. The second parameter, `IEVENT_MYCLOCK_NEWMINUTE`, is the ID that you defined for the `NewMinute` event in the `MYCLOCK.H` file. The third parameter is set to `NULL` because it's not used for the `NewMinute` event. (When an event has arguments, the third parameter is a pointer to a structure that stores the arguments.)

You've finished writing the code that fires the `NewMinute` event! Now, whenever a new minute begins, the code you wrote will fire a `NewMinute` event, and the code that the end user of the VBX control attaches to the `NewMinute` event will be executed automatically.

Note that the code you wrote to detect the `NewMinute` event is not perfect. This code is executed whenever the `DrawTheControl()` function is executed, which is determined by the value of the `UpdateInterval` property. So if the `UpdateInterval` property is set to a value greater than 1,000 milliseconds, there's a chance that a new minute could begin without your code detecting it.

Verify that the code you wrote actually fires the `NewMinute` event:

☐ Select Rebuild All MYCLOCK.VBX from Visual C++'s Project menu.

> *Visual C++ responds by compiling/linking the MYCLOCK project's files and creating the* `MYCLOCK.VBX` *file.*

Switch to the File Manager program (or to DOS) and copy the file that you just created, `C:\VCPROG\PRACTICE\CH35\MYCLOCK.VBX`, to your `C:\WINDOWS\SYSTEM` directory.

☐ Open the TESTVBX.MAK project.

☐ Start App Studio from Visual C++'s Tools menu and use App Studio to display the TESTVBX application's `IDD_DIALOG1` dialog box in design mode.

☐ Make sure that the `Height` property of the MYCLOCK control is set to 10 and the `Width` property is set to 103.

☐ Use ClassWizard add a function for the `VBN_NEWMINUTE` event:

Class Name:	`CTestvbxView`
Object ID:	`IDC_MYCLOCK1`
Message:	`VBN_NEWMINUTE`
Function Name:	`OnNewminuteMyclock1`

☐ Edit the `OnNewminuteMyclock1()` function that you added to the `TESTVVW.CPP` file. After you edit the `OnNewminuteMyclock1()` function, it looks as follows:

```
void CTestvbxView::OnNewminuteMyclock1(UINT, int, CWnd*, LPVOID)
{
// TODO: Add your VBX event notification handler code here

    /////////////////////////
    // MY CODE STARTS HERE
    /////////////////////////

    MessageBeep(-1);
```

```
/////////////////////
// MY CODE ENDS HERE
/////////////////////
```

```
}
```

The code you just attached to the NewMinute event of the MYCLOCK control is made up of one statement:

```
MessageBeep(-1);
```

Thus, whenever the NewMinute event occurs (that is, whenever a new minute begins), the PC speaker will beep.

To hear the code you attached to the NewMinute event in action:

☐ Select Build TESTVBX.EXE from Visual C++'s Project menu and then execute the TESTVBX.EXE application.

The main window of the TESTVBX application appears as shown in Figure 35.40.

☐ Observe the time that MYCLOCK displays and wait for a new minute to begin.

As expected, as soon as a new minute begins, the PC speaker beeps!

☐ Quit the TESTVBX application.

☐ Switch to App Studio and terminate it.

You've finished implementing and testing all the properties and events of the MYCLOCK.VBX control:

> You added a standard property to the control (the ForeColor property).
> You added a custom property to the control (the UpdateInterval property).
> You added a standard event to the control (the DblClick event).
> You added a custom event to the control (the NewMinute event).

In the following section you'll add the final touch to the MYCLOCK.VBX control. You'll customize the MYCLOCK.VBX icon that appears in the Tools window so that it displays a picture of a clock.

Customizing the MYCLOCK.VBX Control's Tool Icon

Currently, the tool icon of the MYCLOCK.VBX control displays a picture of the letter X (see Figure 35.25). That's because you borrowed the bitmap files for the tool icon from the GENVBX directory (the Generic files), and that's what these bitmap files display. Now you'll customize the bitmap files of the MYCLOCK.VBX control so that the Tools window displays a more appropriate image: a picture of a clock.

The bitmap files that are associated with the VBX control are

UP.BMP

DOWN.BMP

UPMONO.BMP

UPEGA.BMP

These files reside in the development directory of the MYCLOCK control (C:\VCPROG\PRACTICE\CH35\MYCLOCK). Recall that when you started the MYCLOCK project, you copied all the Generic directory files to your development directory, and these BMP files were also copied.

The UP.BMP bitmap is displayed in the Tools window when the icon is not selected (see Figure 35.43). As you can see, this bitmap displays the icon in its up position.

The DOWN.BMP bitmap is displayed in the Tools window when the icon control is selected (see Figure 35.44). As you can see, this bitmap displays the icon in its down position. The tool is "selected" when you click it.

Figure 35.43.
The tool's icon when the tool isn't selected.

The tool in its
up position
(UP.BMP)

Figure 35.44.
The tool's icon
when the tool is
selected.

The tool in its
down position
(DOWN.BMP)

The UP.BMP and DOWN.BMP bitmaps are used when the Tools window is displayed on a VGA monitor.

When the Tools window is displayed on a monochrome monitor, the UPMONO.BMP bitmap is used. When the Tools window is displayed on an EGA monitor, the UPEGA.BMP bitmap is used. Note that the down-position bitmaps for monochrome and EGA monitors aren't needed. When the tool is selected on a monochrome or EGA monitor, the up position bitmap is inverted.

Now that you know what the four bitmaps are for, you can customize them for the MYCLOCK control. You can use any bitmap editor. In the following steps, you'll use App Studio's bitmap editor:

☐ Select Close from Visual C++'s Project menu.

It's necessary to close the current project before starting App Studio, because you want to use App Studio only to edit bitmaps. That is, you don't want App Studio to modify the RC file of a project.

☐ Select App Studio from Visual C++'s Tools menu.

Visual C++ responds by running App Studio.

☐ Select Open from App Studio's File menu, and then select the BMP file
C:\VCPROG\PRACTICE\CH35\DOWN.BMP.

App Studio responds by opening the DOWN.BMP bitmap file (see Figure 35.45).

1279

Figure 35.45.
The DOWN.BMP
bitmap file.

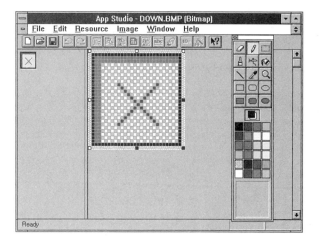

☐ Use the bitmap editor's tools to change the picture of the X to a picture of a clock. Note that you should leave the background pattern of the bitmap as it is. As you can see, the background is made of alternate white and gray pixels. To make your drawing, replace the pixels of the X with white pixels and then do your own drawing.

☐ When you finish drawing the clock, don't forget to save it (select Save from App Studio's File menu).

The DOWN.BMP bitmap is shown in Figure 35.46 after the X has been replaced with a simple drawing of a clock.

Figure 35.46.
The final version of
the DOWN.BMP
bitmap.

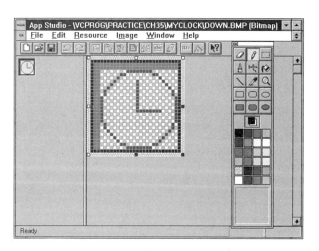

In a similar manner, customize and save the other three bitmap files:

☐ Customize and save `C:\VCPROG\PRACTICE\CH35\UP.BMP`.

☐ Customize and save `C:\VCPROG\PRACTICE\CH35\UPEGA.BMP`.

☐ Customize and save `C:\VCPROG\PRACTICE\CH35\UPMONO.BMP`.

The final versions of the `UP.BMP`, `UPEGA.BMP`, and `UPMONO.BMP` bitmaps are shown in Figures 35.47, 35.48, and 35.49.

Figure 35.47.
The final version
of the UP.BMP
bitmap.

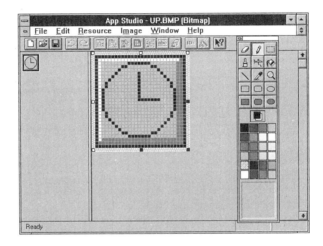

Figure 35.48.
The final version of
the UPEGA.BMP
bitmap.

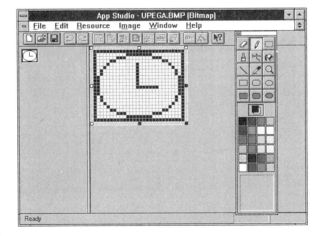

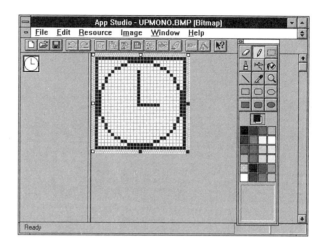

Figure 35.49.
The final version of
the UPMONO . BMP
bitmap.

To see your drawings in action:

☐ Terminate App Studio and switch back to Visual C++.

☐ Open the MYCLOCK.MAK project.

☐ Select Rebuild All MYCLOCK.VBX from Visual C++'s Project menu.

Visual C++ responds by compiling/linking the files of the MYCLOCK project
and creating the MYCLOCK . VBX *file.*

☐ Switch to the File Manager program (or to DOS) and copy the file that you
just created, C : \VCPROG\PRACTICE\CH35\MYCLOCK . VBX, to your
C : \WINDOWS\SYSTEM directory.

☐ Open the TESTVBX.MAK project.

☐ Start App Studio from Visual C++'s Tools menu and use it to display the
TESTVBX application's IDD_DIALOG1 dialog box in design mode.

The dialog box appears as shown in Figure 35.50. As you can see, the
MYCLOCK.VBX tool in the Tools window now displays your drawing.

Figure 35.50.
The MYCLOCK
tool with the clock
drawing.

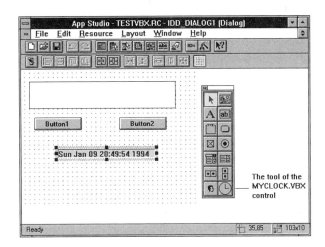

Advanced Multimedia Control Features

This appendix covers several advanced features of the multimedia control. You'll learn how to use the multimedia control to perform the several different tasks.

You'll learn to play a WAV file through the PC speaker while an animation show is running.

You'll learn to play a WAV file through the PC speaker and enable the user to switch to other Windows applications while the WAV file plays in the background.

You'll learn to incorporate multiple multimedia controls in the same application for controlling and playing several multimedia devices.

You'll learn to detect whether the user's PC has a sound card and play sound through either the sound card or the PC speaker accordingly.

The DANCE Application— "PC Speaker" Version

In Chapter 27, "Animation," you used the TegoMM.VBX multimedia control to write the DANCE application. Recall that this application plays a MIDI file through the sound card and simultaneously displays an animation show of a couple dancing.

But what if the user doesn't have a sound card? Is it possible to write an application that plays sound through the PC speaker and at the same time displays an animation show? It sure is! In fact, you don't need to add much code to the DANCE application in Chapter 27 to make it play sound through the PC speaker instead of through a sound card.

A "PC Speaker" version of the DANCE application was copied to your \VCPROG\ORIGINAL\APPENDIX\DANCE directory when you installed the book's CD.

To execute the "PC Speaker" version of the DANCE application:

☐ Use the Run item from the Program Manager's File menu to run
  C:\VCPROG\ORIGINAL\APPENDIX\DANCE\DANCE.EXE.

  Windows responds by executing the "PC Speaker" version of the DANCE application. The DANCE application first displays a limited version message box from the TegoMM.VBX multimedia control (see Figure A.1).

☐ Click the OK button of the message box.

The main window of DANCE.EXE appears as shown in Figure A.2.

Figure A.1.
The limited version
message box of the
TegoMM.VBX
multimedia control.

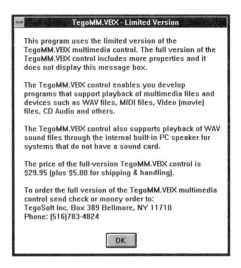

TegoMM.VBX - Limited Version

This program uses the limited version of the TegoMM.VBX multimedia control. The full version of the TegoMM.VBX control includes more properties and it does not display this message box.

The TegoMM.VBX control enables you develop programs that support playback of multimedia files and devices such as WAV files, MIDI files, Video (movie) files, CD Audio and others.

The TegoMM.VBX control also supports playback of WAV sound files through the internal built-in PC speaker for systems that do not have a sound card.

The price of the full-version TegoMM.VBX control is $29.95 (plus $5.00 for shipping & handling).

To order the full version of the TegoMM.VBX multimedia control send check or money order to:
TegoSoft Inc. Box 389 Bellmore, NY 11710
Phone: (516)783-4824

OK

Figure A.2.
The DANCE
("PC Speaker"
version) appli-
cation's main
window.

Dance Windows Application - Dance
File   Help

Start Show   Stop
☐ Multitasking

As you can see, the main window of the "PC Speaker" version of the DANCE application is almost identical to the main window of the original DANCE application in Chapter 27. The only difference is that the "PC Speaker" version has an additional control—a Multitasking check box.

☐ Leave the Multitasking check box in its current status (that is, unchecked) and click the Start Show button.

> *The DANCE application responds by playing music through the PC speaker and changing the mouse pointer to an hourglass. Note that because the Multitasking check box is currently not checked, there is no multitasking. This means that you cannot move the mouse, you cannot switch to another Windows application while the music is being played, and there is no animation show.*

1287

Now start the show with multitasking:

☐ Place a check mark in the Multitasking check box.

☐ Click the Start Show button.

> *The DANCE application responds by playing music through the PC speaker and displaying an animation show. Note that because now the Multitasking check box is checked, the mouse is available and you can switch to other applications while the PC speaker plays in the background.*

☐ Switch to another Windows application (for example, Paintbrush).

> *As you can hear, the PC speaker keeps playing in the background even when another Windows application is active.*

☐ Switch back to the DANCE application and terminate it.

NOTE

As you have just heard and seen, it is possible to write a multitasking application in which the mouse is available while the PC speaker plays a WAV file. The user can even switch to another Windows application and the PC speaker will keep playing the WAV file in the background.

NOTE

The TegoMM.VBX file that is included with the book's CD is the limited version of the TegoMM.VBX multimedia control. The full version of the control has more features. The price of the full version TegoMM.VBX control is $29.95 (plus $5.00 for shipping and handling).

You can order the full version of the TegoMM.VBX control directly from

TegoSoft, Inc.
Box 389
Bellmore, NY 11710
ATTN: TegoMM.VBX for Visual C++
Phone: (516)783-4824

Note that the TegoMM.VBX control enables you to play WAV files through the PC speaker. However, the limited version of this control enables you to play only those WAV files that are included on the book's CD. To play your own WAV files, you have to use the full version.

How the "PC Speaker" Version of the DANCE Application Works

As stated earlier, the "PC Version" of the DANCE application is almost identical to the original DANCE application that you wrote in Chapter 27. Thus, the following discussion covers only the part of the code that is different from the original DANCE application in Chapter 27.

The code that opens the WAV file is inside the function OnInitialUpdate() in the file C:\VCPROG\ORIGINAL\APPENDIX\DANCE\DANCEVW.CPP:

```
/////////////////////////
// MY CODE STARTS HERE
/////////////////////////

void CDanceView::OnInitialUpdate()
{

   // Call the base class function.
   CFormView::OnInitialUpdate();

   // Set the DeviceType property for playback
   // through the PC speaker.
   m_pc->SetStrProperty("DeviceType","PCSpeaker");

   // Disable the timer of the multimedia control.
   m_pc->SetNumProperty("UpdateInterval",0);

   // Set the FileName property.
   m_pc->SetStrProperty("FileName",
                        "\\VCPROG\\WAV\\BOURB2M3.WAV");

   // Make the multimedia control invisible.
   m_pc->SetNumProperty("Visible", FALSE);

   // Issue an Open command to the multimedia control.
   m_pc->SetStrProperty("Command","Open");

   // Load IDB_BITMAP1
   m_pB[0] = new CBitmap;
```

```
m_pB[0]->LoadBitmap(IDB_BITMAP1);

// Load IDB_BITMAP2
m_pB[1] = new CBitmap;
m_pB[1]->LoadBitmap(IDB_BITMAP2);

// Load IDB_BITMAP3
m_pB[2] = new CBitmap;
m_pB[2]->LoadBitmap(IDB_BITMAP3);

// Load IDB_BITMAP4
m_pB[3] = new CBitmap;
m_pB[3]->LoadBitmap(IDB_BITMAP4);

}

/////////////////////
// MY CODE ENDS HERE
/////////////////////
```

This is almost identical to the original DANCE application's `OnInitialUpdate()` function. The only difference is in the two statements that set the `FileName` and `DeviceType` properties of the multimedia control. These statements are

```
m_pc->SetStrProperty("DeviceType","PCSpeaker");
```

```
m_pc->SetStrProperty("FileName", "\\VCPROG\\WAV\\BOURB2M3.WAV");
```

As you can see, the `DeviceType` property of the multimedia control is set to `"PCSpeaker"` (because you want to play through the PC speaker), and the `FileName` property is set to `"\\VCPROG\\WAV\\BOURB2M3.WAV"` (because this is the WAV file you want to play). All the other statements in the `OnInitialUpdate()` function are the same as the statements in the original DANCE application `OnInitialUpdate()` function in Chapter 27.

Another difference between the "PC Speaker" version and the original version of the DANCE application is the Multitasking check box. As shown in Figure A.2, the "PC Speaker" version of the DANCE application has a Multitasking check box. Whenever the user clicks this check box, the function `OnMultitask()` (inside `DANCEVW.CPP`) is automatically executed. Here's the `OnMultitask()` function's code:

```
void CDanceView::OnMultitask()
{
// TODO: Add your control notification handler code here

///////////////////////
// MY CODE STARTS HERE
///////////////////////
```

```
// Update the variable of the Multitasking check box.
UpdateData(TRUE);

// Enable multi-tasking?
if (m_MultiTask==TRUE)
    {
    m_pc->SetNumProperty("pcMouseEnabled", TRUE);
    m_pc->SetNumProperty("pcTaskInterval",400);
    }
else
    {
    m_pc->SetNumProperty("pcMouseEnabled", FALSE);
    m_pc->SetNumProperty("pcTaskInterval",0);
    }

/////////////////////
// MY CODE ENDS HERE
/////////////////////

}
```

The first statement in the OnMultitask() function,

```
UpdateData(TRUE);
```

updates the variable of the Multitasking check box (m_MultiTask) with the current status of the check box. The variable m_MultiTask was attached to the Multitasking check box during the visual implementation.

So at this point, if the Multitasking check box is checked, the value of m_MultiTask is TRUE. Otherwise, the value of m_Multitask is FALSE.

The remaining code in the OnMultitask() function is an if-else statement that sets the multitasking feature on or off, depending on the value of m_Multitask:

```
if (m_MultiTask==TRUE)
    {
    m_pc->SetNumProperty("pcMouseEnabled", TRUE);
    m_pc->SetNumProperty("pcTaskInterval",400);
    }
else
    {
    m_pc->SetNumProperty("pcMouseEnabled", FALSE);
    m_pc->SetNumProperty("pcTaskInterval",0);
    }
```

If m_MultiTask is TRUE (that is, if the Multitasking check box is checked), the two statements under the if are executed:

```
m_pc->SetNumProperty("pcMouseEnabled", TRUE);
m_pc->SetNumProperty("pcTaskInterval",400);
```

The first statement sets the pcMouseEnabled property of the multimedia control to TRUE. This causes the mouse to be available when the PC speaker plays.

The second statement sets the pcTaskInterval property of the multimedia control to 400 milliseconds. What is the pcTaskInterval property? It determines the time slice (in milliseconds) that is allocated to the task that plays through the PC speaker. By setting the pcTaskInterval property to 400 milliseconds, you're telling the multimedia control that it should play the WAV file in sections of 400 milliseconds. Between playback of sections, it will yield control to Windows so that other applications can be run.

If m_MultiTask is FALSE (that is, if the Multitasking check box is not checked), the two statements under the else are executed:

```
m_pc->SetNumProperty("pcMouseEnabled", FALSE);
m_pc->SetNumProperty("pcTaskInterval",0);
```

The first statement sets the pcMouseEnabled property of the multimedia control to FALSE, so the mouse is not available when the PC speaker plays. Whenever the PC speaker plays a WAV file, the mouse pointer becomes an hourglass and the user cannot move it.

The second statement sets the pcTaskInterval property of the multimedia control to 0. This tells the multimedia control that it should disable multitasking when it plays a WAV file through the PC speaker. That is, the processor will play the WAV file through the PC speaker without yielding control to other Windows applications. Thus, when the pcTaskInterval property is set to 0, the user cannot switch to other Windows applications while the WAV file is playing.

The MULTI Application

The MULTI application uses the TegoMM.VBX control to control several multimedia devices. The project files of the MULTI and MULTI.EXE applications were copied to your C:\VCPROG\ORIGINAL\APPENDIX\MULTI directory when you installed the book's CD.

To see and hear the MULTI.EXE application in action:

☐ Use the Run item from the Program Manager's File menu to run
   `C:\VCPROG\ORIGINAL\APPENDIX\MULTI\MULTI.EXE`.

   Windows responds by executing the MULTI.EXE application. The MULTI application first displays a limited version message box from the TegoMM.VBX multimedia control (see Figure A.1).

☐ Click the OK button of the message box.

The main window of MULTI.EXE appears as shown in Figure A.3.

Figure A.3.
The MULTI application's main window.

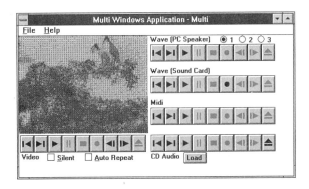

As you can see, the main window of the MULTI application contains five multimedia controls:

> *A Video multimedia control* for playing AVI video files. The video file is displayed in the area above the control. Note that below this multimedia control there are two check boxes, Silent and Auto Repeat. If you check the Silent check box, the video will be played without sound. If you check the Auto Repeat check box, the playback will automatically repeat once it reaches the end of the file.
> *A Wave (PC Speaker) multimedia control* for playing WAV files through the PC speaker. Note that above this multimedia control there are three radio buttons labeled 1, 2, and 3. Depending on which radio button you select, a different WAV file will be played. For example, in Figure A.3, radio button number 1 is selected, so if you click the multimedia control's Play button, WAV file number 1 will be played.
> *A Wave (Sound Card) multimedia control* for playing WAV files through the sound card. Note that if you don't have a sound card, this control will be dimmed (unavailable).

A MIDI multimedia control for playing MIDI files through the sound card. Again, if you don't have a sound card, this control will be dimmed.

A CD Audio multimedia control for playing audio CDs. If you don't have a CD in your CD-ROM drive, this control will be dimmed. Note that below this control there's a Load button. To play an audio CD, you need to insert it into your CD-ROM drive and then click the Load button. Once the CD is loaded, you can play it by clicking the multimedia control's Play button.

The MULTI application is similar to the applications you wrote in Chapters 22 through 25 (the Multimedia chapters). Chapter 22 covers WAV files, Chapter 23 covers MIDI files, Chapter 24 covers AVI (video) files, and Chapter 25 covers CD Audio.

Detecting Whether the PC Has a Sound Card That Can Play WAV Files

If a user runs your application on a system that has a sound card, you should direct the playback of WAV files to the sound card. However, if your user doesn't have a sound card, you should play the WAV files through the PC speaker. The question is, how can your application detect whether or not a sound card is installed in the user's system? The following code shows how:

```
// Set the FileName property.
m_wav->SetStrProperty("FileName", "MySong.WAV");

// Try to open the WAV file for playback
// through a sound card.
m_wav->SetStrProperty("DeviceType","WaveAudio");
m_wav->SetStrProperty("Command","Open");

// If the WAV file did not open successfully for a
// sound card, open it for playback through the
// PC Speaker.
if ( m_wav->GetNumProperty("Error") != 0 )
   {
   m_wav->SetStrProperty("DeviceType","PCSpeaker");
   m_wav->SetStrProperty("Command","Open");
   }
```

This code first tries to open the multimedia control to play a WAV file through a sound card, and if this fails, the multimedia control is opened again to play the WAV file through the PC speaker.

The first statement,

```
m_wav->SetStrProperty("FileName", "MySong.WAV");
```

sets the m_wav multimedia control's FileName property with the name of the WAV file to be played. (This is assuming that during design time the name of the variable that was attached to the multimedia control is m_wav.)

The next two statements are

```
m_wav->SetStrProperty("DeviceType","WaveAudio");
m_wav->SetStrProperty("Command","Open");
```

The first statement sets the DeviceType property to play WAV files through a sound card ("WaveAudio"), and the second statement issues an Open command to the multimedia control.

The next statement is an if statement that examines the multimedia control's Error property:

```
if ( m_wav->GetNumProperty("Error") != 0 )
    {
    m_wav->SetStrProperty("DeviceType","PCSpeaker");
    m_wav->SetStrProperty("Command","Open");
    }
```

If the last multimedia command (the Open command) fails, the multimedia control's Error property is not zero and the if condition is satisfied. As you can see, the statements under the if statement issue another Open command to the multimedia control, but this time the DeviceType property is set to "PCSpeaker".

Index

E

P